See the Difference with LearningCurve!

LearningCurve
macmillan learning

learningcurveworks.com

LearningCurve is a winning solution for everyone: students come to class better prepared and instructors have more flexibility to go beyond the basic facts and concepts in class. LearningCurve's game-like quizzes are book-specific and link back to the textbook in LaunchPad so that students can brush up on the reading when they get stumped by a question. The reporting features help instructors track overall class trends and spot topics that are giving students trouble so that they can adjust lectures and class activities.

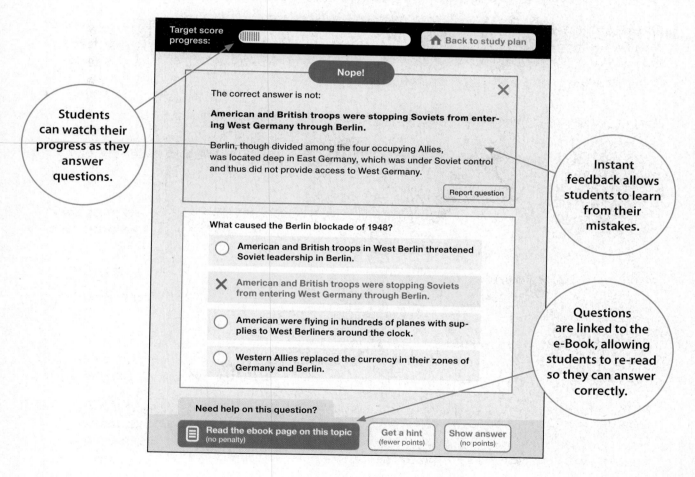

Students can watch their progress as they answer questions.

Instant feedback allows students to learn from their mistakes.

Questions are linked to the e-Book, allowing students to re-read so they can answer correctly.

LearningCurve is easy to assign, easy to customize, and ea[...]
See the difference LearningCurve makes in teaching and l[...]

CONTEMPORARY EUROPE

ATLANTIC OCEAN

North Sea

NORWAY
- Bergen
- Oslo

SWEDEN
- Stockholm
- Göteborg

SCOTLAND
- Edinburgh
- Glasgow

NORTHERN IRELAND
- Belfast

IRELAND
- Dublin
- Cork

UNITED KINGDOM
- Liverpool
- Birmingham

WALES

ENGLAND
Thames R.
- London

English Channel

DENMARK
- Aarhus
- Copenhagen

Baltic Sea

RUSS
- Kaliningra
- Gdańsk

Elbe R.

GERMANY
- Berlin
Oder R.
Vistula R.
- Wa

POLAND
- Kraków

NETHERLANDS
- Amsterdam
- Rotterdam

Rhine R.

- Antwerp
- Brussels

BELGIUM

- Frankfurt

LUXEMBOURG
- Luxembourg

- Prague

CZECH REP.
- Brno

SLOVAK
- Bratislava
- M

Seine R.
- Paris

Loire R.

FRANCE

LIECHTENSTEIN

- Munich
Danube R.
- Vienna

AUSTRIA
- Innsbruck
- Graz

- Budapest

HUNGARY

- Zürich
- Bern
- Vaduz

SWITZERLAND

A L P S

SLOVENIA
- Ljubljana

- Lyons

Rhône R.

- Milan
Po R.

CROATIA
- Zagreb

- Belg

BOSNIA AND HERZEGOVINA
- Sarajevo
- SE

Bay of Biscay

ANDORRA
- Andorra la Vella

PYRENEES

Ebro R.

San Marino

SAN MARINO

A P E N N I N E S

Adriatic Sea

- Split

- Oporto

PORTUGAL

- Madrid

SPAIN

- Barcelona

- Marseilles

MONACO

- Podgorica

MONTENEGRO

- Tirane

ALBA

- Lisbon

- Seville

Corsica

- Rome

ITALY

- Naples

Sardinia

Balearic Is.

- Gibraltar (Gr. Br.)

- Algiers

Tyrrhenian Sea

Ionian Sea

- Palermo

Sicily

- Tunis

- Rabat

- Valletta

MALTA

MOROCCO

TUNISIA

Mediterranean

ALGERIA

- Tripoli

LIBYA

Elevation

Feet	Meters
Over 13,120	Over 4,001
6,561–13,120	2,001–4,000
1,641–6,560	501–2,000
661–1,640	201–500
0–660	0–200
Below sea level	Below sea level

⊛ National capital
• Major city

0   150   300 miles
0   150   300 kilometers

THE CONTEMPORARY WORLD

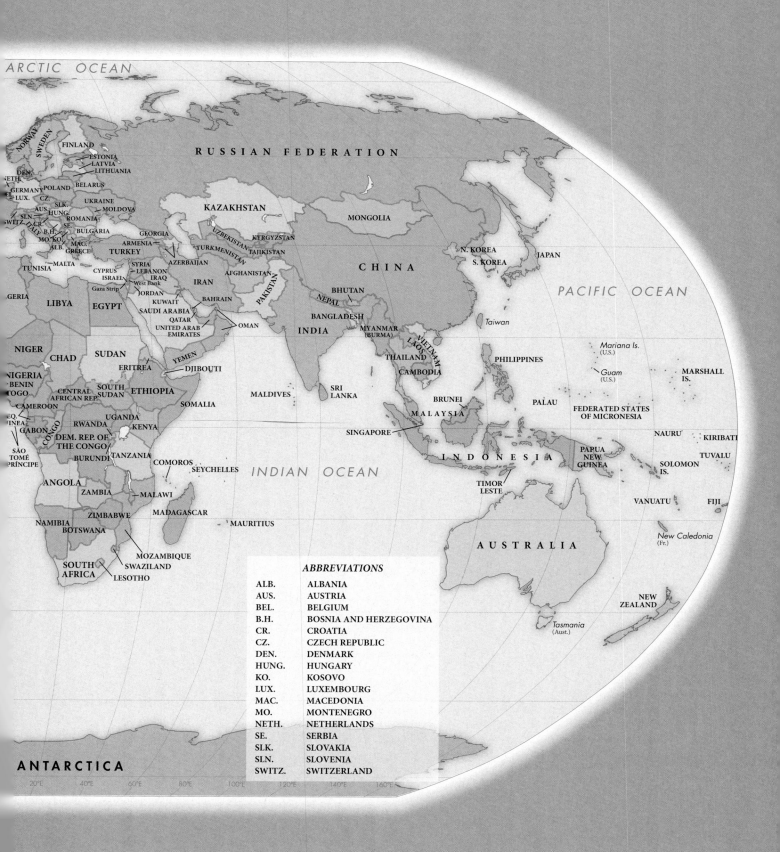

ARCTIC OCEAN

NORWAY
SWEDEN
FINLAND
ESTONIA
LATVIA
LITHUANIA
DEN.
NETH.
GERMANY
POLAND
BELARUS
LUX.
CZ.
UKRAINE
SLK.
AUS.
HUNG.
MOLDOVA
SLN.
ROMANIA
SWITZ.
ITALY
CR.
SE.
MO. KO.
BULGARIA
B.H.
MAC.
ALB.
GREECE
GEORGIA
TUNISIA
MALTA
TURKEY
ARMENIA
AZERBAIJAN
CYPRUS
SYRIA
LEBANON
ISRAEL
IRAQ
West Bank
Gaza Strip
JORDAN
IRAN
GERIA
LIBYA
EGYPT
KUWAIT
BAHRAIN
SAUDI ARABIA
QATAR
UNITED ARAB
EMIRATES
OMAN

RUSSIAN FEDERATION

KAZAKHSTAN

UZBEKISTAN
KYRGYZSTAN
TURKMENISTAN
TAJIKISTAN
AFGHANISTAN
PAKISTAN

MONGOLIA

CHINA

N. KOREA
S. KOREA
JAPAN

PACIFIC OCEAN

BHUTAN
NEPAL
BANGLADESH
INDIA
MYANMAR
(BURMA)
LAOS
VIETNAM
THAILAND
CAMBODIA

Taiwan

Mariana Is.
(U.S.)

Guam
(U.S.)

MARSHALL
IS.

NIGER
CHAD
SUDAN
ERITREA
YEMEN
DJIBOUTI
NIGERIA
BENIN
TOGO
CENTRAL
AFRICAN REP.
SOUTH
SUDAN
ETHIOPIA
SOMALIA
CAMEROON
EQ.
GUINEA
GABON
CONGO
UGANDA
RWANDA
KENYA
DEM. REP. OF
THE CONGO
BURUNDI
TANZANIA
SÃO
TOMÉ
PRÍNCIPE

MALDIVES
SRI
LANKA

BRUNEI
MALAYSIA
SINGAPORE

PHILIPPINES

PALAU

FEDERATED STATES
OF MICRONESIA

NAURU
KIRIBATI

INDONESIA

PAPUA
NEW
GUINEA

TUVALU
SOLOMON
IS.

COMOROS
SEYCHELLES

INDIAN OCEAN

ANGOLA
ZAMBIA
MALAWI
ZIMBABWE
MADAGASCAR
NAMIBIA
BOTSWANA
MOZAMBIQUE
SWAZILAND
SOUTH
AFRICA
LESOTHO

MAURITIUS

TIMOR
LESTE

VANUATU
FIJI

New Caledonia
(Fr.)

AUSTRALIA

NEW
ZEALAND

Tasmania
(Aust.)

ABBREVIATIONS	
ALB.	ALBANIA
AUS.	AUSTRIA
BEL.	BELGIUM
B.H.	BOSNIA AND HERZEGOVINA
CR.	CROATIA
CZ.	CZECH REPUBLIC
DEN.	DENMARK
HUNG.	HUNGARY
KO.	KOSOVO
LUX.	LUXEMBOURG
MAC.	MACEDONIA
MO.	MONTENEGRO
NETH.	NETHERLANDS
SE.	SERBIA
SLK.	SLOVAKIA
SLN.	SLOVENIA
SWITZ.	SWITZERLAND

ANTARCTICA

20°E   40°E   60°E   80°E   100°E   120°E   140°E   160°E

A History of Western Society

TWELFTH EDITION

VOLUME A
From Antiquity to 1500

John P. McKay
University of Illinois at Urbana-Champaign

Bennett D. Hill
Late of *Georgetown University*

John Buckler
Late of *University of Illinois at Urbana-Champaign*

Clare Haru Crowston
University of Illinois at Urbana-Champaign

Merry E. Wiesner-Hanks
University of Wisconsin–Milwaukee

Joe Perry
Georgia State University

bedford/st.martin's
Macmillan Learning

Boston | New York

FOR BEDFORD/ST. MARTIN'S

*Vice President, Editorial, Macmillan Learning
   Humanities:* Edwin Hill
Publisher for History: Michael Rosenberg
Director of Development for History: Jane Knetzger
Acquiring Editor for History: Laura Arcari
Senior Developmental Editor: Leah R. Strauss
Senior Production Editor: Christina M. Horn
Senior Media Producer: Michelle Camisa
Senior Production Supervisor: Jennifer Wetzel
History Marketing Manager: Melissa Famiglietti
Media Editor: Jennifer Jovin
Associate Editor: Tess Fletcher
Editorial Assistant: Melanie McFadyen
Copy Editor: Jennifer Brett Greenstein
Indexer: Leoni Z. McVey

Cartography: Mapping Specialists, Ltd.
Photo Editor: Robin Fadool
Photo Researcher: Bruce Carson
Permissions Editor: Eve Lehmann
Senior Art Director: Anna Palchik
Text Design: Boynton Hue Studio
Cover Design: William Boardman
Volume A Cover Art: Head of a Princess from the family
   of Akhenaton, New Kingdom (painted limestone)
   (see also 116813, 370210, 370211), Egyptian 18th
   Dynasty (ca. 1567–320 B.C.E.)/Louvre, Paris, France/
   Peter Willi/Bridgeman Images
Composition: Jouve
Printing and Binding: RR Donnelley and Sons

Manufactured in the United States of America.

1 0 9 8 7 6
f   e   d   c   b   a

For information, write: Bedford/St. Martin's, 75 Arlington Street, Boston, MA 02116   (617-399-4000)

ISBN 978-1-319-03101-5 (Combined Edition)
ISBN 978-1-319-03102-2 (Volume 1)
ISBN 978-1-319-03103-9 (Volume 2)
ISBN 978-1-319-04041-3 (Volume A)

ISBN 978-1-319-04042-0 (Volume B)
ISBN 978-1-319-04043-7 (Volume C)
ISBN 978-1-319-04040-6 (Since 1300)

ACKNOWLEDGMENTS

*Acknowledgments and copyrights appear on the same page as the text and art selections they cover; these acknowledgments
and copyrights constitute an extension of the copyright page.*

A History of Western Society grew out of the initial three authors' desire to infuse new life into the study of Western Civilization. The three current authors, Clare Haru Crowston, Merry E. Wiesner-Hanks, and Joe Perry, who first used the book as students or teachers and took over full responsibilities with the eleventh edition, continue to incorporate the latest and best scholarship in the field. All three of us regularly teach introductory history courses and thus bring insights into the text from the classroom, as well as from new secondary works and our own research in archives and libraries.

In this new twelfth edition we aimed to enhance the distinctive attention to daily life that sparks students' interest while also providing a number of innovative tools — both print and digital — designed to help students think historically and master the material. In response to the growing emphasis on historical thinking skills in the teaching of history at all levels, as well as to requests from our colleagues and current adopters, we have significantly expanded the book's primary source program to offer a wide variety of sources, both written and visual, presented in several ways. Every chapter now includes **"Thinking Like a Historian"** (one per chapter), which groups at least five sources around a central question, and **"Evaluating the Evidence"** (three per chapter), which features an individual text or visual source.

The Story of *A History of Western Society*: Bringing the Past to Life for Students

At the point when *A History of Western Society* was first conceptualized, social history was dramatically changing the ways we understood the past, and the original authors decided to create a book that would re-create the lives of ordinary people in appealing human terms, while also giving major economic, political, cultural, and intellectual developments the attention they unquestionably deserve. The current authors remain committed to advancing this vision for today's classroom, with a broader definition of social history that brings the original idea into the twenty-first century.

History as a discipline never stands still, and over the last several decades cultural history has joined social history as a source of dynamism. Because of its emphasis on the ways people made sense of their lives, *A History of Western Society* has always included a large amount of cultural history, ranging from foundational works of philosophy and literature to popular songs and stories. This focus on cultural history has been enhanced in recent editions in a way that highlights the interplay between men's and women's lived experiences and the ways men and women reflect on these experiences to create meaning. The joint social and cultural perspective requires — fortunately, in our opinion — the inclusion of objects as well as texts as important sources for studying history, which has allowed us to incorporate the growing emphasis on material culture in the work of many historians. We know that engaging students' interest in the past is often a challenge, but we also know that the text's hallmark approach — the emphasis on daily life and individual experience in its social and cultural dimensions — connects with students and makes the past vivid and accessible.

"Life" Chapters Connect the Past to the Present

Although social and cultural history can be found in every chapter, they are particularly emphasized in the acclaimed "Life" chapters that spark student interest by making the past palpable and approachable in human terms. The five chapters are Chapter 4: Life in the Hellenistic World, 336–30 B.C.E.; Chapter 10: Life in Villages and Cities of the High Middle Ages, 1000–1300; Chapter 18: Life in the Era of Expansion, 1650–1800; Chapter 22: Life in the Emerging Urban Society, 1840–1914; and Chapter 30: Life in an Age of Globalization, 1990 to the Present. Because we know that a key challenge of teaching history — and Western Civilization in particular — is encouraging students to appreciate the relevance of the past to our lives today, these five "Life" chapters each include a feature called **"The Past Living Now"** that examines an aspect of life today with origins in the period covered in that chapter. Featuring engaging topics such as the development of the modern university (Chapter 10) and the dawn of commercialized sports (Chapter 18), these essays were conceived with student interest in mind.

Primary Sources and Historical Thinking

Because understanding the past requires that students engage directly with sources on their own, this edition features a more expansive primary source program within its covers. **"Thinking Like a Historian"** (one in each chapter) groups at least five sources around a central question, with additional questions to guide students' analysis of the evidence and suggestions for essays that will allow them to put these sources together with what they have learned in class. Topics include "Land Ownership and Social Conflict in the Late Republic" (Chapter 5); "The Rights of Which Men?" (Chapter 19); and "The Conservative Reaction to Immigration and Islamist Terrorism" (Chapter 30). **"Evaluating the Evidence"** (three in each chapter) features an individual source, with headnotes and questions that help students understand the source and connect it to the information in the rest of the chapter. Selected for their interest and carefully integrated into their historical context, these sources provide students with firsthand encounters with people of the past along with the means and tools for building historical skills, including chronological reasoning, explaining causation, evaluating context, and assessing perspective. The suggestions for essays based on the primary sources encourage students to further expand their skills as they use their knowledge to develop historical arguments and write historical analyses.

To give students abundant opportunities to hone their textual and visual analysis skills, as well as a sense of the variety of sources on which historians rely, the primary source program includes a mix of canonical and lesser-known sources; a diversity of perspectives representing ordinary and prominent individuals alike; and a wide variety of source types, from tomb inscriptions, diaries, sermons, letters, poetry, and drama to artifacts, architecture, and propaganda posters. In addition, we have quoted extensively from a wide range of primary sources in the narrative, demonstrating that such quotations are the "stuff" of history. We believe that our extensive use of primary source extracts as an integral part of the narrative as well as in extended form in the primary source boxes will give students ample practice in thinking critically and historically.

Finally, the thoroughly revised companion reader, *Sources for Western Society*, Third Edition, provides a rich selection of documents to complement each chapter of the text and is FREE when packaged with the textbook.

Distinctive Essay Features Punctuate Larger Developments

In addition to the expanded primary source program and **"The Past Living Now,"** we are proud of the two unique boxed essay features in each chapter—**"Individuals in Society"** and **"Living in the Past"**—that personalize larger developments and make them tangible.

To give students a chance to see the past through ordinary people's lives, each chapter includes one of the popular **"Individuals in Society" biographical essays**, which offer brief studies of individuals or groups, informing students about the societies in which they lived. We have found that readers empathize with these human beings as they themselves seek to define their own identities. The spotlighting of individuals, both famous and obscure, perpetuates the book's continued attention to cultural and intellectual developments, highlights human agency, and reflects changing interests within the historical profession as well as the development of "microhistory." Features include essays on Aristophanes, the ancient Athenian playwright who mercilessly satirized the demagogues and thinkers of his day; Anna Jansz of

Rotterdam, an Anabaptist martyr; Hürrem, a concubine who became a powerful figure in the Ottoman Empire during the sixteenth century; Rebecca Protten, a former slave and leader in the Moravian missionary movement; Samuel Crompton, the inventor of the spinning mule during the Industrial Revolution who struggled to control and profit from his invention; and Edward Snowden, a former CIA operative who leaked classified documents about American surveillance programs to the world press and was considered by some a hero and by others a traitor.

To introduce students to the study of material culture, **"Living in the Past"** essays use social and cultural history to show how life in the past was both similar to and different from our lives today. These features are richly illustrated with images and artifacts and include a short essay and questions for analysis. We use these essays to explore the deeper ramifications of aspects of their own lives that students might otherwise take for granted, such as consumer goods, factories, and even currency. Students connect to the people of the past through a diverse range of topics such as "Farming in the Hellenistic World," "Roman Table Manners," "Child's Play," "Coffeehouse Culture," "The Immigrant Experience," "Nineteenth-Century Women's Fashion," and "The Supermarket Revolution."

New Coverage and Updates to the Narrative

This edition is enhanced by the incorporation of a wealth of new scholarship and subject areas that immerse students in the dynamic and ongoing work of history. Chapters 1–6 incorporate the exciting cross-disciplinary scholarship that has emerged over the last several decades on the Paleolithic and Neolithic eras, river valley civilizations, and the ancient Mediterranean. For example, archaeologists working at Göbekli Tepe in present-day Turkey have unearthed rings of massive, multi-ton, elaborately carved limestone pillars built around 9000 B.C.E. by groups of foragers, which has led to a rethinking of the links between culture, religion, and the initial development of agriculture. Similarly, new research on the peoples of Mesopotamia, based on cuneiform writing along with other sources, has led scholars to revise the view that Mesopotamians were fatalistic and to emphasize instead that they generally anticipated being well treated by the gods if they behaved morally. Throughout these chapters, material on cross-cultural connections, the impact of technologies, and changing social relationships has been added. In Chapter 14, we have updated and expanded the coverage of the conquest of the Aztec and Inca Empires and the impact of the conquest on indigenous peoples, including new material on the economic exploitation of indigenous people, religious conversion, and European debates about indigenous people. In Chapter 16, there are several significant revisions. First, there is more coverage of global/colonial issues and of the interaction between intellectual ideas and social change. Second, with regard to the Scientific

Revolution, there is a new section called "Why Europe?" that asks why the Scientific Revolution happened in Europe, as well as an expanded discussion of the relationship between religion and science. Third, a new section called "The Social Life of the Enlightenment" draws attention to recent scholarship linking the ideas of the Enlightenment to the social changes of the eighteenth century; this section includes coverage of the impact of contact with non-Europeans, debates on race, and women's role in the Enlightenment. Chapter 20 pays increased attention to the global context of industrialization, including two new sections: "Why Britain?" explains why the Industrial Revolution originated in Britain and not elsewhere in the world, such as China or India; and "The Global Picture" discusses the global spread of industrialization. A new section on living standards for the working class addresses the impact of industrialization on working people.

Other additions include a streamlined discussion of the role of women in classical Athens (Chapter 3); updated coverage of medicine in the Hellenistic period (Chapter 4); new material on the Vikings of western Europe (Chapter 8); expanded treatment of the growth of Russia's land empire to complement attention to western European acquisition of overseas empires and new material on Peter the Great's campaigns against the Ottomans (Chapter 15); increased coverage of communities and identities of the Atlantic world with material on the way colonial contacts help create national European identities as well as "African" and "Indian" identities (Chapter 17); updated coverage of the history of the family, popular culture, and medicine, including material on the use of colonial plants as medicines (Chapter 18); new material on the Congress of Vienna (Chapter 21) and expanded coverage of political ideologies of liberalism, republicanism, and nationalism (Chapters 21 and 23); new material on women's roles in the European colonies and on women and imperialism (Chapter 24); expanded coverage of the First World War in the Middle East, the collapse of the Ottoman Empire, and the postwar mandate system (Chapter 25); new discussion of Jewish resistance to the Holocaust and extended coverage of anti-Semitism and eugenics in Nazi Germany (Chapter 27); new material on violence and decolonization in the Algerian War of Independence (Chapter 28); and up-to-date coverage of contemporary events in the final chapter, including the refugee crisis, the euro crisis and Greek debt relief, Russian expansionism, issues surrounding terrorism and anti-Muslim sentiment in Europe, and the potential fragmentation of the European Union (Chapter 30).

Helping Students Understand the Narrative

We know firsthand and take seriously the challenges students face in understanding, retaining, and mastering so much material that is often unfamiliar. With the goal of making this the most student-centered edition yet, we continued

to enhance the book's pedagogy on many fronts. To focus students' reading, each chapter opens with **a chapter preview with focus questions** keyed to the main chapter headings. These questions are repeated within the chapter and again in the **"Review & Explore" section** at the end of each chapter that provides helpful guidance for reviewing key topics. Each "Review & Explore" section concludes with a **"Suggested Reading and Media Resources"** listing that includes up-to-date readings on the vast amount of new work being done in many fields, as well as recommended documentaries, feature films, television, and Web sites.

To help students understand the bigger picture and prepare for exams, each chapter includes **"Looking Back, Looking Ahead"** conclusions that provide an insightful synthesis of the chapter's main developments, while connecting to events that students will encounter in the chapters to come. In this way students are introduced to history as an ongoing process of interrelated events. These conclusions are followed by **"Make Connections" questions** that prompt students to assess larger developments across chapters, thus allowing them to develop skills in evaluating change and continuity, making comparisons, and analyzing context and causation.

To promote clarity and comprehension, boldface **key terms** in the text are defined in the margins and listed in the chapter review. **Phonetic spellings** are located directly after terms that readers are likely to find hard to pronounce. The **chapter chronologies**, which review major developments discussed in each chapter, mirror the key events of the chapter, and the topic-specific **thematic chronologies** that appear in many chapters provide a more focused timeline of certain developments. Once again, we also provide a **unified timeline** at the end of the text. Comprehensive and easy to locate, this timeline allows students to compare developments over the centuries.

The high-quality art and map program has been thoroughly revised and features hundreds of **contemporaneous illustrations**. To make the past tangible, and as an extension of our attention to cultural history, we include numerous **artifacts**—from swords and fans to playing cards and record players. As in earlier editions, all illustrations have been carefully selected to complement the text, and all include captions that inform students while encouraging them to read the text more deeply. High-quality **full-size maps** illustrate major developments in the narrative, and helpful spot maps are embedded in the narrative to locate areas under discussion. We recognize students' difficulties with geography, and the new edition includes the popular **"Mapping the Past" map activities**. Included in each chapter, these activities give students valuable skills in reading and interpreting maps by asking them to analyze the maps and make connections to the larger processes discussed in the narrative.

In addition, whenever an instructor assigns the **LaunchPad e-Book** (which is free when bundled with the print book), students get full access to **LearningCurve**, an online adaptive learning tool that promotes mastery of the book's content and diagnoses students' trouble spots. With this adaptive quizzing, students accumulate points toward a target score as they go, giving the interaction a game-like feel. Feedback for incorrect responses explains why the answer is incorrect and directs students back to the text to review before they attempt to answer the question again. The end result is a better understanding of the key elements of the text. Instructors who actively assign LearningCurve report their students come to class prepared for discussion and their students enjoy using it. In addition, LearningCurve's reporting feature allows instructors to quickly diagnose which concepts students in their classes are struggling with so they can adjust lectures and activities accordingly. The LaunchPad e-Book with LearningCurve is thus an invaluable asset for instructors who need to support students in all settings, from traditional lectures to hybrid, online, and newer "flipped" classrooms. To learn more about the benefits of LearningCurve and LaunchPad, see the "Versions and Supplements" section on page xv.

Helping Instructors Teach with Digital Resources

As noted, *A History of Western Society* is offered in Macmillan's premier learning platform, **LaunchPad**, an intuitive, interactive e-Book and course space. Free when packaged with the print text or available at a low price when used stand-alone, LaunchPad grants students and teachers access to a wealth of online tools and resources built specifically for our text to enhance reading comprehension and promote in-depth study.

Developed with extensive feedback from history instructors and students, **LaunchPad for *A History of Western Society*** includes the complete narrative of the print book; the companion reader, *Sources for Western Society*; and **LearningCurve**, an adaptive learning tool that is designed to get students to read before they come to class. With **new source-based questions in the test bank and in the LearningCurve**, instructors now have more ways to test students on their understanding of sources and narrative in the book.

This edition also includes **Guided Reading Exercises** that prompt students to be active readers of the chapter narrative and autograded **primary source quizzes** to test comprehension of written and visual sources. These features, plus **additional primary source documents, video sources and tools for making video assignments, map activities, flashcards, and customizable test banks**, make LaunchPad a great asset for any instructor who wants to enliven the history of Western Civilization for students.

These new directions have not changed the central mission of the book, which is to introduce students to the broad sweep of Western Civilization in a fresh yet balanced manner. Every edition has incorporated new research to keep the book up-to-date and respond to the changing needs of readers and instructors, and we have continued to do this in the twelfth edition. As we have made these changes, large and small, we have sought to give students and teachers an integrated perspective so that they can pursue — on their own or in the classroom — the historical questions that they find particularly exciting and significant. To learn more about the benefits of LearningCurve and LaunchPad, see the "Versions and Supplements" section on page xv.

Acknowledgments

It is a pleasure to thank the instructors who read and critiqued the manuscript through its development:

Robert Blackey, California State University, San Bernardino
Kevin Caldwell, Blue Ridge Community College
Amy Colon, SUNY Sullivan
Maia Conrad, Thomas Nelson Community College
Scott Gavorsky, Great Basin College
George Kaloudis, Rivier College
Roy Koepp, University of Nebraska at Kearney
Jesse Lynch, Shasta College
Michael McKeown, Daytona State College
Jennifer Morris, Mount St. Joseph University
Stephen Santelli, Northern Virginia Community College
Calvin Tesler, Lehigh University
Doris Tishkoff, Quinnipiac University

It is also a pleasure to thank the many editors who have assisted us over the years, first at Houghton Mifflin and now at Bedford/St. Martin's. At Bedford/St. Martin's these include senior development editor Leah Strauss, senior production editor Christina Horn, associate editor Tess Fletcher, editorial assistant Melanie McFadyen, director of development Jane Knetzger, and publisher for history Michael Rosenberg. Other key contributors were photo researcher Bruce Carson, text permissions editor Eve Lehmann, text designer Cia Boynton, copy editor Jennifer Brett Greenstein, proofreaders Linda McLatchie and Angela Morrison, indexer Leoni McVey, and cover designer Billy Boardman.

Many of our colleagues at the University of Illinois, the University of Wisconsin–Milwaukee, and Georgia State University continue to provide information and stimulation, often without even knowing it. We thank them for it. We also thank the many students over the years with whom we have used earlier editions of this book. Their reactions and opinions helped shape the revisions to this edition, and we hope it remains worthy of the ultimate praise that they bestowed on it: that it's "not boring like most textbooks." Merry Wiesner-Hanks would, as always, also like to thank her husband, Neil, without whom work on this project would not be possible. Clare Haru Crowston thanks her husband, Ali, and her children, Lili, Reza, and Kian, who are a joyous reminder of the vitality of life that we try to showcase in this book. Joe Perry thanks his colleagues and students at Georgia State for their intellectual stimulation and is grateful to Joyce de Vries for her unstinting support and encouragement.

Each of us has benefited from the criticism of our coauthors, although each of us assumes responsibility for what he or she has written. Merry Wiesner-Hanks intensively reworked John Buckler's Chapters 1–6 and revised Chapters 7–13; Clare Crowston wrote and revised Chapters 14–19 and took responsibility for John McKay's Chapter 20; and Joe Perry took responsibility for John McKay's Chapters 21–24 and wrote and revised Chapters 25–30.

We'd especially like to thank the founding authors, John P. McKay, Bennett D. Hill, and John Buckler, for their enduring contributions and for their faith in each of us to carry on their legacy.

CLARE HARU CROWSTON
MERRY E. WIESNER-HANKS
JOE PERRY

Adopters of *A History of Western Society* and their students have access to abundant print and digital resources and tools, including documents, assessment and presentation materials, the acclaimed Bedford Series in History and Culture volumes, and much more. The LaunchPad course space provides access to the narrative with all assignment and assessment opportunities at the ready. See below for more information, visit **macmillanlearning.com**, or contact your local Bedford/St. Martin's sales representative.

Get the Right Version for Your Class

To accommodate different course lengths and course budgets, *A History of Western Society* is available in several different formats, including a Concise Edition (narrative with select features, maps, and images), a Value Edition (narrative only in two colors with select maps and images), three-hole-punched loose-leaf versions, and low-priced PDF e-Books. And for the best value of all, package a new print book with LaunchPad at no additional charge to get the best each format offers — a print version for easy portability and reading with a LaunchPad interactive e-Book and course space with LearningCurve and loads of additional assignment and assessment options.

- **Combined Edition** (Chapters 1–30): available in paperback, Concise Edition, Value Edition, loose-leaf, e-Book formats, and in LaunchPad

- **Volume 1, From Antiquity to the Enlightenment** (Chapters 1–16): available in paperback, Concise Edition, Value Edition, loose-leaf, e-Book formats, and in LaunchPad

- **Volume 2, From the Age of Exploration to the Present** (Chapters 14–30): available in paperback, Concise Edition, Value Edition, loose-leaf, e-Book formats, and in LaunchPad

- **Volume A, From Antiquity to 1500** (Chapters 1–12): available in paperback, e-Book formats, and in LaunchPad

- **Volume B, From the Later Middle Ages to 1815** (Chapters 11–19): available in paperback, e-Book formats, and in LaunchPad

- **Volume C, From the Revolutionary Era to the Present** (Chapters 19–30): available in paperback, e-Book formats, and in LaunchPad

- **Since 1300** (Chapters 11–30): available in paperback, e-Book formats, and in LaunchPad

As noted below, any of these volumes can be packaged with additional titles for a discount. To get ISBNs for discount packages, visit **macmillanlearning.com** or contact your Bedford/St. Martin's representative.

Assign LaunchPad—an Assessment-Ready Interactive e-Book and Course Space

Available for discount purchase on its own or for packaging with new books at no additional charge, LaunchPad is a breakthrough solution for today's courses. Intuitive and easy to use for students and instructors alike, LaunchPad is ready to use as is and can be edited, customized with your own material, and assigned quickly. LaunchPad for *A History of Western Society* provides Bedford/St. Martin's high-quality content all in one place, including the full interactive e-Book and companion reader, *Sources for Western Society*, plus LearningCurve formative quizzing; guided reading activities designed to help students read actively for key concepts; autograded quizzes for primary sources; and chapter summative quizzes. Through a wealth of formative and summative assessment, including the adaptive learning program of LearningCurve (see the full description ahead), students gain confidence and get into their reading before class. These features, plus additional primary source documents, video tools for making video assignments, map activities, flashcards, and customizable test banks, make LaunchPad an invaluable asset for any instructor.

LaunchPad easily integrates with course management systems, and with fast ways to build assignments, rearrange chapters, and add new pages, sections, or links, it lets teachers build the courses they want to teach and hold students accountable. For more information, visit **launchpadworks.com**, or to arrange a demo, contact us at **history@macmillan.com**.

Assign LearningCurve So Your Students Come to Class Prepared

Students using LaunchPad receive access to LearningCurve for *A History of Western Society*. Assigning LearningCurve in place of reading quizzes is easy for instructors, and the reporting features help instructors track overall class trends and spot topics that are giving students trouble so they can adjust their lectures and class activities. This online learning tool is popular with students because it was designed to help them rehearse content at their own pace in a nonthreatening, game-like environment. The feedback for wrong answers provides instructional coaching and sends students back to the book for review. Students answer as many questions as necessary to reach a target score, with repeated chances to revisit material they haven't mastered. When LearningCurve is assigned, students come to class better prepared.

Take Advantage of Instructor Resources

Bedford/St. Martin's has developed a rich array of teaching resources for this book and for this course. They range from lecture and presentation materials and assessment tools to course management options. Most can be found in LaunchPad or can be downloaded or ordered at **macmillanlearning.com.**

Bedford Coursepack for Blackboard, Canvas, Brightspace by D2L, or Moodle. We can help you integrate our rich content into your course management system. Registered instructors can download coursepacks that include our popular free resources and book-specific content for *A History of Western Society.*

Instructor's Manual. The *Instructor's Manual* offers both experienced and first-time instructors tools for presenting textbook material in engaging ways. It includes content learning objectives, annotated chapter outlines, and strategies for teaching with the textbook, plus suggestions on how to get the most out of LearningCurve and a survival guide for first-time teaching assistants.

Guide to Changing Editions. Designed to facilitate an instructor's transition from the previous edition of *A History of Western Society* to this new edition, this guide presents an overview of major changes as well as of changes in each chapter.

Online Test Bank. The test bank includes a mix of fresh, carefully crafted multiple-choice, matching, short-answer, and essay questions for each chapter. Many of the multiple-choice questions feature a map, an image, or a primary source excerpt as the prompt. All questions appear in easy-to-use test bank software that allows instructors to add, edit, re-sequence, and print questions and answers. Instructors can also export questions into a variety of course management systems.

The Bedford Lecture Kit: **Lecture Outlines, Maps, and Images.** Look good and save time with *The Bedford Lecture Kit.* These presentation materials include fully customizable multimedia presentations built around chapter outlines that are embedded with maps, figures, and images from the textbook and are supplemented by more detailed instructor notes on key points and concepts.

Print, Digital, and Custom Options for More Choice and Value

For information on free packages and discounts up to 50%, visit **macmillanlearning.com** or contact your local Bedford/St. Martin's sales representative.

Sources for Western Society, **Third Edition.** This primary source collection—available in Volume 1, Volume 2, and Since 1300 versions—provides a revised and expanded selection of sources to accompany *A History of Western Society*, Twelfth Edition. Each chapter features five or six written and visual sources by well-known figures and ordinary individuals alike. With over fifty new selections—including a dozen new visual sources—and enhanced pedagogy throughout, this book gives students the tools to engage critically with canonical and lesser-known sources and prominent and ordinary voices. Each chapter includes a "Sources in Conversation" feature that presents differing views on key topics. This companion reader is an exceptional value for students and offers plenty of assignment options for instructors. Available free when packaged with the print text and included in the LaunchPad e-Book. Also available on its own as a downloadable PDF e-Book.

NEW *Bedford Custom Tutorials for History.* Designed to customize textbooks with resources relevant to individual courses, this collection of brief units, each sixteen pages long and loaded with examples, guides students through basic skills such as using historical evidence effectively, working with primary sources, taking effective notes, avoiding plagiarism and citing sources, and more. Up to two tutorials can be added to a Bedford/St. Martin's history survey title at no additional charge, freeing you to spend your class time focusing on content and interpretation. For <u>more</u> information, visit **macmillanlearning.com/historytutorials.**

The Bedford Series in History and Culture. More than one hundred titles in this highly praised series combine first-rate scholarship, historical narrative, and important primary documents for undergraduate courses. Each book is brief, inexpensive, and focused on a specific topic or period. Revisions of several bestselling titles, such as *The Prince by Niccolò Machiavelli with Related Documents*, edited by William J. Connell; *The Enlightenment: A Brief History with Documents*, by Margaret C. Jacob; *Candide by Voltaire with Related Documents*, edited by Daniel Gordon; and *The French Revolution and Human Rights: A Brief History with Documents*, by Lynn Hunt, are now available. For a complete list of titles, visit **macmillanlearning.com.** Package discounts are available.

Rand McNally Atlas of Western Civilization. This collection of over fifty full-color maps highlights social, political, and cross-cultural change and interaction from classical Greece and Rome to the postindustrial Western world. Each map is thoroughly indexed for fast reference. Free when packaged.

Trade Books. Titles published by sister companies Hill and Wang; Farrar, Straus and Giroux; Henry Holt and Company; St. Martin's Press; Picador; and Palgrave Macmillan are available at a 50% discount when packaged with Bedford/St. Martin's textbooks. For more information, visit **macmillanlearning.com/tradeup.**

A Pocket Guide to Writing in History. This portable and affordable reference tool by Mary Lynn Rampolla provides reading, writing, and research advice useful to students in all history courses. Concise yet comprehensive advice on approaching typical history assignments, developing critical reading skills, writing effective history papers, conducting research, using and documenting sources, and avoiding plagiarism — enhanced with practical tips and examples throughout — has made this slim reference a bestseller. Package discounts are available.

A Student's Guide to History. This complete guide to success in any history course provides the practical help students need to be successful. In addition to introducing students to the nature of the discipline, author Jules Benjamin teaches a wide range of skills from preparing for exams to approaching common writing assignments, and explains the research and documentation process with plentiful examples. Package discounts are available.

The Social Dimension of Western Civilization. Combining current scholarship with classic pieces, this reader's forty-eight secondary sources, compiled by Richard M. Golden, hook students with the fascinating and often surprising details of how everyday Western people worked, ate, played, celebrated, worshipped, married, procreated, fought, persecuted, and died. Package discounts are available.

The West in the Wider World: Sources and Perspectives. Edited by Richard Lim and David Kammerling Smith, the first college reader to focus on the central historical question "How did the West become the West?" offers a wealth of written and visual source materials that reveal the influence of non-European regions on the origins and development of Western Civilization. Package discounts are available.

Brief Contents

Contents

1 Origins
to 1200 B.C.E.   2

photo: Deir el-Medina, Thebes, Egypt/Bridgeman Images

photo: British Museum, London, UK/De Agostini Picture Library/Bridgeman Images

photo: National Archaeological Museum, Athens, Greece/De Agostini Picture Library/G. Dagli Orti/Bridgeman Images

photo: Musée du Louvre, Paris, France/Erich Lessing/Art Resource, NY

photo: Wall painting from the Monterozzi Tomb, 6th–4th century B.C.E./Pictures from History/Bridgeman Images

photo: De Agostini Picture Library/A. Dagli Orti/Bridgeman Images

photo: Trier Cathedral Treasury, Trier, Germany/akg-images/Newscom

10 *Life* in Villages and Cities of the High Middle Ages
1000–1300   284

11 The Later Middle Ages
1300–1450   322

photo: Detail from the mosaic *The Triumph of the Cross*, Basilica of St. Clement, Rome, Italy/De Agostini Picture Library/Gianni Dagli Orti/Bridgeman Images

photo: From *Cas de Nobles Hommes et Femmes*, 1465/Musée Condé, Chantilly, France/Bridgeman Images

12 European Society in the Age of the Renaissance
1350–1550   356

photo: By Lorenzo Lotto (ca. 1480–1556), Church of San Michele al Pozzo Bianco,
Bergamo, Italy/Mauro Ranzani Archive/Alinari Archives/Bridgeman Images

Maps, Figures, and Tables

Maps

Figures and Tables

Special Features

A History of
Western Society

1
Origins

TO 1200 B.C.E.

What is history? That seemingly simple question hides great complexities. If history is the story of humans, what does it mean to be human? As they have in the past, philosophers, religious leaders, politicians, physicians, and others wrestle with this question every day, as do scientists using technologies that were unavailable until very recently, such as DNA analysis and radiocarbon dating. Is all of the human past "history"? Previous generations of historians would generally have answered no, that history only began when writing began and everything before that was "prehistory." This leaves out most of the human story, however, and today historians no longer see writing as such a sharp dividing line. They explore all eras of the human past using many different types of sources, although they do still tend to pay more attention to written sources.

For most of their history, humans were foragers moving through the landscape, inventing ever more specialized tools. About 11,000 years ago, people in some places domesticated plants and animals, which many scholars describe as the most significant change in human history. They began to live in permanent villages, some of which grew into cities. They created structures of governance to control their more complex societies, along with military forces and taxation systems. Some invented writing to record taxes, inventories, and payments, and they later put writing to other uses, including the preservation of stories, traditions, and history. The first places where these new technologies and systems were introduced were the Tigris and Euphrates River Valleys of southwest Asia and the Nile Valley of northeast Africa, areas whose history became linked through trade connections, military conquests, and migrations. ◼

CHAPTER PREVIEW

Life in New Kingdom Egypt, ca. 1500–1300 B.C.E.
In this wall painting from the tomb of an official, a man guides a wooden ox-drawn plow through the soil, while the woman walking behind throws seed in the furrow. The painting was designed not to show real peasants working but to depict the servants who would spring to life to serve the deceased in the afterlife. Nevertheless, the gender division of labor and the plow itself are probably accurate. (Deir el-Medina, Thebes, Egypt/Bridgeman Images)

Understanding Western History

FOCUS QUESTION *What do we mean by "the West" and "Western civilization"?*

Most human groups have left some record of themselves. Some left artifacts, others pictures or signs, and still others written documents. In many of these records, groups set up distinctions between themselves and others. Some of these distinctions are between small groups such as neighboring tribes, some between countries and civilizations, and some between vast parts of the world. Among the most enduring of the latter are the ideas of "the West" and "the East."

Describing the West

Ideas about the West and the distinction between West and East derived originally from the ancient Greeks. Greek civilization grew up in the shadow of earlier civilizations to the south and east of Greece, especially Egypt and Mesopotamia. Greeks defined themselves in relation to these more advanced cultures, which they saw as "Eastern." Greeks were also the first to use the word *Europe* for a geographic area, taking the word from the name of a minor goddess. They set Europe in opposition to "Asia" (also named for a minor goddess), by which they meant both what we now call western Asia and what we call Africa.

The Greeks passed this conceptualization on to the Romans, who saw themselves clearly as part of the West. For some Romans, Greece remained in the West, while other Romans came to view Greek traditions as vaguely "Eastern." To Romans, the East was more sophisticated and more advanced, but also decadent and somewhat immoral. Roman value judgments have continued to shape preconceptions, stereotypes, and views of differences between the West and the East — which in the past were also called the "Occident" and the "Orient" — to this day.

Greco-Roman ideas about the West were passed on to people who lived in western and northern Europe, who saw themselves as the inheritors of this classical tradition and thus as the West. When these Europeans established colonies outside of Europe beginning in the late fifteenth century, they regarded what they were doing as taking Western culture with them, even though many aspects of Western culture, such as Christianity, had actually originated in what Europeans by that point regarded as the East. With coloniza-

tion, *Western* came to mean those cultures that included significant numbers of people of European ancestry, no matter where on the globe they were located.

In the early twentieth century educators and other leaders in the United States became worried that many people, especially young people, were becoming cut off from European intellectual and cultural traditions. They encouraged the establishment of college and university courses focusing on "Western civilization," the first of which was taught at Columbia University in 1919. In designing the course, the faculty included cultures that as far back as the ancient Greeks had been considered Eastern, such as Egypt and Mesopotamia. This conceptualization and the course spread to other colleges and universities, developing into what became known as the introductory Western civilization course, a staple of historical instruction for generations of college students.

After World War II divisions between the West and the East changed again. Now there was a new division between East and West within Europe, with *Western* coming to imply a capitalist economy and *Eastern* the Communist Eastern bloc. Thus, Japan was considered Western, and some Greek-speaking areas of Europe became Eastern. The collapse of communism in the Soviet Union and eastern Europe in the 1980s brought yet another refiguring, with much of eastern Europe joining the European Union, originally a Western organization.

At the beginning of the twenty-first century, *Western* still suggests a capitalist economy, but it also has certain cultural connotations, such as individualism and competition, which some see as negative and others as positive. Islamist radicals often describe their aims as an end to Western cultural, economic, and political influence, though Islam itself is generally described, along with Judaism and Christianity, as a Western monotheistic religion. Thus, throughout its long history, the meaning of "the West" has shifted, but in every era it has meant more than a geographical location.

What Is Civilization?

Just as the meaning of the word *Western* is shaped by culture, so is the meaning of the word *civilization*. In the ancient world, residents of cities generally viewed themselves as more advanced and sophisticated than rural folk — a judgment still made today. They saw themselves as more "civilized," a word that comes from the Latin adjective *civilis*, which refers to a citizen, either of a town or of a larger political unit such as an empire.

This depiction of people as either civilized or uncivilized was gradually extended to whole societies. Beginning in the eighteenth century, European scholars

■ **civilization** A large-scale system of human political, economic, and social organizations; civilizations have cities, laws, states, and often writing.

■ **Paleolithic era** The period of human history up to about 9000 B.C.E., when tools were made from stone and bone and people gained their food through foraging.

described any society in which political, economic, and social organizations operated on a large scale, not primarily through families and kin groups, as a **civilization**. Civilizations had cities; laws that governed human relationships; codes of manners and social conduct that regulated how people were to behave; and scientific, philosophical, and theological beliefs that explained the larger world. Civilizations also had some form of political organization, what political scientists call "the state," through which one group was able to coerce resources out of others to engage in group endeavors, such as building large structures or carrying out warfare. States established armies, bureaucracies, and taxation systems. Generally only societies that used writing were judged to be civilizations, because writing allowed more permanent expression of thoughts, ideas, and feelings. Human societies in which people were nomadic or lived in small villages without formal laws, and in which traditions were passed down orally, were not regarded as civilizations.

Until the middle of the twentieth century, historians often referred to the places where writing and cities developed as "cradles of civilization," proposing a model of development for all humanity patterned on that of an individual life span. However, the idea that all human societies developed (or should develop) on a uniform process from a "cradle" to a "mature" civilization has now been largely discredited, and some historians choose not to use the term *civilization* at all because it could imply that some societies are superior to others.

Just as the notion of "civilization" has been questioned, so has the notion of "Western civilization." Ever since the idea of "Western civilization" was first developed, people have debated what its geographical extent and core values are. Are there certain beliefs, customs, concepts, and institutions that set Western civilization apart from other civilizations, and if so, when and how did these originate? How were these values and practices transmitted over space and time, and how did they change? No civilization stands alone, and each is influenced by its neighbors. Whatever Western civilization was—and is—it has been shaped by interactions with other societies, cultures, and civilizations, but the idea that there are basic distinctions between the West and the rest of the world in terms of cultural values has been very powerful for thousands of

Chronology

ca. 250,000 B.C.E.	*Homo sapiens* evolve in Africa
250,000–9000 B.C.E.	Paleolithic era
9000 B.C.E.	Beginning of the Neolithic; crop raising; domestication of sheep and goats
ca. 7000 B.C.E.	Domestication of cattle; plow agriculture
ca. 5500 B.C.E.	Smelting of copper
ca. 3800 B.C.E.	Establishment of first Mesopotamian cities
ca. 3200 B.C.E.	Development of cuneiform and hieroglyphic writing
ca. 3100 B.C.E.	Unification of Upper and Lower Egypt
ca. 3000 B.C.E.	Development of wheeled transport; beginning of bronze technology
ca. 2500 B.C.E.	Bronze technology becomes common in many areas
ca. 2300 B.C.E.	Establishment of the Akkadian empire
ca. 1800 B.C.E.	Hyksos people begin to settle in the Nile Delta
1792–1750 B.C.E.	Hammurabi rules Babylon
1258 B.C.E.	Peace treaty between Egyptian pharaoh Ramesses II and Hittite king Hattusili III
ca. 1200 B.C.E.	"Bronze Age Collapse"; destruction and drought

A note on dates: This book generally uses the terms B.C.E. (Before the Common Era) and C.E. (Common Era) when giving dates, a system of chronology based on the Christian calendar and now used widely around the world.

years, and it still shapes the way many people, including people in power, view the world.

The Earliest Human Societies

FOCUS QUESTION *How did early human societies develop and create new technologies and cultural forms?*

Scientists who study the history of the earth use a variety of systems to classify and divide time. Geologists and paleontologists divide time into periods that last many millions of years, determined by the movements of continents and the evolution and extinction of plant and animal species. During the nineteenth century, archaeologists coined labels for eras of the human past according to the primary material out of which surviving tools had been made. Thus the earliest human era became the Stone Age, the next era the Bronze Age, and the next the Iron Age. They further divided the Stone Age into the **Paleolithic** (Old Stone) **era**, during which people used stone, bone, and other natural products to make tools and gained food largely by foraging—that is, by gathering plant products, trapping or catching small animals and birds, and hunting larger prey. This was followed by the **Neolithic** (New Stone) **era**, which saw the beginning of agricultural and animal domestication. People around the world adopted agriculture at various times, and some never did, but the transition between the Paleolithic and the Neolithic is usually set at about 9000 B.C.E., the point at which agriculture was first developed.

From the First Hominids to the Paleolithic Era

Using many different pieces of evidence from all over the world, archaeologists, paleontologists, and other scholars have developed a view of human evolution that has a widely shared basic outline, though there are disagreements about details. Sometime between 7 and 6 million years ago in southern and eastern Africa, groups of human ancestors (members of the biological "hominid" family) began to walk upright, which allowed them to carry things. About 3.4 million years ago some hominids began to use naturally occurring objects as tools, and around 2.5 million years ago one group in East Africa began to make simple tools, a feat that was accompanied by, and may have spurred, brain development. Groups migrated into much of Africa, and then into Asia and Europe; by about 600,000 years ago there were hominids throughout much of Afroeurasia.

About 200,000 years ago, again in East Africa, some of these early humans evolved into *Homo sapiens* ("thinking humans"), which had still larger and more complex brains that allowed for symbolic language and better social skills. *Homo sapiens* invented highly specialized tools made out of a variety of materials: barbed fishhooks and harpoons, snares and traps for catching small animals, bone needles for sewing clothing, awls for punching holes in leather, sharpened flint pieces bound to wooden or bone handles for hunting and cutting, and slings for carrying infants. They made regular use of fire for heat, light, and cooking, increasing the range of foods that were easily digestible. They also migrated, first across Africa, and by 70,000 years ago out of Africa into Eurasia. Eventually they traveled farther still, reaching Australia using rafts about 50,000 years ago and the Americas by about 15,000 years ago, or perhaps earlier. They moved into areas where other types of hominids lived, interacting with them and in some cases interbreeding with them. Gradually the other types of hominids became extinct, leaving *Homo sapiens* as the only survivors and the ancestors of all modern humans.

In the Paleolithic period humans throughout the world lived in ways that were similar to one another. Archaeological evidence and studies of modern foragers suggest that people generally lived in small groups of related individuals and moved throughout the landscape in search of food. In areas where food resources were especially rich, such as along seacoasts, they settled more permanently in one place, living in caves or building structures. They ate mostly plants, and much of the animal protein in their diet came from foods gathered or scavenged, such as insects and birds' eggs, rather than hunted directly. Paleolithic peoples did, however, hunt large game. Groups working together forced animals over cliffs, threw spears, and, beginning about 15,000 B.C.E., used bows to shoot projectiles so that they could stand farther away from their prey while hunting.

Paleolithic people were not differentiated by wealth, because in a foraging society it was not advantageous to accumulate material goods. Most foraging societies that exist today, or did so until recently, have some type of division of labor by sex, and also by age. Men are more often responsible for hunting, through which they gain prestige as well as meat, and women for gathering plant and animal products. This may or may not have been the case in the Paleolithic era, or there may have been a diversity of patterns.

Early human societies are often described in terms of their tools, but this misses a large part of the story. Beginning in the Paleolithic era, human beings have expressed themselves through what we would now term the arts or culture: painting and decorating walls and objects, making music, telling stories, dancing alone or in groups. Paleolithic evidence, particularly from after about 50,000 years ago, includes flutes, carvings, jewelry, and amazing paintings done on cave walls and rock outcroppings that depict animals, people, and symbols. Burials, paintings, and objects also suggest that people may have developed ideas about supernatural forces that controlled some aspects of the natural world and the humans in it, what we now term spirituality or religion. Spiritually adept men and women communicated with that unseen world, and objects such as carvings or masks were probably thought to have special healing or protective powers. (See "Evaluating the Evidence 1.1: Paleolithic Venus Figures," at right.)

Total human population grew very slowly during the Paleolithic. One estimate proposes that there were perhaps 500,000 humans in the world about 30,000 years ago. By about 10,000 years ago, this number had grown to 5 million—ten times as many people. This was a significant increase, but it took twenty thousand

■ **Neolithic era** The period after 9000 B.C.E., when people developed agriculture, domesticated animals, and used tools made of stone and wood.

■ **Fertile Crescent** An area of mild climate and abundant wild grain where agriculture first developed, in present-day Lebanon, Israel, Jordan, Turkey, and Iraq.

Paleolithic Venus Figures

Written sources provide evidence about the human past only after the development of writing, allowing us to read the words of people long dead. For most of human history, however, there were no written sources, so we "read" the past through objects. Interpreting written documents is difficult, and interpreting archaeological evidence is even more difficult and often contentious. For example, small stone statues of women with enlarged breasts and buttocks dating from the later Paleolithic period (roughly 33,000–9,000 B.C.E.) have been found in many parts of Europe. These were dubbed "Venus figures" by nineteenth-century archaeologists, who thought they represented Paleolithic standards of female beauty just as the goddess Venus represented classical standards. A reproduction of one of these statues, the six-inch-tall Venus of Lespugue made from a mammoth tusk about 25,000 years ago in southern France, is shown here.

EVALUATE THE EVIDENCE

1. As you look at this statue, does it seem to link more closely with fertility or with sexuality? How might your own situation as a twenty-first-century person shape your answer to this question?
2. Some scholars see Venus figures as evidence that Paleolithic society was egalitarian or female dominated, but others point out that images of female deities or holy figures are often found in religions that deny women official authority. Can you think of examples of the latter? Which point of view seems most persuasive to you?

(Museo Civico Palazzo Chiericati, Vicenza, Italy/De Agostini Picture Library/Alfredo Dagli Orti/Bridgeman Images)

years. The low population density meant that human impact on the environment was relatively small, although still significant.

Planting Crops

Foraging remained the basic way of life for most of human history, and for groups living in extreme environments, such as tundras or deserts, it was the only possible way to survive. In a few especially fertile areas, however, the natural environment provided enough food that people could become more settled. About 15,000 years ago, the earth's climate entered a warming phase, and more parts of the world were able to support sedentary or semi-sedentary groups of foragers. In several of these places, foragers began planting seeds in the ground along with gathering wild grains, roots, and other foodstuffs. By observation, they learned the optimum times and places for planting. They removed unwanted plants through weeding and selected the seeds they planted in order to get crops that had favorable characteristics, such as larger edible parts. Through this human intervention, certain crops became domesticated, that is, modified by selective breeding so as to serve human needs.

Intentional crop planting first developed around 9000 B.C.E. in the area archaeologists call the **Fertile Crescent**, which runs from present-day Lebanon, Israel, and Jordan north to Turkey and then south and east to the Iran-Iraq border. In this area of mild climate, wild barley and wheat were abundant, along with fruit and nut trees, migrating ducks, and herds of gazelles and other animals. Over the next two millennia, intentional crop planting emerged for the most part independently in the Nile River Valley, western Africa, China, India, Papua New Guinea, Mesoamerica, and perhaps other places where the archaeological evidence has not survived.

Why, after living successfully as foragers for tens of thousands of years, did humans in so many parts of the world begin raising crops at about the same time? The answer to this question is not clear, but crop raising may have resulted from population pressures in those parts of the world where the warming climate provided more food through foraging. More food meant lower child mortality and longer life spans, which allowed populations to grow. People then had a choice: they could move to a new area—the solution that people had always relied on when faced with the problem of food scarcity—or they could develop ways to increase the food supply. They chose the latter and began to plant more intensively, beginning cycles of expanding population and intensification of land use that have continued to today.

A very recent archaeological find at Göbekli Tepe in present-day Turkey, at the northern edge of the Fertile Crescent, suggests that cultural factors may have played a role in the development of agriculture. Here, around 9000 B.C.E., hundreds of people came together to build rings of massive, multi-ton elaborately carved limestone pillars, and then covered them with dirt and built more. The people who created this site lived some distance away, where archaeological remains indicate that at the time they first carved the pillars, they ate wild game and plants, not crops. We can only speculate about why so many people expended the effort they did to carve these pillars and raise them into place, but the project may have unintentionally spurred the development of new methods of food production that would allow the many workers to be fed efficiently. Indeed, it is very near here that evidence of the world's oldest domesticated wheat has been discovered. Archaeologists speculate that, at least in this case, the symbolic, cultural, or perhaps religious importance of

the structure can help explain why the people building it changed from foraging to agriculture.

Implications of Agriculture

Whatever the reasons for the move from foraging to agriculture, within several centuries of initial crop planting, people in the Fertile Crescent, parts of China, and the Nile Valley were relying primarily on domesticated food products. They built permanent houses near one another in villages and planted fields around the villages. In addition, they invented storage containers for food, such as pottery made from fired clay and woven baskets.

A field of planted and weeded crops yields ten to one hundred times as much food—measured in calories—as the same area of naturally occurring plants. It also requires much more labor, however, which was provided both by the greater number of people in the community and by those people working longer hours. In contrast to the twenty hours a week foragers spent on obtaining food, farming peoples were often in the fields from dawn to dusk. Early farmers were also less healthy than foragers were; their narrower range of foodstuffs made them more susceptible to disease and nutritional deficiencies, such as anemia, and also made them shorter. Still, farmers came to outnumber foragers, and slowly larger and larger parts of Europe, China, South and Southeast Asia, and Africa became home to farming villages, a dramatic human alteration of the environment.

At roughly the same time that they domesticated certain plants, people also domesticated animals. The earliest animal to be domesticated was the dog, which separated genetically as a subspecies from wolves at least 15,000 years ago and perhaps much earlier. In about 9000 B.C.E., at the same time they began to raise crops, people in the Fertile Crescent domesticated wild goats and sheep, probably using them first for meat, and then for milk, skins, and eventually fleece. They began to breed the goats and sheep selectively for qualities that they wanted, including larger size, greater strength, better coats, increased milk production, and more even temperaments. Sheep and goats allow themselves to be herded, and people developed a new form of living, **pastoralism**, based on herding and raising livestock; sometimes people trained dogs to assist them. Eventually other grazing animals, including cattle, camels, horses, yak, and reindeer, also became the basis of pastoral economies in Central and West Asia, many parts of Africa, and far northern Europe.

Crop raising and pastoralism brought significant changes to human ways of life, but the domestication of certain large animals had an even bigger impact. Cattle and water buffalo were domesticated in some parts of Asia and North Africa, in which they occurred

Pillar at Göbekli Tepe The huge limestone pillars arranged in rings at the Paleolithic site Göbekli Tepe are somewhat humanoid in shape, and the carvings are of dangerous animals, including lions, boars, foxes, snakes, vultures, and scorpions. The structure required enormous skill and effort of the people who built it, and clearly had great importance to them. (Vincent J. Musi/National Geographic Creative)

naturally, by at least 7000 B.C.E. Donkeys were domesticated by about 4000 B.C.E., and horses by about 2500 B.C.E. All these animals can be trained to carry people or burdens on their backs and pull against loads dragged behind them, two qualities that are rare among the world's animal species. The domestication of large animals dramatically increased the power available to humans to carry out their tasks, which had both an immediate effect in the societies in which this happened and a long-term effect when these societies later encountered other societies in which human labor remained the only source of power.

Sometime in the seventh millennium B.C.E., people attached wooden sticks to frames that animals dragged through the soil, thus breaking it up and allowing seeds to sprout more easily. These simple scratch plows, pulled by cattle and water buffalo, allowed Neolithic people to produce a significant amount of surplus food, which meant that some people in the community could spend their days performing other tasks, increasing the division of labor. Surplus food had to be stored, and some people began to specialize in making products for storage, such as pots, baskets, bags, bins, and other kinds of containers. Others specialized in making tools, houses, and other items needed in village life or for producing specific types of food. Families and households became increasingly interdependent, trading food for other commodities or services.

The division of labor allowed by plow agriculture contributed to the creation of social hierarchies, that is, the divisions between rich and poor, elites and common people, that have been a central feature of human society since the Neolithic era. Although no written records were produced during this era, archaeological evidence provides some clues about how the hierarchies might have developed. Villagers needed more complex rules about how food was to be distributed and how different types of work were to be valued than did foragers. Certain individuals must have begun to specialize in the determination and enforcement of these rules, and informal structures of power gradually became more formalized. Religious specialists probably developed more elaborate rituals to celebrate life passages and to appeal to the gods for help in times of difficulty, such as illness.

Individuals who were the heads of large families or kin groups had control over the labor of others, and this power became more significant when that labor brought material goods that could be stored. The ability to control the labor of others could also come from physical strength, a charismatic personality, or leadership talents, and such traits may also have led to greater wealth. Material goods — plows, sheep, cattle, sheds, pots, carts — gave one the ability to amass still more material goods, and the gap between those who had them and those who did not widened. Social hierar-

chies were reinforced over generations as children inherited goods and status from their parents. By the time writing was invented, social distinctions between elites — rulers, nobles, hereditary priests, and other privileged groups — and the rest of the population were already in existence.

Along with hierarchies based on wealth and power, the development of agriculture was intertwined with a hierarchy based on gender. In many places, plow agriculture came to be a male task, perhaps because of men's upper-body strength or because plow agriculture was difficult to combine with care for infants and small children. Men's responsibility for plowing and other agricultural tasks took them outside the household more often than women's duties did, enlarging their opportunities for leadership. This role may have led to their being favored as inheritors of family land and the right to farm communally held land, because when inheritance systems were established in later millennia, they often favored sons when handing down land. Accordingly, over generations, women's independent access to resources decreased.

The system in which men have more power and access to resources than women of the same social level, and in which some men are dominant over other men, is called **patriarchy** and is found in every society with written records, although the level of inequality varies. Men's control of property was rarely absolute, because the desire to keep wealth and property within a family or kin group often resulted in women's inheriting, owning, and in some cases managing significant amounts of wealth. Hierarchies of wealth and power thus intersected with hierarchies of gender in complex ways.

Trade and Cross-Cultural Connections

By 7000 B.C.E. or so, some agricultural villages in the Fertile Crescent may have had as many as ten thousand residents. One of the best known of these, Çatal Hüyük in what is now Turkey, shows evidence of trade as well as specialization of labor. Çatal Hüyük's residents lived in densely packed mud-brick houses with walls covered in white plaster that had been made with burned lime. The men and women of the town grew wheat, barley, peas, and almonds and raised sheep and perhaps cattle, though they also seem to have hunted. They made textiles, pots, figurines, baskets, carpets, copper and lead beads, and other goods, and decorated their houses with murals showing animal and human figures. They gathered, sharpened, and polished

■ **pastoralism** An economic system based on herding flocks of goats, sheep, cattle, or other animals beneficial to humans.

■ **patriarchy** A society in which most power is held by older adult men, especially those from the elite groups.

The Iceman

On September 19, 1991, two German vacationers climbing in the Italian Alps came upon a corpse lying facedown and covered in ice. Scientists determined that the Iceman, as the corpse is generally known, died 5,300 years ago. He was between twenty-five and thirty-five years old at the time of his death, and he stood about five feet two inches tall. An autopsy revealed much about the man and his culture. The bluish tinge of his teeth showed a diet of milled grain, which proves that he came from an environment where crops were grown. The Iceman hunted as well as farmed: he was found with a bow and arrows and shoes of straw, and he wore a furry cap and a robe of animal skins that had been stitched together with thread made from grass.

The equipment discovered with the Iceman demonstrates that his people mastered several technologies. He carried a hefty copper ax, made by someone with a knowledge of metallurgy. In his quiver were numerous wooden arrow shafts and two finished arrows. The arrows had sharpened flint heads and feathers attached to the ends of the shafts with resin-like glue. Apparently the people of his culture knew the value of feathers to direct the arrows, and thus had mastered the basics of ballistics. His bow was made of yew, a relatively rare wood in central Europe that is among the best for archers.

Yet a mystery still surrounds the Iceman. When his body was first discovered, scholars assumed that he was a hapless traveler overtaken in a fierce snowstorm. But the autopsy found an arrowhead lodged under his left shoulder. The Iceman was not alone on his last day. Someone was with him, and that someone had shot him from below and behind. The Iceman is the victim in the first murder mystery of Western civilization, and the case will never be solved.

QUESTIONS FOR ANALYSIS

1. What does the autopsy of the corpse indicate about the society in which the Iceman lived?
2. How do the objects found with the Iceman support the generalizations about Neolithic society in this chapter?

The artifacts found with the body tell scientists much about how the Iceman lived. The Iceman's cap, made of bearskin pieces stitched together with sinew, was worn with the fur on the outside. He also had a coat made out of domestic goatskin, in which light and dark stripes alternated in a striking pattern. (discovery of corpse: Paul Hanny/Gamma-Rapho via Getty Images; quiver: S.N.S./Sipa Press; cap and ax: South Tyrol Museum of Archeology, Bolzano, Italy/Wolfgang Neeb/Bridgeman Images)

obsidian, a volcanic rock that could be used for knives, blades, and mirrors, and then traded it with neighboring towns, obtaining seashells and flint. From here the obsidian was exchanged still farther away, for Neolithic societies slowly developed local and then regional networks of exchange and communication.

Among the goods traded in some parts of the world was copper, which people hammered into shapes for jewelry and tools. Like most metals, in its natural state copper usually occurs mixed with other materials in a type of rock called ore, and by about 5500 B.C.E. people in the Balkans had learned that copper could be extracted from ore by heating it in a smelting process. Smelted copper was poured into molds and made into spear points, axes, chisels, beads, and other objects. (See "Living in the Past: The Iceman," at left.) Pure copper is soft, but through experimentation artisans learned that it would become harder if they mixed it with other metals such as zinc, tin, or arsenic during heating, creating an alloy called bronze.

Because it was stronger than copper, bronze had a far wider range of uses, so much so that later historians decided that its adoption marked a new period in human history: the **Bronze Age**. Like all new technologies, bronze arrived at different times in different places, so the dates of the Bronze Age vary. It began about 3000 B.C.E. in some places, and by about 2500 B.C.E. bronze technology was having an impact in many parts of the world. The end of the Bronze Age came with the adoption of iron technology, which also varied from 1200 B.C.E. to 300 B.C.E. (see Chapter 2). All metals were expensive and hard to obtain, however, so stone, wood, and bone remained important materials for tools and weapons long into the Bronze Age.

Objects were not the only things traded over increasingly long distances during the Neolithic period, for people also carried ideas as they traveled on foot, boats, or camels, and in wagons or carts. Knowledge about the seasons and the weather was vitally important for those who depended on crop raising, and agricultural peoples in many parts of the world began to calculate recurring patterns in the world around them, slowly developing calendars. Scholars have demonstrated that people built circular structures of mounded earth or huge upright stones to help them predict the movements of the sun and stars, including Nabta Playa, erected about 4500 B.C.E. in the desert west of the Nile Valley in Egypt, and Stonehenge, erected about 2500 B.C.E. in southern England.

The rhythms of the agricultural cycle and patterns of exchange also shaped religious beliefs and practices. Among foragers, human fertility is a mixed blessing, as too many children can overtax food supplies, but among crop raisers and pastoralists, fertility—of the land, animals, and people—is essential. Thus in many places multiple gods came to be associated with

patterns of birth, growth, death, and regeneration in a system known as **polytheism**. Like humans, the gods came to have a division of labor and a social hierarchy. There were rain-gods and sun-gods, sky goddesses and moon goddesses, gods that ensured the health of cattle or the growth of corn, goddesses of the hearth and home.

Civilization in Mesopotamia

FOCUS QUESTION *What kind of civilization did the Sumerians develop in Mesopotamia?*

The origins of Western civilization are generally traced to an area that is today not seen as part of the West: Mesopotamia (mehs-oh-puh-TAY-mee-uh), the Greek name for the land between the Euphrates (yoo-FRAY-teez) and Tigris (TIGH-grihs) Rivers (Map 1.1). The earliest agricultural villages in Mesopotamia were in the northern, hilly parts of the river valleys, where there is abundant rainfall for crops. Farmers had brought techniques of crop raising southward by about 5000 B.C.E., to the southern part of Mesopotamia, called Sumer. In this arid climate farmers developed irrigation on a large scale, which demanded organized group effort, but allowed the population to grow. By about 3800 B.C.E., one of the agricultural villages, Uruk (OO-rook), had expanded significantly, becoming what many historians view as the world's first city, with a population that eventually numbered more than fifty thousand. People living in Uruk built large temples to honor their chief god and goddess, and also invented the world's first system of writing, through which they recorded information about their society. Over the next thousand years, other cities also grew in Sumer, trading with one another and adopting writing.

Environment and Mesopotamian Development

From the outset, geography had a profound effect on Mesopotamia, because here agriculture is possible only with irrigation. Consequently, the Sumerians and later civilizations built their cities along the Tigris and Euphrates Rivers and their branches. They used the rivers to carry agricultural and trade goods, and also to provide water for vast networks of irrigation channels.

The Tigris and Euphrates flow quickly at certain times of the year and carry silt down from the mountains and hills, causing floods. To prevent major floods, the Sumerians created massive hydraulic projects, including reservoirs, dams, and dikes as well as canals. In stories written later, they described their chief god,

---

■ **Bronze Age** The period in which the production and use of bronze implements became basic to society.

■ **polytheism** The worship of many gods and goddesses.

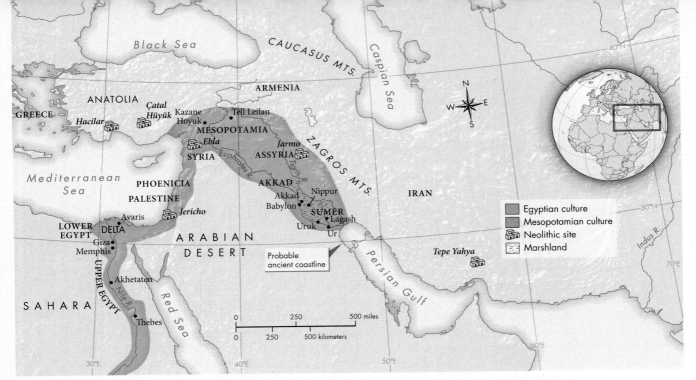

MAP 1.1 Spread of Cultures in the Ancient Near East, ca. 3000–1640 B.C.E.   This map illustrates the spread of the Mesopotamian and Egyptian cultures through the semicircular stretch of land often called the Fertile Crescent. From this area, the knowledge and use of agriculture spread throughout western Asia, North Africa, and Europe.

Enlil, as "the raging flood which has no rival," and believed that at one point there had been a massive flood, a tradition that also gave rise to the biblical story of Noah:

> A flood will sweep over the cult-centers;
> To destroy the seed of mankind . . .
> Is the decision, the word of the assembly of the gods.[1]

Judging by historical records, however, actual destructive floods were few.

In addition to water and transport, the rivers supplied fish, a major element of the Sumerian diet, and reeds, which were used for making baskets and writing implements. The rivers also provided clay, which was hardened to create bricks, the Sumerians' primary building material in a region with little stone. Clay was fired into pots, and inventive artisans developed the potter's wheel so that they could make pots that were stronger and more uniform than those made by earlier methods of coiling ropes of clay. The potter's wheel in turn appears to have led to the introduction of wheeled vehicles sometime in the fourth millennium B.C.E. Exactly where they were invented is hotly contested, but Sumer is one of the first locations in which they appeared. Wheeled vehicles, pulled by domesticated donkeys, led to road building, which facilitated settlement, trade, and conquest, although travel and transport by water remained far easier.

Cities and villages in Sumer and farther up the Tigris and Euphrates traded with one another, and even before the development of writing or kings, it appears that colonists sometimes set out from one city to travel hundreds of miles to the north or west to found a new city or to set up a community in an existing center. These colonies might well have provided the Sumerian cities with goods, such as timber and metal ores, that were not available locally. The cities of the Sumerian heartland continued to grow and to develop governments, and each one came to dominate the surrounding countryside, becoming city-states independent from one another, though not very far apart.

The city-states of Sumer continued to rely on irrigation systems that required cooperation and at least some level of social and political cohesion. The authority to run this system was, it seems, initially assumed by Sumerian priests. Encouraged and directed by their religious leaders, people built temples on tall platforms in the center of their cities. Temples grew into elaborate complexes of buildings with storage space for grain and other products and housing for animals. (Much later, by about 2100 B.C.E., some of the major temple complexes were embellished with a huge stepped pyramid, called a ziggurat, with a shrine on the top.) The Sumerians believed that humans had been created to serve the gods, who lived in the temples. The gods needed not only shelter but food, drink, and clothing. Surrounding the temple and other large buildings were the houses of ordinary citizens, each constructed around a central courtyard. To support the needs of the gods, including the temple con-

■ **cuneiform** Sumerian form of writing; the term describes the wedge-shaped marks made by a stylus.

structions, and to support the religious leaders, temples owned large estates, including fields and orchards. Temple officials employed individuals to work the temple's land, paying the workers in rations of grain, oil, and wool.

By 2500 B.C.E. there were more than a dozen city-states in Sumer. Each city developed religious, political, and military institutions, and judging by the fact that people began to construct walls around the cities and other fortifications, warfare between cities was quite common. Presumably their battles were sometimes sparked by disputes over water, as irrigation in one area reduced or altered the flow of rivers in other areas.

The Invention of Writing and the First Schools

The origins of writing probably go back to the ninth millennium B.C.E., when Near Eastern peoples used clay tokens as counters for record keeping. By the fourth millennium, people had realized that impressing the tokens on clay, or drawing pictures of the tokens on clay, was simpler than making tokens. This breakthrough in turn suggested that more information could be conveyed by adding pictures of still other objects. The result was a complex system of pictographs in which each sign pictured an object, such as "star" (line A of Figure 1.1). These pictographs were the forerunners of the Sumerian form of writing known as **cuneiform** (kyou-NEE-uh-form), from the Latin term for "wedge shaped," used to describe the indentations made by a sharpened stylus in clay.

Scribes could combine pictographs to express meaning. For example, the sign for woman (line B) and the sign for mountain (line C) were combined, literally, into "mountain woman" (line D), which meant "slave woman" because the Sumerians regularly obtained their slave women from wars against enemies

in the mountains. Pictographs were initially limited in that they could not represent abstract ideas, but the development of ideograms—signs that represented ideas—made writing more versatile. Thus the sign for star could also be used to indicate heaven, sky, or even god. The real breakthrough came when scribes started using signs to represent sounds. For instance, the symbol for "water" (two parallel wavy lines) could also be used to indicate "in," which sounded the same as the spoken word for "water" in Sumerian.

The development of the Sumerian system of writing was piecemeal, with scribes making changes and additions as they were needed. The system became so complicated that scribal schools were established, which by 2500 B.C.E. flourished throughout Sumer. Students at the schools were all male, and most came from families

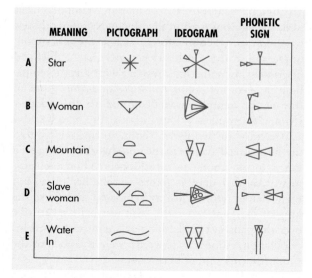

	MEANING	PICTOGRAPH	IDEOGRAM	PHONETIC SIGN
A	Star			
B	Woman			
C	Mountain			
D	Slave woman			
E	Water In			

FIGURE 1.1 Sumerian Writing
(Source: S. N. Kramer, *The Sumerians: Their History, Culture and Character.* Copyright © 1963 by The University of Chicago Press. All rights reserved. Used by permission.)

in the middle range of urban society. Each school had a master, teachers, and monitors. Discipline was strict, and students were caned for sloppy work and misbehavior. One graduate of a scribal school had few fond memories of the joy of learning:

> My headmaster read my tablet, said:
> "There is something missing," caned me.
>
> . . .
>
> The fellow in charge of silence said:
> "Why did you talk without permission,"
>   caned me.
> The fellow in charge of the assembly said:
> "Why did you stand at ease without permission,"
>   caned me.[2]

Scribal schools were primarily intended to produce individuals who could keep records of the property of temple officials, kings, and nobles. Thus writing first developed as a way to enhance the growing power of elites, not to record speech, although it later came to be used for that purpose, and the stories of gods, kings, and heroes were also written down. Hundreds of thousands of hardened clay tablets have survived from ancient Mesopotamia, and from them historians have learned about many aspects of life, including taxes and wages. Sumerians wrote numbers as well as words on clay tablets, and some surviving tablets show multiplication and division problems.

Mathematics was not just a theoretical matter to the people living in Mesopotamia, because the building of cities, palaces, temples, and canals demanded practical knowledge of geometry and trigonometry.

Religion in Mesopotamia

To Sumerians, and to later peoples in Mesopotamia as well, the world was controlled by gods and goddesses, who represented cosmic forces such as the sun, moon, water, and storms. Each city generally had a chief god or goddess, or sometimes several, with a large temple built in his or her honor. In Uruk, for example, one of the central temples was dedicated to the goddess Inanna, the goddess of love and sexuality, who was also associated with the planet Venus. In one widely told myth, Inanna descends to the underworld, setting off a long struggle among her worshippers to find a replacement. Another deity is found to take her place, but then Inanna returns, just as Venus sets and rises. The king of the gods was Enlil, who was believed to rule over the gods just as the king of a city-state ruled his population. Almost as powerful were the gods of the sun, of storms, and of freshwater.

The gods judged good and evil and would punish humans who lied or cheated. Gods themselves suffered for their actions, and sometimes for no reason at all,

just as humans did. People believed that humans had been created to serve the gods and generally anticipated being well treated by the gods if they served them well. The best way to honor the gods was to make the temple as grand and impressive as possible, because the temple's size demonstrated the strength of the community and the power of its chief deity. Once it was built, the temple itself, along with the shrine on the top of the ziggurat, was often off-limits to ordinary people, who did not worship there as a spiritual community. Instead the temple was staffed by priests and priestesses who carried out rituals to honor the god or goddess. Kings and other political leaders might also visit the temple and carry out religious ceremonies from time to time, particularly when they thought the assistance of the gods was especially needed.

The peoples of Mesopotamia had many myths to account for the creation of the universe. According to one told by the Babylonians, in the beginning was the primeval sea, known as the goddess Tiamat, who gave birth to the gods. When Tiamat tried to destroy the gods, Marduk, the chief god of the Babylonians, proceeded to kill her and divide her body and thus created the sky and earth. These myths are the earliest known attempts to answer the question, how did it all begin?

Stories about the gods traveled with people when they moved up and down the rivers, so that gods often acquired new names and new characteristics over the centuries. Myths and stories about them were not written down until long after they had first been told, and often had many variations. Written texts were not an important part of Sumerian religious life, nor were they central to the religious practices of most of the other peoples in this region.

In addition to stories about gods, the Sumerians also told stories about heroes and kings, many of which were eventually reworked into the world's first epic poem, the *Epic of Gilgamesh* (GIL-guh-mesh), which was later written down in Akkadian. An epic poem is a narration of the achievements, the labors, and sometimes the failures of heroes that embodies peoples' ideas about themselves. Historians can use epic poems to learn about various aspects of a society, and to that extent epics can be used as historical sources. The epic recounts the wanderings of Gilgamesh—the semihistorical king of Uruk—and his search for eternal life, and it grapples with enduring questions about life and death, friendship, humankind and deity, and immortality. (See "Evaluating the Evidence 1.2: Gilgamesh's Quest for Immortality," page 16.)

Sumerian Politics and Society

Exactly how kings emerged in Sumerian society is not clear. Scholars have suggested that during times of emergencies, a chief priest or perhaps a military leader assumed what was supposed to be temporary authority over a city. He established an army, trained it, and led it into battle. Temporary power gradually became permanent kingship, and sometime before 2450 B.C.E. kings in some Sumerian city-states began transferring their kingship to their sons, establishing patriarchal hereditary dynasties in which power was handed down through the male line. This is the point at which written records about kingship began to appear. The symbol of royal status was the palace, which came to rival the temple in grandeur.

Military leaders were sometimes able to conquer other cities, and in about 2350 B.C.E. Lugalzagesi, king of the city of Umma, conquered a number of other city-states and created a more unified state. Eventually he conquered Uruk as well, and declared in a long inscription that the god Enlil had given him a realm that extended from the Mediterranean to the Persian Gulf. Like many later rulers in all parts of the world, Lugalzagesi claimed territory far beyond what he actually held.

Kings made alliances with other powerful individuals, often through marriage. Royal family members were depended upon for many aspects of government. Kings worked closely with religious authorities and relied on ideas about the kings' connections with the gods, as well as the kings' military might, for their power. Royal children, both sons and daughters, were sometimes priests and priestesses in major temples. Acting together, priests, kings, and officials in Sumerian cities used force, persuasion, and taxation to maintain order, keep the irrigation systems working, and keep food and other goods flowing.

The king and his officials held extensive tracts of land, as did the temple; these lands were worked by the palace's or the temple's clients, free men and women who were dependent on the palace or the temple. They received crops and other goods in return for their labor. Although this arrangement assured the clients of a livelihood, the land they worked remained the possession of the palace or the temple. Some individuals and families owned land outright and paid their taxes in the form of agricultural products or items they made. At the bottom rung of society were slaves. Slavery predates written records, so like many other aspects of social hierarchies, we are not sure exactly how and when people first began to own other people. Like animals, slaves were a source of physical power for their owners, providing them an opportunity to amass more wealth and influence. Some Sumerian slaves were most likely prisoners of war and criminals who had lost their free-

Mesopotamian Harpist This small clay tablet, carved between 2000 B.C.E. and 1500 B.C.E., shows a seated woman playing a harp. Her fashionable dress and hat suggest that she is playing for wealthy people, perhaps at the royal court. Images of musicians are common in Mesopotamian art, indicating music was important in Mesopotamian culture and social life. (Musée du Louvre, Paris/Erich Lessing/Art Resource, NY)

dom as punishment for their crimes; others perhaps came into slavery to repay debts. Compared to many later societies, slaves were not widely used in Sumer, where most agricultural work was done by dependent clients. Slaves in Sumer also engaged in trade and made profits. They could borrow money, and many slaves were able to buy their freedom.

Each of the social categories included both men and women, but their experiences were not the same, for Sumerian society made distinctions based on gender. Most elite landowners were male, but women who held positions as priestesses or as queens ran their own estates, independently of their husbands and fathers. Some women owned businesses and took care of their own accounts. They could own property and distribute it to their offspring. Sons and daughters inherited from their parents, although a daughter received her inheritance in the form of a dowry, which technically remained hers but was managed by her husband or husband's family after marriage. The Sumerians established the basic social, economic, and intellectual patterns of Mesopotamia, and they influenced their neighbors to the north and east.

Empires in Mesopotamia

FOCUS QUESTION *How did the Akkadian and Old Babylonian empires develop in Mesopotamia?*

The wealth of Sumerian cities also attracted non-Sumerian conquerors from the north, beginning with the Akkadians and then the Babylonians. Both of these peoples created large states in the valley of the Tigris and Euphrates. Hammurabi, one ruler of Babylon, proclaimed an extensive law code. Merchants traveled throughout the Fertile Crescent and beyond, carrying products and facilitating cultural exchange.

Gilgamesh's Quest for Immortality

The human desire to escape the grip of death appears in many cultures. The Epic of Gilgamesh is perhaps the earliest recorded treatment of this topic. The oldest elements of the epic go back to stories told in the third millennium B.C.E. According to tradition, Gilgamesh was a king of the Sumerian city of Uruk. In the story, Gilgamesh is not fulfilling his duties as the king very well and sets out with his friend Enkidu to perform wondrous feats against fearsome agents of the gods. Together they kill several supernatural beings, and the gods decide that Enkidu must die. He foresees his own death in a dream.

Listen again, my friend [Gilgamesh]! I had a dream in the
    night.
The sky called out, the earth replied,
I was standing in between them.
There was a young man, whose face was obscured.
His face was like that of an Anzu-bird.
He had the paws of a lion, he had the claws of an eagle.
He seized me by my locks, using great force against
    me. . . .
He seized me, drove me down to the dark house, dwelling
    of Erkalla's god [the underworld], . . .
On the road where travelling is one way only,
To the house where those who stay are deprived of
    light. . . .

Enkidu sickens and dies. Gilgamesh is distraught and determined to become immortal. He decides to journey to Ut-napishtim and his wife, the only humans who have eternal life. Everyone he meets along the way asks him about his appearance, and Gilgamesh always answers with the same words:

How could my cheeks not be wasted, nor my face dejected,
Nor my heart wretched, nor my appearance worn out,
Nor grief in my innermost being,
Nor my face like that of a long-distance traveller,
Nor my face weathered by wind and heat
Nor roaming open country clad only in a lionskin?
My friend was the hunted mule, wild ass of the mountain,
    leopard of open country,

Enkidu my friend was the hunted mule, wild ass of the
    mountain, leopard of open country.
We who met, and scaled the mountain,
Seized the Bull of Heaven [the sacred bull of the goddess
    Ishtar] and slew it,
Demolished Humbaba [the ogre who guards the forest of
    the gods] who dwelt in the Pine Forest,
Killed lions in the passes of the mountains,
My friend whom I love so much, who experienced every
    hardship with me,
Enkidu my friend whom I love so much, who experienced
    every hardship with me —
The fate of mortals conquered him!
For six days and seven nights I wept over him: I did not
    allow him to be buried
Until a worm fell out of his nose.
I was frightened and
I am afraid of Death, and so I roam open country.
The words of my friend weigh upon me. . . .
I roam open country on long journeys.
How, O how could I stay silent, how, O how could I keep
    quiet?
My friend whom I love has turned to clay: Enkidu my
    friend whom I love has turned to clay.
Am I not like him? Must I lie down too,
Never to rise, ever again?

Gilgamesh finally reaches Ut-napishtim, to whom he tells his story, and who says to him:

Why do you prolong grief, Gilgamesh?
Since [the gods made you] from the flesh of gods and
    mankind,
Since [the gods] made you like your father and mother
[Death is inevitable] . . . ,
Nobody sees the face of Death,
Nobody hears the voice of Death.
Savage Death just cuts mankind down.
Sometimes we build a house, sometimes we make a nest,
But then brothers divide it upon inheritance.
Sometimes there is hostility in [the land],
But then the river rises and brings flood-water. . . .

The Akkadians and the Babylonians

In 2331 B.C.E. Sargon, the king of a city to the north of Sumer, conquered a number of Sumerian cities with what was probably the world's first permanent army and created a large state. The symbol of his triumph was a new capital, the city of Akkad (AH-kahd). Sargon also expanded the Akkadian empire westward to North Syria, which became the breadbasket of the empire. He encouraged trading networks that brought in goods from as far away as the Indus River and what is now Turkey. Sargon spoke a different language than did the Sumerians, one of the many languages that scholars identify as belonging to the Semitic language family, which includes modern-day Hebrew and Arabic. However, Akkadians adapted cuneiform writing to their own language, and

The Anunnaki, the great gods, assembled;
Mammitum [the great mother goddess] who creates
    fate decreed destinies with them.
They appointed death and life.
They did not mark out days for death,
But they did so for life.

*Gilgamesh asks Ut-napishtim how he and his wife
can be immortal like the gods, if death is inevitable.
Ut-napishtim tells him the story of how they survived a
flood sent by the gods and the chief god Enlil blessed
them with eternal life. Gilgamesh wants this as well,
but fails two opportunities Ut-napishtim provides for
him to achieve it. At the end of the epic, he simply
returns to Uruk with the boatman Ur-shanabi, to
whom he points out the glories of the city:*

Go up on to the wall of Uruk, Ur-shanabi, and walk
    around,
Inspect the foundation platform and scrutinize the
    brickwork! Testify that its bricks are baked bricks,
And that the Seven Counsellors must have laid its
    foundations!
One square mile is city, one square mile is orchards,
    one square mile is claypits, as well as the open
    ground of Ishtar's temple.
Three square miles and the open ground comprise
    Uruk.

EVALUATE THE EVIDENCE

1. What does the *Epic of Gilgamesh* reveal about
   attitudes toward friendship in ancient Mesopotamia?
2. What does the epic tell us about views of the
   nature of human life? Where do human beings fit
   into the cosmic world?
3. Although at the end of his quest, Gilgamesh did
   not achieve personal immortality, how can his
   final words to Ur-shanabi be seen as a tribute to
   long-lasting human endeavors?

Source: *Myths from Mesopotamia: Creation, the Flood, Gilgamesh, and
Others,* trans. Stephanie Dalley (Oxford: Oxford University Press, 1989),
pp. 88–89, 103–104, 107, 108–109, 120. Used by permission of Oxford
University Press.

Victory Stele of Naram-Sin, King of Akkad   On this victory
stele carved from sandstone about 2320 B.C.E., King Naram-Sin,
Sargon's grandson, climbs a mountain above his soldiers and
defeated enemies. Naram-Sin, under whose rule Akkad
reached its largest size, is shown here as a god-king in a
horned helmet, twice the size of the other men. (Musée du Louvre,
Paris, France/De Agostini Picture Library/Gianni Dagli Orti/Bridgeman Images)

Akkadian became the diplomatic language used over
a wide area.

Sargon tore down the defensive walls of Sumerian
cities and appointed his own sons as their rulers to help
him cement his power. He also appointed his daughter, Enheduana (2285–2250 B.C.E.), as high priestess
in the city of Ur. Here she wrote a number of hymns,
especially those in praise of the goddess Inanna, becoming the world's first author to put her name to a
literary composition. (See "Thinking Like a Historian:
Addressing the Gods," page 18.) For hundreds of years
Enheduana's works were copied on clay tablets, which
have been found in several cities in the area, indicating
that people may have recited or read them.

Sargon's dynasty appears to have ruled Mesopotamia for about 150 years, during which time the Tigris
and Euphrates Valleys attracted immigrants from
many places. Then his empire collapsed, in part because of a period of extended drought, and the various
city-states became independent again.

One significant city-state that arose in the wake of
the Akkadian empire was settled by the Amorites
(AM-uh-rites), who migrated in from the west, probably starting during the time of Sargon's empire. The
Amorites were initially nomadic pastoralists, not agriculturalists, but they began to raise crops when they

Addressing the Gods

Hymns and incantations to the gods are among the earliest written texts in Mesopotamia and Egypt, and sculpture and paintings also often show people addressing the gods. The sources here are examples of such works. What ideas about the gods and the way humans should address them are shared in all these sources, and how do ideas in Egypt differ from those in Mesopotamia?

1 **Enheduana's "Exaltation of Inanna."** Enheduana (2285–2250 B.C.E.), the daughter of Sargon of Akkad, was appointed by her father as high priestess in the Sumerian city of Ur, where she wrote a number of literary and religious works that were frequently recopied long after her death, including this hymn to the goddess Inanna.

Your divinity shines in the pure heavens. . . . Your torch lights up the corners of heaven, turning darkness into light. The men and women form a row for you and each one's daily status hangs down before you. Your numerous people pass before you, as before Utu [the sun-god], for their inspection. No one can lay a hand on your precious divine powers; all your divine powers. . . . You exercise full ladyship over heaven and earth; you hold everything in your hand. Mistress, you are magnificent, no one can walk before you. You dwell with great An [the god of the heavens] in the holy resting-place. Which god is like you in gathering together . . . in heaven and earth? You are magnificent, your name is praised, you alone are magnificent!

I am En-hedu-ana, the high priestess of the moon god . . . . Mercy, compassion, care, lenience and homage are yours, and to cause flood storms, to open hard ground and to turn darkness into light. My lady, let me proclaim your magnificence in all lands, and your glory! Let me praise your ways and greatness! Who rivals you in divinity? Who can compare with your divine rites? . . . An and Enlil [the chief god of Sumer] have determined a great destiny for you throughout the entire universe. They have bestowed upon you ladyship in the assembly chamber. Being fitted for ladyship, you determine the destiny of noble ladies. Mistress, you are magnificent, you are great! Inanna, you are magnificent, you are great! My lady, your magnificence is resplendent. May your heart be restored for my sake! Your great deeds are unparalleled, your magnificence is praised! Young woman, Inanna, your praise is sweet!

(British Museum, London, UK/Werner Forman Archive/Bridgeman Images)

2 **Babylonian cylinder seal showing a man addressing the deities.** Dating from the Old Babylonian period (1800–1600 B.C.E.), this seal shows a man (second from left) addressing three deities, the one on the right holding the rod and ring, symbols of authority. The cuneiform inscription reads, "Ibni-Amurru, son of Ilima-ahi, servant of the god Amurru."

3 **Pyramid text of King Unas.** This incantation, designed to assist the king's ascent to the heavens after his death, was inscribed on a wall of the royal burial chambers in the pyramid of the Egyptian king Unas (r. 2375–2345) at Saqqara, a burial ground near the Nile.

Re-Atum [the sun-god], this Unas comes
to you,
A spirit indestructible
Who lays claim to the place of the four pillars!
Your son comes to you, this Unas comes to you
May you cross the sky united in the dark,

ANALYZING THE EVIDENCE

1. In Source 1 from Mesopotamia, what powers and qualities of the goddess Inanna does Enheduana praise? In Source 2, what qualities do the deities in the cylinder seal exhibit?
2. In Sources 3–5 from Egypt, what powers and qualities does the sun-god exhibit?
3. What common features do you see across all the sources in the powers ascribed to the gods, and the proper attitude of humans in addressing them?
4. Continuing to think about similarities, bear in mind that Enheduana was a member of the ruling dynasty of Akkad, and Unas and Akhenaton were kings of Egypt. How did their social position shape their relationship to the gods?
5. Thinking about differences, how is the relationship of Unas and Akhenaton to the sun-god distinctive?

May you rise in lightland, the place in which you
    shine!
Osiris, Isis, go proclaim to Lower Egypt's gods
And their spirits:
"This Unas comes, a spirit indestructible,
Like the morning star above Hapy [the god of the
    flooding of the Nile],
Whom the water-spirits worship;
Whom he wishes to live will live,
Whom he wishes to die will die!"
. . .
Thoth [the god of law and science], go proclaim
    to the gods of the west
And their spirits:
"This Unas comes, a spirit indestructible,
Decked above the neck as Anubis
Lord of the western height
He will count hearts, he will claim hearts,
Whom he wishes to live will live,
Whom he wishes to die will die!"

5 **Relief depicting Akhenaton, Nefertiti, and their daughter, Meritaton, making an offering to Aton.** This carved alabaster relief comes from the royal palace at Tell el-Amarna.

(Egyptian National Museum, Cairo, Egypt/Bridgeman Images)

4 **Hymn to Aton.** When the pharaoh Akhenaton (r. 1351–1334 B.C.E.) promoted the worship of the sun-god Aton instead of older Egyptian gods, new hymns were written for the pharaoh to sing in honor of the god.

Thou appearest beautifully on the horizon of heaven
Thou living Aton, the beginning of life!
When thou art risen on the eastern horizon,
Thou hast filled every land with thy beauty.
Thou art gracious, great, glistening, and high over every land;
Thy rays encompass the lands to the limit of all that thou hast made
. . .
Thy rays suckle every meadow.
When thou risest, they live, they grow for thee.
Thou makest the seasons in order to rear all that thou hast made,
The winter to cool them,
And the heat that they may taste thee.
Thou hast made the distant sky in order to rise therein,
In order to see all that thou dost make.
While thou wert alone,
Rising in thy form as the living Aton,

Appearing, shining, withdrawing or approaching,
Thou madest millions of forms of thyself alone.
Cities, towns, fields, road, and river —
Every eye beholds thee over against them,
For thou art the Aton of the day over the earth . . .
Thou art in my heart,
And there is no other that knows thee
Save thy son Nefer-kheperu-Re Wa-en-Re [Akhenaton],
For thou hast made him well versed in thy plans and in thy
    strength . . .
Since thou didst found the earth
And raise them up for thy son
Who came forth from thy body:
The king of Upper and lower Egypt, . . . Akhenaton . . . and the
    Chief Wife of the King . . . Nefertiti, living and youthful forever
    and ever.

PUTTING IT ALL TOGETHER

Using the sources above, along with what you have learned in class and in this chapter, write a short essay that compares ideas about the gods in Mesopotamia and Egypt. How do these reflect the physical environment in which these two cultures developed, and how do they reflect their social and political structures?

Sources: (1) J. A. Black et al., *Electronic Text Corpus of Sumerian Literature* (http://etcsl.orinst.ox.ac.uk/), Oxford 1998–2006, http://etcsl.orinst.ox.ac.uk/cgi-bin/ etcsl.cgi?text=t.4.07.3#. Used by permission of Oxford University, ETCSL Project; (3) Miriam Lichtheim, *Ancient Egyptian Literature: A Book of Readings*, vol. 1, *The Old and Middle Kingdoms* (Berkeley: University of California Press, 1973), p. 31. © 2006 by the Regents of the University of California. Published by the University of California Press; (4) John A. Wilson, trans., in James B. Pritchard, ed., *Ancient Near Eastern Texts Relating to the Old Testament — Third Edition with Supplement*, pp. 370–371. Reproduced with permission of PRINCETON UNIVERSITY PRESS, in the format Book via Copyright Clearance Center.

settled throughout Mesopotamia. One group of Amorites made their home in the city of Babylon along the middle Euphrates, where that river runs close to the Tigris. Positioned to dominate trade on both the Tigris and Euphrates Rivers, the city grew great because of its commercial importance and the sound leadership of a dynasty of Amorite rulers. Like other Amorite kingdoms of the time, Babylon was more than a city-state. It included smaller kingdoms whose rulers recognized the king of Babylon as their overlord.

Life Under Hammurabi

Hammurabi of Babylon (r. 1792–1750 B.C.E.) was initially a typical king of his era. As ruler of Babylon, he fought some of his neighbors, created treaties with others, taxed his people, expanded the city walls, and built temples. After he had ruled for thirty years, Babylon was attacked, and one of Hammurabi's allies did not provide the assistance he expected. Hammurabi defeated the attackers and also conquered his former ally and several other kingdoms, thus uniting most of Mesopotamia under his rule. The era from his reign to around 1595 B.C.E. is called the Old Babylonian period.

As had earlier rulers, Hammurabi linked his success with the will of the gods. He connected himself with the sun-god Shamash, the god of law and justice, and encouraged the spread of myths that explained how Marduk, the primary god of Babylon, had been elected king of the gods by the other deities in Mesopotamia. Marduk later became widely regarded as the chief god

of Mesopotamia, absorbing the qualities and powers of other gods.

Hammurabi's most memorable accomplishment was the proclamation of an extensive law code, introduced about 1755 B.C.E. Hammurabi's was not the first law code in Mesopotamia; the earliest goes back to about 2100 B.C.E. Like the codes of the earlier lawgivers, **Hammurabi's law code** proclaimed that he issued his laws on divine authority "to establish law and justice in the language of the land, thereby promoting the welfare of the people." Hammurabi's code set a variety of punishments for breaking the law, including fines and physical punishment such as mutilation, whipping, and burning.

Hammurabi's code provides a wealth of information about daily life in Mesopotamia, although, like all law codes, it prescribes what the lawgivers hope will be the situation rather than providing a description of real life. We cannot know if its laws were enforced, but we can use it to see what was significant to people in Hammurabi's society. Because of farming's fundamental importance, the code dealt extensively with agriculture. Tenants faced severe penalties for neglecting the land or not working it at all. Since irrigation was essential to grow crops, tenants had to keep the canals and ditches in good repair. Anyone whose neglect of the canals resulted in damaged crops had to bear all the expense of the lost crops. Those tenants who could not pay the costs were forced into slavery.

Hammurabi gave careful attention to marriage and the family. As elsewhere in the Near East, marriage had aspects of a business agreement. The groom or his father offered the prospective bride's father a gift, and if this was acceptable, the bride's father provided his daughter with a dowry. As in Sumer, after marriage the dowry belonged to the woman (although the husband normally administered it) and was a means of protecting her rights and status. No marriage was considered legal without a contract, and although either party could break off the marriage, the cost was a stiff penalty. Fathers often contracted marriages while their children were still young, and once contracted, the children were considered to be wed even if they did not live together. Men were not allowed to take a second wife unless the first wife could not bear children or had a severe illness.

The penalty for adultery, defined as sex between a married woman and a man not her husband, was

Law Code of Hammurabi   Hammurabi ordered his code to be inscribed on stone pillars and set up in public throughout the Babylonian empire. At the top of the pillar, Hammurabi (left) is depicted receiving the rod and ring of authority from Shamash, the god of justice. (Musée du Louvre, Paris, France/De Agostini Picture Library/Gianni Dagli Orti/Bridgeman Images)

death. According to Hammurabi's code, "If the wife of a man has been caught while lying with another man, they shall bind them and throw them into the water."[3] A husband had the power to spare his wife by obtaining a pardon for her from the king. He could, however, accuse his wife of adultery even if he had not caught her in the act. In such a case she could try to clear herself, and if she was found innocent, she could take her dowry and leave her husband.

A father could not disinherit a son without just cause, and the code ordered the courts to forgive a son for his first offense. Men could adopt children into their families and include them in their wills, which artisans sometimes did to teach them the family trade, or wealthy landowners sometimes did to pass along land to able younger men, particularly if they had no children of their own.

The Code of Hammurabi demanded that the punishment fit the crime, calling for "an eye for an eye, and a tooth for a tooth," at least among equals. However, a higher-ranking man who physically hurt a commoner or slave, perhaps by breaking his arm or putting out his eye, could pay a fine to the victim instead of having his arm broken or losing his own eye. The fine for breaking an arm or otherwise hurting a commoner was huge—as much as five years' salary for a laborer—and commoners might have preferred to receive this rather than the less tangible recompense of seeing their assailant injured. As long as criminal and victim shared the same social status, however, the victim could demand exact vengeance.

Hammurabi's code began with legal procedure. There were no public prosecutors or district attorneys, so individuals brought their own complaints before the court. Each side had to produce witnesses to support its case. In cases of murder, the accuser had to prove the defendant guilty; any accuser who failed to do so was to be put to death. Another procedural regulation declared that once a judge had rendered a verdict, he could not change it. Anyone accused of witchcraft, even if the charges were not proved, underwent an ordeal by water. The defendant was thrown into the Euphrates, which was considered the instrument of the gods. A defendant who sank was guilty; a defendant who survived was innocent.

Consumer protection is not a modern idea; it goes back to Hammurabi's day. Merchants had to guarantee the quality of their goods and services. A boat builder who did sloppy work had to repair the boat at his own expense. House builders guaranteed their work with their lives. If inhabitants died when a house collapsed, the builder was put to death. A merchant who tried to increase the interest rate on a loan forfeited the entire

amount. In these ways, Hammurabi's laws tried to ensure that consumers got what they paid for and paid a just price.

The practical impact of Hammurabi's code is much debated. There is disagreement about whether it recorded laws already established, promulgated new laws, recorded previous judicial decisions, or simply proclaimed what was just and proper. It is also unknown whether Hammurabi's proclamation was legally binding on the courts. Nevertheless, Hammurabi's code gives historians a valuable view into the lives of the Mesopotamians, and it influenced other law codes of the Near East, including those later written down in Hebrew Scripture.

Cultural Exchange in the Fertile Crescent

Law codes, preoccupied as they are with the problems of society, provide a bleak view of things, but other Mesopotamian documents give a happier glimpse of life. Countless wills and testaments show that husbands habitually left their estates to their wives, who in turn willed the property to their children. Financial documents prove that many women engaged in business without hindrance.

Mesopotamians found their lives lightened by holidays and religious festivals. Traveling merchants brought news from far away and swapped marvelous tales. The Mesopotamians enjoyed a vibrant and creative culture that left its mark on the entire Fertile Crescent. They made significant and sophisticated advances in mathematics using a numerical system based on units of sixty, ten, and six. They also developed the concept of place value—that the value of a number depends on where it stands in relation to other numbers.

Mesopotamian writing and merchandise, along with other aspects of the culture, spread far beyond the Tigris and Euphrates Valleys. Overland trade connected Sumer, Akkad, and Babylon with the eastern Mediterranean coast. Cities here were mercantile centers rich not only in manufactured goods but also in agricultural produce, textiles, and metals. The cities flourished under local rulers. People in Syria and elsewhere in the Middle East used Akkadian cuneiform to communicate in writing with their more distant neighbors. Cultural exchange remained a mixture of adoption and adaptation.

Southern and central Anatolia presented a similar picture of extensive contact between cultures. Major Anatolian cities with large local populations were also home to colonies of traders from Mesopotamia. Thousands of cuneiform tablets testify to centuries of commercial and cultural exchanges with Mesopotamia, and eventually with Egypt, which rose to power in the Nile Valley.

■ **Hammurabi's law code** A proclamation issued by Babylonian king Hammurabi to establish laws regulating many aspects of life.

The Egyptians

FOCUS QUESTION *How did the Egyptians create a prosperous and long-lasting society?*

At about the same time that Sumerian city-states expanded and fought with one another in the Tigris and Euphrates Valleys, a more cohesive state under a single ruler grew in the valley of the Nile River in North Africa. This was Egypt, which for long stretches of history was prosperous and secure behind desert areas on both sides of the Nile Valley. At various times groups migrated into Egypt seeking better lives or invaded and conquered Egypt. Often these newcomers adopted aspects of Egyptian religion, art, and politics, and the Egyptians also carried their traditions with them when they established an empire and engaged in trade.

The Nile and the God-King

The Greek historian and traveler Herodotus (heh-RAHD-uh-tuhs) in the fifth century B.C.E. called Egypt the "gift of the Nile." No other single geographical factor had such a fundamental and profound impact on the shaping of Egyptian life, society, and history as this river. The Nile flooded once a year for a period of several months, bringing fertile soil and moisture for farming, and agricultural villages developed along its banks by at least 6000 B.C.E. Although the Egyptians worried at times that these floods would be too high or too low, they also praised the Nile as a creative and comforting force:

> Hail to thee, O Nile, that issues from the earth
>   and comes to keep Egypt alive! . . .
> He that waters the meadows which Re [Ra]
>   created,
> He that makes to drink the desert . . .
> He who makes barley and brings emmer [wheat]
>   into being . . .
> He who brings grass into being for the cattle . . .
> He who makes every beloved tree to grow . . .
> O Nile, verdant art thou, who makest man and
>   cattle to live.[4]

The Egyptians based their calendar on the Nile, dividing the year into three four-month periods: *akhet* (flooding), *peret* (growth), and *shemu* (harvest). Herodotus, accustomed to the rigors of Greek agricul-

ture, was amazed by the ease with which the Egyptians seemed to raise crops. Egyptian texts, however, paint a different picture, recognizing the unrelenting work entailed in farming and the diseases from which people suffered. One of these was guinea worm disease, a parasitic illness caused by drinking contaminated water, evidence of which has also been found in Egyptian mummies. Treatment for guinea worm today is exactly the same as that recommended in ancient Egyptian medical texts: when the head of the worm emerges from the large blister it causes, wrap the worm around a stick and gradually pull it out.

Through the fertility of the Nile and their own hard work, Egyptians produced an annual agricultural surplus, which in turn sustained a growing and prosperous population. The Nile also unified Egypt. The river was the region's principal highway, promoting communication and trade throughout the valley.

Egypt was fortunate in that it was nearly self-sufficient — it had most of the materials required to address its basic needs. Besides having fertile soil, Egypt possessed enormous quantities of stone, which served as the raw material of architecture and sculpture, and abundant clay for pottery. The raw materials that Egypt lacked were close at hand. The Egyptians could obtain copper from Sinai (SIGH-nigh) and timber from Lebanon, and they traded with peoples farther away to obtain other materials that they needed.

The political power structures that developed in Egypt came to be linked with the Nile. Somehow the idea developed that a single individual, a king, was responsible for the rise and fall of the Nile. This belief came about before the development of writing in Egypt, so, as with the growth of priestly and royal power in Sumer, the precise details of its origins have been lost. The king came to be viewed as a descendant of the gods, and thus as a god himself. (See "Thinking Like a Historian: Addressing the Gods," page 18.)

Political unification most likely proceeded slowly, but stories told about early kings highlighted one who had united Upper Egypt — the upstream valley in the south — and Lower Egypt — the delta area of the Nile that empties into the Mediterranean Sea — into a single kingdom around 3100 B.C.E. In some sources he is called Narmer and in other sources Menes, but his fame as a unifier is the same, whatever his name, and he is generally depicted in carvings and paintings wearing the symbols of the two kingdoms. Historians later divided Egyptian history into dynasties, or families of kings. For modern historical purposes, however, it is more useful to divide Egyptian history into periods (see "Periods of Egyptian History," at right). The political unification of Egypt in the Archaic Period (3100–2660 B.C.E.) ushered in the period known as the Old Kingdom (2660–2180 B.C.E.), an era remarkable for prosperity and artistic flowering.

■ **pharaoh** The title given to the king of Egypt in the New Kingdom, from a word that meant "great house."

■ **ma'at** The Egyptian belief in a cosmic harmony that embraced truth, justice, and moral integrity; it gave the kings the right and duty to govern.

Periods of Egyptian History

Dates	Period	Significant Events
3100–2660 B.C.E.	**Archaic**	Unification of Egypt
2660–2180 B.C.E.	**Old Kingdom**	Construction of the pyramids
2180–2080 B.C.E.	**First Intermediate**	Political disunity
2080–1640 B.C.E.	**Middle Kingdom**	Recovery and political stability
1640–1570 B.C.E.	**Second Intermediate**	Hyksos migrations; struggles for power
1570–1070 B.C.E.	**New Kingdom**	Creation of an Egyptian empire; growth in wealth
1070–712 B.C.E.	**Third Intermediate**	Political fragmentation and conquest by outsiders (see Chapter 2)

The focal point of religious and political life in the Old Kingdom was the king, who commanded wealth, resources, and people. The king's surroundings had to be worthy of a god, and only a magnificent palace was suitable for his home; in fact, the word **pharaoh**, which during the New Kingdom came to be used for the king, originally meant "great house." Just as the kings occupied a great house in life, so they reposed in great pyramids after death. Built during the Old Kingdom, these massive stone tombs contained all the things needed by the king in his afterlife. The pyramid also symbolized the king's power and his connection with the sun-god. After burial the entrance was blocked and concealed to ensure the king's undisturbed peace, although grave robbers later actually found the tombs fairly easy to plunder.

To ancient Egyptians, the king embodied the concept of **ma'at**, a cosmic harmony that embraced truth, justice, and moral integrity. Ma'at gave the king the right, authority, and duty to govern. To the people, the king personified justice and order—harmony among themselves, nature, and the divine.

Kings did not always live up to this ideal, of course. The two parts of Egypt were difficult to hold together, and several times in Egypt's long history there were periods of disunity, civil war, and chaos. During the First Intermediate Period (2180–2080 B.C.E.), rulers of various provinces asserted their independence from the king, and Upper and Lower Egypt were ruled by rival dynasties. There is evidence that the Nile's floods were unusually low during this period because of drought, which contributed to instability just as it helped bring down the Akkadian empire. Warrior-kings reunited Egypt in the Middle Kingdom (2080–1640 B.C.E.) and expanded Egyptian power southward into Nubia.

Pharaoh Khafre   This statue from around 2570 B.C.E. shows King Khafre seated on his throne, with the wings of the falcon-god Horus wrapped around his head, a visual depiction of the close link between the Egyptian rulers and the gods. Khafre built the second-largest of the great pyramids at Giza as his tomb. (Egyptian National Museum, Cairo, Egypt/De Agostini Picture Library/Alfredo Dagli Orti/Bridgeman Images)

Egyptian Religion

Like the Mesopotamians, the Egyptians were polytheistic, worshipping many gods of all types, some mightier than others. They developed complex ideas of their gods that reflected the world around them, and these views changed over the many centuries of Egyptian history as gods took on new attributes and often merged with one another. During the Old Kingdom, Egyptians considered the sun-god Ra the creator of life. He commanded the sky, earth, and underworld. This giver of life could also take it away without warning. Ra was associated with the falcon-god Horus, the "lord of the sky," who served as the symbol of divine kingship.

Much later, during the New Kingdom (see page 27), the pharaohs of a new dynasty favored the worship of a different sun-god, Amon, whom they described as creating the entire cosmos by his thoughts. Amon brought life to the land and its people, they wrote, and he sustained both. Because he had helped them overthrow their enemies, Egyptians came to consider Amon the champion of fairness and justice, especially for the common people. Called the "vizier of the humble" and the "voice of the poor," Amon was also a magician and physician who cured ills, protected people from natural dangers, and watched over travelers. As his cult grew, Amon came to be identified with Ra, and eventually the Egyptians combined them into one sun-god, Amon-Ra.

The Egyptians likewise developed views of an afterlife that reflected the world around them and that changed over time. During the later part of the Old Kingdom, the walls of kings' tombs were carved with religious texts that provided spells that would bring the king back to life and help him ascend to Heaven, where he would join his divine father, Ra. Toward the end of the Old Kingdom, the tombs of powerful nobles

Funeral Stele of a Wealthy Woman
This painted wooden stele shows Djed-amon-iu-ankh (right), a wealthy Egyptian woman who lived in the Third Intermediate Period, in a thin gown and with a cone of ointment on her head, and the sun-god Ra (left) in the form of Horus the falcon-god. Ra-Horus is holding a scepter in one hand and the ankh, the Egyptian symbol of life, in the other. Djed-amon-iu-ankh offers food and lotus flowers to the god, and the hieroglyphs above them describe the offering. Steles were erected in Egypt for funeral purposes and depicted the person memorialized in an attitude of reverence. (Egyptian National Museum, Cairo, Egypt/photo © Interfoto/Ancient Art & Architecture Collection, Ltd.)

also contained such inscriptions, an indication that more people expected to gain everlasting life, and a sign of the decentralization of power that would lead to the chaos of the First Intermediate Period. In the Middle Kingdom, new types of spells appeared on the coffins of even more people, a further expansion in admissions to the afterlife.

During the New Kingdom, a time when Egypt came into greater contact with the cultures of the Fertile Crescent, Egyptians developed more complex ideas about the afterlife, recording these in funerary manuscripts that have come to be known as the *Book of the Dead*, written to help guide the dead through the difficulties of the underworld. These texts explained that the soul left the body to become part of the divine after death and told of the god Osiris (oh-SIGH-ruhs), who died each year and was then brought back to life by his wife, Isis (IGH-suhs), when the Nile flooded. Osiris eventually became king of the dead, weighing dead humans' hearts to determine whether they had lived justly enough to deserve everlasting life. (See "Thinking Like a Historian: The Moral Life," in Chapter 2 on page 44.) Egyptians also believed that proper funeral rituals, in which the physical body was mummified, were essential for life after death, so Osiris was assisted by Anubis, the jackal-headed god of mummification.

New Kingdom pharaohs came to associate themselves with both Horus and Osiris, and they were regarded as avatars of Horus in life and Osiris in death. The pharaoh's wife was associated with Isis, for both the queen and the goddess were regarded as protectors.

Egyptian Society and Work

Egyptian society reflected the pyramids that it built. At the top stood the king, who relied on a sizable circle of nobles, officials, and priests to administer his kingdom. All of them were assisted by scribes, who used a writing system perhaps adapted from Mesopotamia and perhaps developed independently. Egyptian scribes actually created two writing systems: one called hieroglyphic for engraving important religious or political texts on stone or writing them on papyrus made from reeds growing in the Nile Delta, and a much simpler system called hieratic that allowed scribes to write more quickly. Hieratic writing was used for the documents of daily life, such as letters, contracts, and accounts, and also for medical and literary works. Students learned hieratic first, and only those from well-off families or whose families had high aspirations took the time to learn hieroglyphics. In addition to scribes, the cities of the Nile Valley were home to artisans of all types, along with merchants and other tradespeople. A large group of farmers made up the broad base of the social pyramid.

For Egyptians, the Nile formed an essential part of daily life. During the season of its flooding, from June to October, farmers worked on the pharaoh's building programs and other tasks away from their fields. When the water began to recede, they diverted some of it into ponds for future irrigation and began planting wheat and barley for bread and beer, using plows pulled by oxen or people to part the soft mud. From October to February farmers planted and tended crops, and then from February until the next flood they harvested them. Reapers with wooden sickles fixed with flint teeth cut the grain high, leaving long stubble. Women with baskets followed behind to gather the cuttings. Last came the gleaners — poor women, children, and old men who gathered anything left behind.

As in Mesopotamia, common people paid their obligations to their superiors in products and in labor, and many faced penalties if they did not meet their quota. One scribe described the scene at harvest time:

> And now the scribe lands on the river bank and is about to register the harvest-tax. The janitors carry staves and the Nubians rods of palm, and they say, Hand over the grain, though there is none. The farmer is beaten all over, he is bound and thrown into a well, soused and dipped head downwards. His wife has been bound in his presence and his children are in fetters.[5]

People's labor obligations in the Old Kingdom may have included forced work on the pyramids and canals, although recent research suggests that most people who built the pyramids were paid for their work. Some young men were drafted into the pharaoh's army, which served as both a fighting force and a labor corps.

Egyptian Family Life

The lives of all Egyptians centered around the family. Marriage was a business arrangement, just as in Mesopotamia, arranged by the couples' parents, and seems to have taken place at a young age. Once couples were married, having children, especially sons, was a high priority, as indicated by surviving charms to promote fertility and prayers for successful childbirth. Boys continued the family line, and only they could perform the proper burial rites for their father.

Wealthy Egyptians lived in spacious homes with attractive gardens and walls for privacy. (See "Evaluating the Evidence 1.3: Egyptian Home Life," page 26.) Such a house had an ample living room and a comfortable master bedroom with an attached bathroom.

■ *Book of the Dead* Egyptian funerary manuscripts, written to help guide the dead through the difficulties they would encounter on the way to the afterlife.

Egyptian Home Life

This grave painting depicts an intimate moment in the life of an aristocratic family, with the father and mother in the center and their children around them. Often found in Egyptian tombs are statuettes of cats (see inset), which were both family pets and the symbol of the goddess Bastet.

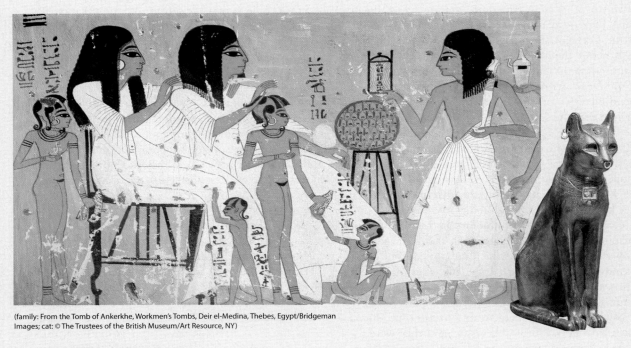

(family: From the Tomb of Ankerkhe, Workmen's Tombs, Deir el-Medina, Thebes, Egypt/Bridgeman Images; cat: © The Trustees of the British Museum/Art Resource, NY)

EVALUATE THE EVIDENCE

1. What evidence do you find in the painting that Egyptian artists based the size of figures on people's status in the household?
2. Based on your reading, how might an image of a poor family differ from this depiction?

Smaller rooms served other purposes, including housing family members and servants, and providing space for cows, poultry, and storage. Poorer people lived in cramped quarters. Excavations at a city now called Tell el-Amarna show that residents' houses were about 16½ feet wide by 33 feet long. The family had narrow rooms for living, including two small rooms for sleeping and cooking. These small houses suggest that most Egyptians lived in small family groups, not as large extended families. The very poor lived in hovels with their animals.

Life in Egypt began at dawn with a bath and clean clothes. The Egyptians bathed several times a day because of the heat and used soda ash for soap. Rich and poor alike used perfumes as deodorants. Egyptians generally wore linen clothes, made from fibers of the flax plant, because there were few sheep in Egypt, and during this period they did not grow cotton. Because of the heat, men often wore only a kilt and women a sheath.

Marriage was apparently not celebrated by any ritual or religious act; it seems to have been purely a legal contract in which a woman brought one-third of her family's property to the marriage. The property continued to belong to her, though her husband managed it. She could obtain a divorce simply because she wanted it. If she did, she took her marriage portion with her and could also claim a share of the profits made during her marriage. Most Egyptian men had only one wife, but among the wealthy some had several wives or concubines. One wife, however, remained primary among the others. A husband could order his wife to her quarters and even beat her, but if a man treated his wife too violently, she could take him to court. If she won, her husband received one hundred lashes from a whip and surrendered his portion of their joint property to her.

A man could dispense with his wife for any reason, just as she could leave him.

Ordinary women were expected to obey their fathers, husbands, and other men, but they possessed considerable economic and legal rights. They could own land in their own names and operate businesses. They could testify in court and bring legal action against men. Information from literature and art depicts a world in which ordinary husbands and wives enjoyed each other's company alone and together with family and friends. They held and attended parties together, and both participated in the festivities after dinner. Egyptian tomb monuments often show the couple happily standing together, arms around each other.

The Hyksos and New Kingdom Revival

While Egyptian civilization flourished in the Nile Valley, various groups migrated throughout the Fertile Crescent and then accommodated themselves to local cultures (Map 1.2). Some settled in the Nile Delta, including a group the Egyptians called Hyksos, which means "rulers of the uplands." Although they were later portrayed as a conquering horde, the Hyksos were actually migrants looking for good land, and their entry into the delta, which began around 1800 B.C.E., was probably gradual and generally peaceful.

The Hyksos brought with them the method of making bronze and casting it into tools and weapons that became standard in Egypt. They thereby brought Egypt fully into the Bronze Age culture of the Mediterranean world. Because bronze tools were sharper and more durable than the copper, stone, or bone tools they replaced, they made farming more efficient. The Hyksos also brought inventions that revolutionized Egyptian warfare, including bronze armor and weapons as well as horse-drawn chariots and the composite bow, made of laminated wood and horn, which was far more powerful than the simple wooden bow.

The migration of the Hyksos, combined with a series of famines and internal struggles for power, led Egypt to fragment politically in what later came to be known as the Second Intermediate Period (1640–1570 B.C.E.). During this time the Egyptians adopted bronze technology and new forms of weaponry from the Hyksos, while the newcomers began to worship Egyptian deities and modeled their political structure on that of the Egyptians.

In about 1570 B.C.E. a new dynasty of pharaohs arose, pushing the Hyksos out of the delta, subduing Nubia in the south, and conquering parts of Canaan in the northeast. In this way, these Egyptian warrior-pharaohs inaugurated what scholars refer to as the New Kingdom—a period in Egyptian history characterized by not only enormous wealth and conscious

imperialism but also a greater sense of insecurity because of new contacts and military engagements. By expanding Egyptian power beyond the Nile Valley, the pharaohs created the first Egyptian empire, and they celebrated their triumphs with monuments on a scale unparalleled since the pyramids of the Old Kingdom. Even today the colossal granite statues of these pharaohs and the rich tomb objects testify to the might and splendor of the New Kingdom. They might also be testimony to an expansion of imported slave labor, although recently some scholars are rethinking the extent of slave labor in the New Kingdom.

The New Kingdom pharaohs include a number of remarkable figures. Among these was Hatshepsut (r. ca. 1479–ca. 1458 B.C.E.), one of the few female pharaohs in Egypt's long history, who seized the throne for herself and used her reign to promote building and trade. Amenhotep III (r. ca. 1388–ca. 1350 B.C.E.) corresponded with other powerful kings in Babylonia and other kingdoms in the Fertile Crescent, sending envoys, exchanging gifts, and in some cases marrying their daughters. The kings promised friendship and active cooperation, referring to each other as "brothers," using this familial term to indicate their connection. They made alliances for offensive and defensive protection and swore to uphold one another's authority. Hence, the greatest powers of the period maintained peace, which facilitated the movement of gifts between kings and trade between ordinary people. Along with his chief royal wife, Tiye, who is known for her correspondence with foreign queens, Amenhotep is depicted on hundreds of statues, vases, amulets, and other objects, including two sixty-foot-tall statues that stood at the gate of his huge mortuary temple.

Amenhotep III was succeeded by his son, who took the name Akhenaton (ah-keh-NAH-tuhn) (r. 1351–1334 B.C.E.). He renamed himself as a mark of his changing religious ideas. Egyptians had long worshipped various sun-gods and aspects of the sun—Ra, Amon, Amon-Ra—but instead Akhenaton favored the worship of the god Aton (also spelled Aten), the visible disk of the sun. (See "Thinking Like a Historian: Addressing the Gods," page 18.) He was not a monotheist (someone who worships only one god), but he did order the erasure of the names of other sun-gods from the walls of buildings, the transfer of taxes from the traditional priesthood of Amon-Ra, and the building of huge new temples to Aton, especially at his new capital in the area now known as Amarna. In these temples Aton was to be worshipped in bright sunlight. Akhenaton also had artists portray him in more realistic ways than they had portrayed earlier pharaohs; he is depicted interacting with his children and especially with his wife Nefertiti (nehf-uhr-TEE-tee), who supported his new religious ideas. (See "Individuals in Society: Hatshepsut and Nefertiti," page 29.)

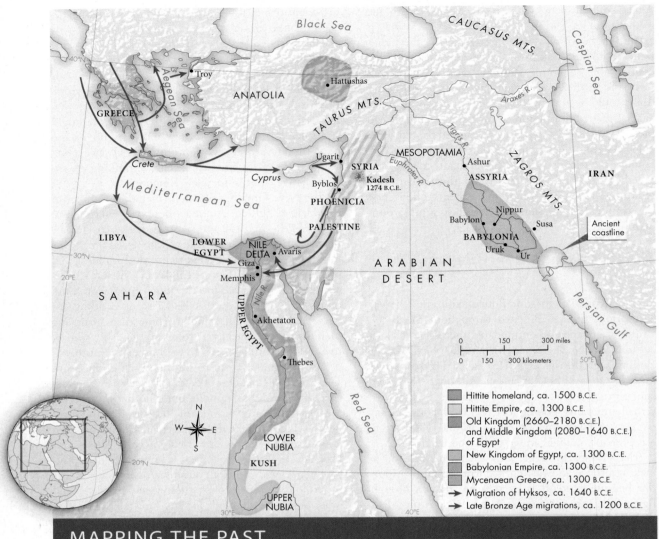

MAP 1.2 Empires and Migrations in the Eastern Mediterranean

The rise and fall of empires in the eastern Mediterranean were shaped by internal developments, military conflicts, and the migration of peoples to new areas.

ANALYZING THE MAP At what point was the Egyptian empire at its largest? The Hittite Empire? What were the other major powers in the eastern Mediterranean at this point?

CONNECTIONS What were the major effects of the migrations of the Hyksos? Of the late Bronze Age migrations? What clues does the map provide as to why the late Bronze Age migrations had a more powerful impact than those of the Hyksos?

Akhenaton's new religion, imposed from above, failed to find a place among the people, however. After his death, traditional religious practices returned and the capital was moved back to Thebes. The priests of Amon-Ra led this restoration, but it was also supported by Akhenaton's son, who rejected the name he had been given that honored Aton and instead chose one that honored the traditional sun-god Amon. This son was Tutankhamon (r. 1333–1323 B.C.E.), whose short reign

was not particularly noteworthy, and whose name would probably not be remembered except for the fact that his was the only tomb of an Egyptian king to be discovered nearly intact. The wealth of "King Tut's tomb," assembled for a boy-king who died unexpectedly at nineteen, can only suggest what must have originally been in the tomb of a truly powerful pharaoh.

The objects in the tomb have been studied intensively since it was first discovered in 1922 and have

Egyptians understood the pharaoh to be an avatar of the god Horus, the source of law and morality, and the mediator between gods and humans. The pharaoh's connection with the divine stretched to members of his family, so that his siblings and children were also viewed as divine in some ways. Because of this, a pharaoh often took his sister or half-sister as one of his wives. This concentrated divine blood set the pharaonic family apart from other Egyptians (who did not generally marry close relatives) and allowed the pharaohs to imitate the gods, who in Egyptian mythology often married their siblings. A pharaoh chose one of his wives, often a relative, to be the "Great Royal Wife," or principal queen.

The familial connection with the divine allowed a handful of women to rule in their own right in Egypt's long history. We know the names of four female pharaohs, of whom the most famous was Hatshepsut (r. ca. 1479–ca. 1458 B.C.E.), the sister and wife of Thutmose II. After he died, she served as regent—adviser and co-ruler—for her young stepson Thutmose III. Hatshepsut sent trading expeditions and sponsored artists and architects, ushering in a period of artistic creativity and economic prosperity. She oversaw the construction of one of the world's great buildings, an elaborate terraced temple at Deir el-Bahri, which eventually served as her mortuary temple. Hatshepsut's status as a powerful female ruler was difficult for Egyptians to conceptualize, and she is often depicted in male dress or with a false beard, thus looking more like the male rulers who were the norm. After her death, Thutmose III tried to destroy all evidence that she had ever ruled, smashing statues and scratching her name off inscriptions, perhaps because of personal animosity and perhaps because he wanted to erase the fact that a woman had once been pharaoh. Only within recent decades have historians and archaeologists begun to (literally) piece together her story.

Though female pharaohs were very rare, many royal women had power through their position as "Great Royal Wives." The most famous was Nefertiti, the wife of Akhenaton. Her name means "the perfect (or beautiful) woman has come," and inscriptions also give her many other titles. Nefertiti used her position to spread the new religion of the sun-god Aton.

Together Nefertiti and Akhenaton built a new palace and capital city at Akhetaton, the present Amarna, away from the old centers of power. There they developed the cult of Aton to the exclusion of the traditional deities. Nearly the only literary survival of their religious belief is the "Hymn to Aton," which declares Aton to be the only god. It describes Nefertiti

Granite head of Hatshepsut. (bpk, Berlin/ Aegyptisches Museum, Staatliche Museen/Margarete Buesing/Art Resource, NY)

Painted limestone bust of Nefertiti.
(Aegyptisches Museum, SMPK, Berlin, Germany/ Bridgeman Images)

as "the great royal consort whom he, Akhenaton, loves. The mistress of the Two Lands, Upper and Lower Egypt."

Nefertiti is often shown as being the same size as her husband, and in some inscriptions she is performing religious rituals that would normally have been carried out only by the pharaoh. The exact details of her power are hard to determine, however. An older theory held that her husband removed her from power, though there is also speculation that after his death she may have ruled secretly in her own right under a different name. Her tomb has long since disappeared. In the last decade individual archaeologists have claimed that several different mummies were Nefertiti, but most scholars dismiss these claims. Because her parentage is not known for certain, DNA testing such as that done on Tutankhamon's corpse would not reveal whether any specific mummy was Nefertiti.

QUESTIONS FOR ANALYSIS

1. Why might it have been difficult for Egyptians to accept a female ruler?
2. What opportunities do hereditary monarchies such as that of ancient Egypt provide for women? How does this fit with gender hierarchies in which men are understood as superior?

yielded much information about New Kingdom Egypt. In 2010 DNA analysis of Tutankhamon's mummy and other mummies from nearby tombs revealed, among other things, that he was the son of Akhenaton (there had been some doubt) and that his mother was probably one of Akhenaton's sisters. Brother-sister marriage was fairly common among Egyptian pharaohs, as it concentrated the family's power and connections with the gods. Marriage to close relatives can also cause genetic defects, however, and Tutankhamon seems to have suffered from several of these, including a malformed foot. Study of Tutankhamon's mummy also revealed that he suffered from malaria and had broken his leg shortly before he died. His high status did not make him immune to physical ailments.

Tutankhamon's short reign was also marked by international problems, including warfare on several of the borders of the Egyptian empire. His grandfather and father had engaged in extensive diplomatic relations with rulers of states dependent on Egypt and with other powerful kings, but Tutankhamon was less successful at these. He also died childless. His successors were court officials, and in 1298 B.C.E. one of them established a new dynasty whose members would reassert Egypt's imperial power and respond to new challenges.

Conflict and Cooperation with the Hittites

One of the key challenges facing the pharaohs after Tutankhamon was the expansion of the kingdom of the Hittites. At about the same time that the Sumerians were establishing city-states, speakers of Indo-European languages migrated into Anatolia. Indo-European is a large family of languages that includes English, most of the languages of modern Europe, Persian, and Sanskrit. It also includes Hittite, the language of a people who seem to have migrated into this area about 2300 B.C.E.

Information about the Hittites comes from archaeological sources, and also from written cuneiform tablets that provide details about politics and economic life. These records indicate that in the sixteenth century B.C.E. the Hittite king Hattusili I led his forces against neighboring kingdoms. Hattusili's grandson and successor, Mursili I, extended the Hittite conquests as far as Babylon. Upon his return home, the victorious Mursili was assassinated by members of his own family, which led to dynastic warfare. This pattern of expansion followed by internal conflict was repeated frequently, but when they were united behind a strong king, the Hittites were extremely powerful.

As the Hittites expanded southward, they came into conflict with the Egyptians, who were re-establishing their empire. The pharaoh Ramesses II engaged in numerous campaigns to retake Egyptian territory in Syria. He assembled a large well-equipped army with thousands of chariots and expected to defeat the Hittites easily, but was ambushed by them at the Battle of Kadesh in 1274 B.C.E. Returning to Egypt, Ramesses declared that he had won and had monuments carved commemorating his victory, including the giant temples at Abu Simbel in Nubia, which were also designed as a demonstration of Egypt's power over its southern neighbors. In reality, neither side gained much by the battle, though both sides seem to have recognized the impossibility of defeating the other.

In 1258 Ramesses II and the Hittite king Hattusili III concluded a peace treaty, which was recorded in both Egyptian hieroglyphics and Hittite cuneiform. Both of these have survived. Although peace treaties are known to have existed since the twenty-fourth century B.C.E., this is one of the best preserved. Returning to the language of cooperation established in earlier royal diplomacy, each side promised not to invade the other and to come to the other's aid if attacked. Each promised peace and brotherhood, and the treaty ended with a long oath to the gods, who would curse the one who broke the treaty and bless the one who kept it.

NOTES

1. J. A. Black et al., *Electronic Text Corpus of Sumerian Literature* (http://etcsl.orinst.ox.ac.uk/), Oxford 1998–2006. Used by permission of Oxford University, ETCSL Project.
2. Quoted in S. N. Kramer, *The Sumerians: Their History, Culture, and Character*, p. 238. Copyright © 1963 by The University of Chicago. All rights reserved. Used by permission of the publisher.
3. James B. Pritchard, ed., *Ancient Near Eastern Texts Relating to the Old Testament — Third Edition with Supplement*, p. 171. © Reproduced with permission of PRINCETON UNIVERSITY PRESS, in the format Book via Copyright Clearance Center.
4. Ibid., p. 372.
5. Quoted in A. H. Gardiner, "Ramesside Texts Relating to the Taxation and Transport of Corn," *Journal of Egyptian Archaeology* 27 (1941): pp. 19–20.

LOOKING BACK LOOKING AHEAD

The political and military story of waves of migrations, battles, and the rise and fall of empires can mask striking continuities across the Neolithic and Bronze Ages. The social patterns set in early agricultural societies — with most of the population farming the land, and a small number of elites who lived off their labor — lasted for millennia. Disrupted peoples and newcomers shared practical concepts of agriculture and metallurgy with one another, and wheeled vehicles allowed merchants to transact business over long distances. Merchants, migrants, and conquerors carried their gods and goddesses with them, and religious beliefs and practices blended and changed. Cuneiform tablets, wall inscriptions, and paintings testify to commercial exchanges and cultural accommodation, adoption, and adaptation.

The treaty of Ramesses II and Hattusili III brought peace between the Egyptians and the Hittites for a time, which was further enhanced by Ramesses II's marriage to a Hittite princess. This stability was not to last, however. Within several decades of the treaty, new peoples were moving into the eastern Mediterranean, disrupting trade and in some cases looting and destroying cities. There is evidence of drought, and some scholars have suggested a major volcanic explosion in Iceland cooled the climate for several years, leading to a series of poor harvests. Both the Egyptian and Hittite Empires shrank dramatically. All of these developments are part of a general "Bronze Age Collapse" that historians see as a major turning point.

Make Connections

Think about the larger developments and continuities within and across chapters.

1. What aspects of life in the Neolithic period continued with little change in the civilizations of Mesopotamia and Egypt? What were the most important differences?

2. Looking at your answers to question 1, do you think the distinction between "civilizations" and human cultures that were not "civilizations" discussed in the first part of this chapter is a valid one? Why or why not?

3. How were the societies that developed in Mesopotamia and Egypt similar to one another? Which of the characteristics you have identified as a similarity do you predict will also be found in later societies, and why?

1 REVIEW & EXPLORE

Identify Key Terms

Identify and explain the significance of each item below.

civilization (p. 5)

Paleolithic era (p. 5)

Neolithic era (p. 6)

Fertile Crescent (p. 7)

pastoralism (p. 8)

patriarchy (p. 9)

Bronze Age (p. 11)

polytheism (p. 11)

cuneiform (p. 13)

Hammurabi's law code (p. 20)

pharaoh (p. 23)

ma'at (p. 23)

Book of the Dead (p. 25)

Review the Main Ideas

Answer the focus questions from each section of the chapter.

◆ What do we mean by "the West" and "Western civilization"? (p. 4)

◆ How did early human societies develop and create new technologies and cultural forms? (p. 5)

◆ What kind of civilization did the Sumerians develop in Mesopotamia? (p. 11)

◆ How did the Akkadian and Old Babylonian empires develop in Mesopotamia? (p. 15)

◆ How did the Egyptians create a prosperous and long-lasting society? (p. 22)

Suggested Reading and Media Resources

BOOKS

◆ Bryce, Trevor. *The Kingdom of the Hittites*, new ed. 2005. The definitive study of the Hittites.

◆ Fagan, Brian M. *People of the Earth: An Introduction to World Prehistory*, 13th ed. 2009. A thorough survey that presents up-to-date scholarship, designed for students.

◆ Harding, A. F. *European Societies in the Bronze Age*. 2000. A comprehensive survey of developments in Europe during the Bronze Age.

◆ Hawass, Zahi. *Silent Images: Women in Pharaonic Egypt*. 2000. Blends text and pictures to draw a history of ancient Egyptian women.

◆ Kriwaczek, Paul. *Babylon: Mesopotamia and the Birth of Civilization*. 2012. Traces Mesopotamia from the first settlements to the fall of Babylon.

◆ Leick, Gwendolyn. *The Babylonians*. 2002. An introduction to all aspects of Babylonian life and culture.

◆ McCarter, Susan Foster. *Neolithic*. 2007. An introductory survey of the development and impact of agriculture, with many illustrations.

◆ McDowell, A. G. *Village Life in Ancient Egypt: Laundry Lists and Love Songs*. 1999. A fascinating study of the basic social and economic factors of the entire period.

◆ Podany, Amanda. *Brotherhood of Kings: How International Relations Shaped the Ancient Near East*. 2010. Examines a thousand years of diplomacy among rulers.

◆ Reeves, Nicholas. *Akhenaten*. 2001. Gives a detailed account of the pharaoh, Nefertiti, and their world.

◆ Tattersall, Ian. *Masters of the Planet: The Search for Our Human Origins*. 2012. An up-to-date survey of how humans evolved, in a lively narrative written for general readers.

◆ Van de Mieroop, Marc. *A History of the Ancient Near East, 3000–332 B.C.E.* 2010. A concise history from Sumerian cities to Alexander the Great.

◆ Visicato, Giuseppe. *The Power and the Writing: The Early Scribes of Mesopotamia*. 2000. Studies the practical importance of early Mesopotamian scribes.

DOCUMENTARIES

- *Ancient Worlds: Come Together* (BBC, 2010). Archaeologist and historian Richard Miles explores the beginning of civilization in the cities of Mesopotamia.
- *Egypt's Golden Empire* (PBS, 2002). This three-part series on the era of the New Kingdom examines the lives of pharaohs, nobles, and ordinary people in Egypt's expanding empire.

FEATURE FILMS

- *Cave of Forgotten Dreams* (Werner Herzog, 2010). Renowned director Werner Herzog goes inside the newly discovered Chauvet caves of southern France to film the oldest-known human artwork from around 32,000 years ago.
- *The Kings: From Babylon to Baghdad* (History Channel, 2004). This feature-length History Channel special surveys the rulers of Mesopotamia from Sargon of Akkad to Saddam Hussein, with special attention to military matters.

WEB SITES

- *Ancient Civilizations, Mesopotamia, and Egypt.* Three interactive sites from the British Museum with objects in the museum's fabulous collection, with maps, essays, and other resources.
  www.ancientcivilizations.co.uk/home_set.html
  www.mesopotamia.co.uk/ancientegypt.co.uk/
- *The Ancient Egypt Film Site.* Egyptian themes abound in horror flicks, mummy movies, cartoon shows, sitcoms, and every other kind of popular entertainment. This Web site covers them all, from the 1890s to today.
  www.ancientegyptfilmsite.nl/

- *Cuneiform Digital Library Initiative.* CDLI offers scholars tens of thousands of pictures of cuneiform texts, many with transcriptions in English, plus a useful wiki written by scholars about Mesopotamian history. Run by UCLA and the Max Planck Institute of the History of Science.
  cdli.ucla.edu/
  cdli.ox.ac.uk/wiki/
- *Eternal Egypt.* A multimedia site with over fifteen hundred examples of Egyptian art and artifacts, along with articles, maps, and animations. Run by the Egyptian Supreme Council of Antiquities, Egyptian Center for Documentation of Cultural and Natural Heritage, and IBM.
  www.eternalegypt.org/EternalEgyptWebsiteWeb /HomeServlet
- *Theban Mapping Project.* An interactive site run by a scholar from the American University in Cairo that highlights the excavations of palaces, tombs, and temples in the Valley of the Kings, with maps, videos, articles, and thousands of photos.
  www.thebanmappingproject.com/

2

Small Kingdoms and Mighty Empires in the Near East

1200–510 B.C.E.

The migrations, drought, and destruction of what scholars call the "Bronze Age Collapse" in the late thirteenth century B.C.E. ended the Hittite Empire and weakened the Egyptians. Much was lost, but the old cultures of the ancient Near East survived to nurture new societies. The technology for smelting iron, which developed in Anatolia as well as other places in the world, improved and spread, with iron weapons and tools becoming stronger and thus more important by about 1000 B.C.E. In the absence of powerful empires, the Phoenicians, Kushites, Hebrews, and many other peoples carved out small independent kingdoms until the Near East was a patchwork of them. The Hebrews created a new form of religious belief with a single god and wrote down their religious ideas and traditions in what later became the most significant written document from this period.

In the tenth century B.C.E. this jumble of small states gave way to an empire that for the first time embraced the entire Near East: the empire of the Assyrians. They assembled a huge army that used sophisticated military technology and brutal tactics, and also developed effective administrative techniques and stunning artistic works. The Assyrian Empire lasted for about three hundred years and then broke apart with the rise of a new empire centered in Babylon. Beginning in 550 B.C.E. the Persians conquered the Medes—nomadic peoples who had settled in Iran—and then the Babylonians and Assyrians, creating the largest empire yet seen, stretching from Anatolia in the west to the Indus Valley in the east. The Persians established effective methods of governing their diverse subjects and built roads for conquest, trade, and communication. ∎

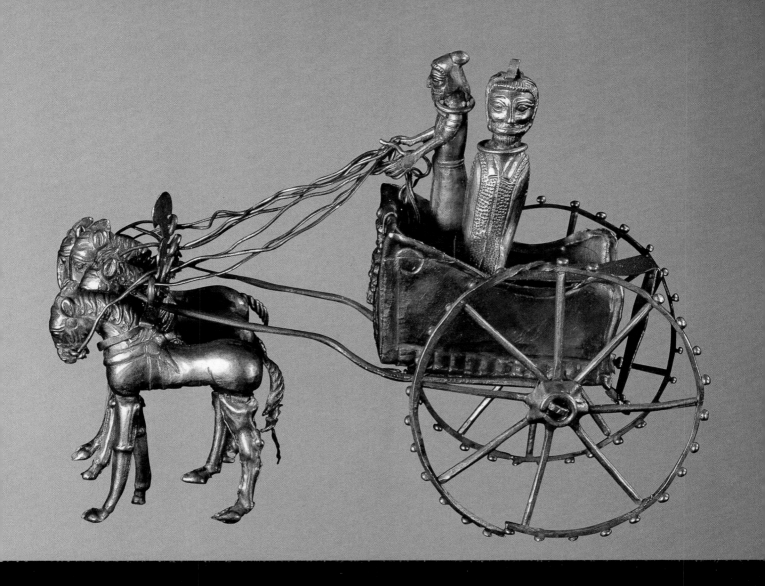

CHAPTER PREVIEW

Iron and the Emergence of New States
How did iron technology shape new states after 1200 B.C.E., including Kush and Phoenicia?

The Hebrews
How did the Hebrews create an enduring religious tradition?

Assyria, the Military Monarchy
What explains the rise and fall of the Assyrians?

The Empire of the Persian Kings
How did the Persians consolidate their power and control and influence the subjects of their extensive empire?

Life in the Persian Empire
Two men dressed in clothing of the Medes, one of the groups conquered by the Persians, drive a four-horse chariot in this small model made entirely of gold. In the nineteenth century a huge collection of silver and gold objects from the fifth and fourth centuries B.C.E. was found on the banks of the Oxus River in what is now Tajikistan. Most likely, the spot had been a ferry crossing and the objects had been buried long ago. (British Museum, London, UK/De Agostini Picture Library/Bridgeman Images)

Iron and the Emergence of New States

FOCUS QUESTION *How did iron technology shape new states after 1200 B.C.E., including Kush and Phoenicia?*

If the Bronze Age Collapse was a time of massive political and economic disruption, it was also a period of the spread of new technologies, especially iron. Even though empires shrank, many small kingdoms survived, each with cultures that combined elements shared across a wide area with local traditions. These states included several that developed on the borders of the shrinking Egyptian empire, including Kush and Phoenicia.

Iron Technology

Along with migration and drought, another significant development in the centuries around 1200 B.C.E. was the spread of iron tools and iron technology. Iron is the most common element in the earth, but most iron found on or near the earth's surface occurs in the form of ore, which must be smelted to extract the metal. This is also true of the copper and tin that are used to make bronze, but these can be smelted at much lower temperatures than iron. As artisans perfected bronze metalworking techniques, they also experimented with iron. They developed a long and difficult process for smelting iron, using charcoal and a bellows (which raised the temperature of the fire significantly) to extract the iron from the ore. This procedure was performed in an enclosed furnace, and the process was repeated a number of times as the ore was transformed into wrought iron, which could be hammered into shapes.

Exactly where and when the *first* smelted iron was produced is a matter of debate — many regions would like this honor — but it happened independently in several different places, including western Africa in what is now Nigeria, Anatolia (modern Turkey), and most likely India. In Anatolia, the earliest smelted weapon has been dated to about 2500 B.C.E., but there may have been some smelting earlier. Most of the iron produced was too brittle to be of much use until about 1100 B.C.E., however, when techniques improved and iron weapons gradually became stronger and cheaper than their bronze counterparts. Thus, in the schema of dividing history into periods according to the main material out of which tools are made (see Chapter 1), the **Iron Age** began in about 1100 B.C.E. Iron weapons became important items of trade around the Mediterranean and throughout the Tigris and Euphrates Valleys, and the technology for making them traveled as well. Iron appears to have been adopted more slowly in Egypt than in other parts of the Near East, so bronze remained important longer there. From Anatolia, iron objects were traded west into Greece and central Europe, and north into western Asia. By 500 B.C.E. knowledge of smelting had traveled these routes as well.

Ironworkers continued to experiment and improve their products. Somewhere in the Near East — again the exact location is disputed — ironworkers discovered that if the relatively brittle wrought iron objects were placed on a bed of burning charcoal and then cooled quickly, the outer layer would form into a layer of much harder material, steel. Goods made of cast or wrought iron were usually traded locally, but fine sword and knife blades of steel traveled long distances, and the knowledge of how to make them followed. Because it was fairly plentiful and relatively cheap when compared with bronze, iron has been called the "democratic metal." The transition from bronze to iron happened over many centuries, but iron (and even more so, steel) would be an important factor in history from this point on.

Nubian Cylinder Sheath   This small silver sheath made about 520 B.C.E., perhaps for a dagger, depicts a winged goddess and the Egyptian god Amon-Ra (not shown in photograph). It and others like it were found in the tombs of Kushite kings and suggest ways that Egyptian artistic styles and religious ideas influenced cultures farther up the Nile. (Cylinder sheath of Amani-natake-lebte. Napatan Period, reign of King Amani-natake-lebte, 538–519 B.C [gilded silver and colored paste]/Nubian/Museum of Fine Arts, Boston, Massachusetts, USA/Harvard University–Boston Museum of Fine Arts Expedition/Bridgeman Images)

■ **Iron Age** Period beginning about 1100 B.C.E., when iron became the most important material for tools and weapons.

■ **Kush** Kingdom in Nubia that adopted hieroglyphics and pyramids, and later conquered Egypt.

The Decline of Egypt and the Emergence of Kush

Although the treaty between the Egyptians and Hittites in 1258 B.C.E. seemed to indicate a future of peace and cooperation, this was not to be. Groups of seafaring peoples whom the Egyptians called "Sea Peoples" raided, migrated, and marauded in the eastern Mediterranean. Just who these people were and where they originated is much debated among scholars. They may have come from Greece, or islands in the Mediterranean such as Crete and Sardinia, or Anatolia (modern Turkey), or from all of these. Wherever they came from, their raids, combined with the expansion of the Assyrians (see page 46), led to the collapse of the Hittite Empire. The Hittite capital city of Hattusa was burned to the ground in 1180 B.C.E. by an army of many different peoples, and though small states re-emerged in Anatolia, these were very much under the influence of Assyria.

In Egypt, the pharaoh Ramesses III (r. 1186–1155 B.C.E.) defeated the Sea Peoples in both a land and sea battle, but these were costly, as were other military engagements. Ramesses appears to have also been the subject of an assassination plot, which he survived, but Egypt entered into a long period of political fragmentation and conquest by outsiders that scholars of Egypt refer to as the Third Intermediate Period (ca. 1070–712 B.C.E.). The long wars against invaders weakened and impoverished Egypt, causing political upheaval and economic decline. Scribes created somber portraits that no doubt exaggerated the negative, but were effective in capturing the mood:

> The land of Egypt was abandoned and every man was a law to himself. During many years there was no leader who could speak for others. Central government lapsed, small officials and headmen took over the whole land. Any man, great or small, might kill his neighbor. In the distress and vacuum that followed . . . men banded together to plunder one another. They treated the gods no better than men, and cut off the temple revenues.[1]

The decline of Egypt allowed new powers to emerge. South of Egypt was a region called Nubia, which as early as 2000 B.C.E. served as a conduit of trade through which ivory, gold, ebony, and other products flowed north from sub-Saharan Africa. Small kingdoms arose in this area, with large buildings and rich tombs. As Egypt expanded during the New King-dom (see Chapter 1), it took over northern Nubia in what were sometimes brutal conquests, incorporating it into the growing Egyptian empire. The Nubians adopted many features of Egyptian culture, including Egyptian gods, the use of hieroglyphics, and the building of pyramids. Many Nubians became officials in the Egyptian bureaucracy and officers in the army, and there was significant intermarriage between the two groups.

With the contraction of the Egyptian empire in the Third Intermediate Period, an independent kingdom, **Kush**, rose in power in Nubia, with its capital at Napata in what is now Sudan. The Kushites conquered southern Egypt, and in 727 B.C.E. the Kushite king Piye (r. ca. 747–716 B.C.E.) swept through the Nile Valley to the delta in the north. United once again, Egypt enjoyed a brief period of peace during which the Egyptian culture continued to influence that of its conquerors. In the seventh century B.C.E. invading Assyrians pushed the Kushites out of Egypt, and the Kushite rulers moved their capital farther up the Nile to

Chronology

ca. 1200 B.C.E.	"Bronze Age Collapse"; end of the Hittite Empire
ca. 1100 B.C.E.	Beginning of the Iron Age; Phoenicians begin to trade in the Mediterranean
ca. 1070–712 B.C.E.	Third Intermediate Period in Egypt
ca. 965–925 B.C.E.	Hebrew kingdom ruled by Solomon
911–609 B.C.E.	Neo-Assyrian Empire
727 B.C.E.	Kushite Dynasty established in Egypt
722 B.C.E.	Kingdom of Israel destroyed by the Assyrians
626–539 B.C.E.	Neo-Babylonian empire
ca. 600 B.C.E.	Ideas of Zoroaster gain prominence in Persia
587 B.C.E.	Kingdom of Judah destroyed by the Neo-Babylonians
587–538 B.C.E.	Babylonian Captivity of the Hebrews
550 B.C.E.	Cyrus the Great conquers the Medes and consolidates the Persian Empire
539 B.C.E.	Persians defeat the Neo-Babylonians
525 B.C.E.	Persians defeat the Egyptians and Nubians

The Kingdom of Kush, 1000 B.C.E.–300 C.E.

Meroë, where they built hundreds of pyramids. Meroë became a center for the production of iron, which was becoming the material of choice for weapons. Iron products from Meroë were the best in the world, smelted using wood from the vast forests in the area. They were traded to much of Africa and across the Red Sea and the Indian Ocean to India.

The Rise of Phoenicia

While Kush expanded in the southern Nile Valley, another group rose to prominence along the Mediterranean coast of modern Lebanon, the northern part of the area called Canaan in ancient sources. These Canaanites established the prosperous commercial centers of Tyre, Sidon, and Byblos, all cities still thriving today, and were master shipbuilders. With their stout ships, between about 1100 and 700 B.C.E. the residents of these cities became the seaborne merchants of the Mediterranean. (See "Evaluating the Evidence 2.1: The Report of Wenamun," at right.) Their most valued products were purple and blue textiles, from which originated their Greek name, **Phoenicians** (fih-NEE-shuhnz), meaning "Purple People."

The trading success of the Phoenicians brought them prosperity. In addition to textiles and purple dye, they began to manufacture goods for export, such as tools, weapons, and cookware. They worked bronze and iron, which they shipped processed or as ores, and made and traded glass products. Phoenician ships often carried hundreds of jars of wine, and the Phoenicians introduced grape growing to new regions around the Mediterranean, dramatically increasing the wine available for consumption and trade. They imported rare goods and materials, including hunting dogs, gold, and ivory, from Persia in the east and their neighbors to the south. They also expanded their trade to Egypt, where they mingled with other local traders.

Phoenician Coin   This silver Phoenician coin shows an animal-headed ship containing soldiers with shields and helmets above the waves, and a hippocampus, a mythical beast, below. Phoenician gold and silver coins have been found throughout the Mediterranean, evidence of the Phoenicians' extensive trading network. This particular coin was most likely not used very often, as the images on it are still sharp; silver is soft, and frequent handling would have rubbed off the edges of the images. (Erich Lessing/Art Resource, NY)

The variety and quality of the Phoenicians' trade goods generally made them welcome visitors. Moving beyond Egypt, they struck out along the coast of North Africa to establish new markets in places where they encountered little competition. In the ninth century B.C.E. they founded, in modern Tunisia, the city of Carthage (meaning "new city" in Phoenician), which prospered to become the leading city in the western Mediterranean, although it would one day struggle with Rome for domination of that region.

The Phoenicians planted trading posts and small farming communities along the coast, founding colonies in Spain and Sicily along with Carthage. Their trade routes eventually took them to the far western Mediterranean and beyond to the Atlantic coast of modern-day Portugal. The Phoenicians' voyages brought them into contact with the Greeks, to whom they introduced many aspects of the older and more urbanized cultures of Mesopotamia and Egypt.

The Phoenicians' overwhelming cultural achievement was the spread of a completely phonetic system of writing—that is, an alphabet. Writers of both cuneiform and hieroglyphics had developed signs that were used to represent sounds, but these were always used with a much larger number of ideograms. Sometime around 1800 B.C.E. workers in the Sinai Peninsula, which was under Egyptian control, began to write only with phonetic signs, with each sign designating one sound. This system vastly simplified writing and

Phoenician Settlements in the Mediterranean

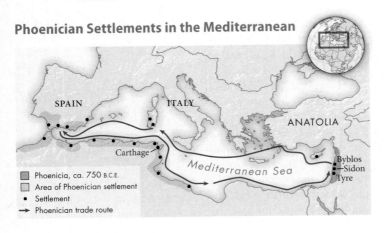

SPAIN   ITALY   ANATOLIA

Carthage

Mediterranean Sea

Byblos
Sidon
Tyre

■ Phoenicia, ca. 750 B.C.E.
□ Area of Phoenician settlement
• Settlement
→ Phoenician trade route

■ **Phoenicians** Seafaring people from Canaan who traded and founded colonies throughout the Mediterranean and spread the phonetic alphabet.

The Report of Wenamun

This account describes the trip of the Egyptian official Wenamun to purchase Lebanese wood to make a large ceremonial boat named Amon-user-he *for the god Amon-Ra. It is unknown whether this text describes a real mission, but the text reflects the political and economic situation in the decade from 1190 to 1180 B.C.E. Wenamun negotiated with the prince of Byblos, a Phoenician city-state in present-day Lebanon, for the timber, encountering great frustrations.*

When morning came, he [the prince of Byblos] sent and brought me up. . . . Then he spoke to me, saying: "On what business have you come?" I said to him: "I have come in quest of timber for the great noble bark of Amon-Ra, King of Gods. What your father did, what the father of your father did, you too will do it." So I said to him. He said to me: "True, they did it. If you pay me for doing it, I will do it. My relations carried out this business after Pharaoh had sent six ships laden with the goods of Egypt, and they had been unloaded into their storehouses. You, what have you brought for me? . . . What are these foolish travels they made you do?"

I said to him: "Wrong! These are not foolish travels that I am doing. There is no ship on the river that does not belong to [the god] Amon. His is the sea and his the Lebanon of which you say, 'It is mine.' It is a growing ground for [the ceremonial ship called] *Amon-user-he*, the lord of every ship. . . . You are prepared to haggle over the Lebanon with Amon, its lord? As to your saying, the former kings sent silver and gold: If they had owned life and health, they would not have sent these things. It was in place of life and health that they sent these things to your fathers! But Amon-Ra, King of Gods, he is the lord of life and health, and he was the lord of your fathers! They passed their lifetimes [making] offering to Amon. You too, you are the servant of Amon!" . . .

He placed my letter in the hand of his messenger; and he loaded the keel, the prow-piece, and the stern-piece, together with four other hewn logs, seven in all, and sent them to Egypt. His messenger who had gone to Egypt returned to me in Syria in the first month of winter, Smendes and Tentamun [the pharaoh and queen of the northern half of Egypt, Wenamun's employers] having sent: four jars and one *kakmen*-vessel of gold; five jars of silver; ten garments of royal linen; ten . . . garments of fine linen; five-hundred smooth linen mats; five-hundred ox-hides; five-hundred ropes; twenty sacks of lentils; and thirty baskets of fish. . . .

The prince rejoiced. He assigned three hundred men and three hundred oxen, and he set supervisors over them to have them fell the timbers. They were felled and they lay there during the winter. In the third month of summer they dragged them to the shore of the sea. The prince came out and stood by them, and he sent to me, saying: "Come!" . . . As I stood before him, he addressed me, saying: "Look, the business my fathers did in the past, I have done it, although you did not do for me what your fathers did for mine. Look, the last of your timber has arrived and is ready. Do as I wish, and come to load it."

EVALUATE THE EVIDENCE

1. How does Wenamun first attempt to get the prince of Byblos to give him the timber? What does the prince send in the first shipment? Why does he eventually provide more timber?
2. How does Wenamun's report reflect the decline of Egyptian power and wealth?

Source: Miriam Lichtheim, *Ancient Egyptian Literature: A Book of Readings,* vol. 2, *The New Kingdom* (Berkeley: University of California Press, 1976), pp. 226–228. © 2006 by the Regents of the University of California. Published by the University of California Press.

reading and spread among common people as a practical way to record things and communicate. Egyptian scribes and officials continued to use hieroglyphics, but the Phoenicians adopted the simpler system for their own language and spread it around the Mediterranean. The Greeks modified this alphabet and then used it to write their own language, and the Romans later based their alphabet—the script we use to write English today—on Greek. Alphabets based on the Phoenician alphabet were also created in the Persian Empire and formed the basis of Hebrew, Arabic, and various alphabets of South and Central Asia. The system invented by ordinary people and spread by Phoenician merchants is the origin of most of the world's phonetic alphabets today.

The Hebrews

FOCUS QUESTION *How did the Hebrews create an enduring religious tradition?*

The legacy of another people who took advantage of Egypt's collapse to found an independent state may have been even more far-reaching than that of the Phoenicians. For a period of several centuries, a people known as the Hebrews controlled first one and then two small states on the western end of the Fertile Crescent, Israel and Judah. Politically unimportant when compared with the Egyptians or Babylonians, the Hebrews created a new form of religious belief, a monotheism based on the worship of an all-powerful god they called **Yahweh** (YAH-way). Beginning in the late 600s B.C.E., they began to write down their religious ideas, traditions, laws, advice literature, prayers, hymns, history, and prophecies in a series of books. These were gathered together centuries later to form the Hebrew Bible, which Christians later adopted and termed the "Old Testament" to parallel specific Christian writings termed the "New Testament." These writings later became the core of the Hebrews' religion, Judaism, a word taken from the kingdom of Judah, the southern of the two Hebrew kingdoms and the one that was the primary force in developing religious traditions. (The word *Israelite*, often used as a synonym for *Hebrew*, refers to all people in this group, and not simply the residents of the northern kingdom of Israel.) Jews today revere these texts, as do many Christians, and Muslims respect them, all of which gives them particular importance.

The Hebrew State

Most of the information about the Hebrews comes from the Bible, which, like all ancient documents, must be used with care as a historical source. Archaeological evidence has supported many of its details, and because it records a living religious tradition, extensive textual and physical research into everything it records

continues, with enormous controversies among scholars about how to interpret findings.

The Hebrews were nomadic pastoralists who may have migrated into the Nile Delta from the east, seeking good land for their herds of sheep and goats. According to the Hebrew Bible, they were enslaved by the Egyptians, but were led out of Egypt by a charismatic leader named Moses. The biblical account is very dramatic, and the events form a pivotal episode in the history of the Hebrews and the later religious practices of Judaism. Moses conveyed God's warning to the pharaoh that a series of plagues would strike Egypt, the last of which was the threat that all firstborn sons in Egypt would be killed. He instructed the Hebrews to prepare a hasty meal of a sacrificed lamb eaten with unleavened bread. The blood of the lamb was painted over the doors of Hebrew houses. At midnight Yahweh spread death over the land, but he passed over the Hebrew houses with the blood-painted doors. This event became known as the Passover, and later became a central religious holiday in Judaism. The next day a terrified pharaoh ordered the Hebrews out of Egypt. Moses then led them in search of what they understood to be the Promised Land, an event known as the Exodus, which was followed by forty years of wandering.

According to scripture, the Hebrews settled in the area between the Mediterranean and the Jordan River known as Canaan. They were organized into tribes, each tribe consisting of numerous families who thought of themselves as all related to one another and having a common ancestor. At first, good farmland, pastureland, and freshwater sources were held in common by each tribe. Common use of land was—and still is—characteristic of nomadic peoples. The Bible divides up the Hebrews at this point into twelve tribes, each named according to an ancestor.

In Canaan, the nomadic Hebrews encountered a variety of other peoples, whom they both learned from and fought. They slowly adopted agriculture, and not surprisingly, at times worshipped the agricultural gods of their neighbors, including Baal, an ancient fertility god represented as a golden calf. This was another example of the common historical pattern of newcomers adapting themselves to the culture of an older, well-established people.

The Bible reports that the greatest danger to the Hebrews came from a group known as the Philistines,

A Golden Calf   According to the Hebrew Bible, Moses descended from Mount Sinai, where he had received the Ten Commandments, to find the Hebrews worshipping a golden calf, which was against Yahweh's laws. In July 1990 an American archaeological team found this model of a gilded calf inside a pot. The figurine, which dates to about 1550 B.C.E., is strong evidence for the existence in Canaan of religious traditions that involved animals as divine symbols. (www.BibleLandPictures.com/Alamy Stock Photo)

who were most likely Greek-speaking people who had migrated to Canaan as part of the movement of the Sea Peoples and established a kingdom along the Mediterranean coast. The Philistines' superior technology and military organization at first made them invincible, but the Hebrews found a champion and a spirited leader in Saul. In the biblical account Saul and his men battled the Philistines for control of the land, often without success. In the meantime Saul established a monarchy over the twelve Hebrew tribes, becoming their king, an event conventionally dated to about 1025 B.C.E.

The Bible includes detailed discussion of the growth of the Hebrew kingdom. It relates that Saul's work was carried on by David of Bethlehem (r. ca. 1005–965 B.C.E.), who pushed back the Philistines and waged war against his other neighbors. To give his kingdom a capital, he captured the city of Jerusalem, which he enlarged, fortified, and made the religious and political center of his realm. David's military successes enlarged the kingdom and won the Hebrews unprecedented security, and his forty-year reign was a period of vitality and political consolidation.

David's son Solomon (r. ca. 965–925 B.C.E.) launched a building program that the biblical narrative describes as including cities, palaces, fortresses, and roads. The most symbolic of these projects was the Temple of Jerusalem, which became the home of the Ark of the Covenant, the chest that contained the holiest of Hebrew religious articles. The temple in Jerusalem was intended to be the religious heart of the kingdom, a symbol of Hebrew unity and Yahweh's approval of the kingdom built by Saul, David, and Solomon.

Evidence of this united kingdom may have come to light in August 1993 when an Israeli archaeologist found an inscribed stone slab that refers to a "king of Israel," and also to the "House of David." This discovery has been regarded by most scholars as the first mention of King David's dynasty outside of the Bible. The nature and extent of this kingdom continue to be disputed among archaeologists, who offer divergent datings and interpretations for the finds that are continuously brought to light.

Along with discussing expansion and success, the Bible also notes problems. Solomon's efforts were hampered by strife. The financial demands of his building program drained the resources of his people, and his use of forced labor for building projects further fanned popular resentment.

The Hebrew Exodus and State, ca. 1250–800 B.C.E.

→ Possible route of the Exodus, ca. 1250 B.C.E.
☐ Solomon's kingdom, ca. 950 B.C.E.
☐ Israel, ca. 800 B.C.E.
☐ Judah, ca. 800 B.C.E.

A united Hebrew kingdom did not last long. At Solomon's death his kingdom broke into political halves. The northern part became Israel, with its capital at Samaria, and the southern half became Judah, with Jerusalem remaining its center. War soon broke out between them, as recorded in the Bible, and the Assyrians wiped out the northern kingdom of Israel in 722 B.C.E. Judah survived numerous calamities until the Babylonians crushed it in 587 B.C.E. The survivors were forcibly relocated to Babylonia, a period commonly known as the Babylonian Captivity. In 539 B.C.E. the Persian king Cyrus the Great (see page 53) conquered the Babylonians and permitted some forty thousand exiles to return to Jerusalem. They rebuilt the temple, although politically the area was simply part of the Persian Empire.

The Jewish Religion

During and especially after the Babylonian Captivity, the most important legal and ethical Hebrew texts were edited and brought together in the **Torah**, the first five books of the Hebrew Bible. Here the exiles redefined their beliefs and practices, thereby establishing what they believed was the law of Yahweh. Fundamental to an understanding of the Jewish religion is the concept of the **Covenant**, an agreement that people believed to exist between themselves and Yahweh. According to the Bible, Yahweh appeared to the tribal leader Abraham, promising him that he would be blessed, as would his descendants, if they followed Yahweh. (Because Judaism, Christianity, and Islam all regard this event as foundational, they are referred to as the "Abrahamic religions.") Yahweh next appeared to Moses during the time he was leading the Hebrews out of Egypt, and Yahweh made a Covenant with the Hebrews: if they worshipped Yahweh as their only god, he would consider them his chosen people and protect them from their enemies. The Covenant was understood to be made with the whole people, not simply a king or an elite, and was renewed again several times in the accounts of

■ **Yahweh** The sole god in Hebrew monotheism; later anglicized as Jehovah.

■ **Torah** The first five books of the Hebrew Bible, containing the most important legal and ethical Hebrew texts; later became part of the Christian Old Testament.

■ **Covenant** An agreement that the Hebrews believed to exist between themselves and Yahweh, in which he would consider them his chosen people if they worshipped him as their only god.

the Hebrew people in the Bible. Individuals such as Abraham and Moses who acted as intermediaries between Yahweh and the Hebrew people were known as "prophets"; much of the Hebrew Bible consists of writings in their voices, understood as messages from Yahweh to which the Hebrews were to listen.

Worship was embodied in a series of rules of behavior that became known as the Ten Commandments, which Yahweh gave to Moses. (See "Thinking Like a Historian: The Moral Life," page 44.) These required certain kinds of religious observances and forbade the Hebrews to steal, kill, lie, or commit adultery, thus creating a system of ethical absolutes. From the Ten Commandments a complex system of rules of conduct was created and later written down as Hebrew law. The earliest part of this code, contained in the Torah, was most likely influenced by Hammurabi's code (see Chapter 1) and often called for harsh punishments. Later tradition, largely the work of the prophets who lived from the eighth to the fifth centuries B.C.E., put more emphasis on righteousness than on retribution.

Like the followers of other religions in the ancient Near East, Jews engaged in rituals through which they showed their devotion. They were also expected to please Yahweh by living up to high moral standards and by worshipping him above all other gods. The first of the Ten Commandments expresses this: "I am the Lord your God . . . you shall have no other gods besides me" (Exodus 20:2–3). Increasingly this was understood to be a commandment to worship Yahweh alone. The later prophets such as Isaiah created a system of ethical monotheism, in which goodness was understood to come from a single transcendent god, and in which religious obligations included fair and just behavior toward other people as well as rituals. They saw Yahweh as intervening directly in history and also working through individuals—both Hebrews and non-Hebrews—he had chosen to carry out his aims. (See "Individuals in Society: Cyrus the Great," page 53.) Judging by the many prophets (and a few prophetesses) in the Bible exhorting the Hebrews to listen to Yahweh, honor the Covenant, stop worshipping other gods, and behave properly, adherence to this system was a difficult challenge.

Like Mesopotamian deities, Yahweh punished people, but the Hebrews also believed he was a loving and forgiving god who would protect and reward all those who obeyed his commandments. A hymn recorded in the book of Psalms captures this idea:

> Blessed is every one who fears the Lord, who
>   walks in his ways!
> You shall eat the fruit of the labor of your hands;
>   you shall be happy, and it shall be well with you.
> Your wife will be like a fruitful vine within your
>   house;

> your children will be like olive shoots around your
>   table.
> Lo, thus shall the man be blessed who fears the
>   Lord. (Psalms 128:1–4)

The religion of the Hebrews was thus addressed to not only an elite but also the individual. Because kings or other political leaders were not essential to its practice, the rise or fall of a kingdom was not crucial to the religion's continued existence. Religious leaders were important in Judaism, but personally following the instructions of Yahweh was the central task for observant Jews in the ancient world.

Hebrew Family and Society

The Hebrews were originally nomadic, but they adopted settled agriculture in Canaan, and some lived in cities. The shift away from pastoralism affected more than just how people fed themselves. Communal use of land gave way to family or private ownership, and devotion to the traditions of Judaism came to replace tribal identity.

Family relationships reflected evolving circumstances. Marriage and the family were fundamentally important in Jewish life; celibacy was frowned upon and almost all major Jewish thinkers and priests were married. Polygamy was allowed, but the typical marriage was probably monogamous. In the codes of conduct written down in the Hebrew Bible, sex between a married woman and a man not her husband was an "abomination," as were incest and sex between men. Men were free to have sexual relations with concubines, servants, and slaves, however.

As in Mesopotamia and Egypt, marriage was a family matter, too important to be left to the whims of young people. (See "Evaluating the Evidence 2.2: A Jewish Family Contract," at right.) Although specific rituals may have been expected to ensure ritual purity in sexual relations, sex itself was viewed as part of Yahweh's creation and the bearing of children was seen in some ways as a religious function. Sons were especially desired because they maintained the family bloodline, while keeping ancestral property in the family. As in Mesopotamia, land was handed down within families, generally from father to son. A firstborn son became the head of the household at his father's death. Mothers oversaw the early education of the children, but as boys grew older, their fathers gave them more of their education. Both men and women were expected to know religious traditions so that they could teach their children and prepare for religious rituals and ceremonies. Women worked in the fields alongside their husbands in rural areas, and in shops in the cities. According to biblical codes, menstruation and childbirth made women ritually

A Jewish Family Contract

During the time of Persian rule in Egypt, Jewish soldiers were stationed in Elephantine, a military post on the Nile. Historians have since recovered papyrus documents from that location, known as the Elephantine papyri, which provide information on all sorts of everyday social and economic matters, including marriage, divorce, property, slavery, and borrowing money. The text below is an agreement by a Jewish father regarding a house he had given to his daughter, probably as part of her dowry. It was written in Aramaic, the language of business in the Persian Empire.

On the 21st of Chisleu, that is the 1st of Mesore, year 6 of King Artaxerxes,* Mahseiah b. Yedoniah, a Jew of Elephantine, of the detachment of Haumadata, said to Jezaniah b. Uriah of the said detachment as follows: There is the site of 1 house belonging to me, west of the house belonging to you, which I have given to your wife, my daughter Mibtahiah, and in respect of which I have written her a deed. The measurements of the house in question are 8 cubits and a handbreadth by 11, *by the measuring-rod.*† Now do I, Mahseiah, say to you, Build and equip that site . . . and dwell thereon with your wife. But you may not sell that house or give it as a present to others; only your children by my daughter Mibtahiah shall have power over it after

you two. If tomorrow or some other day you build upon this land, and then my daughter divorces you and leaves you, she shall have no power to take it or give it to others; only your children by Mibtahiah shall have power over it, in return for the work which you shall have done. If, on the other hand, she recovers from you [in other words, if Jezaniah divorces *her*], she [may] take half the house, and [the] othe[r] half shall be at your disposal in return for the building which you will have done on that house. And again as to that half, your children by Mibtahiah shall have power over it after you. If tomorrow or another day I should institute suit or process against you and say I did not give you this land to build on and did not draw up this deed for you, I shall give you a sum of 10 *karshin* by royal weight, at the rate of 2 *R* to the ten, and no suit or process shall lie. This deed was written by 'Atharshuri b. Nabuzeribni in the fortress of Syene at the dictation of Mahseiah.

Witnesses hereto (signatures)

EVALUATE THE EVIDENCE

1. How does Mahseiah seek to assist his daughter and his future grandchildren?
2. What does this contract reveal about the movement and mixtures of peoples in the Persian Empire, and about Persian methods of governing?

Source: James B. Pritchard, ed., *Ancient Near Eastern Texts Relating to the Old Testament — Third Edition with Supplement.* Reproduced with permission of PRINCETON UNIVERSITY PRESS, in the format Book via Copyright Clearance Center.

*This is the date of the document. Chisleu was a month in the Hebrew calendar, Mesore a seasonal period in the Egyptian calendar. Artaxerxes is most likely Artaxerxes I, king of Persia from 465 to 424 B.C.E., which means the year this agreement was drafted was 459 B.C.E.
†A cubit was the length of a forearm, roughly 20 inches; the house site was thus about 15 by 18 feet.

---

impure, but the implications of this in ancient times are contested by scholars.

Children, according to the book of Psalms, "are a heritage of the lord, and the fruit of the womb is his reward" (Psalms 128:3), and newly married couples were expected to begin a family at once. The desire for children to perpetuate the family was so strong that if a man died before he could sire a son, his brother was legally obliged to marry the widow. The son born of the brother was thereafter considered the offspring of the dead man. If the brother refused, the widow had her revenge by denouncing him to the elders and publicly spitting in his face.

The development of urban life among the Jews created new economic opportunities, especially in crafts and trades. People specialized in certain occupations, such as milling flour, baking bread, making pottery, weaving, and carpentry. As in most ancient societies, these crafts were family trades. Sons worked with their father, daughters with their mother. If the business prospered, the family might be assisted by a few paid workers or slaves. The practitioners of a craft usually lived in a particular section of town, a custom still prevalent in the Near East today. Commerce and trade developed later than crafts. Trade with neighboring countries was handled by foreigners, usually Phoenicians. Jews dealt mainly in local trade, and in most instances craftsmen and farmers sold directly to their customers.

The Torah sets out rules about many aspects of life, including skin diseases, seminal emissions, childbirth, sexual actions, and animal sacrifices. Among these was the set of dietary laws known as *kashrut* (from which we derive the English word *kosher*, which means ritually pure and ready to be eaten), setting out what plants and animals Jews were forbidden to eat and how foods were to be prepared properly. Prohibited animals included pigs, rabbits, many birds, insects (except for locusts), and shellfish, as well as any animal not slaughtered in

The Moral Life

Ancient peoples developed various codes of behavior and morality, which included how they were to treat other humans and often also how they were to act toward the gods. What similarities and differences do you see in the ideas of a moral life for New Kingdom Egyptians, Hebrews, and Zoroastrian Persians?

1 **The Egyptian *Book of the Dead*.** During the New Kingdom and afterward, well-to-do Egyptians were buried with papyrus scrolls on which were written magical and religious texts, now known as the *Book of the Dead*, designed to help the deceased make the crossing to the afterlife. These included a standardized list of things the deceased had not done during life, what modern scholars have called a "negative confession."

To be said on reaching the Hall of the Two Truths so as to purge N [here the name of the deceased was written] of any sins committed and to see the face of every god:

Hail to you, great God, Lord of the Two Truths!
I have come to you, my Lord,
I was brought to see your beauty. . . .

I have not done crimes against people,
I have not mistreated cattle,
I have not sinned in the Place of Truth.
I have not known what should not be known,
I have not done any harm.
I did not begin a day by exacting more than my due,
My name did not reach the bark of the mighty
   ruler.
I have not blasphemed a god,
I have not robbed the poor.
I have not done what the god abhors,
I have not maligned a servant to his master.
I have not caused pain,
I have not caused tears.
I have not killed,

I have not ordered to kill,
I have not made anyone suffer.
I have not damaged the offerings in the temples,
I have not depleted the loaves of the gods,
I have not stolen the cakes of the dead [food left
   for the deceased].
I have not copulated nor defiled myself.
I have not increased nor reduced the measure,
I have not diminished the arura [arable land],
I have not cheated in the fields.
I have not added to the weight of the balance,
I have not falsified the plummet of the scales.
I have not taken milk from the mouth of
   children,
I have not deprived cattle of their pasture.
I have not snared birds in the reeds of the gods,
I have not caught fish in their ponds.
I have not held back water in its season,
I have not dammed a flowing stream,
I have not quenched a needed fire.
I have not neglected the days of meat offerings,
I have not detained cattle belonging to the god,
I have not stopped a god in his procession.
I am pure, I am pure, I am pure, I am pure!

2 **The Ten Commandments.** According to Hebrew Scripture, where they appear twice, the Ten Commandments were given by Yahweh to Moses. HaShem (which means "the Name") is one of the names of God in Judaism, used as a sign of reverence and respect, as is writing "G-d."

EXODUS 20

1: And G-d spoke all these words, saying:
2: I am HaShem thy G-d, who brought thee out of the land of Egypt, out of the house of bondage.
3: Thou shalt have no other gods before Me.
4: Thou shalt not make unto thee a graven image, nor any manner of likeness, of any

thing that is in heaven above, or that is in the earth beneath, or that is in the water under the earth;
5: thou shalt not bow down unto them, nor serve them; for I HaShem thy G-d am a jealous G-d, visiting the iniquity of the fathers upon the children unto the third and fourth generation of them that hate Me;

ANALYZING THE EVIDENCE

1. In Source 1, what religious duties and personal actions does the negative confession suggest were important to Egyptians?
2. In Source 2, the Ten Commandments, what actions were required of or forbidden to Hebrews?
3. What does Zoroaster call on believers to do in Source 3?
4. In these moral codes, what will be the rewards of those who do what they're supposed to do? What will be the fate of those who do not?
5. What seems to be the most important moral duty in each of these codes?

6: and showing mercy unto the thousandth generation of them that love Me and keep My commandments.

7: Thou shalt not take the name of HaShem thy G-d in vain; for HaShem will not hold him guiltless that taketh His name in vain.

8: Remember the sabbath day, to keep it holy.

9: Six days shalt thou labour, and do all thy work;

10: but the seventh day is a sabbath unto HaShem thy G-d, in it thou shalt not do any manner of work, thou, nor thy son, nor thy daughter, nor thy man-servant, nor thy maid-servant, nor thy cattle, nor thy stranger that is within thy gates;

11: in six days HaShem made heaven and earth, the sea, and all that in them is, and rested on the seventh day; wherefore HaShem blessed the sabbath day, and hallowed it.

12: Honour thy father and thy mother, that thy days may be long upon the land which HaShem thy G-d giveth thee.

13: Thou shalt not murder; Thou shalt not commit adultery; Thou shalt not steal; Thou shalt not bear false witness against thy neighbour.

14: Thou shalt not covet thy neighbour's house; thou shalt not covet thy neighbour's wife, nor his man-servant, nor his maid-servant, nor his ox, nor his ass, nor any thing that is thy neighbour's.

3 Zoroaster's teachings in the Avesta.

The sacred texts of the Zoroastrians, collected in the Avesta, include some written by Zoroaster himself as liturgical poems that priests were to recite during divine services. This one tells believers about aspects of Ahuramazda they should understand, such as Right and Good Thought, as they decide what to do in their lives.

Now I will speak, O proselytes, of what ye may bring to the
   attention even of one who knows,
praises for the Lord [Ahuramazda] and Good Thought's acts of
   worship
well considered, and for Right; the gladness beheld by the daylight.
Hear with your ears the best message, behold with lucid mind
the two choices in the decision each man makes for his own person
before the great Supplication, as ye look ahead to the declaration to
   Him.
They are the two Wills, the twins who in the beginning made
   themselves heard through dreaming,
those two kinds of thought, of speech, of deed, the better and the
   evil;
and between them well-doers discriminate rightly, but ill-doers
   do not.
Once those two Wills join battle, a man adopts
life or non-life, the way of existence that will be his at the last:
that of the wrongful the worst kind, but for the righteous one, best
   thought.
Of these two Wills, the Wrongful one chooses to do the worst
   things,
but the most Bounteous Will (chooses) Right, he who clothes
   himself in adamant;
as do those also who committedly please the Lord with genuine
   actions, the Mindful One.

Between those two the very Daevas [the traditional gods of Iran] fail
   to discriminate rightly, because delusion
comes over them as they deliberate, when they choose worst thought;
they scurry together to the violence with which mortals blight the
   world.
But suppose one comes with dominion for Him, with good
   thought and right,
then vitality informs the body, piety the soul:
their ringleader Thou wilt have as if in irons:
and when the requital comes for their misdeeds,
for Thee, Mindful One [Ahuramazda], together with Good Thought,
   will be found dominion
to proclaim to those, Lord, who deliver Wrong into the hands of
   Right.
May we be the ones who will make this world splendid,
Mindful One and Ye Lords, bringers of change, and Right,
as our minds come together where insight is fluctuating.
For then destruction will come down upon Wrong's prosperity,
and the swiftest (steeds) will be yoked from the fair dwelling of
   Good Thought,
of the Mindful One, and of Right, and they will be the winners
   in good repute.
When ye grasp those rules that the Mindful One lays down,
   O mortals,
through success and failure, and the lasting harm that is for
   the wrongful
as furtherance is for the righteous, then thereafter desire will be
   fulfilled.

PUTTING IT ALL TOGETHER

Using the sources above, along with what you have learned in class and in Chapters 1 and 2, write a short essay that discusses similarities and differences in ideas about the moral life for New Kingdom Egyptians, Hebrews, and Zoroastrian Persians. What is the basis of morality for these three groups, and how does this shape how people are supposed to act?

Sources: (1) Miriam Lichtheim, *Ancient Egyptian Literature: A Book of Readings*, vol. 2, *The New Kingdom* (Berkeley: University of California Press, 1976), pp. 124–126. © 2006 by the Regents of the University of California. Published by the University of California Press; (2) *The Tanakh*, JPS Electronic Edition, based on the 1917 JPS translation, https://www.jewishvirtuallibrary.org/jsource/Bible/Exodus20.html; (3) M. L. West, *The Hymns of Zoroaster: A New Translation of the Most Ancient Sacred Texts of Iran* (London: I. B. Tauris, 2010), pp. 51, 53, 55. Used by permission.

the proper way. Meat and dairy products were not to be eaten at the same meal or cooked in the same utensils. Later commentators sought to explain these laws as originating in concerns about health or hygiene, but the biblical text simply gives them as rules coming from Yahweh, sometimes expressed in terms of ritual purity or cleanliness. It is not clear how these rules were followed during the biblical period, because detailed interpretations were written down only much later, during the time of the Roman Empire, in the Talmud, a work that records civil and ceremonial law and Jewish traditions. Most scholars see the written laws as based on earlier oral traditions, but as with any law code, from Hammurabi's to contemporary ones, it is much easier to learn about what people were supposed to do according to the laws of the Torah than what they actually did.

Beliefs and practices that made Jews distinctive endured, but the Hebrew states did not. Small states like those of the Phoenicians and the Hebrews could exist only in the absence of a major power, and the beginning of the ninth century B.C.E. saw the rise of such a power: the Assyrians of northern Mesopotamia. They conquered the kingdom of Israel, the Phoenician cities, and eventually many other states as well.

Hebrew Seal This black stone seal dating from the seventh century B.C.E. depicts an archer shooting an arrow. The inscription beside him in ancient Hebrew letters means "for Hagab." Hagab was most likely the name of the official or army officer who would have used this seal on his letters and documents. Hagab chose to show himself dressed in Assyrian style, an indication of the Assyrian cultural influence that accompanied Assyrian military expansion. (Photo: Clara Amit. Courtesy, Israel Antiquities Authority)

Assyria, the Military Monarchy

FOCUS QUESTION *What explains the rise and fall of the Assyrians?*

The Assyrian kingdom originated in northern Mesopotamia. The Assyrians built up the military and conquered many of their neighbors, including Babylonia, and took over much of Syria all the way to the Mediterranean. The Assyrians then moved into Anatolia, where the pressure they put on the Hittite Empire was one factor in its collapse. Assyria's success allowed it to become the leading power in the Near East, with an army that at times numbered many tens of thousands.

Assyria's Long Road to Power

The Assyrians had inhabited northern Mesopotamia since the third millennium B.C.E., forming a kingdom that grew and shrank in size and power over the centuries. They had long pursued commerce with the Babylonians in the south, and the peoples of northern Syria and Anatolia in the north. During the time of Sargon of Akkad, they were part of the Akkadian empire, then independent, then part of the Babylonian empire under Hammurabi, then independent again (see Chapter 1). Warfare with the Babylonians and other Near Eastern states continued off and on, and in the thirteenth century B.C.E., under the leadership of a series of warrior-kings, the Assyrians slowly began to create a larger state.

The eleventh century B.C.E.—the time of the Bronze Age Collapse—was a period of instability and retrenchment in the Near East. The Assyrians did not engage in any new wars of conquest, but remained fairly secure within their borders. Under the leadership of King Adad-nirari II (r. 911–892 B.C.E.), Assyria began a campaign of expansion and domination, creating what scholars have termed the Neo-Assyrian Empire. Assyrian armies pushed in all directions, conquering, exacting tribute, and building new fortified towns, palaces, and temples. King Shalmaneser III (shal-muh-NEE-zuhr) (r. 858–823 B.C.E.) conquered all of Babylonia, Syria, Phoenicia, and much of the northern half of the Arabian peninsula. The next several turbulent centuries were marked by Assyrian military campaigns, constant efforts by smaller states to maintain or recover their independence, and eventual further Assyrian conquest.

Assyrian history is often told as a story of one powerful king after another, but among the successful Assyrian rulers there was one queen, Shammuramat, whose name in Greek became Semiramis. She ruled with her husband and then as regent for her young son in 810–806 B.C.E. Although not much can be known for certain about the historical Queen Semiramis, many legends grew up about her, which were told

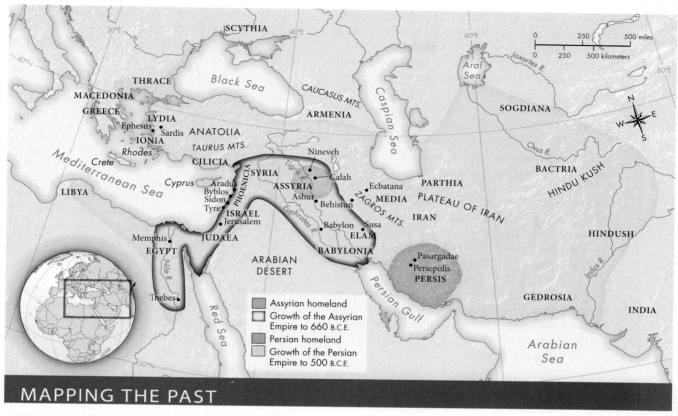

MAP 2.1 The Assyrian and Persian Empires, ca. 1000–500 B.C.E.

The Assyrian Empire at its height around 650 B.C.E. included almost all of the old centers of power in the ancient Near East. By 513 B.C.E., however, the Persian Empire was far larger.

ANALYZING THE MAP How does the Persian Empire compare in size to the Assyrian? What other differences can you identify between the two?

CONNECTIONS Compare this map to Map 1.1 on page 12. What changes and continuities do you see in centers of power in the ancient Near East?

throughout the ancient Near East, and later by Greek and Roman authors. Some emphasized her wisdom, beauty, and patronage of the arts, while others portrayed her as a sex-crazed sorceress. These stories cannot be used as evidence for the lives of women in the Assyrian Empire, but like the stories of Queen Cleopatra of Egypt (see Chapter 5), they can be used as evidence for the continuing fascination with the few women who held political power in the ancient world.

Eighth-century kings continued the expansion of Assyria, which established its capital at Nineveh (NIHN-uh-vuh) on the Tigris River. The kingdom of Israel and many other states fell; others, like the kingdom of Judah, became subservient to the warriors from the Tigris. In 717 B.C.E. Sargon II (r. 721–705 B.C.E.) led his army in a sweeping attack along the coast of the eastern Mediterranean south of Phoenicia, where he defeated the armies of the Egyptian pharaoh. Sargon also lashed out at Assyria's traditional enemies to the north and then turned south against a renewed threat in Babylonia. By

means of almost constant warfare, the Assyrians created an empire that stretched from east and north of the Tigris River to central Egypt (Map 2.1). Revolt against the Assyrians inevitably promised the rebels bloody battles and cruel sieges followed by surrender, accompanied by systematic torture and slaughter, or by deportations. Like many conquerors, the Assyrians recognized that relocated peoples were less likely to rebel because they were forced to create new lives for themselves far from their original homelands, and that simply relocating leaders might be enough to destroy opposition.

Assyrian methods were certainly harsh, but in practical terms Assyria's success was actually due primarily to the size of its army and the army's sophisticated and effective military organization. By Sargon's time, the Assyrians had invented the mightiest military machine the ancient Near East had ever seen, with perhaps seventy thousand men in the field in an era that typically saw armies of under ten thousand. The mainstay of the Assyrian army was the infantryman armed with an iron spear and sword and protected by helmet and armor. The Assyrian army also featured archers, some on foot, others on horseback, and still others in chariots—the latter ready to wield lances once they had expended their supply of arrows. Some infantry archers wore heavy armor. These soldiers served as a primitive field artillery whose job was to sweep the enemy's walls of defenders so that others could storm the defenses. Slingers (warriors who used slingshots) also served as artillery in pitched battles. For mobility on the battlefield, the Assyrians organized a corps of chariots.

Assyrian military genius was remarkable for the development of a wide variety of siege machinery and techniques, including excavation to undermine city walls and battering rams to knock down walls and gates. Never before in the Near East had anyone applied such technical knowledge to warfare. The Assyrians even invented the concept of a corps of engineers, who bridged rivers with pontoons or provided soldiers with inflatable skins for swimming. And the Assyrians knew how to coordinate their efforts, both in open battle and

in siege warfare. Assyrian king Sennacherib's (r. 705–681 B.C.E.) account of his attacks on the kingdom of Judah, which was under the leadership of King Hezekiah (r. ca. 715–686 B.C.E.) in 701 B.C.E., provides a vivid portrait of the Assyrian war machine:

> As to Hezekiah, the Jew, he did not submit to my yoke, I laid siege to 46 of his strong cities, walled forts and to the countless small villages in their vicinity, and conquered them by means of well-stamped earth-ramps, and battering rams brought thus near to the walls combined with the attack by foot soldiers, using mines, breaches as well as sapper work. . . . Himself I made prisoner in Jerusalem, his royal residence, like a bird in a cage. I surrounded him with earthwork in order to molest those who were leaving his city's gate.[2]

What Assyrian accounts do not mention is that the siege of Jerusalem was not successful. Although they had conquered many cities in Judah, the Assyrian armies gave up their attempts to conquer the entire kingdom and went home.

Sennacherib's campaign is also recorded several times in the Hebrew Bible, but there the point is very different. Instead of focusing on Assyrian might, the author stresses King Hezekiah's reliance on Yahweh. The biblical accounts attribute Judah's ability to withstand the Assyrian siege to an angel sent by Yahweh, but they also describe Hezekiah as taking practical measures to counter the Assyrian invasion. He "made weapons and shields in abundance," and also ordered the building of a tunnel that would divert water from the springs outside the walls of Jerusalem into the city, thus both limiting the water available for Assyrian troops and assuring the city of a steady supply:

> When Hezekiah saw that Sennacherib had come and intended to fight against Jerusalem, he planned with his officers and his mighty men to stop the water of the springs that were outside the city; and they helped him. A great many people were gathered, and they stopped all the springs and the brook that flowed through the land. (2 Chronicles 32:2–4)

The tunnel was completed and functioned, and is now a major tourist attraction. An inscription that was originally on the wall recording the way in which it was built has been dated to the eighth century B.C.E., and chemical analysis confirms this dating.

Assyrian Rule and Culture

Although the Assyrians gave up on conquering Judah, they won most of their battles, and they also knew how to use their victories to consolidate their power. The

Hezekiah's Tunnel   When the Assyrians were attacking Jerusalem in the eighth century B.C.E., King Hezekiah ordered the building of a tunnel from the springs outside the city walls to bring freshwater into the city. It was constructed by teams operating from each end, guided by workers above listening for the ways their hammer blows sounded on the rock. The tunnel can still be walked through today, though at certain times of the year this means wading in water. (Photo © Zev Radovan/Bridgeman Images)

Assyrians Besiege a City

In this Assyrian carving made about 700 B.C.E., from the palace of King Sennacherib at Nineveh, troops attack the Jewish fortified town of Lachish using a variety of siege machinery. On the right, defending soldiers crowd a tower, while men and women carry sacks away from the city.

EVALUATE THE EVIDENCE

1. What means of attack do the Assyrians use against the besieged city? How does the artist convey the idea that Assyrian military might was overwhelming?
2. Based on what you have read in this chapter about King Sennacherib, why might he have chosen to have this particular scene portrayed in his palace?

(British Museum, London, UK/De Agostini Picture Library/G. Nimatallah/Bridgeman Images)

key to success in all empires is to get cooperation from some people in the regions you wish to dominate, and the Assyrians did this well. As early as the reign of Tiglath-pileser III, the Assyrian kings began to organize their conquered territories into an empire. The lands closest to Assyria became provinces governed by Assyrian officials. Kingdoms beyond the provinces were not annexed but became dependent states that followed Assyria's lead and also paid Assyria a hefty tribute. The Assyrian king chose these states' rulers either by regulating the succession of native kings or by supporting native kings who appealed to him. Against more distant states the Assyrian kings waged frequent war in order to conquer them outright or make the dependent states secure. (See "Evaluating the Evidence 2.3: Assyrians Besiege a City," above.)

In the seventh century B.C.E. Assyrian power seemed firmly established. Yet the downfall of Assyria was swift and complete. Babylon finally won its independence from Assyria in 626 B.C.E. and joined forces with the Medes, an Indo-European-speaking people from Persia (modern Iran). Together the Babylonians and the Medes destroyed the Assyrian Empire in 612 B.C.E., paving the way for the rise of the Persians. The Hebrew prophet Nahum (NAY-uhm) spoke for many when he asked, "Nineveh is laid waste: who will bemoan her?" (Nahum 3:7). Their cities destroyed and their power shattered, the Assyrians disappeared from history, remembered only as a cruel people of the Old Testament who oppressed the Hebrews. Two hundred years later, when the Greek adventurer and historian Xenophon (ZEH-nuh-fuhn) passed by the ruins of Nineveh, he marveled at the

LIVING IN THE PAST
Assyrian Palace Life and Power

In 1854 the British archaeologist W. K. Loftus uncovered the palace of the Assyrian king Ashurbanipal (r. 668–ca. 627 B.C.E.) at Nineveh in modern Iraq. Among its treasures he found carved reliefs that stunningly illustrated royal life and Assyrian power. The friezes shown here decorated the walls of the palace where visitors to Ashurbanipal's court would see them.

The relief on the left shows Ashurbanipal and his queen enjoying a tranquil banquet in the shade of an arbor. Ele-gantly clothed, they drink first to the gods. Servants fan them. The king reposes on a lavish couch covered with expensive rugs. The queen sits beside him on an ornate chair, and servants carry in an opulent meal. Other servants play music for the royal couple. In true Assyrian style the seemingly peaceful scene gives a bald message of victory and power. Hanging from the tree on the left is the head of Teumann, king of Elam, whom Ashurbanipal has just defeated in battle. The servants are Teumann's captured sons.

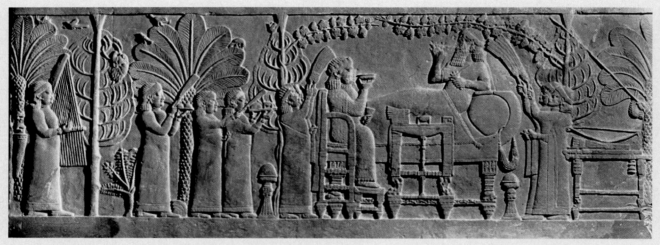

Ashurbanipal and his queen enjoying a banquet. (British Museum, London, UK/Werner Forman Archive/Bridgeman Images)

extent of the former city but knew nothing of the Assyrians. The glory of their empire was forgotten.

Modern archaeology has brought the Assyrians out of obscurity. In 1839 the English archaeologist and traveler A. H. Layard began excavations at Nineveh. His findings electrified the world. Layard's workers unearthed masterpieces, including monumental sculpted figures—huge winged bulls, human-headed lions, and sphinxes—as well as brilliantly sculpted friezes. Among the most renowned of Layard's finds were the Assyrian palace reliefs, whose number has been increased by the discoveries of twentieth-century archaeologists. For the kings' palaces, Assyrian artists carved reliefs that showed scenes of war as a series of episodes that progressed from the time the army marched out until the enemy was conquered. In doing so, they created a visual narrative of events, a form still favored by comic-book artists and the authors of graphic novels. (See "Living in the Past: Assyrian Palace Life and Power," above.)

Equally valuable were the numerous Assyrian cuneiform documents, which ranged from royal accounts of mighty military campaigns to simple letters by common people. The biggest find of these was the library of King Ashurbanipal (r. 668–627 B.C.E.), the last major Assyrian king, in the city of Nineveh. Like many Assyrian kings, Ashurbanipal was described as extremely cruel, but he was also well educated and deeply interested in literary and religious texts, especially those from what was already to him the ancient Mesopotamian past. Included in the tens of thousands of texts in his library were creation accounts from ancient Babylon (some most likely simply confiscated from the city of Babylon, which was part of the Assyrian Empire), the *Epic of Gilgamesh*, and many other mythological and religious texts, as well as word lists, chronicles, and royal documents. Some texts relate to medicine and astronomy, and others to foretelling the future or practicing magic. The clay tablets on which these were written are harder than normal, which many scholars think may have happened as a result of a fire

A frieze of a royal hunt (right) depicts a different display of royal power. Ashurbanipal routinely hunted lions, but only partly as sport. Hunting also enabled him to display symbolically his role as the protector of his people. The hunts often took place in the extensive parks that surrounded the royal court. As part of an elaborate ritual, the lions were let loose from pens. When ready, the king advanced either on foot or on horseback. When on foot, he was armed with bow or lance and accompanied only by a shield-bearer. Like a toreador in a bullfight, the king had to face the lion alone. Here King Ashurbanipal is mounted on a stallion that is wide-eyed from fear of the lion beside him. The king wears only a richly embroidered jacket, a kilt, and riding boots. As the lion lunges, the king plunges his spear down the lion's throat in a public display of his bravery and skill.

QUESTIONS FOR ANALYSIS

1. Based on what you know about the Assyrians, do you think these carved reliefs offer accurate depictions of palace life?
2. Consider the purpose of these two images. What did the king hope to convey with these depictions of himself? How might the reactions of subjects and foreigners have varied?

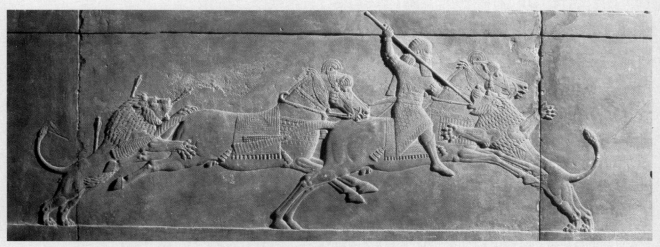

A royal lion hunt. (British Museum, London, UK/Werner Forman Archive/Bridgeman Images)

that destroyed the city of Nineveh shortly after the end of Ashurbanipal's reign. Unfortunately, the English archaeologists who dug up his library in the nineteenth century did not follow the standards of excavation that later archaeologists would, and just shipped the tablets back to London all jumbled together without recording exactly where and how they had been found. Many broke and are still being pieced together more than a century after their discovery. Thus many questions that scholars have about the library are impossible to answer.

The Neo-Babylonian Empire

The decline of Assyria allowed another group of people, the Chaldeans, to create a new dynasty of kings and a somewhat smaller empire centered at Babylon. The Chaldeans were peoples that settled in southern Mesopotamia, where they established their rule, later extending it farther north. They grew strong enough to overthrow Assyrian rule in 626 B.C.E.

with the help of another new people, the Medes, who had established themselves in modern western Iran (see page 52). The Neo- (or new) Babylonian empire they created was marked by an attempt at the restoration of past Babylonian greatness. Their most famous king, Nebuchadnezzar II (neh-buh-kuhd-NEH-zuhr) (r. 604–562 B.C.E.), thrust Babylonian power into Syria and Judah, destroying Jerusalem and forcibly deporting the residents to Babylonia.

The Chaldeans focused on solidifying their power and legitimizing their authority. Kings and priests consciously looked back to the great days of Hammurabi and other earlier kings. They instituted a religious revival that included restoring old temples and sanctuaries, as well as creating new ones in the same tradition. Part of their effort was commercial, as they sought to revive the economy in order to resurrect the image of Babylonian greatness. In their hands the city of Babylon grew and gained a reputation for magnificence and luxury. The city, it was said by later Greek and Roman writers, even housed hanging gardens, one of the "wonders of the ancient world." No contemporary written or archaeological sources confirm the existence of the hanging gardens, but they do confirm that Babylon was a bustling, thriving city.

The Neo-Babylonians preserved many basic aspects of older Babylonian law, literature, and government, yet they failed to bring peace and prosperity to Mesopotamia. Loss of important trade routes to the north and northeast reduced income, and additional misfortune came in the form of famine and plague. The Neo-Babylonian kingdom was weakened and ultimately conquered in 539 B.C.E. by its former allies the Medes, who had themselves found new allies, the Persians.

The Empire of the Persian Kings

FOCUS QUESTION *How did the Persians consolidate their power and control and influence the subjects of their extensive empire?*

The Assyrians rose to power from a base in the Tigris and Euphrates River Valleys of Mesopotamia, which had seen many earlier empires. They were defeated by a coalition that included a Mesopotamian power — Babylon — but also a people with a base of power in a part of the world that had not been the site of earlier urbanized states: Persia (modern-day Iran), a stark land of towering mountains and flaming deserts, with a broad central plateau in the heart of the country (see Map 2.1). The Persians created an even larger empire than the Assyrians did, and one that stretched far to the east. Though as conquerors they willingly used force to accomplish their ends, they also used diplomacy to consolidate their power and generally allowed the peoples that they conquered to practice their existing customs and religions. Thus the Persian Empire was one of political unity and cultural diversity.

Consolidation of the Persian Empire

Iran's geographical position and topography explain its traditional role as the highway between western and eastern Asia. Nomadic peoples migrating south from the broad steppes of Russia and Central Asia have streamed into Iran throughout much of history. Confronting the uncrossable salt deserts, most have turned either westward or eastward, moving on until they reached the advanced and wealthy urban centers of Mesopotamia and India. Cities did emerge along these routes, however, and Iran became the area where nomads met urban dwellers.

Among the nomadic groups were Indo-European-speaking peoples who migrated into this area about 1000 B.C.E. with their flocks and herds. They were also horse breeders, and the horse gave them a decisive military advantage over those who already lived

in the area. One of the Indo-European groups was the Medes, who settled in northern Iran with their capital at Ecbatana, the modern Hamadan. The Medes united under one king and joined the Babylonians in overthrowing the Assyrian Empire. With the rise of the Medes, the balance of power in western Asia shifted for the first time to the area east of Mesopotamia.

In 550 B.C.E. Cyrus the Great (r. 559–530 B.C.E.), king of the Persians and one of the most remarkable statesmen of antiquity, conquered the Medes. (See "Individuals in Society: Cyrus the Great," at right.) Cyrus's conquest of the Medes resulted not in slavery and slaughter but in the union of the two peoples. Having united Persia and Media, Cyrus set out to achieve two goals. First, he wanted to win control of the shore of the Mediterranean and thus of the terminal ports of the great trade routes that crossed Iran and Anatolia. Second, he strove to secure eastern Iran from the pressure of nomadic invaders.

In a series of major campaigns, Cyrus achieved his goals. He conquered the various kingdoms of the Tigris and Euphrates Valleys, including Babylon in 539 B.C.E. A text written in cuneiform on a sixth-century-B.C.E. Babylonian clay cylinder presents Cyrus describing the way in which the main Babylonian god Marduk selected him to conquer Babylon and restore proper government and worship:

> I am Cyrus, king of the universe, the great king, the powerful king, king of Babylon, king of Sumer and Akkad, king of the four quarters of the world. . . . When I went as harbinger of peace i[nt]o Babylon I founded my sovereign residence within the palace amid celebration and rejoicing. Marduk, the great lord, bestowed on me as my destiny the great magnanimity of one who loves Babylon, and I every day sought him out in awe. My vast troops marched peaceably in Babylon, and the whole of [Sumer] and Akkad had nothing to fear. I sought the welfare of the city of Babylon and all its sanctuaries. As for the population of Babylon, . . . [w]ho as if without div[ine intention] had endured a yoke not decreed for them, I soothed their weariness, I freed them from their bonds. . . . Marduk, the great lord, rejoiced at [my good] deeds, and he pronounced a sweet blessing over me, Cyrus, the king who fears him, and over Cambyses, the son [my] issue, [and over] all my troops, that we might proceed further at his exalted command.[3]

We do not know who actually wrote this text, but whoever did made sure to portray Cyrus as someone who triumphed as the result of divine favor, not simply military conquest, and honored the gods of the regions he conquered.

INDIVIDUALS IN SOCIETY

Cyrus the Great

Cyrus (r. 559–530 B.C.E.), known to history as "the Great" and the founder of the Persian Empire, began life as a subject of the Medes, an Iranian people very closely related to the Persians. There are few surviving sources describing his early life, and even the date of his birth is uncertain. There are many legends, however, some originating in Persia and others in Greece, as many later Greek leaders and authors admired Cyrus. The Greek historian Herodotus records the legend that Cyrus was the grandson of Astyages, king of the Medes, who ordered him killed to eliminate him as a future threat. Cyrus, like the biblical Moses, escaped the plot and went on to rule both his own Persians and the Medes.

Another story recounted by Herodotus tells how Cyrus's playmates chose him king. He assigned them specific duties, and when one aristocratic boy refused to obey his orders, Cyrus had him "arrested." The boy's father later demanded that Cyrus explain his haughty behavior. Cyrus replied that the other boys had chosen him king, and he did his duty justly, as a king should. He told the man that if he had done anything wrong, he was there to take his punishment. The man and the other boys admired his calm sense of duty and responsibility. Through this anecdote, the historian projected Cyrus's intelligence and good qualities, revealed later in life, back into his boyhood.

Astyages eventually marched against the grown Cyrus and was defeated. Instead of enslaving the Medes, Cyrus incorporated them into the new kingdom of Persia, thus demonstrating his inclusive concept of rule. This relatively mild rule continued with his later conquests. He won the admiration of many Greeks, whom he allowed to continue their religious rituals and intellectual pursuits.

After conquering Babylonia, Cyrus allowed the Jews who had been in forced exile there to return to Jerusalem. Hebrew Scripture portrays Cyrus as divinely chosen, as evidenced by this biblical passage, probably written in the late sixth century B.C.E., shortly after the end of the Babylonian Captivity:

> Thus said the Lord to Cyrus, His anointed one—
> Whose right hand He has grasped,
> Treading down nations before him,
> Ungirding the loins of kings,
> Opening doors before him, and letting no gate stay shut:
> I will march before you, and level the hills that loom up;
> I will shatter doors of bronze
> And cut down iron bars.
> I will give you treasures concealed in the dark
> And secret hoards—
> So that you may know that it is I the Lord,
> The God of Israel, who call you by name. . . .
> It was I who roused him [Cyrus] for victory
> And who level all roads for him.
> He shall rebuild My city
> And let My exiled people go
> Without price and without payment
>   — said the LORD of hosts. (Isaiah 45:1–3, 13)

Cyrus died in 530 B.C.E. while campaigning in Central Asia. Though much of his life was spent at war, he knew how to govern conquered peoples effectively and acquired a reputation for benevolence and tolerance. Much about his life can never be known, but Cyrus appears to have been a practical man of sound judgment, keenly interested in foreign peoples and their ways of life.

Statue of Cyrus the Great at the Olympic Park in Sydney, Australia. A replica of a bas-relief in Cyrus's capital city of Pasargadae, this monument was erected in 1994 as a testament to the peaceful coexistence of many different peoples in the Persian Empire.
(Visual Connection Archive)

QUESTIONS FOR ANALYSIS

1. How are the Greek stories, as told by Herodotus, and the biblical account similar in their portrayals of Cyrus? How are they different?
2. Herodotus, the Bible, and the inscription on the Cyrus cylinder discussed on page 52 have all been influential in establishing the largely positive historical view of Cyrus. What limitations might there be in using these as historical sources?

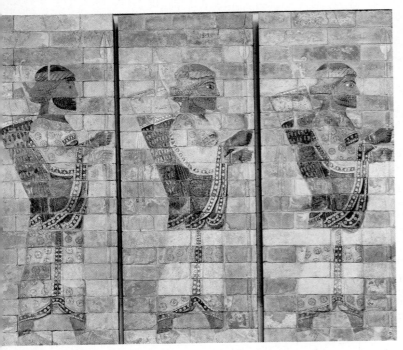

Archers in the King's Palace   In this colorful decorative frieze made of glazed brick, men wearing long Persian robes and laced ankle boots carry spears, bows, and quivers. This reconstruction in the Louvre Museum in Paris was made from material found in the palace of King Darius I of Persia in Susa, built about 510 B.C.E. Enough bricks were found there to suggest that there were originally many archers, perhaps representing Darius's royal guards or symbolizing the entire Persian people. (Musée du Louvre, Paris, France/Erich Lessing/Art Resource, NY)

Cyrus then swept into western Anatolia. Here his forces met those of the young kingdom of Lydia, a small state where gold may have first been minted into coins. Croesus (KREE-suhs), king of the Lydians, considered Cyrus an immediate threat and planned to attack his territory. Greek legends later related that Croesus consulted the oracle at Delphi, that is, the priestess of the temple to the god Apollo at Delphi, who was understood to convey the words of the god when she spoke. Speaking through the priestess, Apollo said of the invasion, "If you make war on the Persians, you will destroy a mighty empire" (Herodotus 1.53.3). Thinking that the oracle meant the Persian Empire, Croesus went ahead and was defeated; the oracle meant that he would destroy his own kingdom.

According to later Greek sources, Cyrus spared the life of Croesus, who then served him as an adviser. To the Greeks, Croesus became synonymous with enormous wealth, giving rise to the phrase "richer than Croesus." Recent scholarship has suggested that stories about Croesus's wealth were based primarily on the fact that Lydia was one of the earliest places where gold coins were minted. Historians studying Persian sources have also noted that the account of Croesus being spared and becoming an adviser to Cyrus might be an embellished story, yet another myth surrounding the kings of Lydia and Persia. The exact date and circumstances of Croesus's death have yet to be determined.

Whatever actually happened to Croesus, Cyrus's generals subdued the Greek cities along the coast of Anatolia, thus gaining him important ports on the Mediterranean. From Lydia, Cyrus marched to the far eastern corners of Iran and conquered the regions of Parthia and Bactria in Central Asia, though he ultimately died on the battlefield there.

After his victories, Cyrus made sure that the Persians were portrayed as liberators, and in some cases he was more benevolent than most conquerors were. According to his own account, he freed all the captive peoples who were living in forced exile in Babylonia. This included the Hebrews. He returned their sacred objects to them and allowed those who wanted to do so to return to Jerusalem, where he paid for the rebuilding of their temple.

Cyrus's successors continued Persian conquests, creating the largest empire the world had yet seen. In 525 B.C.E. Cyrus's son Cambyses (r. 530–522 B.C.E.) subdued the Egyptians and the Nubians. At Cambyses's death (the circumstances of which are disputed), Darius I (r. 521–486 B.C.E.) took over the throne and conquered Scythia in Central Asia, along with much of Thrace and Macedonia, areas north of the Aegean Sea. By 510 B.C.E. the Persians also ruled the western coast of Anatolia and many of the islands of the Aegean. Thus, within forty years, the Persians had transformed themselves from a subject people to the rulers of a vast empire that included all of the oldest kingdoms and peoples of the region, as well as many outlying areas (see Map 2.1). Unsurprisingly, Darius began to call himself "King of Kings." Invasions of Greece by Darius and his son Xerxes were unsuccessful, but the Persian Empire lasted another two hundred years, until it became part of the empire of Alexander the Great (see Chapter 4).

The Persians also knew how to preserve the empire they had won on the battlefield. Learning from the Assyrians, they created an efficient administrative system to govern the empire based in their newly built capital city of Persepolis near modern Shiraz, Iran. Under Darius, they divided the empire into districts and appointed either Persian or local nobles as administrators called **satraps** to head each one. The satrap controlled local government, collected taxes, heard legal cases, and maintained order. He was assisted by a council, and also by officials and army leaders sent from Persepolis who made sure that the satrap knew the will of the king and that the king knew what was going on in the provinces. This system lessened

■ **satraps** Administrators in the Persian Empire who controlled local government, collected taxes, heard legal cases, and maintained order.

■ **Zoroastrianism** Religion based on the ideas of Zoroaster that stressed devotion to the god Ahuramazda alone, and that emphasized the individual's responsibility to choose between good and evil.

opposition to Persian rule by making local elites part of the system of government, although sometimes satraps used their authority to build up independent power.

Communication and trade were eased by a sophisticated system of roads linking the empire from the coast of Asia Minor to the valley of the Indus River. On the roads were way stations where royal messengers could get food and horses, a system that allowed messages to be communicated quickly, much like the famed pony express in the American West. These roads meant that the king was usually in close touch with officials and subjects. The roads also simplified the defense of the empire by making it easier to move Persian armies. In addition, the system allowed the easy flow of trade, which Persian rulers further encouraged by building canals, including one that linked the Red Sea and the Nile.

Persian Religion

Iranian religion was originally tied to nature. Ahuramazda (ah-HOOR-uh-MAZ-duh), the chief god, was the creator of all living creatures. Mithra, the sun-god whose cult would later spread throughout the Roman Empire, saw to justice and redemption. Fire was a particularly important god, and fire was often part of religious rituals. A priestly class, the Magi, developed among the Medes to officiate at sacrifices, chant prayers to the gods, and tend the sacred flame.

Around 600 B.C.E. the ideas of Zoroaster, a thinker and preacher whose dates are uncertain, began to gain prominence. Zoroaster is regarded as the author of key religious texts, later gathered together in a collection of sacred texts called the Avesta. (See "Thinking Like a Historian: The Moral Life," page 44.) He introduced new spiritual concepts to the Iranian people, stressing devotion to Ahuramazda alone and emphasizing the individual's responsibility to choose between the forces of creation, truth, and order and those of nothingness, chaos, falsehood, and disorder. Zoroaster taught that people possessed the free will to decide between these, and that they must rely on their own conscience to guide them through an active life in which they focused on "good thoughts, good words, and good deeds." Their decisions were crucial, he warned, for there would come a time of reckoning. At the end of time the forces of order would win, and the victorious Ahuramazda, like the Egyptian god Osiris (see Chapter 1), would preside over a last judgment to determine each person's eternal fate. Those who had lived according to good and truth would enter a divine kingdom. Liars and the wicked, denied this blessed immortality, would be condemned to eternal pain, darkness, and punishment. Thus Zoroaster preached a last judgment that led to a heaven or a hell.

Scholars—and contemporary Zoroastrians—debate whether Zoroaster saw the forces of disorder as a malevolent deity named Angra Mainyu who was co-eternal with and independent from Ahuramazda, or whether he was simply using this term to mean "evil thoughts" or "a destructive spirit." Later forms of **Zoroastrianism** followed each of these lines of understanding. Most Zoroastrians believed that the good Ahuramazda and the evil Angra Mainyu were locked together in a cosmic battle for the human race, a religious conceptualization that scholars call dualism, which was rejected in Judaism and Christianity. Some, however, had a more monotheistic interpretation and saw Ahuramazda as the only uncreated god.

Whenever he actually lived, Zoroaster's writings were spread by teachers, and King Darius began to use Zoroastrian language and images. Under the protection of the Persian kings, Zoroastrian ideas spread

Persian Saddlecloth   This elaborately painted piece of leather, dating from the fourth or third century B.C.E., shows running goats with huge curved horns. The fact that it survived suggests that it was not actually used, but served a ceremonial function. (Hermitage, St. Petersburg, Russia. Photo © Boltin Picture Library/Bridgeman Images)

Gold Staff Handle   Roaring lions made from lapis lazuli decorate this golden socket from the seventh to sixth century B.C.E. Fragments of bone in the socket indicate this was the handle of a long staff, like that seen held by Assyrian and Persian kings. Then, as now, lions were a symbol of royalty and strength. (British Museum, London, UK/Bridgeman Images)

throughout Iran and the rest of the Persian Empire, and then beyond this into central China. It became the official religion of the later Persian Empire ruled by the Sassanid dynasty, and much later Zoroastrians migrated to western India, where they became known as Parsis and still live today. Zoroastrianism survived the fall of the Persian Empire to influence Christianity, Islam, and Buddhism, largely because of its belief in a just life on earth and a happy afterlife. Good behavior in the world, even though unrecognized at the time, would receive ample reward in the hereafter. Evil, no matter how powerful in life, would be punished after death. In some form or another, Zoroastrian concepts still pervade many modern religions, and Zoroastrianism still exists as a religion.

Persian Art and Culture

The Persians made significant contributions to art and culture. They produced amazing works in gold and silver, often with inlaid jewels and semiprecious stones such as deep blue lapis lazuli. They transformed the Assyrian tradition of realistic monumental sculpture from one that celebrated gory details of slaughter to

King Darius Defeats His Enemies   King Darius of Persia proclaimed victory over his enemies with a written inscription and sculpture high on a cliff near Mount Behistun so all could see. He attributed his victory to Ahuramazda, the god of Zoroastrianism, whose symbol is carved above the chained prisoners. The proclamation itself was inscribed in three different cuneiform script languages, and it has been a vital tool for scholars as they have deciphered these ancient languages. (Photo © Zev Radovan/Bridgeman Images)

one that showed both the Persians and their subjects as dignified. They noted and carved the physical features of their subjects, the way they wore their hair, their clothing, and their tools and weapons. Because they depicted both themselves and non-Persians realistically, Persian art serves as an excellent source for learning about the weapons, tools, clothing, and even hairstyles of many peoples of the area.

These carvings adorned temples and other large buildings in cities throughout the empire, and the Persians also built new cities from the ground up. The most spectacular of these was Persepolis, designed as a residence for the kings and an administrative and cultural center. The architecture of Persepolis combined elements found in many parts of the empire, including large, elegant columns topped by carvings of real and mythical animals. Underneath the city was a system of closed water pipes, drainage canals, and conduits that allowed water from nearby mountains to flow into the city without flooding it; provided water for households and plantings inside the city; and carried away sewage and waste from the city's many residents. The Persians thus further improved the technology for handling water that had been essential in this area since the time of the Sumerians.

The Persians allowed the peoples they conquered to maintain their own customs and beliefs, as long as they paid the proper amount of taxes and did not rebel. Their rule resulted in an empire that brought people together in a new political system, with a culture that blended older and newer religious traditions and ways of seeing the world. Even their opponents, including the Greeks who would stop their expansion and eventually conquer the Persian Empire, admired their art and institutions.

NOTES

1. James H. Breasted, *Ancient Records of Egypt*, vol. 4 (Chicago: University of Chicago Press, 1907), para. 398.
2. James B. Pritchard, ed., *Ancient Near Eastern Texts Relating to the Old Testament —Third Edition with Supplement*, p. 288. Reproduced with permission of PRINCETON UNIVERSITY PRESS, in the format Book via Copyright Clearance Center.
3. Cylinder inscription translation by Irving Finkel, curator of the Cuneiform Collection at the British Museum, www.britishmuseum .org. © The Trustees of the British Museum, 2016. Used by permission of the British Museum.

LOOKING BACK LOOKING AHEAD

During the centuries following the Bronze Age Collapse, natives and newcomers brought order to life across the ancient Near East. As Egypt fell, small kingdoms, including those of the Nubians, Phoenicians, and Hebrews, grew and prospered. Regular trade and communication continued, and new products and ideas were transported by sea and land. Beginning about 900 B.C.E. the Assyrians created a large state through military conquest that was often brutal, though they also developed effective structures of rule through which taxes flowed to their leaders. The Persians, an Iranian people whose center of power was east of Mesopotamia, then established an even larger empire, governing through local officials and building beautiful cities.

The lands on the northern shore of the Mediterranean were beyond the borders of the urbanized cultures and centralized empires of the ancient Near East, but maintained contact with them through trade and migration. As the Persian Empire continued to expand, it looked farther westward toward these lands, including Greece, as possible further conquests. Greek-speaking people living in Anatolia and traveling more widely throughout the area had also absorbed numerous aspects of Persian and other more urbanized cultures they had encountered. They learned of Near Eastern religions and myths, and of the sagas of heroic wars. They also acquired many of the advanced technologies developed by their eastern neighbors, including the use of bronze and later iron, the phonetic alphabet, wine growing, and shipbuilding. The Greeks combined these borrowings with their own traditions, ideas, and talents to create a distinct civilization, one that fundamentally shaped the subsequent development of Western society. Later empires, including the Romans, would adopt techniques of rule developed by the Persians, such as building roads and using local elites to serve as administrators.

Make Connections

Think about the larger developments and continuities within and across chapters.

1. How were the Assyrian and Persian Empires similar to the earlier empires of the Near East (Chapter 1) in terms of their technology and political structure? How were they different? What might explain the pattern of similarities and differences?

2. Most peoples in the ancient world gained influence over others and became significant in history through military conquest and the establishment of empires. By contrast, how did the Phoenicians and the Hebrews shape the development of Western civilization?

2 REVIEW & EXPLORE

Identify Key Terms

Identify and explain the significance of each item below.

Iron Age (p. 36)

Kush (p. 37)

Phoenicians (p. 38)

Yahweh (p. 40)

Torah (p. 41)

Covenant (p. 41)

satraps (p. 54)

Zoroastrianism (p. 55)

Review the Main Ideas

Answer the focus questions from each section of the chapter.

◆ How did iron technology shape new states after 1200 B.C.E., including Kush and Phoenicia? (p. 36)

◆ How did the Hebrews create an enduring religious tradition? (p. 39)

◆ What explains the rise and fall of the Assyrians? (p. 46)

◆ How did the Persians consolidate their power and control and influence the subjects of their extensive empire? (p. 52)

Suggested Reading and Media Resources

BOOKS

* Briant, Pierre. *From Cyrus to Alexander*. 2002. A superb treatment of the entire Persian Empire.

* Clark, Peter. *Zoroastrianism: An Introduction to an Ancient Faith*. 1998. The best introduction to the essence of Zoroastrianism.

* Edwards, David N. *The Nubian Past*. 2004. Studies the history of Nubia and the Sudan, incorporating archaeological evidence to supplement historical sources.

* Foster, Benjamin R. *Civilizations of Ancient Iraq*. 2009. Discusses the development of cities and the empires of Babylonia and Assyria.

* Gates, Charles. *Ancient Cities: The Archaeology of Urban Life in the Ancient Near East and Egypt, Greece, and Rome*. 2003. Provides a survey of ancient life primarily from an archaeological point of view, but also includes cultural and social information.

* Goldenberg, Robert. *The Origins of Judaism: From Canaan to the Rise of Islam*. 2007. Examines the development of Jewish ideas and traditions.

* Kriwaczek, Paul. *In Search of Zarathustra: Across Iran and Central Asia to Find the World's First Prophet*. 2002. An award-winning BBC journalist follows the legacy of Zoroaster back through time.

* Kugel, James. *The God of Old: Inside the Lost World of the Bible*. 2004. A noted biblical scholar surveys the way the ancient Israelites understood God.

* Markoe, Glenn E. *The Phoenicians*. 2000. A fresh investigation of the Phoenicians at home and abroad in the western Mediterranean over their long history, with many illustrations.

* Meyers, Carol. *Rediscovering Eve: Ancient Israelite Women in Context*. 2012. A brief study designed for general readers that draws on archaeology and ethnography along with biblical texts.

* Morkot, Robert G. *The Black Pharaohs: Egypt's Nubian Rulers*. 2000. Examines the growth of the Kushite kingdom and its rule over pharaonic Egypt in the eighth century B.C.E.

* Morris, Ian, and Walter Scheidel, eds. *The Dynamics of Ancient Empires*. 2009. A collection of essays focusing on political developments.

* Pastor, Jack. *Land and Economy in Ancient Palestine*. 1997. Discusses the basics of economic life of the period.

* Provan, Iain, V. Philips Long, and Tremper Longman III. *A Biblical History of Israel*. 2003. A history of ancient Israel that relies primarily on the biblical text.

DOCUMENTARIES

* *The Bible's Buried Secrets* (*Nova*, 2008). In this two-hour special, *Nova* examines the ancient Israelites through biblical and other ancient texts and archaeological artifacts.

* *Engineering an Empire: The Persians* (History Channel, 2006). This hour-long documentary focuses on the engineering of the Persian Empire, especially its canals and roads.

* *Iran, the Forgotten Glory* (Makan Karandish, 2008). This two-part documentary by an independent filmmaker, much of it shot on location, traces the rise and expansion of the Persian Empire.

* *Nubia: The Forgotten Kingdom* (Discovery Channel, 2003). Archaeologists excavate temples and markets of the ancient city of Dangeil and examine Nubia's links with Egypt.

* *Quest for the Phoenicians* (National Geographic, 2004). Scientists use DNA analysis and other modern technologies to examine the migrations and the sailing routes of the ancient Phoenicians.

WEB SITES

* *Ancient Sudan-Nubia*. An informative Web site with information and visual material on Kush, Nubia, and Meroë. **www.ancientsudan.org/**

* *Israel Antiquities Authority*. Official Web site of the Israel Antiquities Authority, with a huge collection of artifacts from many periods in the "National Treasures" section. **www.antiquities.org.il/home_eng.asp**

* *Phoenicia: The Phoenician Ship Expedition*. Traces the building and voyage of a reconstruction of a Phoenician trading vessel that in 2008–2010 retraced the Phoenicians' route around Africa, and in 2012 sailed to London for the Olympics. **phoenicia.org.uk/index.htm**

* *Virtual Interactive Achéménide Museum*. Interactive Web site of more than eight thousand items on the culture of the Persian Empire, from Cyrus the Great to Alexander the Great; in English and French. **www.museum-achemenet.college-de-france.fr/**

3

The Development of Greek Society and Culture

ca. 3000–338 B.C.E.

Humans came into Greece over many thousands of years, in waves of migrants whose place of origin and cultural characteristics have been the source of much scholarly debate. The first to arrive were hunter-gatherers, but techniques of agriculture and animal domestication had spread into Greece from Turkey by about 6500 B.C.E., after which small farming communities worked much of the land. Early settlers to Greece brought skills in making bronze weapons and tools, which became more common around 3000 B.C.E.

Although geographic conditions made farming difficult and limited the growth of early kingdoms, the people of ancient Greece built on the traditions and ideas of earlier societies to develop a culture that fundamentally shaped the intellectual and cultural traditions of Western civilization. They were the first to explore many of the questions about the world around them and the place of humans in it that continue to concern thinkers today. Drawing on their day-to-day experiences as well as logic and empirical observation, they developed ways of understanding and explaining the world around them, which grew into modern philosophy and science. They also created new political forms and new types of literature and art.

The history of the Greeks is divided into three broad periods: the Helladic period, which covered the Bronze Age, roughly 3000 B.C.E. to 1200 B.C.E.; the Hellenic period, from the Bronze Age Collapse to the death in 323 B.C.E. of Alexander the Great, the ruler of Macedonia, which by that point had conquered Greece; and the Hellenistic period, stretching from Alexander's death to the Roman conquest in 30 B.C.E. of the kingdom established in Egypt by Alexander's successors. This chapter focuses on the Greeks in the Bronze (Helladic) Age and most of the Hellenic period, which is further divided into the Dark Age, the Archaic age, and the classical period. Alexander's brief reign and the Hellenistic world are the subject of Chapter 4. ■

CHAPTER PREVIEW

Religious Life in Hellenic Greece
This painted wooden slab from about 540 B.C.E., found in a cave near Corinth, shows adults and children about to sacrifice a sheep to the deities worshipped in this area. The participants are dressed in their finest clothes and crowned with garlands. Music adds to the festivities. Rituals such as this were a common part of religious life throughout Greece.
(National Archaeological Museum, Athens, Greece/De Agostini Picture Library/G. Dagli Orti/Bridgeman Images)

Greece in the Bronze Age

FOCUS QUESTION *How did the geography of Greece shape its earliest kingdoms, and what factors contributed to the decline of those kingdoms?*

During the Bronze Age, which for Greek history is called the "Helladic period," early settlers in Greece began establishing small communities contoured by the mountains and small plains that shaped the land. These communities sometimes joined together to form kingdoms, most prominently the Minoan kingdom on the island of Crete and the Mycenaean kingdom on the mainland. The Minoan and Mycenaean societies flourished for centuries until the Bronze Age Collapse, when Greece entered a period of decline known as the Dark Age (ca. 1100–800 B.C.E.). Epic poems composed by Homer and Hesiod after the Dark Age provide the poets' versions of what life may have been like in these early Greek kingdoms.

Geography and Settlement

Hellas, as the Greeks still call their land, encompassed the Greek peninsula, the islands of the Aegean (ah-GEE-uhn) Sea, and the lands bordering the Aegean, an area known as the Aegean basin (Map 3.1). In ancient times this basin included the Greek settlements in Ionia, the western coast of the area known as Anatolia in modern western Turkey. Geography acts as an enormously divisive force in Greek life; mountains divide the land, and although there are good harbors on the sea, there are no navigable rivers. Much of the land is rocky and not very fertile, which meant that food availability was a constant concern.

The major regions of Greece were Thessaly and Macedonia in the north, and Boeotia (bee-OH-shuh) and the large island of Euboea (YOU-boh-ee-ah) in the center, lands marked by fertile plains that helped to sustain a strong population capable of serving as formidable cavalry and infantry. Immediately to the south

MAP 3.1 Classical Greece, 500–338 B.C.E.   In antiquity, the home of the Greeks included the islands of the Aegean and the western shore of Turkey as well as the Greek peninsula itself. Crete, the home of Minoan civilization, is the large island at the bottom of the map.

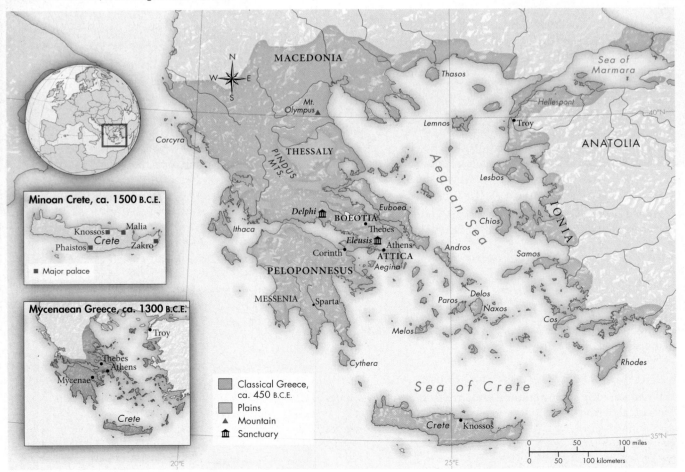

of Boeotia was Attica, an area of thin soil in which olives and wine grapes flourished. Attica's harbors looked to the Aegean, which invited its inhabitants, the Athenians, to concentrate on maritime commerce. Still farther south, the Peloponnesus (peh-luh-puh-NEE-suhs), a large peninsula connected to the rest of mainland Greece by a very narrow isthmus at Corinth, was a patchwork of high mountains and small plains that divided the area into several regions. Beyond the coast, the islands of the Aegean served as stepping-stones to Anatolia.

The geographical fragmentation of Greece encouraged political fragmentation. Communications were poor, with rocky tracks far more common than roads. Early in Greek history several kingdoms did emerge, but the rugged terrain prohibited the growth of a great empire like those of Mesopotamia or Egypt. Instead tiny states became the most common form of government.

The Minoans

On the large island of Crete, Bronze Age farmers and fishermen began to trade their surpluses with their neighbors, and cities grew, housing artisans and merchants. Beginning about 2000 B.C.E. Cretans voyaged throughout the eastern Mediterranean and the Aegean, carrying the copper and tin needed for bronze and many other goods. Social hierarchies developed, and in many cities certain individuals came to hold power, although exactly how this happened is not clear. The Cretans began to use writing about 1900 B.C.E., in a form later scholars called Linear A. This has not been deciphered, but scholars know that the language of Crete was not related to Greek, so they do not consider the Cretans "Greek."

What we can know about the culture of Crete depends on archaeological and artistic evidence, and of this there is a great deal. At about the same time that writing began, rulers in several cities of Crete began to build large structures with hundreds of interconnected rooms. The largest of these, at Knossos (NOH-suhs), has over a thousand rooms along with pipes for bringing in drinking water and sewers to get rid of waste. The archaeologists who discovered these huge structures called them "palaces," and they named the flourishing and vibrant culture of this era **Minoan**, after a mythical king of Crete, Minos.

Chronology

3000 B.C.E.	Bronze tools and weapons become common in Greece
ca. 1900 B.C.E.	Minoan culture begins to thrive on Crete
ca. 1650 B.C.E.	Mycenaean culture develops in Greece
ca. 1300–1100 B.C.E.	"Bronze Age Collapse"; migration, destruction
ca. 1100–800 B.C.E.	Dark Age; population declines; trade decreases; writing disappears
ca. 800–500 B.C.E.	Archaic age; rise of the polis; Greek colonization of the Mediterranean; Homer and Hesiod compose epics and poetry
ca. 750–500 B.C.E.	Sparta expands and develops a military state
ca. 600–500 B.C.E.	Political reforms in Archaic Athens
ca. 600–450 B.C.E.	Pre-Socratics develop ideas about the nature of the universe
500–338 B.C.E.	Classical period; development of drama, philosophy, and major building projects in Athens
499–479 B.C.E.	Persian wars
431–404 B.C.E.	Peloponnesian War
427–347 B.C.E.	Life of Plato
384–322 B.C.E.	Life of Aristotle
371–362 B.C.E.	Thebes, with an alliance of city-states, rules Greece
338 B.C.E.	Philip II of Macedonia gains control of Greece

Few specifics are known about Minoan political life except that a king and a group of nobles stood at its head. Minoan life was long thought to have been relatively peaceful, but new excavations are revealing more and more walls around cities, which has called the peaceful nature of Minoan society into question, although there are no doubts that it was wealthy. In terms of their religious life, Minoans appear to have worshipped goddesses far more than gods. Whether this translated into more egalitarian gender roles for real people is unclear, but surviving Minoan art, including frescoes and figurines, shows women as well as men leading religious activities, watching entertainment, and engaging in athletic competitions, such as leaping over bulls.

Beginning about 1700 B.C.E. Minoan society was disrupted by a series of earthquakes and volcanic eruptions on nearby islands, some of which resulted in large tsunamis. The largest of these was a huge volcanic eruption that devastated the island of Thera to the north of Crete, burying the Minoan town there in lava

■ **Minoan** A wealthy and vibrant culture on Crete from around 1900 B.C.E. to 1450 B.C.E., ruled by a king with a large palace at Knossos.

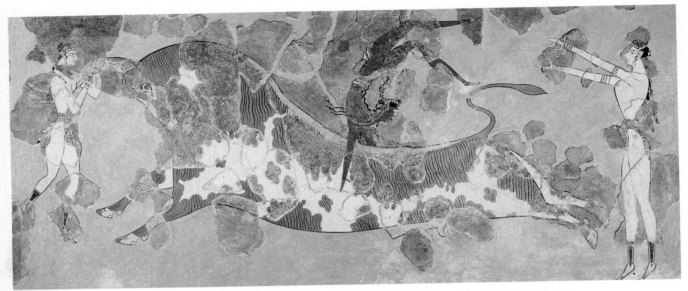

Minoan Bull-Leaping   A colorful fresco dating from around 1600 B.C.E. found at the palace of Knossos on Crete shows three people in a scene of bull-leaping. The outside figures are women, who are generally portrayed with light skin to represent women's association with the household, and the figure leaping over the bull is a man, whose reddish skin associates him with the outdoors. Bulls were venerated in Minoan culture, and this may be a scene of an actual ritual sport done at the palace, a spectacle celebrating human athletic prowess and mastery of nature. (National Archaeological Museum, Athens, Greece/Bridgeman Images)

and causing it to collapse into the sea. This eruption, one of the largest in recorded history, may have been the origin of the story of the mythical kingdom of Atlantis, a wealthy kingdom with beautiful buildings that had sunk under the ocean. The eruption on Thera was long seen as the most important cause of the collapse of Minoan civilization, but scholars using radiocarbon and other types of scientific dating have called this theory into question, as the eruption seems to have occurred somewhat earlier than 1600 B.C.E., and Minoan society did not collapse until more than two centuries later. In fact, new settlements and palaces were often built on Crete following the earthquakes and the eruption of Thera.

The Mycenaeans

As Minoan culture was flourishing on Crete, a different type of society developed on the mainland. This society was founded by groups who had migrated there during the period after 2000 B.C.E., and its members spoke an early form of Greek. By about 1650 B.C.E. one group of these immigrants had raised palaces and established cities at Thebes, Athens, Mycenae (migh-SEE-nee), and elsewhere. These palace-centers ruled by local kings formed a loose hegemony under the authority of the king of Mycenae, and the archaeologists who first discovered traces of this culture called it **Mycenaean** (migh-see-NEE-an).

As in Crete, the political unit in Mycenaean Greece was the kingdom, and the king and his warrior aristocracy stood at the top of society. The seat and symbol of the king's power was his palace, which was also the economic center of the kingdom. Within the palace's walls, royal artisans fashioned gold jewelry and rich ornaments, made and decorated fine pottery, forged weapons, prepared hides and wool for clothing, and manufactured the other goods needed by the king and his supporters. The Mycenaean economy was marked by an extensive division of labor, and at the bottom of the social scale were male and female slaves.

Palace scribes kept records with a script known as Linear B, which scholars realized was an early form of Greek and have learned to read. They thus consider the Mycenaeans the first truly "Greek" culture to emerge in this area. Information on Mycenaean culture comes through inscriptions and other forms of written records as well as buildings and other objects. All of these point to a society in which war was common. Mycenaean cities were all fortified by thick stone walls, and graves contain bronze spears, javelins, swords, helmets, and the first examples of metal armor known in the world. Mycenaean kingdoms appear to have fought regularly with one another.

Contacts between the Minoans and Mycenaeans were originally peaceful, and Minoan culture and trade goods flooded the Greek mainland. But most scholars think that around 1450 B.C.E., possibly in the wake of an earthquake that left Crete vulnerable, the Mycenae-

■ **Mycenaean**   A Bronze Age culture that flourished in Greece from about 1650 B.C.E. to 1100 B.C.E., building fortified palaces and cities.

Mycenaean Dagger Blade　This scene in gold and silver on the blade of an iron dagger depicts hunters armed with spears and protected by shields defending themselves against charging lions. Judging by the number of hunting scenes in surviving Mycenaean art, the Mycenaeans seemed to enjoy the thrill and the danger of hunting. (National Archaeological Museum, Athens, Greece/Ancient Art & Architecture Collection, Ltd./Bridgeman Images)

ans attacked Crete, destroying many towns and occupying Knossos. For about the next fifty years, the Mycenaeans ruled much of the island. The palaces at Knossos and other cities of the Aegean became grander as wealth gained through trade and tribute flowed into the treasuries of various Mycenaean kings. Linear B replaced Linear A as a writing system, a further sign of Mycenaean domination.

Prosperity, however, did not bring peace, and between 1300 and 1100 B.C.E. various kingdoms in and beyond Greece ravaged one another in a savage series of wars that destroyed both the Minoan and Mycenaean civilizations. Among these wars was perhaps one that later became known as the Trojan War, fought by Greeks in Ionia (see page 66).

The fall of the Minoans and Mycenaeans was part of what scholars see as a general collapse of Bronze Age civilizations in the eastern Mediterranean, including the end of the Egyptian New Kingdom and the fall of the Hittite Empire (see Chapters 1 and 2). This collapse appears to have had a number of causes: internal economic and social problems, including perhaps slave revolts; invasions and migrations by outsiders, who destroyed cities and disrupted trade and production; changes in warfare and weaponry, particularly the adoption of iron weapons, which made foot soldiers the most important factor in battles and reduced the power of kings and wealthy nobles fighting from chariots; and natural disasters such as volcanic eruptions, earthquakes, and droughts, which reduced the amount of food and contributed to famines. Mycenaean Greeks joined the migrating Sea Peoples and probably settled in Canaan; here they became the group known in the Bible as Philistines (see Chapter 2).

These factors worked together to usher in a period of poverty and disruption that historians of Greece have traditionally called the Dark Age (ca. 1100–800 B.C.E.). Cities were destroyed, population declined, vil-

lages were abandoned, and trade decreased. Migratory movements continued, including a group that later Greeks called the Dorians, who were originally thought to have been people speaking a language other than Greek invading from the north. Now the Dorians are generally regarded as Greek-speakers from the northern areas of the Greek mainland, and their movement is considered a combination of invasion and migration. Pottery became simpler, and jewelry and other grave goods became less ornate. Even writing, which had not been widespread previously, was a casualty of the chaos, and Linear A and B inscriptions were no longer produced.

The Bronze Age Collapse led to the widespread and prolonged movement of Greek peoples, both within Greece itself and beyond. They dispersed beyond mainland Greece farther south to the islands of the Aegean and in greater strength across the Aegean to the shores of Anatolia, arriving at a time when traditional states and empires had collapsed. By the conclusion of the Dark Age, the Greeks had spread their culture throughout the Aegean basin, and like many other cultures around the Mediterranean and the Near East, they had adopted iron.

Homer, Hesiod, and the Epic

Archaeological sources from the Dark Age are less rich than those from the periods that came after, and so they are often used in conjunction with literary sources written in later centuries to give us a more complete picture of the era. The Greeks, unlike the Hebrews, had no sacred book that chronicled their past. Instead they had epics, poetic tales of legendary heroes and of the times when people believed the gods still walked the earth. Of these, the *Iliad* and the *Odyssey* are the most important. Most scholars think they were composed in the eighth or seventh century B.C.E., with the

Iliad appearing earlier than the *Odyssey*. By the fifth century B.C.E. they were attributed to a poet named Homer, though whether Homer was an actual historical individual is debated. Scholars also disagree about the ways in which the epics combine elements from the Bronze Age, the Dark Age, and the time in which they were written. What is not debated is their long-lasting impact, both on later Greek culture and on the Western world.

The *Iliad* recounts the tale of the Trojan War of the late Bronze Age. As Homer tells it, the Achaeans (uh-KEE-uhnz), the name he gives to the Mycenaeans, send an expedition to besiege the city of Troy to retrieve Helen, who was abducted by Paris, the Trojan king's son. The heart of the *Iliad*, however, concerns the quarrel between the Mycenaean king, Agamemnon, and the stormy hero of the poem, Achilles (uh-KIHL-eez), and how this brought suffering to the Achaeans. The first lines of the *Iliad* capture this well:

> Sing, O goddess, the anger of Achilles son of Peleus, that brought countless ills upon the Achaeans. Many a brave soul did it send hurrying down to Hades [underworld], and many a hero did it yield a prey to dogs and vultures.[1]

Ancient Greeks and Romans believed that the Trojan War was a real event embellished by poetic retelling, but by the modern era most people regarded it as a myth. Then in the late nineteenth century, the German businessman Heinrich Schliemann discovered and excavated the ruins of Troy. The city had actually been destroyed a number of times, including at least once in the late Mycenaean period, which provided evidence of the violence of this era, if not of the Trojan War itself. More recently, geologists studying the landscape features mentioned in the *Iliad* and historians examining written records from the Hittite and Egyptian Empires of the era have also confirmed the general picture portrayed in Homer's epic. Today most scholars think that the core of the story was a composite of many conflicts in Troy's past, although the characters are not historical.

Homer's *Odyssey* recounts the adventures of Odysseus (oh-DIH-see-uhs), a wise and fearless hero of the war at Troy, during his ten-year voyage home. He encounters many dangers, storms, and adventures, but he finally reaches his home and unites again with Penelope, the ideal wife, dedicated to her husband and family.

Both of Homer's epics portray engaging but flawed characters who are larger than life, yet human. The men and women at the center of the stories display the quality known as *arête* (ah-reh-TAY), that is, excellence

and living up to one's fullest potential. Homer was also strikingly successful in depicting the great gods and goddesses, who generally sit on Mount Olympus in the north of Greece and watch the fighting at Troy like spectators at a baseball game, although they sometimes participate in the action.

Greeks also learned about the origin and descent of the gods and goddesses of their polytheistic system from another poet, Hesiod (HEH-see-uhd), who most scholars think lived sometime between 750 and 650 B.C.E. Hesiod made the gods the focus of his poem, the *Theogony*. By combining Mesopotamian myths, which the Hittites had adopted and spread to the Aegean, with a variety of Greek oral traditions, Hesiod forged a coherent story of the origin of the gods. At the beginning was "Chaos," the word Hesiod uses to describe the original dark emptiness. Then came several generations of deities, with the leader of each generation violently overthrowing his father to gain power. Despite this violence, Hesiod viewed the generation of gods who rule from Olympus as more just than those that came before. In another of Hesiod's poems, *Works and Days*, the gods watch over the earth, looking for justice and injustice, while leaving the great mass of men and women to live lives of hard work and endless toil. (See "Evaluating the Evidence 3.1: Hesiod, *Works and Days*," at right.)

The Development of the Polis in the Archaic Age

FOCUS QUESTION *What was the role of the polis in Greek society?*

Homer and Hesiod both lived in the era after the Dark Age, which later historians have termed the Archaic age (800–500 B.C.E.). The most important political change in this period was the development of the **polis** (PAH-luhs; plural *poleis*), a word generally translated as "city-state." With the polis, the Greeks established a new type of political structure. During the Archaic period, poleis established colonies throughout much of the Mediterranean, spreading Greek culture. Two particular poleis, each with a distinctive system of government, rose to prominence on the Greek mainland: Sparta and Athens.

Organization of the Polis

The Greek polis was not the first form of city-state to emerge. The earliest states in Sumer were also city-states, as were many of the small Mycenaean kingdoms. What differentiated the new Greek model from older city-states is the fact that the polis was more than a political institution; it was a community of citizens

---

■ **polis** Generally translated as "city-state," it was the basic political and institutional unit of Greece in the Hellenic period.

Hesiod, *Works and Days*

According to his description of himself in Works and Days (ca. 700 B.C.E.), Hesiod was born in a small village he describes as "bad in winter, godawful in summer, nice never," with one brother, Perses, a lazy and irresponsible swindler who cheated him out of some of his inheritance but later came to him asking for money. Whether these details are true or not, they form the framework for his work, a speech full of advice addressed to his brother, but designed for a larger audience.

And now I will tell a fable for princes who themselves understand. Thus said the hawk to the nightingale with speckled neck, while he carried her high up among the clouds, gripped fast in his talons, and she, pierced by his crooked talons, cried pitifully. To her he spoke disdainfully: "Miserable thing, why do you cry out? One far stronger than you now holds you fast, and you must go wherever I take you, songstress as you are. And if I please I will make my meal of you, or let you go. He is a fool who tries to withstand the stronger, for he does not get the mastery and suffers pain besides his shame." So said the swiftly flying hawk, the long-winged bird.

But you, Perses, listen to right and do not foster violence; for violence is bad for a poor man. Even the prosperous cannot easily bear its burden, but is weighed down under it when he has fallen into delusion. The better path is to go by on the other side towards Justice; for Justice beats Outrage when she comes at length to the end of the race. But only when he has suffered does the fool learn this. For Oath keeps pace with wrong judgements. There is a noise when Justice is being dragged in the way where those who devour bribes and give sentence with crooked judgements, take her. And she, wrapped in mist, follows to the city and haunts of the people, weeping, and bringing mischief to men, even to such as have driven her forth in that they did not deal straightly with her. . . .

To you, foolish Perses, I will speak good sense. Badness can be got easily and in shoals: the road to her is smooth, and she lives very near us. But between us and Goodness the gods have placed the sweat of our brows: long and steep is the path that leads to her, and it is rough at the first; but when a man has reached the top, then is she easy to reach, though before that she was hard. . . .

Do not get base gain: base gain is as bad as ruin. Be friends with the friendly, and visit him who visits you. Give to one who gives, but do not give to one who does not give. A man gives to the free-handed, but no one gives to the close-fisted. Give is a good girl, but Take is bad and she brings death. For the man who gives willingly, even though he gives a great thing, rejoices in his gift and is glad in heart; but whoever gives way to shamelessness and takes something himself, even though it be a small thing, it freezes his heart. . . .

If your heart within you desires wealth, do these things and work with work upon work.

EVALUATE THE EVIDENCE

1. What does Hesiod's advice suggest about his notion of the role of humans in the world and their relationship with the gods?
2. Hesiod lived just after the period of the Greek Dark Age. How does *Work and Days* reflect the situation of his own society?

Source: Hugh G. Evelyn-White, *Works and Days* (Cambridge, Mass.: Harvard University Press; London: Heinemann Ltd, 1914).

with their own customs and laws. With one exception, the poleis that emerged after 800 B.C.E. did not have kings but instead were self-governing. The physical, religious, and political forms of the polis varied from place to place, but everywhere the polis was relatively small, reflecting the fragmented geography of Greece. The very smallness of the polis enabled Greeks to see how they fit individually into the overall system — and how the individual parts made up the social whole.

This notion of community was fundamental to the polis and was the very badge of Greekness.

Poleis developed from Dark Age towns, which were centers of administration, trade, and religion. When fully developed, each polis normally shared a surprisingly large number of features with other poleis. Physically a polis was a society of people who lived in a city (*asty*) and cultivated the surrounding countryside (*chora*). The countryside was essential to the economy of the polis and provided food to sustain the entire population. The city's water supply came from public fountains, springs, and cisterns. By the fifth century B.C.E. the city was generally surrounded by a wall. The city contained a point, usually elevated, called the acropolis, and a public square or marketplace called the agora (ah-guh-RAH). On the acropolis, which in the Dark Age was a place of refuge, people built temples, altars, public monuments, and various dedications to the gods of the polis. The agora was the political center of the polis. In the agora were shops, public buildings, and courts.

All poleis, with one exception, did not have standing armies. Instead they relied on their citizens for protection. Wealthy aristocrats often served as cavalry, which was never very important in military conflicts. The backbone of the army was the heavily armed infantry, or **hoplites**, ordinary citizens rather than members of the elite. Hoplites wore bronze helmets and leather and bronze body armor, which they purchased themselves. They carried heavy, round shields made of wood covered in bronze and armed themselves with iron-tipped spears and swords. They marched and fought in a close rectangular formation known as a phalanx, holding their shields together to form a solid wall, with the spears of the front row sticking out over the tops of the shields. As long as the phalanx stayed in formation, the hoplites presented an enemy with an impenetrable wall. This meant that commanders preferred to fight battles on open plains, where the hoplites could more easily maintain the phalanx, rather than in the narrow mountain passes that were common throughout much of Greece.

Governing Structures

Each Greek polis had one of several different types of government. Monarchy, rule by a king, had been prevalent during the Mycenaean period, but afterward declined. The polis of Sparta (see page 70) had a system with two kings, but they were part of a more broadly based constitution. Sporadic periods of violent political and social upheaval often led to the seizure of power by one man, a type of government the Greeks called **tyranny**. Tyrants generally came to power by using their wealth or by negotiating to win a political following that toppled the existing legal government. In contrast to its contemporary meaning, however, tyranny in ancient Greece did not necessarily mean oppressive

rule. Some tyrants used their power to benefit average citizens by helping to limit the power of the landowning aristocracy, which made them popular.

Other types of government in the Archaic age were democracy and oligarchy. **Democracy** translates as "the power of the people" but was actually rule by citizens, not the people as a whole. Almost all Greek cities defined a citizen as an adult man with at least one or, at some times and places, two citizen parents. Thus citizens shared ancestry as well as a place of residence. Women were citizens for religious and reproductive purposes, but their citizenship did not give them the right to participate in government. Free men who were not children of a citizen, resident foreigners (metics), and slaves were not citizens and had no political voice. Thus ancient Greek democracy did not reflect the modern concept that all people are created equal, but it did permit male citizens to share equally in determining the diplomatic and military policies of the polis, without respect to wealth. This comparatively broad basis of participation made Greek democracy an appealing model to some political thinkers across the ages, although others feared direct democracy and viewed it as "mob rule."

Oligarchy, which literally means "the rule of the few," was government by citizens who met a minimum property requirement. Many Greeks preferred oligarchy because it provided more political stability than democracy did. (Many of the Founding Fathers of the United States agreed, and they established a system in which the most important elections were indirect and only property owners had the right to vote.) Although oligarchy was the government of the prosperous, it left the door open to political and social advancement. If members of the polis obtained enough wealth to meet property or money qualifications, they could enter the governing circle.

Overseas Expansion

The development of the polis coincided with the growth of the Greek world in both wealth and numbers, bringing new problems. The increase in population created more demand for food than the land could supply. The resulting social and political tensions drove many people to seek new homes outside of Greece. In some cases the losers in a conflict within a polis were forced to leave. Other factors, largely intangible, played their part as well: the desire for a new start, a love of excitement and adventure, and curiosity about what lay beyond the horizon.

Greeks from the mainland and Ionia traveled throughout the Mediterranean, sailing in great numbers to Sicily and southern Italy, where there was ample space for expansion (Map 3.2). Here they established prosperous cities and often intermarried with local

■ **hoplites** Heavily armed citizens who served as infantrymen and fought to defend the polis.

■ **tyranny** Rule by one man who took over an existing government, generally by using his wealth to gain a political following.

■ **democracy** A type of Greek government in which all citizens administered the workings of government.

■ **oligarchy** A type of Greek government in which citizens who owned a certain amount of property ruled.

people. Some adventurous Greeks sailed farther west to Sardinia, France, Spain, and perhaps even the Canary Islands. In Sardinia they first established trading stations, and then permanent towns. From these new outposts Greek influence extended to southern France. The modern city of Marseilles, for example, began as a Greek colony and later sent settlers to southern Spain. In the far western Mediterranean the city of Carthage, established by the Phoenicians in the ninth century B.C.E., remained the dominant power. The Greeks traded with the Carthaginians but never conquered them.

Colonization changed the entire Greek world, both at home and abroad. In economic terms the expansion of the Greeks created a much larger market for agricultural and manufactured goods. From the east, especially from the northern coast of the Black Sea, came wheat. In return flowed Greek wine and olive oil, which could not be produced in the harsher climate of the north. Greek-manufactured goods, notably rich jewelry and fine pottery, circulated from southern Russia to Spain. During the same period the Greeks adopted the custom of minting coins from metal, first developed in the kingdom of Lydia in Anatolia. Coins provided many advantages over barter: they allowed merchants to set the value of goods in a determined system, they could be stored easily, and they allowed for more complex exchanges than did direct barter.

Golden Comb   This golden comb, produced about 400 B.C.E. in Scythia (see Map 3.2), shows a battle between three warriors, perhaps the three brothers who are the legendary founders of Scythia. Their dress shows a combination of Greek and Eastern details; the mounted horseman is clothed with largely Greek armor, while the warriors on foot are wearing Eastern dress. The comb may have been made by a Greek craftsman who had migrated to the Black Sea area, as the Greeks had established colonies there, but it was buried in a Scythian burial mound. (Hermitage, St. Petersburg, Russia/Photo © Boltin Picture Library/Bridgeman Images)

MAP 3.2 Greek Colonization, ca. 750–550 B.C.E.   The Greeks established colonies along the shores of the Mediterranean and the Black Sea, spreading Greek culture and creating a large trading network.

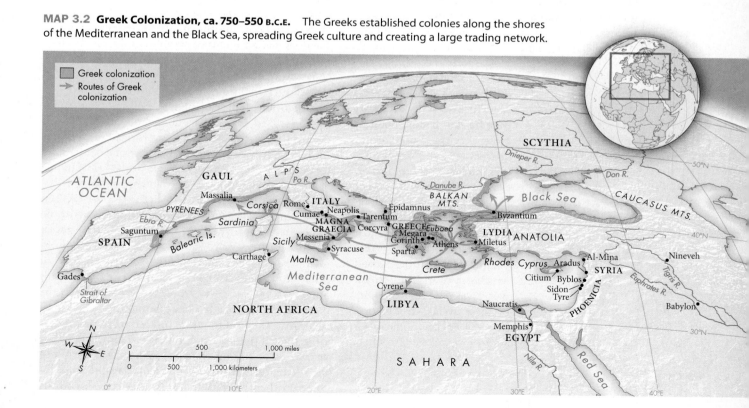

Colonization presented the polis with a huge challenge, for it required organization and planning on an unprecedented scale. The colonizing city, called the *metropolis*, or "mother city," first decided where to establish the colony, how to transport colonists to the site, and who would sail. Sometimes groups of people left willingly, and in other instances they left involuntarily after a civil war or other conflict. Then the metropolis collected and stored the supplies that the colonists would need both to feed themselves and to plant their first crop. All preparations ready, a leader, called an *oikist*, ordered the colonists to sail. Once the colonists landed, the oikist laid out the new polis, selected the sites of temples and public buildings, and established the government. Then he surrendered power to the new leaders. The colony was thereafter independent of the metropolis, a pattern that was quite different from most later systems of colonization. Colonization spread the polis and its values far beyond the shores of Greece.

The Growth of Sparta

Many different poleis developed during the Archaic period, but Sparta became the leading military power in Greece. To expand their polis, the Spartans did not establish colonies but set out in about 750 B.C.E. to conquer Messenia (muh-SEE-nee-uh), a rich, fertile region in the southwestern Peloponnesus. This conflict, called the First Messenian War by later Greek historians, lasted for twenty years and ended in a Spartan triumph. The Spartans appropriated Messenian land and turned the Messenians into **helots** (HEH-luhts), unfree residents forced to work state lands. Residents of coastal areas and the hills surrounding Messenia became a third group, known as *periokoi* (pehr-ee-OI-koi), who were free but had no political voice in the running of Sparta.

In about 650 B.C.E. Spartan exploitation and oppression of the Messenian helots, along with Sparta's defeat at the hands of a rival polis, led to a massive helot revolt that became known as the Second Messenian War. The Spartan poet Tyrtaeus, a contemporary of these events, vividly portrays the violence of the war:

Spartan Expansion, ca. 750–500 B.C.E.

- ⬛ Spartan homeland
- ⬜ Annexed lands
- ⬜ Spartan allies

Euboea

ACHAEA
ELIS   Megara   ATTICA
ARCADIA   Corinth   Athens
                    Argos
PELOPONNESUS
MESSENIA
        Sparta
LACONIA

Cythera

For it is a shameful thing indeed
When with the foremost fighters
An elder falling in front of the young men
Lies outstretched,
Having white hair and grey beard,
Breathing forth his stout soul in the dust,
Holding in his hands his genitals
stained with blood.[2]

Finally, after some thirty years of fighting, the Spartans put down the revolt. Nevertheless, the political and social strain it caused led to a transformation of the Spartan polis. After the war, non-nobles who had shared in the fighting as hoplites appear to have demanded rights equal to those of the nobility and a voice in the government. (In more recent history, similar demands in the United States during the Vietnam War led to a lowering of the voting age to eighteen, to match the age at which soldiers were drafted.) Under intense pressure the aristocrats agreed to remodel the state into a new system.

The plan for the new system in Sparta was attributed to the lawgiver Lycurgus, who may or may not have been an actual person. According to later Greek sources, political distinctions among Spartan men were eliminated, and all citizens became legally equal. Governance of the polis was in the hands of two hereditary kings who were primarily military leaders. The kings were also part of the *Gerousia* (jeh-roo-SEE-ah), a council of men who had reached the age of sixty and thus retired from the Spartan army. The Gerousia deliberated on foreign and domestic matters and prepared legislation for the assembly, which consisted of all Spartan citizens. The real executive power of the polis was in the hands of five ephors (EH-fuhrs), or overseers, elected from and by all the citizens.

To provide for their economic needs, the Spartans divided the land of Messenia among all citizens. Helots worked the land, raised the crops, provided the Spartans with a certain percentage of their harvest, and occasionally served in the army. The Spartans kept the helots in line by means of systematic brutality and oppression.

In the system attributed to Lycurgus every citizen owed primary allegiance to Sparta. Suppression of the individual together with emphasis on military prowess led to a barracks state. Family life itself was sacrificed to the polis. Once Spartan boys reached the age of seven, they were enrolled in separate companies with other boys their age. They were required to live in the barracks and eat together in a common mess hall until age thirty. They slept outside on reed mats and underwent rugged physical and military training until they were ready to become frontline soldiers. For the rest of their lives, Spartan men kept themselves prepared for combat. Their military training never ceased, and the

■ **helots** Unfree residents of Sparta forced to work state lands.

older men were expected to be models of endurance, frugality, and sturdiness. In battle Spartans were supposed to stand and die rather than retreat. Because men often did not see their wives or other women for long periods, not only in times of war but also in peace, their most meaningful relations were same-sex ones. The Spartan military leaders may have viewed such relationships as militarily advantageous because they believed that men would fight even more fiercely for lovers and comrades.

Spartans expected women in citizen families to be good wives and strict mothers of future soldiers. They were prohibited from wearing jewelry or ornate clothes. They, too, were supposed to exercise strenuously in the belief that hard physical training promoted the birth of healthy children. Xenophon (ca. 430–354 B.C.E.), a later Athenian admirer of the Spartans, commented:

> [Lycurgus had] insisted on the training of the body as incumbent no less on the female than the male; and in pursuit of the same idea instituted rival contests in running and feats of strength for women as for men. His belief was that where both parents were strong their progeny would be found to be more vigorous.[3]

An anecdote frequently repeated about one Spartan mother sums up Spartan military values. As her son was setting off to battle, the mother handed him his shield and advised him to come back either victorious, carrying the shield, or dead, being carried on it. Yet Spartan women were freer than many other Greek women. With men in military service much of their lives, women in citizen families owned land and ran the estates and were not physically restricted or secluded.

Along with the emphasis on military values for both sexes, the Spartan system served to instill in society the civic virtues of dedication to the state and a code of moral conduct. These aspects of Spartan society, along with Spartan military successes, were generally admired throughout the Greek world.

The Evolution of Athens

Like Sparta, Athens faced pressing social, economic, and political problems during the Archaic period, but the Athenian response was far different from that of the Spartans. Instead of creating a state devoted to the military, the Athenians created a state that became a democracy.

For Athens the late seventh century B.C.E. was a time of turmoil, the causes of which are unclear. In 621 B.C.E. Draco (DRAY-koh), an Athenian aristocrat, under pressure from small landholders and with the consent of the nobles, published the first law code of the Athenian polis. His code was harsh—and for this reason his name is the origin of the word *draconian*—but it embodied the ideal that the law belonged to all citizens.

Yet the aristocracy still governed Athens oppressively, and the social and economic situation remained dire. Despite Draco's code, noble landholders continued to force small farmers and artisans into economic dependence. Many families were sold into slavery because of debt; others were exiled, and their land was mortgaged to the rich.

One person who recognized these problems clearly was Solon (SOH-luhn), an aristocrat and poet. Reciting his poems in the Athenian agora, where anyone could hear his

Spartan Hoplite   This bronze figurine portrays an armed foot soldier about to strike an enemy. His massive helmet with its full crest gives his head nearly complete protection, while a metal corselet covers his chest and back, and greaves (similar to today's shin guards) protect his lower legs. In his right hand he carries a thrusting spear (now broken off), and in his left a large, round shield. (bpk, Berlin/Antikensammlung, Staatliche Museen/Johannes Laurentius/Art Resource, NY)

call for justice and fairness, Solon condemned his fellow aristocrats for their greed and dishonesty. According to later sources, Solon's sincerity and good sense convinced other aristocrats that he was no crazed revolutionary. Moreover, he gained the trust of the common people, whose problems provoked them to demand access to political life, much as commoners in Sparta had. Around 594 B.C.E. the nobles elected Solon chief *archon* (AHR-kahn), or magistrate of the Athenian polis, with authority over legal, civic, and military issues.

Solon immediately freed all people enslaved for debt, recalled all exiles, canceled all debts on land, and made enslavement for debt illegal. Solon allowed non-nobles into the old aristocratic assembly, where they could take part in the election of magistrates, including the annual election of the city's nine archons.

Although Solon's reforms solved some immediate problems, they did not satisfy either the aristocrats or the common people completely, and they did not bring peace to Athens. During the sixth century B.C.E. the successful general Pisistratus (pigh-SIHS-trah-tuhs) declared himself tyrant, developing a base of followers from among the common people. He was exiled several times, but returned to power each time. Under his rule Athens prospered, and his building program began to transform the city into one of the splendors of Greece. He raised the civic consciousness and prestige of the polis by instituting new cultural festivals that brought people together. Although he had taken over control of the city by force, his reign as tyrant weakened the power of aristocratic families and aroused rudimentary feelings of equality in many Athenian men.

Athens became more democratic under the leadership of Cleisthenes (KLIGHS-thuh-neez), a wealthy and prominent aristocrat who had won the support of lower-status men and became the leader of Athens in 508 B.C.E. Cleisthenes created the *deme* (deem), a unit of land that kept the roll of citizens, or *demos*, within its jurisdiction. Men enrolled as citizens through their deme—much as we would register to vote in the voting district in which we live—instead of through their family group, which brought people of different families together and promoted community and democracy. The demes were grouped into ten tribes, which thus formed the link between the demes and the central government. Each tribe elected a military leader, or *strategos* (plural *strategoi*).

The democracy functioned on the idea that all full citizens were sovereign. In 487 B.C.E. the election of the city's nine archons was replaced by reappointment by lot, which meant that any citizen with a certain amount of property had a chance of becoming an archon. This system gave citizens prestige, although the power of the archons gradually dwindled as the strategoi became the real military leaders of the city. Legislation was in the hands of two bodies, the *boule* (boo-LAY), or council, composed of five hundred members, and the *ecclesia* (ek-lay-SEE-yah), the assembly of all citizens. By supervising the various committees of government and proposing bills to the ecclesia, the boule guided Athenian political life. It received foreign envoys and forwarded treaties to the ecclesia for ratification. It oversaw the granting of state contracts and was responsible for receiving many revenues. It held the democracy together. Nonetheless, the ecclesia had the final word. Open to all male citizens over eighteen years of age—about 10 percent of the population of the city—it met at a specific place to vote on matters presented to it.

War and Turmoil in the Classical Period

FOCUS QUESTION *What were the major wars of the classical period, and how did they shape Greek history?*

From the time of the Mycenaeans, violent conflict was common in Greek society, and this did not change in the fifth century B.C.E., the beginning of what scholars later called the classical period of Greek history, which they date from about 500 B.C.E. to the conquest of Greece by Philip of Macedon in 338 B.C.E. First, the Greeks beat back the armies of the Persian Empire. Then, turning their spears against one another, they destroyed their own political system in a century of warfare culminating in the Peloponnesian War. This war and its aftermath proved that the polis had reached the limits of its success as an effective political institution, with the attempts of various city-states to dominate the others leading only to incessant warfare. Many people went bankrupt, and the quality of life for most people changed for the worse. The Greeks' failure to unify against outsiders led to the rise of a dominant new power: the kingdom of Macedonia.

The Persian Wars

In 499 B.C.E. the Greeks who lived in Ionia unsuccessfully rebelled against the Persian Empire, which had ruled the area for fifty years (see Chapter 2). The Athenians had provided halfhearted help to the Ionians in this failed rebellion, and in 490 B.C.E. the Persians retaliated against Athens, only to be surprisingly defeated by the Athenian hoplites at the Battle of Marathon.

(According to legend, a Greek runner carried the victory message to Athens. When the modern Olympic games were founded in 1896, they included a long-distance running race between Marathon and Athens, a distance of about twenty-five miles, designed to honor the ancient Greeks. The marathon was set at its current distance of 26.2 miles for the London Olympics of 1908, so that the finish would be in front of the royal box in the stadium.)

In 480 B.C.E. the Persian king Xerxes I (r. 485–465 B.C.E.) personally led a massive invasion of Greece. Under the leadership of Sparta, many Greek poleis, though not all, joined together to fight the Persians. The first confrontations between the Persians and the Greeks occurred at the pass of Thermopylae (thuhr-MAWP-uh-lee), where an outnumbered Greek army, including three hundred top Spartan warriors, held off a much larger Persian force for several days. Before the fighting began, a report came in that when the Persian archers shot their bows the arrows darkened the sky. Herodotus (ca. 485–425 B.C.E.), a Greek historian born in the Persian-ruled city of Halicarnassus in Asia Minor, later wrote that one gruff Spartan, upon hearing this report, replied merely, "Fine, then we'll fight in the shade."[4] The Greeks at Thermopylae fought heroically, but the Persians won the battle after a local man showed them a hidden path over the mountains so that they could attack the Greeks from both sides. The victorious Persian army occupied and sacked Athens.

At the same time as the land battle of Thermopylae, Greeks and Persians fought one another in a naval battle at Artemisium off Boeotia. The Athenians, led by the general Themistocles, provided the heart of the naval forces with their fleet of triremes, oar-propelled warships. (See "Living in the Past: Triremes and Their Crews," page 74.) Storms had wrecked many Persian ships, and neither side won a decisive victory. Only a month or so later, the Greek fleet met the Persian armada at Salamis, an island across from Athens. Though outnumbered, the Greek navy won an overwhelming victory by outmaneuvering the Persians. The remnants of the Persian fleet retired, and in 479 B.C.E. the Greeks overwhelmed the Persian army at Plataea.

The wars provided a brief glimpse of what the Greeks could accomplish when they worked together. By defeating the Persians, the Greeks ensured that they would not be ruled by a foreign power. The decisive victories meant that Greek political forms and intellec-

tual concepts would be handed down to later societies. Among the thoughtful Greeks who felt prompted to record and analyze these events was Herodotus, who traveled the Greek world to piece together the rise and fall of the Persian Empire. Like many other authors and thinkers, he was born elsewhere but moved to Athens and lived there for a time.

Growth of the Athenian Empire

The defeat of the Persians created a power vacuum in the Aegean, and the Athenians took advantage of the situation. Led by Themistocles, the Athenians and their allies formed the **Delian League**, a military alliance aimed at protecting the Aegean Islands, liberating Ionia from Persian rule, and keeping the Persians out of Greece. The league took its name from the small island of Delos, on which stood a religious center sacred to all parties. The Delian (DEE-lee-uhn) League was intended to be a free alliance under the leadership of Athens, but as the Athenians drove the Persians out of the Aegean, they also became increasingly imperialistic. Athens began reducing its allies to the status of subjects. Tribute was often collected by force, and the Athenians placed the economic resources of the Delian League under tighter and tighter control. Major allies revolted and were put down.

The aggressiveness of Athenian rule also alarmed Sparta and its allies. Relations between Athens and Sparta grew more hostile, particularly when Pericles (PEHR-uh-kleez) (ca. 494–429 B.C.E.), an aristocrat of solid intellectual ability, became the leading statesman in Athens. Pericles gained support among the ordinary citizens of Athens by introducing measures that broadened democracy, such as lowering the property requirement for the position of archon. Like the democracy he led, Pericles was aggressive and imperialistic. In 459 B.C.E. Sparta and Athens went to war over conflicts between Athens and some of Sparta's allies. The war ended in 445 B.C.E. with a treaty

Map caption:
Areas of Persian control
Greek states at war with Persia
Neutral Greek states

Thermopylae 480 B.C.E.
Artemisium 480 B.C.E.
Plataea 479 B.C.E.
Marathon 490 B.C.E.
Salamis 480 B.C.E.
Crete

The Persian Wars, 499–479 B.C.E.

The Delian League, ca. 478–431 B.C.E.

Delian League
Allied with Delian League, 446 B.C.E.
Athenian military settlement

Thasos
Corcyra
BOEOTIA
Megara　Athens
Corinth　Delos
Sparta
PERSIAN EMPIRE

■ **Delian League**　A military alliance led by Athens aimed at protecting the Aegean Islands, liberating Ionia from Persian rule, and keeping the Persians out of Greece.

Men pulling long oars propelled Greek warships in battle. These ancient mariners were generally free men who earned good wages, although in times of intense warfare cities also used slaves because there were not enough free men available. An experienced rower was valuable because he had learned how to row in rhythm with many other men, and some rowers became professionals who hired themselves out to any military leader. By the sixth century B.C.E. the dominant form of warship in the Mediterranean was the trireme, with three rows of oars on each side and one man per oar. Triremes also had two sails for extra propulsion when the wind was favorable, and large steering oars at the back. The trireme usually carried 186 rowers, 14 soldiers for battles, a steersman who also served as navigator, and a captain.

The hull, or frame, for the trireme was long and narrow like a stiletto blade, and the ship was built for speed, not comfort. A bronze battering ram capped the bow, or front of the ship.

In battle the crews rowed as hard as possible to ram enemy ships. After smashing the enemy's hull, the same rowers or soldiers who were on board the trireme swept over the side to capture the ship. Rowers often had to pull their oars hurriedly in reverse to free themselves from sinking enemy triremes.

Life aboard a trireme was cramped and uncomfortable. The crew sat about eight feet above the waves, and storms proved a constant danger. One captain described a particularly hard night at sea: "It was stormy, the place offered no harbor, and it was impossible to go ashore and get a meal. . . . So we were forced to ride at anchor all night long in the open sea without food and sleep. . . . It was our lot to have by night rain and thunder and a violent wind."* Surviving a naval battle held its own dangers, for a trireme had no space for lifeboats. One sailor described his escape from a sinking ship: "One man said that they had been saved by clinging to a barrel. Others who were drowning told him, if he got away safely, to report

A relief of the middle section of a trireme from the Athenian Acropolis, dated about 410 B.C.E. (Acropolis Museum, Athens, Greece/ Art & Architecture Collection, Ltd./ Bridgeman Images)

promising thirty years of peace, and no serious damage to either side. The treaty divided the Greek world between the two great powers, with each agreeing to respect the other and its allies.

Peace lasted thirteen years instead of thirty. Athens continued its severe policies toward its subject allies and came into conflict with Corinth, one of Sparta's leading supporters, over the island of Corcyra. In this climate of anger and escalation, Pericles decided to punish the city of Megara, which had switched allegiance from Sparta to Athens and then back again. In 432 B.C.E. Pericles persuaded the Athenians to pass a law that excluded the Megarians from trad-

ing with Athens and its empire, a restriction that would have meant economic disaster for the Megarians. In response the Spartans and their allies declared war.

The Peloponnesian War

At the outbreak of the war, which became known as the Peloponnesian (puh-luh-puh-NEE-zhuhn) War, the Spartan ambassador Melesippus warned the Athenians: "This day will be the beginning of great evil for the Greeks." Few men have ever prophesied more accurately. The Peloponnesian War lasted a generation and brought in its wake

that the admirals were doing nothing to rescue men who had fought most gallantly for their country."† Despite such discomforts and dangers, these oared ships and their men ruled the Mediterranean throughout classical antiquity. Greek and later Roman naval architects designed them expertly, and their crews routinely manned them with skill and courage.

QUESTIONS FOR ANALYSIS

1. In the relief from the Acropolis, how does the artist capture the physical effort of the oarsmen?
2. Based on the relief and the photo of the modern reconstruction, why do you think rowing in time was so important?
3. Triremes were well suited for war, but why would they not have worked well for trade?

Source: J. S. Morrison, *Greek and Roman Oared Warships 399–30 B.C.E.* (Oxbow Books, 1996).

*Pseudo-Demosthenes 50.22–23.
†Xenophon, *Hellenika* 1.7.11.

Battering ram on a replica of a trireme, used to bash enemy ships. (© Vito Arcomano/age-fotostock)

disease, famine, civil wars, widespread destruction, and huge loss of life (Map 3.3). During the first Spartan invasion of Attica, which began in 431 B.C.E., many people sought refuge in Athens. Overcrowding and a lack of sanitation or clean water nurtured a dreadful plague that killed huge numbers, eventually claiming Pericles himself. The charismatic and eloquent Cleon became the leader of Athens and urged a more aggressive war strategy, doubling the tribute of Athens's allies to pay for it. Both Cleon and the leading Spartan general were killed in battle. Recognizing that ten years of war had resulted only in death, destruc-

tion, and stalemate, Sparta and Athens concluded the Peace of Nicias (NIH-shee-uhs) in 421 B.C.E.

The Peace of Nicias resulted in a cold war. But even cold war can bring horror and misery. Such was the case when in 416 B.C.E. the Athenians sent a fleet to the largely neutral island of Melos with an ultimatum: the Melians could surrender and pay tribute or perish. The Melians resisted. The Athenians conquered them, killed the men of military age, and sold the women and children into slavery.

The cold war grew hotter, thanks in part to the ambitions of Alcibiades (al-suh-BIGH-uh-dees)

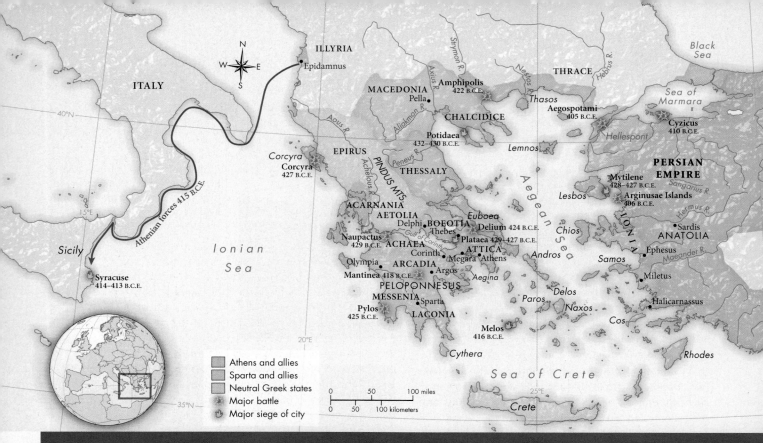

MAP 3.3 The Peloponnesian War, 431–404 B.C.E.

This map shows the alignment of states during the Peloponnesian War.

ANALYZING THE MAP How would you compare the area controlled by Sparta and its allies to that of Athens and its allies? How would you expect these similarities and/or differences to affect the way that each side chose to conduct its military campaigns?

CONNECTIONS What does the location of the major battles and sieges suggest about the impact of the war throughout Greece?

(ca. 450–404 B.C.E.), an aristocrat, a kinsman of Pericles, and a student of the philosopher Socrates (see page 88). An able but overconfident general, Alcibiades widened the war to further his own career and increase the power of Athens. He convinced the Athenians to attack Syracuse, the leading polis in Sicily, which would cut off the grain supply from Sicily to Sparta and its allies, allowing Athens to end the war and become the greatest power in Greece. The undertaking was vast, requiring an enormous fleet and thousands of sailors and soldiers, and ended in disaster. The Athenian historian Thucydides (thoo-SIHD-ih-dees) (ca. 460–ca. 399 B.C.E.), who saw action in the war himself and later tried to understand its causes, wrote the epitaph for the Athenians: "Infantry, fleet, and everything else were utterly destroyed, and out of many few returned home."[5]

The disaster in Sicily ushered in the final phase of the war, which was marked by three major developments: the renewal of war between Athens and Sparta, Persia's intervention in the war, and the revolt of many Athenian subjects. The year 413 B.C.E. saw Sparta's declaration of war against Athens and widespread revolt within the Athenian Empire, both supported by Alcibiades, who had defected to Sparta. The Persians threw their support behind the Spartans and built a fleet of ships for them; in exchange the Persians expected Ionia to be returned to them once the Spartans were successful. Now equipped with a fleet, the Spartans challenged the Athenians in the Aegean, and a long series of inconclusive naval battles followed.

The strain of war prompted the Athenians in 411 B.C.E. to recall Alcibiades from exile. He cheerfully double-crossed the Spartans and Persians, but even he could not restore Athenian fortunes. In 405 B.C.E. Spartan forces destroyed the last Athenian fleet at the Battle of Aegospotami, after which the Spartans blockaded Athens until it was starved into submission. In 404 B.C.E., after twenty-seven years of fighting, the Peloponnesian War was over, and the evils prophesied by the Spartan ambassador Melesippus in 431 B.C.E. had come true.

The Struggle for Dominance

The decades after the end of the Peloponnesian War were turbulent ones. The chief states — Sparta, Athens, and Thebes — each tried to create a political system in which it would dominate. When Athens surrendered to Sparta in 404 B.C.E., the Spartans used their victory to build an empire. Their decision brought them into conflict with Persia, which now demanded the return of Ionia to its control, as Sparta had promised earlier. From 400 to 386 B.C.E. the Spartans fought the Persians for Ionia, a conflict that eventually engulfed Greece itself. After years of stalemate the Spartans made peace with Persia and their own Greek enemies. The result was a treaty, the King's Peace of 386 B.C.E. in which the Greeks and Persians pledged themselves to live in harmony. This agreement cost Sparta its empire but not its position of dominance in Greece.

The Spartans were not long content with this situation, however, and decided to punish cities that had opposed Sparta during the war. They used naked force against old enemies even though they had formally agreed to peace. In 378 B.C.E. the Spartans launched an unprovoked attack on Athens. Together the Thebans and the Athenians created what was called the Second Athenian Confederacy, a federation of states to guarantee the terms of the peace treaty. The two fought Sparta until 371 B.C.E., when due to growing fear of Theban might, Athens made a separate peace with Sparta. Left alone, Thebes defended itself until later that year, when the brilliant Theban general Epaminondas (ih-pah-muh-NAHN-duhs) (ca. 418–362 B.C.E.) routed the Spartan army on the small plain of Leuctra and in a series of invasions eliminated Sparta as a major power.

The defeat of the once-invincible Spartans stunned the Greeks, who wondered how Thebes would use its victory. Epaminondas, also a gifted statesman, immediately grappled with the problem of how to translate military success into political reality. He concluded alliances with many Peloponnesian states but made no effort to dominate them, instead creating a federal league of cities in which people could marshal their resources, both human and material, to defend themselves from outside interference. Although he made Thebes the leader of this federation of cities, other city-states and leagues were bound to Thebes only by voluntary alliances. His premature death at the Battle of Mantinea in 362 B.C.E. put an end to his efforts, however.

Philip II and Macedonian Supremacy

While the Greek states exhausted themselves in endless conflicts, the new power of Macedonia arose in the north. The land, extensive and generally fertile, nurtured a large population. Whether the Macedonians should be considered Greeks is a controversial issue, among both scholars of the ancient world and Greeks and Macedonians living today. Macedonia had strong ties to the Greek poleis, but the government there developed as a kingdom, not a democracy or oligarchy.

The kings of Macedonia slowly built up their power over rival states, and in 359 B.C.E. the brilliant and cultured Philip II ascended to the throne. The young Philip had spent years in Thebes mastering diplomacy and warfare. With decades of effort he secured the borders of Macedonia against invaders from the north, and he then launched a series of military operations in the northwestern Aegean. By clever use of his wealth and superb army, he gained control of the area, and in 338 B.C.E. he won a decisive victory over Thebes and Athens that gave him command of Greece. Because the Greeks could not put aside their quarrels, they fell to an invader, and 338 B.C.E. is often seen as marking the end of the classical period.

After his victory, Philip led a combined army of soldiers from Macedonia and from many Greek states in an attempt to liberate the Ionian Greeks from Persian rule. Before he could launch this campaign, however, Philip fell to an assassin's dagger in 336 B.C.E. His young son Alexander vowed to carry on Philip's mission. He would succeed beyond all expectations.

Classical Greek Life and Culture

FOCUS QUESTION *What were the lasting cultural and intellectual achievements of the classical period?*

Despite the violence that dominated Greece for nearly two centuries beginning in 500 B.C.E., or to some degree because of it, playwrights and thinkers pondered the meaning of the universe and the role of humans in it, and artists and architects created new styles to celebrate Greek achievements. Thus, although warfare was one of the hallmarks of the classical period, intellectual and artistic accomplishments were as well.

Athenian Arts in the Age of Pericles

In the midst of the warfare of the fifth century B.C.E., Pericles turned Athens into the showplace of Greece. He appropriated Delian League funds to pay for a huge building program to rebuild the city that had been destroyed during the Persian occupation in 480 B.C.E., and to display to all Greeks the glory of the Athenian polis. Workers erected temples and other buildings as patriotic memorials housing statues and

The Acropolis of Athens

The natural rock formation of the Acropolis probably had a palace on top as early as the Mycenaean period, when the palace was also surrounded by a defensive wall. Temples were constructed beginning in the sixth century B.C.E., and after the Persian wars Pericles ordered the reconstruction and expansion of many of these, as well as the building of new and more magnificent temples and an extension of the defensive walls. The largest building is the Parthenon, a temple dedicated to the goddess Athena, which originally housed a forty-foot-tall statue of Athena made of ivory and gold sheets attached to a wooden frame. Much of the Parthenon was damaged when it was shelled during a war between Venice and the Ottoman Empire in the seventeenth century C.E., and air pollution continues to eat away at the marble.

(Lingbeek/Getty Images)

EVALUATE THE EVIDENCE

1. Imagine yourself as an Athenian walking up the hill toward the Parthenon. What impression would the setting and the building itself convey?
2. What were the various functions of the Acropolis?

carvings, often painted in bright colors, showing the gods in human form and celebrating the Greek victory over the Persians. (The paint later washed away, leaving the generally white sculpture that we think of as "classical.") Many of the temples were built on the high, rocky Acropolis that stood in the center of the city, on top of the remains of temples that had been burned by the Persians, and sometimes incorporating these into their walls.

The Athenians normally hiked up the long approach to the Acropolis only for religious festivals, of which the most important and joyous was the Great Panathenaea, held every four years to honor the virgin goddess Athena and perhaps offer sacrifices to older deities as well. (See "Evaluating the Evidence 3.2: The Acropolis of Athens," above.) For this festival, Athenian citizens and legal noncitizen residents formed a huge procession to bring the statue of Athena in the Parthenon an exquisite robe, richly embroidered by the citizen women of Athens with mythological scenes. At the head of the procession walked an aristocratic young woman carrying an offering basket. She and other young unmarried women of the city had earlier left their toys and other marks of childhood in caves at the base of the Acropolis. Other richly dressed women followed her, most carrying gold and silver vessels containing wine and perfumes. Young men on horseback came next, followed by older men carrying staffs. Toward the rear came other young men carrying large pitchers of water and wine, or leading the bulls to the sacrifice. After the religious ceremonies, all the people joined in a feast.

Once the procession began, the marchers first saw the Propylaea, the ceremonial gateway whose columns appeared to uphold the sky. On the right was the small temple of Athena Nike, built to commemorate the victory over the Persians. The broad band of sculpture above its columns depicted the struggle between the Greeks and the Persians. To the left of the visitors stood the Erechtheum, a temple that housed several ancient shrines. On its southern side was the famous Portico of the Caryatids, a porch whose roof was supported by huge statues of young women. As visitors walked on, they obtained a full view of the Parthenon, the chief temple dedicated to Athena at the center of the Acropolis, with a huge painted ivory and gold statue of the goddess inside.

The development of drama was tied to the religious festivals of the city, especially those to the god of wine, Dionysus (see page 87). Drama was as rooted in the life of the polis as were the architecture and sculpture of the Acropolis. The polis sponsored the production of plays and required wealthy citizens to pay the expenses of their production. At the beginning of the year, dramatists submitted their plays to the chief archon of the polis. He chose those he considered best and assigned a theatrical troupe to each playwright. Many plays were highly controversial, containing overt political and social commentary, but the archons neither suppressed nor censored them.

Not surprisingly, given the incessant warfare, conflict was a constant element in Athenian drama, and playwrights used their art in attempts to portray, understand, and resolve life's basic conflicts. The Athenian dramatists examined questions about the relationship between humans and the gods, the demands of society on the individual, and the nature of good and evil. Aeschylus (EHS-kuh-lihs) (525–456 B.C.E.), the first of the great Athenian dramatists, was also the first to express the agony of the individual caught in conflict. In his trilogy of plays, *The Oresteia* (ohr-eh-STEE-uh), Aeschylus deals with the themes of betrayal, murder, and reconciliation, urging that reason and justice be applied to reconcile fundamental conflicts. The final play concludes with a prayer that civil dissension never be allowed to destroy the city and that the life of the city be one of harmony and grace.

Sophocles (SOFF-uh-klees) (496–406 B.C.E.) also dealt with matters personal and political. Perhaps his most famous plays are *Oedipus* (EHD-uh-puhs) *the*

The Discus Thrower   This marble statue shows an athlete in mid-throw, capturing the tension in the muscles and tendons. The original was made about 450 B.C.E., perhaps by the sculptor Myron of Athens. As is true of so much Greek statuary, the original is lost, and this is a Roman copy. Athletes in Greece regularly competed nude, including in the Olympic games. (Victoria and Albert Museum, London, UK/Ancient Art and Architecture Collection Ltd./Bridgeman Images)

King and its sequel, *Oedipus at Colonus. Oedipus the King* is the tragic story of a man doomed by the gods to kill his father and marry his mother. Try as he might to avoid his fate, his every action brings him closer to its fulfillment. When at last he realizes that he has unwittingly carried out the decree of the gods, Oedipus blinds himself and flees into exile. In *Oedipus at Colonus*, Sophocles dramatizes the last days of the broken king, whose patient suffering and uncomplaining piety win him an exalted position. In the end the gods honor him for his virtue. The interpretation of these two plays has been hotly debated, but Sophocles seems to be saying that the gods only predict what is going to happen and do not determine it. It is up to the individual, not the gods, to decide whether things turn out tragically or not. (See "Evaluating the Evidence 3.3: Sophocles, *Antigone*," page 80.)

With Euripides (your-IHP-uh-dees) (ca. 480–406 B.C.E.) drama entered a new, and in many ways more personal, phase. To him the gods were far less important than human beings. The essence of Euripides's tragedy is the flawed character—men and women who bring disaster on themselves and their loved ones because their passions overwhelm reason. Although Euripides's plays were less popular in his lifetime than were those of Aeschylus and Sophocles, his work was to have a significant impact on Roman drama.

Sophocles, *Antigone*

The plays of Sophocles concern matters personal, political, and divine. In Antigone *(an-TIH-guh-nee), produced in or before 441 B.C.E., Polyneices (pahl-eh-NIGH-sees) and Eteocles (eh-tee-OH-klees), the sons of King Oedipus of Thebes, have killed each other in a war over who would rule. Creon, the brother of Oedipus's wife, Jocasta (who is also Oedipus's mother, but that's the plot of another play; see page 79), is now king, and orders the body of Polyneices to be left to rot. Polyneices's sister (and Creon's niece) Antigone disobeys him, buries Polyneices, and carries out the proper funeral rituals. Creon condemns her to be walled up, so she hangs herself. Creon's son and Antigone's fiancé, Haemon, then kills himself, as does Creon's wife. The heart of the play is a series of confrontations between Creon and Antigone.*

Creon *(to Antigone):*
You — tell me not at length but in a word.
You knew the order not to do this thing?

Antigone:
I knew, of course I knew. The word was plain.

Creon:
And still you dared to overstep these laws?

Antigone:
For me it was not Zeus who made that order.
Nor did that Justice who lives with the gods below
mark out such laws to hold among mankind.
Nor did I think your orders were so strong
that you, a mortal man, could over-run
the gods' unwritten and unfailing laws.
Not now, nor yesterday's, they always live,
and no one knows their origin in time
So not through fear of any man's proud spirit
would I be likely to neglect these laws,
draw on myself the gods' sure punishment.
I knew that I must die; how could I not?

even without your warning. If I die
before my time, I say it is a gain.
Who lives in sorrows many as are mine
how shall he not be glad to gain his death?
And so, for me to meet this fate, no grief.
But if I left that corpse, my mother's son,
dead and unburied I'd have cause to grieve
as now I grieve not.
And if you think my acts are foolishness
The foolishness may be in a fool's eye.
. . .
I go, without a friend, struck down by fate,
live to the hollow chambers of the dead.
What divine justice have I disobeyed?
Why, in my misery, look to the gods for help?
Can I call any of them my ally?
I stand convicted of impiety,
the evidence my pious duty done.
Should the gods think that this is righteousness,
in suffering I'll see my error clear.
But if it is the others who are wrong
I wish them no greater punishment than mine.
. . .
Look what I suffer, at whose command,
Because I respected the right.

EVALUATE THE EVIDENCE

1. How does Antigone justify what she has done? How does she describe the relationship between divine law and political law?
2. Given what was going on in Athens at the time that this play was performed, how can Antigone's words be seen as political commentary?

Source: *Sophocles I: Antigone*, trans. Elizabeth Wyckoff, in *The Complete Greek Tragedies* (Chicago: Phoenix Books, 1954), pp. 173–174, 190, 191. Copyright © 1954 by The University of Chicago. All rights reserved. Used by permission of the publisher.

Writers of comedy treated the affairs of the polis and its politicians bawdily and often coarsely. Even so, their plays also were performed at religious festivals. Best known are the comedies of Aristophanes (eh-ruh-STAH-fuh-neez) (ca. 445–386 B.C.E.), a merciless critic of cranks and quacks. He commented snidely on Cleon, poked fun at Socrates (see page 88), and hooted at Euripides. (See "Individuals in Society: Aristophanes," page 82.) Like Aeschylus, Sophocles, and Euripides, Aristophanes used his art to convey his ideas about human nature and the values of the polis.

Households and Work

In sharp contrast with the rich intellectual and cultural life of Periclean Athens stands the simplicity of its material life. The Athenians, like other Greeks, lived with comparatively few material possessions in houses that were rather simple. Well-to-do Athenians lived in houses consisting of a series of rooms opening onto a central courtyard, sometimes with bedrooms on an upper floor. Artisans often set aside a room to use as a shop or work area. Larger houses often had a dining room at the front where the men of the family ate and

Blacksmith's Shop　This painting on the side of an amphora from around 500 B.C.E. shows a blacksmith's shop, with the smiths working and other men providing advice. Men often gathered in artisans' shops or on the public square to chat, while women's conversations took place in the home. Although blacksmithing is hot work, a smith would not normally have worked in the nude; showing him naked allowed the painter to demonstrate his ability to depict human musculature. (Two-handled jar [amphora], Late Archaic Period, ca. 500–490 B.C. [ceramic], Plousios Painter [fl. ca. 500–490 B.C.)]/Museum of Fine Arts, Boston, Massachusetts, USA/Henry Lillie Pierce Fund/Bridgeman Images)

entertained guests at drinking parties called *symposia*, and a **gynaeceum** (also spelled *gynaikeion*), a room or section at the back where the women of the family and the female slaves worked, ate, and slept. Other rooms included the kitchen and bathroom. By modern standards there was not much furniture. In the men's dining room were couches, a sideboard, and small tables appropriate for social events. Cups and other pottery were often hung from pegs on the wall, as were hoplites' armor and, for aristocrats, the death masks of their relatives. In the courtyard were the well, a small altar, and a washbasin. If the family lived in the country, the stalls of the animals faced the courtyard. Country dwellers kept oxen for plowing, pigs for slaughtering, sheep for wool, goats for cheese, and mules and donkeys for transportation. Even in the city, chickens and perhaps a goat or two roamed the courtyard along with dogs and cats.

Cooking, done over a hearth in the house, provided welcome warmth in the winter. Baking and roasting were done in ovens. Meals consisted primarily of various grains, especially wheat and barley, as well as lentils, olives, figs, grapes, fish, and a little meat, foods that are now part of the highly touted "Mediterranean diet." The Greeks used olive oil for cooking, and also as an ointment and as lamp fuel.

The Greeks did not eat much meat. On special occasions, such as important religious festivals, the family ate the animal sacrificed to the god. The only Greeks who consistently ate meat were the Spartan warriors. They received a small portion of meat each day, together with the infamous Spartan black broth, a concoction of pork cooked in blood, vinegar, and salt. One Athenian, after tasting the broth, commented that he could easily understand why the Spartans were so willing to die.

In the city a man might support himself as a craftsman—a potter, bronze-smith, sailmaker, or tanner—or he could contract with the polis to work on public buildings. Certain crafts, including spinning and weaving, were generally done by women, who produced cloth for their own families and sold it. Men and women without skills worked as paid laborers but competed with slaves for work.

Slavery was commonplace in Greece, as it was throughout the ancient world. Slaves were usually foreigners and often "barbarians," people whose native language was not Greek. Most citizen households in Athens owned at least one slave. Slaves in Athens ranged widely in terms of their type of work and opportunities for

■ **gynaeceum** Women's quarters at the back of an Athenian house where the women of the family and the female slaves worked, ate, and slept.

In 424 B.C.E., in the middle of the Peloponnesian War, citizens of Athens attending one of the city's regular dramatic festivals watched *The Knights*, in which two slaves complain about their fellow slave's power over their master Demos ("the people" in Greek) and everyone else around him. They run into a sausage seller and tell him that an oracle has predicted he will become more influential than their fellow slave and will eventually dominate the city, becoming what in ancient Greece was called a demagogue. He doesn't think this possible, as he is only a sausage seller, but the men tell him he is the perfect candidate: "Mix and knead together all the state business as you do for your sausages. To win the people, always cook them some savoury that pleases them. Besides, you possess all the attributes of a demagogue; a screeching, horrible voice, a perverse, crossgrained nature and the language of the market-place. In you all is united which is needful for governing." This

Roman copy of a Hellenistic bust depicting what Aristophanes might have looked like. (Musée du Louvre, Paris, France/De Agostini Picture Library/Bridgeman Images)

leads to a series of shouted debates between the influential slave and the sausage maker, each one accusing the other of corruption and indecent behavior, and making ever more elaborate promises to the citizens of Athens. Ultimately the sausage seller wins, and the formerly domineering slave becomes a lowly sausage seller.

Although the forceful slave's name is never mentioned in the play, everyone knew he represented Cleon, at that point the leader of Athens, who had risen to power through populist speeches. The real Cleon may well have been among the thousands in the audience, as front-row seats at festivals were a reward he had just been given by the citizens of Athens for a military victory. Cleon had taken legal action against the playwright two years earlier for another play, accusing him of slandering the polis, but in this case he did nothing.

That playwright was Aristophanes, the only comic playwright in classical Athens from whom whole plays survive. Not much is known about Aristophanes's life, other than a few ambiguous clues in the plays. His first play, now lost, was produced in 427 B.C.E., and his last datable play, also now lost, in 386 B.C.E. (The dates of his life are inferred from these, as there is a comment in one play suggesting he was only eighteen when his first play was produced.) He directed some of his own plays, won the theater competition several times, and had sons who were also comic playwrights. Even in his early plays, Aristophanes seems to have opposed anything that was new in Athens: new types of leaders (like Cleon), new styles in drama (Euripides was a standard target), new kinds of educators (such as the Sophists), new philosophy (especially that of Socrates). Everything and everyone was open to ridicule, and the more obscene the better: poets throw turds at each other, politicians collapse drunk and vomiting in the streets, military leaders walk around with huge erections when their wives refuse to have sex with them until they call off the war. Aristophanes combined kinds of comedy that today are often separated — political satire, complicated wordplay, celebrity slamming, cross-dressing, slapstick, dirty jokes, silly props, absurdity, audience taunting — and was a master at all of these.

QUESTIONS FOR ANALYSIS

1. How might political satires such as those of Aristophanes have both critiqued and reinforced civic values in classical Athens?

2. Can you think of more recent parallels to Aristophanes's political satires? What has been the response to these?

escaping slavery. Some male slaves were skilled workers or well-educated teachers and tutors of writing, while others were unskilled laborers in the city, agricultural workers in the countryside, or laborers in mines, including the Athenian silver mines at Laurium. Female slaves worked in agriculture, or as domestic servants and nurses for children. Slaves received some protection under the law, and those who engaged in skilled labor for which they were paid could buy their freedom.

Gender and Sexuality

Citizenship was the basis of political power for men in ancient Athens and was inherited. After the middle of the fifth century B.C.E., people were considered citizens only if both parents were citizens, except for a few men given citizenship as a reward for service to the city. Adult male citizens were expected to take part in political decisions and be active in civic life, no matter what their occupation. (See "Thinking Like a Historian: Gender Roles in Classical Athens," page 84.) They were also in charge of relations between the household and the wider community. Women in Athens and elsewhere in Greece, like those in Mesopotamia, brought dowries to their husbands upon marriage, which became the husband's to invest or use, though he was supposed to do this wisely.

Women did not play a public role in classical Athens, and we know the names of no female poets, artists, or philosophers. Women in wealthier citizen families probably spent most of their time at home in the gynaeceum, leaving the house only to attend some religious festivals, and perhaps occasionally plays. The main function of women from citizen families was to bear and raise children. Childbirth could be dangerous for both mother and infant, so pregnant women usually made sacrifices or visited temples to ask help from the gods. Women relied on their relatives, on friends, and on midwives to assist in the delivery.

In the gynaeceum women oversaw domestic slaves and hired labor, and together with servants and friends worked wool into cloth. Women personally cared for slaves who became ill and nursed them back to health, and cared for the family's material possessions as well. Women from noncitizen families lived freer lives than citizen women, although they worked harder and had fewer material comforts. They performed manual labor in the fields or sold goods or services in the agora, going about their affairs much as men did.

Among the services that some women and men sold was sex. Women who sold sexual services ranged from poor streetwalkers known as *pornai* to middle-status hired mistresses known as *palakai* to sophisticated courtesans known as *hetaerae,* who added intellectual accomplishments to physical beauty. Hetaerae accom-

Young Man and Hetaera   In this scene painted on the inside of a drinking cup, a hetaera holds the head of a young man who has clearly had too much to drink. Sexual and comic scenes were common on Greek pottery, particularly on objects that would have been used at a private dinner party hosted by a citizen, known as a symposium. Wives did not attend symposia, but hetaerae and entertainers were often hired to perform for the male guests. (Painter: Makron, drinking cup [kylix], Greek, Late Archaic Period, about 490–480 B.C. Place of manufacture: Greece, Attica, Athens; ceramic, Red Figure; Height: 12.8 cm. [5¹⁄₁₆ in.]; Diameter: 33.2 cm. [13¹⁄₁₆ in.]/Museum of Fine Arts, Boston, Massachusetts, USA/Henry Lillie Pierce Fund, 01.8022/Photograph © 2015 Museum of Fine Arts, Boston. All Rights Reserved/Bridgeman Images)

panied men at dinner parties and in public settings where their wives would not have been welcome, serving men as social as well as sexual partners.

Same-sex relations were generally accepted in all of ancient Greece, not simply in Sparta. In classical Athens part of a male adolescent citizen's training might entail a hierarchical sexual and tutorial relationship with an adult man, who most likely was married and may have had female sexual partners as well. These relationships between young men and older men were often celebrated in literature and art, in part because Athenians regarded perfection as possible only in the male. Women were generally seen as inferior to men, dominated by their bodies rather than their minds. The perfect body was that of the young male, and perfect love was that between a young man and a slightly older man, not that between a man and a woman, who was marred by imperfection. The extent to which perfect love was sexual or spiritual was debated among the ancient Greeks. In one of his dialogues, the philosopher Plato (see page 88) argues that the best kind of love is one in which contemplation of the beloved

Gender Roles in Classical Athens

Athenian men's ideas about the proper roles for men and women, conveyed in written and visual form, became a foundation of Western notions of gender. How do the qualities they view as ideal and praiseworthy for men compare with those they view as ideal for women?

1 **Pericles's funeral oration, from Thucydides's *History of the Peloponnesian War*, 430 B.C.E.** In this speech given in honor of those who had died in the war, the Athenian leader Pericles glorifies the achievements of Athenian men and women.

If we look to the laws, they afford equal justice to all in their private differences; if to social standing, advancement in public life falls to reputation for capacity, class considerations not being allowed to interfere with merit; nor again does poverty bar the way, if a man is able to serve the state, he is not hindered by the obscurity of his condition. . . . Further, we provide plenty of means for the mind to refresh itself from business. We celebrate games and sacrifices all the year round, and the elegance of our private establishments forms a daily source of pleasure. . . . [I]n education, where our rivals from their very cradles by a painful discipline seek after manliness, at Athens we live exactly as we please, and yet are just as ready to encounter every legitimate danger. . . . We cultivate refinement without extravagance and knowledge without effeminacy; wealth we employ more for use than for show. . . . Again, in our enterprises we present the singular spectacle of daring and deliberation, each carried to its highest point, and both united in the same persons. . . . In short, I say that as a city we are the school of Hellas; while I doubt if the world can produce a man, who where he has only himself to depend upon, is equal to so many emergencies, and graced by so happy a versatility as the Athenian. . . .

If I must say anything on the subject of female excellence to those of you who will now be in widowhood, it will be all comprised in this brief exhortation: Great will be your glory in not falling short of your natural character; and greatest will be hers who is least talked of among the men whether for good or for bad.

2 **Xenophon, *Oeconomicus*, ca. 360 B.C.E.** In a treatise on household management, the historian, soldier, and philosopher Xenophon creates a character, Isomachus, who provides his much younger wife with advice and informs her about ideal gender roles. "God" in this selection means all of the gods, personified as male; "law" is personified as female ("law gives her consent").

ISOMACHUS: "God made provision from the first by shaping, as it seems to me, the woman's nature for indoor and the man's for outdoor occupations. Man's body and soul He furnished with a greater capacity for enduring heat and cold, wayfaring and military marches; or, to repeat, He laid upon his shoulders the outdoor works. While in creating the body of woman with less capacity for these things," I continued, "God would seem to have imposed on her the indoor works; and knowing that He had implanted in the woman and imposed upon her the nurture of new-born babies, He endowed her with a larger share of affection for the new-born child than He bestowed upon man. And since He imposed on woman the guardianship of the things imported from without, God, in His wisdom, perceiving that a fearful spirit was no detriment to guardianship, endowed the woman with a larger measure of timidity than He bestowed on man. Knowing further that he to whom the outdoor works belonged would need to defend them against malign attack, He endowed the man in turn with a larger share of courage. . . . Law, too, gives her consent—law and the usage of mankind, by sanctioning the wedlock of man and wife; and just as God ordained them to be partners in their children, so the law establishes their common ownership of house and estate. Custom, moreover, proclaims as beautiful those excellences of man and woman with which God gifted them at birth. Thus for a woman to bide tranquilly at home rather than roam abroad is no dishonour; but for a man to remain indoors, instead of devoting himself to outdoor pursuits, is a thing discreditable."

ANALYZING THE EVIDENCE

1. In Sources 1–3, what qualities do the authors see as praiseworthy in men? In women?
2. In Sources 2 and 3, what do Xenophon and Aristotle view as the underlying reasons for gender differences?
3. The two paintings in Sources 4 and 5 show scenes that were normal parts of real Athenian life, but how do they also convey ideals for men and women? What are these ideals?
4. Because no writing or art by Athenian women has survived, we have to extrapolate women's opinions from works by men. What does the body language and expression of the young woman in Source 4 suggest she thought about her situation?

4 **Vase painting showing Athenian woman at home, fifth century B.C.E.** A well-to-do young woman sits on an elegant chair inside a house, spinning and weaving. The bed piled high with coverlets on the left was a symbol of marriage.

(Musée du Louvre, Paris, France/Erich Lessing/Art Resource, NY)

3 **Aristotle, *The Politics*.** In *The Politics*, one of his most important works, Aristotle examines the development of government, which he sees as originating in the power relations in the family and household.

The city belongs among the things that exist by nature, and man is by nature a political animal. . . . The family is the association established by nature for the supply of men's everyday wants. . . .

It is clear that the rule of the soul over the body, and of the mind and the rational element over the passionate, is natural and expedient; whereas the equality of the two or the rule of the inferior is always hurtful. The same holds good of animals in relation to men; for tame animals have a better nature than wild, and all tame animals are better off when they are ruled by man; for then they are preserved. Again, the male is by nature superior, and the female inferior; and the one rules, and the other is ruled; this principle, of necessity, extends to all mankind. . . .

A similar question may be raised about women and children, whether they too have virtues: ought a woman to be temperate and brave and just, and is a child to be called temperate, and intemperate, or not? . . . Here the very constitution of the soul has shown us the way; in it one part naturally rules, and the other is subject, and the virtue of the ruler we maintain to be different from that of the subject; the one being the virtue of the rational, and the other of the irrational part. Now, it is obvious that the same principle applies generally, and therefore almost all things rule and are ruled according to nature. . . . For the slave has no deliberative faculty at all; the woman has, but it is without authority, and the child has, but it is immature. So it must necessarily be supposed to be with the moral virtues also; all should partake of them, but only in such manner and degree as is required by each for the fulfillment of his duty. . . . Clearly, then, moral virtue belongs to all of them; but the temperance of a man and of a woman, or the courage and justice of a man and of a woman, are not, as Socrates maintained, the same; the courage of a man is shown in commanding, of a woman in obeying. . . . All classes must be deemed to have their special attributes; as the poet says of women, "Silence is a woman's glory," but this is not equally the glory of man.

5 **Lekythos (oil flask), with a wedding scene, attributed to the Amasis Painter, ca. 550 B.C.E.** In this early representation of an Attic wedding procession, the bearded groom drives the cart to his home, while the bride (right) pulls her veil forward in a gesture associated with marriage in Greek art.

(Lekythos by Amasis Painter/Metropolitan Museum of Art, New York, New York, USA/De Agostini Picture Library/Bridgeman Images)

PUTTING IT ALL TOGETHER

Using the sources above, along with what you have learned in class and in Chapter 3, write a short essay that compares ideals for men and women in classical Athens. How did these ideas about gender roles both reflect and shape Athenian society and political life?

Sources: (1) Thucydides, *The Peloponnesian War* (London: J. M. Dent; New York, E. P. Dutton, 1910), at Perseus Digital Library; (2) Xenophon, *The Economist*, trans. H. G. Dakyns, at http://www.gutenberg.org/files/1173/1173-h/1173-h.htm; (3) Aristotle, *Politics*, Book One, translated by Benjamin Jowett, at http://classics.mit.edu/Aristotle/politics.1.one.html.

leads to contemplation of the divine, an intellectualized love that came to be known as "platonic." Plato was suspicious of the power of sexual passion because it distracted men from reason and the search for knowledge.

Along with praise of intellectualized love, Greek authors also celebrated physical sex and desire. The soldier-poet Archilochus (d. 652 B.C.E.) preferred "to light upon the flesh of a maid and ram belly to belly and thigh to thigh."[6] The lyric poet Sappho, who lived on the island of Lesbos in the northern Aegean Sea in the sixth century B.C.E., wrote often of powerful desire. One of her poems describes her reaction on seeing her beloved talking to someone else:

> He appears to me, that one, equal to the gods,
> the man who, facing you,
> is seated and, up close, that sweet voice of yours
> he listens to
>
> And how you laugh your charming laugh. Why it
> makes my heart flutter within my breast,
> because the moment I look at you, right then, for
>   me,
> to make any sound at all won't work any more.
>
> My tongue has a breakdown and a delicate
> —all of a sudden—fire rushes under my skin.
> With my eyes I see not a thing, and there is a roar
> that my ears make.
> Sweat pours down me and a trembling
> seizes all of me; paler than grass
> am I, and a little short of death
> do I appear to me.[7]

Sappho's description of the physical reactions caused by love—and jealousy—reaches across the centuries. The Hellenic, and even more the Hellenistic, Greeks regarded her as a great lyric poet, although because some of her poetry is directed toward women, over the last century she has become better known for her sexuality than her writing. Today the English word *lesbian* is derived from Sappho's home island of Lesbos.

Same-sex relations did not mean that people did not marry, for Athenians saw the continuation of the family line as essential. Sappho, for example, appears to have been married and had a daughter. Sexual desire and procreation were both important aspects of life, but ancient Greeks did not necessarily link them.

Public and Personal Religion

Like most peoples of the ancient world, the Greeks were polytheists, worshipping a variety of gods and goddesses who were immortal but otherwise acted just like people. Migration, invasion, and colonization brought the Greeks into contact with other peoples and caused their religious beliefs to evolve. How much these contacts shaped Greek religion and other aspects of culture has been the subject of a fierce debate since the late 1980s, when in *Black Athena: The Afroasiatic Roots of Classical Civilization*, Martin Bernal proposed that the Greeks owed a great deal to the Egyptians and Phoenicians, and that scholars since the nineteenth century had purposely tried to cover this up to make the Greeks seem more European and less indebted to cultures in Africa and Asia.[8] Bernal's ideas are highly controversial, and most classicists do not accept his evidence, but they are part of a larger tendency among scholars in the last several decades—including those who vigorously oppose Bernal—to see the Greeks less in isolation from other groups and more in relation to the larger Mediterranean world.

Greek religion was primarily a matter of ritual, with rituals designed to appease the divinities believed to control the forces of the natural world. Processions, festivals, and sacrifices offered to the gods were frequently occasions for people to meet together socially, times of cheer or even drunken excess.

By the classical era the primary gods were understood to live metaphorically on Mount Olympus, the highest mountain in Greece. Zeus was the king of the gods and the most powerful of them, and he was married to Hera, who was also his sister (just as, in Egypt, Isis was Osiris's wife and sister; see Chapter 2). Zeus and Hera had several children, including Ares, the god of war. Zeus was also the father of the god Apollo, who represented the epitome of youth, beauty, and athletic skill, and who served as the patron god of music and poetry. Apollo's half sister Athena was a warrior-goddess who had been born from the head of Zeus.

The Greeks also honored certain heroes. A hero was born of a union of a god or goddess and a mortal and was considered an intermediate between the divine and the human. A hero displayed his divine origins by performing deeds beyond the ability of human beings. Herakles (or Hercules, as the Romans called him), the son of Zeus and the mortal woman Alcmene, was the most popular of the Greek heroes, defeating mythical opponents and carrying out impossible (or "Herculean") tasks. Devotees to Hercules believed that he, like other heroes, protected mortals from supernatural dangers and provided an ideal of vigorous masculinity.

The polis administered cults and festivals, and everyone was expected to participate in events similar to today's patriotic parades or ceremonies. Much religion was local and domestic, and individual families honored various deities privately in their homes. Many people also believed that magic rituals and spells were effective and sought the assistance of individuals reputed to have special knowledge or powers to cure disease, drive away ghosts, bring good weather, or influence the actions of others. Even highly educated Greeks sought the assistance of fortune-tellers and soothsayers, from the oracle at Delphi to local figures who examined the flights of birds or the entrails of recently slaughtered chickens for clues about what was going to happen in the future.

Along with public and family forms of honoring the gods, some Greeks also participated in what later historians have termed **mystery religions**, in which participants underwent an initiation ritual and gained secret knowledge that they were forbidden to reveal to the uninitiated. The Eleusinian mysteries, held at Eleusis in Attica, are one of the oldest of these. They centered on Demeter, the goddess of the harvest, whose lovely daughter Persephone (Per-SEH-foh-nee), as the story goes, was taken by the god Hades to the underworld. In mourning, Demeter caused drought, and ultimately Zeus allowed Persephone to return to her, though she had to spend some months of the year in Hades. There is evidence of an agrarian ritual celebrating this mythological explanation for the cycle of the seasons as early as the Bronze Age, and in the sixth century B.C.E. the rulers of nearby Athens made the ritual open to all Greeks, women and slaves included. Many people flocked to the annual ceremonies and learned the mysteries, which by the fourth century B.C.E. appear to have promised life after death to those initiated into them.

Another somewhat secret religion was that of Dionysus (digh-uh-NIGH-suhs), the god of wine and powerful emotions. Dionysus appears to have been a god of non-Greek origin, though stories evolved to fit him into the Olympian system as a son of Zeus. He was killed and then reborn, which is why he, like Persephone, became the center of mystery religions offering rebirth. As the god of wine, he also represented freedom from the normal constraints of society, and his worshippers were reported to have danced ecstatically and even to have become a frenzied and uncontrolled mob. Whether or how often this actually happened is impossible to know, as contemporary Athenian writers who did not approve may have embellished their accounts of these wild rituals, and later scholars sometimes regarded them simply as fiction because chaotic orgies did not fit with their notions of the rational and orderly Greeks.

Greeks also shared some public Pan-Hellenic festivals, the chief of which were held at Olympia in honor of Zeus and at Delphi in honor of Apollo. The festivities at Olympia included athletic contests that have inspired the modern Olympic games. Held every four years, these games were for the glory of Zeus. They attracted visitors from all over the Greek world and lasted until the fourth century C.E., when they were banned by a Christian emperor because they were pagan. The Pythian (PIH-thee-uhn) games at Delphi were also held every four years and emphasized musical and literary contests as well as athletic prowess. Both the Olympic and the Pythian games were unifying factors in Greek life, bringing Greeks together culturally as well as religiously.

The Flowering of Philosophy

Just as the Greeks developed rituals to honor the gods, they spun myths and epics to explain the origin of the universe. Over time, however, as Greeks encountered other peoples with different beliefs, some of them began to question their old gods and myths, and they sought rational rather than supernatural explanations for natural phenomena. These Greek thinkers, based in Ionia, are called the Pre-Socratics because their rational efforts preceded those of the Athenian. They took individual facts and wove them into general theories that led them to conclude that, despite appearances, the universe is actually simple and subject to natural laws. Although they had little impact on the average Greek of their day, the Pre-Socratics began an intellectual revolution with their idea that nature was predictable, creating what we now call philosophy and science.

Drawing on their observations, the Pre-Socratics speculated about the basic building blocks of the universe. Thales (THAY-leez) (ca. 600 B.C.E.) thought the basic element of the universe was water, and Heraclitus (hehr-uh-KLIGH-tuhs) (ca. 500 B.C.E.) thought it was fire. Democritus (dih-MAW-kruh-tuhs) (ca. 460 B.C.E.) broke this down further and created the atomic theory, the idea that the universe is made up of invisible, indestructible particles. The culmination of Pre-Socratic thought was the theory that four simple substances make up the universe: fire, air, earth, and water.

The stream of thought started by the Pre-Socratics branched into several directions. Hippocrates (hih-PAW-kruh-teez) (ca. 470–400 B.C.E.), who lived on the island of Kos near present-day Turkey, became the most prominent physician and teacher of medicine of his time. He appears to have written several works, and his followers wrote many more. These medical writings became known as the "Hippocratic corpus," although it is impossible to say who actually wrote any specific work. Hippocrates sought natural explanations for diseases and seems to have advocated letting nature take its course and not intervening too much. Illness was caused not by evil spirits, he asserted, but by physical problems in the body, particularly by imbalances in what he saw as four basic bodily fluids: blood, phlegm, black bile, and yellow bile. In a healthy body these fluids, called humors, were in perfect balance, and the goal of medical treatment of the ill was to help the body bring them back into balance.

■ **mystery religions** Belief systems that were characterized by secret doctrines, rituals of initiation, and sometimes the promise of rebirth or an afterlife.

The **Sophists** (SOFF-ihsts), a group of thinkers in fifth-century-B.C.E. Athens, applied philosophical speculation to politics and language, questioning the beliefs and laws of the polis to understand their origin. They believed that excellence in both politics and language could be taught, and they provided lessons for the young men of Athens who wished to learn how to persuade others in the often-tumultuous Athenian democracy. Their later opponents criticized them for charging fees and also accused them of using rhetoric to deceive people instead of presenting the truth. (Today the word *sophist* is usually used in this sense, describing someone who deceives people with clever-sounding but false arguments.)

Socrates (SOK-ruh-teez) (ca. 469–399 B.C.E.), whose ideas are known only through the works of others, also applied philosophy to politics and to people. He seemed to many Athenians to be a Sophist because he also questioned Athenian traditions, although he never charged fees. His approach when exploring ethical issues and defining concepts was to start with a general topic or problem and to narrow the matter to its essentials. He did so by continuously questioning participants in a discussion or argument through which they developed critical thinking skills, a process known as the **Socratic method**. Because he posed questions rather than giving answers, it is difficult to say exactly what Socrates thought about many things, although he does seem to have felt that through knowledge people could approach the supreme good and thus find happiness. He clearly thought that Athenian leaders were motivated more by greed and opportunism than by a desire for justice in the war with Sparta, and he criticized Athenian democracy openly.

Socrates was viewed with suspicion by many because he challenged the traditional beliefs and values of Athens. The playwright Aristophanes satirized him and his followers in the riotously funny *The Clouds*, performed around 420 B.C.E. Twenty years later, after Athens's disastrous defeat at the hands of Sparta in the Peloponnesian War, Socrates came into serious conflict with the government. Charges were brought against him for corrupting the youth of the city, and for impiety, that is, for not believing in the gods honored in the city. Thus he was essentially charged with being unpatriotic because he criticized the traditions of the city and the decisions of government leaders. He was tried and imprisoned, and though he had several opportuni-

ties to escape, in 399 B.C.E. he drank the poison ordered as his method of execution and died.

Most of what we know about Socrates, including the details of his trial and death, comes from his student Plato (427–347 B.C.E.), who wrote dialogues in which Socrates asks questions and who also founded the Academy, a school dedicated to philosophy. Plato developed the theory that there are two worlds: the impermanent, changing world that we know through our senses, and the eternal, unchanging realm of "forms" that constitute the essence of true reality. According to Plato, true knowledge and the possibility of living a virtuous life come from contemplating ideal forms—what later came to be called **Platonic ideals**—not from observing the visible world. Thus if you want to understand justice, asserted Plato, you should think about what would make perfect justice, not study the imperfect examples of justice around you. Plato believed that the ideal polis could exist only when its citizens were well educated. From education came the possibility of determining all of the virtues of life and combining them into a system that would lead to an intelligent, moral, and ethical life.

Plato's student Aristotle (384–322 B.C.E.) also thought that true knowledge was possible, but he believed that such knowledge came from observation of the world, analysis of natural phenomena, and logical reasoning, not contemplation. Aristotle thought that everything had a purpose, so that to know something, one also had to know its function. Excellence—*arête* in Greek—meant performing one's function to the best of one's ability, whether one was a horse or a person. To the qualities of courage and strength that Homer had seen as essential to arête in people (see page 66), Aristotle added justice, generosity, temperance, and other moral virtues. The range of Aristotle's thought is staggering. His interests embraced logic, ethics, natural science, physics, politics, poetry, and art. He studied the heavens as well as the earth and judged the earth to be the center of the universe, with the stars and planets revolving around it.

Plato's idealism profoundly shaped Western philosophy, but Aristotle came to have an even wider influence; for many centuries in Europe, the authority of Aristotle's ideas was second only to the Bible's. His works—which are actually a combination of his lecture notes and those of his students, copied and recopied many times—were used as the ultimate proof that something was true, even if closer observation of the phenomenon indicated that it was not. Thus, ironically, Aristotle's authority was sometimes invoked in a way that contradicted his own ideas. Despite these limitations, the broader examination of the universe and the place of humans in it that Socrates, Plato, and Aristotle engaged in is widely regarded as Greece's most important intellectual legacy.

■ **Sophists**   A group of thinkers in fifth-century-B.C.E. Athens who applied philosophical speculation to politics and language and were accused of deceit.

■ **Socratic method**   A method of inquiry used by Socrates based on asking questions, through which participants developed their critical thinking skills and explored ethical issues.

■ **Platonic ideals**   In Plato's thought, the eternal unchanging ideal forms that are the essence of true reality.

NOTES

1. Homer, *The Iliad*, trans. Samuel Butler (London: Longmans, Green, and Co., 1898), book 1, lines 1–5.
2. J. M. Edmonds, *Greek Elegy and Iambus* (Cambridge, Mass.: Harvard University Press, 1931), I.70, frag. 10.
3. *The Works of Xenophon*, trans. Henry G. Dakyns (London: Macmillan and Co., 1892), p. 296.
4. Herodotus, *Histories* 7.226.2. Works in Greek with no translator noted were translated by John Buckler.
5. Thucydides, *History of the Peloponnesian War* 7.87.6.
6. G. Tarditi, *Archilochus Fragmenta* (Rome: Edizioni dell'Ateno, 1968), frag. 112.
7. Gregory Nagy, *The Ancient Greek Hero in 24 Hours* (Cambridge, Mass.: Harvard University Press, 2013), p. 119. Used by permission of Gregory Nagy, Center for Hellenic Studies.
8. Martin Bernal, *Black Athena: The Afroasiatic Roots of Classical Civilization* (New Brunswick, N.J.: Rutgers University Press, 1991). Essays by classical scholars refuting Bernal can be found in Mary R. Lefkowitz and Guy Maclean Rogers, *Black Athena Revisited* (Durham: University of North Carolina Press, 1996).

LOOKING BACK LOOKING AHEAD

The ancient Greeks built on the endeavors of earlier societies in the eastern Mediterranean, but they also added new elements, including drama, philosophy, science, and naturalistic art. They created governments that relied on the participation of citizens. These cultural and political achievements developed in a society that for many centuries was almost always at war, with the Persians and with each other. Those conflicts led many to wonder whether democracy was really a good form of government, and to speculate more widely about abstract ideals and the nature of the cosmos. The Greeks carried these ideas with them as they colonized much of the Mediterranean, in migrations that often resulted from the conflicts that were so common in Greece.

The classical Greeks had tremendous influence not only on the parts of the world in which they traveled or settled, but also on all of Western civilization from that point on. As you will see in Chapter 5, Roman art, religion, literature, and many other aspects of culture relied on Greek models. And as you will see in Chapter 12, European thinkers and writers made conscious attempts to return to classical ideals in art, literature, and philosophy during the Renaissance. In America political leaders from the Revolutionary era on decided that important government buildings should be modeled on the Parthenon or other temples, complete with marble statuary of their own heroes. In some ways, capitol buildings in the United States are perfect symbols of the legacy of Greece — gleaming ideals of harmony, freedom, democracy, and beauty that (as with all ideals) do not always correspond with realities.

Make Connections

Think about the larger developments and continuities within and across chapters.

1. What were the effects of the Bronze Age Collapse in Egypt, the Hittite Empire, Kush, Phoenicia, and Greece, and how did interactions among these societies change in this period of turmoil?

2. How were Greek understandings of the role of the gods in public and private life similar to those of the Egyptians and Sumerians? How were they different?

3. Looking at your own town or city, what evidence do you find of the cultural legacy of ancient Greece?

3 REVIEW & EXPLORE

Identify Key Terms

Identify and explain the significance of each item below.

Minoan (p. 63)

Mycenaean (p. 64)

polis (p. 66)

hoplites (p. 68)

tyranny (p. 68)

democracy (p. 68)

oligarchy (p. 68)

helots (p. 70)

Delian League (p. 73)

gynaeceum (p. 81)

mystery religions (p. 87)

Sophists (p. 88)

Socratic method (p. 88)

Platonic ideals (p. 88)

Review the Main Ideas

Answer the focus questions from each section of the chapter.

◆ How did the geography of Greece shape its earliest kingdoms, and what factors contributed to the decline of those kingdoms? (p. 62)

◆ What was the role of the polis in Greek society? (p. 66)

◆ What were the major wars of the classical period, and how did they shape Greek history? (p. 72)

◆ What were the lasting cultural and intellectual achievements of the classical period? (p. 77)

Suggested Reading and Media Resources

BOOKS

◆ Beard, Mary. *The Parthenon.* 2010. A cultural history of Athens's most famous building, including the many controversies that surround it.

◆ Cartledge, Paul. *The Spartans: The World of the Warrior Heroes of Ancient Greece.* 2002. A solid general book on the history and legacy of Sparta.

◆ Davidson, James. *Courtesans and Fishcakes: The Consuming Passions of Classical Athens.* 1999. A witty examination of sex, wine, food, and other objects of desire, based on plays, poems, speeches, and philosophical treatises.

◆ Fantham, Elaine, et al. *Women in the Classical World.* 1994. Uses written sources and visual materials to present women of all classes in the cultural context of their times.

◆ Fisher, N. R. E. *Slavery in Classical Greece.* 2001. A brief study that puts slavery into its social, political, and intellectual contexts.

◆ Hansen, Mogens Herman. *Polis: An Introduction to the Ancient Greek City-State.* 2006. The authoritative study of the polis.

◆ Hanson, Victor Davis. *The Other Greeks: The Family Farm and the Agrarian Roots of Western Civilization.* 1999. Argues that it was Greek rural residents rather than city dwellers who really created Greek culture.

◆ Holland, Tom. *Persian Fire: The First World Empire and the Battle for the West.* 2007. Designed for general audiences, a dramatic retelling of conflict between the Greeks and the Persians.

◆ Kagan, Donald. *The Peloponnesian War.* 2003. A comprehensive yet accessible study that focuses on leaders and battles, but also the human costs.

◆ Osborne, Robin. *Greece in the Making, 1200–479 B.C.* 2003. Traces the evolution of Greek communities from villages to cities and the development of their civic institutions.

- Roochnik, David. *Retrieving the Ancients: An Introduction to Greek Philosophy.* 2004. A sophisticated and well-written narrative of ancient Greek thought designed for students.
- Shelmerdine, Cynthia. *The Cambridge Companion to the Aegean Bronze Age.* 2008. A collection of essays by leading scholars on the history and the material culture of Crete, Greece, and the Aegean Islands from ca. 3000 B.C.E. to 1100 B.C.E.
- Thomas, Carol G. *Myth Becomes History.* 1993. An excellent treatment of early Greece and modern historical attitudes toward it.
- Worthington, Ian. *Philip II of Macedonia.* 2010. Examines Philip's life and legacy, based on literary and archaeological sources.

DOCUMENTARIES

- *Ancient Apocalypse: Mystery of the Minoans* (BBC, 2008). Explores the role of the volcanic eruption on the nearby island of Thera in ending Minoan civilization; shot on location in Crete.
- *Athens: The Truth About Democracy* (BBC, 2007). Historian Bettany Hughes takes a critical look at classical Athens, with attention to slavery, imperialism, the flow of money, and restrictions on women.
- *The Rise and Fall of the Spartans* (History Channel, 2003). Examines the creation, maintenance, and end of Sparta's distinctive military/political system.

FEATURE FILMS

- *The Odyssey* (Andrey Konchalovskiy, 1997). Originally made as a television miniseries, this film portrays many of Odysseus's adventures much as Homer wrote them, as they need no enhancing. Shot on location in the Mediterranean and with an international cast.
- *Troy* (Wolfgang Petersen, 2004). A fairly decent Hollywood film that focuses, as did Homer in his epic, on the personalities and motivations of the characters as well as on the Trojan War itself.

WEB SITES

- *Diotima: Materials for the Study of Women and Gender in the Ancient World.* Contains an extensive anthology of translated Greek, Latin, Egyptian, and Coptic texts, along with articles, book reviews, databases, and images. **www.stoa.org/diotima/**
- *Metropolitan Museum Timeline of Art History, Ancient Greece.* The Metropolitan Museum's timeline of art history is excellent for every era, but especially for the classical world; the site includes specialized essays on many topics, all linked to items in the museum's collection. **www.metmuseum.org/toah/ht/?period =04&region=eusb**
- *Perseus Digital Library.* The premier site for accessing the literature and archaeology of ancient Greek culture and now Roman as well, with hundreds of primary texts in Greek, Latin, and English translation, and thousands of images from museum collections and archaeological sites. **www.perseus.tufts.edu/hopper/**

4

Life in the Hellenistic World

336–30 B.C.E.

When his father was assassinated in 336 B.C.E., twenty-year-old Alexander inherited not only Philip's crown but also his determination to lead a united Greek force in fighting Persia. Alexander's invasion of the Persian Empire led to its downfall, but he died while planning his next campaign, only a little more than a decade after he had started. He left behind an empire that quickly broke into smaller kingdoms, but more important, his death ushered in an era, the Hellenistic, in which Greek culture, the Greek language, and Greek thought spread as far as India, blending with local traditions. The end of the Hellenistic period is generally set at 30 B.C.E., the year of the death of Cleopatra VII—a Greek ruler—and the Roman conquest of her kingdom of Egypt. The Romans had conquered much of what had been Alexander's empire long before this, but many aspects of Hellenistic culture continued to flourish under Roman governance, adapting to Roman ways of life. Thus rather than coming to an abrupt end in one specific year, the Hellenistic world gradually evolved into the Roman.

In many ways, life in the Hellenistic world was not much different from life in Hellenic Greece or from that in any other Iron Age agricultural society: most people continued to be farmers, raising crops and animals for their own needs and for paying rents and taxes to their superiors. Those who lived in cities, however, often ate foods and drank wine that came from far away, did business with people who were quite unlike them, and adopted religious practices and ways of thinking unknown to their parents. Hellenistic cities thus offer striking parallels to those of today. ■

CHAPTER PREVIEW

Hellenistic Married Life
This small terra-cotta figurine from Myrina in what is now Turkey, made in the second century B.C.E., shows a newly married couple sitting on a bridal bed. The groom is drawing back the bride's veil, and she is exhibiting the modesty that was a desired quality in young women. Figurines representing every stage of life became popular in the Hellenistic period and were used for religious offerings in temples and sacred places. This one was found in a tomb. (Musée du Louvre, Paris, France/Erich Lessing/Art Resource, NY)

Alexander's Conquests and Their Political Legacy

FOCUS QUESTION *How and why did Alexander the Great create an empire, and what was its political legacy?*

Fully intending to carry out Philip's designs to lead the Greeks against the Persians, Alexander (r. 336–323 B.C.E.) proclaimed to the Greek world that the invasion of Persia was to be a mighty act of revenge for Xerxes's invasion of Greece in 480 B.C.E. (see Chapter 3) and more recent Persian interference in Greek affairs. Although he could not foresee this, Alexander's invasion ended up being much more. His campaign swept away the Persian Empire, which had ruled the area for over two hundred years. In its place Alexander established a Macedonian monarchy, and although his rule over these vast territories was never consolidated due to his premature death, he left behind a legacy of political and cultural influence, and a long period of war. Macedonian kings established dynasties and Greek culture spread in this Hellenistic era.

Military Campaigns

Despite his youth, Alexander was well prepared to invade Persia. Philip had groomed his son to become king and had given him the best education possible, hiring the Athenian philosopher Aristotle to be his tutor. In 334 B.C.E. Alexander led an army of Macedonians and Greeks into Persian territory in Asia Minor. With him went a staff of philosophers to study the people of these lands, poets to write verses praising Alexander's exploits, scientists to map the area and study strange animals and plants, and a historian to write an account of the campaign. Alexander intended not only a military campaign but also an expedition of discovery.

In the next three years Alexander moved east into the Persian Empire, winning major battles at the Granicus River and Issus (Map 4.1). He moved into Syria and took most of the cities of Phoenicia and the eastern coast of the Mediterranean without a fight. His army successfully besieged the cities that did oppose him, including Tyre and Gaza, executing the men of military age afterwards and enslaving the women and children. He then turned south toward Egypt, which had earlier

MAP 4.1 Alexander's Conquests, 334–324 B.C.E. This map shows the course of Alexander's invasion of the Persian Empire. More important than the great success of his military campaigns were the founding of new cities and expansion of existing ones by Alexander and the Hellenistic rulers who followed him.

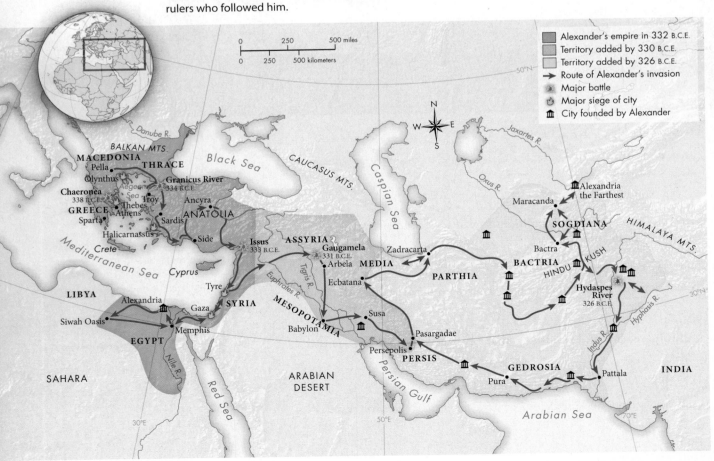

been conquered by the Persians. The Egyptians saw Alexander as a liberator, and he seized it without a battle. After honoring the priestly class, Alexander was proclaimed pharaoh, the legitimate ruler of the country. He founded a new capital, Alexandria, on the coast of the Mediterranean, which would later grow into an enormous city. He next marched to the oasis of Siwah, west of the Nile Valley, to consult the famous oracle of Zeus-Amon, a composite god who combined qualities of the Greek Zeus and the Egyptian Amon (see Chapter 1). No one will ever know what the priest told him, but henceforth Alexander called himself the son of Zeus.

Alexander left Egypt after less than a year and marched into Assyria, where at Gaugamela he defeated the Persian army. After this victory the principal Persian capital of Persepolis fell to him in a bitterly fought battle. There he performed a symbolic act of retribution by burning the royal buildings of King Xerxes, the invader of Greece during the Persian wars 150 years earlier. Alexander continued to pursue Darius, who appears to have been killed by Persian conspirators.

The Persian Empire had fallen and the war of revenge was over, but Alexander had no intention of stopping. Many of his troops had been supplied by Greek city-states that had allied with him; he released these troops from their obligations of military service,

but then rehired them as mercenaries. Alexander then began his personal odyssey. With his Macedonian soldiers and Greek mercenaries, he set out to conquer more of Asia. He plunged deeper into the East, into lands completely unknown to the Greek world. It took his soldiers four additional years to conquer Bactria (in today's Afghanistan) and the easternmost parts of the now-defunct Persian Empire, but still Alexander was determined to continue his march.

Chronology

ca. 342–291 B.C.E.	Life of comedy writer Menander
340–270 B.C.E.	Life of Epicurus, on whose ideas Epicureanism was based
335–262 B.C.E.	Life of Zeno, on whose ideas Stoicism was based
334–324 B.C.E.	Alexander the Great's military campaigns
ca. 330–200 B.C.E.	Establishment of new Hellenistic cities
323 B.C.E.	Alexander dies at age thirty-two
323–ca. 300 B.C.E.	War of succession leads to the establishment of Antigonid, Ptolemaic, and Seleucid dynasties
ca. 287–212 B.C.E.	Life of Archimedes
ca. 280 B.C.E.	Founding of the library of Alexandria by the Ptolemies
168 B.C.E.	Roman overthrow of the Antigonid dynasty
166–164 B.C.E.	Revolt of the Maccabees in Judaea
30 B.C.E.	Roman conquest of Egypt; Ptolemaic dynasty ends

Amphora with Alexander and Darius at the Battle of Issus Alexander, riding bareback, charges King Darius III, who is standing in a chariot. This detail from a jug was made within a decade after the battle, in a Greek colony in southern Italy, beyond the area of Alexander's conquests, a good indication of how quickly Alexander's fame spread. (Apulian amphora, ca. 330—320 B.C., by Darius Painter, from Ruvo in Magna Graecia, Italy/Museo Archeologico Nazionale, Naples, Italy/De Agostini Picture Library/ Alfredo Dagli Orti/Bridgeman Images)

Arrian on Alexander the Great

Arrian (ca. 86–160 C.E.) was a Greek military leader and historian who rose high in the ranks of the Roman army. He spent most of his career on the eastern border of the Roman Empire and thus lived in the heart of what had been Alexander's empire four hundred years earlier. He wrote a long history of Alexander's military campaigns based on accounts of Alexander's contemporaries, all of which are now lost, and modeled on the classical histories of war by Thucydides and Herodotus.

8. When [Alexander] arrived at Opis, he collected the Macedonians and announced that he intended to discharge from the army those who were useless for military service either from age or from being maimed in the limbs; and he said he would send them back to their own abodes. . . . [They were] offended by the speech which he delivered, thinking that now they were despised by him. . . . When Alexander heard this . . . , he ordered the most conspicuous of the men who had tried to stir up the multitude to sedition to be arrested. He himself pointed out with his hand to the shield-bearing guards those whom they were to arrest, to the number of thirteen; and he ordered these to be led away to execution. When the rest, stricken with terror, became silent, he mounted the platform again, and spoke as follows: . . .

10. ". . . Most of you have golden crowns, the eternal memorials of your valour and of the honour you receive from me. Whoever has been killed has met with a glorious end and has been honoured with a splendid burial. Brazen statues of most of the slain have been erected at home, and their parents are held in honour, being released from all public service and from taxation. But no one of you has ever been killed in flight under my leadership. And now I was intending to send back those of you who are unfit for service, objects of envy to those at home; but since you all wish to depart, depart all of you! Go back and report at home that your king Alexander, the conqueror of the Persians, Medes, Bactrians, and Sacians; . . . report that when you returned to Susa you deserted him and went

away, handing him over to the protection of conquered foreigners. . . . Depart!"

11. Having thus spoken, he leaped down quickly from the platform, and entered the palace, where . . . on the third day he summoned the select Persians within, and among them he distributed the commands of the brigades. . . . But the Macedonians who heard the speech were thoroughly astonished. . . . [T]hey were no longer able to restrain themselves; but running in a body to the palace, they cast their weapons there in front of the gates as signs of supplication to the king. Standing in front of the gates, they shouted, beseeching to be allowed to enter, and saying that they were willing to surrender the men who had been the instigators of the disturbance. . . . When he [Alexander] was informed of this, he came out without delay. . . . After this Alexander offered sacrifice to the gods to whom it was his custom to sacrifice, and gave a public banquet, over which he himself presided, with the Macedonians sitting around him; and next to them the Persians; after whom came the men of the other nations, preferred in honour for their personal rank or for some meritorious action.

EVALUATE THE EVIDENCE

1. According to Arrian, how does Alexander react when his Macedonian troops disagree with his decision about sending some of them home? How do they then respond to his actions?
2. Arrian is generally favorable toward Alexander. In your opinion, does the incident related here show Alexander in a good light? Why might he have done what Arrian describes?

In 326 B.C.E. Alexander crossed the Indus River and entered India (in the area that is now Pakistan). There, too, he saw hard fighting, and finally at the Hyphasis (HIH-fuh-sihs) River his troops refused to go farther. Alexander was enraged by the mutiny, for he believed he was near the end of the world. Nonetheless, the army stood firm, and Alexander relented. Still eager to explore the limits of the world, Alexander turned south to the Arabian Sea, and he waged a bloody and ruthless war against the people of the area. After reaching the Arabian Sea and turning west, he led his army through the

grim Gedrosian Desert (now part of Pakistan and Iran). The army and those who supported the troops with supplies suffered fearfully, and many soldiers died along the way. Nonetheless, in 324 B.C.E. Alexander returned to Susa in the Greek-controlled region of Assyria, and in a mass wedding married the daughter of Darius as well as the daughter of a previous Persian king, a ceremony that symbolized both his conquest and his aim to unite Greek and Persian cultures. His mission was over, but Alexander never returned to his homeland of Macedonia. He died the next year in Babylon from fever, wounds, and excessive drinking. He was only thirty-two, but in just thirteen years he had created an empire that stretched from his homeland of Macedonia to India, gaining the title "the Great" along the way.

Alexander so quickly became a legend that he still seems superhuman. That alone makes a reasoned interpretation of his goals and character very difficult. His contemporaries from the Greek city-states thought he was a bloody-minded tyrant, but later Greek and Roman writers and political leaders admired him and even regarded him as a philosopher interested in the common good. That view influenced many later European and American historians, but this idealistic interpretation has generally been rejected after a more thorough analysis of the sources. The most common view today is that Alexander was a brilliant leader who sought personal glory through conquest, and who tolerated no opposition. (See "Evaluating the Evidence 4.1: Arrian on Alexander the Great," at left.)

The Political Legacy

The main question at Alexander's death was whether his vast empire could be held together. Although he fathered a successor, the child was not yet born when Alexander died, and was thus too young to assume the duties of kingship. (Later he and his mother, Roxana, were murdered by one of Alexander's generals, who viewed him as a threat.) This meant that Alexander's empire was a prize for the taking. Several of the chief Macedonian generals aspired to become sole ruler, which led to a civil war lasting for decades that tore Alexander's empire apart. By the end of this conflict, the most successful generals had carved out their own smaller monarchies, although these continued to be threatened by internal splits and external attacks.

Alexander's general Ptolemy (ca. 367–ca. 283 B.C.E.) was given authority over Egypt, and after fighting off rivals, established a kingdom and dynasty there, called the Ptolemaic (TAH-luh-MAY-ihk). In 304 B.C.E. he took the title of pharaoh, and by the end of his long life he had a relatively stable realm to pass on to his son. For these successes he was later called Ptolemy Soter, "Ptolemy the Savior." The Ptolemaic dynasty would rule Egypt for nearly three hundred years, until the death of the last Ptolemaic ruler, Cleopatra VII, in 30 B.C.E. (see Chapter 5). Seleucus (ca. 358–281 B.C.E.), another of Alexander's officers, carved out a large kingdom, the Seleucid (SUH-loo-suhd), that stretched from the coast of Asia Minor to India, for which he was later called Seleucus Nicator, "Seleucus the Victor." He was assassinated in 281 B.C.E. on the order of the ruler of the Ptolemaic kingdom, but his son succeeded him, founding a dynasty that also lasted for centuries, although the kingdom itself shrank as independent states broke off in Pergamum, Bactria, Parthia, and elsewhere.

Royal Couple Cameo   This Hellenistic cameo, designed to be worn as a necklace, probably portrays King Ptolemy II and his sister Arsinoe II, rulers of the Ptolemaic kingdom of Egypt. During the Hellenistic period portraits of queens became more common because of the increased importance of hereditary monarchies. (Kunsthistorisches Museum, Vienna, Austria/ Erich Lessing/Art Resource, NY)

Antigonus I (382–301 B.C.E.), a third general, became king of Macedonia and established the Antigonid (an-TIH-guh-nuhd) dynasty, which lasted until it was overthrown by the Romans in 168 B.C.E. Rome would go on to conquer the Seleucid and Ptolemaic kingdoms as well (see Chapters 5 and 6).

Hellenistic rulers amassed an enormous amount of wealth from their large kingdoms, and royal patronage provided money for the production of literary works and the research and development that allowed discoveries in science and engineering. To encourage obedience, Hellenistic kings often created ruler cults that linked the king's authority with that of the gods, or they adopted ruler cults that already existed, as Alexander did in Egypt. These deified kings were not considered gods as mighty as Zeus or Apollo, and the new ruler cults probably had little religious impact on the people being ruled. The kingdoms never won the deep emotional loyalty that Greeks had once felt for the polis, but the ruler cult was an easily understandable symbol of unity within the kingdom.

Hellenistic kingship was hereditary, which gave women who were members of royal families more power than any woman had in democracies such as Athens, where citizenship was limited to men. Wives and mothers of kings had influence over their husbands and sons, and a few women ruled in their own right when there was no male heir.

■ **Hellenistic** A term that literally means "like the Greek," used to describe the period after the death of Alexander the Great, when Greek culture spread.

Greece itself changed politically during the Hellenistic period. To enhance their joint security, many poleis organized themselves into leagues of city-states, of which the two most extensive were the Aetolian (ee-TOH-lee-uhn) League in western and central Greece and the Achaean (uh-KEE-uhn) League in southern Greece. Until the arrival of the Romans in the eastern Mediterranean in the second century B.C.E. (see Chapter 5), the Hellenistic monarchies and Greek leagues of city-states waged frequent wars with one another that brought no lasting results. In terms of political stability and peace, these forms of government were no improvement on the Greek polis.

Building a Hellenized Society

FOCUS QUESTION *How did Greek ideas and traditions spread across the eastern Mediterranean and Near East?*

Alexander's most important legacy was clearly not political unity. Instead it was the spread of Greek ideas and traditions across a wide area, a process scholars later called **Hellenization**. To maintain contact with the Greek world as he moved farther eastward, he founded new cities and military colonies and expanded existing cities, settling Greek and Macedonian troops and veterans in them. Besides keeping the road back to Greece open, these settlements helped secure the countryside around them. This practice continued after his death, with more than 250 new cities founded in North Africa, West and Central Asia, and southeastern Europe. These cities and colonies became powerful instruments in the spread of Hellenism and in the blending of Greek and other cultures.

Urban Life

In many respects the Hellenistic city resembled a modern city. It was a cultural center with theaters, temples, and libraries. It was a seat of learning, a home of poets, writers, teachers, and artists. City dwellers could find amusement through plays, musical performances, animal fights, and gambling. The Hellenistic city was also an economic center that provided a ready market for grain and produce raised in the surrounding countryside. In short, the Hellenistic city offered cultural and economic opportunities for rich and poor alike.

To the Greeks, civilized life was unthinkable outside of a city, and Hellenistic kings often gave cities all the external trappings of a polis. Each had an assembly of citizens, a council to prepare legislation, and a board of magistrates to conduct political business. Yet, however

similar to the Greek polis it appeared, such a city could not engage in diplomatic dealings, make treaties, pursue its own foreign policy, or wage its own wars. The city was required to follow royal orders, and the king often placed his own officials in it to see that his decrees were followed.

A Hellenistic city differed from a Greek polis in other ways as well. The Greek polis had one body of law and one set of customs. In the Hellenistic city Greeks represented an elite class. Natives and non-Greek foreigners who lived in Hellenistic cities usually possessed lesser rights than Greeks and often had their own laws. In some instances this disparity spurred natives to assimilate Greek culture in order to rise politically and socially.

The city of Pergamum in northwestern Anatolia is a good example of an older city that underwent changes in the Hellenistic period. Previously an important strategic site, Pergamum was transformed by its new Greek rulers into a magnificent city complete with all the typical buildings of the polis, including gymnasia, baths, and one of the finest libraries in the entire Hellenistic world. The new rulers erected temples to the traditional Greek deities, but they also built imposing temples to other gods. There was a Jewish population in the city, who may have established a synagogue. Especially in the agora, Greeks and indigenous people met to conduct business and exchange goods and ideas. Greeks felt as though they were at home, and the evolving culture mixed Greek and local elements.

The Bactrian city of Ay Khanoum on the Oxus River, on the border of modern Afghanistan, is a good example of a brand-new city where cultures met. Bactria and Parthia had been part of the Seleucid kingdom, but in the third century B.C.E. their governors overthrew the Seleucids and established independent kingdoms in today's Afghanistan and Turkmenistan (Map 4.2). Bactria became an outpost of Hellenism, from which the rulers of China and India learned of sophisticated societies other than their own. It had Greek temples and administration buildings, and on a public square was a long inscription in Greek verse carved in stone, erected by a man who may have been a student of Aristotle and taken from a saying of the Oracle at Delphi:

> In childhood, learn good manners
> In youth, control your passions
> In middle age, practice justice
> In old age, be of good counsel
> In death, have no regrets.[1]

Along with this very public display of Greek ideals, the city also had temples to local deities and artwork that blended Greek and local styles (for an example, see the metal plate on page 100).

■ **Hellenization** The spread of Greek ideas, culture, and traditions to non-Greek groups across a wide area.

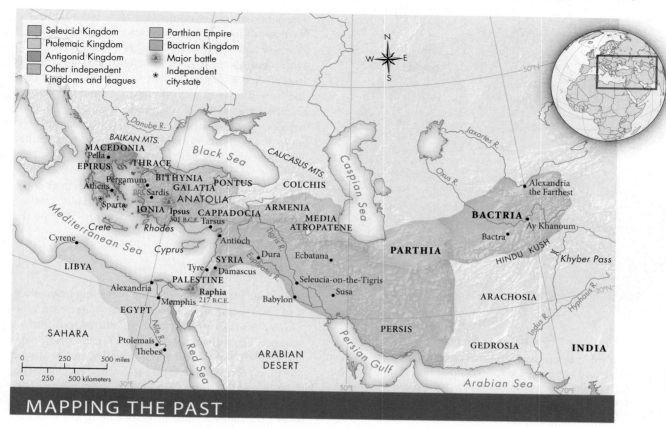

MAP 4.2 The Hellenistic World, ca. 263 B.C.E.

This map depicts the Hellenistic world after Alexander's death.

ANALYZING THE MAP Compare this map to Map 4.1 on page 94. After Alexander's death, were the Macedonians and Greeks able to retain control of most of the land he had conquered? What areas were lost?

CONNECTIONS What does this map suggest about the success or failure of Alexander's dreams of conquest?

Greeks in Hellenistic Cities

The ruling dynasties of the Hellenistic world were Macedonian, and Macedonians and Greeks filled all the important political, military, and diplomatic positions. Besides building Greek cities, Hellenistic kings offered Greeks land and money as lures to further immigration.

The Hellenistic monarchy, unlike the Greek polis, did not depend solely on its citizens to fulfill its political needs, but instead relied on professionals. Talented Greek men had the opportunity to rise quickly in the government bureaucracy. Appointed by the king, these administrators did not have to stand for election each year, unlike many officials of Greek poleis. Since they held their jobs year after year, they had ample time to create new administrative techniques, and also time to develop ways to profit personally from their positions.

Greeks also found ready employment in the armies and navies of the Hellenistic monarchies. Alexander had proved the Greco-Macedonian style of warfare to be far superior to that of other peoples, and Alexander's successors, themselves experienced officers, realized the importance of trained soldiers. Hellenistic kings were reluctant to arm the local populations or to allow them to serve in the army, fearing military rebellions among their conquered subjects. The result was the emergence of professional armies and navies consisting primarily of Greeks, although drawn from many areas of Greece and Macedonia, not simply from one polis. Unlike the citizen hoplites of classical Greece, these men were full-time soldiers. Hellenistic kings paid them well, often giving them land or leasing it to them as an incentive to remain loyal.

Greeks were able to dominate other professions as well. Hellenistic kingdoms and cities recruited Greek writers and artists to create Greek literature, art, and culture. Greek architects, engineers, and skilled craftsmen found themselves in great demand to produce the Greek-style buildings commissioned by the Hellenistic monarchs. Architects and engineers would sometimes design and build whole cities, which they laid out in checkerboard fashion and filled with typical Greek

Metal Plate from Ay Khanoum This spectacular metal plate, made in the Bactrian city of Ay Khanoum in the second century B.C.E., probably depicts the goddess Cybele being pulled in a chariot by lions with the sun-god above. Worship of Cybele, an earth-mother goddess, spread into Greece from the east, and was then spread by her Greek followers as they traveled and migrated. (National Museum of Afghanistan, Kabul/Pictures from History/Bridgeman Images)

buildings. An enormous wave of construction took place during the Hellenistic period.

Increased physical and social mobility benefited some women as well as men. More women learned to read than before, and they engaged in occupations in which literacy was beneficial, including care of the sick. During the Hellenistic period women continued to be required to have male guardians to buy, sell, or lease land; to borrow money; and to represent them in other commercial transactions. (The requirement of a male guardian was later codified in Roman law and largely maintained in Europe into the nineteenth century.) Yet often such a guardian was present only to fulfill the letter of the law. The woman was the real agent and handled the business being transacted.

Because of the opportunities the Hellenistic monarchies offered, many people moved frequently. These were generally individual decisions, not part of organized colonization efforts such as those that had been common in Archaic Greece (see Chapter 3). Once a Greek man had left home to take service with, for instance, the army or the bureaucracy of the Ptolemies, he had no incentive beyond his pay and the comforts of life in Egypt to keep him there. If the Seleucid king offered him more money or a promotion, he might well accept it and take his talents to Asia Minor. Thus professional

Greek soldiers and administrators were very mobile and were apt to look to their own interests, not their kingdom's. Linguistic changes further facilitated the ease with which people moved. Instead of the different dialects spoken in Greece itself, a new Greek dialect called the *koine* (koy-NAY), which means "common," became the spoken language of traders, the royal court, the bureaucracy, and the army across the Hellenistic world.

As long as Greeks continued to migrate, the kingdoms remained stable and strong. In the process they drew an immense amount of talent from the Greek peninsula. However, the Hellenistic monarchies could not keep recruiting Greeks forever, in spite of their wealth and willingness to spend lavishly. In time the huge surge of immigration slowed greatly.

Greeks and Non-Greeks

Across the Hellenistic world the prevailing institutions and laws became Greek. Everyone, Greek or non-Greek, who wanted to find an official position or compete in business had to learn Greek. Those who did gained an avenue of social mobility, and as early as the third century B.C.E. local people in some Hellenistic cities began to rise in power and prominence. They adopted a Greek name and, if they were male, went to Greek educational institutions or sent their sons there. Hoping to impress the Greek elite, priests in Babylon and Alexandria composed histories of their areas in Greek. Once a man knew Greek, he could move more easily to another area for better opportunities, and perhaps even hide his non-Greek origins. He could also join a military unit and perhaps be deployed far from his place of origin. Thus learning Greek was an avenue of geographic mobility as well.

Cities granted citizenship to Hellenized local people and sometimes to Greek-speaking migrants, although there were fewer political benefits of citizenship than there had been in the classical period, because real power was held by monarchs, not citizens. Even a few women received honorary citizenship in Hellenistic cities because of aid they had provided in times of crisis. Being Greek became to some degree a matter of culture, not bloodlines.

Cultural influences in the other direction occurred less frequently, because they brought fewer advantages. Few Greeks learned a non-Greek language, unless they were required to because of their official position. Greeks did begin to worship local deities, but often these were somewhat Hellenized and their qualities blended with those of an existing Greek god or goddess. Greeks living in Egypt generally cremated their dead while Egyptians continued to mummify them, although by the first century B.C.E. Greeks and Romans sometimes mummified their dead as well, attaching realistic portraits painted on wooden panels to the mummies that have served as important sources about clothing and hairstyles.

Yet the spread of Greek culture was wider than it was deep. Hellenistic kingdoms were never entirely unified in language, customs, and thought. The principal reason for this phenomenon is that Greek culture generally did not extend far beyond the reaches of the cities. Many urban residents adopted the aspects of Hellenism that they found useful, but people in the countryside generally did not embrace it, nor were they encouraged to.

Ptolemaic Egypt provides an excellent example of this situation. The indigenous people were the foundation of the kingdom: they fed it by their labor in the fields and financed its operations with their taxes. Because of this, the Ptolemies tied local people to the land more tightly than they had been before, making it nearly impossible for them to leave their villages. The Ptolemies maintained separate legal systems for Greeks and Egyptians. The bureaucracy of the Ptolemies was relatively efficient, and the indigenous population was viciously and cruelly exploited. Even in times of hardship, the king's taxes came first, although payment might mean starvation. The people's desperation was summed up by one Egyptian, who scrawled the warning, "We are worn out; we will run away."[2] To many Egyptians, revolt or a life of banditry was preferable to working the land under the harsh Ptolemies.

The situation was somewhat different in the booming city of Alexandria, founded by Alexander to be a new seaport, where there had been a small village earlier. Within a century of its founding, it was probably the largest city in the world, with a population numbering in the hundreds of thousands. The ruling elite was primarily Greek, and the Ptolemies tried to keep the Greek and Egyptian populations apart, but this was not always possible. Although the Ptolemies encouraged immigration from Greece, the number of immigrants was relatively low, so intermarriage increased. And the Ptolemies themselves gave privileges to local priests, building temples and sponsoring rituals honoring the local gods. Priestly families became owners of large landed estates and engaged in other sorts of business as well, becoming loyal supporters of the Ptolemaic regime. Even the processions honoring local gods still celebrated Greekness, however, and sometimes became a flash point sparking protests by Egyptians.

In about 280 B.C.E. the Ptolemies founded a library in Alexandria that both glorified Greek culture and sponsored new scholarship. It came to contain hundreds of thousands of papyrus scrolls of Greek writings, including copies of such classic works as the poems of Homer, the histories of Herodotus and Thucydides, and the philosophical works of Plato and Aristotle, as well as newer accounts of scientific discoveries. The Ptolemies sent representatives to Greece to buy books, paid for copies made of any Greek books that were brought to Alexandria, and supported scholars who edited multiple versions of older books into a single authoritative version. The library became one of the foremost intellectual centers of the ancient world, pulling in Greek-speaking writers, scholars, scientists, and thinkers from far away and preserving Greek writings.

Greek culture spread more deeply in the Seleucid kingdom than in Egypt, although this was not because the Seleucids had an organized plan for Hellenizing the local population. The primary problem for the Seleucids was holding on to the territory they had inherited. To do this, they established cities and military colonies throughout the region to nurture a vigorous and large Greek-speaking population and to defend the kingdom from their Persian neighbors. Seleucid military colonies were generally founded near existing villages, thus exposing even rural residents to all aspects of Greek life. Many local people found Greek political and cultural forms attractive and imitated them. In Asia Minor and Syria, for instance, numerous

Head of a Young Nubian This bust, carved in black porphyry rock, was most likely made in Alexandria in the second or first century B.C.E. Hellenistic sculptors depicted the wide range of migrants to the city in stone, bronze, and marble. (From Alexandria, Egypt/Private Collection/De Agostini Picture Library/Gianni Dagli Orti/Bridgeman Images)

villages and towns developed along Greek lines, and some of them grew into Hellenized cities.

The kings of Bactria and Parthia spread Greek culture even further. Some of these rulers converted to Buddhism, and the Buddhist ruler of the Mauryan Empire in northern India, Ashoka (ca. 269–233 B.C.E.), may have ordered translations of his laws into Greek for the Greek-speaking residents of Bactria and Parthia. In the second century B.C.E., after the collapse of the Mauryan Empire, Bactrian armies conquered part of northern India, establishing several small Indo-Greek states where the mixing of religious and artistic traditions was particularly pronounced.

The Economy of the Hellenistic World

FOCUS QUESTION *What new economic connections were created in the Hellenistic period?*

Alexander's conquest of the Persian Empire not only changed the political face of the ancient world and led to a shared urban culture, but also brought the Near East and Egypt fully into the sphere of Greek economics. The Hellenistic period, however, did not see widespread improvements in the way people lived and worked. Cities flourished, but many people who lived in rural areas were actually worse off than they had been before, because of higher levels of rents and taxes. Alexander and his successors did link East and West in a broad commercial network, however. The spread of Greeks throughout the Near East and Egypt created new markets and stimulated trade.

Agriculture and Industry

Much of the revenue for the Hellenistic kingdoms was derived from agricultural products, rents paid by the tenants of royal land, and taxation of land. Trying to improve productivity, the rulers sponsored experiments on seed grain, selecting seeds that seemed the most hardy and productive. Egypt had a strong tradition of central authority dating back to the pharaohs, which the Ptolemies inherited and tightened. They had the power to mobilize local labor into the digging and maintenance of canals and ditches, and they even attempted to decree what crops Egyptian farmers would plant and what animals would be raised. Such centralized planning was difficult to enforce at the local level, however, especially because the officials appointed to do so switched positions frequently and concentrated most on extracting taxes. Thus, despite royal interest in agriculture and a more studied approach to it in the Hellenistic period, there is no evidence that agricultural productivity increased

or that practices changed. Technology was applied to military needs, but not to those of food production.

Diodorus Siculus, a Greek historian who apparently visited Ptolemaic Egypt around 60 B.C.E., was surprised that Egyptians could feed all their children instead of resorting to the selective exposure of infants practiced in Greece. He decided that this was because of their less formal child-rearing habits:

> They feed their children in a sort of happy-go-lucky fashion that in its inexpensiveness quite surpasses belief; for they serve them with stews made of any stuff that is ready to hand and cheap, and give them such stalks as the byblos plant [the reeds from which papyrus is made] as can be roasted in the coals and the roots and the stems of marsh plants, either raw or boiled or baked. And since most of the children are reared without shoes or clothing because of the mildness of the climate of the country, the entire expense incurred by the parents of a child until it comes to maturity is not more than twenty drachmas. These are the leading reasons why Egypt has such an extraordinarily large population.[3]

Egyptian parents would probably have given other reasons, such as rents and taxes, for why their children had simple food and no shoes.

As with agriculture, although demand for goods increased during the Hellenistic period, no new techniques of production appear to have developed. Manual labor, not machinery, continued to turn out the raw materials and manufactured goods the Hellenistic world used. (See "Living in the Past: Farming in the Hellenistic World," page 104.)

Diodorus gives a picture of this hard labor, commenting about life in the gold mines owned by the kings:

> At the end of Egypt is a region bearing many mines and abundant gold, which is extracted with great pain and expense. . . . For kings of Egypt condemn to the mines criminals and prisoners of war, those who were falsely accused and those who were put into jail because of royal anger, not only them but sometimes also all of their relatives. Rounding them up, they assign them to the gold mines, taking revenge on those who were condemned and through their labors gaining huge revenues. The condemned—and they are very many—all of them are put in chains; and they work persistently and continually, both by day and throughout the night, getting no rest and carefully cut off from escape. For the guards, who are barbarian soldiers and who speak a different language, stand watch over them so that no man can either by conversation or friendly contact corrupt any of them.[4]

Apart from gold and silver, which were used primarily for coins and jewelry, bronze continued to be used for shields. Iron was utilized for weapons and tools.

Pottery remained an important commodity, and most of it was produced locally. The coarse pottery used in the kitchen for plates and cups changed little. Fancier pots and bowls, decorated with a shiny black glaze, came into use during the Hellenistic period. This ware originated in Athens, but potters in other places began to imitate its style, heavily cutting into the Athenian market. In the second century B.C.E. a red-glazed ware, often called Samian, burst on the market and soon dominated it. Pottery was often decorated with patterns and scenes from mythology, legend, and daily life. Potters often portrayed heroic episodes, such as battles from the *Iliad*, or gods, such as Dionysus at sea. Pots journeyed with Greek merchants, armies, and travelers, so these images spread knowledge of Greek religion and stories west as far as Portugal and east as far as Southeast Asia. Pottery thus served as a means of cultural exchange—of ideas as well as goods—among people scattered across huge portions of the globe.

Commerce

Alexander's conquest of the Persian Empire had immediate effects on trade. In the conquered Persian capitals Alexander had found vast sums of gold, silver, and other treasure. This wealth financed the creation of new cities, the building of roads, and the development of harbors. It also provided the thousands who participated in his expeditions with booty, with which they could purchase commodities. Whole new fields lay open to Greek merchants, who eagerly took advantage of the new opportunities. Commerce itself was a leading area where Greeks and non-Greeks met on grounds of common interest.

Trade was facilitated by the coining of money. Most of the great monarchies coined their money according to a uniform system, which meant that much of the money used in Hellenistic kingdoms had the same value. Traders were less in need of money changers than in the days when each major power coined money on a different standard.

Overland trade was conducted by caravan, and the backbone of this caravan trade was the camel—a shaggy, ill-tempered, but durable animal ideally suited to the harsh climate of the caravan routes. Luxury goods that were light, rare, and expensive traveled over the caravan routes to Alexandria or to the harbors of Phoenicia and Syria, from which they were shipped to Greece, Italy, and Spain. In time these luxury items became more commonplace, in part as the result of an increased volume of trade. Due to the prosperity of the period, more people could afford to buy gold, silver, ivory, precious stones, spices, and a host of other easily transportable

goods. Perhaps the most prominent good in terms of volume was silk, and the trade in silk later gave the major east-west route its name: the Great Silk Road. In return the Greeks and Macedonians sent east manufactured goods, especially metal weapons, cloth, wine, and olive oil. Although these caravan routes can trace their origins to earlier times, they became far more prominent in the Hellenistic period. Business customs and languages of trade developed and became standardized, so that merchants from different nationalities could communicate in a way understandable to all of them.

The durability and economic importance of the caravan routes are amply demonstrated by the fact that the death of Alexander, the ensuing wars of his successors, and later regional conflicts had little effect on trade. Numerous mercantile cities grew up along these routes, and commercial contacts brought people from far-flung regions together, even if sometimes indirectly. The merchants and the caravan cities were links in a chain that reached from the Mediterranean Sea to India and beyond to China, along which ideas as well as goods were passed.

More economically important than the trade in luxury goods were commercial dealings in essential commodities like raw materials and grain and such industrial products as pottery. The Hellenistic monarchies usually raised enough grain for their own needs as well as a surplus for export. This trade in grain was essential for the cities of Greece and the Aegean, many of which could not grow enough. Fortunately for them, abundant wheat supplies were available nearby in Egypt and in the area north of the Black Sea (see Map 4.2).

Most trade in bulk commodities was seaborne, and the Hellenistic merchant ship was the workhorse of the day. The merchant ship had a broad beam and relied on sails for propulsion. It was far more seaworthy than the contemporary warship, the trireme (see Chapter 3), which was long, narrow, and built for speed. A small crew of experienced sailors could handle the merchant vessel easily. Maritime trade provided opportunities for workers in other industries and trades: sailors, shipbuilders, dockworkers, accountants, teamsters, and pirates. Piracy was always a factor in the Hellenistic world, so ships' crews had to be ready to defend their cargoes as well as transport them.

Cities in Greece often paid for their grain by exporting olive oil and wine. When agriculture and oil production developed in Syria, Greek products began to encounter competition from the Seleucid monarchy. Later in the Hellenistic period, Greek oil and wine, shipped in mass-produced pottery jugs called amphoras, found a lucrative market in Italy and throughout the Mediterranean. (See "The Past Living Now: Container Shipping," page 106.)

Another significant commodity was fish, which for export was salted, pickled, or dried. This trade was

The robust urbanism of the Hellenistic period depended on a thriving agricultural base. Consequently, farming remained an essential part of the economy. Most people in this period worked on small family farms that they owned or rented, or on larger farms owned by wealthy absentee landlords. The mainstay of Hellenistic agriculture remained the triad of grain, vine, and olive.

Farmers relied on a simple plow pulled by oxen to break the ground and prepare the soil for planting. Plowing also controlled weeds and preserved soil moisture. Farmers further broke up the land with mattocks, a tool similar to a pickax. At harvest time they reaped the grain with sickles. Barley was more common than wheat because it was hardier and could grow in poorer soil; it was generally eaten as a cooked grain.

Wheat, on the other hand, was the preferred grain for making bread. Lentils and beans served as food for both people and animals, and as fertilizer for the soil. Olive trees grew even in poor earth, and fruit trees added welcome sweets to the family diet. Whenever possible, farmers grew grapevines, as wine was a common drink in the Hellenistic world, where it was generally drunk mixed with water because the wine was so rough.

Men tended to do the plowing, while women and children hoed and weeded. Plowing and seeding were usually done in the autumn. Winter rains encouraged growth, and farmers harvested their crops in early summer. After the harvest, grain was spread over a circular threshing floor, where donkeys harnessed to a pole crushed the kernels. Grapes were harvested in early fall and left sitting for two weeks before being crushed into wine.

A bronze model of a team of oxen pulling a cart, dating from the second century B.C.E. to the first century C.E. This figure was part of a group of miniature farm animals found together, which could have been toys (the animals can fit in a child's hand) or an offering to the gods for a successful harvest. (Image copyright © The Metropolitan Museum of Art, New York, New York, USA/Art Resource, NY)

An olive mill from the town of Capernaum on the Mediterranean. Olives would have been placed in the trough, and the large millstone would have been rolled on top of them to extract the oil, using human or animal power. (Erich Lessing/Art Resource, NY)

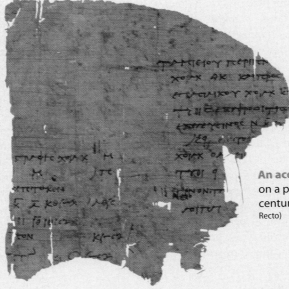

An accounting of agricultural produce, on a papyrus manuscript from the third century B.C.E. (ONB/Vienna, Picture Archive, G 42359 Recto)

A small pottery figurine of Ceres, the goddess of the harvest, holding fruit and accompanied by a wild boar, made in the Hellenistic period. Pottery figurines were cheap and were often sold at the entrance to temples so that people could use them as religious offerings instead of presenting crops or animals. (Musée du Louvre, Paris, France/Erich Lessing/Art Resource, NY)

At harvest time people offered some of their crops to the gods in thanks and set aside another—no doubt larger—portion for paying their rents and taxes. Another portion was saved as seed for the next year, but the largest portion was stored to be eaten over the next months. With what was left, farmers treated themselves to a festive meal, enjoyed along with music and dancing as a short break from work.

QUESTIONS FOR ANALYSIS

1. Why would ox-drawn carts and olive mills be common features of the rural economy in the Hellenistic world?
2. Given what you have read in this chapter, why do you think written records of agriculture, such as the papyrus manuscript shown at left, are rare historical sources for this period? Why would images of agricultural gods and goddesses, such as the figurine of Ceres shown above, be more common?

especially important because fish provided poor people with protein, an essential element of their diet. Salt, too, was often imported, and there was a very small trade in salted meat, which was a luxury item. Far more important was the trade in honey, dried fruit, nuts, and vegetables. Of raw materials, wood was high in demand, but little trade occurred in manufactured goods.

Slaves were a staple of Hellenistic trade, traveling in all directions on both land and sea routes. A few lists of slaves owned by a single individual have survived, and these indicate that slaves in one area often came from far away, and from many different regions. Ancient authors cautioned against having too many slaves from one area together, as this might encourage them to revolt. War provided prisoners for the slave market; to a lesser extent, so did kidnapping and capture by pirates, although the origins of most slaves are unknown. Both old Greek states and new Hellenistic kingdoms were ready slave markets, and throughout the Mediterranean world slaves were almost always in demand. Slaves were to be found in the cities and temples of the Hellenistic world; in the shops, fields, armies, and mines; and in the homes of wealthier people. Their price varied depending on their age, sex, health, and skill level, and also—as with any commodity—on market conditions. Large-scale warfare increased the number of slaves available, so the price went down; during periods of relative peace, fewer people were enslaved through conquest, so the price went up.

Religion and Philosophy in the Hellenistic World

FOCUS QUESTION *How did religion and philosophy shape everyday life in the Hellenistic world?*

The mixing of peoples in the Hellenistic era influenced religion and philosophy. The Hellenistic kings built temples to the old Olympian gods and promoted rituals and ceremonies like those in earlier Greek cities, but new deities also gained prominence. More people turned to mystery religions, which blended Greek and non-Greek elements. Others turned to practical philosophies that provided advice on how to live a good life.

Religion and Magic

When Hellenistic kings founded cities, they also built temples, staffed by priests and supported by taxes, for the Olympian gods of Greece. The transplanted religions, like those in Greece itself, sponsored literary, musical, and athletic contests, which were staged in beautiful surroundings among impressive new Greek-style buildings.

Container Shipping

At the beginning of the twentieth century, goods carried in the world's ships were packed in a variety of types of containers—barrels, boxes, bags, pallets, and cartons—which were loaded into and unloaded from the holds of ships by skilled longshoremen. At the beginning of the twenty-first century, the vast majority of goods are packed in standardized steel shipping containers, which are loaded and unloaded by huge cranes directly onto trucks and railcars. In 2005 there were nearly 20 million containers in use around the world, which had made about 200 million trips. Containers radically changed shipping, which moved to ports where giant ships could dock, and dramatically lowered transport costs, contributing to the globalization of production.

The history of standardized shipping containers is actually much longer than a century, however. In the fourth millennium B.C.E. large two-handled pottery jars called amphoras first appeared in the Mediterranean. They had a wide mouth, a round belly, and a base and became the workhorse of maritime shipping because they protected contents from water and rodents. They were easy and cheap to produce, were surprisingly durable, and could easily be reused. Amphoras contained all sorts of goods—wine, olive oil, spices, unguents, dried fish, olives, grapes, and the pine pitch used to caulk ships so that they would not leak. The amphora's dependability and versatility kept it in use until the seventh century C.E.

In the Hellenistic period amphoras became ubiquitous throughout the Mediterranean and carried goods eastward to the Black Sea, Persian Gulf, and Red Sea. The Ptolemies of Egypt sent amphoras and their contents farther still, to Arabia, eastern Africa, and India. Thus merchants and mariners who had never seen the Mediterranean depended on these containers, just as people today depend on goods sent in shipping containers from places they have never been. Like modern containers, amphoras often had stamps, inscriptions, or other markings indicating where they were made, where they were going, and what their contents were. These markings and the remains of the amphoras' contents have provided marine archaeologists and historians with much of their information about trade in the Hellenistic world. Amphoras made specifically for wine seem to have been standardized in size and shape so that they could fit on racks in ships, making long-distance shipping of wine cheaper and easier, just as steel containers have made the shipping of breakable wine bottles—and every other commodity—cheaper and easier today.

QUESTIONS FOR ANALYSIS

1. Why would standardized containers be an impetus to trade?
2. The Hellenistic period is often described as a time of "globalization." How would you compare Hellenistic globalization to that of today?

Amphoras Underwater Ancient amphoras can be found in many parts of the Mediterranean, particularly near well-traveled shipping routes. These jars date from the second century B.C.E., found at a site near the small town of Kas on the Turkish coast, a port in the Hellenistic period.
(© Helmut Corneli/imageBROKER/age-fotostock)

These festivities offered bright and lively entertainment, both intellectual and physical. They fostered Greek culture and traditional sports and were attractive to socially aspiring individuals who adopted Greek culture.

Along with the traditional Olympian gods, Greeks and non-Greeks in the Hellenistic world also honored and worshipped deities that had not been important in the Hellenic period or that were a blend of imported Greek and indigenous gods and goddesses. Tyche (TIGH-kee), for example, was a new deity, the goddess and personification of luck, fate, chance, and fortune. Temples to her were built in major cities of the eastern Mediterranean, including Antioch and Alexandria, and her image was depicted on coins and bas-reliefs. Contemporaries commented that when no other cause could be found for an event, Tyche was responsible. Like the Olympians, she was unpredictable and sometimes malevolent.

Tyche could be blamed for bad things that happened, but Hellenistic people did not simply give in to fate. Instead they honored Tyche with public rituals and more-private ceremonies, and they also turned to professionals who offered spells for various purposes. We generally make a distinction between religion and magic, but for Greeks there was not a clear line. Thus these people would write spells using both ordinary Greek words and special "magical" language known only to the gods, often instructing those who purchased them to carry out specific actions to accompany their words. Thousands of such spells survive, many of which are curse tables, intended to bring bad luck to a political, business, or athletic rival; or binding spells, meant to force a person to do something against his or her will. These binding spells included hundreds intended to make another person love the petitioner. They often invoke a large number of deities to assist the petitioner, reflecting the mixture of gods that was common in Hellenistic society. (See "Evaluating the Evidence 4.2: A Hellenistic Spell of Attraction," page 109.)

Hellenistic kings generally did not suppress indigenous religious practices. Some kings limited the power of existing priesthoods, but they also subsidized them with public money. Priests continued to carry out the rituals that they always had, perhaps now adding the name "Zeus" to that of the local deity or composing their hymns in Greek.

Some Hellenistic kings intentionally sponsored new deities that mixed Egyptian and Greek elements. When Ptolemy I Soter established the Ptolemaic dynasty in Egypt, he thought that a new god was needed who would appeal to both Greeks and Egyptians. Working together, an Egyptian priest and a Greek priest combined elements of the Egyptian god Osiris (god of the afterlife) with aspects of the Greek gods Zeus, Hades (god of the underworld), and Asclepius (god of medicine) to create a new god, Serapis. Like Osiris, Serapis came to be regarded as the judge of souls, who rewarded

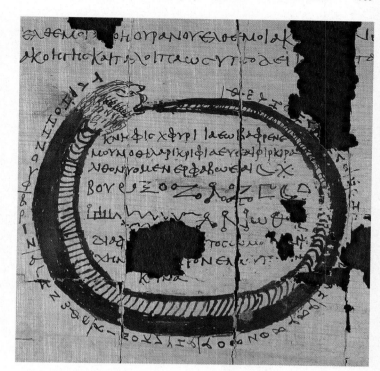

Hellenistic Magical Text   This text, written in Greek and Egyptian on papyrus, presents a magical incantation surrounded by a lion-headed snake. Both Hellenic and Hellenistic Greeks sought to know the future through various means of divination and to control the future through rituals and formulas that called on spirits and gods. (© British Library Board, PAP.121 fr 3)

virtuous and righteous people with eternal life. Like Asclepius, he was also a god of healing. Ptolemy I's successors made Serapis the protector and patron of Alexandria and built a huge temple in the god's honor in the city. His worship spread as intentional government policy, and he was eventually adopted by Romans as well, who blended him with their own chief god, Jupiter.

Increasingly, many people were attracted to mystery religions, so called because at the center of each was an inexplicable event that brought union with a god and was not to be divulged to anyone not initiated into them. Early mystery religions in the Hellenic period, such as those of Eleusis, were linked to specific gods in particular places, which meant that people who wished to become members had to travel (see Chapter 3). But new mystery religions, like Hellenistic culture in general, were not tied to a particular place; instead they were spread throughout the Hellenistic world. People did not have to undertake long and expensive pilgrimages just to become members. In that sense the mystery religions came to the people, for temples of the new deities sprang up wherever Greeks lived.

Mystery religions incorporated aspects of both Greek and non-Greek religions and claimed to save their adherents from the worst that fate could do. Most taught that by the rites of initiation, in which the secrets of the religion were shared, devotees became united with a deity who had also died and risen from the dead. The sacrifice of the god and his victory over death saved the devotee from eternal death. Similarly, mystery religions demanded a period of preparation in which the converts strove to become pure and holy, that is, to live by the religion's precepts. Once aspirants had prepared themselves, they went through the initiation, usually a ritual of great emotional intensity symbolizing the entry into a new life.

Isis and Horus In this small statue from Egypt, the goddess Isis is shown suckling her son Horus. Worship of Isis spread throughout the Hellenistic world; her followers believed that Isis offered them life after death, just as she had brought Horus's father, Osiris, back to life. (Musée du Louvre, Paris, France/Peter Willi/The Bridgeman Art Library)

Among the mystery religions the Egyptian cult of Isis spread widely. In Egyptian mythology Isis brought her husband Osiris back to life (see Chapter 1), and during the Hellenistic era this power came to be understood by her followers as extending to them as well. She promised to save any mortal who came to her, and her priests asserted that she had bestowed on humanity the gift of civilization and founded law and literature. Isis was understood to be a devoted mother as well as a devoted wife, and she became the goddess of marriage, conception, and childbirth. She became the most important goddess of the Hellenistic world, where Serapis was often regarded as her consort instead of Osiris. Devotion to Isis, and to many other mystery religions, later spread to the Romans as well as to the Greeks and non-Greeks who lived in Hellenistic cities.

Hellenism and the Jews

Jews in Hellenistic cities were generally treated the same as any other non-Greek group. At first they were seen as resident aliens. As they grew more numerous, they received permission to form a political corporation, a *politeuma* (pah-lih-TOO-mah), which gave them a great deal of autonomy. The Jewish politeuma, like the rest of the Hellenistic city, was expected to obey the king's commands, but there was virtually no royal interference with the Jewish religion. The Seleucid king Antiochus III (ca. 242–187 B.C.E.), for instance, recognized that most Jews were loyal subjects, and in his efforts to solidify his empire he endorsed their religious customs and ensured their autonomy.

Antiochus IV Epiphanes (r. 175–ca. 164 B.C.E.) broke with this pattern. He expanded the Seleucid kingdom and nearly conquered Egypt, but while he was there a revolt broke out in Judaea, led by Jews who opposed the Hellenized Jewish leader he had designated for them. Antiochus attacked Jerusalem, killing many, and restored his leader. According to Hebrew Scripture, he then banned Jewish practices and worship, ordered copies of the Torah burned, and set up altars to the Greek gods in Jewish temples. This sparked a widespread Jewish revolt that began in 166 B.C.E., called the Revolt of the Maccabees after the name of one of its leaders. Using guerrilla tactics, the Maccabees fought Syrian troops who were fighting under Seleucid commanders, retook Jerusalem, and set up a semi-independent state in 164 B.C.E. This state lasted for about a century, until it was conquered by the Romans. (The rededication of the temple in Jerusalem after the Maccabee victory is celebrated in the Jewish holiday of Hanukkah.)

Jews living in Hellenistic cities often embraced many aspects of Hellenism. The Revolt of the Maccabees is seen by some historians, in fact, as primarily a dispute between Hellenized Jews and those who wanted to retain traditional practices. So many Jews learned Greek,

A Hellenistic Spell of Attraction

Spells that have survived from the Hellenistic world include hundreds that are intended to make another person love the petitioner. Most of these are heterosexual, but a few involve men seeking men or women seeking women. This spell, inscribed on a lead tablet, is directed toward Anubis, the Egyptian dog-headed god of the underworld, and mentions a number of Egyptian and Greek deities associated with the underworld. Through this spell a woman named Sophia seeks to attract a woman named Gorgonia, although the spell itself is formulaic and was most likely written by a professional.

Fundament of the gloomy darkness, jagged-toothed dog, covered with coiling snakes, turning three heads, traveler in the recesses of the underworld, come, spirit-driver, with the Erinyes [or Furies, Greek goddesses of vengeance, often shown with snake hair and whips], savage with their stinging whips; holy serpents, maenads [frenzied female followers of Dionysus], frightful maidens, come to my wroth incantations. Before I persuade by force this one and you, render him immediately a fire-breathing daemon. Listen and do everything quickly, in no way opposing me in the performance of this action; for you are the governors of the earth. . . . By means of this corpse-daemon inflame the heart, the liver [which people also saw as a location of emotions], the spirit of Gorgonia, whom Nilogenia bore, with love and affection for Sophia, whom Isara bore. Constrain Gorgonia, whom

Nilogenia bore, to cast herself into the bath-house for the sake of Sophia, whom Isara bore; and you, become a bath-woman.* Burn, set on fire, inflame her soul, heart, liver, spirit with love for Sophia, whom Isara bore. Drive Gorgonia, whom Nilogenia bore, drive her, torment her body night and day, force her to rush forth from every place and every house, loving Sophia, whom Isara bore, she, surrendered like a slave, giving herself and all her possessions to her, because this is the will and command of the great god. . . . Blessed lord of the immortals, holding the scepters of Tartaros and of terrible, fearful Styx (?) and of life-robbing Lethe, the hair of Kerberos trembles in fear of you, you crack the loud whips of the Erinyes; the couch of Persephone delights you, when you go to the longed bed, whether you be the immortal Serapis, whom the universe fears, whether you be Osiris, star of the land of Egypt; your messenger is the all-wise boy; yours is Anubis, the pious herald of the dead. Come hither, fulfill my wishes, because I summon you by these secret symbols.

EVALUATE THE EVIDENCE

1. In the spell, what feelings does Sophia direct Anubis to create in Gorgonia, and what behavior is the expected result of these feelings?
2. What aspects of this spell appear distinctively Hellenistic? What aspects fit with modern understandings of sexual attraction?

*Public baths were common in Hellenistic and Roman society as places where people went for recreation and relaxation as well as cleansing, much like today's spas. Here Sophia wants Gorgonia to meet her in a public bath, and Anubis wants to change himself into a female bath attendant so he can cast his spell on her more easily.

Source: Bernadette J. Brooten, *Love Between Women: Early Christian Responses to Female Homoeroticism* (Chicago: University of Chicago Press, 1996), pp. 83–87. Copyright © 1966 by The University of Chicago. All rights reserved. Used by permission of the publisher.

especially in Alexandria, that the Hebrew Bible was translated into Greek and services in the synagogue there came to be conducted in Greek. Jews often took Greek names, used Greek political forms, adopted Greek practice by forming their own trade associations, and put inscriptions on graves as the Greeks did. Some Jews were given the right to become full citizens of Hellenistic cities, although relatively few appear to have exercised that right. Citizenship would have allowed them to vote in the assembly and serve as magistrates, but it would also have obliged them to worship the gods of the city—a practice few Jews chose to follow.

Philosophy and the People

Philosophy during the Hellenic period was the exclusive province of the wealthy and educated, for only they had

leisure enough to pursue philosophical studies (see Chapter 3). During the Hellenistic period, however, although philosophy was still directed toward the educated elite, it came to touch the lives of more men and women than ever before. There were several reasons for this development. First, much of Hellenistic life, especially in the new cities of the East, seemed unstable and without venerable traditions. Greeks were far more mobile than they had ever been before, but their very mobility left them feeling uprooted. Second, traditional religions had declined and there was a growing belief that one could do relatively little to change one's fate. One could honor Tyche, the goddess of fortune, through rituals in the hope that she would be kind, but to protect against the worst that Tyche could do, many Greeks also looked to philosophy. Philosophers themselves became much more numerous, and several new schools of

Boy with a Goose   In the Hellenistic culture that developed across a huge area after Alexander the Great's conquests, wealthy urban residents wanted art that showed real people rather than gods. This statue of a little boy wrestling a goose, originally carved about 200 B.C.E., no doubt found an eager buyer. (Glyptothek, Staatliche Antikensammlung, Munich, Germany/photo © Vanni Archive/Art Resource, NY)

philosophical thought caught the minds and hearts of many contemporary Greeks and some non-Greeks.

One of these was **Epicureanism** (eh-pih-kyou-REE-uh-nih-zuhm), a practical philosophy of serenity in an often-tumultuous world. Epicurus (eh-pih-KYOUR-uhs) (340–270 B.C.E.) was influenced by the atomic theory developed by the Pre-Socratic philosopher Democritus (see Chapter 3). Like Democritus, he thought that the world was made up of small pieces of matter that move in space, which determine the events of the world. Although he did not deny the existence of the gods, Epicurus taught that they had no effect on human life. Epicurus used observation and logic to study the world, and also to examine the human condition. He decided that the principal goods of human life were contentment and pleasure, which he defined as the absence of pain, fear, and suffering. By encouraging the pursuit of pleasure, he was not advocating drunken revels or sexual excess, which he thought caused pain, but moderation in food, clothing, and shelter.

The writings of Epicurus survive only in fragments, but the third-century-C.E. biographer Diogenes Laertes quotes several of his letters. It is impossible to know if these are actual letters or not, but they express sentiments that fit with Epicurus's ideas, including these from a letter written at the end of his life, when he apparently suffered from kidney stones:

> I have written this letter to you on a happy day to me, which is also the last day of my life. For I have been attacked by a painful inability to urinate, and also dysentery, so violent that nothing can be added to the violence of my sufferings. But the cheerfulness of my mind, which comes from the recollection of all my philosophical contemplation, counterbalances all these afflictions. And I beg you to take care of the children of Metrodorus, in a manner worthy of the devotion shown by the young man to me, and to philosophy.[5]

Epicurus also taught that individuals could most easily attain peace and serenity by ignoring the outside world and looking into their personal feelings and reactions. This ideal was one to which anyone could aspire, no matter what their social standing. Epicurus is reported to have allowed slaves and even women to attend his school, a sharp contrast with the earlier philosopher Plato. Epicureanism taught its followers to ignore politics and issues, for politics led to tumult, which would disturb the soul. Although the Epicureans thought that the state originated through a social contract among individuals, they did not care about the political structure of the state. They were content to live under a democracy, oligarchy, monarchy, or any other form of government, and they never speculated about the ideal state.

Zeno (335–262 B.C.E.), a philosopher from Cyprus, advanced a different concept of human beings and the universe. Zeno first came to Athens to form his own school, the Stoa, named after the covered walkways where he preferred to teach, and his philosophy, **Stoicism** (STOH-uh-sih-zuhm), in turn, came to be named for his school. Zeno and his followers considered nature an expression of divine will; in their view people could be

■ **Epicureanism**   A system of philosophy based on the teachings of Epicurus, who viewed a life of contentment, free from fear and suffering, as the greatest good.

■ **Stoicism**   A philosophy, based on the ideas of Zeno, that people could be happy only when living in accordance with nature and accepting whatever happened.

■ **natural law**   A Stoic concept that a single law that was part of the natural order of life governed all people.

happy only when living in accordance with nature. They stressed the unity of humans and the universe, stating that all people were obliged to help one another.

Unlike the Epicureans, the Stoics taught that people should participate in politics and worldly affairs. Yet this idea never led to the belief that individuals should try to change the order of things. The Stoics used the image of an actor in a play: the Stoic plays an assigned part but never tries to change the play. Like the Epicureans, they were indifferent to specific political forms. They believed that people should do their duty to the state in which they found themselves. To the Stoics, the important question was not whether they achieved anything, but whether they lived virtuous lives. The patient self-control and fortitude that the Stoics advocated made this a popular philosophy among the Romans later, and gave rise to the modern adjective *stoic* to convey these virtues.

The Stoics' most significant practical achievement was the creation of the concept of **natural law**. They concluded that because all people were kindred, partook of divine reason, and were in harmony with the universe, one law governed them all. This law was a part of the natural order of life, not something created by individual states or rulers. Thus natural law was an abstract matter of ethics, and applicable everywhere, not something that applied to everyday political or social life.

Individualistic and individualized themes emerge in Hellenistic art and literature as well as in philosophy. Sculptors looked to the works of the classical period such as the reliefs and statuary on the Athenian Acropolis for their models in terms of composition, but then created works that show powerful emotions and straining muscles. In contrast to the classical preference for the perfect human form, the artists and the people who bought their works wanted art that showed real people, including those suffering from trauma, disease, and the physical problems that came with aging. Hellenistic art was more naturalistic than Hellenic art—portraying the poor, old, and ugly as well as the young and beautiful.

As had Athens in the classical period, Hellenistic cities offered theater performances to their residents, paid for by the government. People tended to prefer revivals of the tragedies of Aeschylus, Sophocles, and Euripides (see Chapter 3) over newly written tragic works, but in comedy they wanted new material. This was provided by Menander (ca. 342–291 B.C.E.), whose more than one hundred comedies poked fun at current philosophies and social trends, including love, luck, money, and marriage. Menander's comedies tended to be less political than those of Aristophanes, but they still commented on the ruler cults developed by Hellenistic kings, the dangers of the new professionalized mercenary armies to older values, and the conspicuous consumption of the newly rich.

Hellenistic Science and Medicine

FOCUS QUESTION *How did science and medicine serve the needs of Hellenistic society?*

In the scholarly realm, Hellenistic thinkers made advances in mathematics, astronomy, and mechanical design. Physicians used observation and dissection to better understand the way the human body works and to develop treatments for disease. Many of these developments occurred in Alexandria, where the Ptolemies did much to make the city an intellectual, cultural, and scientific center.

Science

The main advances in Hellenistic science came in astronomy, geography, and mechanics. The most notable of the Hellenistic astronomers was Aristarchus (a-ruh-STAHR-kuhs) of Samos (ca. 310–230 B.C.E.). Aristarchus concluded that the sun is far larger than the earth and that the stars are enormously distant from the earth. He argued against the commonsense observation, which Aristotle had supported, that the earth was the center of the universe. Instead, Aristarchus developed the heliocentric theory—that the earth and planets revolve around the sun. His theory was discussed for several centuries, but was later forgotten when another astronomer working in Alexandria, Claudius Ptolemy (ca. 90–ca. 168 C.E.)—probably no relation to the ruling Ptolemies, as the name was a common one—returned to an earth-centered universe. Aristarchus's heliocentric theory was resurrected in the sixteenth century C.E. by the brilliant Polish astronomer Nicolaus Copernicus.

In geometry Hellenistic thinkers discovered little that was new, but Euclid (YOU-kluhd) (ca. 300 B.C.E.), a mathematician who lived in Alexandria, compiled a valuable textbook of existing knowledge. His *Elements of Geometry* rapidly became the standard introduction to geometry. Generations of students from the Hellenistic period to the twentieth century learned the essentials of geometry from it.

The greatest thinker of the Hellenistic period was Archimedes (ca. 287–212 B.C.E.), a native of Syracuse who was interested in nearly everything. (See "Individuals in Society: Archimedes, Scientist and Inventor," page 112.) A clever inventor, he devised new artillery for military purposes. In peacetime he perfected the water screw to draw water from a lower to a higher level. He also invented the compound pulley to lift heavy weights. His chief interest, however, lay in pure mathematics. He founded the science of hydrostatics (the study of fluids at rest) and discovered

Archimedes (ca. 287–212 B.C.E.) was born in the Greek city of Syracuse in Sicily, an intellectual center where he pursued scientific interests. He was the most original thinker of his time and a practical inventor. In his book *On Plane Equilibriums* he dealt for the first time with the basic principles of mathematics, including the principle of the lever. He once said that if he were given a lever and a suitable place to stand, he could move the world. He also demonstrated how easily his compound pulley could move huge weights with little effort:

> A three-masted merchant ship of the royal fleet had been hauled on land by hard work and many hands. Archimedes put aboard her many men and the usual freight. He sat far away from her; and without haste, but gently working a compound pulley with his hand, he drew her towards him smoothly and without faltering, just as though she were running on the surface.*

He perfected what became known as the Archimedean screw, a pump to bring subterranean water up to irrigate fields, which he had observed in Egypt and which later came into wider use. He worked on issues involved with solid geometry, and in his treatise *On Floating Bodies* he founded the science of hydrostatics. He concluded that an object will float if it weighs less than the water it displaces, and that whenever a solid floats in a liquid, the volume of the solid equals the volume of the liquid displaced. The way he made his discovery has become famous:

> When he was devoting his attention to this problem, he happened to go to a public bath. When he climbed down into the bathtub there, he noticed that water in the tub equal to the bulk of his body flowed out. Thus, when he observed this method of solving the problem, he did not wait. Instead, moved with joy, he sprang out of the tub, and rushing home naked he kept indicating in a loud voice that he had indeed discovered what he was seeking. For while

running he was shouting repeatedly in Greek, "Eureka, eureka" ("I have found it, I have found it").†

War between Rome and Syracuse interrupted Archimedes's scientific life. In 213 B.C.E. during the Second Punic War, the Romans besieged the city. Hiero, its king and Archimedes's friend, asked the scientist for help in repulsing Roman attacks. Archimedes began to design and build remarkable devices that served as artillery. One weapon shot missiles to break up infantry attacks, and others threw huge masses of stones that fell on the enemy. For use against Roman warships, he is said to have designed a machine with beams from which large claws dropped onto the hulls of warships, hoisted them into the air, and dropped them back into the sea. Later Greek writers reported that he destroyed Roman ships with a series of polished mirrors that focused sunlight and caused the ships to catch fire. Modern experiments re-creating Archimedes's weapons have found that the claw might have been workable, but the mirrors probably were not, as they required a ship to remain stationary for the fire to ignite. It is not certain whether his war machines were actually effective, but later people recounted tales that the Romans became so fearful that whenever they saw a bit of rope or a stick of timber projecting over the wall, they shouted, "There it is — Archimedes is trying some engine on us," and fled. After many months the Roman siege was successful, however, and Archimedes was killed by a Roman soldier.

QUESTIONS FOR ANALYSIS

1. How did Archimedes combine theoretical mathematics and practical issues in his work?
2. What applications do you see in the world around you for the devices Archimedes improved or invented, such as the lever, the pulley, and artillery?

*Plutarch, *Life of Marcellus*. †Vitruvius, *On Architecture*, 9 Preface, 10.

Several of Archimedes's treatises were found on a palimpsest, a manuscript that had been scraped and washed so that another text could be written over it, thus reusing the expensive parchment. Reusing parchment was a common practice in the Middle Ages, but the original text can sometimes be reconstructed. Using digital processing with several types of light and X-rays to study this thirteenth-century-C.E. prayer book, scientists were slowly able to decipher the texts by Archimedes that were underneath, including one that had been completely lost. (Image by the Rochester Institute of Technology. Copyright resides with the owner of the Archimedes Palimpsest)

the principle that the volume of a solid floating in a liquid is equal to the volume of the liquid displaced by the solid.

Archimedes was willing to share his work with others, among them Eratosthenes (ehr-uh-TAHS-thuh-neez) (285–ca. 204 B.C.E.). Like Archimedes, he was a man of almost universal interests. From his native Cyrene in North Africa, Eratosthenes traveled to Athens, where he studied philosophy and mathematics. He refused to join any of the philosophical schools, for he was interested in too many things to follow any particular dogma. Around 245 B.C.E. King Ptolemy III invited Eratosthenes to Alexandria and made him the head of the library there. Eratosthenes continued his mathematical work and by letter struck up a friendship with Archimedes.

Eratosthenes used mathematics to further the geographical studies for which he is most famous. He concluded that the earth was a spherical globe and calculated the circumference of the earth geometrically, estimating it as about 24,675 miles. He was not wrong by much: the earth is actually 24,860 miles in circumference. He drew a map of the earth and discussed the shapes and sizes of land and ocean and the irregularities of the earth's surface. His idea that the earth was divided into large landmasses influenced other geographers and later shaped ordinary people's understanding of the world as well. Using geographical information gained by Alexander the Great's scientists, Eratosthenes declared that to get to India, a ship could sail around Africa or even sail directly westward, an idea that would not be tested until the end of the fifteenth century.

Other Greek geographers also turned their attention southward to Africa. During this period the people of the Mediterranean learned of the climate and customs of Ethiopia and gleaned some information about sub-Saharan Africa from Greek sailors and merchants who had traveled there. (See "Evaluating the Evidence 4.3: The Periplus of the Erythraean Sea," page 116.) Geographers incorporated these travelers' reports into their more theoretical works.

As the new artillery devised by Archimedes indicates, Hellenistic science was used for purposes of war as well as peace. Theories of mechanics were used to build machines that revolutionized warfare. Fully realizing the practical possibilities of the first effective artillery in Western history, Philip of Macedonia had introduced the machines to the broader world in the middle of the fourth century B.C.E. The catapult became the first and most widely used artillery piece, shooting ever-larger projectiles. Generals soon realized that they could also hurl burning bundles over the walls to start fires in the city. As the Assyrians had earlier, engineers built siege towers, large wooden structures that served as artillery platforms, and put

them on wheels so that soldiers could roll them up to a town's walls. Once there, archers stationed on top of the siege towers swept the enemy's ramparts with arrows, while other soldiers manning catapults added missile fire. As soon as the walls were cleared, soldiers from the siege towers swept over the enemy's ramparts and into the city. To augment the siege towers, generals added battering rams that consisted of long, stout shafts housed in reinforced shells. Inside the shell the crew pushed the ram up to the wall and then heaved the shaft against the wall. Rams proved even more effective than catapults in bringing down large portions of walls.

Diodorus provided a description of these machines in his discussion of Philip's attack on the city of Perinthos in 340 B.C.E.:

> Philip launched a siege of Perinthos, advancing engines to the city and assaulting the walls in relays day after day. He built towers 120 feet tall that rose far above the towers of Perinthos. From their superior height he kept wearing down the besieged. He mined under the wall and also rocked it with battering-rams until he threw down a large section of it. The Perinthians fought stoutly and threw up a second wall. Philip rained down great destruction through his many and various arrow-shooting catapults. . . . Philip continually battered the walls with his rams and made breaches in them. With his arrow-firing catapults clearing the ramparts of defenders, he sent his soldiers in through the breaches in tight formation. He attacked with scaling-ladders the parts of the walls that had been cleared.[6]

For the Perinthians this grim story had a happy ending when their allies arrived to lift the siege, but many cities were successfully besieged and conquered with the new machines. Over time, Hellenistic generals built larger, more complex, and more effective machines. The earliest catapults could shoot only large arrows and small stones. By the time Alexander the Great besieged Tyre in 332 B.C.E., his catapults could throw stones big enough to knock down city walls.

If these new engines made waging war more efficient, they also added to the misery of the people, as war often directly involved the populations of cities. As it had in Periclean Athens (see Chapter 3), war often contributed to the spread of disease, and battlefields gave surgeons and physicians plenty of opportunities to test their ideas about how the human body would best heal.

Medicine

Doctors as well as scientists combined observation with theory during the Hellenistic period. (See "Thinking Like a Historian: Hellenistic Medicine," page 114.)

Hellenistic Medicine

Hellenistic medical specialists based their ideas about the body and their handling of illness on observation, and also on the writings ascribed to the Greek physician Hippocrates and his followers. These were copied, recopied, edited, and expanded over the centuries, so it is impossible to say who wrote any specific work, but they contain ideas that were widely shared. How did Hellenistic physicians view the healthy body, and what did they recommend to maintain good health and treat sickness?

1 **Hippocratic Writings, *The Nature of Man*.** This treatise discusses the structure of the human body and the causes of disease.

The human body contains blood, phlegm, yellow bile and black bile. These are the things that make up its constitution and cause its pains and health. Health is primarily that state in which these constituent substances are in the correct proportion to each other, both in strength and quantity, and are well mixed. Pain occurs when one of the substances presents either a deficiency or an excess, or is separated in the body and not mixed with the others. . . .

Now the quantity of the phlegm in the body increases in winter because it is that bodily substance most in keeping with the winter, seeing that it is the coldest. . . . The following signs show that winter fills the body with phlegm: people spit and blow from their noses the most phlegmatic mucus in winter; swellings become white especially at that season and other diseases show phlegmatic signs. . . .

And just as the year is governed at one time by winter, then by spring, then by summer, and then by autumn; so at one time in the body phlegm predominates, at another time blood, at another time yellow bile and this is followed by a preponderance of black bile. In these circumstances it follows that the diseases which increase in winter should decrease in summer and vice versa. . . .

Some diseases are produced by the manner of life that is followed; others by the life-giving air that we breathe. That there are these two types must be demonstrated in the following way. When a large number of people all catch the same disease at the same time, the cause must be ascribed to something common to all and which they all use; in other words to what they all breathe. In such a disease, it is obvious that individual bodily habits cannot be responsible because the malady attacks one after another, young and old, men and women alike.

2 **Hippocratic Writings, *Prognosis*.** This treatise provides guidance about how to examine a patient and determine if a disease will be fatal or not.

It seems to be highly desirable that a physician pay much attention to prognosis. If he is able to tell his patients when he visits them not only about their past and present symptoms, but also to tell them what is going to happen, as well as to fill in the details they have omitted, he will increase his reputation as a medical practitioner and people will have no qualms in putting themselves in his care. . . .

The signs to watch for in acute diseases are as follows: First, study the patient's face; whether it has a healthy look and in particular whether it is exactly as it normally is. If the patient's normal appearance is preserved, this is best; just as the more abnormal it is, the worse it is. . . .

Rapid breathing indicates either distress or inflammation of the organs above the diaphragm. Deep breaths taken at long intervals are a sign of delirium. If the expired air from the mouth and nostrils is cold, death is close at hand. . . .

The most helpful kinds of vomiting is that in which the matter consists of phlegm and bile, as well-mixed as possible, and is neither thick nor particularly great in quantity. If it is not well-mixed, it is less good. The vomiting of dark green, livid or dark material, no matter which of these colours, must be considered a bad sign.

In all disease of the lungs, running at the nose and sneezing is bad.

ANALYZING THE EVIDENCE

1. In Source 1, what are the basic substances in the body, and how do they create pain and illness? How is health shaped by the seasons and by people's actions? By things in the air (which we would call germs, though the Greeks thought of them as poisons)?
2. In Source 2, what does the author suggest that a physician pay attention to when diagnosing illness, and why is prognosis important? How does the technique of the physician in Source 3 fit with this advice?
3. How does the author of Source 4 suggest infections in the pleural cavity be handled?
4. What does the author of Source 5 recommend for people who want to stay healthy, and how does this advice differ for different types of individuals?
5. Taking the sources together, what do these authors see as the most important role of physicians in preventing and treating illness? What do they see as the most important role of people themselves in maintaining their own health?

(Hulton Archive/Getty Images)

3 **Physician with young patient.** This plaster cast from ca. 350 B.C.E. shows a physician examining a child, while Asclepius, the god of healing, observes.

4 **Hippocratic Writings, *Diseases*.** In this section of a long treatise, the author discusses treatment of people who have pus in the pleural cavity surrounding the lungs, which today is often linked with emphysema.

First cut the skin between the ribs with a knife with a rounded blade. Then take a sharp-pointed knife wrapped in a strip of cloth with its tip exposed a thumb-nail's length and make an incision. Next, having drained away as much pus as seems appropriate, drain the wound with a drain of raw linen, attached to a cord. Let out the pus once a day. On the tenth day, after having let out all the pus, drain the wound with a piece of fine linen. Then inject warm wine and oil through a small tube, so that the lung accustomed to being moistened by the pus might not suddenly be dried out. Let out the morning's infusion toward evening, and the evening one in the morning. When the pus becomes thick like water, sticky to the finger when touched, and scanty, insert a hollow tin drainage tube. When the [pleural] cavity is completely drained, gradually cut the drain shorter, and allow the wound to heal until you finally take out the drain.

5 **Hippocratic Writings, *A Regimen for Health*.** In this treatise the author provides suggestions for preventing illness.

People with a fleshy, soft, or ruddy appearance are best kept on a dry diet for the greater part of the year as they are constitutionally moist. Those with firm and tight-drawn skins, and those with tawny and dark complexions should keep to a diet containing plenty of fluids most of the time, as such people are naturally dry. The softest and most moist diets suit young bodies best as at that age the body is dry and has set firm. Older people should take a drier diet most of the time, for at that age bodies are moist, soft, and cold. Diets then must be conditioned by age, the time of year, habit, country and constitution. They should be opposite in character to the prevailing climate, whether winter or summer. Such is the best road to health. . . .

Fat people who want to reduce should take their exercise on an empty stomach and sit down to their food out of breath. . . . [T]hey should take only one meal a day, go without baths, sleep on hard beds and walk about with as little clothing as may be. Thin people who want to get fat should do exactly the opposite. . . . A wise man ought to realize that health is his most valuable possession and learn how to treat his illnesses by his own judgment.

PUTTING IT ALL TOGETHER

Using the sources above, along with what you have learned in class and in the chapters in this book, write a short essay that analyzes ideas about health and illness in the Hellenistic world, and the treatments that resulted from these. What characterized a healthy body, and how was good health to be regained in the case of illness? Many of the ideas and treatments may seem strange, given how we understand the body today, but do any sound familiar?

Sources: (1) *Hippocratic Writings*, ed. G. E. R. Lloyd, trans. J. Chadwick and W. N. Mann (Harmondsworth, U.K.: Penguin, 1983), pp. 262, 264. Reproduced by permission of Penguin Books Ltd; (2) *Hippocratic Writings*, pp. 170–171, 172, 177; (4) James Longrigg, *Greek Medicine: From the Heroic to the Hellenistic Age: A Source Book* (London: Duckworth, 1998), 139; (5) *Hippocratic Writings*, p. 274.

The Periplus of the Erythraean Sea

A periplus was a manuscript that described a shoreline, along with ports and the distance between them; it was similar to the sailing logs used until the advent of modern navigation technology, or to the driving directions found through map Web sites today. The earliest peripli that survive (in later copies) date from the fifth century B.C.E. This particular periplus, written by a Greek-speaking merchant of Alexandria in the first century C.E., describes the coasts of the Red Sea, eastern Africa, and India, all of which the author appears to have visited personally.

1. Of the designated ports on the Erythraean Sea, and the market-towns around it, the first is the Egyptian port of Mussel Harbor. To those sailing down from that place, on the right hand, after eighteen hundred stadia [about two hundred miles], there is Berenice. The harbors of both are at the boundary of Egypt, and are bays opening from the Erythraean Sea.

2. On the right-hand coast next below Berenice is the country of the Berbers [or Barbaroi, that is, people who do not speak Greek]. . . . [A]nd behind them, further inland, in the country toward the west, there lies a city called Meroe. . . .

6. There are imported into these places, undressed cloth made in Egypt for the Berbers; robes from Arsinoe; cloaks of poor quality dyed in colors; double-fringed linen mantles; many articles of flint glass, and others of murrhine [a substance used to make glass], made in Diospolis; and brass, which is used for ornament and in cut pieces instead of coin; sheets of soft copper, used for cooking-utensils and cut up for bracelets and anklets for the women; iron, which is made into spears used against the elephants and other wild beasts, and in their wars. Besides these, small axes are imported, and adzes and swords; copper drinking-cups, round and large; a little coin for those coming to the market; wine of Laodicea [southern Turkey] and Italy, not much; olive oil, not much; for the king, gold and silver plate made after the fashion of the country, and for clothing, military cloaks, and thin coats of skin, of no great value. Likewise from the district of Ariaca [in India] across this sea, there are imported Indian iron, and steel, and Indian cotton cloth; the broad cloth called *monaché* and that called *sagmatogênê*, and girdles [wide belts], and coats of skin and mallow-colored cloth, and a few muslins, and colored lac [lacquer ware]. There are exported from these places ivory, and tortoise-shell and rhinoceros-horn. . . .

8. After Avalites there is another market-town, better than this, called Malao, distant a sail of about eight hundred stadia. The anchorage is an open roadstead, sheltered by a spit running out from the east. Here the natives are more peaceable. There are imported into this place the things already mentioned, and many tunics, cloaks from Arsinoe, dressed and dyed; drinking-cups, sheets of soft copper in small quantity, iron, and gold and silver coin, not much. There are exported from these places myrrh, a little frankincense (that known as far-side), the harder cinnamon, *duaca*, Indian copal and *macir*, which are imported into Arabia; and slaves, but rarely.

EVALUATE THE EVIDENCE

1. What types of merchandise are being traded along the east coast of Africa, and for what purposes?
2. What does this document suggest about consumers in the Hellenistic world, including those in Africa?

Source: Wilfred H. Schoff, trans., *The Periplus of the Erythraean Sea: Travel and Trade in the Indian Ocean by a Merchant of the First Century* (New York: Longmans, Green, and Co., 1912), pp. 22, 24–25.

They studied the writings attributed to Hippocrates (see Chapter 3) and generally accepted his theory of the four humors, but they also approached the study of medicine in a systematic, scientific fashion. The physician Herophilus (ca. 335–280 B.C.E.), for example, who lived in Alexandria, was the first to accurately describe the nervous system, and he differentiated between nerves and blood vessels and between motor and sensory nerves. Herophilus also closely studied the brain, which he considered the center of intelligence, and discerned the cerebrum and cerebellum. His younger contemporary Erasistratus (ca. 304–250 B.C.E.) also conducted research on the brain and nervous system and improved on Herophilus's work. To learn more about human anatomy, Herophilus and Erasistratus dissected human cadavers while their students watched. Human dissection was seen as unacceptable in most parts of the Hellenistic world, so they were probably the only scientists in antiquity to dissect human bodies, although animal dissection became very common in the Roman period. The story later spread that they had dissected living criminals, provided for them by the Ptolemaic kings of Egypt, but this may have just been a legend. They wrote works on various medical and anatomical topics, but only the titles and a few fragments quoted by later authors survive.

Because Herophilus and Erasistratus followed the teachings of Hippocrates, later writers on medicine labeled them "Dogmatists" or the "Dogmatic school," from the Greek word *dogma*, or philosophical idea. Along with their hands-on study of the human body, the Dogmatists also speculated about the nature of disease and argued that there were sometimes hidden causes for illness. Opposing them was an "Empiric school" begun by a student of Herophilus; these doctors held observation and experiment to be the only way to advance medical knowledge and viewed the search for hidden causes as useless. Later Greek and Roman physicians sometimes identified themselves with one or the other of these ways of thinking, but the labels were also sometimes simply used as insults to dismiss the ideas of a rival.

Whether undertaken by Dogmatists or Empiricists, medical study did not lead to effective cures for the infectious diseases that were the leading cause of death for most people, however, and people used a variety of ways to attempt to combat illness. Medicines prescribed by physicians or prepared at home often included natural products blended with materials understood to work magically. One treatment for fever, for example, was the liver of a cat killed when the moon was waning and preserved in salt. People also invoked Asclepius, the god of medicine, in healing rituals, or focused on other deities who were understood to have power over specific illnesses.

They paid specialists to devise spells that would cure them or prevent them from becoming ill in the first place (see page 109). Women in childbirth gathered their female friends and relatives around them, and in larger cities could also hire experienced midwives who knew how to decrease pain and assist in the birthing process if something went wrong. People in the Hellenistic world may have thought that fate determined what would happen, but they also actively sought to make their lives longer and healthier.

NOTES

1. Ahmad Hasan Dani et al., *History of Civilizations of Central Asia* (Paris: UNESCO, 1992), p. 107.
2. Quoted in W. W. Tarn and G. T. Griffith, *Hellenistic Civilizations*, 3d ed. (Cleveland and New York: Meridian Books, 1961), p. 199.
3. All quotations from Diodorus are reprinted by permission of the publishers and the Trustees of the Loeb Classical Library from Diodorus of Sicily, *Biblioteca historica* 1.80–36, Loeb Classical Library Volume 279, with an English translation by C. H. Oldfather, pp. 275, 277. Cambridge, Mass.: Harvard University Press. First published 1933. Loeb Classical Library® is a registered trademark of the President and Fellows of Harvard College.
4. Ibid., 3.12.1–3.
5. Diogenes Laertius, *Lives of Eminent Philosophers* 10.22, trans. C. D. Yonge, at Attalus (http://www.attalus.org/old/diogenes10a.html#22).
6. Diodorus 3.12.2–3.

LOOKING BACK LOOKING AHEAD

The conquests of Philip and Alexander broadened Greek and Macedonian horizons, but probably not in ways that they had intended. The empire that they created lasted only briefly, but the Hellenistic culture that developed afterwards took Greeks even beyond the borders of Alexander's huge empire as conquerors, merchants, artists, and sailors.

The Hellenistic world was largely conquered by the Romans, but in cultural terms the conquest was reversed: The Romans derived their alphabet from the Greek alphabet, though they changed the letters somewhat. Roman statuary was modeled on Greek and was often, in fact, made by Greek sculptors, who found ready customers among wealthy Romans. Furthermore, the major Roman gods and goddesses were largely the same as the Greek ones, though they had different names. Although the Romans did not seem to have been particularly interested in the speculative philosophy of Socrates and Plato, they were drawn to the more practical philosophies of the Epicureans and Stoics. And like the Hellenistic Greeks, many Romans turned from traditional religions to mystery religions that offered secret knowledge and promised eternal life. Among these was Christianity, a new religion that grew in the Roman Empire and whose most important early advocate was Paul of Tarsus, a well-educated Hellenized Jew who wrote in Greek. Significant aspects of

Greek culture thus lasted long after the Hellenistic monarchies and even the Roman Empire were gone, shaping all subsequent societies in the Mediterranean and Near East.

Make Connections

Think about the larger developments and continuities within and across chapters.

1. How was Greek society in the Hellenistic era similar to that of the earlier Hellenic era examined in Chapter 3? How was it different? What would you judge to be more significant, the continuities or the changes?

2. Cities had existed in the Tigris and Euphrates Valleys and the Near East long before Alexander's conquests. What would residents of Sumer (Chapter 1), Babylon (Chapters 1 and 2), and Pergamum find unusual about one another's cities? What would seem familiar?

3. How would you compare religion in Egypt in the Old and New Kingdoms (Chapter 1) with religion in Hellenistic Egypt? What provides the best explanation for the differences you have identified?

4 REVIEW & EXPLORE

Identify Key Terms

Identify and explain the significance of each item below.

Hellenistic (p. 97)

Hellenization (p. 98)

Epicureanism (p. 110)

Stoicism (p. 110)

natural law (p. 111)

Review the Main Ideas

Answer the focus questions from each section of the chapter.

◆ How and why did Alexander the Great create an empire, and what was its political legacy? (p. 94)

◆ How did Greek ideas and traditions spread across the eastern Mediterranean and Near East? (p. 98)

◆ What new economic connections were created in the Hellenistic period? (p. 102)

◆ How did religion and philosophy shape everyday life in the Hellenistic world? (p. 105)

◆ How did science and medicine serve the needs of Hellenistic society? (p. 111)

Suggested Reading and Media Resources

BOOKS

- Bowden, Hugh. *Mystery Cults of the Ancient World.* 2010. Examines the main mystery religions of the ancient Mediterranean, using artistic and literary evidence.
- Carney, Elizabeth D. *Women and Monarchy in Macedonia.* 2000. Studies the queens of Macedonia and their influence on the exercise of power.
- Chaniotis, Angelos. *War in the Hellenistic World.* 2005. Covers the wars of this period, the reasons behind them, and how they were waged.
- Connelly, Joan. *Portrait of a Priestess: Women and Ritual in Ancient Greece.* 2009. A survey of the important public roles of priestesses, with many illustrations.
- Errington, R. Malcolm. *A History of the Hellenistic World, 323–30 B.C.* 2008. Easily the best coverage of the period: full, scholarly, and readable.
- Erskine, Andrew. *A Companion to the Hellenistic World.* 2003. An edited collection with chapters on many of the issues discussed here.
- Freeman, Philip. *Alexander the Great.* 2010. Designed for general readers, this excellent biography portrays Alexander as both ruthless and cultured.
- Jaeger, Mary. *Archimedes and the Roman Imagination.* 2008. Puts the discovery of the new manuscript into the context of Archimedes's other scientific works.
- Manning, J. G. *The Last Pharaohs: Egypt Under the Ptolemies, 305–30 B.C.* 2009. Examines the impact of the Ptolemies on Egyptian society and the way their state blended Greek and Egyptian elements.
- Sharples, R. W. *Stoics, Epicureans, and Sceptics.* 1996. Provides a brief synthesis of these three major branches of Hellenistic philosophy, written for students.
- Shipley, Graham. *The Greek World After Alexander, 323–30 B.C.* 2000. A very thorough discussion of political, socioeconomic, intellectual, and cultural developments.
- Waterfield, Robin. *Dividing the Spoils: The War for Alexander the Great's Empire.* 2011. A cultural and political narrative of this turbulent period based on up-to-date research.

DOCUMENTARIES

- *Ancient Mysteries: The Lost Treasures of the Alexandria Library* (History Channel, 2004). Presents the building of the library and its collection, the research undertaken there, and the destruction of the library at the hands of a Christian mob in the fourth century C.E.
- *Cleopatra's Alexandria* (BBC, 2000). Explores the history of Alexandria from its construction through the time of Cleopatra, highlighting the findings of marine archaeologists.
- *Infinite Secrets: The Genius of Archimedes* (*Nova*, 2004). Excellent *Nova* special that explores Archimedes's ideas, theories, and writings, and tells the story of the lost manuscript featured in this chapter.
- *In the Footsteps of Alexander the Great* (BBC, 2010). Michael Wood follows Alexander's two-thousand-mile journey from Greece to India, tracing his conquests and the meaning these have for the peoples of these areas today.
- *The True Story of Alexander the Great* (History Channel, 2005). Examines the life and career of Alexander, with on-site re-enactments and computer graphics.

WEB SITES

- *Ancient History Sourcebook.* Well-organized collection of ancient Mediterranean texts and art and archaeological sources. Organized chronologically and topically, with materials from 2000 B.C.E. to 500 C.E. **www.fordham .edu/Halsall/ancient/asbook.html**
- *Brought to Life: Exploring the History of Medicine.* Interactive Web site from the Science Museum in London offering a thematic approach to the past three thousand years in the history of medicine that foregrounds objects and material culture. Includes many items from the ancient Mediterranean. **www.sciencemuseum.org.uk /broughttolife**
- *Pothos.* Long-standing user-generated Web site with articles, debates, a blog, and visual materials about Alexander the Great. **www.pothos.org/content/**

5

The Rise of Rome

ca. 1000–27 B.C.E.

The Hellenistic monarchies that arose after Alexander's conquests extended eastward and southward from Greece. The Greek colonies that had been established in southern Italy were not part of these monarchies, but culturally they became part of the Hellenistic world. To the north of the Greek city-states in the Italian peninsula, other people built their own societies. Among these were the people who later became the Romans, who settled on hills along the Tiber River in central Italy. Beginning in the sixth century B.C.E., the Romans gradually took over more and more territory in Italy through conquest and annexation. At about the same time, a group of aristocrats revolted against the kings ruling Rome and established a republican government in which the main institution of power was a political assembly, the Senate. Under the direction of the Senate, the Romans continued their political and military expansion, first to all of Italy, then throughout the western Mediterranean basin, and then to areas in the east that had been part of Alexander's empire. As they did, they learned about and incorporated Greek art, literature, philosophy, and religion, but the wars of conquest also led to serious problems that the Senate proved unable to handle.

Roman history is generally divided into three periods: the monarchical period, traditionally dated from 753 B.C.E. to 509 B.C.E., in which the city of Rome was ruled by kings; the republic, traditionally dated from 509 B.C.E. to 27 B.C.E., in which it was ruled by the Senate and expanded its power first to all of Italy and then beyond; and the empire, from 27 B.C.E. to 476 C.E., in which the vast Roman territories were ruled by an emperor. This chapter covers the first two of these periods. The Roman Empire will be discussed in Chapters 6 and 7. ■

Life in Etruscan Society
A fresco from an Etruscan tomb, painted about 470 B.C.E., shows dancers in an idyllic setting with olive trees, while other walls depict musicians and a banquet. The scenes are based on those on Greek pottery, evidence of the connections between the Etruscans and their Greek neighbors to the south. This tomb is one among many thousands in the Necropolis of Monterozzi in Tarquinia, just north of Rome, now a UNESCO World Heritage site. (Wall painting from the Monterozzi Tomb, 6th–4th century B.C.E./Pictures from History/Bridgeman Images)

Rome's Rise to Power

FOCUS QUESTION *How did the Romans become the dominant power in Italy?*

The colonies established by Greek poleis (city-states) in the Hellenic era (see Chapter 3) included a number along the coast of southern Italy and Sicily, an area already populated by a variety of different groups that farmed, fished, and traded. So many Greek settlers came to this area and the Greek settlements there became so wealthy that it later became known as Magna Graecia—Greater Greece. Although Alexander the Great (see Chapter 4) created an empire that stretched from his homeland of Macedonia to India, his conquests did not reach as far as southern Italy and Sicily. Thus the Greek colonies there remained politically independent. They became part of the Hellenistic cultural world, however, and they transmitted much of that culture to people who lived farther north in the Italian peninsula. These included the Etruscans, who built the first cities north of Magna Graecia, and then the Romans, who eventually came to dominate the peninsula.

MAP 5.1 Roman Italy and the City of Rome, ca. 218 B.C.E. As Rome expanded, it built roads linking major cities and offered various degrees of citizenship to the territories it conquered or with which it made alliances. The territories outlined in green that are separate from the Italian peninsula were added by 218 B.C.E., largely as a result of the Punic Wars.

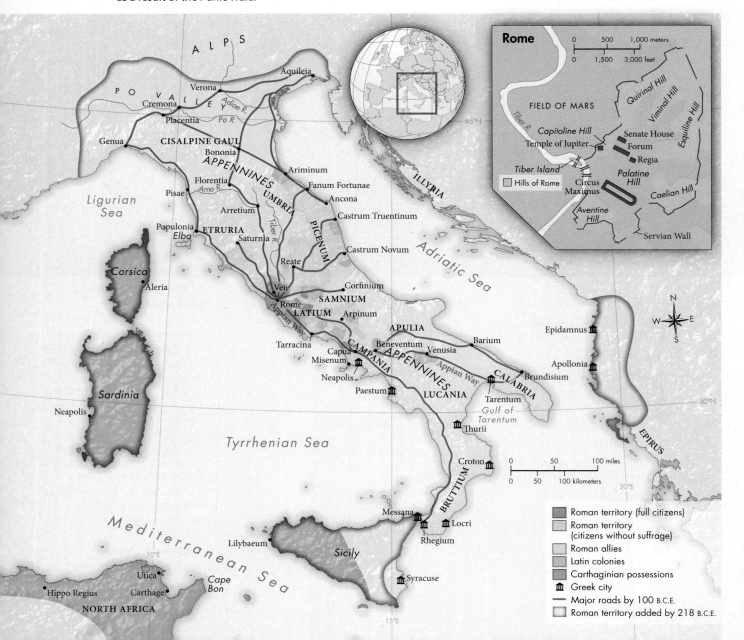

The Geography of Italy

The boot-shaped peninsula of Italy, with the island of Sicily at its toe, occupies the center of the Mediterranean basin (Map 5.1). To the south lies Africa; the distance between southwestern Sicily and the northern African coast is at one point only about a hundred miles. Italy and Sicily literally divide the Mediterranean into two basins and form the focal point between the two halves.

Like Greece and other Mediterranean lands, Italy enjoys a largely pleasant climate. The winters are rainy, but the summer months are dry. Because of the climate, the rivers of Italy usually carry little water during the summer, and some go entirely dry. Most of Italy's other rivers are unsuitable for regular large-scale shipping and never became major thoroughfares for commerce and communications. Yet the rivers nourished a bountiful agriculture that could produce enough crops for a growing population.

Geography encouraged Italy to look to the Mediterranean. In the north Italy is protected by the Alps, which form a natural barrier. The Alps retarded but did not prevent peoples from entering Italy by this route. From the north the Apennine Mountains run southward for the entire length of the Italian boot, cutting off access to the Adriatic Sea for those to their west. This barrier induced Italy to look west to Spain and Carthage rather than east to Greece, but it did not carve up the land in a way that would prevent the development of political unity.

In their southward course the Apennines leave two broad and fertile plains to their west: Latium and Campania. These plains attracted settlers and invaders from the time that peoples began to move into Italy. Among these peoples were those who would found Rome on the Tiber River in Latium.

This site enjoyed several advantages. The Tiber provided Rome with a constant source of water. Located at an easy crossing point on the Tiber, Rome thus stood astride the main avenue of communications between northern and southern Italy. Positioned amid seven hills, Rome was defensible and safe from the floods of the Tiber. It was also close to the sea through the port of Ostia. Thus Rome was in an excellent position to develop the resources of Latium and maintain contact with the rest of Italy.

Chronology

ca. 1000 B.C.E.	Earliest settlements in the area that became the city of Rome
753 B.C.E.	Traditional founding of the city of Rome
509 B.C.E.	Traditional date of establishment of the Roman Republic
451–449 B.C.E.	Laws of the Twelve Tables written and issued
387 B.C.E.	Gauls sack Rome
367 B.C.E.	Licinian-Sextian laws passed
ca. 265 B.C.E.	Romans control most of Italy
264–201; 149–146 B.C.E.	Punic Wars
133–121 B.C.E.	Reforms of the Gracchi
107–31 B.C.E.	Turmoil in the late republic (see timeline, page 144)
44 B.C.E.	Julius Caesar assassinated
31 B.C.E.	Octavian defeats Antony and Cleopatra at the Battle of Actium
27 B.C.E.	Senate issues decrees giving Octavian great power

The Etruscans

The culture that is now called Etruscan developed in north-central Italy about 800 B.C.E. Recent studies of DNA evidence have indicated that the Etruscans most likely originated in Turkey or elsewhere in the Near East, but migrated to Italy by at least 3000 B.C.E., and developed their culture there. The Etruscans spoke a language that was very different from Greek and Latin, although they adopted the Greek alphabet to write it. We know they wrote letters, records, and literary works, but once the Romans conquered them, knowledge of how to read and write Etruscan died out. Also, the writings themselves largely disappeared because many were written on linen books that did not survive; what remain are inscriptions on stone or engravings in metal. Modern

The Etruscans, ca. 500 B.C.E.

- Etruscan homeland
- Areas of expansion
- Etruscan city

scholars have learned to read Etruscan to some degree, but most of what we know about their civilization comes from archaeological evidence and from the writings of other peoples who lived around them at the same time.

The Etruscans established permanent settlements that evolved into cities resembling the Greek city-states, and they thereby built a rich cultural life, full of art and music, that became the foundation of civilization in much of Italy. The Etruscans spread their influence over the surrounding countryside, which they farmed and mined for its rich mineral resources. They traded natural products, especially iron, with their Greek neighbors to the south and with other peoples throughout the Mediterranean, including the Phoenicians, in exchange for a variety of goods.

Etruscan cities appear to have been organized in leagues, and beginning about 750 B.C.E. the Etruscans expanded southward into central Italy through military actions on land and sea and through the establishment of colony cities. Written records of battles all come from the side of the Etruscans' opponents, but objects found in graves indicate that military values were important in their society, as wealthy men were buried with bronze armor and shields and iron weapons. In the process of expansion they encountered a small collection of villages subsequently called Rome.

The Founding of Rome

Archaeological evidence indicates that the ancestors of the Romans began to settle on the hills east of the Tiber during the early Iron Age, around 1000 B.C.E. to 800 B.C.E. Archaeological sources provide the most important information about this earliest period of Roman history, but later Romans told a number of stories about the founding of Rome. These mix legend and history, but they illustrate the traditional ethics, morals, and ideals of Rome.

The Romans' foundation myths were told in a number of different versions. In the most common of these, Romulus and Remus founded the city of Rome, an event later Roman authors dated precisely to 753 B.C.E. These twin brothers were the sons of the war god Mars, and their mother, Rhea Silvia, was a descendant of Aeneas, a brave and pious Trojan who left Troy after it was destroyed by the Greeks in the Trojan War (see Chapter 3). The brothers, who were left to die by a jealous uncle, were raised by a female wolf. When they were grown, they decided to build a city in the hills that became part of Rome, but they quarreled over which hill should be the site of the city. Romulus chose one hill and started to build a wall around it, and Remus chose another. After Remus jumped mockingly over Romulus's wall, Romulus killed him and named the city after himself. He also established a council of

Etruscan Figure of a Mother and Son   This bronze Etruscan sculpture from the sixth to fourth century B.C.E. shows a mother and child. The influence of Hellenistic Greek art is evident in the musculature of the little boy and the drape of the woman's clothing. The holders at the sides may have held candles. (Candelabra-shaped cymatium, bronze, 6th–4th century B.C.E./Museo Civico Archeologico, Bologna, Italy/De Agostini Picture Library/akg-images)

advisers later called the Senate, which means "council of old men."

Romulus and his mostly male followers expanded their power over the neighboring Sabine peoples, in part by abducting and marrying their women. The Sabine women then arranged a peace by throwing themselves between their brothers and their husbands, convincing them that killing kin would make the men cursed. The Romans, favored by the gods, continued their rise to power. Despite its tales of murder and kidnapping, this founding myth ascribes positive traits to the Romans: they are descended from gods and heroes, can thrive in wild and tough settings, will defend their boundaries at all costs, and mix with other peoples rather than simply conquering them. Also, the story portrays women who were ancestors of Rome as virtuous and brave.

Later Roman historians continued the story by describing a series of kings after Romulus—the traditional number is seven—each elected by the Senate. According to tradition, the last three kings were Etruscan, and another tale about female virtue was told to explain why the Etruscan kings were overthrown. In this story, of which there are several versions, the son of King Tarquin, the Etruscan king who ruled Rome, raped Lucretia, a virtuous Roman wife, in her own home. As related by the historian Livy (59 B.C.E.–17 C.E.) in his massive history of the Roman Republic, Lucretia summoned her husband and father to the house, told them what had happened, and demanded they seek vengeance:

> One after another they tried to comfort her. They told her she was helpless, and therefore innocent; that he alone was guilty. It was the mind, they said, that sinned, not the body: without intention there could never be guilt. "What is due to him," Lucretia said, "is for you to decide. As for me I am innocent of fault, but I will take my punishment. Never shall Lucretia provide a precedent for unchaste women to escape what they deserve." With these words she drew a knife from under her robe, drove it into her heart, and fell forward, dead.[1]

Her father and husband and the other Roman nobles, continued Livy, swore on the bloody knife to avenge Lucretia's death by throwing out the Etruscan kings, and they did. Whether any of this story was true can never be known, but Romans generally accepted it as history, and dated the expulsion of the Etruscan kings to 509 B.C.E. They thus saw this year as marking the end of the monarchical period and the dawn of the republic, which had come about because of a wronged woman and her demands.

Most historians today view the idea that Etruscan kings ruled the city of Rome as legendary, but they stress the influence of the Etruscans on Rome. The Etruscans transformed Rome from a relatively large town to a real city with walls, temples, a drainage system, and other urban structures. The Romans adopted the Etruscan alphabet, which the Etruscans themselves had adopted from the Greeks. Romans adopted the use of a bundle of rods tied together with an ax emerging from the center, which symbolized the Etruscan kings' power. This ceremonial object was called the fasces (FAS-eez), and was carried first by Etruscan officials and then by Romans. (In the twentieth century Mussolini would use the fasces as the symbol of his political party, the Fascists, and it is also used by many other governmental groups, including some in the United States.) Even the toga, the white woolen robe worn by citizens, came from the Etruscans, as did gladiatorial combat honoring the dead. In engineering and

architecture the Romans adopted some design elements and the basic plan of their temples, along with paved roads, from the Etruscans.

In this early period the city of Rome does appear to have been ruled by kings, as were most territories in the ancient world. A hereditary aristocracy also developed—again, an almost universal phenomenon—which advised the kings and may have played a role in choosing them. And sometime in the sixth century B.C.E. a group of aristocrats revolted against these kings and established a government in which the main institution of power would be in the **Senate**, an assembly of aristocrats, rather than a single monarch. Executive power was in the hands of Senate leaders called **consuls**, but there were always two of them and they were elected for one-year terms only, not for life. Rome thereby became a republic, not a monarchy. Thus at the core of the myths was a bit of history.

Under kings and then the Senate, the villages along the Tiber gradually grew into a single city, whose residents enjoyed contacts with the larger Mediterranean world. Temples and public buildings began to grace Rome, and the Forum (see Map 5.1), a large plaza between two of Rome's hills, became a public meeting place similar to the Greek agora (see Chapter 3). The Capitoline Hill became the city's religious center when the temple of Jupiter Optimus Maximus (Jupiter the Best and Greatest) was built there. In addition, trade in metalwork became common, and wealthier Romans began to import fine Greek vases and other luxuries.

The Roman Conquest of Italy

In the years following the establishment of the republic, the Romans fought numerous wars with their neighbors on the Italian peninsula. The Roman army was made up primarily of citizens of Rome conscripted through an annual levy; any man aged sixteen to forty-six was eligible for the military draft and was then assigned to a legion for a particular campaign, with a maximum of six years. Those who could afford it bought their own weapons and armor. War also involved diplomacy, at which the Romans became masters. At an early date they learned the value of alliances, which became a distinguishing feature of Roman expansion in Italy. Alliances with the towns around them in Latium provided a large population that could be tapped for military needs; men from these towns were organized into troops called auxiliaries who fought with the legions.

■ **Senate**   The assembly that was the main institution of power in the Roman Republic, originally composed only of aristocrats.

■ **consuls**   Primary executives in the Roman Republic, elected for one-year terms, who commanded the army in battle, administered state business, and supervised financial affairs.

These wars of the early republic later became the source of legends that continued to express Roman values. One of these involved the aristocrat Cincinnatus, who had been expelled from the Senate and forced to pay a huge fine because of the actions of his son. As the story goes, in 458 B.C.E. he was plowing the fields of his small farm when the Senate asked him to return and assume the office of dictator. This position, which had been created very early in the republic, was one in which one man would be given ultimate powers for six months in order to handle a serious crisis such as an invasion or rebellion. (Like the word *tyrant* in ancient Greece, *dictator* did not have its current negative meaning in the early Roman Republic.) At this point the armies of the Aequi, a neighboring group, had surrounded Roman forces commanded by both consuls, and Rome was in imminent danger of catastrophe. Cincinnatus, wiping his sweat, listened to the appeal of his countrymen and led the Roman infantry in victory over the Aequi. He then returned to his farm, becoming a legend among later Romans as a man of simplicity who put his civic duty to Rome before any consideration of personal interest or wealth, and who willingly gave up power for the greater good. The Roman Senate actually chose many more men as dictator in the centuries after Cincinnatus, and not until the first century B.C.E. would any try to abuse this position. No subsequent dictator achieved the legendary reputation of Cincinnatus, however. For George Washington and other leaders of the American War of Independence, he became the symbolic model of a leader who had performed selfless service but then stepped down from power. When in 1783 they decided to form a patriotic society, they named it after him: the Society of the Cincinnati (from which the Ohio city takes its name).

In 387 B.C.E. the Romans suffered a major setback when the Celts—or Gauls, as the Romans called them—invaded the Italian peninsula from the north, destroyed a Roman army, and sacked the city of Rome. (For more on the Gauls, see Chapter 7.) More intent on loot than on conquest, the Gauls agreed to abandon Rome in return for a thousand pounds of gold. As the story was later told, when the Gauls provided their own scale, the Romans howled in indignation. The Gallic chieftain Brennus then threw his sword on the scale, exclaiming "*Vae victis*" (woe to the conquered). These words, though legendary, were used by later Romans as an explanation for why they would not surrender, and the city of Rome was not sacked again until 410 C.E.

The Romans rebuilt their city and recouped their losses. They brought Latium and their Latin allies fully under their control and conquered Etruria (see Map 5.1). Starting in 343 B.C.E. they turned south and grappled with the Samnites in a series of bitter wars for the possession of Campania. The Samnites were a formidable enemy and inflicted serious losses on the Romans, and in response the Romans reorganized their army to create the mobile legion, a flexible unit of soldiers capable of fighting anywhere. The Romans won out in the end and continued their expansion southward.

In 280 B.C.E., alarmed by Roman expansion, the Greek city of Tarentum in southern Italy called for help from Pyrrhus (PIHR-uhs), king of Epirus in western Greece. A relative of Alexander the Great and an excellent general, Pyrrhus won two furious battles but suffered heavy casualties—thus the phrase "Pyrrhic victory" is still used today to describe a victory involving severe losses. According to the later historian Plutarch, Roman bravery and tenacity led Pyrrhus to comment: "If we win one more battle with the Romans, we'll be completely washed up."[2]

The Romans and the Carthaginians had made a series of treaties to help one another (see page 130), and the Carthaginians attacked Sicily, drawing the armies of Pyrrhus away from Italy for a while and relieving pressure on the Romans. The Romans threw new legions against Pyrrhus's army, which in the end left southern Italy. The Romans made formal alliances with many of the cities of Magna Graecia and then turned north again. Their superior military institutions, organization, and large supply of soldiers allowed them to conquer or take into their sphere of influence most of Italy by about 265 B.C.E.

As they expanded their territory, the Romans spread their religious traditions throughout Italy, blending them with local beliefs and practices. Religion for the Romans was largely a matter of honoring the state and the family. The main goal of religion was to secure the peace of the gods, what was termed *pax deorum*, and to harness divine power for public and private enterprises. Religious rituals were an important way of expressing common values, which for Romans meant those evident in their foundation myths: bravery, morality, seriousness, family, and home. The sacred fire at the shrine of the goddess Vesta in the city of Rome, for example, was attended by the vestal virgins, young women chosen from aristocratic families. Vesta was the goddess of hearth and home, whose protection was regarded as essential to Roman well-being. The vestal virgins were important figures at major public rituals, though at several times of military loss and political crisis they were also charged with negligence of duty or unchastity, another link between female honor and the Roman state. Along with the great gods, the Romans believed in spirits who inhabited fields, forests, crossroads, and even the home itself. These were to be honored with rituals and gifts so that they would remain favorable instead of becoming hostile.

The Temple of Hercules Victor

This round temple, dating from the second century B.C.E., is the oldest surviving marble building in Rome and was imported from Greece. It once contained a statue of the mythical hero Hercules and was dedicated to him at this spot where legend told he killed a monster who had stolen some cattle.

EVALUATE THE EVIDENCE

1. Looking at the picture of the temples on the Acropolis in Athens on page 78, what stylistic similarities do you see between those buildings and this temple?

2. How do those similarities, and the fact that this temple was dedicated to Hercules, provide evidence for Roman adoption of Greek religion and culture?

(© Justin Kase z12z/Alamy Stock Photo)

Victorious generals made sure to honor the gods of people they had conquered and by doing so transformed them into gods they could also call on for assistance in their future campaigns. Greek deities and mythical heroes were absorbed into the Roman pantheon. Their names were changed to Roman names, so that Zeus (the king of the gods), for example, became Jupiter, and Herakles (the semidivine hero) became Hercules, but their personal qualities and powers were largely the same. (See "Evaluating the Evidence 5.1: The Temple of Hercules Victor," above.)

Once they had conquered an area, the Romans built roads, many of which continued to be used for centuries and can still be seen today. These roads provided an easy route for communication between the capital and outlying areas, allowed for the quick movement of armies, and offered an efficient means of trade. They were the tangible sinews of unity, and many were marvels of engineering, as were the stone bridges the Romans built over Italy's many rivers.

In politics the Romans shared full Roman citizenship with many of their oldest allies, particularly the inhabitants of the cities of Latium. In other instances they granted citizenship without the franchise, that is, without the right to vote or hold Roman office. These allies were subject to Roman taxes and calls for military service, but ran their own local affairs. The extension of Roman citizenship strengthened the state and increased its population and wealth, although limitations on this extension would eventually become a source of conflict (see page 129).

The Roman Republic

FOCUS QUESTION **What were the key institutions of the Roman Republic?**

Along with citizenship, the republican government was another important institution of Roman political life. Unlike the Greeks, the Romans rarely speculated on the ideal state or on political forms. Instead they created institutions, magistracies, and legal concepts to deal with practical problems and govern their ever-expanding state. These institutions were not static, but changed over time to allow a broader access to power and address new problems.

The Roman State

The Romans summed up their political existence in a single phrase: *senatus populusque Romanus*, "the Senate and the Roman people," which they abbreviated "SPQR." This sentiment reflects the republican ideal of shared government rather than power concentrated in a monarchy. It stands for the beliefs, customs, and laws of the republic—the unwritten constitution that evolved over two centuries to meet the demands of the governed. SPQR became a shorthand way of saying "Rome," just as U.S.A. says "the United States of America."

In the early republic social divisions determined the shape of politics. Political power was in the hands of a hereditary aristocracy—the **patricians**, whose privileged legal status was determined by their birth as members of certain families. Patrician men dominated the affairs of state, provided military leadership in time of war, and monopolized knowledge of law and legal procedure. The common people of Rome, the **plebeians** (plih-BEE-uhns), were free citizens with a voice in politics, but they had few of the patricians' political and social advantages. While some plebeian merchants increased their wealth in the course of Roman expansion and came to rival the patricians economically, most plebeians were poor artisans, small farmers, and landless urban dwellers.

The Romans created several assemblies through which men elected high officials and passed legislation. The earliest was the Centuriate Assembly, in which citizens were organized into groups called centuries based loosely around their status in the military. Each citizen was assigned to a century depending on his status and amount of wealth, and the patricians possessed the majority of centuries. When an election was ordered, each century met separately and voted as a bloc, which meant that the patricians could easily outvote the plebeians. In 471 B.C.E. plebeian men won the right to meet in an assembly of their own, the *concilium plebis*, and to pass ordinances.

The highest officials of the republic were the two consuls, who were elected for one-year terms by the Centuriate Assembly. At a later time Romans believed that the consulship had initially been open only to patrician men, although surviving lists of consuls actually show that a few early consuls were plebeians. The consuls commanded the army in battle, administered state business, presided over the Senate and assemblies, and supervised financial affairs. In effect, they ran the state. The consuls appointed quaestors (KWEH-stuhrs) to assist them in their duties, and in 421 B.C.E. the quaestorship became an elective office open to plebeian men. The quaestors took charge of the public treasury and investigated crimes, reporting their findings to the consuls.

In 366 B.C.E. the Romans created a new office, that of praetor (PREE-tuhr). When the consuls were away from Rome, the praetors could act in their place; they could also command armies, be governors in the provinces, interpret law, and administer justice. Other officials included the powerful censors who had many responsibilities, the most important being supervision of public morals, the power to determine who lawfully could hold public office and sit in the Senate, the registration of citizens, the taking of a census, and the leasing of public contracts.

The most important institution of the republic was the Senate, a political assembly that by tradition was established by Romulus and in reality most likely originated in the monarchical period as a council of the heads of powerful families who advised the king. By the time written records begin for Roman history, the Senate was already in existence. During the republic the Senate grew to several hundred members, all of whom had previously been elected to one of the high positions, which automatically conferred Senate membership. Because the Senate sat year after year with the same members, while high officials changed annually, it provided stability and continuity. It passed formal decrees that were technically "advice" to the magistrates, who were not bound to obey them but usually did. It directed the magistrates on the conduct of war and had the power over the expenditure of public money. In times of emergency it could name a dictator. Technically the Senate could not pass binding legislation during the republican period. Its decisions had to be put to the Centuriate Assembly for a vote before they could become law, but patricians dominated both groups and generally agreed on legislative matters.

■ **patricians** The Roman hereditary aristocracy, who held most of the political power in the republic.

■ **plebeians** The common people of Rome, who were free but had few of the patricians' advantages.

Within the city of Rome itself the Senate's powers were limited by laws and traditions, but as Rome expanded, the Senate had greater authority in the outlying territories. The Romans divided the lands that they conquered into provinces, and the Senate named the governors for these, most of whom were former consuls or praetors. Another responsibility of the Senate was to handle relations between Rome and other powers.

A lasting achievement of the Romans was their development of law. Roman civil law, the *ius civile*, consisted of statutes, customs, and forms of procedure that regulated the lives of citizens. As the Romans came into more frequent contact with foreigners, the consuls and praetors applied a broader *ius gentium*, the "law of the peoples," to such matters as peace treaties, the treatment of prisoners of war, and the exchange of diplomats. In the ius gentium all sides were to be treated the same regardless of their nationality. By the late republic Roman jurists had widened this principle still further into the concept of *ius naturale*, "natural law," based in part on Stoic beliefs (see Chapter 4). Natural law, according to these thinkers, is made up of rules that govern human behavior that come from applying reason rather than customs or traditions, and so apply to all societies. In reality, Roman officials generally interpreted the law to the advantage of Rome, of course, at least to the extent that the strength of Roman armies allowed them to enforce it. But Roman law came to be seen as one of the most important contributions Rome made to the development of Western civilization.

Social Conflict in Rome

Inequality between plebeians and patricians led to a conflict known as the **Struggle of the Orders**. In this conflict the plebeians sought to increase their power by taking advantage of the fact that Rome's survival depended on its army, which needed plebeians to fill the ranks of the infantry. According to tradition, in 494 B.C.E. the plebeians literally walked out of Rome and refused to serve in the army. Their general strike worked, and the patricians grudgingly made important concessions. They allowed the plebeians to elect their own officials, the **tribunes**, who presided over the concilium plebis, could bring plebeian grievances to the Senate for resolution, and could also veto the decisions of the consuls. Thus, as in Archaic age Greece (see Chapter 3), political rights were broadened because of military needs for foot soldiers.

The law itself was the plebeians' primary target. Only the patricians knew what the law was, and only they could argue cases in court. All too often they used the law for their own benefit. The plebeians wanted the law codified and published, but many patricians, including Cincinnatus and his son, vigorously opposed attempts by plebeians to gain legal rights. After much struggle, in 449 B.C.E. the patricians surrendered their legal monopoly and codified and published the Laws of the Twelve Tables, so called because they were inscribed on twelve bronze plaques. The Laws of the Twelve Tables covered many legal issues, including property ownership, guardianship, inheritance, procedure for trials, and punishments for various crimes. The penalty set for debt was strict:

> Unless they make a settlement [with their creditor], debtors shall be held in bonds for sixty days. During that time they shall be brought before the praetor's court in the meeting place on three successive market days, and the amount for which they are judged liable shall be announced; on the third market day they shall suffer capital punishment or be delivered for sale abroad, across the Tiber.[3]

Debtors no doubt made every effort to settle with their creditors. The patricians also made legal procedures public so that plebeians could argue cases in court. Later, in 445 B.C.E., the patricians passed a law, the *lex Canuleia*, that for the first time allowed patricians and plebeians to marry one another.

Licinius and Sextius were plebeian tribunes in the fourth century B.C.E. who mounted a sweeping assault on patrician privilege. Wealthy plebeians wanted the opportunity to provide political leadership for the state. After a ten-year battle the Licinian-Sextian laws passed in 367 B.C.E., giving wealthy plebeians access to all the offices of Rome, including the right to hold one of the two consulships. Once plebeians could hold the consulship, they could also sit in the Senate and advise on policy. They also gained such cosmetic privileges as wearing the purple-bordered toga, the symbol of aristocracy. Though decisive, this victory did not end the Struggle of the Orders. That happened only in 287 B.C.E. with the passage of the *lex Hortensia*, which gave the resolutions of the concilium plebis, the plebeian assembly, the force of law for patricians and plebeians alike.

The long Struggle of the Orders had resulted in an expansion of power to wealthy plebeians, but once certain plebeian families could hold the consulship and become members of the Senate, they became as guarded of their privileges and as uninterested in the problems of the average plebeian as the patricians had formerly been. Theoretically, all men could aspire to

■ **Struggle of the Orders** A conflict in which the plebeians sought political representation and safeguards against patrician domination.

■ **tribunes** Plebeian-elected officials; tribunes brought plebeian grievances to the Senate for resolution and protected plebeians from the arbitrary conduct of patrician magistrates.

the highest political offices. In reality, political power had been expanded only slightly and still resided largely in a group of wealthy families, some of whom happened to be plebeian. Access to the highest political offices was still difficult for any plebeian, who often had to get the support of patrician families if he wanted a political career.

Networks of support were actually important for all Romans involved in public life, not simply aspiring plebeians. Roman politics operated primarily through a **patron-client system** whereby free men promised their votes to a more powerful man in exchange for his help in legal or other matters. The more powerful patron looked after his clients, and his clients' support helped the patron advance his career.

Roman Expansion

FOCUS QUESTION *How did the Romans take control of the Mediterranean world?*

As the republican government was developing, Roman territory continued to expand. Unlike Alexander the Great, the Romans did not map out grandiose strategies to conquer the world. Rather they responded to situations as they arose. This meant, however, that they sought to eliminate any state they saw as a military threat.

The Punic Wars

As they pushed southward, incorporating the southern Italian peninsula into their growing territory, the Romans confronted another great power in the western Mediterranean, the Carthaginians. The city of Carthage had been founded by Phoenicians as a trading colony in the eighth century B.C.E. (see Chapter 2). It commanded one of the best harbors on the northern African coast and was surrounded by fertile farmland. By the fourth century B.C.E. the Carthaginians began to expand their holdings, and they engaged in war with the Etruscans and with the Greek cities of southern Italy and Sicily. They had one of the largest navies in the Mediterranean and were wealthy enough to hire mercenaries to do much of their fighting. At the end of a long string of wars, the Carthaginians had created and defended a mercantile empire that stretched from western Sicily to the western end of the Mediterranean (see Map 5.1).

Beginning in the fifth century B.C.E. the Romans and the Carthaginians made a series of treaties with one another that defined their spheres of influence, and they worked together in the 270s B.C.E. to defeat Pyrrhus. But the Greek cities that became Roman allies in southern Italy and Sicily, including Syracuse, saw Carthage as a competitor in terms of trade. This competition led to the first of the three **Punic Wars** between Rome and Carthage. The First Punic War lasted for twenty-three years (264–241 B.C.E.). The Romans quickly learned that they could not hold Sicily unless they controlled the sea. Thus they hired Greeks from Syracuse to build and sail ships for them, engineering some of their vessels based on wrecked Carthaginian warships. The Romans adapted what they knew best, land warfare, to fighting at sea, rigging gangplanks to cross over to the Carthaginian ships and seize them. Of the seven major naval battles they fought with the Carthaginians, the Romans won six and finally wore their opponents down with superior resources and military might. In 241 B.C.E. the Romans took possession of Sicily, which became their first real province.

The peace treaty between Rome and Carthage brought no peace, as both powers had their sights set on dominating the western half of the Mediterranean. In 238 B.C.E. the Romans took advantage of Carthaginian weakness to seize Sardinia and Corsica. The Carthaginians responded by expanding their holdings in Spain, under the leadership of the commander Hamilcar Barca. With him he took his ten-year-old son, Hannibal, whom he had earlier led to an altar where he had made the boy swear to be an enemy to Rome forever. In the following years Hamilcar and his son-in-law Hasdrubal (HAHZ-droo-buhl) subjugated much of southern Spain and in the process rebuilt Carthaginian power. Rome first made a treaty with Hasdrubal setting the boundary between Carthaginian and Roman interests at the Ebro River, and then began to extend its own influence in Spain.

In 221 B.C.E. Hannibal became the Carthaginian commander in Spain and laid siege to Saguntum (suh-GUHN-tum), a Roman-allied city that lay within the sphere of Carthaginian interest and was making raids into Carthaginian territories. The Romans declared war, claiming that Carthage had attacked a friendly city. So began the Second Punic War, one of the most desperate wars ever fought by Rome. In 218 B.C.E. Hannibal marched an army of tens of thousands of troops—and, more famously, several dozen war elephants—from Spain across what is now France and over the Alps into Italy. Once there, he defeated one Roman army after another, and in 216 B.C.E. he won his greatest victory at the Battle of Cannae (KAH-nee). The exact number of Roman deaths is unknown, but ancient historians place it between fifty thousand and seventy thousand. Hannibal then spread devastation throughout the Italian peninsula, and a number of cities in central and southern Italy rebelled against Rome because it appeared to them that Hannibal would be victorious. Syracuse, Rome's ally during the First Punic War, also went over to the Carthaginians. Yet Hannibal was not able to win areas near Rome in central Italy, as Roman allies there, who had been extended citizenship rights, remained loyal. Hannibal's allies, who included Philip V, the Antigonid king of Macedonia (see Chapter 4), did not supply him with enough food and supplies to sustain his troops, and Rome fought back.

In 210 B.C.E. Rome found its answer to Hannibal in the young commander Scipio Africanus. Scipio copied Hannibal's methods of mobile warfare and guerrilla tactics and made more extensive use of cavalry than had earlier Roman commanders. In the following years Scipio operated in Spain, which in 207 B.C.E. he wrested from the Carthaginians. That same year the Romans sealed Hannibal's fate in Italy. At the Battle of Metaurus the Romans destroyed a major Carthaginian army coming to reinforce Hannibal. Scipio then struck

directly at Carthage itself, prompting the Carthaginians to recall Hannibal from Italy to defend their homeland.

In 202 B.C.E., at the town of Zama near Carthage (Map 5.2), Scipio defeated Hannibal in a decisive battle. The Carthaginians sued for peace and the Roman Senate agreed, on terms that were very favorable to the Romans. Hannibal himself later served as a military adviser at the Seleucid court in its battle with Rome, and then as an adviser to one of the small kingdoms in Anatolia.

The Second Punic War contained the seeds of still other wars. Unabated fear of Carthage combined with the encouragement of Cato the Elder (see page 137) led to the Third Punic War, a needless, unjust, and savage conflict that ended in 146 B.C.E. when Scipio Aemilianus, the grandson by adoption of Scipio Africanus, destroyed the hated rival and burned Carthage to the ground. Scipio's friend Polybius, a Greek historian and military leader, later reported that as the Roman conqueror watched the city burn, he said, "I fear and foresee that someday someone will give the same order about my fatherland."[4] It would, however, be centuries before an invader would stand before the gates of Rome.

During the war with Hannibal, the Romans had invaded the Iberian Peninsula, an area rich in material resources and the home of fierce warriors. They met with bloody and determined resistance. Not until 133 B.C.E., after years of brutal and ruthless warfare, did Scipio Aemilianus finally conquer Spain. Scipio's victory meant that Roman language, law, and culture, fertilized by Greek influences, would in time permeate this entire region, although it would be another century before the Iberian Peninsula was completely pacified.

Rome Turns East

During the Second Punic War, King Philip V of Macedonia made an alliance with Hannibal against Rome. The Romans, in turn, allied themselves with the Aetolian League of Greek city-states. The cities of the league bore the brunt of the fighting on the Greek peninsula until after the Romans had defeated Hannibal in 202 B.C.E. Then the Roman legions were deployed against Macedonian phalanxes, and the Macedonians were defeated in a series of wars. Roman

Triumphal Column of Gaius Duilius This is a replica of a monument celebrating Rome's first naval victory in the First Punic War in 260 B.C.E., a battle in which the admiral Gaius Duilius destroyed fifty Carthaginian ships. Models of the prows of the enemy ships are shown projecting from the column. The original was erected in the Roman Forum several centuries after the war to look back to earlier Roman glories, a common practice among Roman military and political leaders. (Museo della Civiltà Romana/© Vanni Archive/Art Resource, NY)

North Sea
Baltic Sea
BRITAIN
ATLANTIC OCEAN
BELGICA
GERMANY
Rhine R.
Elbe R.
Vistula R.
Dnieper R.
Don R.
BOSPORAN KINGDOM
GAUL
RAETIA
Lugdunum
ALPS
CISALPINE GAUL
Trebia 218 B.C.E.
Po R.
PANNONIA
DACIA
NARBONENSIS
Narbo
Massilia
FARTHER SPAIN
Numantia
Ebro R.
Adriatic Sea
ILLYRICUM
Danube R.
MOESIA
Black Sea
Arretium
Lake Trasimene 217 B.C.E.
Corsica
ITALY
Rome
Capua
Cannae 216 B.C.E.
Brundisium
Tarentum
MACEDONIA
THRACE
Byzantium
BITHYNIA AND PONTUS
NEARER SPAIN
Saguntum
Corduba
Balearic Is.
Sardinia
New Carthage
Gades
Gibraltar
EPIRUS
Actium
Cynoscephalae 197 B.C.E.
Pergamum
ASIA
GALATIA
CAPPADOCIA
ANATOLIA
Tigris R.
PARTHIA
Drepana 249 B.C.E.
Sicily
Messana
Syracuse
Corinth
Athens
Sparta
ACHAEA
Ephesus
PAMPHYLIA
LYCIA
CILICIA
Tarsus
Carrhae 53 B.C.E.
Antioch
Euphrates R.
MAURETANIA
Carthage
Zama 202 B.C.E.
NUMIDIA
AFRICA PROCONSULARIS
Rhodes
SYRIA
Cyprus
Damascus
Crete
Mediterranean Sea
JUDAEA
Jerusalem
NORTH AFRICA
Cyrene
CYRENAICA
Alexandria
Petra
SINAI
EGYPT
Nile R.
Red Sea
SAHARA
Roman territory in 264 B.C.E.
Roman territory added by 133 B.C.E.
Roman territory added by 44 B.C.E.
Major battle of the Punic Wars
Other major battle
0 250 500 miles
0 250 500 kilometers
50°N
40°N
30°N
0°
10°E
20°E
30°E
40°E
N
S
E
W

MAPPING THE PAST

MAP 5.2 Roman Expansion During the Republic, ca. 282–44 B.C.E.

Rome expanded in all directions, first west and then east, eventually controlling every shore of the Mediterranean.

ANALYZING THE MAP Which years saw the greatest expansion of Roman power during the republic? How might the different geographic features have helped or hindered the expansion into certain areas?

CONNECTIONS What allowed the Romans to maintain their power across such a wide and diverse area?

armies also won significant victories against the forces of the Seleucid emperors, and that empire shrank. After the Battle of Pydna in 168 B.C.E., the Romans deported the important Macedonian leaders to Rome and reshaped the Macedonian kingdom to their liking. In 148 B.C.E. they made Macedonia into a Roman province. Another decisive victory came in 146 B.C.E., when the Romans attacked the city of Corinth, which was part of another league of Greek city-states, the Achaean League. Just as they had at Carthage earlier that year, the Romans destroyed the city, looting it for treasure. In 133 B.C.E. the king of Pergamum bequeathed his kingdom to the Romans. The Ptolemies of Egypt retained formal control of their kingdom, but they obeyed Roman wishes in terms of trade policy.

The Romans had used the discord and disunity of the Hellenistic world to divide and conquer it. Once they had done so, they faced the formidable challenge of governing it without further warfare, which they met by establishing the first Roman provinces in the East. Declaring the Mediterranean *mare nostrum*, "our sea," the Romans began to create political and administrative machinery to hold the Mediterranean together under a political system of provinces ruled by governors sent from Rome. Not all Romans were joyful over Rome's conquest of the Mediterranean world; some considered the victory a misfortune. The historian Sallust (86–34 B.C.E.), writing from hindsight, complained that the acquisition of an empire was the beginning of Rome's troubles:

> But when through labor and justice our Republic grew powerful, great kings defeated in war, fierce nations and mighty peoples subdued by force, when Carthage the rival of the Roman people was wiped out root and branch, all the seas and lands lay open, then fortune began to be harsh and to throw everything into confusion. The Romans had easily borne labor, danger, uncertainty, and hardship. To them leisure, riches—otherwise desirable—proved to be burdens and torments. So at first money, then desire for power grew great. These things were a sort of cause of all evils.[5]

Roman Society

FOCUS QUESTION *How did expansion affect Roman society and culture?*

Sallust was not alone in his feelings. By the second century B.C.E. the Romans ruled much of the Mediterranean world, and tremendous wealth poured into Rome. Roman institutions, social patterns, and ways of thinking changed to meet the new era. Some looked nostalgically back at what they fondly considered the good old days and idealized the traditional agrarian and family-centered way of life. Others embraced the new urban life and eagerly accepted Greek culture.

Roman Families

The core of traditional Roman society was the family, although the word "family" (*familia*) in ancient Rome actually meant all those under the authority of a male head of household, including nonrelated slaves and servants. In poor families this group might be very small, but among the wealthy it could include hundreds of slaves and servants.

The male head of household was called the **paterfamilias**. Just as slave owners held power over their slaves, fathers held great power over their children, which technically lasted for their children's whole lives. Initially this seems to have included power over life and death, but by the second century B.C.E. that had been limited by law and custom. Fathers continued to have the power to decide how family resources should be spent, however, and sons did not inherit until after their fathers had died.

In the early republic, legal authority over a woman generally passed from her father to her husband on marriage, but the Laws of the Twelve Tables allowed it to remain with her father even after a marriage. That was advantageous to the father, and could also be to the woman, for her father might be willing to take her side in a dispute with her husband, and she could return to her birth family if there was quarreling or abuse. By the late republic more and more marriages were of this type, and during the time of the empire (27 B.C.E.–476 C.E.) almost all of them were.

In order to marry, both spouses had to be free Roman citizens. Most citizens did marry, with women of wealthy families marrying in their midteens and non-elite women in their late teens. Grooms were generally somewhat older than their brides. Marital agreements, especially among the well-to-do, were stipulated with contracts between the families involved. According to Roman law, marriage required a dowry, a payment of money, property, and/or goods that went from the bride's family to the groom. Roman law also prohibited marriages between slaves, between a slave and a free person, and initially between plebeians and patricians, although that changed in the fifth century B.C.E. (see page 129). If their owner allowed it, slaves could enter a marriage-like relationship called *contubernium*, which benefited their owner, as any children produced from it would be his. People who were not slaves or citizens certainly lived together in marriage-like relationships, but these had no standing before the law and their children could not legally inherit.

Weddings were central occasions in a family's life, with spouses chosen carefully by parents, other family members, or marriage brokers. Professional fortune-tellers were frequently consulted to determine whether a match was good or what day would be especially lucky or auspicious for a couple to marry. The ceremony typically began with the bride welcoming the groom and the wedding party to her home for a feast, and then later the whole group progressed with much noise to the groom's household. It would be very unlucky if the bride tripped while going into the house, so the groom often carried her across the doorstep. The bride's entrance into the groom's house marked the point at which the two were married. As elsewhere in the ancient world, no public officials or priests were involved.

Women could inherit and own property under Roman law, though they generally received a smaller portion of any family inheritance than their brothers did. A woman's inheritance usually came as her dowry on marriage. In the earliest Roman marriage laws, men could divorce their wives without any grounds while women could not divorce their husbands, but by the second century B.C.E. these laws had changed, and both men and women could initiate divorce. By then women

■ **paterfamilias** The oldest dominant male of the family, who held great power over the lives of family members.

A Woman's Actions in the Turia Inscription

Because they were carved in stone, most funeral inscriptions from ancient Rome are very short. One of the few surviving long inscriptions about a woman is from a tombstone from the first century B.C.E. Neither she nor her husband — the speaker in the inscription — has been identified with certainty, though she is traditionally called "Turia," and he may have been a Roman official named Quintus Lucretius Vespillo. Both of them were caught up in the unrest of the civil wars of the late republic.

You became an orphan suddenly before the day of our wedding, when both your parents were murdered together in the solitude of the countryside. It was mainly due to your efforts that the death of your parents was not left unavenged. I had left for Macedonia, and your sister's husband Cluvius had gone to the Province of Africa.

So strenuously did you perform your filial duty by your persistent demands and your pursuit of justice that we could not have done more if we had been present. But these merits you have in common with that most virtuous lady your sister.

. . . Then pressure was brought to bear on you and your sister to accept the view that your father's will, by which you and I were heirs, had been invalidated by his having contracted a [fictitious purchase] with his wife. If that was the case, then you together with all your father's property would necessarily come under the guardianship of those who pursued the matter; your sister would be left without any share at all of that inheritance. . . .

You defended our common cause by asserting the truth, namely, that the will had not in fact been broken. . . .

They gave way before your firm resolution and did not pursue the matter any further. Thus you on your own brought to a successful conclusion the defence you took up of your duty to your father, your devotion to your sister, and your faithfulness towards me. . . .

You provided abundantly for my needs during my flight [into political exile] and gave me the means for a dignified manner of living, when you took all the gold and jewellery from your own body and sent it to me and over and over again enriched me in my absence with servants, money and provisions, showing great ingenuity in deceiving the guards posted by our adversaries.

You begged for my life when I was abroad — it was your courage that urged you to this step — and because of your entreaties I was shielded by the clemency of those against whom you marshalled your words. But whatever you said was always said with undaunted courage.

Meanwhile when a troop of men collected by Milo, whose house I had acquired by purchase when he was in exile, tried to profit by the opportunities provided by the civil war and break into our house to plunder, you beat them back successfully and were able to defend our home.

EVALUATE THE EVIDENCE

1. What actions does the Roman woman in this tombstone inscription take to defend and support her family and husband?
2. How did the military campaigns and civil wars of the Roman Republic affect women's lives, and how did they shape what were regarded as admirable qualities in Roman women?

Source: Mary R. Lefkowitz and Maureen B. Fant, eds., *Women's Life in Greece and Rome: A Source Book in Translation*, Second Edition, pp. 135–137. © 1982, 1992 M. B. Fant and M. R. Lefkowitz. Reprinted with permission of The Johns Hopkins University Press and Bloomsbury Publishing Plc.

had also gained greater control over their dowries and other family property, perhaps because Rome's military conquests meant that many husbands were away for long periods of time and women needed some say over family finances. (See "Evaluating the Evidence 5.2: A Woman's Actions in the Turia Inscription," above.)

Although marriages were arranged by families primarily for the handing down of property to legitimate children, the Romans, somewhat contradictorily, viewed the model marriage as one in which husbands and wives were loyal to one another and shared interests and activities. The Romans praised women, like Lucretia of old, who were virtuous and loyal to their husbands and devoted to their children. Such praises emerge in literature, and also in epitaphs on tombstones, such as this one from around 130 B.C.E.:

Stranger, my message is short. Stand by and read it through. Here is the unlovely tomb of a lovely woman. Her parents called her Claudia by name. She loved her husband with all her heart. She bore two sons; of these she leaves one on earth; under the earth she has placed the other. She was charming in converse, yet gentle in bearing. She kept house, she made wool. That's my last word. Go your way.[6]

Household Shrine to the Gods and Ancestors Two protector deities (lares), each holding a container for liquid, flank an ancestor-spirit (which the Romans called the "genius"), his head covered as a sign of reverence, who holds a box for incense and bowl for offerings. At the bottom a snake, symbol of fertility and prosperity, approaches an altar. This elaborate shrine in the entryway of the house of two wealthy freedmen in Pompeii was a symbol of their prosperity and upward mobility, but even poor families had a designated space for protective lares figures. (House of the Vettii, Pompeii, Italy/Werner Forman Archive/Bridgeman Images)

Traditionally minded Romans thought that mothers should nurse their own children and personally see to their welfare. Non-elite Roman women did nurse their own children, although wealthy women increasingly employed slaves as wet nurses and to help them raise the children. Very young children were under their mother's care, and most children learned the skills they needed from their own parents. For children from wealthier urban families, opportunities for formal education increased in the late republic. Boys and girls might be educated in their homes by tutors, who were often Greek slaves, and boys also might go to a school, paid for by their parents.

Most people in the expanding Roman Republic lived in the countryside. Farmers used oxen and donkeys to plow their fields, collecting the dung of the animals for fertilizer. Besides spreading manure, some farmers fertilized their fields by planting lupines and beans and plowing them under when they began to pod. Forage crops for animals to eat included clover, vetch, and alfalfa. Along with crops raised for local consumption and to pay their rents and taxes, many farmers raised crops to be sold. These included wheat, flax for making linen cloth, olives, and wine grapes.

Most Romans worked long days, and an influx of slaves from Rome's wars and conquests provided additional labor for the fields, mines, and cities. To the Romans, slavery was a misfortune that befell some people, but it did not entail any racial theories. Slave boys and girls were occasionally formally apprenticed in trades such as leatherworking, weaving, or metalworking. Well-educated slaves served as tutors or accountants, ran schools, and designed and made artwork and buildings. For loyal slaves the Romans always held out the possibility of freedom, and **manumission**, the freeing of individual slaves by their masters, was fairly common, especially for household slaves. Nonetheless, slaves rebelled from time to time, sometimes in large-scale revolts put down by Roman armies (see page 144).

Membership in a family did not end with death, as the spirits of the family's ancestors were understood to remain with the family. They and other gods regarded as protectors of the household—collectively these were called the *lares* and *penates*—were represented by small statues that stood in a special cupboard or a niche in the wall. The statues were taken out at meals and given small bits of food, or food was thrown into the household's hearth for them. The lares and penates represented the gods at family celebrations such as weddings, and families took the statues with them when they moved. They were honored in special rituals

■ **manumission** The freeing of individual slaves by their masters.

and ceremonies, although the later Roman poet Ovid (43 B.C.E.–17 C.E.) commented that these did not have to be elaborate:

> The spirits of the dead ask for little.
> They are more grateful for piety than for an
>   expensive gift—
> Not greedy are the gods who haunt the Styx [the
>   river that bordered the underworld] below.
> A rooftile covered with a sacrificial crown,
> Scattered kernels, a few grains of salt,
> Bread dipped in wine, and loose violets—
> These are enough.[7]

Greek Influence on Roman Culture

Many aspects of life did not change greatly during the Roman expansion. Most people continued to marry and form families, and to live in the countryside with the rhythm of their days and years determined by the needs of their crops. But with the conquest of the Mediterranean world, Rome became a great city, and many other cities emerged as well. The spoils of war

went to build theaters, stadiums, and other places of amusement. Romans and Italian townspeople began to spend more of their time in leisure pursuits.

This new urban culture reflected Hellenistic influences. Romans developed a liking for Greek literature, and it became common for an educated Roman to speak both Latin and Greek. The poet Horace (64–8 B.C.E.) summed it up well: "Captive Greece captured her rough conqueror and introduced the arts into rustic Latium."[8]

The new Hellenism profoundly stimulated the growth and development of Roman art and literature. The Roman conquest of the Hellenistic East resulted in wholesale confiscation of Greek paintings and sculpture to grace Roman temples, public buildings, and private homes. Roman artists copied many aspects of Greek art, but used art, especially portraiture, to communicate Roman values. Portrait busts in stone were a favored art form. Those who commissioned them wanted to be portrayed as individuals, but also as representing certain admirable qualities, such as wisdom or dignity.

In literature the Greek influence was also strong. Roman authors sometimes wrote histories and poetry in Greek, or translated Greek classics into Latin. The

Roman Bath   This Roman bath in Bath, England (a city to which it gave its name), was built beginning in the first century C.E. around a natural hot spring. The Romans spread the custom of bathing, which they had adopted from the Greeks, to the outer reaches of their empire. In addition to hot water, bathers used oil for massage and metal scrapers (inset) to clean and exfoliate their skin. Many Roman artifacts have been unearthed at Bath, including a number of curse tablets, small tablets made of lead calling on the gods to harm someone, which were common in the Greco-Roman world. Not surprisingly, many of the curse tablets found at Bath relate to the theft of clothing while people were bathing. (bath: Photo © Neil Holmes/Bridgeman Images; artifact: © The Trustees of the British Museum/Art Resource, NY)

poet Ennius (EHN-ee-uhs) (239–169 B.C.E.), the father of Latin poetry, studied Greek philosophy, wrote comedies in Latin, and adapted many of Euripides's tragedies for the Roman stage. Plautus (ca. 254–184 B.C.E.) brought a bawdy humor to his reworkings of Greek plays. The Roman dramatist Terence (ca. 195–159 B.C.E.), a follower of Scipio, wrote comedies of refinement and grace that owed their essentials to Greek models. All early Roman literature was derived from that of the Greeks, but it flourished because it also spoke to Roman ways of thinking.

The conquest of the Mediterranean world and the wealth it brought gave the Romans leisure, and Hellenism influenced how they spent their free time. Many rich urban dwellers changed their eating habits by consuming elaborate meals of exotic dishes. (See "Living in the Past: Roman Table Manners," page 138.) During the second century B.C.E. the Greek custom of bathing also gained popularity in the Roman world. In the early republic Romans had bathed infrequently, especially in the winter. Increasingly Romans built large public buildings containing pools and exercise rooms, and by the period of the early empire baths had become an essential part of any Roman city. Architects built intricate systems of aqueducts to supply the bathing establishments with water. The baths contained hot-air rooms to induce a good sweat and pools of hot and cold water to finish the actual bathing.

Conservative Romans railed against this Greek custom, calling it a waste of time and an encouragement to idleness and immorality. They were correct in that bathing establishments were more than just places to take a bath. They came to include gymnasia where men exercised and played ball, snack bars where people dined and chatted, and even libraries and lecture halls. Women also had opportunities to bathe, generally in separate facilities or at separate times.

The baths were socially important places where men and women went to see and be seen. Social climbers tried to talk to the right people and wangle invitations to dinner; politicians took advantage of the occasion to discuss the affairs of the day; marriages were negotiated by wealthy fathers. Baths were also places where people could buy sex, as the women and men who worked in bathhouses often made extra income through prostitution. Because of this, moralists portrayed them as dens of iniquity, but they were seen by most Romans as a normal part of urban life.

Opposing Views: Cato the Elder and Scipio Aemilianus

In addition to disagreeing over public baths, Romans differed greatly in their opinions about Hellenism and other new social customs. Two men, Marcus Cato (234–149 B.C.E.) and Scipio Aemilianus (185–129 B.C.E.), both of whom were military commanders and consuls, the highest office in the Roman Republic, can serve as representatives of these opposing views.

Marcus Cato, called Cato the Elder, was a plebeian and owned a small rural estate, but his talent caught the eye of high patrician officials and he became their client. He fought in the Second Punic War under Scipio Africanus and then returned to Rome, where he worked his way up through various offices. In 195 B.C.E. he was elected consul. A key issue facing Cato was the heated debate over the repeal of the Oppian Law, which had been passed twenty years earlier, right after Rome's disastrous loss to Carthage at the Battle of Cannae. Rome needed money to continue the war, and the law decreed that no woman was to own more than a small amount of gold, or wear clothing trimmed in purple, or drive a chariot in the city of Rome itself. These were all proclaimed to be luxuries that wasted money and undermined the war effort. The law was passed in part for financial reasons, but also had gendered social implications, as there was no corresponding law limiting men's conspicuous consumption. By 195 B.C.E. the war was over and this restriction on women's spending had lost its economic rationale. Roman women publicly protested against it, and Cato led the battle to prevent its repeal. He declared that women were like animals and would engage in an orgy of shopping if the law were lifted, and that Roman society would be destroyed by women's spending. The women's actions were more effective than Cato's speeches, however, and the law was lifted, although later in his political career Cato pushed for other laws forbidding women from wearing fancy clothing or owning property.

Women's spending was not the only problem destroying Roman society, according to Cato. Although he made certain his older son learned Greek as an essential tool in Roman society, he instructed the boy not to take Greek ideas too seriously and viewed the influx of Greek culture in general as dangerous. Cato set himself up as the defender of what he saw as traditional Roman values: discipline, order, morality, frugality, and an agrarian way of life. He even criticized his superior Scipio Africanus for being too lenient toward his troops and spending too much money. Cato proclaimed his views in speeches at the Senate, through his decisions when acting as a military commander, and also in his written works, which were all in Latin. His only work to survive in its entirety is a manual for running large agricultural estates written for the absentee landowners who were becoming more common. In this he advises the adoption of any measures that would increase efficiency and profitability, including selling off old or sickly slaves as soon as possible.

LIVING IN THE PAST
Roman Table Manners

Until the late republic most Romans, rich and poor, ate the same plain meals of bread, olives, vegetables, and a little meat or fish, with fruit for dessert. They used fingers and wooden spoons to serve themselves from simple pottery or wooden bowls and plates. They usually drank water or wine mixed with water from clay cups. Drinking unmixed wine was considered a sign of degeneracy. The Romans took three meals a day: an early breakfast, a main meal or dinner in the middle of the day, and a light supper in the evening. Dinner was also a social event, the main time for Romans to visit, chat, and exchange news. Afterward everyone who could afford the time took a long nap, especially during the hot summer months.

The conquest of the Mediterranean world and the spread of Hellenism changed Roman table manners. As many urban dwellers grew richer and more sophisticated, they began to dine more elegantly. By the late republic and early empire, Romans dined formally on couches around a circular table. Tableware became more varied and refined. Metal spoons took the place of wooden ones, and silver and bronze platters took the place of pottery. In the early first century B.C.E. artisans in Syria developed glassblowing, a technique they took to Rome when Syria was conquered by the Romans in 64 B.C.E. Glassblowing revolutionized glass production, and glass drinking cups could soon be seen on nearly every Roman

This simple pottery plate was made in the mid-first century C.E. but is similar to the standard tableware of the early republic. (Terracotta marbled slipware bowl made by the potter Castus of southern Gaul/Image copyright © The Metropolitan Museum of Art, New York, New York, USA/Image source: Art Resource, NY)

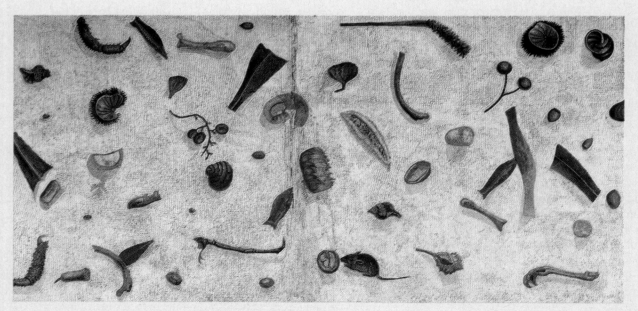

This mosaic from the floor of a second-century-C.E. villa whimsically suggests what a dining room floor looked like after a lavish dinner and also tells us something about the menu. (Asarotos Oikos, "Unswept Room" from Vigna Lupi, Rome/Vatican Museums and Galleries, Vatican State/De Agostini Picture Library/V. Pirozzi/Bridgeman Images)

table. Dinner was now served in three courses. It began with an appetizer, ordinarily composed of vegetables and eggs. Next came the main course of young goat, chicken, pork, or fish, which was followed by a dessert of fruit, including new varieties from the provinces.

For the richest Romans, dinners consisted of many courses of exotic dishes such as the livers of rare fish, the brains and tongues of flamingos and pheasants mixed in sauce, and seafood of every description. The more outlandish the dish, the more the wealthy Romans appreciated it. Nuts and berries completed the meal, which the Romans washed down with vintage wines drawn from all over the empire. All of the scraps ended up on the floor.

QUESTIONS FOR ANALYSIS

1. What social purposes did the elaborate meals of wealthy Romans in the late republic serve?
2. How are changes in Roman eating habits, as described here and reflected in the two pieces of tableware, symptomatic of social and cultural changes in the late republic? What do you imagine Cato the Elder would have said about the fancy glass and the mosaic floor?

A glass drinking cup from the first century C.E., made by blowing hot glass into a reusable carved mold and then removing it to smooth the lip and base. (© The Trustees of the British Museum/Art Resource, NY)

Cato held the office of censor, and he attempted to remove from the lists of possible officeholders anyone who did not live up to his standards. Late in life he was a diplomat to Carthage, and after seeing that the city had recovered economically from the war with Rome, he came home declaring, "Carthage must be destroyed." He repeated this often enough that shortly after his death the Romans decided to do just this in the Third Punic War.

Ironically, the mission to Carthage was led by Scipio Aemilianus, the grandson of Scipio Africanus and an avid devotee of Hellenism. Like his grandfather, Scipio believed that broader views had to replace the old Roman narrowness. Rome was no longer a small city on the Tiber; it was the capital of the world, and Romans had to adapt themselves to that fact. Scipio became an innovator in both politics and culture. He developed a more personal style of politics that looked unflinchingly at the broader problems that the success of Rome brought to its people. He embraced Hellenism wholeheartedly. Perhaps more than anyone else of his day, Scipio represented the new Roman—imperial, cultured, and independent.

In his education and interests, too, Scipio broke with the past. As a boy he had received the traditional Roman training, learning to read and write Latin and becoming acquainted with the law. He mastered the fundamentals of rhetoric and learned how to throw the javelin, fight in armor, and ride a horse. But as a young man he formed a lasting friendship with the historian Polybius, who after being brought to Rome as a war hostage was his tutor. Polybius actively encouraged him in his study of Greek and in his intellectual pursuits. In later life Scipio's love of Greek learning, rhetoric, and philosophy became legendary. Scipio also promoted the spread of Hellenism in Roman society, and his views became more widespread than those of Cato. In general, Rome absorbed and added what it found useful from Hellenism, just as earlier it had absorbed aspects of Etruscan culture.

The Late Republic

FOCUS QUESTION *What led to the fall of the Roman Republic?*

The wars of conquest created serious problems for the Romans. The republican constitution had suited the needs of a simple city-state but was inadequate to meet the requirements of Rome's new position in international affairs. New armies had to be provided for defense, and systems of administration and tax collection had to be created to support the republic. Moreover, the people of the Roman Republic came away from the war with differing needs and expectations. Roman generals, who had commanded huge numbers of troops for long periods of time, acquired great power and ambition and were becoming too mighty for the state to control. At the same time, non-Roman inhabitants of Italy who had fought in the wars of expansion began to agitate for full Roman citizenship, including the right to vote. Some individuals, including military contractors, profited greatly from the foreign wars, while average soldiers gained little.

These problems, complex and explosive, largely account for the turmoil of the late republic (133–27 B.C.E.). This era produced some of Rome's most famous figures: the Gracchi brothers, Marius, Sulla, Cicero, Crassus, Pompey, and Julius Caesar, among others.

Reforms for Poor and Landless Citizens

Hannibal's operations and the warfare in Italy had left the countryside a shambles. The prolonged fighting had also drawn untold numbers of Roman and Italian men away from their farms for long periods. Conscripted legionaries were required to serve in their units until a military campaign was over, which might be many years. Women often ran the farms in their absence, but with so many men away fighting they did not have enough workers to keep the land under full cultivation. When the legionaries returned to their farms in Italy, they encountered an appalling situation. All too often their farms looked like those they had destroyed in their wars of conquest: land was untilled, buildings were falling down, and animals were wandering.

The wars of conquest had also made some men astoundingly rich, and the newly wealthy invested their money in land. Land won by conquest was generally declared public land, and although officially there was a limit on how much public land one individual could hold, this law was often ignored. Wealthy people rented public land—though rents were frequently not

collected—and bought up small farms, often at very low prices, to create huge estates, which the Romans called **latifundia** (lah-tuh-FUHN-dee-uh). The owners of the latifundia occasionally hired free men as day laborers, but they preferred to use slaves, who could not strike or be drafted into the army. Using slave labor, and farming on a large scale, owners of latifundia could raise crops at a lower cost than could small farmers.

Confronted by these conditions, veterans and their families took what they could get for their broken and bankrupt farms and tried their luck elsewhere. Sometimes large landowners simply appropriated public land and the small farms of former soldiers, and there was little that veterans could do about it. Gradually agriculture in Italy was transformed from subsistence farming to an important source of income for the Roman ruling class.

Most veterans migrated to the cities, especially to Rome. Although some found work, most did not. Industry and small manufacturing were generally in the hands of slaves, and even when work was available, slave labor kept the wages of free men low. Instead of a new start, veterans and their families encountered slum-like living conditions and continued dependency on others. If they were Roman citizens, they could vote in citizens' assemblies, however, and tended to back anyone who offered them better prospects.

Growing numbers of landless citizens held ominous consequences for the strength of Rome's armies. The Romans had always believed that only landowners should serve in the army, for only they had something to fight for. Landless men, even if they were Romans and lived in Rome, could not be conscripted into the army. These landless men may have been veterans of major battles and numerous campaigns, but once they lost their land, they became ineligible for further military service. The landless ex-legionaries wanted to be able to serve in the army again, and they were willing to support any leader who would allow them to.

Coin Showing a Voter   This coin from 63 B.C.E. shows a citizen wearing a toga dropping a voting tablet into a voting urn, the Roman equivalent of today's ballot box. The tablet has a *V* on it, meaning a yes vote, and the coin has an inscription giving the name of the moneyer, the official who controlled the production of coins and decided what would be shown on them. Here the moneyer, Lucius Cassius Longinus, depicted a vote held fifty years earlier regarding whether an ancestor of his should be named prosecutor in a trial charging three vestal virgins with unchastity. As was common among moneyers, Longinus chose this image as a means to advance his political career, in this case by suggesting his family's long history of public office. (Bibliothèque Nationale de France [BnF]/Snark/Art Resource, NY)

One man who recognized the plight of Rome's veterans, peasant farmers, and urban poor was the aristocratic military leader Tiberius Gracchus (tigh-BEER-ee-uhs GRAK-uhs) (163–133 B.C.E.). After his election as tribune in 133 B.C.E., Tiberius proposed reforms that would help make land ownership more equitable. (See "Thinking Like a Historian: Land Ownership and Social Conflict in the Late Republic," page 142.) Although his reforms enjoyed the support of some distinguished and popular members of the Senate, they angered those who had usurped large tracts of public land for their own use, who bitterly resisted Tiberius's efforts. This was to be expected, yet he unquestionably made additional problems for himself by making decisions and taking actions in ways that, while within his rights as a tribune, were unprecedented.

Many powerful Romans became suspicious of Tiberius's growing influence with the people. Some considered him a tyrant, a concept that came from the Greeks for someone who gained power outside the normal structures and against the traditional ruling class. When he sought to be re-elected as tribune, riots erupted among his opponents and supporters, and a group of senators beat Tiberius to death in cold blood. Thus some of the very people who directed the affairs of state and administered the law had taken the law into their own hands. The death of Tiberius was the beginning of an era of political violence.

Although Tiberius was dead, his land bill was law. Furthermore, Tiberius's brother Gaius Gracchus (153–121 B.C.E.) took up the cause of reform. Gaius (GAY-uhs) was a veteran soldier with an enviable record, and when he became tribune he demanded even more extensive reform than had his brother. To help the urban poor, Gaius pushed legislation to provide them with cheap grain for bread. He defended his brother's land law and proposed that Rome send many of its poor and propertyless people out to form colonies, including one on the site where Carthage had once stood. The prospect of new homes, land, and a fresh start gave the urban poor new hope and made Gaius popular among them.

Like his brother Tiberius, Gaius aroused a great deal of personal and factional opposition. When Gaius failed in 121 B.C.E. to win the tribunate for the third time, he feared for his life. In desperation he armed his staunchest supporters, whereupon the Senate ordered the consul to restore order. Gaius was killed, and many of his supporters died in the turmoil.

Political Violence

The death of Gaius brought little peace, and trouble came from two sources: the outbreak of new wars in the Mediterranean basin and further political unrest in Rome. In 112 B.C.E. Rome declared war against the re-bellious Jugurtha (joo-GUHR-thuh), king of Numidia in North Africa. Numidia had been one of Rome's client kingdoms, a kingdom still ruled by its own king but subject to Rome. Client kingdoms followed Rome's lead in foreign affairs but conducted their own internal business according to their own laws and customs. The benefits of these relationships were mutual, for the client kingdoms enjoyed the protection of Rome while defending Rome's borders, but they were not relationships between equals: Rome always remained the senior partner. In time many of these states became provinces of the Roman Empire (see Chapters 6 and 7).

The Roman legions made little headway against Jugurtha until 107 B.C.E., when Gaius Marius (MEHR-ee-uhs), a politician not from the traditional Roman aristocracy, became consul and led troops to Numidia. A man of fierce vigor and courage, Marius saw the army as the tool of his ambition. He took the unusual but not wholly unprecedented step of recruiting an army by permitting landless men to serve in the legions, thus tapping Rome's vast reservoir of poor citizens; the state provided them with weapons and armor and promised them pay. Marius was unable to defeat Jugurtha directly, but his assistant, Sulla, bribed Jugurtha's father-in-law to betray him, and Jugurtha was captured and later executed in Rome. Marius later claimed this as a victory.

Fighting was also going on at Rome's northern border, where two German peoples, the Cimbri and Teutones, were moving into Gaul and later into northern Italy. After the Germans had defeated Roman armies sent to repel them, the Senate sent Marius to lead the campaign against them. Before engaging the Germans, Marius encouraged enlistments by promising his volunteers land after the war. Poor and landless citizens flocked to him. Marius and his army conquered the Germans, but when Marius proposed a bill to grant land to his troops once they had retired from military service, the Senate refused to act, in effect turning its back on the soldiers of Rome. It was a disastrous mistake. Henceforth the legionaries expected their commanders—not the Senate or the state—to protect their interests, and the Roman army gradually changed from an army of citizen conscripts into an army of paid soldiers.

Rome was dividing into two political factions, both of whom wanted political power. The *populares* attempted to increase their power through the plebeian assembly and the power of the tribunes, while the *optimates* employed the traditional means of patron-client relationships and working primarily through the Senate. Both of these factions were represented in the Senate, and both had their favored general. Marius was the general backed by the populares, who from 104 B.C.E. to 100 B.C.E. elected him consul every year, although this was technically illegal and put unprecedented power into a Roman military commander's hands.

■ latifundia Huge agricultural estates owned by wealthy absentee landowners and worked by slaves.

Land Ownership and Social Conflict in the Late Republic

The increasing concentration of land ownership was a serious social problem and a hot-button political issue in the late republic. Traditionally only landowners could be conscripted into the army, and as families lost their property to wealthy absentee owners, the number of possible soldiers declined and many impoverished landless people flocked to the city of Rome. How did political leaders of the late republic seek to solve the problem, and why were their measures unsuccessful?

1 **Speech by Tiberius Gracchus.** The general and tribune Tiberius Gracchus gave an eloquent public speech outlining the problem in 133 B.C.E., as related by the later Roman biographer Plutarch.

He took his place and spoke on behalf of the poor. "The wild beasts that roam over Italy have their dens, each has a place of repose and refuge. But the men who fight and die for Italy enjoy nothing but the air and light. Without house or home they wander about with their wives and children. Their commanders lie when they exhort the soldiers in their battles to defend sepulchres and shrines from the enemy, for not one of these many Romans has either hereditary altar or ancestral tomb; they fight and die to protect the wealth and luxury of others; they are styled masters of the world, and have not a single clod of earth they can call their own." About this time King Attalus Philometor [of Pergamum] died, and Eudemus of Pergamum brought to Rome his last will, in which the Roman people was named the king's heir. Tiberius proposed a law of popular appeal providing that the king's money, when brought to Rome, should be distributed among those of the citizens receiving allotments of public land, to provide them with equipment and give them a start in farming. As for cities that were in the kingdom of King Attalus, he declared that the disposal of them was not the senate's business, but that he himself would put a resolution before the people. By this he offended the senate more than ever.

2 **Reforms proposed by Tiberius Gracchus.** Along with the small allotments of land for veterans paid for by King Attalus's money, Tiberius Gracchus proposed other measures, as reported by the Roman historian Appian.

After speaking thus he again brought forward the existing law providing that nobody should hold more than 500 *iugera* [about 300 acres] of public domain. But he added a provision to the former law that two sons of the occupiers might each hold one half of that amount [in addition to that held by their father] and that the remainder should be divided among the poor. This was extremely disturbing to the rich because . . . they could no longer disregard the law as they had done before. . . . They collected together in groups, and made lamentation, and accused the poor of appropriating their fields of long standing, their vineyards, and their buildings. Some said they had paid the price of the land to their neighbors. Were they to lose the money with the land? . . . Others said that their wives' dowries had been expended on these estates, or that the land had been give to their own daughters as dowry. Moneylenders could show loans made on their security. All kinds of wailing and expressions of indignation were heard at once. On the other side were heard the lamentations of the poor — that they were being reduced from competence to extreme poverty, because they were unable to rear their offspring. They recounted the military services they had rendered, by which this very land had been acquired, and were angry that they should be robbed of their share of the common property. [The law was passed through procedures that many senators regarded as illegal.] Gracchus, immensely popular by reason of the law, was escorted home by the multitude as though he were the founder, not of a single city or people, but of all the nations of

ANALYZING THE EVIDENCE

1. In Sources 1–3, what measures do Tiberius and Gaius Gracchus propose to create a more equitable distribution of land? What values seem to underlie these measures?
2. Who opposes these reforms, and why? What values underlie their opposition?
3. In Source 4, how does the Senate seek to prevent reforms like those of the Gracchi from happening again?
4. In Source 5, what does the Flavian Bill propose, and why does the Senate oppose it? How and why is Cicero attempting to play both sides of the issue?
5. These sources stretch over more than seventy years. Why do you think this issue persisted over this long period?

Italy.... The defeated ones remained in the city and talked the matter over, feeling aggrieved and saying that as soon as Gracchus should become a private citizen he would be sorry that he had done outrage to the sacred and inviolable office of tribune, and had sown in Italy so many seeds of future strife.

3 The reforms of Gaius Gracchus. Tiberius Gracchus was assassinated by a group of senators, but his brother Gaius became tribune and continued reforms, as related by Plutarch.

Of the laws which he now proposed with the object of gratifying the people and destroying the power of the senate, the first concerned public lands, which were to be divided among the poor citizens; another provided that common soldiers were to be clothed at public expense without any reduction in pay, and that no one under seventeen years of age should be conscripted into military service; another concerned the allies, giving the Italians equal suffrage rights with the citizens of Rome; a fourth related to grain, lowering the market price for the poor; a fifth, dealing with the courts of justice, was the greatest blow to the power of the senators, for hitherto they alone could sit on juries, and were therefore much feared by the plebs and *equites* [wealthy commoners].... He also proposed measures for sending out colonies, for constructing roads, and for building public granaries.

4 The Agrarian Law of 111 B.C.E. After Gaius Gracchus was killed by his opponents in 121 B.C.E., the Senate passed several laws overturning the Gracchan reforms.

With respect to the public land belonging to the Roman people within Italy... whatever portion of such public land or ground within Italy, or outside the city of Rome, or in a city, town, or village a land commissioner has granted or assigned and any individual shall hold or possess at the time when this measure becomes law... excluding such land or ground specially excepted as aforesaid, shall be private land, and for all such land, ground, or buildings there shall be the same right of purchase or sale as for other private lands, grounds, or buildings.... Nor shall any person take steps whereby an individual who rightfully holds or shall hold the said land, ground, or building in accordance with the law or plebiscite shall be prevented from using, enjoying, holding, or possessing the said land, ground, or building... nor shall any person make a proposal to that effect in the senate.

5 Cicero discusses the Flavian Bill, 60 B.C.E. After the law of 111 B.C.E. made almost all land in Italy private property, land for soldiers or veterans could only be found by turning to the newly conquered provinces or by using state funds to buy private land in Italy to distribute to them. In a private letter, Cicero (see page 146) discusses a bill to do this.

[The bill proposed] that land be purchased with the windfall which will come in from the new foreign revenues in the next five years. The senate was opposed to this whole agrarian scheme, suspecting that Pompey was aimed at getting some new powers. Pompey set his heart on carrying the law through. I, with the full approval of the applicants for land, was for confirming the holdings of all private persons—for, as you know, our strength lies in the rich landed gentry; at the same time I satisfied Pompey and the populace—which I also wanted to do—by supporting the purchase of land, thinking that if it were faithfully carried out, the dregs of the city population could be drained off and the deserted parts of Italy peopled.

PUTTING IT ALL TOGETHER

Using the sources above, along with what you have learned in class and in this chapter, write a short essay that analyzes land reform and social conflict in the later Roman Republic. How did political leaders of the late republic seek to solve the problem of increasing landlessness and a concentration of wealth, and why were their measures unsuccessful? How did this issue play into the power struggle between the Senate and charismatic military leaders during this period?

Sources: (1) Plutarch, *Life of Tiberius Gracchus*, 4.1–2; (2) Appian, *Civil Wars*, 1.i.9–2.16. Loeb Classical Library. Cambridge, Mass.: Harvard University Press. Loeb Classical Library® is a registered trademark of the President and Fellows of Harvard College.; (3) Plutarch, *Life of Gaius Gracchus*, 3–9; (4) The Agrarian Law of 111 B.C., *Corpus Inscriptionum Latinarum*, 2d ed., vol. 1 (Berlin, 1865–), no. 585; (5) Cicero, *Letters to Atticus*, book 1, no. 29. Loeb Classical Library. Cambridge, Mass.: Harvard University Press. Loeb Classical Library® is a registered trademark of the President and Fellows of Harvard College.

Turmoil in the Late Republic

107 B.C.E.	Marius, with the aid of Sulla, defeats Jugurtha
104–100 B.C.E.	Marius, backed by populares, is elected consul
90 B.C.E.	Social War
88 B.C.E.	Sulla, backed by optimates, is elected consul
86 B.C.E.	Marius leads his own troops into Rome, killing Sulla's supporters and seizing consulship
81 B.C.E.	Sulla is elected dictator
79 B.C.E.	Sulla abdicates
73–71 B.C.E.	Spartacus leads major slave revolt
70 B.C.E.	Pompey and Crassus are elected consuls
60 B.C.E.	Pompey, Crassus, and Caesar form the First Triumvirate; Caesar is elected consul
49 B.C.E.	Caesar crosses the Rubicon and takes Rome
48 B.C.E.	Caesar defeats Pompey at the Battle of Pharsalus
44 B.C.E.	Caesar is killed by a group of senators

of his opponents. He then attempted to turn back the clock, returning all power to the Senate and restoring the conservative constitution as it had been before the Gracchan reforms. In 81 B.C.E. he was granted the office of dictator and, in sharp contrast to Cincinnatus, used his position as a tool to gain personal power. Dictators were supposed to step down after six months—and many had done so in Roman history—but Sulla held this position for two years. In 79 B.C.E. Sulla abdicated his dictatorship because he was ill and believed his policies would last. Yet civil war was to be the constant lot of Rome for the next forty-eight years, and Sulla's abuse of political office became the blueprint for later leaders.

The favored general of the optimates was Sulla, who had earlier been Marius's assistant. In 90 B.C.E. many Roman allies in the Italian peninsula rose up against Rome because they were expected to pay taxes and serve in the army, but they had no voice in political decisions because they were not full citizens. This revolt became known as the Social War, so named from the Latin word *socius*, or "ally." Sulla's armies gained a number of victories over the Italian allies, and Sulla gained prestige through his success in fighting them. In the end, however, the Senate agreed to give many allies Roman citizenship in order to end the fighting.

Sulla's military victories led to his election as consul in 88 B.C.E., and he was given command of the Roman army in a campaign against Mithridates, the king of a state that had gained power and territory in what is now northern Turkey and was expanding into Greece. Before he could depart, however, the populares gained the upper hand in the assembly, revoked his consulship, and made Marius the commander of the troops against Mithridates. Riots broke out. Sulla fled the city and returned at the head of an army, an unprecedented move by a Roman general. He quelled the riots, put down his opponents, made some political changes that reduced the power of the assembly, and left again, this time to fight Mithridates.

Sulla's forces were relatively successful against Mithridates, but meanwhile Marius led his own troops into Rome in 86 B.C.E., undid Sulla's changes, and killed many of his supporters. Although Marius died shortly after his return to power, the populares who supported him continued to hold Rome. Sulla returned in 83 B.C.E., and after a brief but intense civil war he entered Rome and ordered a ruthless butchery

Civil War

The history of the late republic is the story of power struggles among many famous Roman figures against a background of unrest at home and military campaigns abroad. This led to a series of bloody civil wars that raged from Spain across northern Africa to Egypt.

Sulla's political heirs were Pompey, Crassus, and Julius Caesar, all of them able military leaders and brilliant politicians. Pompey (106–48 B.C.E.) began a meteoric rise to power as a successful commander of troops for Sulla against Marius in Italy, Sicily, and Africa. He then suppressed a rebellion in Spain, led naval forces against pirates in the Mediterranean, and in 67 B.C.E. was sent by the Senate to command Roman forces in the East. He defeated Mithridates and the forces of other rulers as well, transforming their territories into Roman provinces and providing wealth for the Roman treasury. (See "Thinking Like a Historian: Land Ownership and Social Conflict in the Late Republic," page 142.)

Crassus (ca. 115–53 B.C.E.) also began his military career under Sulla and became the wealthiest man in Rome through buying and selling land. In 73 B.C.E. a major slave revolt broke out in Italy, led by Spartacus, a former gladiator. The slave armies, which eventually numbered in the tens of thousands, defeated several Roman units sent to quash them. Finally Crassus led a large army against them and put down the revolt. Spartacus was apparently killed on the battlefield, and the slaves who were captured were crucified, with thousands of crosses lining the main road to Rome.

Pompey and Crassus then made an informal agreement with the populares in the Senate. Both were elected consuls in 70 B.C.E. and began to dismantle

Sulla's constitution and initiate economic and political reforms once again. They and the Senate moved too slowly for some people, however, who planned an uprising. This plot was discovered, and the forces of the rebels were put down in 63 B.C.E. by an army sent by Cicero (106–43 B.C.E.), a leader of the optimates who was consul at the time. The rebellion and Cicero's skillful handling of it discredited the populares.

The man who cast the longest shadow over these troubled years was Julius Caesar (100–44 B.C.E.). Born of a noble family, he received an excellent education, which he furthered by studying in Greece with some of the most eminent teachers of the day. He had serious intellectual interests and immense literary ability. His account of his military operations in Gaul (present-day France), the *Commentaries on the Gallic Wars*, became a classic of Western literature. Caesar was a superb orator, and his personality and wit made him popular. Military service was an effective stepping-stone to politics, and Caesar was a military genius who knew how to win battles and turn victories into permanent gains. He was also a shrewd politician of unbridled ambition, who knew how to use the patron-client system to his advantage. He became a protégé of Crassus, who provided cash for Caesar's needs, and at the same time helped the careers of other politicians, who in turn looked to Caesar's interests in Rome when he was away from the city. Caesar launched his military career in Spain, where his courage won the respect and affection of his troops.

In 60 B.C.E. Caesar returned to Rome from Spain and Pompey returned from military victories in the east. Together with Crassus, the three concluded an informal political alliance later termed the **First Triumvirate** (trigh-UHM-veh-ruht), in which they agreed to advance one another's interests. Crassus's money helped Caesar be elected consul, and Pompey married Caesar's daughter Julia. Crassus was appointed governor of Syria, Pompey of Hispania (present-day Spain), and Caesar of Gaul.

Personal ambitions undermined the First Triumvirate. While Caesar was away from Rome fighting in Gaul, his supporters formed gangs that attacked the supporters of Pompey. These were countered by supporters of Pompey, and there were riots in the streets of Rome. The First Triumvirate disintegrated. Crassus died in battle while trying to conquer Parthia, and Caesar and Pompey accused each other of treachery. Fearful of Caesar's popularity and growing power, the Senate sided with Pompey and ordered Caesar to disband his army. He refused, and instead in 49 B.C.E. he crossed the Rubicon River in northern Italy—the boundary of his territorial command—with soldiers. ("Crossing the Rubicon" is still used as an expression for committing to an irreversible course of action.) Although their forces outnumbered Caesar's, Pompey and the Senate fled Rome, and Caesar entered the city without a fight.

Julius Caesar In this bust from the first century B.C.E., the sculptor portrays Caesar as a man of power and intensity. Showing individuals as representing certain virtues was common in Roman portraiture. (Museo e Gallerie Nazionali di Capodimonte, Naples, Italy/The Bridgeman Images)

Caesar then led his army against those loyal to Pompey and the Senate in Spain and Greece. In 48 B.C.E., despite being outnumbered, he defeated Pompey and his army at the Battle of Pharsalus in central Greece. Pompey fled to Egypt, which was embroiled in a battle for control not between two generals, but between a brother and sister, Ptolemy XIII and Cleopatra VII (69–30 B.C.E.). Caesar followed Pompey to Egypt, Cleopatra allied herself with Caesar, and Caesar's army defeated Ptolemy's army, ending the power struggle. Pompey was assassinated in Egypt, Cleopatra and Caesar became lovers, and Caesar brought Cleopatra to Rome. (See "Individuals in Society: Queen Cleopatra," page 148.) Caesar put down a revolt against Roman control by the king of Pontus in northern Turkey, then won a major victory over Pompey's army—now commanded by his sons—in Spain.

In the middle of defeating his enemies in battles all around the Mediterranean (see Map 5.2), Julius Caesar returned to Rome several times and was elected or appointed to various positions, including consul and

■ **First Triumvirate** The name later given to an informal political alliance among Caesar, Crassus, and Pompey in which they agreed to advance one another's interests.

Cicero and the Plot to Kill Caesar

Marcus Tullius Cicero was born in January 106 B.C.E. After an excellent education, he settled in Rome to practice law. He held a series of ever-higher public offices, ending with the consulship in 63 B.C.E. By the time of Caesar's return to Rome in 49 B.C.E., Cicero was a senior statesman with great importance as a lawyer and thinker and powerful influence through his skills at oratory. Caesar wrote Cicero a flattering letter stating, "[Y]our approval of my actions elates me beyond words. . . . As for yourself, I hope I shall see you at Rome so that I can avail myself as usual of your advice and resources in all things."* Cicero tended to favor Pompey, however, thinking that Caesar was a greater danger to traditional republican institutions. He was not involved in the plot to assassinate Caesar, perhaps because the conspirators did not trust him to keep the matter quiet. He was involved in the jockeying for power that followed, however, as evidenced by the following letters and speeches.

Trebonius, one of the assassins, wrote to Cicero describing the murder, and on February 2, 43 B.C.E., Cicero gave this frank opinion of the events:

Would to heaven you had invited me to that noble feast that you made on the ides of March: no remnants, most assuredly, should have been left behind. Whereas the part you unluckily spared gives us so much perplexity that we find something to regret, even in the godlike service that you and your illustrious associates have lately rendered to the republic. To say the truth, when I reflect that it was owing to the favor of so worthy a man as yourself that Antony now lives to be our general bane, I am sometimes inclined to be a little angry with you for taking him aside when Caesar fell as by this means you have occasioned more trouble to myself in particular than to all the rest of the whole community.†

By the "part you unluckily spared" he meant Mark Antony, Caesar's firm supporter and a fierce enemy of the assassins, whom Cicero feared. Still undecided about what to do after the assassination, Cassius, one of the leaders of the plot, wrote to Cicero asking for advice. Cicero responded, again emphasizing that the conspirators should have killed Antony as well, and clearly miffed that he was not consulted:

Where to advise you to begin to restore order I must acknowledge myself at a loss. To say the truth, it is the tyrant alone, and not the tyranny, from which we seem to be delivered: for although the man [Caesar] is destroyed, we still servilely maintain all his despotic ordinances. We do more: and under the pretence of carrying his designs into execution, we approve of measures which even he himself would never have pursued. . . . This outrageous man [Antony] represents me as the principal advisor and promoter of your glorious efforts. Would to heaven the charge were true! For had I been a party in your councils, I should have put it out of his power thus to bother and embarrass our plans. But this was a point that depended on yourselves to decide; and since the opportunity is now over, I can only wish that I were capable of giving you any effective advice. But the truth is that I am utterly at a loss in how to act myself. For what is the purpose of resisting where one cannot oppose force by force?‡

At this stage the young Octavian, Caesar's designated heir, sought Cicero's advice. In a series of letters to his close friend Atticus, Cicero discussed the situation, upset that Decimus Brutus, a general who was one of the conspirators, was not taking charge of the situation:

On the second or third of November 44 B.C.E. a letter arrived from Octavian. He has great schemes afoot. He has won the veterans at Casilinum and Calatia over to his views, and no wonder since he gives them 500 denarii apiece. He plans to make a round of the other colonies. His object is plain: war with Antony and himself as commander-in-chief. So it looks to me as though in a few

* *To Atticus* 9.16.2 in D. R. Shackleton-Bailey, *Cicero's Letters to Atticus*, vol. 4 (Cambridge: Cambridge University Press, 1968), pp. 203–205.

† *To Trebonius* in T. de Quincy, *Cicero: Offices, Essays, and Letters* (New York: Everyman's Library), pp. 328–329.

‡ *To Cassius*, ibid., pp. 324–325.

dictator. He was acclaimed imperator, a title given to victorious military commanders and a term that later gave rise to the word *emperor*. Sometimes these elections happened when Caesar was away fighting; they were often arranged by his chief supporter and client in Rome, Mark Antony (83–30 B.C.E.), who was himself a military commander. Whatever Caesar's official position, after he crossed the Rubicon he simply made changes on his own authority, though often with the approval of the

Senate, which he packed with his supporters. The Senate transformed his temporary positions as consul and dictator into ones he would hold for life.

Caesar began to make a number of legal and economic reforms. He issued laws about debt, the collection of taxes, and the distribution of grain and land. Families who had many children were to receive rewards, and Roman allies in Italy were to have full citizenship. He reformed the calendar, which had been

days' time we shall be in arms. But whom are we to follow? Consider his name; consider his age. . . . In short, he proffers himself as our leader and expects me to back him up. For my part I have recommended him to go to Rome. I imagine he will have the city rabble behind him, and the honest men too if he convinces them of his sincerity. Ah Brutus, where are you? What a golden opportunity you are losing! I could not foretell *this*, but I thought something of the kind would happen.§

Four days later Cicero records news of the following developments:

~

Two letters for me from Octavian in one day! Now he wants me to return to Rome at once, says he wants to work through the Senate. . . . In short, he presses and I play for time. I don't trust his age and I don't know what he's after. . . . I'm nervous of Antony's power and don't want to leave the coast. But I'm afraid of some star performance during my absence. Varro [an enemy of Antony] doesn't think much of the boy's plan, I take a different view. He has a strong force at his back and *can* have Brutus. And he's going to work quite openly, forming companies at Capua and paying out bounties. War is evidently coming any minute now.**

Even though he contemptuously called him a "boy," Cicero decided to openly side with Octavian. On April 21, 43 B.C.E., he denounced Antony in a speech to the Senate. He reminded his fellow senators how they had earlier opposed Antony:

~

Do you not remember, in the name of the immortal gods, what resolutions you have made against these men [Antony and his supporters]? You have repealed the acts of Antony. You have taken down his law. You have voted that they were carried by violence and with a disregard of the auspices. You have called out the troops throughout all Italy. You have pronounced that colleague and ally of all wickedness [Antony] a public enemy. What peace can there be with this man? Even if he were a foreign enemy, still, after such actions as have taken place, it would be scarcely possible by any means whatever to have peace. Though seas and mountains and vast regions lay between you, still you would hate such a man without seeing him. But these men will stick to your eyes, and when they can to your very throats; for what fences will be strong enough for us to restrain savage beasts? Oh, but the result of war is uncertain. It is at all events in the power of brave men such as you ought to be to display your valor, for certainly brave men can do that, and not to fear the caprice of fortune.††

Antony and Octavian briefly reconciled and formed the Third Triumvirate. An ill and aging Cicero was declared an enemy of the state and sought to leave Italy, but was intercepted by Antony's men. When Cicero stretched his head out of the window of the litter in which he was being carried, indicating he would surrender, a centurion slit his throat. His head and hands were cut off on Antony's orders and displayed in the Roman Forum. Octavian's opinion about all this as it happened is disputed, but years later he said of Cicero: "A learned man, learned and a lover of his country."‡‡

EVALUATE THE EVIDENCE

1. What can you infer from these letters about how well prepared the conspirators and other leaders in the Senate such as Cicero were to take control of the government after Caesar's death?

2. What do these sources suggest about Cicero's importance and the role of his speeches in the Senate?

§ *To Atticus* 16.8.1–2 in D. R. Shackleton-Bailey, *Cicero's Letters to Atticus*, vol. 6 (Cambridge: Cambridge University Press, 1967), pp. 185–187.

** *To Atticus* 16.9, ibid., p. 189.

†† *The Fourteenth Phillipic* in C. D. Yonge, *Cicero, Select Orations* (New York: Harper and Brothers, 1889), p. 499.

‡‡ Plutarch, *Cicero* 49.15.

based on the cycles of the moon, by replacing it with one based on the sun, adapted from the Egyptian calendar. He sponsored celebrations honoring his victories, had coins struck with his portrait, and founded new colonies, which were to be populated by veterans and the poor. He planned even more changes, including transforming elected positions such as consul, tribune, and provincial governor into ones that he appointed.

Caesar was wildly popular with most people in Rome, and even with many senators. Other senators, led by Brutus and Cassius, two patricians who favored the traditional republic, opposed his rise to what was becoming absolute power. In 44 B.C.E. they conspired to kill him and did so on March 15 — a date called the "Ides of March" in the Roman calendar — stabbing him multiple times on the steps of the theater of Pompey, where the Senate was meeting that day.

INDIVIDUALS IN SOCIETY

Queen Cleopatra

Cleopatra VII (69–30 B.C.E.) was a member of the Ptolemy dynasty, the Hellenistic rulers of Egypt who had established power in the third century B.C.E. Although she was a Greek, she was passionately devoted to her Egyptian subjects and was the first in her dynasty who could speak Egyptian in addition to Greek. Just as ancient pharaohs had linked themselves with the gods, she had herself portrayed as the goddess Isis and may have seen herself as a reincarnation of Isis (see Chapter 4).

At the time civil war was raging in the late Roman Republic, Cleopatra and her brother Ptolemy XIII were in a dispute over who would be supreme ruler in Egypt. Julius Caesar captured the Egyptian capital of Alexandria, Cleopatra arranged to meet him, and the two became lovers, although Cleopatra was much younger and Caesar was married. The two apparently had a son, Caesarion, and Caesar's army defeated Ptolemy's army, ending the power struggle. In 46 B.C.E. Cleopatra arrived in Rome, where Caesar put up a statue of her as Isis in one of the city's temples. The Romans hated her because they saw her as a decadent Eastern queen and a threat to what were considered traditional Roman values.

After Caesar's assassination, Cleopatra returned to Alexandria. There she became involved in the continuing Roman civil war that now pitted Octavian, Caesar's grand-nephew and heir, against Mark Antony, who commanded the Roman army in the East. When Antony visited Alexandria in 41 B.C.E., he met Cleopatra, and though he was already married to Octavian's sister, he became her lover. He abandoned (and later divorced) his Roman wife, married Cleopatra in 37 B.C.E., and changed his will to favor his children by Cleopatra. Antony's wedding present to Cleopatra was a huge grant of territory, much of it Roman, that greatly increased her power and that of all her children, including Caesarion. Antony also declared Caesarion to be Julius Caesar's rightful heir.

Octavian used the wedding gift as the reason to declare Antony a traitor. He and other Roman leaders described Antony as a romantic fool captivated by the seductive Cleopatra. Roman troops turned against Antony and joined with Octavian, and at the Battle of Actium in 31 B.C.E. Octavian defeated the army and navy of Antony and Cleopatra. Antony committed suicide, as did Cleopatra shortly afterward. Octavian ordered the teenage Caesarion killed, but the young children of Antony and Cleopatra were allowed to go back to Rome, where they were raised by Antony's ex-wife. In another consequence of Octavian's victory, Egypt became a Roman province.

Roman sources are viciously hostile to Cleopatra, and she became the model of the alluring woman whose sexual attraction led men to their doom. Stories about her beauty, sophistication, lavish spending, desire for power, and ruthlessness abounded and were retold for centuries. The most dramatic story was that she committed suicide through the bite of a poisonous snake, which may have been true and which has been the subject of countless paintings. Her tumultuous relationships with Caesar and Antony have been portrayed in plays, novels, movies, and television programs.

QUESTIONS FOR ANALYSIS

1. How did Cleopatra benefit from her relationships with Caesar and Antony? How did they benefit from their relationships with her?
2. How did ideas about gender and Roman suspicion of the more sophisticated Greek culture combine to shape Cleopatra's fate and the way she is remembered?
3. In Chapter 1, "Individuals in Society: Hatshepsut and Nefertiti" (see page 29) also focuses on leading female figures in Egypt, but these two women lived more than a thousand years before Cleopatra. How would you compare their situation with hers?

The only portraits of Cleopatra that date from her own lifetime are on the coins that she issued. This one, made at the mint of Alexandria, shows her as quite plain, reinforcing the point made by Cicero that her attractiveness was based more on intelligence and wit than on physical beauty. The reverse of the coin shows an eagle, a symbol of rule. (© The Trustees of the British Museum/Art Resource, NY)

The conspiring senators called themselves the "Liberators" and said they were defending the liberties of the Roman Republic, but their support for the traditional power of the Senate could do little to save Rome from its pattern of misgovernment. The result of the assassination was another round of civil war. (See "Evaluating the Evidence 5.3: Cicero and the Plot to Kill Caesar," page 146.) Caesar had named his eighteen-year-old grandnephew and adopted son, Octavian, as his heir. In 43 B.C.E. Octavian joined forces with Mark Antony and another of Caesar's lieutenants, Lepidus (LEH-puh-duhs), in a formal pact known later as the **Second Triumvirate**. Together they hunted down Caesar's killers and defeated the military forces loyal to Pompey's sons and to the conspirators. They agreed to divide the provinces into spheres of influence, with Octavian taking most of the west, Antony the east, and Lepidus the Iberian Peninsula and North Africa. The three came into conflict, and Lepidus was forced into exile by Octavian, leaving the other two to confront one another.

Both Octavian and Antony set their sights on gaining more territory. Cleopatra had returned to rule Egypt after Caesar's death, and supported Antony, who became her lover as well as her ally. In 31 B.C.E. Octavian's forces defeated the combined forces of Antony and Cleopatra at the Battle of Actium in Greece, but the two escaped. Octavian pursued them to Egypt, and they committed suicide rather than fall into his hands. Octavian's victory at Actium put an end to an age of civil war. For his success, the Senate in 27 B.C.E. gave Octavian the name Augustus, meaning "revered one." Although the Senate did not mean this to be a decisive break with tradition, that date is generally used to mark the end of the Roman Republic and the start of the Roman Empire.

NOTES

1. Aubrey de Sélincourt, trans., *Livy: The Early History of Rome, Books 1–5 of the History of Rome from Its Foundation* (Baltimore: Penguin Books, 1960), p. 58.
2. Plutarch, *Pyrrhos* 21.14. In this chapter, works in Latin with no translator noted were translated by John Buckler.
3. Naphtali Lewis and Meyer Reinhold, eds., *Roman Civilization: Sourcebook 1: The Republic* (New York: Harper Torchbooks, 1951), p. 104.
4. Polybius, *The Histories* 38.21.
5. Sallust, *War with Catiline* 10.1–3.
6. Lewis and Reinhold, *Roman Civilization*, p. 489.
7. Ovid, *Fasti* 2.535–539.
8. Horace, *Epistles* 2.1.156.

■ **Second Triumvirate** A formal agreement in 43 B.C.E. among Octavian, Mark Antony, and Lepidus to defeat Caesar's murderers.

LOOKING BACK LOOKING AHEAD

As the Greeks were creating urban culture and spreading it around the Mediterranean, other peoples, including the Etruscans and the people who later became the Romans, built their own societies on the Italian peninsula. The Romans spread their way of life throughout Italy by means of conquest and incorporation. After wars in which they defeated the wealthy city of Carthage, they expanded their political dominance throughout the western Mediterranean basin. Then they conquered in the East until they came to view the entire Mediterranean as *mare nostrum*, "our sea." Yet their successes brought war and civil unrest, and they also brought transformations of Roman society and culture as these became Hellenized.

The final days of the republic were filled with war and chaos, and the republican institutions did not survive. Rome became an empire ruled by one man. The laws and administrative practices of the republic shaped those of the empire, however, as well as those of later states in Europe and beyond. Lyons, Marseilles, Paris, Córdoba, and other modern European cities began as Roman colonies or expanded from small settlements into cities during the period of the republic. When the American Constitution was drafted in 1783, its authors — well read in Roman history and law — favored a balance of powers like those they idealized in the Roman Republic, and they chose to call the smaller and more powerful deliberative assembly the Senate. They, too, were divided into those who favored rule by traditional elites and those who favored broader political power, much like the optimates and populares of the Roman Republic. That division is reflected in the fact that the American Congress has two houses, the House of Representatives, elected directly by voters, and the Senate, originally elected indirectly by state legislatures.

Make Connections

Think about the larger developments and continuities within and across chapters.

1. How would you compare ideals for male and female behavior in republican Rome with those of classical Sparta and classical Athens in Chapter 3? What are some possible reasons for the differences and similarities you have identified?

2. The Phoenicians, the Greeks, and the Romans all established colonies around the Mediterranean. How did these colonies differ, and how were they the same, in terms of their economic functions and political situations?

3. Looking over the long history of the Roman Republic, do interactions with non-Romans or conflicts among Romans themselves appear to be the most significant drivers of change? Explain your answer.

5 REVIEW & EXPLORE

Identify Key Terms

Identify and explain the significance of each item below.

Senate (p. 125)

consuls (p. 125)

patricians (p. 128)

plebeians (p. 128)

Struggle of the Orders (p. 129)

tribunes (p. 129)

patron-client system (p. 130)

Punic Wars (p. 130)

paterfamilias (p. 133)

manumission (p. 135)

latifundia (p. 140)

First Triumvirate (p. 145)

Second Triumvirate (p. 149)

Review the Main Ideas

Answer the focus questions from each section of the chapter.

- How did the Romans become the dominant power in Italy? (p. 122)
- What were the key institutions of the Roman Republic? (p. 128)
- How did the Romans take control of the Mediterranean world? (p. 130)
- How did expansion affect Roman society and culture? (p. 133)
- What led to the fall of the Roman Republic? (p. 139)

Suggested Reading and Media Resources

BOOKS

- Boatwright, Mary T., et al. *The Romans: From Village to Empire*, 2d ed. 2012. An excellent survey of Roman history that emphasizes everyday life as well as political developments.
- Canfora, Luciano. *Julius Caesar: The Life and Times of the People's Dictator.* 2007. Provides a new interpretation of Caesar that puts him fully into the context of his times.
- Cornell, T. J. *The Beginnings of Rome: Italy and Rome from the Bronze Age to the Punic Wars.* 1995. Extremely influential study that led to a major rethinking of early Roman history.
- Eckstein, Arthur M. *Mediterranean Anarchy, Interstate War, and the Rise of Rome.* 2006. Places the rise of the Roman Republic in the context of the wars of contemporary Hellenistic states.
- Evans, J. K. *War, Women, and Children in Ancient Rome.* 2000. Provides a concise survey of how war affected the home front in wartime.
- Everitt, Anthony. *The Rise of Rome: The Making of the World's Greatest Empire.* 2012. An engaging and thorough narrative written for general readers.
- Forsythe, Gary A. *A Critical History of Early Rome from Prehistory to the First Punic War.* 2005. Uses archaeological findings as well as written sources to examine the political, social, and religious developments of early Rome.
- Haynes, Sybille. *Etruscan Civilization: A Cultural History.* 2005. Deals with cultural history, giving special emphasis to Etruscan women.
- Holland, Tom. *Rubicon: The Last Years of the Roman Republic.* 2005. A dramatic account of the disintegration of the republic from the Gracchi to Caesar's death.
- Matz, David. *Daily Life of the Ancient Romans.* 2008. A brief but valuable account of the ordinary things in Roman life.
- Miles, Richard. *Carthage Must Be Destroyed: The Rise and Fall of a Civilization.* 2011. A lively narrative of the rise and fall of Carthage, based on early sources and archaeological evidence.
- Murell, John. *Cicero and the Roman Republic.* 2008. Looks at the late republic through Cicero's life and political career.
- Warrior, Valerie. *Roman Religion.* 2006. A relatively brief study that examines the actual practices of Roman religion in their social contexts.

DOCUMENTARIES

- *Ancient Rome: The Rise and Fall of an Empire* (BBC, 2006). A six-part docudrama; each part focuses on a turning point, with one on the Gracchi and another on Julius Caesar.
- *Great Generals of the Ancient World: Alexander the Great, Hannibal, Julius Caesar* (History Channel, 2006). Three-part set examining the military careers, battles, and personalities of the most successful generals in the ancient world.
- *Lost Worlds: The Etruscans* (Discovery Channel, 2002). An examination of Etruscan society and culture centering on the unexpected discovery of a 2,500-year-old Etruscan ship filled with artifacts.
- *Secrets of Lost Empires: Roman Bath* (*Nova*, 2000). In Turkey *Nova* re-creates a working Roman bath, complete with hot tubs, cold plunges, and underfloor heating, using original techniques and examining the social context of public baths.

FEATURE FILMS AND TELEVISION

- *Rome* (HBO and BBC, 2005, 2007). British-American historical-drama television series set in the transition from republic to empire, with real historical figures and invented characters.
- *Spartacus* (Stanley Kubrick, 1960). Oscar-winning epic tells the story of the slave revolt led by Spartacus; starring and produced by Kirk Douglas, who considered the movie in part a response to McCarthy-era blacklisting.

WEB SITES

- *Aquae Urbis Romae.* An interactive cartographic history of Roman hydraulic systems and their impact on the urban development of Rome, including aqueducts, fountains, sewers, bridges, and conduits. **www3.iath.virginia.edu/waters/**
- *LacusCurtius: Into the Roman World.* Primary and secondary resources on ancient Rome, including photographs, inscriptions, maps, and links to other Roman Web sites. **penelope.uchicago.edu/Thayer/E/Roman/home.htm**
- *Mysterious Etruscans.* Informative, well-illustrated Web site with information on Etruscan language, art, religion, and lifestyle. **www.mysteriousetruscans.com/**

6

The Roman Empire

27 B.C.E.–284 C.E.

In 27 B.C.E. the civil wars were largely over, at least for a time. With peace came prosperity, stability, and a new vision of Rome's destiny. In his epic poem the *Aeneid* celebrating the founding of Rome, the Roman poet Virgil expressed this vision:

> You, Roman, remember—these are your arts:
> To rule nations, and to impose the ways of peace,
> To spare the humble and to conquer the proud.[1]

This was an ideal, of course, but Augustus, now the ruler of Rome, recognized that ideals and traditions were important to Romans. Instead of creating a new form of government, he left the republic officially intact, but held all real power himself. The rulers that followed him continued to transform Rome into an empire. The boundaries of the Roman Empire expanded in all directions, and the army became an important means of Romanization through its forts, camps, and cities. Gaul, Germany, Britain, and eastern Europe were introduced to Greco-Roman culture. A new religion, Christianity, developed in the eastern Roman province of Judaea, and spread on the roads and sea-lanes used by Roman traders and troops. By the third century C.E. civil wars had returned, however, and it seemed as if Augustus's creation would collapse. ■

CHAPTER PREVIEW

Life in Imperial Rome
In this terra-cotta relief from the third century C.E., a woman sells fruit in a shop while customers line up in front of her. Shops like this one, where goods were sold and neighbors met each other for conversation, were common in imperial Rome. (De Agostini Picture Library/A. Dagli Orti/Bridgeman Images)

Augustus's Reign

FOCUS QUESTION *How did Augustus create a foundation for the Roman Empire?*

After Augustus (r. 27 B.C.E.–14 C.E.) ended the civil wars that had raged off and on for decades, he faced the monumental problems of reconstruction. He first had to reconstruct the constitution and the organs of government. Next he had to pay his armies for their services, and care for the welfare of the provinces. Then he had to address the danger of various groups on Rome's European frontiers.

Augustus was highly successful in meeting these challenges. The result of this work was a system of government in which the emperor held all executive power in both the civil government and the military. The Senate remained as a prestigious advisory body whose members functioned at the desire and request of the emperor.

The Principate

Augustus claimed that he was restoring the republic, but he actually transformed the government into one in which all real power was held by a single ruler. As he did this, however, he maintained the illusion that the republic still existed, and he linked his rule with the traditional idea of SPQR (see Chapter 5).

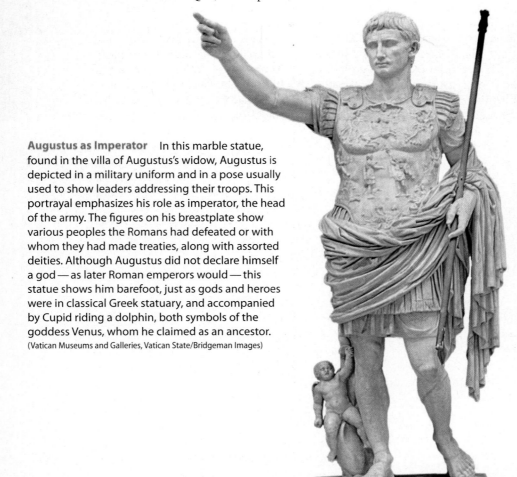

Augustus as Imperator   In this marble statue, found in the villa of Augustus's widow, Augustus is depicted in a military uniform and in a pose usually used to show leaders addressing their troops. This portrayal emphasizes his role as imperator, the head of the army. The figures on his breastplate show various peoples the Romans had defeated or with whom they had made treaties, along with assorted deities. Although Augustus did not declare himself a god — as later Roman emperors would — this statue shows him barefoot, just as gods and heroes were in classical Greek statuary, and accompanied by Cupid riding a dolphin, both symbols of the goddess Venus, whom he claimed as an ancestor. (Vatican Museums and Galleries, Vatican State/Bridgeman Images)

Augustus fit his own position into the republican constitution not by creating a new office for himself but by gradually taking over many of the offices that traditionally had been held by separate people. The Senate named him often as both consul and tribune. As consul, Augustus had the right to call the Senate into session and present legislation to the citizens' assemblies, and as tribune he presided over the *concilium plebis* (see Chapter 5). He was also named **imperator**, a title with which the Senate customarily honored a general after a major victory. He held control of the army, which he made a permanent standing organization. Furthermore, recognizing the importance of religion, he had himself named *pontifex maximus*, or chief priest.

An additional title that Augustus had the Senate bestow on him was *princeps civitatis* (prihn-KEHPS cih-vee-TAH-tees), "first citizen of the state." This title had no official powers attached to it and had been used as an honorific for centuries, so it was inoffensive to Roman ears. One of Augustus's cleverest tactics was to use noninflammatory language for himself and the changes he was making. Only later would *princeps civitatis* become the basis of the word *prince*, meaning "sovereign ruler," although "prince" quite accurately describes what Augustus actually was.

Considering what had happened to Julius Caesar, Augustus wisely wielded all his power in the background, and the government he created is called the **principate**. Although principate leaders were said to be "first among equals," Augustus's tenure clearly marked the end of the republic. Still, for a generation that had known only civil war, the shift away from republican government may have seemed minor compared to the benefits brought by the stability of Augustus's rule.

Augustus curtailed the power of the Senate, but it continued to exist as the chief deliberative body of the state, and it continued to act as a court of law. Under Augustus and his successors, it provided officials to administer Rome and its provinces. The Senate's relations with particular emperors were often hostile, and senators were involved in plots to overthrow various emperors. In general, however, the Senate adapted itself to the new reality and cooperated in running the empire. Governors sent to the provinces were often members of the Senate, and they took the Roman legal system with them.

Without specifically saying so, Augustus created the office of emperor. The English word *emperor* is derived from the Latin word *imperator*, an origin that reflects the fact that Augustus's command of the army was the main source of his power. Augustus governed the provinces where troops were needed for defense and guarded the frontiers from attack. He could declare war, he controlled deployment of the Roman army, and he paid the soldiers' wages. He granted bonuses and gave veterans retirement benefits. Augustus never shared control of the army, and no Roman found it easy to defy him militarily.

Augustus professionalized the military even more than it had been in the late republic, and made the army a recognized institution of government. Soldiers were generally volunteers; they received a salary and training under career officers who advanced in rank according to experience, ability, valor, and length of service. (See "Thinking Like a Historian: Army and Empire," page 156.) Soldiers served twenty-year terms, plus five in the reserves, and on retiring were to be given a discharge bonus of cash or a piece of land. To pay for this, Augustus ordered a tax on inheritance and on certain types of sales. Those soldiers who were Roman citizens were organized into legions, units of about five thousand men. The legions were backed up by auxiliaries, military forces of noncitizens, some conscripts but mostly volunteers who also served twenty- or twenty-five-year terms. Auxiliaries were paid—though at a lower rate than legionaries—and were granted Roman citizenship when they retired, which gave them legal, social, and economic privileges. Legions were often transferred from place to place as the need arose. Auxiliaries were more likely to stay near the area where they had been recruited, but sometimes they served far away from home as well.

Grants of land to veterans had originally been in Italy, but by Augustus's time there was not enough land for this. Instead he gave veterans land in the frontier provinces that had been taken from the people the Romans conquered, usually near camps with active army units. Some veterans objected, and at Augustus's death they briefly revolted, but these colonies of veterans continued to play an important role in securing the Roman Empire's boundaries and controlling its newly won provinces. Augustus's veterans took abroad with them their Latin language and Roman culture, becoming important agents of Romanization.

Chronology

27 B.C.E.–68 C.E.	Julio-Claudian emperors; expansion into northern and western Europe
ca. 50 B.C.E.–20 C.E.	"Golden age" of Latin literature
ca. 3 B.C.E.–ca. 29 C.E.	Life of Jesus
69–96 C.E.	Flavian emperors; restoration of order
70 C.E.	Rebellion crushed in Judaea
96–180 C.E.	Era of the "five good emperors," with relative peace and prosperity
193–211 C.E.	Emperor Septimius Severus expands Rome's borders in Africa and western Asia
212 C.E.	Edict of Caracalla makes all free males living in Roman Empire citizens
235–284 C.E.	Barracks emperors; civil war; breakdown of the empire; economic decline

The army that Augustus developed was loyal to him as a person, not as the head of the Roman state. This would lead to trouble later, but the basics of the political and military system that Augustus created lasted fairly well for almost three centuries.

Roman Expansion

One of the most significant aspects of Augustus's reign was Roman expansion into northern and western Europe (Map 6.1). Augustus began his work in the west and north by completing the conquest of Spain begun by Scipio Africanus in the third century B.C.E. (see Chapter 5). In Gaul he founded twelve new towns, and the Roman road system linked new settlements with one another and with Italy. The German frontier along the Rhine River was the scene of hard fighting. In 12 B.C.E. Augustus ordered a major invasion of Germany beyond the Rhine. Roman legions advanced to the Elbe River, and the area north of the Main River and west of the Elbe was on the point of becoming Roman. But in 9 C.E. some twenty thousand Roman troops were annihilated at the Battle of the Teutoburg Forest and their general Varus was killed on the battlefield.

Meanwhile Roman troops penetrated the area of modern Austria, southern Bavaria, and western Hungary. Thereafter the Rhine and the Danube remained the Roman frontier in central Europe. The Romans began to build walls, forts, and watchtowers to firm up their defenses, especially in the area between the two rivers, where people could more easily

■ **imperator** Title given to a Roman general after a major victory that came to mean "emperor."

■ **principate** Official title of Augustus's form of government, taken from *princeps*, meaning "first citizen."

Army and Empire

Military might made it possible for the Romans to conquer and hold a huge empire. As the empire grew, the Romans needed to recruit troops from conquered areas and make these soldiers effective, loyal, and dependable. How did the Romans turn countless individuals from diverse cultures into the most powerful fighting force the Mediterranean world had ever seen?

1 Julius Caesar, *The Gallic War,* 50 B.C.E. In his account of his successful campaigns in Gaul, designed to present himself as the consummate Roman military leader, Caesar (writing of himself in the third person) describes his efforts to rally his wavering troops.

Such a terrible panic suddenly seized our whole army as severely affected everyone's courage and morale. Our men started asking questions, and the Gauls and traders replied by describing how tall and strong the Germans were, how unbelievably brave and skilful with weapons. . . . The panic began among the military tribunes and prefects, and the other men who, having no great military experience, had followed Caesar from Rome to court his friendship. . . . They hid themselves away in their tents and bemoaned their fate. . . . As soon as Caesar was aware of the situation he called a council, ordered centurions of all ranks to attend, and severely reprimanded them. . . . Why did they despair of their own courage, or of his anxious concern for their well-being? The danger posed by this enemy had already been experienced in the time of our fathers, when the Cimbri and Teutoni were expelled by Gaius Marius. On that occasion it was clear that the army had deserved as much credit as its commander. . . . From all this, said Caesar, they could see how crucial was firmness of purpose. . . . The Germans were the same people who had often clashed with the Helvetii — and the Helvetii had frequently beaten them, not only within their own borders but also in Germany itself — and yet the Helvetii had proved no match for our army. . . . And so, Caesar concluded, he would do at once what he had intended to put off till a later date. The very next night, during the fourth watch, they would strike camp. Then he would know as soon as possible whether their sense of shame and duty was stronger than their fear. . . . At the end of this speech the change of attitude was quite remarkable, and there arose an immense enthusiasm and eagerness to start the campaign.

2 Titus Flavius Josephus, *The Jewish War,* ca. 75 C.E. Josephus was a commander in the Jewish revolt against the Romans in 66 C.E. who after he was taken prisoner went over to the Roman side. Here he describes how he used the Romans as a model for the Jewish army. Like Caesar in Source 1, he writes of himself in the third person.

Josephus knew that the invincible might of Rome was chiefly due to unhesitating obedience and to practice in arms. He despaired of providing similar instruction, demanding as it did a long period of training; but he saw that the habit of obedience resulted from the number of their officers, and he now reorganized his army on the Roman model, appointing more junior commanders than before. He divided the soldiers into different classes, and put them under decurions and centurions, those being subordinate to tribunes, and the tribunes to commanders of larger units. He taught them how to pass on signals, how to sound the advance and the retreat, how to make flank attacks and encircling movements, and how a victorious unit could relieve one in difficulties and assist any who were hard pressed. He explained all that contributed to toughness of body or fortitude of spirit. Above all he trained them for war by stressing Roman discipline at every turn: they would be facing men who by physical prowess and unshakable determination had conquered almost the entire world.

ANALYZING THE EVIDENCE

1. How does Julius Caesar use history and tradition in Source 1 to convince his troops to fight, and what do you think his purpose was in relating this incident as he did?
2. What aspects of the Roman military does Josephus use as a model for his own forces in Source 2? How do these compare with the qualities Vegetius identifies in Source 5 as ideal in the perfect recruit?
3. Why would the promise of eventual citizenship recorded in military diplomas, like the one in Source 3, have been an effective recruiting tool?
4. What does the roof plaque in Source 4 suggest about the self-identity of the soldiers who made it?

3 Roman military diploma, 71 C.E.

Military diplomas were bronze sheets, wired together, on which a former soldier's tours of duty, record of service, and status as a citizen were recorded. One copy stayed in Rome, and one was sent to the soldier himself, much as members of the military today receive discharge papers.

(The Israel Museum, Jerusalem/Acquired in memory of Chaim Herzog, Sixth President of the State of Israel, by his family and Yad Chaim Herzog; the Carmen and Louis Warschaw Fund of Archeological Acquisitions; David and Genevieve Hendin, New York/Bridgeman Images)

5 Vegetius, *Epitome of Military Science*, ca. 380–390 C.E.

Vegetius seems to have been a Roman imperial bureaucrat who set out what he saw as ideal military recruitment and training at a point when the Roman Empire was in decline and the army faced many challenges.

In every battle it is not numbers and untaught bravery so much as skill and training that generally produce the victory. For we see no other explanation of the conquest of the world by the Roman People than their drill-at-arms, camp-discipline and military expertise. . . . But what succeeded against all [enemies] was careful selection of recruits, instruction in the rules, so to speak, of war, toughening in daily exercises, prior acquaintance in field practice with all possible eventualities in war and battle, and strict punishment of cowardice. Scientific knowledge of warfare nurtures courage in battle. No one is afraid to do what he is confident of having learned well. A small force which is highly trained in the conflicts of war is more apt to victory: a raw and untrained horde is always exposed to slaughter. . . . The rural populace is better suited for arms. They are nurtured under the open sky in a life of work, enduring the sun, careless of shade, unacquainted with bathhouses, ignorant of luxury, simple souled, content with a little, with limbs toughened to endure every kind of toil. . . . If ancient custom is to be retained, everyone knows that those entering puberty should be brought to the levy. For those things are taught not only more quickly but even more completely which are learned from boyhood. Secondly military alacrity, jumping and running should be attempted before the body stiffens with age. . . . You need not greatly regret the absence of tall stature. It is more useful that soldiers be strong than big. . . . The youth in whose hands is to be placed the defence of provinces, the fortune of battles, ought to be of outstanding breeding if numbers suffice, and morals. Decent birth makes a suitable soldier, while a sense of shame prevents flight and makes him a victor.

4 Roman legion roof plaque.

The legionaries of the Twentieth Legion (Leg. XX) stationed in Britain, whose symbol was a charging boar, made this clay plaque for the roof of one of their buildings.

(British Museum, London, UK/Erich Lessing/Art Resource, NY)

PUTTING IT ALL TOGETHER

Using the sources above, along with what you have learned in class and in Chapters 5 and 6, write a short essay that analyzes the military's role in the empire's expansion. How did the Romans turn countless individuals from diverse cultures into the most powerful fighting force the Mediterranean world had ever seen? How would you assess the relative importance of various factors in this transformation, and why might your assessment be different from that of the authors cited here?

Sources: (1) Julius Caesar, *Seven Commentaries on the Gallic War*, trans. Carolyn Hammond (New York: Oxford University Press, 1998), pp. 24–27. By permission of Oxford University Press; (2) Josephus, *The Jewish War*, trans. G. A. Williamson (Baltimore: Penguin Books, 1972), p. 172; (5) N. P. Milner, trans., *Vegetius: Epitome of Military Science* (Liverpool: Liverpool University Press, 1996), pp. 2–8.

MAP 6.1 Roman Expansion Under the Empire, 44 B.C.E.–180 C.E. Following Roman expansion during the republic, Augustus added vast tracts of Europe to the Roman Empire, which the emperor Trajan later enlarged by assuming control over parts of central Europe, the Near East, and North Africa.

enter Roman territory. The regions of modern Serbia, Bulgaria, and Romania in the Balkans fell, and the Romans created a land-based link between the eastern and western Mediterranean.

Within the area along the empire's northern border the legionaries and auxiliaries built fortified camps. Roads linked the camps with one another, and settlements grew up around the camps. Traders began to frequent the frontier and to do business with the people who lived there. Thus Roman culture—the rough-and-ready kind found in military camps—gradually spread into the north. As a result, for the first time central and northern Europe came into direct and continuous contact with Mediterranean culture. Many Roman camps grew into cities, transforming the econ-

omy of the area around them. Roman cities were the first urban developments in most parts of central and northern Europe.

As a political and religious bond between the provinces and Rome, Augustus encouraged the cult of **Roma et Augustus** (Rome and Augustus) as the guardians of the state and the source of all benefits to society. In praying for the good health and welfare of the emperor, Romans and provincials were praying for the empire itself. The cult spread rapidly, especially in the eastern Mediterranean, where it built on the ideas of divine kingship developed in the Hellenistic monarchies (see Chapter 4). Worshipping Roma et Augustus became a symbol of Roman unity, and Roman officials could often judge the degree of loyalty of a province by noting the extent of public temple activities.

To make his presence felt further, Augustus had himself portrayed on coins standing alongside the goddess Victory, and on celebratory stone arches built to com-

■ **Roma et Augustus** Patriotic cult encouraged by Augustus and later emperors in which the good of Rome and the good of the emperor were linked.

■ **pax Romana** The "Roman peace," a period during the first and second centuries C.E. of political stability and relative peace.

memorate military victories. In addition, he had temples, stadiums, marketplaces, and public buildings constructed in Rome and other cities. Later emperors expanded this imperial cult, erecting statues, triumphal arches, columns, temples, and other buildings to honor themselves, their family members, or their predecessors. Many of these were decorated with texts as well as images. Shortly after Augustus's death, for example, an inscription detailing his achievements, known as the *Res Gestae Divi Augusti* (The deeds of the divine Augustus), was carved on monuments throughout the Roman Empire. (See "Evaluating the Evidence 6.1: Augustus, *Res Gestae*," page 160.)

In the late eighteenth century the English historian Edward Gibbon dubbed the stability and relative peace within the empire that Augustus created the **pax Romana**, the "Roman peace," which he saw as lasting about two hundred years, until the end of the reign of Marcus Aurelius in 180 C.E. Those outside the empire might not have agreed that things were so peaceful. The Roman historian Tacitus wrote of a speech delivered by the Scottish chieftain Calcagus before a battle with an invading Roman army in which Calcagus says, "The Romans make a desert and call it peace." The speech may be an invention by Tacitus—this was a common practice for ancient historians—but it captures the idea that not everyone saw the Roman Empire as a positive force. Gibbon's term has stuck, however, because, especially for those living away from contested frontier areas, this two-hundred-year stretch of Roman history was much more stable and prosperous than what came before or after.

The pax Romana was enforced by troops who remained on active duty or as reserves in the provinces and on the frontier, ready to respond to any resistance to Roman dominance. In general, however, Augustus respected local customs and ordered his governors to do the same. Roman governors applied Roman law to Romans living in their territories, but they let local people retain their own laws. As long as they provided taxes and did not rebel, they could continue to run their political and social lives as they had before Roman conquest.

While Romans did not force their culture on local people in Roman territories, local elites with aspirations knew that the best way to rise in stature and power was to adopt aspects of Roman culture. Thus, just as ambitious individuals in the Hellenistic world embraced Greek culture and learned to speak Greek, those determined to get ahead now learned Latin, and sometimes Greek as well if they wished to be truly well educated.

Especially in cities, Roman culture blended with local traditions. The Roman city of Lugdunum, modern Lyons in southern France, provides an example of this process. The site was originally the capital of a state that had existed before the Roman conquest of Gaul,

Organist and Horn Player   Games, gladiatorial contests, and other events in the cities of the Roman Empire were often accompanied by music. In this floor mosaic from a villa in Nennig, Germany, built in the third century, a horn player plays a large curved instrument known as a *cornu*, which was also used by the military to call troops. The organist plays a water organ (*hydraulis*) in which water stored in the hexagonal podium was pumped through tubes and the force of the water pushed air through the organ pipes. (Museum für Vor und Frühgeschichte, Saarbrücken, Germany/Bridgeman Images)

named for the Gallic god Lug. Julius Caesar made it a Roman military settlement. In 12 B.C.E. Augustus made it a political and religious center, with responsibilities for administering the area and for honoring the gods of both the Romans and Gauls. Physical symbols of this fusion of two cultures can still be seen today. The extensive remains of the amphitheater and other buildings testify to the fact that the city was prosperous enough to afford expensive Roman construction and the style of life that it represented. Many such towns were eventually granted Roman citizenship due to their embrace of Roman culture and government and their importance to the Roman economy. Ambitious young men flocked to provincial capitals such as Lugdunum, for it was here, and not in the countryside, that one could make one's mark.

The Flowering of Latin Literature

Many poets and prose writers were active in the late republic and the principate, and scholars of literature later judged their work to be of such high quality that they called the period from about 50 B.C.E. to 20 C.E.

Augustus, *Res Gestae*

During his lifetime Augustus wrote an official account of his long career that began in 44 B.C.E., when he was nineteen years old. He included the work with his will, which told the Senate to set it up as a public inscription. The original document, which no longer survives, was engraved on two bronze columns in front of the Mausoleum of Augustus, a large tomb erected in Rome by Augustus that is still standing. In many other places throughout the Roman Empire copies were carved into monuments, some of which survive, and the text became known as the Res Gestae Divi Augusti *(The deeds of the divine Augustus). In this work Augustus offers his readers a firsthand account of his public life. He stresses that he has always acted according to the authority that the Romans bestowed upon him. However, Augustus's publicized opinions of his actions and aims were not always shared by others.*

In the opening section Augustus lists his accomplishments and the honors bestowed upon him by the Roman Senate and people.

1. At the age of nineteen, on my own initiative and at my own expense, I raised an army by means of which I restored liberty to the republic, which had been oppressed by the tyranny of a faction. . . .

2. Those who slew my father [Julius Caesar, his adoptive father] I drove into exile, punishing their deed by due process of law, and afterwards when they waged war upon the republic I twice defeated them in battle.

3. Wars, both civil and foreign, I undertook throughout the world, on sea and land, and when victorious I spared all citizens who sued for pardon. The foreign nations which could with safety be pardoned I preferred to save rather than to destroy. The number of Roman citizens who bound themselves to me by military oath was about 500,000. Of these I settled in colonies or sent back into their own towns, after their term of service, something more than 300,000, and to all I assigned lands, or gave money as a reward for military service. I captured six hundred ships, over and above those which were smaller than triremes.

4. . . . For successful operations on land and sea, conducted either by myself or by my lieutenants under my auspices, the Senate on fifty-five occasions decreed that thanks should be rendered to the immortal gods. The days on which such thanks were rendered by decree of the Senate numbered 890. . . .

6. . . . When the Senate and the Roman people unanimously agreed that I should be elected overseer of laws and morals, without a colleague and with the fullest power, I refused to accept any power offered me which was contrary to the traditions of our ancestors.

In the next section Augustus tells of his personal donations to the republic.

20. The Capitolium and the theatre of Pompey, both works involving great expense, I rebuilt without any inscription of my own name. I restored the channels of the aqueducts which in several places were falling into disrepair through age, and doubled the capacity of the aqueduct called the Marcia by turning a new spring into its channel. . . . I rebuilt in the city eighty-two temples of the gods, omitting none which at that time stood in need of repair. . . .

22. Three times in my own name I gave a show of gladiators, and five times in the name of my sons or grandsons; in these shows there fought about ten thousand men. Twice in my own name I furnished for the people an exhibition of athletes gathered from all parts of the world, and a third time in the name of my grandson. Four times I gave games in my own name; as representing other

---

the "golden age" of Latin literature. Roman poets and prose writers celebrated the physical and emotional joys of a comfortable life. Their works were highly polished, elegant in style, and intellectual in conception. Roman poets referred to the gods often and treated mythological themes, but the core subject matter of their work was human, not divine.

Rome's greatest poet was Virgil (70–19 B.C.E.), who drew on earlier traditions, but gave them new twists. The *Georgics*, for example, is a poem about agriculture that used Hellenistic models to capture both the peaceful pleasures and the day-to-day violence of rural life. In vivid language Virgil depicts the death of one of the bulls pulling a plow and the farmer unyoking the remaining animal:

> Look, the bull, shining under the rough plough,
> falls to the ground
> and vomits from his mouth blood mixed with
>   foam,
> and releases his dying groan.
> Sadly moves the ploughman, unharnessing the
> young steer grieving for the death of his brother
> and leaves in the middle of the job
> the plough stuck fast.[2]

magistrates twenty-three times. . . . [O]n twenty-six occasions I gave to the people, in the circus, in the forum, or in the amphitheatre, hunts of African wild beasts, in which about three thousand five hundred beasts were slain.

He then discusses his military actions and founding of colonies.

~

25. I freed the sea from pirates. About thirty thousand slaves, captured in that war, who had run away from their masters and had taken up arms against the republic, I delivered to their masters for punishment. The whole of Italy voluntarily took oath of allegiance to me and demanded me as its leader in the war in which I was victorious at Actium. The provinces of the Spains, the Gauls, Africa, Sicily, and Sardinia took the same oath of allegiance. . . .

26. I extended the boundaries of all the provinces which were bordered by races not yet subject to our empire. The provinces of the Gauls, the Spains, and Germany, bounded by the ocean from Gades to the mouth of the Elbe, I reduced to a state of peace. The Alps, from the region such lies nearest to the Adriatic as far as the Tuscan Sea, I brought to a state of peace without waging on any tribe an unjust war. . . . On my order and under my auspices two armies were led, at almost the same time, into Ethiopia and into Arabia, which is called the "Happy," and very large forces of the enemy of both races were cut to pieces in battle and many towns were captured. . . .

28. I settled colonies of soldiers in Africa, Sicily, Macedonia, both Spains, Achaia, Asia, Syria, Gallia Narbonensis, Pisidia. Moreover, Italy has twenty-eight colonies founded under my auspices which have grown to be famous and populous during my lifetime.

Augustus concludes by describing the titles given to him by the Senate.

~

34. In my sixth and seventh consulships, when I had extinguished the flames of civil war, after receiving by universal consent the absolute control of affairs, I transferred the republic from my own control to the will of the Senate and the Roman people. For this service on my part I was given the title of Augustus by decree of the Senate, and the doorposts of my house were covered with laurels by public act, and a civic crown was fixed above my door, and a golden shield was placed in the Curia Julia whose inscription testified that the Senate and the Roman people gave me this in recognition of my valour, my clemency, my justice, and my piety. . . .

35. While I was administering my thirteenth consulship the Senate and the equestrian order and the entire Roman people gave me the title of Father of my Country, and decreed that this title should be inscribed upon the vestibule of my house and in the Senate-house and in the Forum Augustum. . . . At the time of writing this I was in my seventy-sixth year.

EVALUATE THE EVIDENCE

1. What major themes does Augustus address in his account of his career?
2. How does Augustus portray himself in this document?
3. Why do you think Augustus mentions the Senate, the Roman people, and the people of Italy so often?

Source: *Velleius Paterculus*, Loeb Classical Library, Volume 152, translated by Frederick W. Shipley; pp. 345, 347, 349, 351, 355, 377, 379, 381, 383, 385, 387, 389, 393, 399, 401. Cambridge, Mass.: Harvard University Press. First published 1924. The Loeb Classical Library® is a registered trademark of the President and Fellows of Harvard College.

Virgil's masterpiece is the *Aeneid* (uh-NEE-ihd), an epic poem that is the Latin equivalent of the Greek *Iliad* and *Odyssey* (see Chapter 3). Virgil's account of the founding of Rome and the early years of the city gave final form to the legend of Aeneas, the Trojan hero (and ancestor of Romulus and Remus) who escaped to Italy at the fall of Troy:

> Arms and the man I sing, who first made way,
> predestined exile, from the Trojan shore
> to Italy, the blest Lavinian strand.
> Smitten of storms he was on land and sea

> by violence of Heaven, to satisfy
> stern Juno's sleepless wrath; and much in war
> he suffered, seeking at the last to found
> the city, and bring o'er his fathers' gods
> to safe abode in Latium; whence arose
> the Latin race, old Alba's reverend lords,
> and from her hills wide-walled, imperial Rome.[3]

As Virgil told it, Aeneas became the lover of Dido, the widowed queen of Carthage, but left her because his destiny called him to found Rome. Swearing the destruction of Rome, Dido committed

Ovid, *The Art of Love*

The Art of Love is a humorous guide for lovers written by the Roman poet Ovid. Ovid addresses the first two parts to men, instructing them on how to seduce and keep women — look good, give them compliments, don't be too obvious. The third part is his corresponding advice for women, which in its main points is the same. The section below comes from the beginning of part one, advising men on where and how to meet women.

~

While you are footloose and free to play the field at your
    pleasure,
Watch for the one you can tell, "I want no other but you!"
She is not going to come to you floating down from the
    heavens:
For the right kind of a girl you must keep using your eyes.
Hunters know where to spread their nets for the stag in
    his cover,
Hunters know where the boar gnashes his teeth in the
    glade.
Fowlers know brier and bush, and fishermen study the
    waters
Baiting the hook for the cast just where the fish may be
    found.
So you too, in your hunt for material worthy of loving,
First will have to find out where the game usually goes.

. . .

. . . The theater's curve is a very good place for your
    hunting,
More opportunity here, maybe, than anywhere else.
Here you may find one to love, or possibly only to have
    fun with,
Someone to take for a night, someone to have and to
    hold.

. . .

Furthermore, don't overlook the meetings when horses
    are running;
In the crowds at the track opportunity waits.

There is no need for a code of finger-signals or nodding,
Sit as close as you like; no one will stop you at all.
In fact, you will have to sit close — that's one of the rules,
    at a race track.
Whether she likes it or not, contact is part of the game.
Try to find something in common, to open the
    conversation;
Don't care too much what you say, just so that every one
    hears
Ask her, "Whose colors are those?" — that's good for an
    opening gambit.
Put your own bet down, fast, on whatever she plays.

. . .

Often it happens that dust may fall on the blouse of the
    lady.
If such dust should fall, carefully brush it away.
Even if there's no dust, brush off whatever there isn't.
Any excuse will do: why do you think you have hands?

. . .

There is another good ground, the gladiatorial shows.
On that sorrowful sand Cupid has often contested,
And the watcher of wounds often has had it himself.
While he is talking, or touching a hand, or studying
    entries,
Asking which one is ahead after his bet has been laid,
Wounded himself, he groans to feel the shaft of the arrow;
He is victim himself, no more spectator, but show.

EVALUATE THE EVIDENCE

1. What metaphors and symbols does Ovid use to describe finding a lover and falling in love?
2. What does this poem indicate about leisure activities in the Rome of Ovid's day?

Source: Ovid, *The Art of Love*, trans. Rolfe, pp. 106–110. Copyright © 1957 Indiana University Press. Reprinted with permission of Indiana University Press.

suicide, and according to Virgil, her enmity helped cause the Punic Wars. In leaving Dido, an "Eastern" queen, Aeneas put duty and the good of the state ahead of marriage or pleasure. The parallels between this story and the very recent real events involving Antony and Cleopatra were not lost on Virgil's audience. Making the public aware of these parallels, and of Virgil's description of Aeneas as an ancestor of Julius Caesar, fit well with Augustus's aims. Therefore, Augustus encouraged Virgil to write the *Aeneid* and made sure it was circulated widely immediately after Virgil died.

The poet Horace (65–8 B.C.E.) rose from humble beginnings to friendship with Augustus. The son of an ex-slave and tax collector, Horace nonetheless received an excellent education, which he finished in Athens. After Augustus's victory Horace returned to Rome and became Virgil's friend. His most important works are a series of odes, short lyric poems often focusing on a single individual or event. One of these commemorated Augustus's victory over Antony and Cleopatra at Actium in 31 B.C.E. Horace depicted Cleopatra as a frenzied queen, drunk with desire to destroy Rome, a view that has influenced opinions about Cleopatra until today.

The historian Livy (59 B.C.E.–17 C.E.) was a friend of Augustus and a supporter of the principate. He especially approved of Augustus's efforts to restore what he saw as republican virtues. Livy's history of Rome, titled simply *Ab Urbe Condita* (From the founding of the city), began with the legend of Aeneas and ended with the reign of Augustus. Livy used the works of earlier Greek and Roman writers, as well as his own experiences, as his source material.

Augustus actively encouraged poets and writers, but he could also turn against them. The poet Ovid (AH-vuhd) (43 B.C.E.–17 C.E.) wrote erotic poetry about absent lovers and the joys of seduction, as well as other works about religious festivals and mythology. His best-known work is *The Art of Love*, a satire of the serious instructional poetry that was common in Rome at the time. *The Art of Love* provides advice to men about how to get and keep women, and for women about how to get and keep men. (See "Evaluating the Evidence 6.2: Ovid, *The Art of Love*," at left.) This work was so popular, Ovid relates, that shortly after completing it he felt compelled to write *The Cure for Love*, advising people how to fall out of love and forget their former lovers. Have lots of new lovers, it advises, and don't hang around places, eat foods, or listen to songs that will make you remember your former lover. In 8 B.C.E. Augustus banished Ovid to a city on the Black Sea far from Rome. Why he did so is a mystery, and Ovid himself states only that the reason was "a poem and a mistake." Some scholars argue that Augustus banished Ovid because his poetry celebrated adultery at a time when Augustus was promoting marriage and childbearing, and others say it was because the poet knew about political conspiracies. Whatever its causes, the exile of Ovid became a symbol of misunderstood poetic genius for many later writers.

Marriage and Morality

Augustus's banishing of Ovid may have simply been an excuse to get rid of him, but concern with morality and with what were perceived as traditional Roman virtues was a matter not just for literature in Augustan Rome, but also for law. Augustus promoted marriage and childbearing through legal changes that released free women and freedwomen (female slaves who had been freed) from male guardianship if they had given birth to a certain number of children. Men and women who were unmarried or had no children were restricted in the inheritance of property. Adultery, defined as sex with a married woman or with a woman under male guardianship, was made a crime, not simply the private family matter it had been.

In imperial propaganda, Augustus had his own family depicted as a model of traditional morality, with his wife Livia at his side and dressed in conservative and somewhat old-fashioned clothing rather than the more daring Greek styles that wealthy women were actually wearing in Rome at the time. (See "Evaluating the Evidence 6.3: Ara Pacis," page 164.) In fact, Augustus's family did not live up to this ideal. Augustus had his daughter Julia arrested and exiled for adultery and treason. Although it is impossible to tell what actually happened, she seems to have had at least one affair after her father forced her to marry a second husband—her stepbrother Tiberius—whom she hated.

Same-sex relationships among men in Rome followed a variety of patterns: some were between social equals and others between men and their slaves. Moralists denounced sexual relationships in which men squandered family money or became subservient to those of lower social status, but no laws were passed against same-sex relationships. We do not know very much about same-sex relationships among women in Rome, though court gossip and criticism of powerful women, including the wives of Augustus's successors, sometimes included charges of such relationships, along with charges of heterosexual promiscuity and other sexual slander.

Augustus's Successors

FOCUS QUESTION *How did the Roman state develop after Augustus?*

Augustus's success in creating solid political institutions was tested by the dynasty he created, the Julio-Claudians, whose members schemed against one another trying to win and hold power. The incompetence of one of the Julio-Claudians, Nero, and his failure to deal with the army generals allowed a military commander, Vespasian (veh-SPAY-zhuhn), to claim the throne and establish a new dynasty, the Flavians. The Flavians were followed by the "five good emperors," who were relatively successful militarily and politically. Rome entered a period of political stability, prosperity, and relative peace that lasted until the end of the second century C.E.

The Julio-Claudians and the Flavians

Because the principate was not technically an office, Augustus could not legally hand it to a successor. There were various plots surrounding the succession, including the one for which Ovid was banished. Augustus dealt firmly with plotters, sometimes having them executed, and he also found a way to solve the succession issue. Just as his great-uncle Julius Caesar had adopted him, he adopted his stepson Tiberius (who was also his son-in-law) as his son. Adoption of

Ara Pacis

In the middle years of Augustus's reign, the Roman Senate ordered a huge altar, the Ara Pacis, built to honor him and the peace he had brought to the empire. This was decorated with life-size reliefs of Augustus and members of his family, prominent Romans, and other people and deities. One side, shown here, depicts a goddess figure, most likely the goddess Peace herself, with twin babies on her lap, flanked by nymphs representing land and sea, and surrounded by plants and animals.

(DEA/Gianni Dagli Orti/De Agostini/Getty Images)

EVALUATE THE EVIDENCE

1. What do the elements depicted here most likely symbolize?
2. The Ara Pacis and the *Res Gestae* (see page 160) were both works of public art designed to commemorate the deeds of Augustus. Why might the Senate and Augustus have commissioned such works? Can you think of contemporary parallels?

an heir was a common practice among members of the elite in Rome, who used this method to pass on property to a chosen younger man—often a relative—if they had no sons. Long before Augustus's death he shared his consular and tribunician powers with Tiberius, thus grooming him for the principate. In his will Augustus left most of his vast fortune to Tiberius, and the Senate formally requested Tiberius to assume the burdens of the principate. Formalities apart, by the time of his death in 14 C.E. Augustus had succeeded in creating a dynasty.

For fifty years after Augustus's death the dynasty that he established—known as the Julio-Claudians because all were members of the Julian and Claudian clans—provided the emperors of Rome. Two of the Julio-Claudians who followed Augustus, Tiberius and Claudius, were sound rulers and able administrators. The other two, Caligula and Nero, were weak and frivolous men who exercised their power poorly and to the detriment of the empire.

Augustus's creation of an imperial bodyguard known as the **Praetorians** (pree-TAWR-ee-uhnz) had repercussions for his successors. In 41 C.E. the Praetorians murdered Caligula and forced the Senate to ratify their choice of Claudius as emperor. The events were repeated frequently. During the first three centuries of the empire, the Praetorian Guard all too often murdered emperors they were supposed to protect, and raised to emperor men of their own choosing.

In his early years Nero ruled fairly well, but he became increasingly paranoid about the power of those around him. In 68 C.E. his erratic actions and his policies led to a revolt by several generals, which was supported by the Praetorian Guard and members of the Senate. He was declared an enemy of the people and committed suicide. This opened the way to widespread disruption and civil war. In 69 C.E., the "year of the four emperors," four men claimed the position of emperor in quick succession. Roman armies in Gaul, on the Rhine, and in the east marched on Rome to make their commanders emperor. The man who emerged triumphant was Vespasian, commander of the eastern armies.

Vespasian restored the discipline of the armies. To prevent others from claiming the throne, Vespasian designated his sons Titus and Domitian as his successors, thus establishing the Flavian dynasty. Although Roman policy was to rule by peaceful domination whenever possible, he used the army to suppress the rebellions that had begun erupting at the end of Nero's reign. The most famous of these was one that had burst out in Judaea in 66 C.E., sparked by long-standing popular unrest over taxes. Jewish rebels initially defeated the Roman troops stationed in Judaea, but a larger army under the leadership of Vespasian and his son Titus put down the revolt. They destroyed much of the city of Jerusalem, including the Jewish temple, in 70 C.E., and took thousands of Jews as military captives and slaves, dispersing them throughout the empire. The military conquest of Judaea represented a failure of official Roman policy, but it is a good example of the way in which the Romans maintained clear control over their subjects, a control backed by military force if initial attempts at negotiation failed.

The Flavians carried on Augustus's work in Italy and on the frontiers. During the brief reign of Vespasian's son Titus, Mount Vesuvius in southern Italy erupted, destroying Pompeii and other cities and killing thousands of people. (See "Individuals in Society: Pliny the Elder," page 166.) Titus gave money and sent officials to organize the relief effort. His younger brother Domitian, who followed him as emperor, won additional territory in Germany, consolidating it into two new provinces. Later in life he became more autocratic, however, and he was killed in 96 C.E. in a plot that involved his own wife, ending the Flavian dynasty.

The Julio-Claudians and the Flavians

■ The Julio-Claudians		■ The Flavians	
27 B.C.E.–14 C.E.	Augustus	69 C.E.–79 C.E.	Vespasian
14 C.E.–37 C.E.	Tiberius	79 C.E.–81 C.E.	Titus
37 C.E.–41 C.E.	Caligula	81 C.E.–96 C.E.	Domitian
41 C.E.–54 C.E.	Claudius		
54 C.E.–68 C.E.	Nero		

The Age of the "Five Good Emperors"

The Flavians were succeeded by a line of relatively competent emperors, whom the political philosopher Niccolò Machiavelli in the sixteenth century termed the **"five good emperors"**— Nerva, Trajan, Hadrian, Antoninus Pius, and Marcus Aurelius. Machiavelli praised them because they all adopted able men as their successors during their lifetimes instead of relying on birth to provide an heir, thus giving Rome stability. None except Marcus Aurelius had a legitimate son, however, so they actually had little choice. They were also following the pattern set by Julius Caesar and Augustus, not breaking new ground. The last four "good emperors" were, in fact, related members of the Antonine family. Historians since Machiavelli have also noted that in some cases their choices were the result of pressure by the army or members of their family, rather than their own political astuteness. Whatever the reasons for the pattern, however, because all of these emperors were experienced generals and members of the Senate, Rome was provided with a stable series of well-trained political and military leaders for nearly a century, from 96 C.E. to 180 C.E.

Augustus had claimed that his influence arose from the collection of offices the Senate had bestowed on him and that he was merely the first citizen. Already during his rule many recognized that this was a façade, but the Senate continued to exist as a deliberative body and Rome remained officially a republic. Gradually the rulers expanded their individual powers, however, and Rome became in fact an empire, in which increasing amounts of power were held by one man. Although they never adopted the title "king"—this would have been seen as too great a break with Roman traditions—the rulers of Rome are conventionally called emperors. And as emperors took on new tasks

■ **Praetorians** Imperial bodyguard created by Augustus.

■ **"five good emperors"** The five Roman emperors (Nerva, Trajan, Hadrian, Antoninus Pius, and Marcus Aurelius) of the second century C.E. whose reigns were relatively prosperous and stable.

Pliny the Elder

"My uncle was stationed at Misenum, in active command of the fleet. On 24 August, in the early afternoon, my mother drew his attention to a cloud of unusual size and appearance.... My uncle's scholarly acumen saw at once that it was important enough for a closer inspection, and he ordered a boat to be made ready." So begins a letter from the statesman and writer Pliny the Younger to the historian Tacitus, describing what happened when Mount Vesuvius erupted in 79 C.E. Pliny provided terrifying details of clouds of hot ash, raining pumice stones, and sheets of fire, and then sang the praises of his uncle, also named Pliny, whose actions, "begun in a spirit of inquiry, [were] completed as a hero." According to Pliny the Younger's account, his uncle "steer[ed] his course straight for the danger zone with the intention of bringing help to many more people.... He was entirely fearless, describing each new movement and phase of the portent to be noted down exactly as he observed them . . . and when his helmsman advised him to turn back he refused, telling him that Fortune stood by the courageous." The elder Pliny (23 C.E.–79 C.E.) died on the beach near Pompeii, most likely from inhaling fumes that aggravated his asthma. His body was discovered several days later when the smoke and ash cleared.

The younger Pliny used this letter to portray his uncle as a model of traditional Roman virtues, but some of what he related was not an exaggeration. Like many young men of his social class—the equestrian—Pliny the Elder studied law and then joined the army as an officer. He was involved in several military campaigns in Germany and also found time to write books, including a volume on military tactics and several biographies. He left military service during Nero's reign and kept out of the limelight, writing noncontroversial books on grammar and rhetoric. After Nero committed suicide and Vespasian came to power, Pliny went back into government service, serving as the procurator (governor) of several different provinces. He again wrote biographies and histories, all of which are now lost, and the work that became his masterpiece, *Natural History*, an encyclopedia in which he sought to cover everything that was known to ancient Romans. In thirty-seven volumes, *Natural History* covers what we would now term biology, geology, astronomy, mineralogy, geography, ethnography, comparative anthropology, medicine, painting, building techniques, and many other subjects. Pliny's "spirit of inquiry" shines through this work, which he researched through the study of hundreds of sources (all carefully cited) and wrote while he was traveling around in government service. It is one of the largest works to have survived from the Roman Empire and served as a source of knowledge into the Renaissance, when it was one of the very first classical books to be published after the invention of the printing press in the fifteenth century. Pliny finished a first draft in about 77 C.E. and was working on revisions when he was appointed fleet commander in the Roman navy and sent to Misenum, near Naples. There the cloud of smoke from the erupting Vesuvius was too interesting for him to ignore, and he set off in a boat to investigate, with deadly results.

QUESTIONS FOR ANALYSIS

1. What Roman ideals does the younger Pliny portray his uncle as exemplifying through his conduct during the eruption?
2. How did army and government service in the Roman Empire provide opportunities for men of broad interests like Pliny?

Source: Quotations from Pliny the Younger, *Letters* 6.16, translated with an introduction by Betty Radice, vol. 1, pp. 166, 168 (Penguin Classics 1963, reprinted 1969). Reproduced by permission of Penguin Books Ltd.

No contemporary portrait of Pliny the Elder survives, but his nephew reports that when his body was discovered, it was "still fully clothed and looking more like sleep than death." When Pompeii was excavated, archaeologists used plaster to fill the voids in layers of ash that once held human bodies, allowing us to see the exact position a person was in when he or she died. This plaster cast is not Pliny but is as close to him in death as we can come. (© SZ Photo/Manfred Storck/ Bridgeman Images)

and functions, their influence was felt in more areas of life and government.

Hadrian is typical of the emperors of the second century C.E. He received a solid education in Rome and became an ardent admirer of Greek culture. He caught the attention of his elder cousin Trajan, the future emperor, who started him on a military career. At age nineteen Hadrian served on the Danube frontier, where he learned the details of how the Roman army lived and fought and saw for himself the problems of defending the frontiers. When Trajan became emperor in 98 C.E., Hadrian was given important positions in which he learned how to defend and run the empire. Although Trajan did not officially declare Hadrian his successor, at Trajan's death in 117 Hadrian assumed power.

Hadrian built a number of buildings, including the circular Pantheon in Rome and new temples in Athens. He established more formal imperial administrative departments and separated civil service from military service. Men with little talent or taste for the army could instead serve the state as administrators. These innovations made for more efficient running of the empire and increased the authority of the emperor.

Under Trajan the boundaries of the Roman Empire were expanded to their farthest extent, and Hadrian worked to maintain most of these holdings, although he pulled back Roman armies from areas in the East he considered indefensible. No longer a conquering force, the army was expected to defend what had already been won. Forts and watch stations guarded the borders. Outside the forts the Romans built a system of roads that allowed the forts to be quickly supplied and reinforced in times of rebellion or unrest. Trouble for the Romans included two major revolts by Jews in the eastern part of the empire, which resulted in heavy losses on both sides and the exile of many Jews from Judaea.

Roman soldiers also built walls, of which the most famous was one across northern England built primarily during Hadrian's reign. Hadrian's Wall, as it became known, protected Romans from attacks from the north, and also allowed them to regulate immigration and trade through the many gates along the wall. Like all walls around cities or across territory, it served as a symbol and means of power and control as well as a defensive strategy. The later emperor Antoninus Pius built a second wall one hundred miles north, but this was quickly abandoned. Thousands of troops patrolled Hadrian's Wall until the Romans pulled out of the area in the late fourth century.

Roman Britain, ca. 130 C.E.

"Five Good Emperors" (the Antonines)	
96–98	Nerva
98–117	Trajan
117–138	Hadrian
138–161	Antoninus Pius
161–180	Marcus Aurelius

As the empire expanded, the army grew larger, and more and more troops were auxiliary forces of noncitizens. Because army service could lead to citizenship, men from the provinces and even from beyond the borders of the Roman Empire joined the army willingly to gain this, receive a salary, and learn a trade. The army evolved into a garrison force, with troops guarding specific areas for long periods. Soldiers on active duty had originally been prohibited from marrying, but this restriction was increasingly ignored, and some troops brought their wives and families along on their assignments.

Rome and the Provinces

FOCUS QUESTION *What was life like in the city of Rome, and what was it like in the provinces?*

The expansion and stabilization of the empire brought changes to life in the city of Rome and also to life in the provinces in the first two centuries C.E. The city grew to a huge size, bringing the problems that plague any crowded urban area but also opportunities for work and leisure. Roads and secure sea-lanes linked the empire in one vast web, creating a network of commerce and communication. Trade and production flourished in the provinces, and Romans came into indirect contact with China.

Life in Imperial Rome

Rome was truly an extraordinary city, and with a population of over a million it may have been the largest city in the world. Although it boasted stately palaces and beautiful residential areas, most people lived in shoddily constructed houses. They took whatever work was available, producing food, clothing, construction materials, and the many other items needed by the city's residents, or selling these products from small shops or at the city's many marketplaces.

Many residents of the city of Rome were slaves, who ranged from highly educated household tutors or government officials and widely sought sculptors to workers who engaged in hard physical tasks. Slaves sometimes attempted to flee their masters, but those who failed in their escape attempts were returned to their masters and often branded on their foreheads. Others had metal collars fastened around their necks. One collar discovered near Rome read: "I have run away. Capture me. If you take me back to my master Zoninus, you will receive a gold coin."[4]

A story told about the author Plutarch reveals Roman attitudes toward slavery. One of Plutarch's educated slaves had read some of his master's philosophical writings and began to talk back to his master, for which Plutarch had him flogged. The slave accused his master of not acting very philosophically. Plutarch told the man with the whip to continue while he and the slave discussed philosophy. We have no idea whether this actually happened, but it demonstrates the reality of life for most slaves: lofty ideals did not interfere with their actual treatment.

Romans used the possibility of manumission as a means of controlling the behavior of their slaves, and individual Romans did sometimes free their slaves. Often these were house slaves who had virtually become members of the family and who often stayed with their former owner's family after being freed. The example of Helene, the slave of Marcus Aurelius Ammonio, is typical: the master "manumitted in the presence of friends his house-born female Helene, about 34 years old, and ordered her to be free."[5] Ammonio then gave her a gift of money. Manumission was limited by law, however, in part because freeing slaves made them citizens, allowing them to receive public grain and gifts of money, which some Romans thought debased pure Roman citizenship.

A typical day for the Roman family began with a modest breakfast, as in the days of the republic. Afterward came a trip to the outdoor market for the day's provisions. Seafood was a favorite item, as the Romans normally ate meat only at festivals. While poor people ate salt fish, the more prosperous dined on rare fish, oysters, squid, and eels. Wine was the common drink, and the rich often enjoyed rare vintages imported from abroad. Rich or poor, Romans mixed their wine with water, because drinking wine straight was seen as vulgar.

As in the republic, children began their education at home, where parents emphasized moral conduct, especially reverence for the gods and the law and respect for elders. Daughters learned how to manage the house, and sons learned the basics of their future calling from their fathers, who also taught them the use of weapons for military service. Boys boxed, swam, and learned to ride when possible, all to increase their strength, while giving them basic skills. Wealthy boys gained formal education from tutors or schools, generally favoring rhetoric and law for a political career. The lawyer and educator Quintilian (ca. 35–ca. 100 C.E.) expressed a widely held belief that public speaking was the most important academic subject for active citizenship and public life, and that school was the best place to learn this skill:

> The man who can really play his part as a citizen and is capable of meeting the demands both of public and private business, the man who can guide a state by his counsels, give it a firm basis by his legislation and purge its vices by his decisions as a judge, is assuredly no other than the orator. . . . It is above all things necessary that our future orator, who will have to live in the utmost publicity and in the broad daylight of public life, should become accustomed from his childhood to move in society without fear and habituated to a life far removed from that of the pale student, the solitary, and the recluse. His mind requires constant stimulus and excitement, whereas retirement such as has just been mentioned induces languor and the mind becomes mildewed like things that are left in the dark, or else flies to the opposite extreme and becomes puffed up with empty conceit; for he who has no standard of comparison by which to judge his own powers will necessarily rate them too high. . . . Further, at home he can only learn what is taught to himself, while at school he will learn what is taught others as well.[6]

Approaches to Urban Problems

Fire and crime were serious problems in the city, even after Augustus created urban fire and police forces. Streets were narrow, drainage was inadequate, and sanitation was poor. Numerous inscriptions record prohibitions against dumping human refuse and even cadavers on the grounds of sanctuaries and cemeteries. Private houses generally lacked toilets, so people used chamber pots.

In the second century C.E. urban planning and new construction improved the situation. For example, engineers built an elaborate system that collected sewage from public baths, the ground floors of buildings, and public latrines. They also built hundreds of miles of **aqueducts**, sophisticated systems of canals, channels,

■ **aqueducts** Canals, channels, and pipes that brought freshwater into cities.

Roman Architecture   These three structures demonstrate the beauty and utility of Roman architecture. The Pont du Gard at Nîmes in France (above) is a bridge over a river carrying an aqueduct that supplied millions of gallons of water per day to the Roman city of Nîmes in Gaul; the water flowed in a channel at the very top. Although this bridge was built largely without mortar or concrete, many Roman aqueducts and bridges relied on concrete and sometimes iron rods for their strength. The Pantheon in Rome (left), a temple dedicated to all the gods, was built in its present form around 130 C.E., after earlier temples on this site burned down. Its dome, 140 feet in diameter, remains the largest unreinforced concrete dome in the world. Romans also used concrete for more everyday purposes. The Coliseum in Rome (below), a sports arena that could seat fifty thousand spectators built between 70 and 80 C.E., was the site of gladiatorial games, animal spectacles, and executions. For a brief time it was also used for mock naval battles, but this proved to be impractical.

(Pont du Gard: © Masterfile Royalty Free; Pantheon: Gianni Dagli Orti/The Art Archive at Art Resource, NY; Coliseum: © Gerard Degeorge/Bridgeman Images)

and pipes, most of them underground, that brought freshwater into the city from the surrounding hills. The aqueducts, powered entirely by gravity, required regular maintenance, but they were a great improvement and helped make Rome a very attractive place to live. Building aqueducts required thousands and sometimes tens of thousands of workers, who were generally paid out of the imperial treasury. Aqueducts became a feature of Roman cities in many parts of the empire.

Better disposal of sewage was one way that people living in Rome tried to maintain their health, and they also used a range of treatments to stay healthy and cure illness. This included treatments based on the ideas of the Greek physician Hippocrates; folk remedies; prayers and rituals at the temple of the god of medicine, Asclepius; surgery; and combinations of all of these.

The most important medical researcher and physician working in imperial Rome was Galen (ca. 129–ca. 200 C.E.), a Greek born in modern-day Turkey. Like anyone hoping to rise in stature and wealth, he came to Rome. Building on the work of Hellenistic physicians (see Chapter 4), Galen wrote a huge number of treatises on anatomy and physiology, and became the personal physician of many prominent Romans, including several emperors. He promoted the idea that imbalances among various bodily fluids caused illness, and recommended bloodletting as a cure. This would remain a standard treatment in Western medicine until the eighteenth century. His research into the nervous system and the operation of muscles—most of which he conducted on animals, because the Romans forbade dissections of human cadavers—proved to be more accurate than did his ideas about the circulation of fluids. So did his practical advice on the treatment of wounds, much of which grew out of his and others' experiences with soldiers on the battlefield.

Neither Galen nor any other Roman physician could do much for infectious diseases, and in 165 C.E. troops returning from campaigns in the East brought a new disease with them, which spread quickly in the city and then beyond into other parts of the empire. Modern epidemiologists think this was most likely smallpox, but in the ancient world it became known simply as the Antonine plague, because it occurred during the reigns of emperors from the Antonine family. Whatever it was, it appears to have been extremely virulent in the city of Rome and among the Roman army for a decade or so.

Along with fire and disease, food was an issue in the ever more crowded city. Because of the danger of starvation, the emperor, following republican practice, provided the citizen population with free grain for bread and, later, oil and wine. By feeding the citizenry, the emperor prevented bread riots caused by shortages and high prices. For those who did not enjoy the rights of citizenship, the emperor provided grain at low prices.

This measure was designed to prevent speculators from forcing up grain prices in times of crisis. By maintaining the grain supply, the emperor kept the favor of the people and ensured that Rome's poor did not starve.

Popular Entertainment

In addition to supplying grain, the emperor and other wealthy citizens also entertained the Roman populace, often at vast expense. This combination of material support and popular entertainment to keep the masses happy is often termed "bread and circuses." The most popular forms of public entertainment were gladiatorial contests and chariot racing. Gladiatorial combat had begun as a private event during the republic, sponsored by men seeking new ways to honor their ancestors. By the early empire it had grown into a major public spectacle, with sponsors sometimes offering hundreds of gladiator fights along with battles between animals or between animals and humans. Games were advertised on billboards, and spectators were given a program with the names and sometimes the fighting statistics of the pairs, so that they could place bets more easily.

Men came to be gladiators through a variety of ways. Many were soldiers captured in war, sent to Rome or other large cities to be gladiators instead of being killed. Some were criminals, especially slaves found guilty of various crimes. By the imperial period increasing numbers were volunteers, often poor immigrants who saw gladiatorial combat as a way to support themselves. All gladiators were trained in gladiatorial schools and were legally slaves, although they could keep their winnings and a few became quite wealthy. The Hollywood portrayal of gladiatorial combat has men fighting to their death, but this was increasingly rare, as the owners of especially skilled fighters wanted them to continue to compete. Many—perhaps most—did die at a young age from their injuries or later infections, but some fought more than a hundred battles over long careers, retiring to become trainers in gladiatorial schools. Sponsors of matches sought to offer viewers ever more unusual spectacles: left-handed gladiators fighting right-handed ones, dwarf gladiators, and for a brief period even female gladiators. For a criminal condemned to die, the arena was preferable to the imperial mines, where convicts worked digging ore and died under wretched conditions. At least in the arena the gladiator might fight well enough to win freedom. Some Romans protested gladiatorial fighting, but the emperors recognized the political value of such spectacles, and most Romans enjoyed them.

The Romans were even more addicted to chariot racing than to gladiatorial shows. Under the empire four permanent teams competed against one another. Each had its own color—red, white, green, or blue.

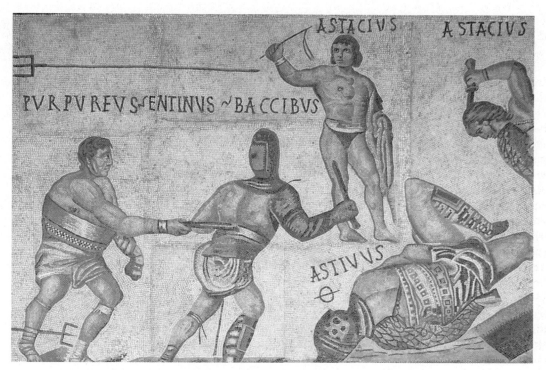

Gladiator Mosaic　Made in the first half of the fourth century, this mosaic from an estate outside Rome includes the name of each gladiator next to the figure. In the back a gladiator stands in a victory pose, while the fallen gladiator in the front is marked with the symbol Ø, indicating that he has died in combat. Many of the gladiators in this mosaic, such as those at the left, appear less fit and fearsome than the gladiators depicted in movies, more closely reflecting the reality that gladiatorial combat was a job undertaken by a variety of people. (Galleria Borghese, Rome, Italy/Alinari/Bridgeman Images)

Two-horse and four-horse chariots ran a course of seven laps, about five miles. One charioteer, Gaius Appuleius Diocles, raced for twenty-four years, with over 4,000 starts and nearly 1,500 wins. His admirers honored him with an inscription that proclaimed him champion of all charioteers. Other winning charioteers were also idolized, just as sports stars are today.

Roman spectacles such as gladiator fights and chariot racing are fascinating subjects for movies and computer games, but they were not everyday activities for Romans. As is evident on tombstone inscriptions, ordinary Romans were proud of their work and accomplishments and affectionate toward their families and friends. An impression of them can be gained from their epitaphs. (See "Living in the Past: Roman Epitaphs: Death Remembers Life," page 172.)

Prosperity in the Roman Provinces

As the empire grew and stabilized, many Roman provinces grew prosperous. Peace and security opened Britain, Gaul, and the lands of the Danube to settlers from other parts of the Roman Empire (Map 6.2). Veterans were given small parcels of land in the provinces, becoming tenant farmers.

The rural population throughout the empire left few records, but the inscriptions that remain point to a melding of cultures. One sphere where this occurred was language. People used Latin for legal and state religious purposes, but gradually Latin blended with the original language of an area and with languages spoken by those who came into the area later. Slowly what would become the Romance languages of Spanish, Italian, French, Portuguese, and Romanian evolved. Religion was another site of cultural exchange and mixture. Romans moving into an area learned about and began to venerate local gods, and local people learned about Roman ones. Gradually hybrid deities and rituals developed. The process of cultural exchange was at first more urban than rural, but the importance of cities and towns to the life of the wider countryside ensured that its effects spread far afield.

The garrison towns that grew up around provincial military camps became the centers of organized political life, and some grew into major cities, including Eburacum (modern-day York), Lutetia Parisiorum (Paris), and Londinium (London). In order to supply these administrative centers with food, land around them was cultivated more intensively.

LIVING IN THE PAST
Roman Epitaphs: Death Remembers Life

Romans who could afford them used tombstones and sarcophagi—stone coffins—to commemorate their own lives or those of the deceased and often to share their personal philosophies. They ordinarily expressed themselves seriously in inscriptions that are also intimate in tone. A simple tombstone reads: "To the spirits of the dead. T. Aelius Dionysius the freedman made this while he was alive both for Aelia Callitycena, his most blessed wife with whom he lived for thirty years with never a quarrel, an incomparable woman, and also for Amelius Perseus, his fellow freedman, and for their freedmen and those who come after them."* Paprius Vitalis paid tribute to his deceased wife: "If there is anything good in the lower regions—I, however, finish a poor life without you—be happy there too, sweetest Thelassia . . . married to me for forty years."† A tombstone from Roman Britain (opposite) reads: "Volusia Faustina, a citizen of Lindum, lived 26 years, 1 month, 26 days. Aurelius Senecio, a councillor, set this up to his well-deserving wife. Claudia Catiotua lived 60 years."

Others enjoyed their prosperity with wry gratitude. His sarcophagus shows Lucius Valerianus calmly looking over his very prosperous estates where the workers most likely included slaves (below). Yet his epitaph states: "I've escaped; got clean away. Good-bye Lady Hope and Fortune. I have nothing more to do with you. Work your worst on other people."‡ Marcus Antonius Encolpus left a similarly blunt message for the living: "Do not pass by this epitaph, wayfarer, but stop, listen, hear, then go. There is no boat in Hades, no ferryman Charon. No caretaker Aecus, no Cerberus dog. All we dead below have become bones and ashes, nothing more. I have spoken the truth to you. Go now, wayfarer, lest even in death I seem garrulous to you."§ All of these people felt that their lessons in life were valuable enough to share with others.

QUESTIONS FOR ANALYSIS

1. Examine the tombstone and sarcophagus illustrated here. How do the images on them fit with the epitaphs inscribed on them quoted here?

2. Consider all the epitaphs. What do they tell us about Roman attitudes toward life and death?

Sarcophagus of Lucius Valerianus. (Vatican Museums and Galleries, Vatican State/Alinari/Art Resource, NY)

*Elaine Fantham et al., *Women in the Classical World* (New York: Oxford University Press, 1994), pp. 369–370.

†Naphtali Lewis and Meyer Reinhold, *Roman Civilization*, vol. 2 (New York: Harper Torchbooks, 1955), p. 285. Copyright © 1990 Columbia University Press. Reprinted by permission of Columbia University Press.

‡Mary Johnston, *Roman Life* (Chicago: Scott, Foresman, and Co., 1957), p. 405.

§Lewis and Reinhold, *Roman Civilization*, vol. 2, pp. 284–285. Copyright © 1990 Columbia University Press. Reprinted by permission of Columbia University Press.

Roman merchants became early bankers, loaning money to local people and often controlling them financially. Wealthy Roman officials also sometimes built country estates in rural areas near the city, where they did grow crops but also escaped from the stresses of city life.

During the first and second centuries C.E., Roman Gaul became more prosperous than ever before, and prosperity attracted Roman settlers. Roman veterans mingled with the local population and sometimes married into local families. There was not much difference in many parts of the province between the original Celtic villages and their Roman successors.

In Britain, Roman influence was strongest in the south, where more towns developed. Archaeological evidence, such as coins and amphoras that held oil or wine, indicates healthy trading connections with the north, however, as Roman merchandise moved through the gates of Hadrian's Wall in exchange for food and other local products.

Across eastern Europe, Roman influence was weaker than it was in Gaul or southern Britain, and there appears to have been less intermarriage. In Illyria (ih-LIHR-ee-uh) and Dalmatia, regions of modern Albania, Croatia, and Montenegro, the local population never widely embraced either Roman culture or urban life. To a certain extent, however, Romanization occurred simply because the peoples lived in such close proximity.

The Romans were the first to build cities in northern Europe, but in the eastern Mediterranean they ruled cities that had existed before Rome itself was even a village. Here there was much continuity in urban life from the Hellenistic period. There was less construction than in the Roman cities of northern and western Europe because existing buildings could simply be put to new uses.

The well-preserved ruins of the ancient city of Aspendos, at the mouth of the Eurymedon (now Kopru) River on the south coast of modern Turkey (see Map 6.2), give a picture of life in one of these older Eastern cities. Built sometime before 500 B.C.E., the city was an important economic center in the Persian Empire and the site of a major battle in the wars between the Persian Empire and the Greek city-states. It sat among fertile fields, and the resources of the land provided raw materials for industry and trade. Trade along the river and in the port, especially salt, oil, horses, and wool, provided wealth to merchants. Aspendos was one of the earliest cities to mint coins. It was conquered by Alexander the Great and then by the Romans, but it remained prosperous. Romans and indigenous people mixed at the city's central marketplace and in temples and public buildings. The Romans built an aqueduct to bring water into the city, although this was later destroyed in an earthquake. Over the river

Tombstone of two women, Volusia Faustina and Claudia Catiotua, from the Roman city of Lindum (now Lincoln) in England. (© The Trustees of the British Museum/Art Resource, NY)

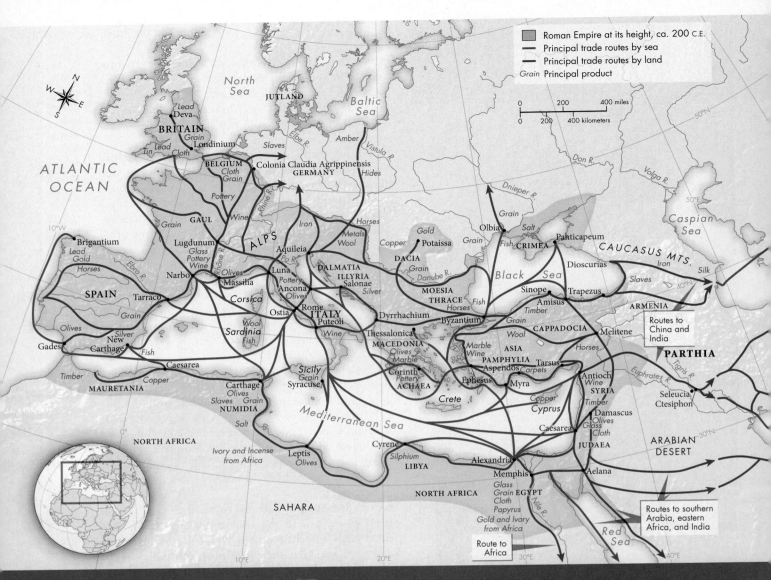

Map labels (within image):

North Sea · JUTLAND · Baltic Sea · Elbe R. · Vistula R. · Amber · Don R. · Volga R. · Dnieper R. · Caspian Sea

Roman Empire at its height, ca. 200 C.E.
Principal trade routes by sea
Principal trade routes by land
Grain Principal product

0 200 400 miles
0 200 400 kilometers

BRITAIN · Lead Deva · Grain · Londinium · Lead · Tin · Cloth · Slaves

ATLANTIC OCEAN

BELGIUM · Cloth · Grain · Colonia Claudia Agrippinensis · GERMANY · Hides · Pottery · Wine · Rhine R. · Iron · Horses · Metals · Wool · Copper · Gold · Potaissa · Grain · Olbia · Salt · Grain · CRIMEA · Fish · Panticapeum · CAUCASUS MTS. · Iron · Silk

GAUL · Grain · Lugdunum · Glass · Pottery · Wine · Narbo · Massilia · Luna · Pottery · Ancona · Olives · Olives · Rhône R. · Aquileia · DALMATIA · ILLYRIA · Salonae · Silver · DACIA · Grain · Danube R. · MOESIA · THRACE · Horses · Fish · Black Sea · Sinope · Amisus · Timber · Trapezus · Dioscurias · Slaves · ARMENIA

Brigantium · Lead · Gold · Horses · Ebro R. · SPAIN · Tarraco · Grain · Olives · Silver · New Carthage · Gades · Fish · Corsica · Sardinia · Wool · Fish · Ostia · Rome · ITALY · Puteoli · Wine · Dyrrhachium · Byzantium · Grain · Wool · CAPPADOCIA · Horses · Melitene · Routes to China and India · PARTHIA

Caesarea · Timber · Copper · MAURETANIA · Carthage · Olives · Slaves · Grain · NUMIDIA · Salt · Sicily · Grain · Syracuse · Thessalonica · MACEDONIA · Olives · Marble · Marble · Wine · ACHAEA · Corinth · Pottery · Crete · ASIA · PAMPHYLIA · Aspendos · Carpets · Tarsus · Ephesus · Myra · Copper · Cyprus · Antioch · Wine · SYRIA · Timber · Damascus · Glass · Olives · Cloth · Caesarea · JUDAEA · Seleucia · Ctesiphon · Euphrates R. · Tigris R. · ARABIAN DESERT

Mediterranean Sea · Leptis · Olives · Cyrene · Silphium · LIBYA · NORTH AFRICA · SAHARA · Ivory and Incense from Africa · Alexandria · Memphis · Glass · Grain · EGYPT · Cloth · Papyrus · Gold and Ivory from Africa · Nile R. · Aelana · Route to Africa · Red Sea · Routes to southern Arabia, eastern Africa, and India

ALPS · ATLANTIC OCEAN

MAPPING THE PAST

MAP 6.2 Production and Trade in the Pax Romana, ca. 27 B.C.E.–180 C.E.

This map gives a good idea of the principal products of various parts of the Roman Empire at its height and the trade routes connecting these regions. Map 10.2 on page 302 is a similar map that shows products and trade in roughly the same area nearly a millennium later. Examine both maps and answer the following questions.

ANALYZING THE MAP What similarities and differences do you see in products during these two periods?

CONNECTIONS To what extent did Roman trade routes influence later European trade routes?

they also built an arched stone bridge, about thirty feet wide so that carts and chariots could easily travel on it. This may have also collapsed in an earthquake, but its foundations were so sturdy that a thousand years later the area's Turkish rulers used them to build a new bridge, which still stands. In 155 C.E. a local architect built a magnificent theater that probably held seven thousand spectators, who sat under a retractable awning that provided shade. Here men and women enjoyed the great plays of the past and those popular in their own day.

They also watched gladiatorial contests, for these were popular in Eastern cities, as was horse racing.

More than just places to live, cities like Aspendos were centers of intellectual and cultural life. Their residents were in touch with the ideas and events of the day, in a network that spanned the entire Mediterranean and reached as far north as Britain. As long as the empire prospered and the revenues reached the imperial coffers, life in provincial cities—at least for the wealthy—could be nearly as pleasant as that in Rome.

174

Glass Beaker by Ennion This exquisite mold-blown glass beaker from the first century C.E. with relief decorations of leaves and basketry has an inscription in Greek: "Ennion made it." Ennion came from the coastal city of Sidon in modern Lebanon and is one of a very few artisans from the ancient world whose name we know. The fine detail and precision of his work led him to have a powerful influence on the Roman glass industry. (The Israel Museum, Jerusalem/Bridgeman Images)

Trade and Commerce

The expansion of trade during the pax Romana made the Roman Empire an economic as well as a political force in the provinces (see Map 6.2). Britain and Belgium became prime grain producers, with much of their harvests going to the armies of the Rhine, and Britain's wool industry probably got its start under the Romans. Italy and southern Gaul produced huge quantities of wine, which was shipped in large pottery jugs wherever merchant vessels could carry it. Roman colonists introduced the olive to southern Spain and northern Africa, which soon produced most of the oil consumed in the western part of the empire. In the East the olive oil production of Syrian farmers reached an all-time high, and Egypt produced tons of wheat that fed the Roman populace.

The growth of industry in the provinces was another striking development of this period. Cities in Gaul and Germany eclipsed the old Mediterranean manufacturing centers. Lyons in Gaul and later Cologne in Germany became the new centers of the glassmaking industry, and the cities of Gaul were nearly unrivaled in the manufacture of bronze and brass. The Romans took the manufacture of pottery to an advanced stage by introducing a wider range of vessels and making some of these on an industrial scale in kilns that were large enough to fire tens of thousands of pots at once. The most prized pottery was *terra sigillata*, reddish decorated tableware with a glossy surface. Methods for making terra sigillata spread from Italy northwards into Europe, often introduced by soldiers in the Roman army who had been trained in potterymaking in Italy. These craftsmen set up facilities to make roof tiles, amphoras, and dishes for their units, and local potters began to copy their styles and methods of manufacturing. Terra sigillata often portrayed Greco-Roman gods and heroes, so this pottery spread Mediterranean myths and stories. Local artisans added their own distinctive flourishes and sometimes stamped their names on the pots; these individual touches have allowed archaeologists to trace the pottery trade throughout the Roman Empire in great detail. Aided by all this growth in trade and industry, Europe and western Asia were linked in ways they had not been before.

As the Romans drove farther eastward, they encountered the Parthians, who had established a kingdom in what is now Afghanistan and Iran in the Hellenistic period. In the second century C.E. the Romans tried unsuccessfully to drive out the Parthians, who came to act as a link between Roman and Chinese merchants. Chinese merchants sold their wares to the Parthians, who then carried the goods overland to Mesopotamia or Egypt, from which they were shipped throughout the Roman Empire. Silk was a major commodity traded from the East to the West, along with other luxury goods. In return the Romans traded glassware, precious gems, and slaves.

The pax Romana was also an era of maritime trade, and Roman ships sailed from Egyptian ports to the mouth of the Indus River, where they traded local merchandise and wares imported by the Parthians. In the late first century C.E. the Chinese emperor sent an ambassador, Gan Ying, to make contact with the Roman Empire. Gan Ying made it as far as the Persian Gulf ports, where he heard about the Romans from Parthian sailors and reported back to his emperor that the Romans were wealthy, tall, and strikingly similar to the Chinese. His report became part of a group of accounts about the Romans and other "Western" peoples that circulated widely among scholars and officials in Han China. Educated Romans did not have a corresponding interest in China. For them, China remained more of a mythical than a real place, and they never bothered to learn more about it.

The Coming of Christianity

FOCUS QUESTION *How did Christianity grow into a major religious movement?*

During the reign of the emperor Tiberius (r. 14–37 C.E.), in the Roman province of Judaea, which had been created out of the Jewish kingdom of Judah, a Jewish man named Jesus of Nazareth preached, attracted a following, and was executed on the order of the Roman prefect Pontius Pilate. At the time this was a minor event, but Christianity, the religion created by Jesus's followers, came to have an enormous impact first in the Roman Empire and later throughout the world.

Factors Behind the Rise of Christianity

The civil wars that destroyed the Roman Republic left their mark on Judaea, where Jewish leaders had taken sides in the conflict. The turmoil created a climate of violence throughout the area, and among the Jews movements in opposition to the Romans spread. Some of these, such as the Zealots, encouraged armed rebellion against Roman rule, which would, indeed, break

out several times in the first and second centuries C.E. Many Jews came to believe that a final struggle was near, and that it would lead to the coming of a savior, or **Messiah**, a descendant of King David who would destroy the Roman legions and inaugurate a period of peace, happiness, and prosperity for Jews. This apocalyptic belief was an old one among Jews, but by the first century C.E. it had become more widespread than ever, with many people prophesying the imminent coming of a Messiah and readying themselves for a cataclysmic battle.

The pagan world also played its part in the story of early Christianity. The term **pagan**, derived from a Latin word meaning "rural dweller," came to refer to those who practiced religions other than Judaism or Christianity. (Christianity was initially an urban religion, and those who lived in the countryside were less likely to be converts.) This included religions devoted to the traditional Roman gods of the hearth, home, and countryside; syncretistic religions that blended Roman and indigenous deities; the cult of the emperor spread through the erection of statues, temples, and monuments; and mystery religions that offered the promise of life after death (see Chapter 4). Many people in the Roman Empire practiced all of these, combining them in whatever way seemed most beneficial or satisfying to them.

The Life and Teachings of Jesus

Into this climate of Messianic hope and Roman religious blending came Jesus of Nazareth (ca. 3 B.C.E.–ca. 29 C.E.). According to Christian Scripture, he was born to deeply religious Jewish parents and raised in Galilee, the stronghold of the Zealots and a trading center where Greeks and Romans interacted with Jews. His ministry began when he was about thirty, and he taught by preaching and telling stories.

Like Socrates, Jesus left no writings. Accounts of his sayings and teachings first circulated orally among his followers and were later written down. The principal evidence for his life and deeds are the four Gospels of the Bible (Matthew, Mark, Luke, and John), books that are part of what Christians later termed the New Testament. These Gospels—the name means "good news"—are records of Jesus's teachings, written to build a community of faith sometime in the late first century C.E. The Gospels were among the most widely copied and circulated early accounts of Jesus's life, and by the fourth century officials in the Christian Church decided that they, along with other types of writing such as letters and prophecies, would form Christian Scripture. The four Gospels included in the Bible are called canonical, from the Greek word that means "the rule" or "the standard." Other early documents also circulated, some of which have been rediscovered in modern times, and their interpretation is often a source of controversy.

■ **Messiah** In Jewish belief, a savior who would bring a period of peace and happiness for Jews.

■ **pagan** Originally referring to those who lived in the countryside, it came to mean those who practiced religions other than Judaism or Christianity.

Earliest Known Depiction of Jesus
This mural, from a Roman camp at Dura-Europos on the Euphrates River, may be the earliest known depiction of Jesus. Dating to 235 C.E., it depicts Jesus healing a paralytic man, an incident described in the New Testament. Early Christians used art to spread their message. (Yale University Art Gallery, Dura-Europos Collection)

The Gospels include certain details of Jesus's life, but they were not meant to be biographies. Their authors had probably heard many different people talk about what Jesus said and did, and there are discrepancies among the four accounts. These differences indicate that early followers had a diversity of beliefs about Jesus's nature and purpose. This diversity of beliefs about Jesus continues today. Some see him as a moral teacher, some as a prophet, and many as the son of God who rose from the dead and is himself divine.

However, almost all the early sources agree on certain aspects of Jesus's teachings: He preached of a heavenly kingdom of eternal happiness in a life after death, and of the importance of devotion to God and love of others. His teachings were based on Hebrew Scripture and reflected a conception of God and morality that came from Jewish tradition. Jesus's orthodoxy enabled him to preach in the synagogue and the temple, but he deviated from orthodoxy in insisting that he taught in his own name, not in the name of Yahweh (the Hebrew name for God). The Greek translation of the Hebrew word *Messiah* is *Christos*, the origin of the English word *Christ*. Was Jesus the Messiah, the Christ? A small band of followers thought so, and Jesus claimed that he was. Yet Jesus had his own conception of the Messiah. He would establish a spiritual kingdom, not

an earthly one. As recounted in one of the Gospels, he commented:

> Do not lay up for yourselves treasures on earth, where moth and rust consume and where thieves break in and steal, but lay up for yourselves treasures in heaven, where neither moth nor rust consumes and where thieves do not break in and steal. For where your treasure is, there will your heart be also.[7]

The Roman official Pontius Pilate, who had authority over much of Judaea, knew little about Jesus's teachings. Like all Roman officials, he was concerned with maintaining peace and order, which was a difficult task in restive Judaea. According to the New Testament, crowds followed Jesus into Jerusalem at the time of Passover, a highly emotional time in the Jewish year that marked the Jewish people's departure from Egypt under the leadership of Moses (see Chapter 2). The prospect that these crowds would spark violence no doubt alarmed Pilate. Some Jews believed that Jesus was the long-awaited Messiah. Others hated and feared him because they thought him religiously dangerous. The four Gospels differ somewhat on exactly what actions Jesus took in the city and what Jesus and Pilate said to each other after Jesus was arrested. They agree that Pilate condemned Jesus to death by crucifixion, and his soldiers carried out the sentence. On the third day after Jesus's crucifixion, some of his followers claimed that he had risen from the dead. For his earliest followers and for generations to come, the resurrection of Jesus became a central element of faith.

The Spread of Christianity

The memory of Jesus and his teachings survived and flourished. Believers in his divinity met in small assemblies or congregations, often in one another's homes, to discuss the meaning of Jesus's message and to celebrate a ritual (later called the Eucharist or Lord's Supper) commemorating his last meal with his disciples before his arrest. Because they expected Jesus to return to the world very soon, they regarded earthly life and institutions as unimportant. Only later did these congregations evolve into what came to be called the religion of Christianity, with a formal organization and set of beliefs.

The catalyst in the spread of Jesus's teachings and the formation of the Christian Church was Paul of Tarsus, a well-educated Hellenized Jew who was comfortable in both the Roman and the Jewish worlds. The New Testament reports that at first he persecuted members of the new sect, but then on the road to the city of Damascus in Syria he was struck blind by a vision of light and heard Jesus's voice. He converted to belief in Jesus, regained his sight, and became a vigorous promoter of Jesus's ideas. Paul traveled all over the Roman Empire and wrote letters of advice to many groups. These letters were copied and widely circulated, transforming Jesus's ideas into more specific moral teachings. He recognized that Christianity would not grow if it remained within Judaism, and connected it with the non-Jewish world. As a result of his efforts, Paul became the most important figure in changing Christianity from a Jewish sect into a separate religion, and many of his letters became part of Christian Scripture.

The breadth of the Roman Empire was another factor behind the spread of Christianity. If all roads led to Rome, they also led outward to the provinces. This enabled early Christians to spread their faith easily throughout the known world, as Jesus had told his followers to do in the Gospels, thus making his teachings universal. The pagan Romans also considered their secular empire universal, and the early Christians combined the two concepts of universalism.

Though most of the earliest converts seem to have been Jews, or Greeks and Romans who were already interested in Jewish moral teachings, Paul urged that Gentiles, or non-Jews, be accepted on an equal basis. The earliest Christian converts included people from all social classes. These people were reached by missionaries and others who spread the Christian message through family contacts, friendships, and business networks. Many women were active in spreading Christianity. Paul greeted male and female converts by name in his letters and noted that women often provided financial support for his activities. The growing Christian communities differed about the extent to which women should participate in the workings of the religion; some favored giving women a larger role in church affairs, while others were more restrictive, urging women to be silent on religious matters.

People were attracted to Christian teachings for a variety of reasons. It was in many ways a mystery religion, offering its adherents special teachings that would give them immortality. But in contrast to traditional mystery religions, Christianity promised this immortality widely, not only to a select few.

Most early Christians believed that they would rise in body, not simply in spirit, after a final day of judgment, so they favored burial of the dead rather than the more common Roman practice of cremation. They retained the Roman belief that the dead were polluting and so had to be buried outside city walls, however, and in the second century began to dig tunnels in the soft rock around Rome for burials. The bodies were placed in niches along the walls of these underground chambers and then sealed up. Gradually huge complexes of burial passageways called catacombs were dug. Memorial services for martyrs were sometimes held in or near catacombs, but they were not regular places of worship. Many catacombs contain some of the earliest examples of Christian art, and others, dug by Jews or pagans who chose to bury rather than cremate their own dead, contain examples of Jewish and secular Roman art from this period.

Along with the possibility of life after death, Christianity also offered rewards in this world to adherents. One of these was the possibility of forgiveness, for believers accepted that human nature is weak and that even the best Christians could fall into sin. But Jesus loved sinners and forgave those who repented. Christianity was also attractive to many because it gave the Roman world a cause. Instead of passivity, Christians stressed the ideal of striving for a goal. By spreading the word of Christ, Christians played their part in God's plan for the triumph of Christianity on earth. Christianity likewise gave its devotees a sense of community, which was very welcome in the often highly mobile world of the Roman Empire. To stress the spiritual kinship of this new type of community, Christians often called one another "brother" and "sister." Also, many Christians took Jesus's commandment to love one another as a guide and provided support for widows, orphans, and the poor, just as they did for family members. Such material support

■ **bishops** Christian Church officials with jurisdiction over certain areas and the power to determine the correct interpretation of Christian teachings.

■ **heresy** A religious practice or belief judged unacceptable by church officials.

became increasingly attractive as Roman social welfare programs broke down in the third century.

The Growing Acceptance and Evolution of Christianity

At first most Roman officials largely ignored the followers of Jesus, viewing them simply as one of the many splinter groups within Judaism. Slowly some Roman officials and leaders came to oppose Christian practices and beliefs. They considered Christians to be subversive dissidents because they stopped practicing traditional rituals venerating the hearth and home and they objected—often publicly or in writing—to the cult of the emperor. Some Romans thought that Christianity was one of the worst of the mystery religions, with immoral and indecent rituals. For instance, they thought that the ritual of the Lord's Supper, at which Christians said that they ate and drank the body and blood of Jesus, was an act of cannibalism involving the ritual murder of Roman boys. Many in the Roman Empire also feared that the traditional gods would withdraw their favor from the Roman Empire because of the Christian insistence that these gods either did not exist or were evil spirits. The Christian refusal to worship Roman gods, in their opinion, endangered Roman lives and society. Others worried that Christians were trying to destroy the Roman family with their insistence on a new type of kinship, and they pointed to Jesus's words in the Gospels saying that salvation was far more important than family relationships. A woman who converted, thought many Romans, might use her new faith to oppose her father's choice of marital partner or even renounce marriage itself, an idea supported by the actions of a few female converts.

Persecutions of Christians, including torture and executions, were organized by governors of Roman provinces and sometimes by the emperor, beginning with Nero. Most persecutions were local and sporadic in nature, however, and some of the gory stories about the martyrs are later inventions, designed to strengthen believers with accounts of earlier heroes. Christians differed in their opinions about how to respond to persecution. Some sought out martyrdom, while others thought that doing so went against Christian teachings.

Responses to Christianity on the part of Roman emperors varied. The emperor Trajan forbade his governors to hunt down Christians. Though admitting that he considered Christianity an abomination, he decided it was better policy to leave Christians in peace. Later emperors, including Septimius Severus at the very end of the second century, Decius in the third century, and Diocletian in the fourth century, increased persecutions again, ordering Christians to sac-

Christian Oil Lamp When Christianity spread in the Roman Empire, many believers purchased household goods with Christian symbols. This pottery lamp for an ordinary home, dating from the fourth century, is marked with a common symbol for Jesus, the letters *XP* (chi rho), the first two letters in Greek for *Christos*, "Christ." (Photo by Zev Radovan/© www.BibleLand Pictures.com/Alamy Stock Photo)

rifice to the emperor and the Roman gods or risk death. Executions followed their edicts, although estimates of how many people were actually martyred in any of these persecutions vary widely.

By the second century C.E. Christianity was also changing. The belief that Jesus was soon coming again gradually waned, and as the number of converts increased, permanent institutions were established instead of simple house churches. These included buildings and a hierarchy of officials often modeled on those of the Roman Empire. **Bishops**, officials with jurisdiction over a certain area, became especially important. They began to assert that they had the right to determine the correct interpretation of Christian teachings and to choose their successors. Councils of bishops determined which writings would be considered canonical, and lines were increasingly drawn between what was considered correct teaching and what was considered incorrect, or **heresy**.

Christianity also began to attract more highly educated individuals, who developed complex theological interpretations of issues that were not clear in scripture. Often drawing on Greek philosophy and Roman legal traditions, they worked out understandings of such issues as how Jesus could be both divine and human, and how God could be both a father and a son (and later a spirit as well, a Christian doctrine known as the Trinity). Bishops and theologians often modified teachings that seemed upsetting to Romans, such as Jesus's harsh words about wealth and family ties. Given all these changes, Christianity became more formal in the second century, with power more centralized.

The Empire in Disarray

FOCUS QUESTION *What explains the chaos of the third century C.E.?*

The prosperity and political stability of the second century gave way to a period of domestic upheaval and foreign invasion. The third century saw a long series of able but ambitious military commanders who used their legions to make themselves emperors. Law yielded to the sword, and the office of the emperor lost legitimacy. The nature of the army changed, and the economy weakened because of unsound policies.

Civil Wars and Military Commanders

The reign of Marcus Aurelius (r. 161–180 C.E.), the last of the "five good emperors," was marked by problems. The Tiber River flooded in 162, destroying crops and killing animals, which led to famine. Soldiers returning from wars in the East brought the Antonine plague back to Rome (see page 170) and then carried it northward. Germanic-speaking groups attacked along the Rhine and Danube borders, and the emperor himself took over the campaign against them in 169. He spent most of the rest of his life in military camps along Rome's northern border, where in addition to leading troops he wrote a series of personal reflections in Greek. These *Meditations*, as they later came to be known, are advice to himself about doing one's duty and acting in accordance with nature, ideas that came from Stoic philosophy (see Chapter 4). He wrote:

> Do not act unwillingly nor selfishly nor without self-examination. . . . Take heed not to be transformed into a Caesar, not to be dipped in the purple dye [a color only the emperor could wear]. Keep yourself therefore simple, good, pure, grave, unaffected, the friend of justice, religious, kind, affectionate, strong for your proper work. Wrestle to continue to be the man Philosophy wished to make you. Reverence the gods, save men.[8]

The *Meditations* are a good key to Marcus Aurelius's character, but they appear not to have circulated very much during the centuries immediately after they were written. Certainly very few later emperors took this advice to heart.

After the death of Marcus Aurelius, misrule by his successors led to a long and intense spasm of fighting. Marcus Aurelius's son Commodus was strangled by a conspiracy that included his wife, and in 193 five men claimed the throne in quick succession. Two of

The Emperor Marcus Aurelius   This larger-than-life bronze equestrian statue, sculpted to celebrate his military victories or shortly after his death in 180 C.E., shows the emperor holding up his hand in the conventional imperial greeting. More than twenty equestrian statues could be seen in late imperial Rome, but this is the only one to survive. In the sixteenth century Michelangelo built one of the major plazas of Rome around it, although now the original has been moved to a museum for better preservation and a copy stands outdoors. (Piazza Campodoglio, Rome, Italy/Prisma/UIG via Getty Images)

them were also assassinated, and Septimius Severus (r. 193–211) emerged as the victor. He restored order, expanded the borders of the Roman Empire in Africa and western Asia, and invaded Scotland. He increased the size of the army significantly and paid the soldiers better. This made him popular with soldiers, though it also increased the taxes on civilians. Some of his policies regarding the army created additional problems in the long run. Changes in recruiting practices that emphasized local recruiting of non-Romans created a Roman army that became less acculturated to Roman values. This army was no longer the vehicle for Romanization that it had been in earlier centuries. In part to increase the tax base, in 212 Septimius Severus's son Caracalla (r. 198–217) issued an edict making all free male residents of the Roman Empire citizens. This made them eligible to serve in the legions—which may

■ **barracks emperors** The emperors of the middle of the third century, so called because they were military commanders.

have been why Caracalla did this—but also made serving in the army less attractive, and reduced the number of men willing to join.

More than twenty different emperors seized power in the forty-nine years between 235 and 284, a period scholars call the "crisis of the third century." These emperors were generally military commanders from the border provinces, and there were so many that the middle of the third century has become known as the age of the **barracks emperors**. Almost all were either assassinated or died in civil wars, and their concentration on overthrowing the ruling emperor left the borders unguarded. Non-Roman groups on the frontiers took full advantage of the chaos to overrun vast areas. When they reached the Rhine and the Danube, they often found gaping holes in the Roman defenses.

Turmoil in Economic Life

This chaos also disrupted areas far away from the borders of the empire. Renegade soldiers and corrupt imperial officials, together with many greedy local agents, preyed on local people. In some places in the countryside, officials requisitioned villagers' livestock and compelled them to do forced labor. Farmers appealed to the government for protection so that they could cultivate the land. Although some of those in authority were unsympathetic and even violent to villagers, many others tried to maintain order. Yet even the best of them also suffered. If officials could not meet their tax quotas, which were rising to support the costs of civil war, they had to pay the deficits from their own pockets. Because the local officials were themselves so hard-pressed, they squeezed what they needed from rural families. Many farmers, unable to pay, were driven off their land, and those remaining faced ruin. As a result, agricultural productivity declined.

In response to the economic crisis, the emperors reduced the amount of silver used in coins, replacing it with less valuable metals such as copper, so that they could continue to pay their troops. This tactic, however, led to crippling inflation, which wiped out savings and sent prices soaring.

The Romans still controlled the Mediterranean, which nurtured commerce. The road system remained largely intact, though often roads were allowed to fall into disrepair. Trade still flowed, but with reduced efficiency and high costs.

By 284 C.E. the empire had reached a crisis that threatened its downfall. The position of emperor was gained no longer by lawful succession but rather by victory in civil war. The empire had failed at the top, and the repercussions of the disaster spread throughout the empire with dire effects.

NOTES

1. Virgil, *Aeneid*, trans. Theodore C. Williams (Boston: Houghton Mifflin, 1910), 6.851–853.
2. Virgil, *Georgics* 3.515–519. In this chapter, works in Latin with no translator noted were translated by John Buckler.
3. Virgil, *Aeneid* 1.1–11.
4. Text in Mary Johnston, *Roman Life* (Chicago: Scott, Foresman, and Co., 1957), p. 172.
5. Napthali Lewis and Meyer Reinhold, *Roman Civilization*, vol. 2 (New York: Harper Torchbooks, 1955), p. 262.
6. H. E. Butler, trans., *The Institutio Oratoria of Quintilian*, vol. 1 (Cambridge, Mass.: Harvard University Press and Loeb Classical Library, 1920), pp. 10–11, 41, 49.
7. Matthew 6:19–21.
8. Marcus Aurelius, *Meditations* 3.5, 6.30, trans. A. S. L. Farquharson (New York: Everyman's Library, 1961), pp. 12, 5.

LOOKING BACK LOOKING AHEAD

The period of the Roman Empire was a rich era in both economic and cultural terms. Roman emperors developed a system of government that ruled over vast areas of diverse people fairly effectively. The resulting stability and peace encouraged agriculture and production. Goods and people moved along roads and sea-lanes, as did ideas, including the new religion of Christianity. All the while, the Romans incorporated indigenous peoples into their way of life as the empire expanded into northern and western Europe. Yet during a long period of internal crisis, civil war, and invasions in the third century, it seemed as if the empire would collapse.

The Roman Empire did not disintegrate in the third century, however. Although emperors came and went in quick and violent succession, the basic institutions and infrastructure of the empire remained intact. Even during the worst of the ordeal, many lower-level officials and ordinary soldiers continued to do their jobs, embodying the principles of duty that Marcus Aurelius advocated. People like this would be key to passing Roman traditions on to institutions that developed later in Europe, including law courts, city governments, and nations.

Make Connections

Think about the larger developments and continuities within and across chapters.

1. What allowed large empires in the ancient world, including the Persians (Chapter 2) and the Romans, to govern vast territories and many different peoples successfully?

2. How was slavery in the Roman Empire different from that of earlier societies? How was it similar? What might account for the continuities and changes in slavery you have identified?

3. If a male resident of Athens during the time of Pericles (Chapter 3) had time-traveled to Rome during the time of Augustus, what might he have found familiar? What might have seemed strange? How might these observations have differed if the time traveler were a female resident of Athens?

6 REVIEW & EXPLORE

Identify Key Terms

Identify and explain the significance of each item below.

imperator (p. 154)

principate (p. 154)

Roma et Augustus (p. 158)

pax Romana (p. 159)

Praetorians (p. 164)

"five good emperors" (p. 165)

aqueducts (p. 168)

Messiah (p. 176)

pagan (p. 176)

bishops (p. 179)

heresy (p. 179)

barracks emperors (p. 181)

Review the Main Ideas

Answer the focus questions from each section of the chapter.

- How did Augustus create a foundation for the Roman Empire? (p. 154)
- How did the Roman state develop after Augustus? (p. 163)
- What was life like in the city of Rome, and what was it like in the provinces? (p. 167)
- How did Christianity grow into a major religious movement? (p. 176)
- What explains the chaos of the third century C.E.? (p. 180)

Suggested Reading and Media Resources

BOOKS

- Aldrete, Gregory S. *Daily Life in the Roman City.* 2004. Reveals the significance of ordinary Roman life in the cities of Rome, its port Ostia, and Pompeii.
- Campbell, Brian. *War and Society in Imperial Rome, 31 B.C.–A.D. 284.* 2002. Shows how Roman warfare and military life influenced and was influenced by Roman society.
- Clark, Gillian. *Christianity and Roman Society.* 2004. Surveys the evolution of Christian life among Christians and with their pagan neighbors.
- D'Ambra, Eve. *Roman Women.* 2006. Treats the lives of women of all social ranks.
- Everitt, Anthony. *Augustus: The Life of Rome's First Emperor.* 2007. A lively biography that traces Augustus's rise to power.
- Freeman, Charles. *A New History of Early Christianity.* 2010. A survey of the first four centuries of Christianity, written for a general audience.
- Joshel, Sandra R. *Slavery in the Roman World.* 2010. An overview of Roman slavery, including the social and family lives of slaves, designed for students.
- Knapp, Robert. *Invisible Romans.* 2011. A view of Roman life that focuses on ordinary men and women: soldiers, slaves, laborers, housewives, gladiators, and outlaws.
- Kyle, Donald G. *Sport and Spectacle in the Ancient World.* 2007. Examines the nature and meaning of sports from Mesopotamia through Rome, including running races, fighting, and chariot racing.
- Nutton, Vivian. *Ancient Medicine.* 2005. A comprehensive analysis of health and disease that examines different approaches to medicine and the role of physicians.
- Potter, David, and David J. Mattingly. *Life, Death, and Entertainment in the Roman Empire,* 2d ed. 2010. Discusses family and gender, slavery, food, religion, and entertainment.
- Roth, Jonathan P. *Roman Warfare.* 2010. Surveys arms, tactics, strategy, and logistics from republican to imperial times.
- Woolf, Greg. *Becoming Roman: The Origins of Provincial Civilization in Gaul.* 2000. Examines how and why a blended culture emerged in the Roman provinces.

DOCUMENTARIES

- *From Jesus to Christ: The First Christians* (PBS, 1998). A four-part documentary exploring the life and death of Jesus and the transformation of Christianity from a small group to an established church. With commentary by theologians, archaeologists, and historians on many key issues.
- *The Roman Empire in the First Century* (PBS, 2001). A four-part documentary that examines the building of the Roman Empire, highlighting ordinary people as well as emperors.
- *Rome: The Rise and Fall of an Empire* (History Channel, 2008). A thirteen-part documentary, with re-enactments—especially of battle scenes, power struggles, and lavish banquets—that trace Rome from the second century B.C.E. to the fifth century C.E.

FEATURE FILMS AND TELEVISION

- *Ben-Hur* (William Wyler, 1959). The story of a fictional Jewish merchant condemned to the galleys who becomes a champion chariot racer and witnesses the crucifixion of Jesus; includes an amazing chariot-race sequence and spectacular sets.
- *Gladiator* (Ridley Scott, 2000). The Academy Award–winning historical epic about a Roman general who becomes a gladiator and avenges the murder of his family by a power-crazy emperor.
- *I, Claudius* (BBC, 1976). A highly acclaimed fictionalized version of the political intrigue in the first century, told from the viewpoint of the emperor Claudius; with Derek Jacobi and Patrick Stewart.

WEB SITES

- *Rome Reborn: A Digital Model of Ancient Rome.* Three-dimensional digital models by an international team of scholars illustrating the urban development of ancient Rome; includes a fascinating video tour of the streets of Rome in 320 C.E. **www.romereborn.virginia.edu/**
- *Vindolanda Tablets Online.* A highly unusual find of wooden writing tablets from the second century C.E., discovered at the Roman fortress of Vindolanda behind Hadrian's Wall in Britain, reveals many aspects of non-elite Roman society and military life. The site includes text images, transliterated texts, English translations, and historical background. **vindolanda.csad.ox.ac.uk/**

7

Late Antiquity

250–600

The Roman Empire, with its powerful — and sometimes bizarre — leaders, magnificent buildings, luxurious clothing, and bloody amusements, has long fascinated people. Politicians and historians have closely studied the reasons for its successes and have even more closely analyzed the weaknesses that led to its eventual collapse. From the third century onward, the Western Roman Empire slowly disintegrated. Scholars have long seen this era as one of the great turning points in Western history, a time when the ancient world was transformed into the very different medieval world. During the past several decades, however, focus has shifted to continuities as well as changes, and what is now usually termed "late antiquity" has been recognized as a period of creativity and adaptation, not simply of decline and fall.

The two main agents of continuity in late antiquity were the Christian Church and the Byzantine or Eastern Roman Empire. Missionaries and church officials spread Christianity within and far beyond the borders of the Roman Empire, bringing with them the Latin language and institutions based on Roman models. The Byzantine Empire lasted until 1453, a thousand years longer than the Western Roman Empire, and preserved and transmitted much of ancient Greco-Roman law, philosophy, and institutions. The main agents of change in late antiquity were groups the Romans labeled barbarians migrating into the Roman Empire. They brought different social, political, and economic structures with them, but as they encountered Roman culture and became Christian, their own ways of doing things were also transformed. ■

Life in Late Antiquity
In this sixth-century ivory carving, a procession of people carry relics of a saint to a Christian church under construction. New churches often received holy items when they were dedicated, and processions were common ways in which people expressed community devotion. (Trier Cathedral Treasury, Trier, Germany/akg-images/Newscom)

Reconstruction Under Diocletian and Constantine

FOCUS QUESTION *How did Diocletian and Constantine try to reform the empire?*

In the middle of the third century, the Roman Empire faced internal turmoil and external attacks. Civil wars tore the empire apart as emperors rose and fell in quick succession, and barbarian groups migrated and marauded deep within the boundaries of the empire (see Chapter 6). Wars and invasions disrupted normal commerce and agriculture, the primary sources of tax revenues. The barracks emperors of the third century dealt with economic hardship by cutting the silver content of coins until money was virtually worthless. The immediate result was crippling inflation throughout the empire, made worse by the corruption of many officials. Many Romans had become Christian, but the followers of traditional Roman religion were divided in their views of what this meant for the empire. In the early fourth century the emperor Diocletian (r. 284–305), who was born of low-status parents and had risen through the ranks of the military to become emperor, restored order, and the later emperor

Constantine (r. 306–337) continued his work. How Diocletian, Constantine, and their successors responded to the problems facing the empire influenced later developments.

Political Measures

Under Diocletian, Augustus's polite fiction of the emperor as first among equals gave way to the emperor as absolute autocrat. The princeps became *dominus* (lord). The emperor claimed that he was "the elect of god"—that he ruled because of divine favor. To underline the emperor's exalted position, Diocletian and Constantine adopted the gaudy court ceremonies and trappings of the Persian Empire. People entering the emperor's presence prostrated themselves before him and kissed the hem of his robes.

Diocletian recognized that the empire had become too large for one man to handle and divided it into a western half and an eastern half (Map 7.1). Diocletian assumed direct control of the eastern part; he gave the rule of the western part to a colleague, along with the title *augustus*. Around 293 Diocletian further delegated power by appointing two men to assist the augustus and him; each of the four men was given the title *caesar*, and the system was known as the **tetrarchy** (TEH-trahr-kee), meaning "rule of four." He further divided each part of the empire into administrative units called **dioceses**, which were in turn subdivided into small provinces, all governed by an expanded bureaucracy. Although four men ruled the empire, Diocletian was clearly the senior partner and final source of authority.

Diocletian's political reforms were a momentous step. The reorganization made the empire easier to administer and placed each of the four central military commands much closer to borders or other trouble spots, so that troops could be sent more quickly when needed. Diocletian hoped that the tetrarchy would supply a clearly defined order of succession and end struggles for power over the emperorship. That did not happen, but much of Diocletian's reorganization remained.

Like Diocletian, Constantine came up through the army, and took control after a series of civil wars. He eventually had authority over the entire empire, but ruled from the East, where he established a new capital for the empire at Byzantium, an old Greek city on the Bosporus, naming it "New Rome," though it was soon called Constantinople. Constantine sponsored a massive building program of palaces, warehouses, public buildings, and even a hippodrome for horse racing, modeling these on Roman buildings. He built defensive works along the borders of the empire, trying hard to keep it together, and used various means to strengthen the army, as did his successors. The emperors ruling

MAP 7.1 The Division of the Roman World, 293 Under Diocletian, the Roman Empire was first divided into a western and an eastern half, a development that foreshadowed the medieval division between the Latin West and the Byzantine East.

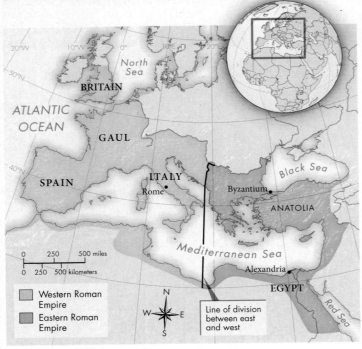

Western Roman Empire

Eastern Roman Empire

Line of division between east and west

from Constantinople could not provide enough military assistance to repel invaders in the western half of the Roman Empire, however, and Roman authority there slowly disintegrated.

Economic Issues

Diocletian and Constantine were faced with a number of economic problems, including inflation and declining tax revenues, and their attempts to solve them illustrate the methods and limitations of absolute monarchy. In a move unprecedented in Roman history, Diocletian issued an edict that fixed maximum prices and wages throughout the empire. He and his assistant emperors dealt with the tax system just as strictly and inflexibly. Taxes became payable in kind, that is, in goods such as grain, sheep, or cloth instead of money, which made them difficult to transport to central authorities. Constantine continued these measures and also made occupations more rigid: all people involved in the growing, preparation, and transportation of food and other essentials were locked into their professions. A baker, for example, could not go into any other business, and his son took up the trade at his death. In this period of severe depression many individuals and communities could not pay their taxes. In such cases local tax collectors, who were also bound to their occupations, had to make up the difference from their own funds. This system soon wiped out a whole class of moderately wealthy people and set the stage for the lack of social mobility that was a key characteristic of European society for many centuries to follow.

The emperors' measures did not really address Rome's central economic problems, however. Because of worsening conditions during the third and fourth centuries, many free farmers and their families were killed by invaders or renegade soldiers, fled the land to escape the barbarians, or abandoned farms ravaged in the fighting. Consequently, large tracts of land lay deserted. Landlords with ample resources began at once to reclaim as much of this land as they could, often hiring back the free farmers who had previously worked the land as paid labor or tenants. The huge villas that resulted were self-sufficient and became islands of stability in an unsettled world.

Chronology

ca. 293	Diocletian establishes the tetrarchy
313	Edict of Milan, allowing practice of all religions in the Roman Empire
325	Council of Nicaea
354–430	Life of Saint Augustine
378	Visigoths defeat the Roman army at Adrianople
380	Theodosius makes Christianity the official religion of the Roman Empire
410	Visigoths sack Rome
429	Vandals begin their conquest of North Africa
476	Odoacer deposes the last Roman emperor in the West
ca. 481–511	Reign of Clovis
493	Theoderic establishes an Ostrogothic state in Italy
527–565	Reign of Justinian
529	*The Rule of Saint Benedict*
535–572	Byzantines reconquer and rule Italy
597	Pope Gregory I sends missionaries to Britain

Gold Coin Showing Constantine
In this gold coin, minted at Ticinum in northern Italy in 316, Constantine is shown with a halo, a symbol of his sacred character and connection to the sun-god. This iconography was later adopted in Christian art to signify divinity or sanctity. (Ashmolean Museum, University of Oxford, UK/Bridgeman Images)

Free farmers who remained on the land were exposed to the raids of barbarians or robbers and to the tyranny of imperial officials. In return for the protection and security landlords could offer, small landholders gave over their lands and their freedom. To guarantee a supply of labor, landlords denied them freedom to move elsewhere. Henceforth they and their families worked their patrons' land, not their own. Free men and women were becoming tenant farmers bound to the land, what would later be called serfs.

■ **tetrarchy** Diocletian's four-part division of the Roman Empire.

■ **diocese** An administrative unit in the later Roman Empire; adopted by the Christian Church as the territory under the authority of a bishop. **187**

The Acceptance of Christianity

The turmoil of the third century seemed to some emperors, including Diocletian, to be the punishment of the gods. Diocletian stepped up persecution of Christians who would not sacrifice to Rome's traditional deities, portraying them as disloyal to the empire in an attempt to wipe out the faith. These persecutions lasted only a few years, however. Increasing numbers of Romans, including members of prominent families, were converting to Christianity, and many who followed traditional Roman religions no longer saw Christianity as un-Roman (see Chapter 6). Constantine reversed Diocletian's policy and instead ordered toleration of all religions in the Edict of Milan, issued in 313. Whether Constantine was himself a Christian by this point is hotly debated. His later biographer, the Christian bishop Eusebius, reported that he had been converted on a battlefield in 312 after seeing a vision, and other sources attribute his conversion to his Christian mother, Helena. On the other hand, he continued to worship the sun-god, and in 321 proclaimed that Sunday, "the Day of the Sun," would be the official day

of rest. He was baptized only shortly before he died, although this was not uncommon for high officials. Whatever his personal beliefs at different stages of his life, there is no debate that he recognized the growing numbers of Christians in the empire and financially supported the church. He freed the clergy from imperial taxation and endowed the building of Christian churches. One of his gifts—the Lateran Palace in Rome—remained the official residence of the popes until the fourteenth century. He allowed others to make gifts to the church as well, decreeing in 321, "Every man, when dying, shall have the right to bequeath as much of his property as he desires to the holy and venerable Catholic Church. And such wills are not to be broken."[1] In return for his support, Constantine expected the assistance of church officials in maintaining order. Helped in part by its favored position in the empire, Christianity slowly became the leading religion (Map 7.2).

Christians disagreed with one another about many issues, which led to schisms (SKIH-zuhms), denunciations, and sometimes violence. In the fourth and fifth centuries disputes arose over the nature of Christ. For

MAP 7.2 The Spread of Christianity, to 600 Originating in Judaea, the southern part of modern Israel and Jordan, Christianity first spread throughout the Roman world and then beyond it in all directions.

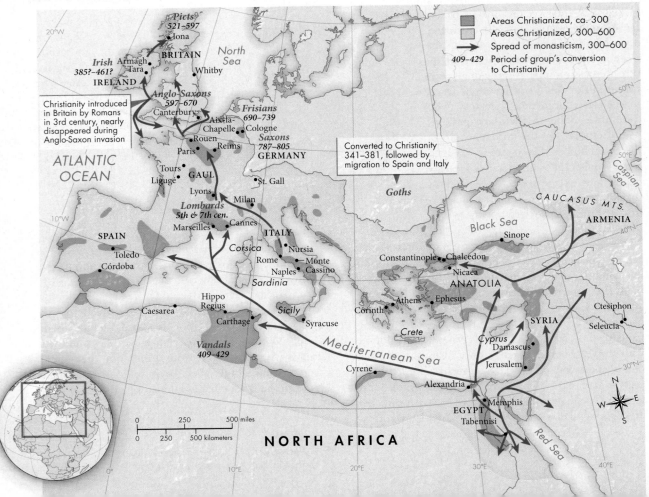

Sarcophagus of Helena This marble sarcophagus was made for Helena, the mother of Emperor Constantine, at her death. Its detailed carvings show victorious Roman horsemen and barbarian prisoners. Helena became a Christian before her son did and may have influenced his conversion. She was sent by Constantine on a journey to bring sacred relics from Jerusalem to Constantinople as part of his efforts to promote Christianity in the empire. (Museo Pio Clementino, Vatican Museums and Galleries, Vatican State/© Vanni Archive/Art Resource, NY)

example, **Arianism** (AI-ree-uh-nih-zuhm), developed by Arius (ca. 250–336), a priest of Alexandria, held that Jesus was created by the will of God the Father and thus was not co-eternal with him. Arian Christians reasoned that Jesus the Son must be inferior to God the Father because the Father was incapable of suffering and did not die. Arianism enjoyed such popularity and provoked such controversy that Constantine, who declared that "internal strife within the Church of God is far more evil and dangerous than any kind of war and conflict," interceded. In 325 he summoned church leaders to a council in Nicaea (nigh-SEE-uh) in Asia Minor and presided over it personally, referring to himself as "your fellow servant of our common Lord and Savior."[2] The council produced the Nicene (nigh-SEEN) Creed, which defined the position that Christ is "eternally begotten of the Father" and of the same substance as the Father. Arius and those who refused to accept Nicene Christianity were banished. Their interpretation of the nature of Christ was declared a heresy, that is, a belief that contradicted the interpretation the church leaders declared was correct, which was termed orthodoxy. These actions did not end Arianism, however. Several later emperors were Arian Christian, and Arian missionaries converted many barbarian tribes, who were attracted by the idea that Jesus was God's first-in-command, which fit well with their own warrior hierarchies and was less complicated than the idea of two persons with one substance. The Nicene Creed says little specifically about the Holy Spirit, but in the following centuries the idea that the Father, Son, and Holy Spirit are "one substance in three persons"—the Trinity—became a central doctrine in Christianity, though again there were those who disagreed. Disputes about

the nature of Christ also continued, with factions establishing themselves as separate Christian groups. The Nestorians, for example, regarded the divine and human natures in Jesus as distinct from one another, whereas the orthodox opinion was that they were united. The Nestorians split from the rest of the church in the fifth century after their position was outlawed, and settled in Persia. Nestorian Christian missionaries later founded churches in Central Asia, India, and China.

Religious and secular authorities tried in various ways to control this diversity as well as promote Christianity. In 380 the emperor Theodosius (thee-uh-DOH-shee-uhs) made Nicene Christianity the official religion of the empire. Theodosius stripped Roman pagan temples of statues, made the practice of the old Roman state religion a treasonable offense, and persecuted Christians who dissented from orthodox doctrine. Most significant, he allowed the church to establish its own courts and to use its own body of law, called canon law. The church courts, not the Roman government, had jurisdiction over the clergy and ecclesiastical disputes. At the death of Theodosius, the Christian Church was considerably independent of the Roman state. The foundation for later growth in church power had been laid.

Later emperors continued the pattern of active involvement in church affairs. They appointed the highest officials of the church hierarchy; the emperors or their representatives presided at ecumenical councils; and the emperors controlled some of the material resources of the church—land, rents, and dependent peasantry.

■ **Arianism** A theological belief that originated when Arius, a priest of Alexandria, denied that Christ was co-eternal with God the Father.

The Growth of the Christian Church

FOCUS QUESTION *How did the Christian Church become a major force in the Mediterranean and Europe?*

As the emperors changed their policies about Christianity from persecution to promotion, the church grew, gradually becoming the most important institution in the Mediterranean and Europe. The able administrators and creative thinkers of the church developed permanent institutions and complex philosophical concepts that drew on the Greco-Roman tradition, which attracted learned Romans.

The Church and Its Leaders

The early Christian Church benefited from the administrative abilities of church leaders. With the empire in decay, educated people joined and worked for the church in the belief that it was the one institution able to provide some stability. Bishop Ambrose of Milan (339–397) is typical of the Roman aristocrats who held high public office, were converted to Christianity, and subsequently became bishops. Like many bishops, Ambrose had a solid education in classical law and rhetoric, which he used to become an eloquent preacher. He had a strong sense of his authority and even stood up to Emperor Theodosius, who had ordered Ambrose to hand over his major church—called a basilica—to the emperor:

> At length came the command, "Deliver up the Basilica"; I reply, "It is not lawful for us to deliver it up, nor for your Majesty to receive it. By no law can you violate the house of a private man, and do you think that the house of God may be taken away? . . . But do not burden your conscience with the thought that you have any right as Emperor over sacred things. . . . It is written, God's to God and Caesar's to Caesar. The palace is the Emperor's, the churches are the Bishop's. To you is committed jurisdiction over public, not over sacred buildings."[3]

The emperor relented. Ambrose's assertion that the church was supreme in spiritual matters and the state in secular issues was to serve as the cornerstone of the church's position on church-state relations for centuries. Ambrose came to be regarded as one of the fathers of the church, that is, early Christian thinkers whose authority was seen as second only to the Bible in later centuries.

Gradually the church adapted the organizational structure of the Roman Empire begun during the reign of Diocletian. The territory under the authority of a bishop was also called a diocese, with its center a cathe-

Saint Jerome and Saint Ambrose   This wood carving shows Saint Jerome and Saint Ambrose, two of the most important early church fathers, hard at work writing. Divine inspiration appears in the form of an angel and a dove. (Duomo, Modena, Italy/Photo: Ghigo Roli, 1999. Franco Cosimo Panini Editore © Management Fratelli Alinari/Alinari/Art Resource, NY)

dral (from the Latin *cathedra*, meaning "chair"), the church that contained the bishop's official seat of power. A bishop's jurisdiction extended throughout the diocese, and he came to control a large amount of land that was given to or purchased by the church. Bishops generally came from prominent families and had both spiritual and political power; as the Roman Empire disintegrated, they became the most important local authority on many types of issues. They claimed to trace their spiritual ancestry back to Jesus's apostles, a doctrine called **apostolic succession**. Because of the special importance of their dioceses, five bishops—those of Antioch, Alexandria, Jerusalem, Constantinople, and Rome—gained the title of patriarch.

After the capital and the emperor moved to Constantinople, the power of the bishop of Rome grew because he was the only patriarch in the Western Roman Empire. The bishops of Rome stressed that Rome had special significance because of its history as the capital of a worldwide empire. More significantly, they asserted, Rome had a special place in Christian history. According to tradition, Saint Peter, chief of Jesus's disciples, had lived in Rome and been its first bishop. Thus, as successors of Peter, the bishops of Rome—known as popes, from the Latin word *papa*, meaning "father"—claimed a privileged position in the church hierarchy, an idea called the **Petrine Doctrine** that built on the notion of apostolic succession. They stressed their supremacy over other Christian communities and urged other churches to appeal to Rome for the resolution of disputed doctrinal issues. Not surprisingly, the other patriarchs did not agree. They continued to exercise authority in their own regions, and local churches did as well, but the groundwork had been laid for later Roman predominance on religious matters.

In the fifth century the popes also expanded the church's secular authority. Pope Leo I (pontificate 440–461) made treaties with several barbarian leaders who threatened the city of Rome. Gregory I (pontificate 590–604), later called "the Great," made an agreement with the barbarian groups who had cut off Rome's food supply, reorganized church lands to increase production, and then distributed the additional food to the poor. He had been an official for the city of Rome before he became a church official, and his administrative and diplomatic talents helped the church expand. He sent missionaries to the British Isles (see page 208) and wrote letters and guides instructing bishops on practical and spiritual matters. He promoted the ideas of Augustine (see page 193), particularly those that defined church rituals as essential for salvation. The Western Christian Church headed by the pope in Rome would become the most enduring nongovernmental institution in world history.

The Development of Christian Monasticism

Christianity began and spread as a city religion. Since the first century, however, some especially pious Christians had felt that the only alternative to the decadence of urban life was complete separation from the world. They believed that the Christian life as set forth in the Gospel could not be lived in the midst of the immorality of Roman society.

This desire to withdraw from ordinary life led to the development of the monastic life. Monasticism began in third-century Egypt, where individuals like Saint Anthony (251?–356) and small groups first withdrew from cities and from organized society to seek God through prayer in desert or mountain caves and shelters, giving up all for Christ. Gradually large colonies of monks gathered in the deserts of Upper Egypt, and

Christians came to believe that monks, like the early Christian martyrs executed by Roman authorities before them, could speak to God and that their prayers had special influence. These monks were called hermits, from the Greek word *eremos*, meaning "desert." Many devout women also were attracted to this eremitical (ehr-uh-MIH-tihk-uhl) type of monasticism.

The Egyptian ascetic Pachomius (puh-KOH-mee-uhs) (290–346?) drew thousands of men and women to the monastic life at Tabennisi on the Upper Nile. There were too many for them to live as hermits, so Pachomius organized communities of men and women, creating a new type of monasticism, known as cenobitic (seh-nuh-BIH-tik), that emphasized communal living. Saint Basil (329?–379), an influential bishop from Asia Minor and another of the fathers of the church, encouraged cenobitic monasticism. He and much of the church hierarchy thought that communal living provided an environment for training the aspirant in the virtues of charity, poverty, and freedom from self-deception.

Starting in the fourth century, information about Egyptian monasticism came to the West, and both men and women sought the monastic life. Because of the dangers of living alone in the forests of northern Europe, where wild animals, harsh climate, and barbarian tribes posed ongoing threats, the eremitical form of monasticism did not take root. Most of the monasticism that developed in Gaul, Italy, Spain, England, and Ireland was cenobitic.

Monastery Life

In 529 Benedict of Nursia (480–543), who had experimented with both eremitical and communal forms of monastic life, wrote a brief set of regulations for the monks who had gathered around him at Monte Cassino between Rome and Naples. Benedict's guide for monastic life, known as *The Rule of Saint Benedict*, came to influence all forms of organized religious life in the Western Christian Church. Men and women in monastic houses all followed sets of rules, first those of Benedict and later those written by other individuals. Because of this, men who lived a communal monastic life came to be called **regular clergy**, from the Latin word *regulus* (rule). Priests and bishops who staffed churches in which people worshipped and who were not cut off

---

■ **apostolic succession** The doctrine that all bishops can trace their spiritual ancestry back to Jesus's apostles.

■ **Petrine Doctrine** A doctrine stating that the popes (the bishops of Rome) were the successors of Saint Peter and therefore heirs to his highest level of authority as chief of the apostles.

■ **regular clergy** Men and women who lived in monastic houses and followed sets of rules, first those of Benedict and later those written by other individuals.

from the world were called **secular clergy**. According to official church doctrine, women were not members of the clergy, but this distinction was not clear to most people.

The Rule of Saint Benedict outlined a monastic life of regularity, discipline, and moderation in an atmosphere of silence. Each monk had ample food and adequate sleep. The monk spent part of each day in formal prayer, which consisted of chanting psalms and other prayers from the Bible in the part of the monastery church called the choir. The rest of the day was passed in manual labor, study, and private prayer. The monastic life as conceived by Saint Benedict struck a balance between asceticism (extreme material sacrifice, including fasting and the renunciation of sex) and activity. It thus provided opportunities for men of entirely different abilities and talents—from mechanics to gardeners to literary scholars. The Benedictine form of religious life also appealed to women, because it allowed them to show their devotion and engage in study. Benedict's twin sister Scholastica (480–543) adapted the *Rule* for use by her community of nuns.

Benedictine monasticism also succeeded partly because it was so materially successful. In the seventh and eighth centuries monasteries pushed back forests and wastelands, drained swamps, and experimented with crop rotation. Benedictine houses thus made a significant contribution to the agricultural development of Europe.

Finally, monasteries conducted schools for local young people, and monks and nuns copied manuscripts, preserving classical as well as Christian literature. Local and royal governments drew on the services of the literate men and able administrators the monasteries produced. This was not what Saint Benedict had intended, but perhaps the effectiveness of the institution he designed made it inevitable.

Christianity and Classical Culture

The growth of Christianity was not simply a matter of institutions such as the papacy and monasteries, but also a matter of ideas. The earliest Christian thinkers sometimes rejected Greco-Roman culture, but as Christianity grew from a tiny persecuted group to the official religion of the Roman Empire, its leaders and thinkers gradually came to terms with classical culture (see Chapter 6). They incorporated elements of Greek and Roman philosophy and learning into Christian teachings, modifying them to fit with Christian notions.

Saint Jerome (340–419), for example, a distinguished theologian and linguist regarded as a father of the church, translated the Old and New Testaments

from Hebrew and Greek into vernacular Latin. Called the Vulgate, his edition of the Bible served as the official translation until the sixteenth century, and scholars rely on it even today. Familiar with the writings of classical authors, Saint Jerome believed that Christians should study the best of ancient thought because it would direct their minds to God. He maintained that the best ancient literature should be interpreted in light of the Christian faith.

Christian Notions of Gender and Sexuality

Early Christians both adopted and adapted the then-contemporary views of women, marriage, and sexuality. In his plan of salvation, Jesus considered women the equal of men. Women were among the earliest converts to Christianity and took an active role in its spread, preaching, acting as missionaries, being martyred alongside men, and perhaps even baptizing believers. Because early Christians believed that the Second Coming of Christ was imminent, they devoted their energies to their new spiritual family of co-believers. Early Christians often met in people's homes and called one another "brother" and "sister," a metaphorical use of family terms that was new to the Roman Empire. Women and men joyously accepted the ascetic life, renouncing marriage and procreation to use their bodies for a higher calling. Some women, either singly or in monastic communities, declared themselves "virgins in the service of Christ." All this initially made Christianity seem dangerous to many Romans, who viewed marriage as the foundation of society and the proper patriarchal order.

Not all Christian teachings about gender were radical, however. In the first century C.E. male church leaders began to place restrictions on female believers. Women were forbidden to preach and were gradually excluded from holding official positions in Christianity other than in women's monasteries. Women who chose lives of virginity in the service of God were to be praised; Saint Jerome commented that a woman "who wishes to serve Christ more than the world . . . will cease to be a woman and will be called man," the highest praise he could bestow.[4] Even such women were not to be too independent, however. Both Jewish and classical Mediterranean culture viewed women's subordination as natural and proper, so in limiting the activities of female believers the Christian Church was following well-established patterns, just as it did in modeling its official hierarchy after that of the Roman Empire.

Christian teachings about sexuality built on and challenged classical models. The rejection of sexual activity involved an affirmation of the importance of a

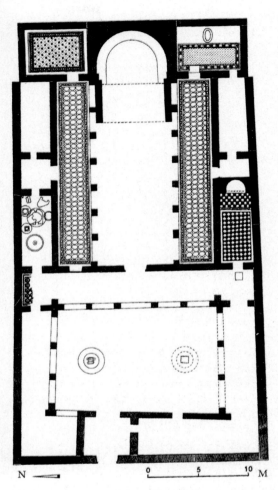

Floor Plan and Foundation of Kursi Monastery Church   Built on the eastern shore of the Sea of Galilee in the fifth century at a major pilgrimage site, this walled monastery had living quarters for the monks, a guesthouse, and a bath for pilgrims. It contained a church modeled on the type of Roman public building known as a basilica, with an open courtyard with two wells (near the bottom in the pictures), mosaic floors, and a central nave separated from side aisles by rows of arched columns. In one side chapel (on the left in the pictures) was a small baptismal font, and in another a press for olive oil, a major source of income for the monastery. The skeletons of thirty monks were found in a crypt when the site was uncovered during road construction in 1970. (Private Collection/Photo © Zev Radovan/Bridgeman Images)

spiritual life, but it also incorporated the hostility toward the body found in some Hellenistic philosophies and some of the other religions that had spread in the Roman Empire in this era, such as Manichaeism (MAN-ih-kee-ih-zuhm). Manichaeism, a dualistic religion based on the ideas of the third-century Persian thinker Mani, taught that the spiritual world was good and the material world was evil, so salvation came through education and self-denial. Christian teachings affirmed that God had created the material world and sanctioned marriage, but most Christian thinkers also taught that celibacy was the better life, and that anything that took one's attention from the spiritual world performed an evil function. For most

clerical writers (who themselves were male) this temptation came from women, and in some of their writings women themselves are depicted as evil, the "devil's gateway." Thus the writings of many church fathers contain a strong streak of misogyny (hatred of women), which was passed down to later Christian thinkers.

Saint Augustine on Human Nature, Will, and Sin

The most influential church father in the West was Saint Augustine of Hippo (354–430). Saint Augustine was born into an urban family in what is now Algeria

Heaven in Augustine's *City of God*   Augustine's writings were copied and recopied for many centuries in all parts of Europe, and they remained extremely influential. In this copy from a twelfth-century Czech illuminated manuscript of Augustine's *City of God*, the Czech king Wenceslaus and his grandmother are portrayed in the lower right corner; they probably paid for the manuscript. (Archives, Hradcany Castle, Prague, Czech Republic/ Erich Lessing/Art Resource, NY)

torical style and language of late Roman antiquity, it marks the synthesis of Greco-Roman forms and Christian thought. *The Confessions* describes Augustine's moral struggle, the conflict between his spiritual and intellectual aspirations and his sensual and material self. Many Greek and Roman philosophers had taught that knowledge would lead to virtue. Augustine came to reject this idea, claiming that people do not always act on the basis of rational knowledge. As he notes in *The Confessions*, even before he became a Christian he had decided that chastity was the best possible life, so he prayed to God for "chastity and continency," yet always added "but not yet." His education had not made him strong enough to avoid lust or any other evil; that would come only through God's power and grace.

Augustine's ideas on sin, grace, and redemption became the foundation of all subsequent Western Christian theology, Protestant as well as Catholic. He wrote that the basic force in any individual is the will, which he defined as "the power of the soul to hold on to or to obtain an object without constraint." The end or goal of the will determines the moral character of the individual. When Adam ate the fruit forbidden by God in the Garden of Eden (Genesis 3:6), he committed the "original sin" and corrupted the will. Adam's sin was not simply his own—it was passed on to all later humans through sexual intercourse; even infants were tainted. Original sin thus became a common social stain, in Augustine's opinion, transmitted by sexual desire. Coitus was theoretically good because it was created by God, but it had been corrupted by sin, so every act of intercourse was evil and every child was conceived through a sinful act. By viewing sexual desire as the result of Adam and Eve's disobedience to divine instructions, Augustine linked sexuality even more clearly with sin than had earlier church fathers. Because Adam disobeyed God and fell, all human beings have an innate tendency to sin: their will is weak. But according to Augustine, God restores the strength of

in North Africa. His father, a minor civil servant, was a pagan; his mother, Monica, was a devout Christian. He gained an excellent classical education in philosophy and rhetoric and, as was normal for young Roman men, began relations with a concubine, who later had his son. Interested in new religious ideas, he became a Manichaean.

Augustine took teaching positions first in Rome and then in Milan, where he had frequent conversations with Bishop Ambrose. Through his discussions with Ambrose and his own reading, Augustine rejected his Manichaeism and became a Christian. He returned to Africa and later became bishop of the seacoast city of Hippo Regius. He was a renowned preacher to Christians there, a vigorous defender of orthodox Christianity, and the author of more than ninety-three books and treatises.

Augustine's autobiography, *The Confessions*, is a literary masterpiece and one of the most influential books in the history of Europe. Written in the rhe-

the will through grace, which is transmitted in certain rituals that the church defined as **sacraments**. Grace results from God's decisions, not from any merit on the part of the individual.

When Visigothic forces captured the city of Rome in 410, horrified pagans blamed the disaster on the Christians. In response, Augustine wrote *City of God*. This original work contrasts Christianity with the secular society in which it exists. According to Augustine, history is the account of God acting in time. Human history reveals that there are two kinds of people: those who live the life of the flesh, and those who live the life of the spirit in what Augustine called the City of God. The former will endure eternal hellfire; the latter will enjoy eternal bliss.

Augustine maintained that states came into existence as the result of Adam's fall and people's inclination to sin. He believed that the state was a necessary evil with the power to do good by providing the peace, justice, and order that Christians need to pursue their pilgrimage to the City of God. States' legitimate power included the ability to wage war, and Augustine's ideas were later used to develop notions of just warfare.

Barbarian Society

FOCUS QUESTION *What were the key characteristics of barbarian society?*

Augustine's *City of God* was written in response to the conquest of Rome by an army of Visigoths, one of the many peoples the Romans—and later historians—labeled "barbarians." The word *barbarian* comes from the Greek *barbaros*, meaning someone who did not speak Greek. (To the Greeks, others seemed to be speaking nonsense syllables; *barbar* is the Greek equivalent of "blah-blah" or "yada-yada.") The Greeks used this word to include people such as the Egyptians, whom the Greeks respected. The Romans usually used the Latin version of *barbarian* to mean the peoples who lived beyond the northeastern boundary of Roman territory, whom they regarded as unruly, savage, and primitive. That value judgment is generally also present when we use "barbarian" in English, but there really is no other word to describe the many different peoples who lived to the north of the Roman Empire. Thus historians of late antiquity use the word *barbarian* to designate these peoples, who spoke a variety of languages, but had similarities in their basic social, economic, and political structures. Many of these historians find much to admire in barbarian society.

Scholars have been hampered in investigating barbarian society because most groups did not write and thus kept no written records before Christian missionaries introduced writing. Greek and Roman authors did describe barbarian society, but they were not always objective observers, instead using barbarians to highlight what they thought was right or wrong about their own cultures. Thus written records must be combined with archaeological evidence to gain a more accurate picture. In addition, historians are increasingly deciphering and using the barbarians' own written records that do exist, especially inscriptions carved in stone, bone, and wood and written in the **runic alphabet**. Runic inscriptions come primarily from Scandinavia and the British Isles. Most are short and limited to names, such as inscriptions on tombstones, but some describe the actions of kings and other powerful individuals, and a few of them mention the activities of more ordinary people.

Barbarians included many different ethnic groups with social and political structures, languages, laws, and beliefs that developed in central and northern Europe over many centuries. Among the largest groups were Celts (whom the Romans called Gauls) and Germans; Germans were further subdivided into various groups, such as Ostrogoths, Visigoths, Burgundians, and Franks. *Celt* and *German* are often used as ethnic terms, but they are better understood as linguistic terms, a Celt being a person who spoke a Celtic language, an ancestor of the modern Gaelic or Breton language, and a German one who spoke a Germanic language, an ancestor of modern German, Dutch, Danish, Swedish, and Norwegian. Celts, Germans, and other barbarians brought their customs and traditions with them when they moved southward, and these gradually combined with classical and Christian patterns to form new types of societies.

Village and Family Life

Barbarian groups usually resided in small villages, and climate and geography determined the basic patterns of how they lived off the land. Many groups lived in small settlements on the edges of clearings where they raised barley, wheat, oats, peas, and beans. Men and women tilled their fields with simple wooden plows and harvested their grains with small iron sickles. The vast majority of people's caloric intake came from grain in some form; the kernels of grain were eaten as porridge, ground up for flour, or fermented into strong, thick beer. (See "Evaluating the Evidence 7.1: Tacitus on Germanic Society," page 197.)

Within the villages, there were great differences in wealth and status. Free men and their families constituted the largest class. The number of cattle a man possessed indicated his wealth and determined his social

---

■ **sacraments** Certain rituals defined by the church in which God bestows benefits on the believer through grace.

■ **runic alphabet** Writing system developed in some barbarian groups that helps give a more accurate picture of barbarian society.

Whalebone Chest This eighth-century chest made of whalebone, depicting warriors, other human figures, and a horse, tells a story in both pictures and words. The runes along the border are one of the varieties from the British Isles. Contact with the Romans led to the increasing use of the Latin alphabet, though runes and Latin letters were used side by side in some parts of northern Europe for centuries. (Museo Nazionale del Bargello, Florence, Italy/Erich Lessing/Art Resource, NY)

status. Free men also shared in tribal warfare. Slaves acquired through warfare worked as farm laborers, herdsmen, and household servants.

Ironworking represented the most advanced craft; much of northern Europe had iron deposits, and the dense forests provided wood for charcoal, which was used to provide the clean fire needed to make iron. The typical village had an oven and smiths who produced agricultural tools and instruments of war—one-edged swords, arrowheads, and shields. By the second century C.E. the swords produced by barbarian smiths were superior to the weapons of Roman troops.

In the first two centuries C.E. the quantity and quality of material goods increased dramatically. Goods were used locally and for gift giving, a major social custom. Gift giving conferred status on the giver, whose giving showed his higher (economic) status, cemented friendship, and placed the receiver in his debt. Goods were also traded, though commercial exchange was less important than in the Roman Empire.

Families and kin groups were the basic social units in barbarian society. Families were responsible for the debts and actions of their members and for keeping the peace in general. Barbarian law codes set strict rules of inheritance based on position in the family and often set aside a portion of land that could not be sold or given away by any family member so that the family always retained some land.

Barbarian society was patriarchal: within each household the father had authority over his wife, children, and slaves. Some wealthy and powerful men had more than one wife, a pattern that continued even after they became Christian, but polygamy was not widespread among ordinary people. Women worked alongside men in the fields and forests, and the Roman

historian Tacitus reported that at times they joined men on the battlefield, urging them to fight harder. Once women were widowed, they sometimes assumed their husbands' rights over family property and held the guardianship of their children.

Tribes and Hierarchies

The basic social and political unit among barbarian groups was the tribe or confederation, a group whose members believed that they were all descended from a common ancestor and were thus kin. Tribes were led by chieftains. The chief was the member recognized as the strongest and bravest in battle and was elected from among the male members of the most powerful family. He led the group in war, settled disputes among its members, conducted negotiations with outside powers, and offered sacrifices to the gods. The period of migrations and conquests of the Western Roman Empire witnessed the strengthening of the power of chiefs, who often adopted the title of king, though this title implies broader power than they actually had.

Closely associated with the chief in some tribes was the **comitatus**, or war band. These warriors swore loyalty to the chief, fought with him in battle, and were not supposed to leave the battlefield without him; to do so implied cowardice, disloyalty, and social disgrace. These oaths of loyalty were later more formalized in the development of feudalism (see Chapter 8).

Although initially a social egalitarianism appears to have existed among members of the comitatus because they regarded each other as kin, during the migrations and warfare of the third and fourth centuries, the war band was transformed into a system of stratified ranks. Among the Ostrogoths, for example, a warrior nobility evolved. Contact with the Romans stimulated demand

■ **comitatus** A war band of young men in a barbarian tribe who were closely associated with the chief, swore loyalty to him, and fought with him in battle.

Tacitus on Germanic Society

Toward the end of the first century, the Roman historian Tacitus wrote an account of Germanic society based on the works of earlier authors and most likely interviews with Romans who had traveled beyond the northern borders of the empire. His descriptions are not accurate in all respects, but evidence from other written sources and from archaeological excavations has supported a number of them.

Warlike Ardour of the People. When they go into battle, it is a disgrace for the chief to be surpassed in valour, a disgrace for his followers not to equal the valour of the chief. And it is an infamy and a reproach for life to have survived the chief, and returned from the field. . . .

Arrangement of their towns, subterranean dwellings. It is well known that the nations of Germany have not cities, and that they do not even tolerate closely contiguous dwellings. They live scattered and apart, just as a spring, a meadow, or a wood has attracted them. Their village they do not arrange in our fashion, with the buildings connected and joined together, but every person surrounds his dwelling with an open space, either as a precaution against the disasters of fire, or because they do not know how to build. No use is made by them of stone or tile; they employ timber for all purposes, rude masses without ornament or attractiveness. Some parts of their buildings they stain more carefully with a clay so clear and bright that it resembles painting, or a coloured design. They are wont also to dig out subterranean caves, and pile on them great heaps of dung as shelter from winter and as a receptacle for the year's produce. . . .

Their children. In every household the children, naked and filthy, grow up with those stout frames and limbs which we so much admire. Every mother suckles her own offspring and never entrusts it to servants and nurses. The master is not distinguished from the slave by being brought up with greater delicacy. Both live amid the same flocks and lie on the same ground till the freeborn are distinguished by age and recognised by merit. The young men marry late, and their vigour is thus unimpaired. Nor are the maidens hurried into marriage; the same age and a similar stature is required; well-matched and vigorous they wed, and the offspring reproduce the strength of the parents. . . .

Food. A liquor for drinking is made of barley or other grain, and fermented into a certain resemblance to wine. The dwellers on the river-bank also buy wine. Their food is of a simple kind, consisting of wild fruit, fresh game, and curdled milk. They satisfy their hunger without elaborate preparation and without delicacies. In quenching their thirst they are equally moderate. If you indulge their love of drinking by supplying them with as much as they desire, they will be overcome by their own vices as easily as by the arms of an enemy.

EVALUATE THE EVIDENCE

1. What does Tacitus praise, and what does he criticize, about Germanic warriors, food, houses, and child rearing?
2. Tacitus's work was written in part to criticize his fellow Romans, whom he saw as becoming weak from the influx of wealth into the empire. How does this perspective inform his description of Germanic customs? How might such attitudes shape the way Romans responded to the barbarian migrations?

Source: Tacitus, *The Agricola and Germania*, trans. A. J. Church and W. J. Brodribb (London: Macmillan, 1877), pp. 87ff.

---

for goods such as metal armbands, which the Romans produced for trade with barbarian groups. Armbands were of different widths and value, and they became a symbol of hierarchy among warriors, much as the insignia of military rank function today. During the Ostrogothic conquest of Italy, warrior-nobles also began to acquire land as both a mark of prestige and a means to power. As land and wealth came into the hands of a small elite class, social inequalities within the group emerged and gradually grew stronger. These inequalities help explain the origins of the European noble class.

Customary and Written Law

Early barbarian tribes had no written laws. Law was custom, but certain individuals were often given special training in remembering and retelling laws from generation to generation. Beginning in the late fifth century, however, some chieftains and rulers began to collect, write, and publish lists of their customs and laws. (See "Thinking Like a Historian: Slavery in Roman and Germanic Society," page 198.)

The law code of the Salian Franks, one of the barbarian tribes, included a feature common to

Slavery in Roman and Germanic Society

Slavery continued to be a common condition in the late Roman Empire, and the Germanic tribes were also slave-owning cultures. In both societies, slavery was based not on racial distinctions, but on one's personal status as free or unfree, which was increasingly regulated by law. How could a person cross the border between slave and free in these two societies, and what larger social values do laws regarding slavery reflect?

1 **Theodosian Code, 435–438.** Under Emperor Theodosius II (r. 408–450), imperial decrees issued since the time of Constantine that were still in effect were brought together in a single law code.

If a father, forced by need, shall sell any free-born child whatsoever, the child cannot remain in perpetual slavery, but if he has made compensation by his slavery, he shall be restored to his freeborn status without the repayment of the purchase price. . . . It is established that children born from the womb of a slave woman are slaves, according to the law. . . . We have subjected the Scyrae, a barbarian nation, to Our power. Therefore We grant to all persons the opportunity to supply their own fields with men of the aforesaid race. . . . If any person should take up a boy or girl child that has been cast out of its home with the knowledge and consent of its father or owner, and if he should rear this child to strength with his own sustenance, he shall have the right to keep the said child under the same status as he wished it to have when he took charge of it, that is, as his child or as a slave, whichever he should prefer. . . . We exhort slaves, that as soon as possible they shall offer themselves for the labors of war, and if they receive their arms as men fit for military service, they shall obtain the reward of freedom. . . . [In the case of deserters] if the slave should surrender such a deserter, he shall be given his freedom.

2 **Roman tombstone.** The tombstone at right shows a man reclining on a couch, being served a drink by a small slave boy. The inscription identifies the man as a twenty-year-old soldier and freed slave, and it gives his name simply as Victor, with no family name or patronymic.

3 **Justinian's Code, 529–534.** The law code of Emperor Justinian includes many provisions regarding slaves.

Liberty is the natural power of doing whatever anyone wishes to do unless he is prevented in some way, by force or by law. Slavery is an institution of the Law of Nations by means of which anyone may subject one man to the control of another, contrary to nature. Slaves are so called for the reason that military commanders were accustomed to sell their captives, and in this manner to preserve

(Arbeia Roman Fort, South Shields, UK/© Tyne & Wear Archives & Museums/Bridgeman Images)

ANALYZING THE EVIDENCE

1. According to the Roman laws (Sources 1 and 3), how could a person become a slave in Roman society? According to the Germanic laws (Sources 4–6), how could this happen in Germanic society? Which of these methods established more permanent conditions of servitude?
2. How could a slave become free in Roman society? In Germanic?
3. How did the man in the tombstone (Source 2) obtain his freedom?
4. According to Justinian's Code (Source 3), is slavery natural? What types of laws establish it, and how do these laws reflect Roman notions of law?
5. In Germanic society, the kin group was responsible for the actions of its members. How do the laws in Sources 4–6 reflect this principle? From Sources 1–3 and your reading in this and earlier chapters, how did family and kin shape slavery in Roman society?

them, instead of putting them to death. . . . Slaves are brought under our ownership either by the Civil Law or by that of Nations. This is done by the Civil Law where anyone who is over twenty years of age permits himself to be sold for the sake of sharing in his own price [that is, for debt]. Slaves become our property by the Law of Nations when they are either taken from the enemy, or are born of our female slaves. . . . Where a fugitive slave betakes himself to the arena [as a gladiator], he cannot escape the power of his master by exposing himself to this danger, which is only that of the risk of death; such a slave must, by all means, be restored to his master, either before or after the combat with wild beasts.

4 The Burgundian Code, ca. 500. King Gundobad (r. 474–516), who ruled the Burgundian kingdom in what is now southeastern France, drew up one of the earliest Germanic law codes for his subjects.

~ If anyone shall buy another's slave from the Franks [with whom the Burgundians were at war], let him prove with suitable witnesses how much and what sort of price he paid and when the witnesses have been sworn in, they shall make oath in the following manner, "We saw him pay the price in our presence, and he who purchased the slave did not do so through any fraud or connivance with the enemy." . . . If anyone wishes to manumit a slave, he may do so by giving him his liberty through a legally competent document; or if anyone wishes to give freedom to a bondservant without a written document, let the manumission thus be conferred with the witness of not less than five or seven native freemen.

5 Lombard laws, 643–735. The Lombards invaded Italy in 568, conquered Germanic tribes that were already there, and established a kingdom that lasted until 774. Various Lombard kings issued laws on many topics.

~ In the case of a natural son who is born to another man's woman slave, if the father purchases him and gives him his freedom by the formal procedure he shall remain free. But if the father does not free him, the natural son shall be a slave to him to whom the mother slave belongs. . . . He who renders false testimony against anyone else, or sets his hand knowingly to a false charter, and this fraud becomes evident, shall pay restitution, half to the king and half to him whose case it is. If the guilty party does not have enough to pay restitution, a public official ought to hand him over as a slave to him who was injured, and he [the offender] shall serve him as a slave. . . . If a man who is prodigal and ruined, or who has sold or dissipated his substance, or for other reasons does not have that with which to pay restitution, commits theft or adultery or a breach of the peace, or injures another man and the restitution for this is twenty solidi or more, then a public representative ought to hand him over as a slave to the man who committed such illegal acts. . . . If a freeman has a man and woman slave, or freedman and freedwoman, who are married, and inspired by hatred of the human race, he has intercourse with that woman whose husband is the slave or with the freedwoman whose husband is the freedman, he has committed adultery and we decree that he shall lose that slave or freedman with whose wife he committed adultery and the woman as well, for it is not pleasing to God that any man should have intercourse with the wife of another.

6 Laws of the Anglo-Saxon kings, early tenth century. The Anglo-Saxon rulers in England issued law codes; this law is from the code of Edward the Elder (r. 899–925), king of Wessex and Mercia.

~ If a man, through [being found guilty of] an accusation of stealing, forfeits his freedom and gives up his person to his lord, and his kinsmen forsake him, and he knows no one who will make legal amends for him, he shall do such servile labour as may be required and his kinsmen shall have no right to his wergeld [if he is slain].

PUTTING IT ALL TOGETHER

Using the sources above, along with what you have learned in class and in Chapters 5, 6, and 7, write a short essay that analyzes ways in which the boundary between slave and free was established, protected, and traversed in Roman and Germanic society. How could a person cross the border between slave and free in these two societies, and what larger social values do laws regarding slavery reflect? How did the laws regarding slavery differ in Roman and Germanic society, and how were they similar?

Sources: (1) Clyde Pharr, ed., *The Theodosian Code* (Princeton, N.J.: Princeton University Press, 1952), 3.3.1, 5.6.3, 5.9.1, 7.13.16, 7.18.4; (3) S. P. Scott, trans., *The Civil Law* (Cincinnati: The Central Trust Company, 1932), vol. 2, p. 228; vol. 4, p. 82; (4) Katherine Fischer Drew, trans., *The Burgundian Code* (Philadelphia: University of Pennsylvania Press, 1972), Constitutiones Extravagantes 21.9; (5) Katherine Fischer Drew, trans., *The Lombard Laws* (Philadelphia: University of Pennsylvania Press, 1973), Rothair 156, Luitprand 63, Luitprand 140, Luitprand 152; (6) F. L. Attenborough, *Laws of the Earliest English Kings* (Cambridge: Cambridge University Press, 1922), Laws of Edward the Elder 6.

Visigothic Work and Play
This page comes from one of the very few manuscripts from late antiquity to have survived, a copy of the first five books of the Old Testament — the Pentateuch — made around 600, perhaps in Visigothic Spain or North Africa. The top shows biblical scenes, while the bottom shows people engaged in everyday activities — building a wall, drawing water from a well, and trading punches. (Illuminated page from the Ashburnham Pentateuch/Bibliothèque Nationale, Paris, France/De Agostini/Getty Images)

many barbarian codes. Any crime that involved a personal injury, such as assault, rape, and murder, was given a particular monetary value, called the **wergeld** (WUHR-gehld) (literally "man-money" or "money to buy off the spear"), that was to be paid by the perpetrator to the victim or the family. The Salic law lists many of these:

> If any person strike another on the head so that the brain appears, and the three bones which lie above the brain shall project, he shall be sentenced to 1200 denars, which make 300 shillings. . . .
> If any one have killed a free woman after she has begun bearing children, he shall be sentenced to 2400 denars, which make 600 shillings.[5]

The wergeld varied according to the severity of the crime and also the social status of the victim. The fine for the murder of a woman of childbearing years was the same value as that attached to military officers of the king, to priests, and to boys preparing to become warriors, which suggests the importance of women in Frankish society, at least for their childbearing capacity.

The wergeld system aimed to prevent or reduce violence. If a person accused of a crime agreed to pay the wergeld and if the victim and his or her family accepted the payment, there was peace. If the accused refused to pay the wergeld or if the victim's family refused to accept it, a blood feud ensued. At first, Romans had been subject to Roman law and barbarians to barbarian custom. As barbarian kings accepted Christianity and as Romans and barbarians increasingly intermarried and assimilated culturally, the distinction between the two sets of law blurred and, in the course of the seventh and eighth centuries, disappeared. The result would be the new feudal law, to which all who lived in certain areas were subject.

■ **wergeld** Compensatory payment for death or injury set in many barbarian law codes.

Celtic and Germanic Religion

Like Greeks and Romans, barbarians worshipped hundreds of gods and goddesses with specialized functions. They regarded certain mountains, lakes, rivers, or groves of trees as sacred because these were linked to deities. Rituals to honor the gods were held outdoors rather than in temples or churches, often at certain points in the yearly agricultural cycle. Presided over by a priest or priestess understood to have special abilities to call on the gods' powers, rituals sometimes involved animal (and perhaps human) sacrifice. Among the Celts, religious leaders called druids (DROO-ihds) had legal and educational as well as religious functions, orally passing down laws and traditions from generation to generation. Bards singing poems and ballads also passed down myths and stories of heroes and gods, which were written down much later.

The first written records of barbarian religion came from Greeks and Romans who encountered barbarians or spoke with those who had. They understood barbarian traditions through their own belief systems, often equating barbarian gods with Greco-Roman ones and adapting stories and rituals to blend the two. This assimilation appears to have gone both ways, at least judging by the names of the days of the week. In the Roman Empire the days took their names from Roman deities or astronomical bodies, and in the Germanic languages of central and northern Europe the days acquired the names of corresponding barbarian gods. Jupiter's day, for example, became Thor's day (Thursday); both of these powerful gods were associated with thunder.

Celtic Brooch   This magnificent silver and gold brooch, used to hold a heavy wool cape in place, is adorned with red garnets and complex patterns of interlace. Made in Ireland, the brooch has patterns similar to those found in Irish manuscripts from this era. (National Museum of Ireland, Dublin/ Photo © Boltin Picture Library/Bridgeman Images)

Migration, Assimilation, and Conflict

FOCUS QUESTION *What were some of the causes and consequences of the barbarian migrations?*

Migrating groups that the Romans labeled barbarians had moved southward and eastward off and on since about 100 B.C.E. (see Chapters 5 and 6). As their movements became more organized in the third and fourth centuries C.E., Roman armies sought to defend the Rhine-Danube border of the Roman Empire, but with troop levels low because Italians were increasingly unwilling to serve in the army, generals were forced to recruit barbarians to fill the ranks. Barbarian refugees and enslaved prisoners of war joined Roman units, and free barbarian units, called *foederati*, allied themselves with Rome. Some barbarian leaders rose to the highest ranks of the Roman army and often assimilated into Roman culture, incorporating their own traditions and intermarrying with Roman families. By the fourth century barbarians made up the majority of those fighting both for and against Rome, and climbed higher and higher in the ranks of the Roman military. Toward the end of the fifth century this barbarian assumption of authority stretched all the way to the top, and the last person with the title of emperor in the Western Roman Empire was deposed by a Gothic general.

Why did the barbarians migrate? In part they were searching for more regular supplies of food, better farmland, and a warmer climate. In part they were pushed by groups living farther eastward, especially by the Huns from Central Asia in the fourth and fifth centuries. Conflicts within and among barbarian groups also led to war and disruption, which motivated groups to move (Map 7.3).

Celtic and Germanic People in Gaul and Britain

The Celts present a good example of both assimilation and conflict. Celtic-speaking peoples had lived in central Europe since at least the fifth century B.C.E. and spread out from there to the Iberian Peninsula in the west, Hungary in the east, and the British Isles in the north. As Julius Caesar advanced northward into what he termed Gaul (present-day France) between 58 and 50 B.C.E. (see Chapter 5), he defeated many Celtic tribes. Celtic peoples conquered by the Romans often assimilated Roman ways, adapting the Latin language and other aspects of Roman culture. In Roman Gaul and then in Roman Britain, towns were planned in the Roman fashion, with temples, public baths, theaters, and amphitheaters. In the countryside large manors controlled the surrounding lands. Roman merchants brought Eastern luxury goods

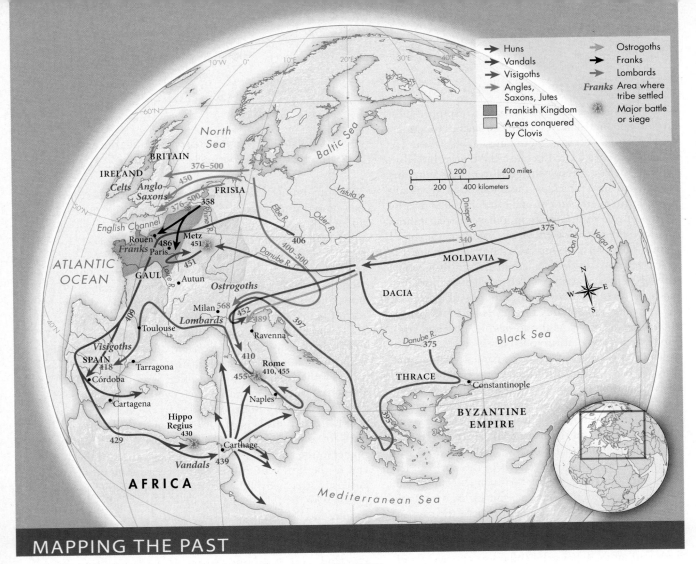

Huns → | Ostrogoths →
Vandals → | Franks →
Visigoths → | Lombards →
Angles, Saxons, Jutes →
Frankish Kingdom | *Franks* Area where tribe settled
Areas conquered by Clovis | Major battle or siege

MAPPING THE PAST

MAP 7.3 The Barbarian Migrations, ca. 340–500

This map shows the migrations of various barbarian groups in late antiquity and can be used to answer the following questions.

ANALYZING THE MAP The movements of barbarian peoples used to be labeled "invasions" and are now usually described as "migrations." How do the dates on the map support the newer understanding of these movements?

CONNECTIONS Human migration is caused by a combination of push factors—circumstances that lead people to leave a place—and pull factors—things that attract people to a new location. Based on the information in this and earlier chapters, what push and pull factors might have shaped the migration patterns you see on the map?

and Eastern religions—including Christianity. The Romans suppressed the Celtic chieftains, and a military aristocracy made up of Romans—some of whom intermarried with Celtic families—governed. In the course of the second and third centuries, many Celts became Roman citizens and joined the Roman army. Celtic culture survived only in areas beyond the borders of the empire. (The modern Welsh, Bretons, Scots, and Irish are all peoples of Celtic descent.)

By the fourth century C.E. Gaul and Britain were under pressure from Germanic groups moving westward, and Rome itself was threatened (see Map 7.3). Imperial troops withdrew from Britain in order to

defend Rome, and the Picts from Scotland and the Scots from Ireland (both Celtic-speaking peoples) invaded territory held by the Britons. According to the eighth-century historian Bede (beed), the Briton king Vortigern invited the Saxons from Denmark to help him against his rivals. However, Saxons and other Germanic tribes from the area of modern-day Norway, Sweden, and Denmark turned from assistance to conquest. Their goal was plunder, and at first their invasions led to no permanent settlements. As more Germanic peoples arrived, however, they took over the best lands and eventually conquered most of Britain. Historians have labeled the years 500 to 1066 (the year of the Norman Conquest) the Anglo-Saxon period of English history, after the two largest Germanic groups in England, the Angles and the Saxons.

Anglo-Saxon England was divided along ethnic and political lines. The Germanic kingdoms in the south, east, and center were opposed by the Britons in the west, who wanted to get rid of the invaders. The Anglo-Saxon kingdoms also fought among themselves, causing boundaries to shift constantly. Finally, in the ninth century, under pressure from the Viking invasions, King Alfred of Wessex (r. 871–899) created a more unified state with a reorganized army and system of fortresses for defense.

The Anglo-Saxon invasion gave rise to a rich body of Celtic mythology, particularly legends about King Arthur, who first appeared in Welsh poetry in the sixth century and later in histories, epics, and saints' lives. Most scholars see Arthur as a composite figure that evolved over the centuries in songs and stories. In their earliest form as Welsh poems, the Arthurian legends may represent Celtic hostility to Anglo-Saxon invaders, but they later came to be more important as representations of the ideal of medieval knightly chivalry and as compelling stories whose retelling has continued to the present.

Visigoths and Huns

On the European continent, the Germanic peoples included a number of groups with very different cultural traditions. The largest Germanic group was the Goths, who were further subdivided by scholars into Ostrogoths (eastern Goths) and Visigoths (western Goths) based on their migration patterns. Both of these groups played important roles in the political developments of late antiquity.

Pressured by defeat in battle, starvation, and the movement of other groups, the Visigoths moved westward from their homeland north of the Black Sea, and in 376 they petitioned the Roman emperor Valens to admit them to the empire. They offered to fight for Rome in exchange for the province of Thrace in what is now Greece and Bulgaria. Seeing in the hordes of warriors the solution to his manpower problem, Valens agreed. However, the deal fell apart when crop failures led to famine and Roman authorities exploited the Visigoths' hunger by forcing them to sell their own people as slaves in exchange for dog flesh: "the going rate was one dog for one Goth." The Visigoths revolted, joined with other barbarian enemies of Rome, and defeated the Roman army at the Battle of Adrianople in 378, killing Valens and thousands of Roman soldiers in the process. This left a large barbarian army within the borders of the Roman Empire, and not that far from Constantinople.

Valens's successor made peace with the Visigoths, but relations worsened as the Visigoths continued mi-

Anglo-Saxon Helmet This ceremonial bronze helmet from seventh-century England was found inside a ship buried at Sutton Hoo. The nearly 100-foot-long ship was dragged overland before being buried completely. It held one body and many grave goods, including swords, gold buckles, and silver bowls made in Byzantium. The unidentified person who was buried here was clearly wealthy and powerful. (© The Trustees of the British Museum/Art Resource, NY)

grating westward (see Map 7.3). The Visigothic king Alaric I, who had also been a general in one of the Roman armies in the east, invaded Italy and sacked Rome in 410. The Visigoths burned and looted the city for three days, which caused many Romans to wonder whether God had deserted them. (See "Evaluating the Evidence 7.2: Battle Between Romans and Goths," page 205.) Seeking to stabilize the situation at home, the imperial government pulled its troops from the British Isles and many areas north of the Alps, leaving these northern areas vulnerable to other migrating groups. A year later Alaric died, and his successor led his people into southwestern Gaul, where they established the Visigothic kingdom.

One significant factor in the migration of the Visigoths and other Germanic peoples was pressure from nomadic steppe peoples from Central Asia. They included the Alans, Avars, Bulgars, Khazars, and most prominently the Huns, who attacked the Black Sea area and the Byzantine Empire beginning in the fourth century. The Roman officer and historian Ammianus

Marcellinus fought the Huns and later described them with both admiration and scorn:

> They are not at all adapted to battles on foot, but they are almost glued to their horses, which are hardy, it is true, but ugly. From their horses by night or day every one of the nation buys and sells, eats and drinks, and bowed over the narrow neck of the animal relaxes into a sleep so deep as to be accompanied by many dreams. . . . They are subject to no royal restraint, but they are content with the disorderly government of important men, and led by them they force their way through every obstacle. No one in their country ever plows a field or touches a plowhandle. They are all without fixed abode, without hearth, or law, or settled mode of life. . . . In wagons their wives weave for them their hideous garments, in wagons they cohabit with their husbands, bear children, and rear them. . . . Like unreasoning beasts, they are utterly ignorant of the difference between right and wrong.[6]

Under the leadership of their warrior-king Attila, the Huns attacked the Byzantine Empire in 447 and then turned westward. Several Germanic groups allied with them, as did the sister of the Roman emperor, who hoped to take over power from her brother. Their troops combined with those of the Huns, and a huge army took the city of Metz, now in eastern France. A combined army of Romans and Visigoths stopped the advance of the Huns at Châlons, and they retreated. The following year they moved into the Western Roman Empire again, crossing the Alps into Italy, and a papal delegation, including Pope Leo I himself, asked Attila not to attack Rome. Though papal diplomacy was later credited with stopping the advance of the Huns, their dwindling food supplies and a plague that spread among their troops were probably much more important. The Huns retreated from Italy, and within a year Attila was dead. Later leaders were not as effective, and the Huns were never again an important factor in European history. Their conquests had pushed many Germanic groups together, however, transforming smaller bands into larger, more unified peoples who could more easily pick the Roman Empire apart.

Germanic Kingdoms and the End of the Roman Empire

After they conquered an area, barbarians generally established states ruled by kings. However, the kingdoms did not have definite geographical borders, and their locations shifted as tribes moved. In the fifth century the Burgundians ruled over lands roughly circumscribed by the old Roman army camps in what is now central France and western Switzerland. The Visigoths exercised a weak domination over southern France and much of the Iberian Peninsula (modern Spain) until a Muslim victory at Guadalete in 711 ended Visigothic rule. The Vandals, another Germanic tribe whose destructive ways are commemorated in the word *vandal*, swept across Spain into North Africa in 429 and took over what had been Rome's breadbasket. (See "Living in the Past: The Horses of Spain," page 206.) They established a state that lasted about a century, raided many coastal cities, and even sacked the city of Rome itself in 455.

Barbarian states eventually came to include Italy itself. The Western Roman emperors were generally chosen by the more powerful successors of Constantine in the East, and they increasingly relied on barbarian commanders and their troops to maintain order. In the 470s a series of these commanders took over authority in name as well as in reality, deposing several Roman emperors. In 476 the barbarian chieftain Odoacer (OH-duh-way-suhr) deposed Romulus Augustus, the last person to have the title of Roman emperor in the West. Odoacer did not take on the title of emperor, calling himself instead the king of Italy, so that this date marks the official end of the Roman Empire in the West. Emperor Zeno, the Roman emperor in the East ruling from Constantinople, worried about Odoacer's growing power and promised Theoderic (r. 471–526), the leader of the Ostrogoths who had recently settled in the Balkans, the right to rule Italy if he defeated Odoacer. Theoderic's forces were successful, and in 493 Theoderic established an Ostrogothic state in Italy, with his capital at Ravenna.

For centuries, the end of the Roman Empire in the West was seen as a major turning point in history, the fall of the sophisticated and educated classical world to uncouth and illiterate tribes. This view was further promoted by the English historian and member of Parliament Edward Gibbon, whose six-volume *The History of the Decline and Fall of the Roman Empire*, published in 1776–1788, was required reading for university students well into the twentieth century. Over the last several decades, however, many historians have put greater stress on continuities. The Ostrogoths, for example, maintained many Roman ways. Old Roman families continued to run the law courts and the city governments, and well-educated Italians continued to study the Greek classics. Theoderic's adviser Boethius (ca. 480–524) translated Aristotle's works on logic from Greek into Latin. While imprisoned after falling out of royal favor, Boethius wrote *The Consolation of Philosophy*, which argued that philosophical inquiry was valuable for understanding God. This became one of the most widely read books in the Middle Ages, though its popularity did not prevent Boethius from being executed for treason.

Battle Between Romans and Goths

Rome's wars with the Germanic-speaking groups along its northern border come to life in this relief from a Roman sarcophagus of the third century C.E., discovered in a tomb in the city of Rome. The Romans are wearing helmets, and the soldier at the right is wearing iron or bronze chain mail, a defensive technology that the Romans adapted from the Celts.

(Ludovisi sarcophagus from Livia's Villa/Terme Museum, Rome, Italy/Bridgeman Images)

EVALUATE THE EVIDENCE

1. How would you describe this depiction of war? How does the artist show Roman superiority over the barbarians through the placement, dress, and facial features of the soldiers?
2. How does this funeral sculpture reinforce or challenge what you have learned about Roman expansion and the Romans' treatment of the peoples they conquered?

In other barbarian states, as well, aspects of classical culture continued. Barbarian kings relied on officials trained in Roman law, and Latin remained the language of scholarly communication. Greco-Roman art and architecture still adorned the land, and people continued to use Roman roads, aqueducts, and buildings. The Christian Church in barbarian states modeled its organization on that of Rome, and many bishops were from upper-class families that had governed the empire.

Very recently some historians and archaeologists have returned to an emphasis on change. They note that people may have traveled on Roman roads, but the roads were rarely maintained, and travel itself was much less secure than during the Roman Empire. Merchants no longer traded over long distances, so people's access to goods produced outside their local area plummeted. Knowledge about technological processes such as the making of glass and roof tiles declined or disap-

peared. There was intermarriage and cultural assimilation among Romans and barbarians, but there was also violence and great physical destruction.

The kingdom established by the Franks is a good example of this combination of peaceful assimilation and violent conflict. The Franks were a confederation of Germanic peoples who originated in the marshy lowlands north and east of the northernmost part of the Roman Empire (see Map 7.3). In the fourth and fifth centuries they settled within the empire and allied with the Romans, some attaining high military and civil positions. The Franks believed that Merovech, a man of supernatural origins, founded their ruling dynasty, which was thus called Merovingian (mehr-uh-VIHN-jee-uhn).

The reign of Clovis (KLOH-vis) (r. ca. 481–511) marks the decisive period in the development of the Franks as a unified people. Through military campaigns, Clovis acquired the central provinces of Roman

Horses were first domesticated around 4000 B.C.E. in Central Asia, probably initially for their meat, but soon afterward for transportation and warfare. By 2000 B.C.E. warriors' graves in what is now southern Russia contained full-size wood and metal chariots and the skeletons of the horses that pulled them. Paintings from Egypt and Mesopotamia show warriors shooting arrows from horse-drawn chariots. Saddles and stirrups, which allow riders to sit securely on a horse's back, were developed much later, probably in India or Central Asia. By 200 C.E. mounted archers were an important part of the barbarian armies, both Germanic and Central Asian, that threatened the Roman Empire. The Romans also used horses, and bred them selectively for speed and sturdiness. Owners of large villas ran horse-breeding operations, supplying the Roman army with horses as they supplied the cities with grain.

All of these uses of the horse came together in the Iberian Peninsula, an area the Romans termed Hispania: the Romans raised horses there, and the Vandals and Suevi (two Germanic tribes) and the Alans (a Central Asian steppe people) conquered the area with horses in the fifth century. Later in that century the Visigoths (another Germanic tribe) took over much of the peninsula in campaigns where their skill with horses proved a decisive factor. This would be true for the next conquest of Spain as well, in the eighth century by Muslims, whose Arabian horses—bred for endurance, speed, and intelligence—had allowed them to sweep swiftly across North Africa.

Horses were a weapon of war, but they were also a place to display artistic skill and cultural values. Metal ornaments for horse harnesses are among the relatively few Visigothic artifacts that have survived, providing a glimpse of an early version of the horse culture that Spanish conquerors brought to the New World in the sixteenth century and that still remains important in Spain.

Bronze Visigothic harness pendant from Spain, produced in the sixth century C.E. (The Metropolitan Museum of Art, New York, NY, USA/Rogers Fund, 1990 [1990.77]/Image copyright © The Metropolitan Museum of Art/Image source: Art Resource, NY)

Gaul and began to conquer southern Gaul from the Burgundians and Visigoths. Clovis's conversion to Roman Christianity brought him the crucial support of the bishops of Gaul in his campaigns against tribes that were still pagan or had accepted the Arian version of Christianity. Along with brutal violence, however, the next two centuries witnessed the steady assimilation of Franks and Romans, as many Franks adopted the Latin language and Roman ways, and Romans copied Frankish customs and Frankish personal names.

From Constantinople, Eastern Roman emperors worked to hold the empire together and to reconquer at least some of the West from barbarian tribes. The emperor Justinian (r. 527–565) waged long and hard-fought wars against the Ostrogoths and temporarily regained Italy and North Africa, but his conquests had disastrous consequences. Justinian's wars exhausted the resources of the state, destroyed Italy's economy, and killed a large part of Italy's population. The wars also paved the way for the easy conquest of Italy by another Germanic tribe, the Lombards, shortly after Justinian's death. In the late sixth century the territory of the Western Roman Empire came once again under barbarian sway.

Christian Missionaries and Conversion

FOCUS QUESTION *How did the church convert barbarian peoples to Christianity?*

The Mediterranean served as the highway over which Christianity spread to the cities of the Roman Empire. Christian teachings were initially carried by all types of converts, but they were often spread into the countryside and into areas beyond the borders of the empire by those who had dedicated their lives to the church, such as monks. Such missionaries were often sent by popes specifically to convert certain groups. As they preached to barbarian peoples, the missionaries developed new techniques to convert them.

Throughout barbarian Europe, religion was not a private or individual matter; it was a social affair, and the religion of the chieftain or king determined the religion of the people. Thus missionaries concentrated their initial efforts not on ordinary people, but on kings or tribal chieftains and the members of their families, who then ordered their subjects to convert. Because they had more opportunity to spend

1. Looking at the photograph of the bit, how do you think the use of horses might have served as a stimulus to the development and improvement of metal technology?

2. What do the decorations on the horse harness pendant and bit shown here suggest about Visigothic values and technical abilities?

3. Thinking more speculatively, would you expect the use of horses in war to enhance or diminish social and political hierarchies?

In this mosaic, a Vandal landowner rides out from his Roman-style house. (From Carthage/© The Trustees of the British Museum/Art Resource, NY)

Visigothic horse bit from the seventh century C.E., made of iron with silver inlay. Bits allowed riders to control horses more effectively. (The Metropolitan Museum of Art, New York, NY, USA/Fletcher Fund, 1947 [1947.100.24]/Image copyright © The Metropolitan Museum of Art/Image source: Art Resource, NY)

time with missionaries, queens and other female members of the royal family were often the first converts in an area, and they influenced their husbands and brothers. Germanic kings sometimes accepted Christianity because they came to believe that the Christian God was more powerful than pagan gods and that the Christian God—in either its Arian or Roman version—would deliver victory in battle. They also appreciated that Christianity taught obedience to kingly as well as divine authority. Christian missionaries were generally literate, and they taught reading and writing to young men who became priests or officials in the royal household, a service that kings appreciated.

Missionaries' Actions

During the Roman occupation, small Christian communities were scattered throughout Gaul and Britain. The leaders of some of these, such as Bishop Martin of Tours (ca. 316–397), who founded a monastery and established a rudimentary parish system in his diocese, supported Nicene Christianity (see page 189). Other missionaries were Arian Christians, who also founded dioceses and converted many barbarian groups. Bishop Ulfilas (ca. 310–383), for example,

an Ostrogoth himself, translated the Bible from the Greek in which it was normally written into the Gothic language, creating a new Gothic script in order to write it down. The Ostrogoths, Visigoths, Lombards, and Vandals were all originally Arian Christians, though over the sixth and seventh centuries most of them converted to Roman Christianity, sometimes peacefully and sometimes as a result of conquest.

Tradition identifies the conversion of Ireland with Saint Patrick (ca. 385–461). Born in England to a Christian family of Roman citizenship, Patrick was captured and enslaved by Irish raiders and taken to Ireland, where he worked as a herdsman for six years. He escaped and returned to England, where a vision urged him to Christianize Ireland. In preparation, Patrick studied in Gaul and was consecrated a bishop in 432. He returned to Ireland, where he converted the Irish tribe by tribe, first baptizing the chief of each tribe. By the time of Patrick's death, the majority of the Irish people had received Christian baptism.

In his missionary work, Patrick had the strong support of Bridget of Kildare (ca. 450–528), daughter of a wealthy chieftain. Bridget defied parental pressure to marry and became a nun. She and the other nuns at Kildare instructed relatives and friends in basic Christian doctrine, made religious vestments (clothing) for churches, copied books, taught children, and above all set a religious example by their lives of prayer. In this way, in Ireland and later in continental Europe, women like the nuns at Kildare shared in the process of conversion.

The Christianization of the English began in earnest in 597, when Pope Gregory I sent a delegation of monks under the Roman Augustine to Britain. Augustine's approach, like Patrick's, was to concentrate on converting those who held power. When he succeeded in converting Ethelbert, king of Kent, the baptism of Ethelbert's people took place as a matter of course. Augustine established his headquarters, or *see*, at Canterbury, the capital of Kent in southern England.

In the course of the seventh century, two Christian forces competed for the conversion of the pagan Anglo-Saxons: Roman-oriented missionaries traveling north from Canterbury, and Celtic monks from Ireland and northwestern Britain. The Roman and Celtic church organizations, types of monastic life, and methods of arriving at the date of the central feast of the Christian calendar, Easter, differed completely. Through the influence of King Oswiu of Northumbria and the dynamic abbess Hilda of Whitby, the Synod (ecclesiastical council) held at Hilda's convent of Whitby in 664 opted to follow the Roman practices. The conversion of the English and the close attachment of the English Church to Rome had far-reaching consequences because Britain later served as a base for the Christianization of the European continent (see Map 7.2), spreading Roman Christian teachings among both pagans and Arians.

The Process of Conversion

When a ruler marched his people to the waters of baptism, the work of Christianization had only begun. Christian kings could order their subjects to be baptized, married, and buried in Christian ceremonies, and people complied increasingly across Europe. Churches could be built, and people could be required to attend services and belong to parishes, but the process of conversion was a gradual one.

How did missionaries and priests get masses of pagan and illiterate peoples to understand Christian ideals and teachings? They did so through preaching, assimilation, the ritual of penance, and the veneration of saints. Missionaries preached the basic teachings of Christianity in simplified Latin or translated them into the local language. In monasteries and cathedrals, men—and a few women—wrote hymns, prayers, and stories about the lives of Christ and the saints. People heard these and slowly became familiar with Christian notions.

Deeply ingrained pagan customs and practices could not be stamped out by words alone, however, or even by royal edicts. Christian missionaries often pursued a policy of assimilation, easing the conversion of pagan men and women by stressing similarities between their customs and beliefs and those of Christianity. In the same way that classically trained scholars such as Jerome and Augustine blended Greco-Roman and Christian ideas, missionaries and converts mixed pagan ideas and practices with Christian ones. Bogs and lakes sacred to Germanic gods became associated with saints, as did various aspects of ordinary life, such as traveling, planting crops, and worrying about a sick child. Aspects of existing midwinter celebrations, which often centered on the return of the sun as the days became longer, were incorporated into celebrations of Christmas. Spring rituals involving eggs and rabbits (both symbols of fertility) were added to Easter.

The ritual of penance was also instrumental in teaching people Christian ideas. Christianity taught that certain actions and thoughts were sins, meaning that they were against God's commands. Only by confessing these sins and asking forgiveness could a sinning believer be reconciled with God. Confession was initially a public ritual, but by the fifth century individual confession to a parish priest was more common. The person knelt before the priest, who questioned him or her about sins he or she might have committed. The priest then set a penance such as fasting or saying specific prayers to allow the person to atone for

St. John's Crucifixion Plaque
One of the earliest depictions of the crucifixion in Irish art, this gilt and bronze plaque from the late seventh or early eighth century shows Christ flanked by two Roman soldiers while angels hover overhead, with the figures decorated with swirls and interlace. Made by hammering a bronze sheet from behind, the plaque might have originally been on a book cover, wooden cross, or panel in a shrine. (National Museum of Ireland, Dublin/Photo © Boltin Picture Library/Bridgeman Images)

■ **relics** Bones, articles of clothing, or other objects associated with the life of a saint.

the sin. The priest and penitent were guided by manuals known as penitentials (peh-nuh-TEHN-shuhlz), which included lists of sins and the appropriate penance. The seventh-century English penitential of Theodore, for example, stipulated that "if a lay Christian vomits because of drunkenness, he shall do penance for fifteen days," while drunken monks were to do penance for thirty days. Those who "commit fornication with a virgin" were to do penance for a year, as were those who perform "divinations according to the custom of the heathens." Penance for killing someone depended on the circumstances. Usually it was seven years, but if the murder was "in revenge for a brother," it was three years; if it was by accident, one year; and if it was "by command of [the killer's] lord" or in "public war," only forty days.[7] Penance gave new Christians a sense of expected behavior, encouraged the private examination of conscience, and offered relief from the burden of sinful deeds.

Most religious observances continued to be community matters, as they had been in the ancient world. People joined with family members, friends, and neighbors at their parish church to attend baptisms, weddings, and funerals presided over by a priest. The parish church often housed the **relics** of a saint, that is, bones, articles of clothing, or other objects associated with a person who had lived (or died) in a way that was spiritually heroic or noteworthy. This patron saint was understood to provide protection and assistance for those who came to worship, and the relics served as a link between the material world and the spiritual. (See "Evaluating the Evidence 7.3: Gregory of Tours on the Veneration of Relics," page 210.)

Christians came to venerate the saints as powerful and holy. They prayed to saints or to the Virgin Mary to intercede with God, or they simply asked the saints to assist and bless them. The entire village participated in processions marking saints' days or points in the agricultural year, often carrying images of saints or their relics around the houses and fields. The decision to become Christian was often made first by an emperor or king, but actual conversion was a local matter, as people came to feel that the parish priest and the patron saint provided them with benefits in this world and the world to come.

The Byzantine Empire

FOCUS QUESTION *How did the Byzantine Empire preserve the legacy of Rome?*

Barbarian migrations and Christian conversions occurred throughout all of Europe in late antiquity, but their impact was not the same in the western and eastern halves of the Roman Empire. The Western Roman Empire gradually disintegrated, but the Roman Empire continued in the East (Map 7.4). The Byzantine or Eastern Roman Empire preserved the forms, institutions, and traditions of the old Roman Empire, and its people even called themselves Romans. Byzantine emperors traced their lines back past Constantine to Augustus, and the Senate in Constantinople carried on the traditions of the old Roman Senate. Most important, however, is how Byzantium protected the

MAP 7.4 The Byzantine Empire, ca. 600   The strategic position of Constantinople on the waterway between the Black Sea and the Mediterranean was clear to Constantine when he chose the city as the capital of the Eastern Roman Empire. Byzantine territories in Italy were acquired in Emperor Justinian's sixth-century wars and were held for several centuries.

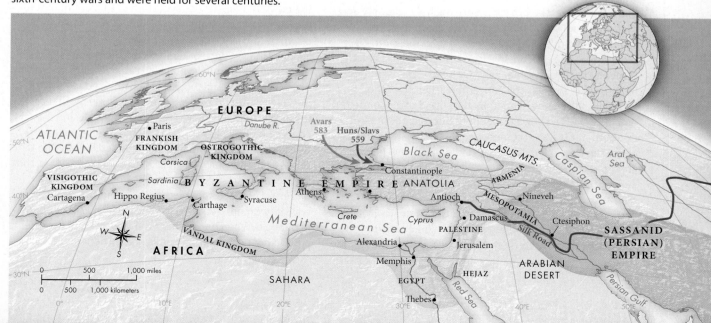

Gregory of Tours on the Veneration of Relics

Accounts of the miracles associated with the relics of saints were an important part of Christian preaching and writing, designed to win converts and strengthen their faith, and to provide spiritual guidance. Gregory of Tours (ca. 539–594), a bishop in the Frankish kingdom, described events surrounding relics in Glory of the Martyrs. *He begins with a discussion of relics associated with the cross on which Jesus had been crucified, the discovery of which was attributed to Emperor Constantine's mother, Helena, who gathered many relics in and around Jerusalem and brought them back to Constantinople. Pieces of this relic were distributed widely throughout Europe, and elaborately decorated reliquaries were made to hold them. As Gregory notes here, some went to the convent in Poitiers (in west-central France) that had been founded by the Merovingian Frankish queen Radegund shortly before Gregory wrote this.*

The cross of the Lord that was found by the empress Helena at Jerusalem is venerated on Wednesday and Friday. Queen Radegund, who is comparable to Helena in both merit and faith, requested relics of this cross and piously placed them in a convent at Poitiers that she founded out of her own zeal. She repeatedly sent servants to Jerusalem and throughout the entire region of the East. These servants visited the tombs of holy martyrs and confessors and brought back relics of them all. After placing them in the silver reliquary with the holy cross itself, she thereafter deserved to see many miracles. . . .

A girl named Chrodigildis was punished by the loss of her eyesight while she was living in the territory of Le Mans after the death of her father. Later, however, while the blessed Queen Radegund was still alive, at the command of King Chilperic she entered the rule of the aforementioned convent. With the most blessed Radegund as a guide, she bowed before the holy reliquary and there kept vigils with the other nuns. When morning came and the others left, she remained in the same place prostrate on the ground. In a vision it seemed to her as if someone had opened her eyes. One eye was restored to health; while she was still concerned about the other, suddenly she was awakened by the sound of a door being unlocked and regained the sight of one eye. There is no doubt that this was accomplished by the power of the cross. The possessed, the lame, and also other ill people are often cured at this place. Enough on this topic. . . .

Through their confession [that is, their not being deterred by persecution] the glorious martyrs have earned the unspeakable benefits of gifts that are always salutary. To petitioners they have revealed themselves by this power that the Lord Creator shared with them. I know

that this happened just as my deacon recently told me. This deacon received relics of some martyrs and confessors [heroic believers] from pope Pelagius [II] of Rome [pontificate 579–590]. A large chorus of monks who were chanting psalms and a huge crowd of people escorted him to Ostia. After he boarded a ship the sails were unfurled and hoisted over the rigging of a mast that presented the appearance of a cross. As the wind blew, they set out on the high seas. When they were sailing to reach the port of Marseilles, they began to approach a certain place where a mountain of stone rose from the shore of the sea and, sinking a bit, stretched into the sea to the top of the water. As the wind forced them on, the ship was lifted by a mighty blast into danger. When the ship was shaken as if struck by the rock, the sailors recognized their peril and announced their death. The deacon lifted the reliquary with the holy relics. He groaned and in a loud voice began to invoke the names of the individual saints. He prayed that their power might liberate from danger those who were about to die. The ship, as I said, sailed closer and closer to the rock. Suddenly, out of respect for the holy relics, a wind blew from that spot with great force against the other wind. It crushed the waves and repulsed the opposing wind. By recalling the ship to the deep sea, the wind freed everyone from the danger of death. So they circumvented this impending danger, and by the grace of the Lord and the protection of the saints they arrived at the port they had hoped for. . . .

Because he [Gregory's father] wished himself to be protected by relics of saints, he asked a cleric to grant him something from these relics, so that with their protection he might be kept safe as he set out on this long journey. He put the sacred ashes in a gold medallion and carried it with him. Although he did not even know the names of the blessed men, he was accustomed to recount that he had been rescued from many dangers. He claimed that often, because of the powers of these relics, he had avoided the violence of bandits, the dangers of floods, the threats of turbulent men, and attacks from swords.

I will not be silent about what I witnessed regarding these relics. After the death of my father my mother carried these relics with her. It was the time for harvesting the crops, and huge piles of grain had been collected on the threshing floors. . . . The threshers kindled fires for themselves from the straw. . . . Quickly, fanned by the wind, the fire spread to the piles of grain. The fire became a huge blaze and was accompanied by the shouts of men, the wails of women, and the crying of children. This happened in our field. When my mother, who was wearing these relics around her neck, learned of this, she rushed from the meal and held the sacred relics in front of the balls of flames. In a moment the entire fire so died down that no sparks were found among the piles of burned straw and the seeds. The grain the fire had touched had suffered no harm.

Many years later I received these relics from my mother. While I was travelling from Burgundy to Clermont, a huge storm appeared in my path. The storm frequently flashed with lightning in the sky and rumbled with loud crashes of thunder. Then I took the holy relics from my pocket and raised my hand before the cloud. The cloud immediately divided into two parts and passed by on the right and the left; it threatened neither me nor anyone else. Then, as a presumptuous young man is expected to behave, I began to be inflated by the arrogance of vainglory. I silently thought that this concession had been made especially for me, rather than because of the merits of the saints. I boasted to my travelling companions and insisted that I had deserved that which God had bestowed upon my naïveté. Immediately my horse suddenly slipped beneath me and threw me to the ground. I was so seriously bruised during this accident that I could hardly get up. I understood that this accident had happened because of my pride; and it was sufficient to note that afterwards the urge of vainglory did not bother me. For if it happened that I was worthy to observe some manifestations of the powers of saints, I have proclaimed that they were due to the gift of God through the faith of the saints.

EVALUATE THE EVIDENCE

1. According to Gregory, what gives relics their power, and why should they be venerated?
2. The veneration of relics involved both public display for community devotion and personal ownership for private needs. What examples of each do you see in Gregory's text?
3. Gregory was a historian who wrote chronicles of the Frankish kingdom as well as spiritual works such as this one. How does he use the techniques of a historian, such as identifying his sources, in this work? How do these support his assertions about the power of relics?

Source: Gregory of Tours, *Glory of the Martyrs*, trans. Raymond Van Dam (Liverpool: Liverpool University, 1988), pp. 22, 24, 106–109. Reprinted with permission of Liverpool University Press.

intellectual heritage of Greco-Roman civilization and then passed it on to the rest of Europe.

Sources of Byzantine Strength

While the western parts of the Roman Empire gradually succumbed to barbarian invaders, the Byzantine Empire survived Germanic, Persian, and Arab attacks. In 540 the Huns and Bulgars crossed the Danube and raided as far as southern Greece. In 559 a force of Huns and Slavs reached the gates of Constantinople. In 583 the Avars, a mounted Mongol people who had swept across Russia and southeastern Europe, seized Byzantine forts along the Danube and reached the walls of Constantinople. Between 572 and 630 the Sassanid Persians posed a formidable threat, and the Greeks were repeatedly at war with them. Beginning in 632 Muslim forces pressured the Byzantine Empire (see Chapter 8).

Why didn't one or a combination of these enemies capture Constantinople as the Ostrogoths had taken Rome? The answer lies in strong military leadership and even more in the city's location and its excellent fortifications. Justinian's generals were able to reconquer much of Italy and North Africa from barbarian groups, making them part of the Eastern Roman Empire. The Byzantines ruled most of Italy from 535 to 572 and the southern part of the peninsula until the eleventh century; they ruled North Africa until it was conquered by Muslim forces in the late seventh century. Under the skillful command of General Priskos (d. 612), Byzantine armies inflicted a severe defeat on the Avars in 601, and under Emperor Heraclius I (r. 610–641) they crushed the Persians at Nineveh in Iraq. Massive triple walls, built by the emperors Constantine and Theodosius II (r. 408–450) and kept in good repair, protected Constantinople from sea invasion. Within the walls huge cisterns provided water, and vast gardens and grazing areas supplied vegetables and meat, so the defending people could hold out far longer than the besieging army. Attacking Constantinople by land posed greater geographical and logistical problems than a seventh- or eighth-century government could solve. The site was not absolutely impregnable—as the Venetians demonstrated in 1204 and the Ottoman Turks in 1453—but it was almost so. For centuries the Byzantine Empire served as a bulwark for the West, protecting it against invasions from the East.

The Law Code of Justinian

One of the most splendid achievements of the Byzantine emperors was the preservation of Roman law for the medieval and modern worlds. Roman law had developed from many sources—decisions by judges, edicts of the emperors, legislation passed by the Senate, and the opinions of jurists. By the fourth century it

Greek Fire   In this illustration from a twelfth-century manuscript, sailors shoot Greek fire toward an attacking ship from a pressurized tube that looks strikingly similar to a modern flamethrower. The exact formula for Greek fire has been lost, but it was probably made from a petroleum product because it continued burning on water. Greek fire was particularly important in Byzantine defenses of Constantinople from Muslim forces in the late seventh century. (Prado, Madrid/Bridgeman Images)

had become a huge, bewildering mass, and its sheer bulk made it almost unusable.

Sweeping and systematic codification took place under the emperor Justinian. He appointed a committee of eminent jurists to sort through and organize the laws. The result was the *Corpus Juris Civilis* (KAWR-puhs JOOR-uhs sih-VIH-luhs) (Body of Civil Law), a multipart collection of laws and legal commentary issued from 529 to 534, and often called simply "Justinian's Code." The first part of this work, the *Codex*, brought together all the existing imperial laws into a coherent whole, eliminated outmoded laws and contradictions, and clarified the law itself. It began with laws ordering the interpretation of Christian doctrine favored by the emperor in opposition to groups such as the Arians and Nestorians, and affirming the power of the emperor in matters of religion, such as this decree first issued by the emperor Theodosius:

> We desire that all peoples subject to Our benign Empire shall live under the same religion that the Divine Peter, the Apostle, gave to the Romans, and which the said religion declares was introduced by himself . . . that is to say, in accordance with the rules of apostolic discipline and the evangelical doctrine, we should believe that the Father, Son, and Holy Spirit constitute a single Deity, endowed with equal majesty, and united in the Holy Trinity.
>
> We order all those who follow this law to assume the name of Catholic Christians, and considering others as demented and insane, We order that they shall bear the infamy of heresy; and when the Divine vengeance which they merit has been appeased, they shall afterwards be punished in accordance with our resentment, which we have acquired from the judgment of Heaven.[8]

The rest of the *Codex* was structured by topic and included provisions on every aspect of life, including economic issues, social concerns, and family life. (See "Thinking Like a Historian: Slavery in Roman and Germanic Society," page 198.)

The second part of Justinian's Code, the *Digest*, is a collection of the opinions of foremost Roman jurists on complex legal problems, and the third part, the *Institutes*, is a handbook of civil law designed for students and beginning jurists. All three parts were given the force of law and formed the backbone of Byzantine jurisprudence from that point on. Like so much of classical culture, the *Corpus Juris Civilis* was lost in western Europe with the end of the Roman Empire, but it was rediscovered in the eleventh century and came to form the foundation of law for nearly every modern European nation.

Byzantine Intellectual Life

The Byzantines prized education; because of them, many masterpieces of ancient Greek literature have survived to influence the intellectual life of the modern

INDIVIDUALS IN SOCIETY

Theodora of Constantinople

The most powerful woman in Byzantine history was the daughter of a bear trainer for the circus. Theodora (ca. 497–548) grew up in what her contemporaries regarded as an undignified and morally suspect atmosphere, and she worked as a dancer and burlesque actress, both dishonorable occupations in the Roman world. Despite her background, she caught the eye of Justinian, who was then a military leader and whose uncle (and adoptive father) Justin had himself risen from obscurity to become the emperor of the Byzantine Empire. Under Justinian's influence, Justin changed the law to allow an actress who had left her disreputable life to marry whom she liked, and Justinian and Theodora married in 525. When Justinian was proclaimed co-emperor with his uncle Justin on April 1, 527, Theodora received the rare title of *augusta*, or empress. Thereafter her name was linked with Justinian's in the exercise of imperial power.

Most of our knowledge of Theodora's early life comes from the *Secret History*, a tell-all description of the vices of Justinian and his court written around 550 by Procopius (pruh-KOH-pee-uhs), who was the official court historian and thus spent his days praising those same people. In the *Secret History* he portrays Theodora and Justinian as demonic, greedy, and vicious, killing courtiers to steal their property. In scene after detailed scene, Procopius portrays Theodora as particularly evil, sexually insatiable, depraved, and cruel, a temptress who used sorcery to attract men, including the hapless Justinian.

In one of his official histories, *The History of the Wars of Justinian*, Procopius presents a very different Theodora. Riots

The empress Theodora (center) shown with a halo, symbolizing piety, and a crown, symbolizing power, in an intricate mosaic of thousands of cubes of colored glass and stone, created in Ravenna, Italy, in the sixth century. Like Justinian, Theodora had power over secular and religious institutions, much to the dismay of many at Justinian's court. (San Vitale, Ravenna, Italy/Universal History Archive/UIG via Getty Images)

between the supporters of two teams in chariot races — who formed associations somewhat like both street gangs and political parties — had turned deadly, and Justinian wavered in his handling of the perpetrators. Both sides turned against the emperor, besieging the palace while Justinian was inside it. Shouting "N-I-K-A" (victory), the rioters swept through the city, burning and looting, and destroyed half of Constantinople. Justinian's counselors urged flight, but, according to Procopius, Theodora rose and declared:

> For one who has reigned, it is intolerable to be an exile. . . . If you wish, O Emperor, to save yourself, there is no difficulty: we have ample funds and there are the ships. Yet reflect whether, when you have once escaped to a place of security, you will not prefer death to safety. I agree with an old saying that the purple [that is, the color worn only by emperors] is a fair winding sheet [to be buried in].

Justinian rallied, had the rioters driven into the hippodrome, and ordered between thirty thousand and thirty-five thousand men and women executed. The revolt was crushed and Justinian's authority was restored, an outcome approved by Procopius.

Other sources describe or suggest Theodora's influence on imperial policy. Justinian passed a number of laws that improved the legal status of women, such as allowing women to own property the same way that men could and to be guardians over their own children. Justinian is reputed to have consulted her every day about all aspects of state policy, including religious policy regarding the doctrinal disputes that continued throughout his reign. Theodora's influence over her husband and her power in the Byzantine state continued until she died, perhaps of cancer, twenty years before Justinian. Her influence may have even continued after death, for Justinian continued to pass reforms favoring women and, at the end of his life, accepted her interpretation of Christian doctrine. Institutions that she established, including hospitals, orphanages, houses for the rehabilitation of prostitutes, and churches, continued to be reminders of her charity and piety.

Theodora has been viewed as a symbol of the manipulation of beauty and cleverness to attain position and power, and also as a strong and capable co-ruler who held the empire together during riots, revolts, and deadly epidemics. Just as Procopius expressed both views, the debate has continued to today among writers of science fiction and fantasy as well as biographers and historians.

QUESTIONS FOR ANALYSIS

1. How would you assess the complex legacy of Theodora?
2. Since the official and unofficial views of Procopius are so different regarding the empress, should he be trusted at all as a historical source?

world. The literature of the Byzantine Empire was predominantly Greek, although politicians, scholars, and lawyers also spoke and used Latin. Justinian's Code was first written in Latin. More people could read in Byzantium than anywhere else in Christian Europe at the time, and history was a favorite topic.

The most remarkable Byzantine historian was Procopius (ca. 500–562), who left a rousing account praising Justinian's reconquest of North Africa and Italy, but also wrote the *Secret History*, a vicious and uproarious attack on Justinian and his wife, the empress Theodora. (See "Individuals in Society: Theodora of Constantinople," page 213.)

Although the Byzantines discovered little that was new in mathematics and geometry, they made advances in terms of military applications. For example, they invented an explosive liquid that came to be known as "Greek fire." The liquid was heated and propelled by a pump through a bronze tube, and as the jet left the tube, it was ignited—somewhat like a modern flamethrower. Greek fire saved Constantinople from Arab assault in 678 and was used in both land and sea battles for centuries, although modern military experts still do not know the exact nature of the compound. In mechanics Byzantine scientists improved and modified artillery and siege machinery.

The Byzantines devoted a great deal of attention to medicine, and the general level of medical competence was far higher in the Byzantine Empire than in western Europe. Yet their physicians could not cope with the terrible disease, often called the "Justinian plague," that swept through the Byzantine Empire and parts of western Europe between 542 and about 560. Probably originating in northwestern India and carried to the Mediterranean region by ships, the disease was similar to what was later identified as the bubonic plague. Characterized by high fever, chills, delirium, and enlarged lymph nodes, or by inflammation of the lungs that caused hemorrhages of black blood, the Justinian plague claimed the lives of tens of thousands of people. The epidemic had profound political as well as social consequences: it weakened Justinian's military resources, thus hampering his efforts to restore unity to the Mediterranean world.

By the ninth or tenth century most major Greek cities had hospitals for the care of the sick. The hospitals might be divided into wards for different illnesses, and hospital staff included surgeons, practitioners, and aids with specialized responsibilities. The imperial Byzantine government bore the costs of these medical facilities.

The Orthodox Church

The continuity of the Roman Empire in the East meant that Christianity developed differently there than it did in the West. The emperors in Constantinople were understood to be Christ's representative on earth; their palace was considered holy and was filled with relics and religious images, called icons. Emperors convened councils, appointed church officials, and regulated the income of the church. As in Rome, there was a patriarch in Constantinople, but he did not develop the same powers that the pope did in the West because there was never a similar power vacuum into which he needed to step. The **Orthodox Church**, the name generally given to the Eastern Christian Church, was more subject to secular control than the Western Christian Church, although some churchmen did stand up to the emperor. Saint John Chrysostom (ca. 347–407), for example, a bishop and one of the church fathers, thunderously preached against what he saw as the luxury and decadence of the emperor's court and its support of pagan practices, such as erecting statues of rulers. He was banished—twice—but his sermons calling for an ascetic life and support for the poor were copied and recopied for centuries.

Monasticism in the Orthodox world differed in fundamental ways from the monasticism that evolved in western Europe. First, while *The Rule of Saint Benedict* gradually became the universal guide for all western European monasteries, each individual house in the Byzantine world developed its own set of rules for organization and behavior. Second, education never became a central feature of Orthodox monasteries. Monks and nuns had to be literate to perform the appropriate rituals, but no Orthodox monastery assumed responsibility for the general training of the local young.

There were also similarities between Western and Eastern monasticism. As in the West, Eastern monasteries became wealthy property owners, with fields, pastures, livestock, and buildings. Since bishops and patriarchs of the Orthodox Church were recruited only from the monasteries, these religious leaders also exercised cultural influence.

Like their counterparts in the West, Byzantine missionaries traveled far beyond the boundaries of the empire in search of converts. In 863 the emperor Michael III sent the brothers Cyril (826–869) and Methodius (815–885) to preach Christianity in Moravia (a region in the modern Czech Republic). Other missionaries succeeded in converting the Russians in the tenth century. Cyril invented a Slavic alphabet using Greek characters, later termed the Cyrillic (suh-RIH-lihk) alphabet in his honor. In the tenth century other missionaries spread Christianity, the Cyrillic alphabet, and Byzantine art and architecture to Russia. The Byzantines were so successful that the Russians would later claim to be the successors of the Byzantine Empire. For a time Moscow was even known as the "Third Rome" (the second Rome being Constantinople).

■ **Orthodox Church** Eastern Christian Church in the Byzantine Empire.

NOTES

1. Maude Aline Huttman, ed. and trans., *The Establishment of Christianity and the Proscription of Paganism* (New York: AMS Press, 1967), p. 164.

2. Eusebius, *Life of Constantine the Great*, trans. Ernest Cushing Richardson (Grand Rapids, Mich.: Eerdmans, 1979), p. 534.

3. R. C. Petry, ed., *A History of Christianity: Readings in the History of Early and Medieval Christianity* (Englewood Cliffs, N.J.: Prentice Hall, 1962), p. 70.

4. Saint Jerome, *Commentaries on the Letter to the Ephesians*, book 16, cited in Vern Bullough, *Sexual Variance in Society and History* (Chicago: University of Chicago Press, 1976), p. 365.

5. E. F. Henderson, ed., *Select Historical Documents of the Middle Ages* (London: G. Bell and Sons, 1912), pp. 176–189.

6. Reprinted by permission of the publishers and the Trustees of the Loeb Classical Library from Ammianus Marcellinus, *The History*, Volume 1, Loeb Classical Library, translated by John C. Rolfe; book 31, pt. 2, pp. 383, 385, 387. Cambridge, Mass.: Harvard University Press. First published 1939. The Loeb Classical Library® is a registered trademark of the President and Fellows of Harvard College.

7. John McNeill and Helena M. Gamer, *Medieval Handbooks of Penance: A Translation of the Principal Libri Poenitentiales and Selections from Related Documents* (New York: Columbia University Press, 1938).

8. Justinian's Code 1.1.1, in S. P. Scott, trans., *The Civil Law*, vol. 12 (Cincinnati: The Central Trust Company, 1932), p. 9.

LOOKING BACK LOOKING AHEAD

The Christian Church and the barbarian states absorbed many aspects of Roman culture, and the Roman Empire continued to thrive in the East as the Byzantine Empire, but western Europe in 600 was very different than it had been in 250. The Western Roman Empire had slowly disintegrated under pressure from barbarian groups. Barbarian kings ruled small states from Italy to Norway, while churches and monasteries rather than emperors and wealthy individuals took on the role of constructing new buildings and providing education. The city of Rome no longer attracted a steady stream of aspiring immigrants and had shrunk significantly, as had many other cities, which were no longer centers of innovation. As the vast network of Roman urban centers dissolved, economies everywhere became more localized. Commentators such as Augustine advised people to put their faith in the eternal City of God rather than in worldly cities, because human history would always bring great change. People who lived with Augustine in Hippo would have certainly understood such counsel, for they watched the Vandals besiege their city in 430, move swiftly across North Africa, and bring an end to Roman rule there. Although Justinian's Byzantine forces reclaimed the area a little over a century later, the culture that survived was as much barbarian as Roman, with smaller cities, less trade, and fewer schools.

Two hundred years after the Vandal attack, the residents of Byzantine North Africa confronted another fast-moving army of conquest, Arabian forces carrying a new religion, Islam. This Arabic expansion dramatically shaped the development of Western civilization. Though the end of the Roman Empire in 476 has long been seen as a dramatic break in European history, the expansion of Islam two centuries later may have been even more significant. Many of the patterns set in late antiquity continued, however. Warrior values such as physical prowess, bravery in battle, and loyalty to one's lord remained central and shaped the development of the political system known as feudalism. The Frankish kingdom established by Clovis continued to expand, becoming the most important state in Europe. The economic and political power of the Christian Church expanded as well, with monasteries and convents providing education for their residents. The vast majority of people continued to live in small villages, trying to raise enough grain to feed themselves and their families, and asking the saints for help to overcome life's difficulties.

Make Connections

Think about the larger developments and continuities within and across chapters.

1. The end of the Roman Empire in the West in 476 has long been viewed as one of the most important turning points in history. Do you agree with this idea? Why or why not?

2. In what ways was the role of the family in barbarian society similar to that of the family in classical Athens (Chapter 3) and republican Rome (Chapter 5)? In what ways was it different? What might account for the similarities and differences that you identify?

3. How did the Christian Church adapt to Roman and barbarian society? How was it different in 600 from how it had been in 100?

7 REVIEW & EXPLORE

Identify Key Terms

Identify and explain the significance of each item below.

tetrarchy (p. 186)

diocese (p. 186)

Arianism (p. 189)

apostolic succession (p. 190)

Petrine Doctrine (p. 191)

regular clergy (p. 191)

secular clergy (p. 192)

sacraments (p. 195)

runic alphabet (p. 195)

comitatus (p. 196)

wergeld (p. 200)

relics (p. 209)

Orthodox Church (p. 214)

Review the Main Ideas

Answer the focus questions from each section of the chapter.

◆ How did Diocletian and Constantine try to reform the empire? (p. 186)

◆ How did the Christian Church become a major force in the Mediterranean and Europe? (p. 190)

◆ What were the key characteristics of barbarian society? (p. 195)

◆ What were some of the causes and consequences of the barbarian migrations? (p. 201)

◆ How did the church convert barbarian peoples to Christianity? (p. 206)

◆ How did the Byzantine Empire preserve the legacy of Rome? (p. 209)

Suggested Reading and Media Resources

BOOKS

- Brown, Peter. *Augustine of Hippo*, rev. ed. 2000. The definitive biography of Saint Augustine, who is viewed here as a symbol of change.

- Brown, Peter. *The World of Late Antiquity*, A.D. *150–750*, rev. ed. 1989. A lavishly illustrated survey that stresses social and cultural changes and continuities, and provides clearly written introductions to the entire period.

- Burns, Thomas S. *Rome and the Barbarians, 100 B.C.–A.D. 400.* 2003. Argues that Germanic and Roman cultures assimilated with each other more than they conflicted.

- Clark, Gillian. *Late Antiquity: A Very Short Introduction.* 2011. A compact survey of the era, portraying it as a period of great transformation rather than simply decline.

- Clark, Gillian. *Women in Late Antiquity: Pagan and Christian Lifestyles.* 1994. Explores law, marriage, and religious life.

- Dunn, Marilyn. *The Emergence of Monasticism: From the Desert Fathers to the Early Middle Ages.* 2003. A thorough study of the beginnings of monasticism.

- Fletcher, Richard. *The Barbarian Conversion: From Paganism to Christianity.* 1998. A superbly written analysis of conversion to Christianity.

- Goldsworthy, Adrian. *How Rome Fell: Death of a Superpower.* 2009. A detailed narrative that emphasizes internal weaknesses caused by civil war and struggles for power.

- Heather, Peter. *The Fall of the Roman Empire: A New History of Rome and the Barbarians.* 2006. A masterful analysis that asserts the centrality of barbarian military actions in the end of the Roman Empire.

- Herrin, Judith. *Byzantium: The Surprising Life of a Medieval Empire.* 2008. Written for a general audience, this book portrays a tradition-based yet dynamic empire and discusses its signifiance for today.

- Herrin, Judith. *The Formation of Christendom.* 1987. An excellent synthesis of the development of the Christian Church from the third to the ninth centuries.

- Todd, Malcolm. *The Early Germans*, 2d ed. 2004. Uses archaeological and literary sources to analyze Germanic social structure, customs, and religion and to suggest implications for an understanding of migration and ethnicity.

- Ward-Perkins, Bryan. *The Fall of Rome and the End of Civilization.* 2006. Uses material evidence to trace the physical destruction and economic dislocation that accompanied the barbarian migrations.

- Wells, Peter S. *The Barbarians Speak: How the Conquered Peoples Shaped Roman Europe.* 1999. Presents extensive evidence of Celtic and Germanic social and technical development.

DOCUMENTARIES

- *Barbarians II* (History Channel, 2007). A four-part documentary with many battle re-enactments that views the Vandals, Saxons, Franks, and Lombard barbarians as warrior hordes with savage tactics that "drove the empire to its knees."

- *The Germanic Tribes: The Complete Four-Part Saga* (Kultur, 2003). Using computer graphics and re-enactments, this documentary examines the settlements and religion of the German tribes as well as their warfare, and argues that they actually preserved much of the Roman legacy.

- *I, Caesar* (BBC, 1997). Each part of this six-part documentary series focuses on one Roman emperor, beginning with Julius Caesar and including both Constantine and Justinian; the films examine both their private lives and their public careers.

- *Terry Jones' Barbarians* (BBC, 2007). A witty and lively four-part documentary by a member of the Monty Python comedy troupe that sees the barbarians as less important for Rome's fall than other factors.

WEB SITES

- *CELT: Corpus of Electronic Texts.* Ireland's longest-running humanities computing project, this database includes writing by and about Saint Patrick and chronicles of the early Irish kings. **www.ucc.ie/celt/**

- *Christian Classics Ethereal Library.* Hosted by Calvin College, this site has hundreds of primary sources in the public domain on all aspects of the history of Christianity, and is especially strong in the writings of the church fathers, including Jerome, Ambrose, Augustine, and Benedict. **www.ccel.org**

- *Explore Byzantium.* Developed in New Zealand, this site offers a variety of resources on the Byzantine Empire: historical overviews, timelines, maps, articles, bibliographic material, and an extensive collection of photographs of surviving examples of Byzantine architecture and public art. **byzantium.seashell.net.nz /index.php**

- *Internet Medieval Sourcebook: Byzantium.* Includes actual sources and links to sources elsewhere on many aspects of Byzantine politics and religion. **www.fordham.edu/halsall/sbook1c.asp**

8

Europe in the Early Middle Ages

600–1000

By the fifteenth century, scholars in the growing cities of northern Italy began to think that they were living in a new era, one in which the glories of ancient Greece and Rome were being reborn. What separated their time from classical antiquity, in their opinion, was a long period of darkness, to which a seventeenth-century professor gave the name "Middle Ages." In this conceptualization, Western history was divided into three periods—ancient, medieval, and modern—an organization that is still in use today.

For a long time the end of the Roman Empire in the West was seen as the division between the ancient period and the Middle Ages, but, as we saw in the last chapter, there was continuity as well as change, and the transition from ancient to medieval was a slow process, not a single event. The agents in this process included not only the barbarian migrations that broke the Roman Empire apart but also the new religion of Islam, Slavic and steppe peoples in eastern Europe, and Christian officials and missionaries. The period from the end of antiquity (ca. 600–1000), conventionally known as the "early Middle Ages," was a time of disorder and destruction, but it also marked the creation of a new type of society and a cultural revival that influenced later intellectual and literary traditions. While agrarian life continued to dominate Europe, political and economic structures that would influence later European history began to form, and Christianity continued to spread. People at the time did not know that they were living in an era that would later be labeled "middle" or sometimes even "dark," and we can wonder whether they would have shared this negative view of their own times. ■

CHAPTER PREVIEW

The Spread of Islam
What were the origins of Islam, and what impact did it have on Europe as it spread?

Frankish Rulers and Their Territories
How did the Franks build and govern a European empire?

Early Medieval Culture
What were the significant intellectual and cultural changes in Charlemagne's era?

Invasions and Migrations
What were the consequences of the ninth-century invasions and migrations?

Political and Economic Decentralization
How did internal conflict and outside threats shape European political and economic development in this period?

Life in the Early Middle Ages
In this manuscript illumination from Spain, Muslim fishermen take a rich harvest from the sea. Fish were an important part of the diet of all coastal peoples in medieval Europe and were often salted and dried to preserve them for later use. (From *Cantigas de Santa Maria*, manuscript made under the direction of Alfonso X [1221–1284], King of Castile and Leon/Granger, NYC — All rights reserved)

The Spread of Islam

FOCUS QUESTION *What were the origins of Islam, and what impact did it have on Europe as it spread?*

In the seventh century C.E. two empires dominated the area today called the Middle East: the Byzantine-Greek-Christian empire and the Sassanid-Persian-Zoroastrian empire. Between the two lay the Arabian peninsula, where a merchant called Muhammad began to have religious visions around 610. By the time he died in 632, all Arabia had accepted his creed of Islam. A century later his followers controlled what is now Syria, Palestine, Egypt, North Africa, Spain, and part of France. This Arab expansion profoundly affected the development of Western civilization as well as the history of Africa and Asia.

The Arabs

In Muhammad's time Arabia was inhabited by various tribes, many of them Bedouins (BEH-duh-wuhnz). These nomadic peoples grazed goats and sheep on the sparse patches of grass that dotted the vast semiarid peninsula. The power of the Bedouins came from their fighting skills, toughness, ability to control trade, and possession of horses and camels. Other Arabs lived more settled lives in the southern valleys and coastal towns along the Red Sea, such as Yemen, Mecca, and Medina, supporting themselves by agriculture and trade. Caravan routes crisscrossed Arabia and carried goods to Byzantium, Persia, and Syria. The wealth produced by business transactions led to luxurious living for many residents in the towns.

For all Arabs, the basic social unit was the clan—a group of blood relations connected through the male line. Clans expected loyalty from their members and in turn provided support and protection. Although the nomadic Bedouins condemned the urbanized lifestyle of the cities as immoral and corrupt, Arabs of all types respected certain aspects of one another's customs and had some religious rules and rituals in common. For example, all Arabs kept three months of the year as sacred; during that time any fighting stopped so that everyone could attend holy ceremonies in peace. The city of Mecca was the major religious and economic center of western Arabia. For centuries before the rise of Islam, many Arabs prayed at the Ka'ba (KAH-buh), a temple in Mecca containing a black stone thought to be the dwelling place of a god, as well as objects connected to other gods. Economic links also connected Arab peoples, but what eventually molded the diverse Arab tribes into a powerful political and social unity was a new religion based on the teachings of Muhammad.

The Prophet Muhammad

Except for a few vague remarks in the **Qur'an** (kuh-RAHN), the sacred book of Islam, Muhammad (ca. 571–632) left no account of his life. Arab tradition accepts some of the sacred stories that developed about him as historically true, but those accounts were not written down until about a century after his death. (Similarly, the earliest accounts of the life of Jesus, the Christian Gospels, were not written until forty to sixty years after his death.) Orphaned at the age of six, Muhammad was raised by his grandfather. As a young man he became a merchant in the caravan trade. Later he entered the service of a wealthy widow, and their subsequent marriage brought him financial independence.

The Qur'an reveals Muhammad to be an extremely devout man, ascetic, self-disciplined, and literate, but not formally educated. He prayed regularly, and when he was about forty he began to experience religious visions. Unsure for a time about what he should do, Muhammad discovered his mission after a vision in which the angel Gabriel instructed him to preach. Muhammad described his visions in a stylized and often rhyming prose and used this literary medium as his *Qur'an*, or "prayer recitation." Muhammad's revelations were written down by his followers during his lifetime and organized into chapters, called *sura*, shortly after his death. In 651 Muhammad's third successor arranged to have an official version published. The Qur'an is regarded by Muslims as the direct words of God to his Prophet Muhammad and is therefore especially revered. (When Muslims around the world use translations of the Qur'an, they do so alongside the original Arabic, the language of Muhammad's revelations.) At the same time, other sayings and accounts of Muhammad, which gave advice on matters that went beyond the Qur'an, were collected into books termed *hadith* (huh-DEETH). Muslim tradition (*Sunna*) consists of both the Qur'an and the hadith.

Muhammad's visions ordered him to preach a message of a single God and to become God's prophet, which he began to do in his hometown of Mecca. He gathered followers slowly, but also provoked a great deal of resistance because he urged people to give up worship of the gods whose sacred objects were in the Ka'ba and also challenged the power of the local elite. In 622 he migrated with his followers to Medina, an event termed the *hijra* (hih-JIGH-ruh) that marks the beginning of the Muslim calendar. At Medina Muhammad was much more successful, gaining converts and working out the basic principles of the faith. That same year, through the Charter of Medina, Muhammad formed the first *umma*, a community that united his followers from different tribes and set religious ties above clan loyalty. The charter also extended

■ **Qur'an** The sacred book of Islam.

rights to non-Muslims living in Medina, including Jews and Christians, which set a precedent for the later treatment of Jews and Christians under Islam.

In 630 Muhammad returned to Mecca at the head of a large army, and he soon united the nomads of the desert and the merchants of the cities into an even larger umma of Muslims, a word meaning "those who comply with God's will." The religion itself came to be called Islam, which means "submission to God." The Ka'ba was rededicated as a Muslim holy place, and Mecca became the most holy city in Islam. According to Muslim tradition, the Ka'ba predates the creation of the world and represents the earthly counterpart of God's heavenly throne, to which "pilgrims come dishevelled and dusty on every kind of camel."[1]

By the time Muhammad died in 632, the crescent of Islam, the Muslim symbol, prevailed throughout the Arabian peninsula. During the next century one rich province of the old Roman Empire after another came under Muslim domination — first Syria, then Egypt, and then all of North Africa (Map 8.1). Long and bitter wars (572–591, 606–630) between the Byzantine and Persian Empires left both so weak and exhausted that they easily fell to Muslim attack.

Chronology

481–752	Merovingian dynasty
ca. 571–632	Life of the Prophet Muhammad
651	Official version of the Qur'an published
711	Muslim forces defeat Visigothic kingdom
711–720	Muslim conquest of Spain
ca. 760–840	Carolingian Renaissance
768–814	Reign of Charlemagne
800	Imperial coronation of Charlemagne
800–900	Free peasants in western Europe increasingly tied to the land as serfs
843	Treaty of Verdun divides Carolingian kingdom
850–1000	Most extensive Viking voyages and conquests
ca. 900	Establishment of Kievan Rus
911	Vikings establish Normandy
950	Muslim Córdoba is Europe's largest and most prosperous city
1000	Stephen crowned first king of Hungary

Dome of the Rock, Jerusalem   Completed in 691 and revered by Muslims as the site where Muhammad ascended to Heaven, the Dome of the Rock is the third-holiest place in Islam, after Mecca and Medina. Influenced by Byzantine and Persian architecture, it also has distinctly Arab features, such as Qur'anic inscriptions. (imageBROKER.net/SuperStock)

The Teachings and Expansion of Islam

Muhammad's religion eventually attracted great numbers of people, partly because of the straightforward nature of its doctrines. The strictly monotheistic theology outlined in the Qur'an has only a few central tenets: Allah, the Arabic word for God, is all-powerful and all-knowing. Muhammad, Allah's prophet, preached his word and carried his message. Muhammad described himself as the successor both of the Jewish patriarch Abraham and of Christ, and he claimed that his teachings replaced theirs. He invited and won converts from Judaism and Christianity.

Because Allah is all-powerful, believers must submit themselves to him. All Muslims have the obligation of the *jihad* (literally, "self-exertion") to strive or struggle to lead a virtuous life and to spread God's rule and law. In some cases striving is an individual struggle against sin; in others it is social and communal and could involve armed conflict, though this is not an essential part of jihad (jee-HAHD). The Islamic belief of "striving in the path of God" is closely related to the central feature of Muslim doctrine, the coming Day of Judgment. Muslims believe with conviction that the Day of Judgment will come; consequently, all of a Muslim's thoughts and actions should be oriented toward the Last Judgment and the rewards of Heaven.

To merit the rewards of Heaven, a person must follow the strict code of moral behavior that Muhammad prescribed. The Muslim must recite a profession of faith in God and in Muhammad as God's prophet: "There is no god but God and Muhammad is his prophet." The believer must pray five times a day, fast and pray during the sacred month of Ramadan, and contribute alms to the poor and needy. If possible, the believer must make a pilgrimage to Mecca once during his or her lifetime. According to the Muslim *shari'a* (shuh-REE-uh), or sacred law, these five practices—the profession of faith, prayer, fasting, giving alms to the poor, and pilgrimage to Mecca—constitute the **Five Pillars of Islam**. The Muslim who faithfully observes the laws of the Qur'an can hope for salvation.

The Qur'an forbids alcoholic beverages and gambling, as well as a number of foods, such as pork, a dietary regulation adopted from the Mosaic law of the Hebrews. It condemns business usury—that is, lending money at interest rates or taking advantage of market demand for products by charging high prices for them.

Polygyny, the practice of men having more than one wife, was common in Arab society before Muhammad, though for economic reasons the custom was limited to the well-to-do. The Qur'an limited the number of wives a man could have, however: "[Of] women who seem good in your eyes, marry but

MAP 8.1 The Spread of Islam, 622–900   The rapid expansion of Islam in a relatively short span of time testifies to the Arabs' superior fighting skills, religious zeal, and economic organization as well as to their enemies' weakness.

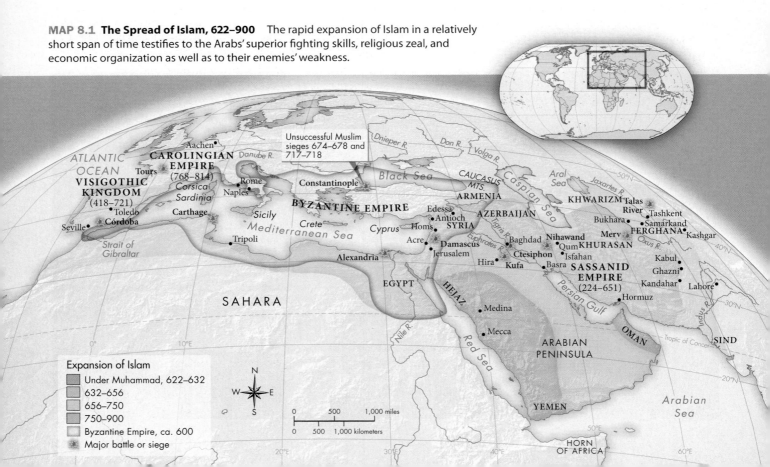

two, three, or four; and if ye still fear that ye shall not act equitably then only one" (Sura 4:3).

The Qur'an sets forth a strict sexual morality and condemns immoral behavior on the part of men as well as women: "The whore and the fornicator: whip each of them a hundred times. . . . The fornicator shall not marry other than a whore; and the whore shall not marry other than a fornicator" (Sura 24:2–3).

The Qur'an also set out rules for inheritance:

> Men who die and leave wives behind shall bequeath to them a year's maintenance. . . . And your wives shall have a fourth part of what you leave, if you have no issue [offspring]; but if you have issue, then they shall have an eighth part. . . . With regard to your children, God commands you to give the male the portion of two females. (Sura 4:11–12)

With respect to matters of property, Muslim women of the early Middle Ages had more rights than Western women. For example, a Muslim woman retained complete jurisdiction over one-third of her property when she married and could dispose of it in any way she wished. Women in most European countries and the United States did not gain these rights until the nineteenth century.

Sunni and Shi'a Divisions

Every Muslim hoped that by observing the laws of the Qur'an, he or she could achieve salvation, and it was the tenets of Islam preached by Muhammad that bound all Arabs together. Despite the clarity and unifying force of Muslim doctrine, however, divisions developed within the Islamic faith within decades of Muhammad's death. Neither the Qur'an nor the hadith gave clear guidance about how successors to Muhammad were to be chosen, but, according to tradition, in 632 a group of Muhammad's closest followers chose Abu Bakr (uh-BOO BAH-kuhr), who was a close friend of the Prophet's and a member of a clan affiliated with the Prophet's clan, as **caliph** (KAY-luhf), a word meaning "successor." He was succeeded by two other caliphs, but these provoked opposition, which coalesced around Ali, Muhammad's cousin and son-in-law. Ali was chosen as the fourth caliph in 656, but was assassinated only five years later by backers of the initial line of caliphs. Ali's supporters began to assert that the Prophet had designated Ali as *imam*, or leader, and that he should rightly have been the first caliph; thus, any caliph who was not a descendant of Ali was a usurper. These supporters of Ali—termed Shi'ites (SHEE-ights) or Shi'a (SHEE-ah) from Arabic terms meaning "supporters" or "partisans" of Ali—saw Ali and subsequent imams as the divinely inspired leaders of the community. The larger body of Muslims who

accepted the first elections—termed Sunnis, a word derived from *Sunna*, the practices of the community derived from Muhammad's example—saw the caliphs as political leaders. Since Islam did not have an organized priesthood, the caliphs had an additional function of safeguarding and enforcing the religious law (shari'a) with the advice of scholars (*ulama*), particularly the jurists, judges, and scholastics who were knowledgeable about the Qur'an and hadith. Over the centuries enmity between Sunni and Shi'a Muslims has sometimes erupted into violence, and discord still exists today.

After the assassination of Ali, the caliphate passed to members of the Umayyad (oo-MIGH-uhd) clan, who asserted control and brought stability to the growing Muslim empire. They established their capital at Damascus in Syria, and the Muslim faith continued to expand eastward to India and westward across North Africa. That expansion was facilitated everywhere by three main factors: military strength, trade connections, and tolerance toward non-Muslims. By the early tenth century a Muslim proverb spoke of the Mediterranean Sea as a Muslim lake, though the Greeks at Constantinople contested that notion.

Life in Muslim Spain

In Europe, Muslim political and cultural influence was felt most strongly in the Iberian Peninsula. In 711 a Muslim force crossed the Strait of Gibraltar and easily defeated the weak Visigothic kingdom. (See "Evaluating the Evidence 8.1: The Muslim Conquest of Spain," page 224.) A few Christian princes supported by the Frankish rulers held out in northern mountain fortresses, but by 720 the Muslims controlled most of Spain. A member of the Umayyad Dynasty, Abd al-Rahman (r. 756–788) established a kingdom in Spain with its capital at Córdoba (KAWR-doh-buh).

Throughout the Islamic world, Muslims used the term **al-Andalus** to describe the part of the Iberian Peninsula under Muslim control. The name probably derives from the Arabic for "land of the Vandals," the Germanic people who swept across Spain in the fifth century (see Chapter 7). In the eighth century al-Andalus included the entire peninsula from Gibraltar in the south to the Cantabrian Mountains in the north (see Map 8.1). Today we often use the word *Andalusia* (an-duh-LOO-zhuh) to refer especially to southern Spain, but eighth-century Christians throughout Europe called the peninsula "Moorish Spain" because the

■ **Five Pillars of Islam** The five practices Muslims must fulfill according to the shari'a, or sacred law, including the profession of faith, prayer, fasting, giving alms to the poor, and pilgrimage to Mecca.

■ **caliph** A successor, as chosen by a group of Muhammad's closest followers.

■ **al-Andalus** The part of the Iberian Peninsula under Muslim control in the eighth century, encompassing most of modern-day Spain.

The Muslim Conquest of Spain

There are no contemporary descriptions from either Muslim or Christian authors of the Muslim conquest of the Iberian Peninsula that began in 711. One of the few existing documents is a treaty from 713 between 'Abd al-'Aziz, the son of the conquering Muslim governor and general Musa ibn Nusair, and Tudmir, the Visigothic Christian ruler of the city of Murcia in southern Spain. Treaties such as this, and military aspects of the conquest, were also described in the earliest surviving account, an anonymous Latin chronicle written by a Christian living in Muslim Spain in 754.

1. A Treaty from 713

In the name of God, the merciful and the compassionate.

This is a document [granted] by 'Abd al-'Aziz ibn Musa ibn Nusair to Tudmir, son of Ghabdush, establishing a treaty of peace and the promise and protection of God and his Prophet (may God bless him and grant him peace). We ['Abd al-'Aziz] will not set special conditions for him or for any among his men, nor harass him, nor remove him from power. His followers will not be killed or taken prisoner, nor will they be separated from their women and children. They will not be coerced in matters of religion, their churches will not be burned, nor will sacred objects be taken from the realm, [so long as] he [Tudmir] remains sincere and fulfills the [following] conditions that we have set for him. He has reached a settlement concerning seven towns: Orihuela, Valentilla, Alicante, Mula, Bigastro, Ello, and Lorca. He will not give shelter to fugitives, nor to our enemies, nor encourage any protected person to fear us, nor conceal news of our enemies. He and [each of] his men shall [also] pay one dinar every year, together with four measures of wheat, four measures of barley, four liquid measures of concentrated fruit juice, four liquid measures of vinegar, four of honey, and four of olive oil. Slaves must each pay half of this amount.

2. Chronicle of 754

In Justinian's time [711], . . . Musa . . . entered the long plundered and godlessly invaded Spain to destroy it. After forcing his way to Toledo, the royal city, he imposed on the adjacent regions an evil and fraudulent peace. He decapitated on a scaffold those noble lords who had remained, arresting them in their flight from Toledo with the help of Oppa, King Egica's son [a Visigothic Christian prince]. With Oppa's support, he killed them all with the sword. Thus he devastated not only [the former Roman province of] Hispania Ulterior, but [the former Roman province of] Hispania Citerior up to and beyond the ancient and once flourishing city of Zaragoza, now, by the judgment of God, openly exposed to the sword, famine, and captivity. He ruined beautiful cities, burning them with fire; condemned lords and powerful men to the cross; and butchered youths and infants with the sword. While he terrorized everyone in this way, some of the cities that remained sued for peace under duress and, after persuading and mocking them with a certain craftiness, the Saracens [Muslims] granted their requests without delay.

EVALUATE THE EVIDENCE

1. What conditions and guarantees are set for Christians living under Muslim rule in the treaty, and how does the author of the chronicle view treaties such as this?
2. What evidence do these documents provide for coexistence between Christians and Muslims in Spain and for hostility between the two groups?

Source: Olivia Remie Constable, ed., *Medieval Iberia: Readings from Christian, Muslim, and Jewish Sources* (Philadelphia: University of Pennsylvania Press, 1997), pp. 37–38, 30–31. Reprinted by permission of the University of Pennsylvania Press.

Muslims who invaded and conquered it were Moors—Berbers from northwest Africa.

The ethnic term *Moorish* can be misleading, however, because the peninsula was home to sizable numbers of Jews and Christians as well as Muslim Moors. In business transactions and in much of daily life, all peoples used the Arabic language. With Muslims, Christians, and Jews trading with and learning from one another and occasionally intermarrying, Moorish Spain and Norman Sicily (see Chapter 9) were the only distinctly pluralistic societies in medieval Europe.

Some scholars believe that the eighth and ninth centuries in Andalusia were an era of remarkable inter-faith harmony. Jews in Muslim Spain were generally treated well, and Córdoba became a center of Jewish as well as Muslim learning. Many Christians adopted Arab patterns of speech and dress, gave up eating pork, and developed an appreciation for Arab music and poetry. Some Christian women of elite status chose the Muslim practice of veiling their faces in public. Records describe Muslim and Christian youths joining in celebrations and merrymaking.

From the sophisticated centers of Muslim culture in Baghdad, Damascus, and Cairo, al-Andalus seemed a provincial backwater, a frontier outpost with little significance in the wider context of Islamic civilization. On the other hand, "northern barbarians," as

Muslim Garden in Spain   Tranquil gardens such as this one built by Muslim rulers in Granada represented paradise in Islamic culture, perhaps because of the religion's desert origins. Muslim architectural styles shaped those of Christian Spain and were later taken to the New World by Spanish conquerors. (Tower of the Ladies and Partal Gardens, The Alhambra, Grenada, Spain/Photo © Tarker/Bridgeman Images)

Muslims called the European peoples, acknowledged the splendor of Spanish culture. The Saxon nun and writer Hroswitha of Gandersheim (roz-WEETH-uh of GAHN-duhr-shighm) called the city of Córdoba "the ornament of the world." By 950 the city had a population of about a half million, making it Europe's largest and most prosperous city. Many residents lived in large houses and easily purchased the silks and brocades made by the city's thousands of weavers. The streets were well paved and well lit—a sharp contrast to the dark and muddy streets of other cities in Europe—and there was an abundance of freshwater for drinking and bathing. The largest library contained four hundred thousand volumes, a vast collection, particularly when compared with the largest library in northern Europe at the Benedictine abbey of St. Gall in Switzerland, which had only six hundred books.

In Spain, as elsewhere in the Arab world, the Muslims had an enormous impact on agricultural development. They began the cultivation of rice, sugarcane, citrus fruits, dates, figs, eggplants, carrots, and, after the eleventh century, cotton. These crops, together with new methods of field irrigation, provided the population with food products unknown in the rest of Europe. Muslims also brought technological innovations westward, including new kinds of sails and navigational instruments, as well as paper. (See "Living in the Past: Muslim Technology: Advances in Papermaking," page 226.)

Muslim-Christian Relations

What did early Muslims think of Jesus? Jesus is mentioned many times in the Qur'an, which affirms that he was born of Mary the Virgin. He is described as a righteous prophet chosen by God who performed miracles and continued the work of Abraham and Moses, and he was a sign of the coming Day of Judgment. But Muslims held that Jesus was an apostle only, not God, and that people (that is, Christians) who called Jesus divine committed blasphemy (showing contempt for God). The Christian doctrine of the Trinity—that there is one God in three persons (Father, Son, and Holy Spirit)—posed a powerful obstacle to Muslim-Christian understanding because of Islam's emphasis on the absolute oneness of God. Muslims esteemed the Judeo-Christian Scriptures as part of God's revelation, although they believed that the Qur'an superseded them.

Muslims call Jews and Christians *dhimmis*, or "protected people," because they were "people of the book," that is, the Hebrew Scriptures. Christians and Jews in the areas Muslims conquered were allowed to continue practicing their faith, although they did have to pay a special tax. This toleration was sometimes accompanied by suspicion, however. In Spain, Muslim teachers increasingly feared that close contact with Christians and Jews would lead to Muslim contamination and threaten the Islamic faith. Thus, beginning in the late tenth century, Muslim regulations began to officially prescribe what Christians, Jews, and Muslims could do. A Christian or Jew, however much assimilated, remained an **infidel**. An infidel was an unbeliever, and the word carried a pejorative or disparaging connotation.

By about 950 Caliph Abd al-Rahman III (912–961) of the Umayyad Dynasty of Córdoba ruled most of the Iberian Peninsula from the Mediterranean in the south to the Ebro River in the north. Christian Spain consisted of the tiny kingdoms of Castile, León,

■ **infidel**   A disparaging term used for a person who does not believe in a particular religion.

Along with scientific and medical knowledge, technological advances often entered Europe through Muslim Spain. One of these was papermaking. Ancient Egyptians had made a writing surface by weaving pounded papyrus stalks (the origin of the word *paper*), and sometime before 100 B.C.E. the Chinese invented paper that could be made from many different materials. They shredded and mashed rags and woody plant fibers in water to make a pulp, dipped a large, flat wire screen into this pulp to form a mat of fibers, and pressed the resulting sheet between layers of felt to dry. The Chinese used paper for wrapping and writing, and merchants and Buddhist missionaries carried the skills of papermaking to Samarkand in Central Asia (see Map 8.1). When this area was conquered by Arab armies, papermaking techniques spread into Muslim areas. Muslim papermakers improved on Chinese techniques, producing thicker and smoother sheets by using starch to fill the pores in the surfaces of the sheets. They carried this new method to Iraq, Syria, Egypt, and the Maghrib (North Africa), from where it entered Spain. Paper mills that produced large quantities were opened in Baghdad around 800 and in Muslim Spain around 1100.

By that point, paper was the most common writing surface in the Muslim world, though Christian Europeans were still largely using parchment or vellum, both made in a time-consuming process from stretched animal skins. The oldest surviving Christian text on paper is the *Missal of Silos*, a prayer book written in the eleventh century by Christian monks at the abbey of Santo Domingo de Silos in northern

Poem on paper, composed by the important Cordoban poet Ibn Quzman and spread widely in the Muslim world, as with this thirteenth-century copy from Syria. (Poem by Ibn Quzman, 13th century Syrian copy of a 12th century original, ink on paper/Institute of Oriental Studies, St. Petersburg, Russia/Bridgeman Images)

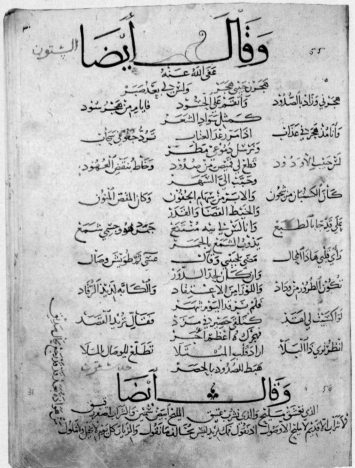

Thirteenth-century Qur'an written on paper in southern Spain, with colorful ornamented letters. (Leaf from a 13th-century Qur'an written in Maghribi Kufi script on pink-tinted paper/Pictures from History/Bridgeman Images)

Late medieval engraving of a paper mill, where workers are using the process developed by Muslim papermakers. At the right rear a cogged wooden wheel (probably driven by water) drives large wooden hammers that break up fibers, while in the foreground workers dip the screen of fibers in water and stack finished sheets. (Wood engraving from Elias Porzelius, *Curioser Spiegel*, Nürnberg, 1689/akg-images)

Spain on paper made in Muslim mills. The first paper mill in Christian Europe was opened in Fabriano, Italy, around 1200, and other cities quickly followed. Paper allowed the expansion of business and government record keeping, providing an important tool for bureaucrats as well as scholars.

QUESTIONS FOR ANALYSIS

1. What advantages did paper offer over other writing materials?
2. Consider the traditions and rapid expansion of Islam. How might these factors have contributed to the use and spread of paper technology?
3. Based on the description and the illustration of the papermaking process, why do you think paper mills were generally located along streams?

Catalonia, Aragon, Navarre, and Portugal. Civil wars among al-Rahman's descendants weakened the caliphate, and the small northern Christian kingdoms began to expand southward, sometimes working together. When Christian forces conquered Muslim territory, Christian rulers regarded their Muslim and Jewish subjects as infidels and enacted restrictive measures similar to those imposed on Christians in Muslim lands. Christian bishops worried that even a knowledge of Islam would lead to ignorance of essential Christian doctrines, and interfaith contacts declined. Christians' perception of Islam as a menace would help inspire the Crusades of the eleventh through thirteenth centuries (see Chapter 9).

Cross-Cultural Influences in Science and Medicine

Despite growing suspicions on both sides, the Islamic world profoundly shaped Christian European culture in Spain and elsewhere. Toledo, for example, became an important center of learning through which Arab intellectual achievements entered and influenced western Europe. Arab knowledge of science and mathematics, derived from the Chinese, Greeks, and Hindus, was highly sophisticated. The Muslim mathematician al-Khwarizmi (al-KHWAHR-uhz-mee) (d. 830) wrote the important treatise *Algebra*, the first work in which the word *algebra* is used mathematically. Al-Khwarizmi adopted the Hindu system of numbers (1, 2, 3, 4), used it in his *Algebra*, and applied mathematics to problems of physics and astronomy. (Since our system of numbers is actually Indian in origin, the term *Arabic numerals*, coined about 1847, is a misnomer.) Scholars in Baghdad translated Euclid's *Elements*, the basic text for plane and solid geometry (see Chapter 4). Muslims also instructed Westerners in the use of the zero, which permitted the execution of complicated problems of multiplication and long division.

Middle Eastern Arabs translated and codified the scientific and philosophical learning of Greek and Persian antiquity. In the ninth and tenth centuries that knowledge was brought to Spain, where between 1150 and 1250 it was translated into Latin. Europeans' knowledge of Aristotle (see Chapter 3) changed the entire direction of European philosophy and theology.

Muslim medical knowledge far surpassed that of the West. By the ninth century Arab physicians had translated most of the treatises of the ancient Greek physician Hippocrates and produced a number of important works of their own. Arab science reached its peak in the physician, philologist, philosopher, poet, and scientist ibn-Sina of Bukhara (980–1037), known in the West as Avicenna (ah-vuh-SEH-nuh). His *Canon of Medicine*

Astrolabe Made by al-Zarqali
Abu Ishaq Ibrahim al-Zarqali (1029–1087) was an astronomer, inventor, and instrument maker who lived in Toledo, the most important center of learning in Muslim Spain. He wrote works on geography and astronomy that were later translated into Hebrew and Latin, and designed and built instruments, including sophisticated astrolabes, instruments used by astronomers, astrologers, navigators, and surveyors for locating and predicting the positions of the heavenly bodies and determining local time and latitude. (Pictures from History/Bridgeman Images)

codified all Greco-Arab medical thought, described the contagious nature of tuberculosis and the spreading of diseases, and listed 760 pharmaceutical drugs.

Unfortunately, many of these treatises came to the West as translations from Greek to Arabic and then to Latin and inevitably lost a great deal in translation. Nevertheless, in the ninth and tenth centuries Arab knowledge and experience in anatomy and pharmaceutical prescriptions much enriched Western knowledge.

Frankish Rulers and Their Territories

FOCUS QUESTION *How did the Franks build and govern a European empire?*

Over two centuries before the Muslim conquest of Spain, the Frankish king Clovis converted to Roman Christianity and established a large kingdom in what had been Roman Gaul (see Chapter 7). Though at that time the Frankish kingdom was simply one barbarian kingdom among many, it grew to become the most important state in Europe, expanding to become an empire. Rulers after Clovis used a variety of tactics to enhance their authority and create a stable system. Charles the Great (r. 768–814), generally known by the French version of his name, Charlemagne (SHAHR-luh-mayne), built on the military and diplomatic foundations of his ancestors and on the administrative

machinery of the Merovingian kings. He expanded the Frankish kingdom into what is now Germany and Italy and, late in his long reign, was crowned emperor by the pope.

The Merovingians

Clovis established the Merovingian dynasty in about 481 (see Chapter 7), and under him the Frankish kingdom included much of what is now France and a large section of southwestern Germany. Following Frankish traditions in which property was divided among male heirs, at Clovis's death the kingdom was divided among his four sons. Historians have long described Merovingian Gaul in the sixth and seventh centuries as wracked by civil wars, chronic violence, and political instability as Clovis's descendants fought among themselves. So brutal and destructive were these wars and so violent the conditions of daily life that the term *Dark Ages* was at one time used to designate the entire Merovingian period, although more recently historians have noted that the Merovingians also created new political institutions, so the era was not uniformly bleak.

Merovingian rulers also developed diverse sources of income. These included revenues from the royal estates and the "gifts" of subject peoples, such as plunder and tribute paid by peoples east of the Rhine River. New lands might be conquered and confiscated, and served to replace lands donated as monastic or religious endowments. All free landowners paid a land tax, although some landowners gradually gained immunity from doing so. Fines imposed for criminal offenses and tolls and customs duties on roads, bridges, and waterways (and the goods transported over them) also yielded income. As with the Romans, the minting of coins was a royal monopoly, with drastic penalties for counterfeiting.

The Franks also based some aspects of their government on Roman principles. For example, the basis of the administrative system in the Frankish kingdom was the **civitas** (SIH-vih-tahs)—Latin for a city and surrounding territory—similar to the political organization of the Roman Empire. A **comites** (KOH-meh-tehs)—a senior official or royal companion, later called a count—presided over the civitas, as had governors in Rome. He collected royal revenue, heard lawsuits, enforced justice, and raised troops. Many comites were not conquerors from outside, but came from families that had been administrators in Roman Gaul and were usually native to the regions they administered and knew their areas well. Frankish royal administration involved another official, the *dux* (dooks) or duke. He was a military leader, commanding troops in the territory of several civitas, and thus responsible for all defensive and offensive strategies. Clovis and his descendants also issued capitularies—Roman-style administrative and legislative orders—in an attempt

Saint Radegund and King Clotaire This eleventh-century manuscript shows the Germanic princess Radegund (ca. 520–586) led before the Merovingian king Clotaire, who became her husband. They had no children, and after Clotaire had Radegund's brother killed, she left him and founded a convent, where she lived the rest of her life. Convents were islands of learning and safety in Merovingian society; from here Radegund corresponded with learned church officials and wrote Latin poems, a few of which have survived. (From the *Life of St. Radegund*/Bibliothèque Municipale, Poitiers, France/Bridgeman Images)

to maintain order in Merovingian society. Some of these laws were designed to protect the clergy and church property from violence, others were meant to define ownership and inheritance, and still others set out to punish crimes such as drunkenness, robbery, arson, rape, and murder.

Within the royal household, Merovingian politics provided women with opportunities, and some queens not only influenced but occasionally also dominated events. Because the finances of the kingdom were merged with those of the royal family, queens often had control of the royal treasury just as more ordinary women controlled household expenditures. The status of a princess or queen also rested on her diplomatic importance, with her marriage sealing or her divorce breaking an alliance with a foreign kingdom or powerful noble family; on her personal relationship with her husband and her ability to give him sons and heirs; and on her role as the mother and guardian of princes who had not reached legal adulthood.

Queen Brunhilda (543?–613), for example, married first one Frankish king and at his death another. When her second husband died, Brunhilda overcame the objections of the nobles and became regent, ruling on behalf of her son until he came of age. Later she governed as regent for her grandsons and, when she was nearly seventy, for her great-grandson. Stories of her ruthlessness spread during her lifetime and were later much embellished by Frankish historians

uncomfortable with such a powerful woman. The evil Brunhilda, they alleged, killed ten Frankish kings in pursuit of her political goals, and was finally executed by being torn apart by horses while cheering crowds looked on. How much of this actually happened is impossible to say, but Brunhilda's legend became a model for the wicked queen in European folklore.

Merovingian rulers and their successors led peripatetic lives, traveling constantly to check up on local administrators and peoples. Merovingian kings also relied on the comites and bishops to gather and send local information to them. The court or household of Merovingian kings included scribes who kept records, legal officials who advised the king on matters of law, and treasury agents responsible for aspects of royal finance. These officials could all read and write Latin. Over them all presided the mayor of the palace, the most important secular figure after the king, who governed the palace and the kingdom in the king's absence. Mayors were usually from one of the great aristocratic families, which increasingly through intermarriage blended Frankish and Roman elites. These families possessed landed wealth—villas over which they exercised lordship, dispensing local customary, not royal, law—and they often had rich and lavish lifestyles.

■ **civitas** The city and surrounding territory that served as a basis of the administrative system in the Frankish kingdoms, based on Roman models.

■ **comites** A senior official or royal companion, later called a count, who presided over the civitas.

The Rise of the Carolingians

From this aristocracy one family gradually emerged to replace the Merovingian dynasty. The rise of the Carolingians—whose name comes from the Latin *Carolus*, or Charles, the name of several important members of the family—rests on several factors. First, the Carolingian Pippin I (d. 640) acquired the powerful position of mayor of the palace and passed the title on to his heirs. As mayors of the palace and heads of the Frankish bureaucracy, Pippin I and his descendants were entrusted with extraordinary amounts of power and privilege by the Merovingian kings. Although the mayor of the palace was technically employed by the ruling family, the Carolingians would use their influential position to win support for themselves and eventually subvert Merovingian authority. Second, a series of advantageous marriage alliances brought the family estates and influence in different parts of the Frankish world, and provided the Carolingians with landed wealth and treasure with which to reward their allies and followers. Third, military victories over supporters of the Merovingians gave the Carolingians a reputation for strength and ensured their dominance. Pippin I's great-grandson, Charles Martel (r. 714–741), waged war successfully against the Saxons, Frisians, Alamanni, and Bavarians, which further enhanced the family's prestige. In 732 Charles Martel defeated a Muslim force near Poitiers (pwah-tee-AY) in central France. Muslims and Christians have interpreted the battle differently. To the Muslims it was a minor skirmish won by the Franks because of Muslim difficulties in maintaining supply lines over long distances and the distraction of ethnic conflicts and unrest in Islamic Spain. For Christians the Frankish victory was one of the great battles of history, halting Muslim expansion in Europe. Charles Martel and later Carolingians used it to enhance their reputation, portraying themselves as defenders of Christendom against the Muslims.

The Battle of Poitiers helped the Carolingians acquire the support of the church, perhaps their most important asset. Charles Martel and his son Pippin III (r. 751–768) further strengthened their ties to the church by supporting the work of Christian missionaries. The most important of these missionaries was the Englishman Boniface (BAH-nuh-fays) (680–754), who had close ties to the Roman pope. Boniface ordered the oak of Thor, a tree sacred to many pagans, cut down and used the wood to build a church. When the god Thor did not respond by killing him with his lightning bolts, Boniface won many converts. As missionaries preached, baptized, and established churches, they included the Christian duty to obey secular authorities as part of their message, thus extending to Frankish rulers the church's support of secular power that had begun with Constantine (see Chapter 7).

As mayor of the palace, Charles Martel had exercised the power of king of the Franks. His son Pippin III aspired to the title as well as the powers it entailed. Pippin's diplomats were able to convince an embattled Pope Zacharias to rule in his favor against the Merovingians in exchange for military support against the Lombards, who were threatening the papacy. Zacharias invoked his apostolic authority as pope, deposed the Merovingian ruler Chilperic in 752, and declared that Pippin should be king "in order to prevent provoking civil war [between the Merovingians and Carolingians] in Francia."[2] An assembly of Frankish magnates elected Pippin king, and Boniface anointed him. When in 754 Lombard expansion again threatened the papacy, Pope Stephen II journeyed to the Frankish kingdom seeking help. On this occasion, he personally anointed Pippin with the sacred oils and gave him the title "Patrician of the Romans," thus linking him symbolically with the ruling patrician class of ancient Rome. Pippin promised restitution of the papal lands and later made a gift of estates in central Italy.

Because of his anointment, Pippin's kingship took on a special spiritual and moral character. Prior to Pippin only priests and bishops had received anointment. Pippin became the first to be anointed with the sacred oils and acknowledged as *rex et sacerdos* (rehks eht SAHK-ehr-dohse), meaning king and priest. Anointment, not royal blood, set the Christian king apart. By having himself anointed, Pippin cleverly eliminated possible threats to the Frankish throne by other claimants, and the pope promised him support in the future. An important alliance had been struck between the papacy and the Frankish monarchs. When Pippin died, his son Charles, generally known as Charlemagne, succeeded him.

The Warrior-Ruler Charlemagne

Charlemagne's adviser and friend Alcuin (ca. 735–804; see page 235) wrote that "a king should be strong against his enemies, humble to Christians, feared by pagans, loved by the poor and judicious in counsel and maintaining justice."[3] Charlemagne worked to realize that ideal in all its aspects. Through brutal military expeditions that brought wealth—lands, booty, slaves, and tribute—and by peaceful travel, personal appearances, and the sheer force of his personality, Charlemagne sought to awe newly conquered peoples and rebellious domestic enemies.

If an ideal king was "strong against his enemies" and "feared by pagans," Charlemagne more than met the standard. In continuing the expansionist policies of his ancestors, his reign was characterized by con-

MAP 8.2 Charlemagne's Conquests, ca. 768–814
Though Charlemagne's hold on much of his territory was relatively weak, the size of his empire was not equaled again until the nineteenth-century conquests of Napoleon.

stant warfare; according to the chroniclers of the time, only seven years between 714 and 814 were peaceful. Charlemagne fought more than fifty campaigns and became the greatest warrior of the early Middle Ages. He subdued all of the north of modern France, but his greatest successes were in today's Germany, where he fought battles he justified as spreading Christianity to pagan peoples. In the course of a bloody thirty-year war against the Saxons, he added most of the northwestern German peoples to the Frankish kingdom. In his biography of the ruler, Charlemagne's royal secretary Einhard reported that Charlemagne ordered more than four thousand Saxons killed on one day and deported thousands more. Those who surrendered were forced to become

Christian, often in mass baptisms. He established bishoprics in areas he had conquered, so church officials and church institutions became important means of imposing Frankish rule.

Charlemagne also achieved spectacular results in the south, incorporating Lombardy into the Frankish kingdom. He ended Bavarian independence and defeated the nomadic Avars, opening eastern Germany for later settlement by Franks. He successfully fought the Byzantine Empire for Venetia, Istria, and Dalmatia and temporarily annexed those areas to his kingdom. Charlemagne's only defeat came at the hands of the Basques of northwestern Spain. By around 805 the Frankish kingdom included all of northwestern Europe except Scandinavia and Britain (Map 8.2). Not since the Roman emperors of the third century C.E. had any ruler controlled so much of the Western world. Other than brief periods under Napoleon and Hitler, Europe would never again see as large a unified state as it had under Charlemagne, which is one reason he has become an important symbol of European unity in the twenty-first century.

Carolingian Government and Society

Charlemagne's empire was not a state as people today understand that term; it was a collection of peoples and clans. For administrative purposes, Charlemagne divided his entire kingdom into counties based closely on the old Merovingian civitas. Each of the approximately six hundred counties was governed by a count (or in his absence by a viscount), who published royal orders, held courts and resolved legal cases, collected taxes and tolls, raised troops for the army, and supervised maintenance of roads and bridges. (See "Evaluating the Evidence 8.2: The Capitulary de Villis," page 232.) Counts were originally sent out from the royal court; later a person native to the region was appointed. As a link between local authorities and the central government, Charlemagne appointed officials called *missi dominici* (mih-see doh-MEH-nee-chee), "agents of the lord king," who checked up on the counts and held courts to handle judicial and financial issues.

Considering the size of Charlemagne's empire, the counts and royal agents were few and far between, and the authority of the central government was weak. The abbots and bishops who served as Charlemagne's advisers envisioned a unified Christian society presided over by a king who was responsible for maintaining peace, law, and order and administering justice. This remained a vision, however, not reality. Instead, society was held together by alliances among powerful families, along with dependent relationships cemented by oaths promising faith and loyalty.

The Capitulary de Villis

Charlemagne and other Frankish rulers issued sets of instructions and decisions, called capitularies, to their officials on legal, military, political, and economic matters. Like all instructions or sets of rules, capitularies describe an ideal, not the way things really were, but we can still use them as sources for many aspects of life. The Capitulary de Villis, issued in about 800, describes the wide variety of activities envisioned for royal manors, which were run by individuals called stewards.

We desire that each steward shall make an annual statement of all our income, giving an account of our lands cultivated by the oxen which our own plowmen drive and of our lands which the tenants of farms ought to plow; of the pigs, of the rents, of the obligations and fines; of the game taken in our forests without our permission; of the various compositions [things that have been made]; of the mills, of the forest, of the fields, of the bridges and ships; of the free men and the districts under obligations to our treasury; of markets, vineyards, and those who owe wine to us; of the hay, firewood, torches, planks, and other kinds of lumber; of the waste lands; of the vegetables, millet, panic [a type of millet]; of the wool, flax, and hemp; of the fruits of the trees; of the nut trees, larger and smaller; of the grafted trees of all kinds; of the gardens; of the turnips; of the fish ponds; of the hides, skins, and horns; of the honey and wax; of the fat, tallow [fat used for candles], and soap; of the mulberry wine, cooked wine, mead, vinegar, beer, and wine, new and old; of the new grain and the old; of the hens and eggs; of the geese; of the number of fishermen, workers in metal, sword makers, and shoemakers; of the bins and boxes; of the turners and saddlers; of the forges and mines, — that is, of iron, lead, or other substances; of the colts and fillies. They shall make all these known to us, set forth separately and in order, at Christmas, so that we may know what and how much of each thing we have.

The greatest care must be taken that whatever is prepared or made with the hands, — that is, bacon, smoked meat, sausage, partially salted meat, wine, vinegar, mulberry wine, cooked wine, garum [fermented fish sauce], mustard, cheese, butter, malt, beer, mead, honey, wax, flour, — all should be prepared and made with the greatest cleanliness.

Each steward on each of our domains shall always have, for the sake of ornament, peacocks, pheasants, ducks, pigeons, partridges, and turtle-doves. . . .

For our women's work they are to give at the proper time, as has been ordered, the materials [for clothmaking], — that is, the linen, wool, woad [for making blue dye], vermilion [for making red dye], madder [for making yellow dye], wool combs, teasels, soap, grease, vessels, and the other objects which are necessary. . . .

Each steward shall have in his district good workmen, namely, blacksmiths, a goldsmith, a silversmith, shoemakers, turners, carpenters, sword makers, fishermen, fowlers, soap makers, men who know how to make beer, cider, perry [pear cider], or other kind of liquor good to drink, bakers to make pastry for our table, net makers who know how to make nets for hunting, fishing, and fowling, and other sorts of workmen too numerous to be designated.

EVALUATE THE EVIDENCE

1. What tasks were men expected to do on Charlemagne's estates? What tasks were seen as women's work?
2. How does this listing of the work on medieval estates support the idea that the Carolingian economy was more localized than the economy of the Roman Empire had been (see Chapter 6)?

Source: James Harvey Robinson, ed., *Readings in European History*, vol. 1 (Boston: Ginn and Company, 1904), pp. 137–139.

Family alliances were often cemented by sexual relations, including those of Charlemagne himself. Charlemagne had a total of four legal wives, most from other Frankish tribes, and six concubines. Charlemagne's personal desires certainly shaped his complicated relationships — even after the age of sixty-five he continued to sire children — but the security and continuation of his dynasty and the need for diplomatic alliances were also important motives. Despite all the women bearing his children, only three of Charlemagne's sons born in wedlock reached adulthood, and only one outlived him. Four surviving legitimate grandsons did ensure perpetuation of the family, however, and the marriages themselves linked Charlemagne with other powerful families even in the absence of sons. Several of his children born out of wedlock became abbots or abbesses of major monasteries, connecting his family with the church as well as the secular hierarchy.

In terms of social changes, the Carolingian period witnessed moderate population growth. The highest aristocrats and church officials lived well, with fine clothing and at least a few rooms heated by firewood. Male nobles hunted and managed their estates, while female nobles generally oversaw the education of their children and sometimes inherited and controlled land on their own. Craftsmen and craftswomen on manorial estates manufactured textiles, weapons, glass, and pottery, primarily for local consumption. Sometimes abbeys and manors served as markets; goods were shipped away to towns and fairs for sale; and a good deal of interregional commerce existed. In the towns, artisans and merchants produced and traded luxury goods for noble and clerical patrons. When compared with earlier Roman cities or with Muslim cities of the time, such as Córdoba and Baghdad, however, Carolingian cities were small; few north of the Alps had more than seven thousand people. Even in Charlemagne's main political center at Aachen, most buildings were made of wood and earth, streets were narrow and muddy, and beggars were a common sight.

The modest economic expansion benefited townspeople and nobles, but it did not significantly alter the lives of most people, who continued to live in a vast rural world dotted with isolated estates and small villages. Here life was precarious. Crops could easily be wiped out by hail, cold, or rain, and transporting food from other areas was impossible. People's diets centered on grain, which was baked into bread, brewed into beer, and especially cooked into gruel. To this were added seasonal vegetables such as peas, cabbage, and onions, and tiny amounts of animal protein, mostly cheese. Clothing and household goods were just as simple, and houses were drafty, smoky, and often shared with animals. Lice, fleas, and other vermin spread disease, and the poor diet led to frequent stomach disorders. Work varied by the season, but at all times of the year it was physically demanding and yielded relatively little. What little there was had to be shared with landowners, who demanded their taxes and rents in the form of crops, animals, or labor.

The Imperial Coronation of Charlemagne

In autumn of the year 800, Charlemagne paid a momentous visit to Rome. Einhard gives this account of what happened:

> His last journey there [to Rome] was due to another factor, namely that the Romans, having inflicted many injuries on Pope Leo—plucking out his eyes and tearing out his tongue, he had been compelled to beg the assistance of the king. Accordingly, coming to Rome in order that he might set in order those things which had exceedingly disturbed the condition of the Church, he remained there the whole winter. It was at the time that he accepted the name of Emperor and Augustus. At

> first he was so much opposed to this that he insisted that although that day was a great [Christian] feast, he would not have entered the Church if he had known beforehand the pope's intention. But he bore very patiently the jealousy of the Roman Emperors [that is, the Byzantine rulers] who were indignant when he received these titles. He overcame their arrogant haughtiness with magnanimity, . . . by sending frequent ambassadors to them and in his letters addressing them as brothers.[4]

For centuries scholars have debated the reasons for the imperial coronation of Charlemagne. Did Charlemagne plan the ceremony in Saint Peter's on Christmas Day, or did he merely accept the title of emperor? What did he have to gain from it? If, as Einhard implies, the coronation displeased Charlemagne, was that because it put the pope in the superior position of conferring power on the emperor? What were Pope Leo's motives in arranging the coronation?

Though definitive answers will probably never be found, several things seem certain. First, after the coronation Charlemagne considered himself an emperor ruling a Christian people. Through his motto, *Renovatio romani imperi* (Revival of the Roman Empire), Charlemagne was consciously perpetuating old Roman imperial notions while at the same time identifying with the new Rome of the Christian Church. In this sense, Charlemagne might be considered a precursor of the eventual Holy Roman emperor, although that term didn't come into use for two more centuries. Second, Leo's ideas about gender and rule undoubtedly influenced his decision to crown Charlemagne. In 800 the ruler of the Byzantine Empire was the empress Irene, the first woman to rule Byzantium in her own name, but Leo did not regard her authority as legitimate because she was female. He thus claimed to be placing Charlemagne on a vacant throne. Third, both parties gained: the Carolingian family received official recognition from the leading spiritual power in Europe, and the papacy gained a military protector.

Not surprisingly, the Byzantines regarded the papal acts as rebellious and Charlemagne as a usurper. The imperial coronation thus marks a decisive break between Rome and Constantinople. From Baghdad, however, Harun al-Rashid (r. 786–809), caliph of the Abbasid (uh-BAH-suhd) Empire, congratulated the Frankish ruler with the gift of an elephant. It was named Abu'l Abbas after the founder of the Abbasid Dynasty and may have served as a symbol of the diplomatic link Harun al-Rashid hoped to forge with the Franks against Byzantium. Having plodded its way to Charlemagne's court at Aachen, the elephant survived for nine years, and its death was considered important enough to be mentioned in the Frankish *Royal Annals*, the official chronological record of events, for the year 810. Like everyone else at Aachen, the elephant lived in a city that was far less sophisticated, healthy, and beautiful than the Baghdad of Harun al-Rashid.

The coronation of Charlemagne, whether planned by the Carolingian court or by the papacy, was to have a profound effect on the course of German history and on the later history of Europe. In the centuries that followed, German rulers were eager to gain the imperial title and to associate themselves with the legends of Charlemagne and ancient Rome. Ecclesiastical authorities, on the other hand, continually cited the event as proof that the dignity of the imperial crown could be granted only by the pope.

Carolingian Minuscule In the Carolingian period books played a large role in the spread of Christianity and in the promotion of learning. The development of the clearer script known as Carolingian minuscule shown here made books more legible and copying more efficient because more words could fit on the page. (The initial "C" with the Ascension of Christ, book illumination on parchment from the Drogo Sacramentary, Lorraine [Metz], 850–855 A.D./akg-images)

Early Medieval Culture

FOCUS QUESTION *What were the significant intellectual and cultural changes in Charlemagne's era?*

As he built an empire through conquest and strategic alliances, Charlemagne also set in motion a cultural revival that had long-lasting consequences. The stimulus he gave to scholarship and learning may, in fact, be his most enduring legacy, although at the time most people continued to live in a world where knowledge was transmitted orally.

The Carolingian Renaissance

In Roman Gaul through the fifth century, the culture of members of the elite rested on an education that stressed grammar, Greco-Roman works of literature and history, and the legal and medical treatises of the Roman world. Beginning in the seventh and eighth centuries, a new cultural tradition common to Gaul, Italy, the British Isles, and to some extent Spain emerged. This culture was based primarily on Christian sources. Scholars have called the new Christian and ecclesiastical culture of the period from about 760 to 840, and the educational foundation on which it was based, the "Carolingian Renaissance" because Charlemagne was its major patron.

Charlemagne directed that every monastery in his kingdom should cultivate learning and educate the monks and secular clergy so that they would have a better understanding of the Christian writings. He also urged the establishment of cathedral and monastic schools where boys might learn to read and to pray properly. Thus the main purpose of this rebirth of learning was to promote an understanding of the Scriptures and of Christian writers and to instruct people to pray and praise God in the correct manner.

Women shared with men the work of evangelization and the new Christian learning. Rulers, noblemen, and noblewomen founded monasteries for nuns, each governed by an abbess. The abbess oversaw all aspects of life in the monastery. She handled the business affairs, supervised the copying of manuscripts, and directed the daily round of prayer and worship. Women's monasteries housed women who were unmarried, and also often widows, children being taught to read and recite prayers and chants, elderly people seeking a safe place to live, and travelers needing hospitality. Some female houses were, in fact, double monasteries in which the abbess governed two adjoining establishments, one for women and one for men. Monks provided protection from attack and did the heavy work on the land in double monasteries, but nuns handled everything else.

In monasteries and cathedral schools, monks, nuns, and scribes copied books and manuscripts and built up libraries. They developed the beautifully clear handwriting known as "Carolingian minuscule," with both uppercase and lowercase letters, from which modern Roman type is derived. In this era before printed books, works could survive only if they were copied. Almost all of the works of Roman authors that we are now able to read, both Christian and secular, were preserved by the efforts of Carolingian scribes. Some scholars went beyond copying to develop their own ideas, and by the middle years of the ninth century there was a great outpouring of more sophisticated original works. Ecclesiastical writers imbued with the legal ideas of ancient Rome and the theocratic ideals of Saint Augustine instructed the semibarbaric rulers of the West.

The most important scholar at Charlemagne's court was Alcuin (al-KYOO-ihn), who came from Northumbria, one of the kingdoms in England. He was the leader of a palace school at Aachen, where Charlemagne assembled learned men from all over Europe. From 781 until his death, Alcuin was the emperor's chief adviser on religious and educational matters. Alcuin's letters to Charlemagne set forth political theories on the authority, power, and responsibilities of a Christian ruler.

Through monastic and cathedral schools, basic literacy in Latin was established among some of the clergy and even among some of the nobility, a change from Merovingian times. By the tenth century the patterns of thought and the lifestyles of educated western Europeans were those of Rome and Latin Christianity. Most people, however, continued to live in an oral world. They spoke local languages, which did not have a written form. Christian services continued to be conducted in Latin, but not all village priests were able to attend a school, and many simply learned the service by rote. Some Latin words and phrases gradually penetrated the various vernacular languages, but the Carolingian Renaissance did not trickle down to ordinary people.

This division between a learned culture of Latin that built on the knowledge of the ancient world and a vernacular culture of local traditions can also be seen in medicine. Christian teaching supported concern for the poor, sick, and downtrodden. Churchmen taught that all knowledge came from God, who had supplied it for people to use for their own benefit. The foundation of a medical school at Salerno in southern Italy in the ninth century gave a tremendous impetus to medical study. The school's location attracted Arab, Greek, and Jewish physicians from all over the Mediterranean region. Students flocked there even from northern Europe.

Despite the advances at Salerno, however, physicians were few in the early Middle Ages, and only

Saint Matthew   This manuscript illumination shows Saint Matthew hard at work writing the Gospel that bears his name. He is holding a horn with ink in one hand and a quill in the other. Produced around 800 for Ebbo, the archbishop of the Frankish city of Reims, the illustrations in these Gospels seem strikingly modern in their portrayal of human emotion. (Bibliothèque Municipale, Epernay, France/Erich Lessing/Art Resource, NY)

the rich could afford them. Local folk medicine practiced by nonprofessionals provided help for commoners, with treatments made from herbs, bark, and other natural ingredients. Infants and children were especially susceptible to a range of illnesses, and about half of the children born died before age five. Although a few people lived into their seventies, most did not, and a forty-year-old was considered old.

Northumbrian Learning and Writing

Charlemagne's court at Aachen was not the only center of learning in early medieval Christian Europe. Another was the Anglo-Saxon kingdom of Northumbria, situated at the northernmost tip of the old Roman world. Northumbrian creativity owed a great deal to

INDIVIDUALS IN SOCIETY

The Venerable Bede

The finest representative of Northumbrian, and indeed all Anglo-Saxon, scholarship is Bede (ca. 673–735). He was born into a noble family, and when he was seven his parents sent him to Benet Biscop's monastery at Wearmouth as a sign of their religious devotion. Later he was sent to the new monastery at Jarrow five miles away. Surrounded by the hundreds of pagan and Christian books Benet Biscop had brought from Italy, Bede spent the rest of his life there, studying and writing. He wrote textbooks on grammar and writing designed to help students master the intricacies of Latin, commentaries on the Old and New Testaments, historical works relating the lives of abbots and the development of the church, and scientific works on time. His biblical commentaries survive in hundreds of manuscripts, indicating that they were widely studied throughout the Middle Ages. His doctrinal works led him to be honored after his death with the title "Venerable," and centuries after his death to be named a "doctor of the church" by the pope.

Bede's religious writings were actually not that innovative, but his historical writings were, particularly his best-known work, the *Ecclesiastical History of the English People*, written about 720. As the title suggests, Bede's main topic is the growth of Christianity in England. The book begins with a short discussion of Christianity in Roman Britain, then skips to Augustine of Canterbury's mission to the Anglo-Saxons (see Chapter 7). Most of the book tells the story of Christianity's spread from one small kingdom in England to another, with missionaries and the kings who converted as its heroes, and the narrative ends with Bede's own day. Bede searched far and wide for his information, discussed the validity of his evidence, compared various sources, and exercised critical judgment. He includes accounts of miracles, but, like the stories of valiant missionaries, these are primarily related to provide moral lessons, which all medieval writers thought was the chief purpose of history.

One of the lessons that Bede sought to impart with his history is that Christianity should be unified, and one feature of the *Ecclesiastical History of the English People* inadvertently provided a powerful model for this. In his history, Bede adopted a way of reckoning time proposed by an earlier monk

A manuscript portrait of Bede, set within the first letter of a copy of his *Life of St. Cuthbert*. This is the letter *d*, with the monster's head forming the upward line and Bede's foot the short downward line. There are no contemporary descriptions of Bede, so the later manuscript illuminator was free to imagine what he looked like. (The Bodleian Library, University of Oxford, Ms Digby 20, folio 194r)

that would eventually provide a uniform chronology for all Christians. He dated events from the incarnation of Christ, rather than from the foundation of the city of Rome, as the Romans had done, or from the regnal years of kings, as the Germans did. His history was recopied by monks in many parts of Europe, who used this dating method, *anno Domini*, "in the year of the Lord" (later abbreviated A.D.), for their own histories as well. (Though Bede does talk about "before the time of the incarnation of our Lord," the reverse dating system of B.C., "before Christ," does not seem to have been widely used before 1700.) Disputes about whether the year began with the incarnation (that is, the conception) of Christ or his birth, and whether these occurred in 1 B.C. or A.D. 1 (the Christian calendar does not have a year zero), continued after Bede, but his method prevailed.

QUESTIONS FOR ANALYSIS

1. How do the career and accomplishments of Bede fit with the notion of an early medieval "renaissance" of learning?
2. Does Bede's notion that history has a moral purpose still shape the writing of history? Do you agree with him?
3. The Christian calendar dates from a midpoint rather than from a starting point, the way many of the world's calendars do. What advantages does this create in reckoning time? What would you see as the primary reason that the Christian calendar has now been widely adopted worldwide?

the intellectual curiosity and collecting zeal of Saint Benet Biscop (ca. 628–689), who brought manuscripts and other treasures back from Italy. These formed the library on which much later study rested.

Northumbrian monasteries produced scores of books: missals (used for the celebration of the Mass); psalters (SAL-tuhrs), which contained the 150 psalms and other prayers used by the monks in their devotions; commentaries on the Scriptures; illuminated manuscripts; law codes; and collections of letters and sermons. (See "Individuals in Society: The Venerable Bede," at left.) The finest product of Northumbrian art is probably the Gospel book produced at Lindisfarne monastery around 700. The book was produced by a single scribe working steadily over a period of several years, with the expenses involved in the production of such a book—for vellum, coloring, and gold leaf—probably supplied by the monastery's aristocratic patrons.

As in Charlemagne's empire, women were important participants in Northumbrian Christian culture. Perhaps the most important abbess of the early medieval period anywhere in Europe was Saint Hilda (d. 680). A noblewoman of considerable learning and administrative ability, she ruled the double monastery of Whitby on the Northumbrian coast, advised kings and princes, and encouraged scholars and poets. Hilda played a key role in the adoption of Roman practices by Anglo-Saxon churches (see Chapter 7).

At about the time the monks at Lindisfarne were producing their Gospel book, another author was probably at work on a nonreligious epic poem, *Beowulf* (BAY-uh-woolf). The poem tells the story of the hero Beowulf's progress from valiant warrior to wise ruler. (See "Evaluating the Evidence 8.3: The Death of Beowulf," page 238.) In contrast to most writings of this era, which were in Latin, *Beowulf* was written in the vernacular Anglo-Saxon. The identity of its author (or authors) is unknown, and it survives only in a single copy. The poem includes descriptions of real historical events that took place in fifth- and sixth-century Denmark and Sweden, which have been confirmed by archaeological excavations. These are mixed in with legends, oral traditions, and material from the Bible; though it tells a story set in pagan Denmark and Sweden, it was written in Christian England sometime in the eighth to tenth centuries. *Beowulf* provides evidence of the close relationship between England and the northern European continent in the early Middle Ages, for the North Sea was no barrier to regular contact and cultural exchange. The movements of people and ideas that allowed a work like *Beowulf* to be written only increased in the ninth century, when the North Sea became even more of a highway.

Invasions and Migrations

FOCUS QUESTION *What were the consequences of the ninth-century invasions and migrations?*

Charlemagne left his vast empire to his sole surviving son, Louis the Pious (r. 814–840), who attempted to keep the empire intact. This proved to be impossible. Members of the nobility engaged in plots and open warfare against the emperor, often allying themselves with one of Louis's three sons, who were in conflict with their father and with one another. In 843, shortly after Louis's death, his sons agreed to the **Treaty of Verdun** (vehr-DUHN), which divided the empire into three parts: Charles the Bald received the western part; Lothair the middle part and the title of emperor; and Louis the eastern part, from which he acquired the title "the German." Though no one knew it at the time, this treaty set the pattern for political boundaries in Europe that has been maintained until today.

The Treaty of Verdun, 843

After the Treaty of Verdun, continental Europe was fractured politically. All three kingdoms controlled by the sons of Louis the Pious were torn by domestic dissension and disorder. The frontier and coastal defenses erected by Charlemagne and maintained by Louis the Pious were neglected. No European political power was strong enough to put up effective resistance to external attacks. Beginning around 850 three main groups invaded western Europe: Vikings from Scandinavia, representing the final wave of Germanic migrants; Muslims from the Mediterranean; and Magyars from central Europe forced westward by other peoples (Map 8.3).

Vikings in Western Europe

From the moors of Scotland to the mountains of Sicily, there arose in the ninth century the prayer, "Save us, O God, from the fury of the Northmen." The feared Northmen were Germanic peoples from the area of modern-day Norway, Sweden, and Denmark who originally lived by farming and fishing. They began to make overseas expeditions, which they themselves called *vikings*, a word that probably derives from

■ **Treaty of Verdun** Treaty signed in 843 by Charlemagne's grandsons dividing the Carolingian Empire into three parts and setting the pattern for political boundaries in Europe still in use today.

The Death of Beowulf

In the long Anglo-Saxon epic poem that bears his name, the hero Beowulf fights and kills the monster Grendel and then Grendel's mother. He then becomes the king of the Geats, one of the Germanic groups that lived in western Sweden, and takes arms late in life against a dragon that was threatening his people.

He ruled it well for fifty winters — that was an aged king, a veteran guardian of his people, — until in the dark nights a certain one began to have power, — a dragon, who on an upland heath kept watch over a hoard. . . .

Then the fiend began to vomit forth flames, to burn the noble dwellings; the gleam of fire blazed forth, a terror to the sons of men; the hateful creature flying in the air would leave there no thing with life. . . .

Beowulf discoursed, — spoke a last time with words of boasting: — "I ventured on many battles in my younger days; once more will I, the aged guardian of the people, seek combat and get renown." . . .

Then rose the doughty champion by his shield; bold under his helmet, he went clad in his war-corslet to beneath the rock cliffs, and trusted in his own strength — not such is the coward's way. Then he who, excellent in virtues, had lived through many wars, — the tumult of battles, when armies dash together, — saw by the rampart a rocky arch whence burst a stream out from the mound; hot was the welling of the flood with deadly fire. He could not any while endure unscorched the hollow near the hoard, by reason of the dragon's flame. . . .

Never a whit [Not in the least] did his comrades, those sons of nobles, stand round him in a body, doing deeds of warlike prowess; but they shrank back into the wood and took care of their lives. . . . [One of Beowulf's warriors assists him, and together they kill the dragon, though Beowulf is mortally wounded in the fight.]

Then the chieftain wise in thought went on until he sat on a seat by the rampart. . . . Beowulf discoursed: despite his hurt, his grievous deadly wound, he spoke, — he knew full well that he had used up his time of earthly joy. . . . "I have ruled over this people fifty winters; there was not one of the kings of the neighbouring tribes who dared encounter me with weapons, or could weigh me down with fear. In my own home I awaited what the times destined for me, kept my own well, did not pick treacherous quarrels, nor have I sworn unjustly any oaths. In all this may I, sick with deadly wounds, have solace; because the Ruler of men may never charge me with the murder of kinsfolk, when my life parts from my body. . . .

"I utter in words my thanks to the Ruler of all, the King of Glory, the everlasting Lord. . . . Bid the war-veterans raise a splendid barrow [mound of earth] after the funeral fire, on a projection by the sea, which shall tower high on Hronesness as a memorial for my people, so that seafarers who urge their tall ships from afar over the spray of ocean shall thereafter call it Beowulf's barrow.

EVALUATE THE EVIDENCE

1. Based on Beowulf's actions and words, what were the qualities of an ideal leader in the early Middle Ages?
2. How do these sections of *Beowulf* provide evidence for the assimilation of Germanic and Christian values discussed in Chapter 7? For the distinctive aspects of early medieval culture discussed in this chapter?

Source: *Beowulf and the Finnesburg Fragment*, trans. John R. Clark Hall, rev. C. L. Wrenn (London: George Allen and Unwin, 1940), pp. 132, 137, 147, 148, 150, 156, 157, 160.

a unit of maritime distance. *Viking* came to be used both for the activity ("to go a-viking") and for the people who went on such expeditions. Propelled either by oars or by sails, deckless, and about sixty-five feet long, a Viking ship could carry between forty and sixty men — enough to harass an isolated monastery or village. These ships, navigated by experienced and fearless sailors, moved through complicated rivers, estuaries, and waterways in Europe. Their targets were initially often isolated monasteries, as these had gold, silver, and other goods that could be easily plundered, but later the Vikings turned to more substantial targets. The Carolingian Empire, with no navy, was helpless. The Vikings moved swiftly, attacked, and escaped to return again.

Scholars disagree about the reasons for Viking attacks and migrations. A very unstable Danish kingship and disputes over the succession led to civil war and disorder, which may have driven warriors abroad in search of booty and supporters. The population of Scandinavia may have grown too large for the available land to support, and cities on the coasts of northern Europe offered targets for plunder. Goods plundered could then be sold, and looting raids turned into trading ventures. Some scholars assert that the Vikings were looking for trade and new commercial contacts from the beginning. (See "Thinking Like a Historian: Vikings Tell Their Own Story," page 240.)

Whatever the motivations, Vikings burned, looted, and did extensive property damage, although there is

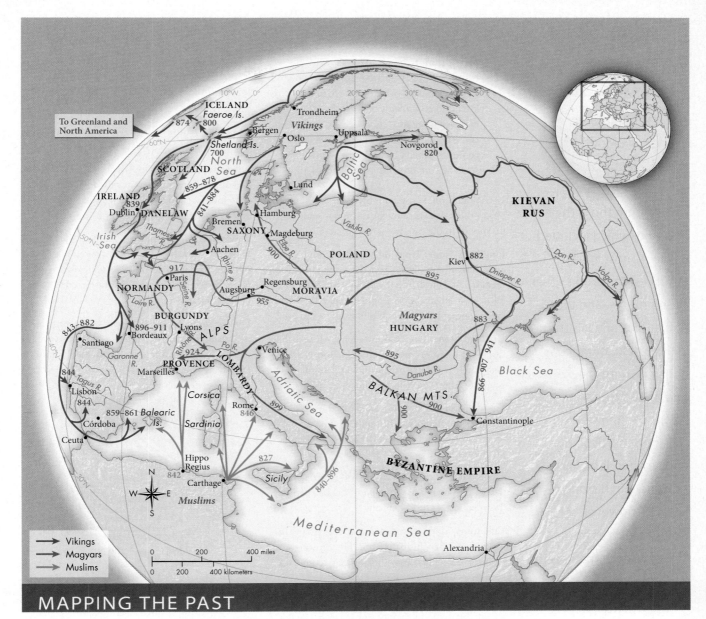

MAPPING THE PAST

MAP 8.3 Invasions and Migrations of the Ninth and Tenth Centuries

This map shows the Viking, Magyar, and Arab invasions and migrations in the ninth and tenth centuries. Compare it with Map 7.3 (page 202) on the barbarian migrations of late antiquity to answer the following questions.

ANALYZING THE MAP What similarities do you see in the patterns of migration in these two periods? What significant differences?

CONNECTIONS How did the Vikings' expertise in shipbuilding and sailing make their migrations different from those of earlier Germanic tribes? How did this set them apart from the Magyar and Muslim invaders of the ninth century?

Vikings Tell Their Own Story

The traditional view of Vikings as bloodthirsty and ruthless marauders driven by fury comes largely from those they attacked, which included Europe's most literate group—monks and other churchmen—and the nobles and officials the Vikings held for ransom or from whom they demanded tribute. Relying on the views of outsiders, particularly hostile ones, is always a problem in historical analysis, however. How do sources from Scandinavians themselves in this era portray Viking actions, motivations, and values?

1 Inscriptions from runestones. The only existing written texts from Scandinavians themselves from before 1050 are runic inscriptions, primarily on memorial stones, of which thousands survive. The ones below come from the tenth and early eleventh centuries, when Christianity was spreading, so some contain Christian references.

Veda Stone, Uppland, Sweden: "Irenmuder set up this stone. He bought this estate and made his money in the east, in Gardar [eastern Russia]."

Lingsberg Stone, Uppland, Sweden: "And Danr and Húskarl and Sveinn had the stone erected in memory of Ulfríkr, their father's father. He had taken two payments in England. May God and God's mother help the souls of the father and son."

Uppland Stone, Uppland, Sweden: "Áli had this stone put up in his own honour. He took Knútr's *danegeld* [the tribute paid to Danish invaders] in England. May God help his soul!"

Fjuckby Stone, Uppland, Sweden: "Liótr set up this stone in memory of his son, Áki. He was master of a freighter, docking in the harbors of Greece. He died at home."

Ada Stone, Sweden: "Hermóðr had (the rock) cut in memory of Bergviðr/Barkviðr, his brother. He drowned in Lífland [Livonia]."

Vallentuna Stone, Sweden: "... and Ingibjôrg in memory of her husbandman. He drowned in Holmr's sea—his cargo-ship drifted to the sea-bottom—only three came out (alive)."

Gripsholm Stone, Södermanland, Sweden: "Tola set up this stone in memory of her son Haraldt, Ingvarr's brother. Like men they went far to seek gold, and in the east they fed the eagle. Died south, in Serkland ['Saracen land,' or Muslim territory]."

Uppland Stone 1011, Uppland, Sweden: "Vigmund had this stone carved in memory of himself, the cleverest of men. May God help the soul of Vigmund, the ship captain. Vigmund and Åfrid carved this memorial while he lived."

Sigurd Stone, Södermanland, Sweden: "Sigrid, Alrik's mother, Orm's daughter made this bridge for her husband Holmgers, father of Sigoerd."

Odenslunda Stone, Uppland, Sweden: "Véketill and Ôzurr had this stone raised in memory of Eysteinn, ... good father. He perished abroad with all the seamen. May God help (his) spirit."

Ingvar Stone 778, Uppland, Sweden: "Thjalfi and Holmlaug had all of these stones raised in memory of Banki/Baggi, their son, who alone owned a ship and steered to the east in Ingvarr's retinue. May God help Banki's/Baggi's spirit. Áskell carved."

Dynna Stone, Gran, Norway: "Gunnvor, Thrydrik's daughter, made a bridge in memory of her daughter, Ástrídr. She was the most skillful girl in Hadeland."

2 Silver coin. This silver coin, minted in Hedeby in Denmark, was unearthed at Birka, an archaeological site on an island in Lake Mälaren in eastern Sweden, which in Viking times was a trading center handling goods from as far away as Byzantium and the Abbasid caliphate. (10th century, minted in Hedeby, Denmark/De Agostini/Getty Images)

ANALYZING THE EVIDENCE

1. What activities do the runic inscriptions in Source 1 highlight? What personal qualities do they praise? What do they say about people's motivations for what they undertake?
2. How are the activities and qualities desribed in Source 1 reflected in the scenes shown in Sources 2–5?
3. What information do the runic inscriptions in Source 1 provide about relations among family members?
4. What do the written and visual sources suggest about gender roles in Viking society?
5. Why would memorial inscriptions and burials be good sources for studying social values? For what aspects of life would they *not* be good sources?

(Viking Ship Museum, Bygdoy, Oslo, Norway/Werner Forman Archive/ Bridgeman Images)

4 **Carving from the side of the Oseberg cart.** The Oseberg ship burial (see page 242), from early ninth century Norway, contains a decoratively carved wooden cart, one side of which shows a woman with streaming hair apparently restraining a man striking at a horseman with his sword.

3 **Memorial stone.** This memorial stone from Gotland, Sweden, carved and erected in the eighth century, shows scenes common on early Viking memorial stones, with a mounted warrior carrying a shield above, and a ship below.
(Private Collection/Ancient Art & Architecture Collection, Ltd./Bridgeman Images)

(Viking Ship Museum, Bygdoy, Oslo, Norway/Bridgeman Images)

5 **Tapestry found with the Oseberg ship.** A tapestry fragment found with the Oseberg ship shows animals pulling carts; other tapestry fragments show groves of trees, battle scenes, women riding horses, houses with dragons on their gables, and ships.

PUTTING IT ALL TOGETHER

Using the sources above, along with what you have learned in class and in this chapter, write a short essay that assesses the traditional view of the Vikings. How do sources from Scandinavians themselves in this era portray Viking actions, motivations, and values? What judgments of outsiders are supported, and which are refuted, in sources from insiders?

Source: (1) English translations from R. I. Paige, Runes: Reading the Past (Berkeley: University of California Press, 1987), pp. 46–51. © 1987 by the Regents of the University of California; and Rundata, the Scandinavian Runic database: www.nordiska.uu.se/forskn/samnord.htm, Department of Scandinavian Languages, Uppsala University.

little evidence that they caused long-term physical destruction—perhaps because, arriving in small bands, they lacked the manpower to do so. They seized nobles and high churchmen and held them for ransom; they also demanded tribute from kings. In 844–845 Charles the Bald had to raise seven thousand pounds of silver, and across the English Channel Anglo-Saxon rulers collected a land tax, the *Danegeld*, to buy off the Vikings. In the Seine and Loire Valleys the frequent presence of Viking war bands seems to have had economic consequences, stimulating the production of food and wine and possibly the manufacture (for sale) of weapons and the breeding of horses.

The slave trade represented an important part of Viking plunder and commerce. Slaves, known as *thralls*, were common in Scandinavian society, and Vikings took people from the British Isles and territories along the Baltic Sea as part of their booty. They sold them as slaves in the markets of Magdeburg and Regensburg, at the fairs of Lyons, and in seaports of the Muslim world. Dublin became a center of the Viking slave trade, with hundreds and sometimes thousands of young men and women bought and sold there in any one year.

In the early tenth century Danish Vikings besieged Paris with fleets of more than a hundred highly maneuverable ships, and the Frankish king Charles the Simple bought them off in 911 by giving them a large part of northern France. There the Vikings established the province of "Northmanland," or Normandy as it was later known, intermarrying with the local population and creating a distinctive Norman culture. From there they sailed around Spain and into the Mediterranean, eventually seizing Sicily from the Muslim Arabs in 1060–1090, while other Normans crossed the English Channel, defeating Anglo-Saxon forces in 1066. Between 850 and 1000 Viking control of northern Europe reached its zenith. Norwegian Vikings moved farther west than any Europeans had before, establishing permanent settlements on Iceland and short-lived settlements in Greenland and Newfoundland in what is now Canada.

The Vikings made positive contributions to the areas they settled. They carried their unrivaled knowledge of shipbuilding and seamanship everywhere. The northeastern and central parts of England where the Vikings settled became known as the *Danelaw* because Danish, not English, laws and customs prevailed there. Scholars believe that some legal institutions, such as the ancestor of the modern grand jury, originated in the Danelaw. Exports from Ireland included iron tools and weapons manufactured there by Viking metal-smiths.

Slavs and Vikings in Eastern Europe

Vikings also brought change in eastern Europe, which was largely populated by Slavs. In antiquity the Slavs lived in central Europe, farming with iron technology, building fortified towns, and worshipping a variety of deities. With the start of the mass migrations of the late Roman Empire, the Slavs moved in different directions and split into what historians later identified as three groups: West, South, and East Slavs.

Oseberg Ship   This well-preserved and elaborately decorated Viking ship, discovered in a large burial mound in southern Norway, could be powered by sail or oars. Boatbuilders recently constructed a full-scale replica using traditional building methods and materials, and sailed it on the open ocean in 2014, reaching a speed of ten knots. The burial mound contained the skeletons of two older women, one wearing a dress made of fine wool and silk, along with a cart, several sleighs, horses, dogs, and many artifacts, suggesting that this was the grave of a powerful and prominent woman, though her identity is unknown. (Viking Ship Museum, Bygdoy, Norway/Werner Forman Archive/Bridgeman Images)

The group labeled the West Slavs included the Poles, Czechs, Slovaks, and Wends. The South Slavs, comprising peoples who became the Serbs, Croats, Slovenes, Macedonians, and Bosnians, migrated southward into the Balkans. In the seventh century Slavic peoples of the west and south created the state of Moravia along the banks of the Danube River. By the tenth century Moravia's residents were Roman Christian, along with most of the other West and South Slavs. The pattern of conversion was similar to that of the Germanic tribes: first the ruler was baptized, and then missionaries preached, built churches, and spread Christian teachings among the common people. The ruler of Poland was able to convince the pope to establish an independent archbishopric there in 1000, the beginning of a long-lasting connection between Poland and the Roman Church. In the Balkans the Serbs accepted Orthodox Christianity, while the Croats became Roman Christian, a division with a long-standing impact; it was one of the factors in the civil war in this area in the late twentieth century.

Between the fifth and ninth centuries the eastern Slavs moved into the vast areas of present-day European Russia and Ukraine. This enormous area consisted of an immense virgin forest to the north, where most of the eastern Slavs settled, and an endless prairie grassland to the south. In the tenth century Ibrahim Ibn Jakob, a learned Jew from the Muslim caliphate in Córdoba in Spain, traveled in Slavic areas. He found the Slavs to be "violent and inclined to aggression," but far cleaner than Christians in other parts of Europe in which he had traveled, "who wash only once or twice a year." Such filthy habits were unacceptable to someone raised in Muslim Spain, but the Slavs had an ingenious way of both getting clean and staying healthy: "They have no bathhouses as such, but they do make use of wooden huts [for bathing]. They build a stone stove, on which, when it is heated, they pour water. . . . They hold a bunch of grass in their hands, and waft the stream around. Then their pores open, and all excess matter escapes from their bodies."[5]

In the ninth century the Vikings appeared in the lands of the eastern Slavs. Called "Varangians" in the old Russian chronicles, the Vikings were interested primarily in gaining wealth through plunder and trade, and the opportunities were good. Moving up and down the rivers, they soon linked Scandinavia and northern Europe to the Black Sea and to the

Byzantine Empire's capital at Constantinople. They raided and looted the cities along the Caspian Sea several times in the tenth century, taking booty and slaves, which they then sold elsewhere; thus raiding turned into trading, and the Scandinavians later established settlements, intermarried, and assimilated with Slavic peoples.

In order to increase and protect their international commerce and growing wealth, the Vikings declared themselves the rulers of the eastern Slavs. According to tradition, the semi-legendary chieftain Ruirik founded a princely dynasty about 860. In any event, the Varangian ruler Oleg (r. 878–912) established his residence at Kiev in modern-day Ukraine. He and his successors ruled over a loosely united confederation of Slavic territories known as Rus, with its capital at Kiev, until 1054. (The word *Russia* comes from *Rus*, though the origins of *Rus* are hotly debated, with some historians linking it with Swedish words and others with Slavic words.)

Oleg and his clansmen quickly became assimilated into the Slavic population, taking local wives and emerging as the noble class. Missionaries of the Byzantine Empire converted the Vikings and local Slavs to Eastern Orthodox Christianity, accelerating the unification of the two groups. Thus the rapidly Slavified Vikings left two important legacies for the future: in about 900 they created a loose unification of Slavic territories, **Kievan Rus**, under a single ruling prince and dynasty, and they imposed a basic religious unity by accepting Orthodox Christianity, as opposed to Roman Catholicism, for themselves and the eastern Slavs.

Even at its height under Great Prince Iaroslav (YAHR-uh-slahv) the Wise (r. 1019–1054), the unity of Kievan Rus was extremely tenuous. Trade, not government, was the main concern of the rulers. Moreover, the Slavified Vikings failed to find a way to peacefully transfer power from one generation to the next. In early Rus there were apparently no fixed rules, and much strife accompanied each succession. Possibly to avoid such chaos, Great Prince Iaroslav, before his death in 1054, divided Kievan Rus among his five sons, who in turn divided their properties when they died. Between 1054 and 1237, Kievan Rus disintegrated into more and more competing units, each ruled by a prince claiming to be a descendant of Ruirik. The princes divided their land like

Kievan Rus, ca. 1050

L. Onega
L. Ladoga
Baltic Sea
Dvina R.
• Novgorod
LITHUANIA
Smolensk •
Dnieper R.
Kiev •
Dniester R.
Don R.
CARPATHIAN MTS.
HUNGARY
Black Sea

■ Area settled by Varangians, ca. 880
□ Kievan Rus, 1054

■ **Kievan Rus** A confederation of Slavic territories, with its capital at Kiev, ruled by descendants of the Vikings.

private property because they thought of it as private property. A prince owned a certain number of farms or landed estates and had them worked directly by his people, mainly slaves, called *kholops* in Russian. Outside of these estates, which constituted the princely domain, the prince exercised only limited authority in his principality. Excluding the clergy, two kinds of people lived there: the noble boyars and the commoner peasants.

The **boyars** were descendants of the original Viking warriors, and they also held their lands as free and clear private property. Although the boyars normally fought in princely armies, the customary law declared that they could serve any prince they wished. The ordinary peasants were also truly free. They could move at will wherever opportunities were greatest. In a touching phrase of the times, theirs was "a clean road, without boundaries."[6] In short, fragmented princely power, private property, and personal freedom all went hand in hand.

Magyars and Muslims

Groups of central European steppe peoples known as Magyars also raided villages in the late ninth century, taking plunder and captives, and forcing leaders to pay tribute in an effort to prevent further looting and destruction. Moving westward, small bands of Magyars on horseback reached as far as Spain and the Atlantic coast. They subdued northern Italy, compelled Bavaria and Saxony to pay tribute, and even penetrated into the Rhineland and Burgundy (see Map 8.3). Because of their skill with horses and their Eastern origins, the Magyars were often identified with the earlier Huns by those they conquered, though they are probably unrelated ethnically. This identification, however, may be the origin of the word *Hungarian*.

Magyar forces were defeated by a combined army of Frankish and other Germanic troops at the Battle of Lechfeld near Augsburg in southern Germany in 955, and the Magyars settled in the area that is now Hungary in eastern Europe. Much as Clovis had centuries earlier, the Magyar ruler Géza (GEE-zuh) (r. 970–997), who had been a pagan, became a Roman Christian. This gave him the support of the papacy and offered prospects for alliances with other Roman Christian rulers against the Byzantine Empire, Hun-

gary's southern neighbor. Géza's son Stephen I (r. 997–1038) was officially crowned the king of Hungary by a papal representative on Christmas Day of 1000. He supported the building of churches and monasteries, increased royal power, and encouraged the use of Latin and the Roman alphabet. Hungary's alliance with the papacy shaped the later history of eastern Europe just as Charlemagne's alliance with the papacy shaped western European history. The Hungarians adopted settled agriculture, wrote law codes, and built towns, and Hungary became an important crossroads of trade for German and Muslim merchants.

The ninth century also saw invasions into Europe from the south. In many ways these were a continuation of the earlier Muslim conquests in the Iberian Peninsula, but now they focused on Sicily and mainland Italy. Muslim fleets had attacked Sicily, which was part of the Byzantine Empire, beginning in the seventh century, and by the end of the ninth century they controlled most of the island. The Muslims drove northward, reached Rome in 846 by sailing up the Tiber River and sacked the city, and captured towns along the Adriatic coast almost all the way to Venice. They attacked Mediterranean settlements along the coast of Provence and advanced on land as far as the Alps. In the tenth century Frankish, papal, and Byzantine forces were able to retake much territory, though the Muslims continued to hold Sicily. Under their rule, agricultural innovations from elsewhere in the Muslim world led to new crops such as cotton and sugar, and fortified cities became centers of Muslim learning. Disputes among the Muslim rulers on the island led one faction to ask the Normans for assistance, and between 1060 and 1090 the Normans gradually conquered all of Sicily.

What was the impact of these invasions? From the perspective of those living in what had been Charlemagne's empire, Viking, Magyar, and Muslim attacks contributed to increasing disorder and violence. Italian, French, and English sources often describe this period as one of terror and chaos: "Save us, O God," in the words of the prayer on page 237. People in other parts of Europe might have had a different opinion, however. In Muslim Spain scholars worked in thriving cities, and new crops such as rice enhanced ordinary people's lives. In eastern Europe, states such as Moravia and Hungary became strong kingdoms. A Viking point of view might be the most positive, for by 1100 descendants of the Vikings not only ruled their homelands in Denmark, Norway, and Sweden, but also ruled Normandy, England, Sicily, Iceland, and Kievan Rus, with an outpost in Greenland and occasional voyages to North America.

■ **boyars** High-ranking nobles in Russia who were descendants of Viking warriors and held their lands as free and clear private property.

■ **vassal** A warrior who swore loyalty and service to a noble in exchange for land, protection, and support.

■ **fief** A piece of land granted by a feudal lord to a vassal in return for service and loyalty.

■ **feudalism** A term devised by later scholars to describe the political system in which a vassal was generally given a piece of land in return for his loyalty.

Political and Economic Decentralization

FOCUS QUESTION *How did internal conflict and outside threats shape European political and economic development in this period?*

The large-scale division of Charlemagne's empire into three parts in the ninth century led to a decentralization of power at the local level. Civil wars weakened the power and prestige of kings, who could do little about domestic violence. Likewise, the great invasions, especially those of the Vikings, weakened royal authority. The western Frankish kings were unable to halt the invaders, and the local aristocracy had to assume responsibility for defense. Thus, in the ninth and tenth centuries great aristocratic families increased their authority in the regions of their vested interests. They built private castles for defense and to live in, and they governed virtually independent territories in which distant and weak kings could not interfere. Common people turned for protection to the strongest power, the local counts, whom they considered their rightful rulers, and free peasants sank to the level of serfs.

Decentralization and the Origins of "Feudalism"

The political power of the Carolingian rulers had long rested on the cooperation of the dominant social class, the Frankish aristocracy. Charlemagne and his predecessors relied on the nobles to help wage wars of expansion and suppress rebellions, and in return these families were given a share of the lands and riches confiscated by the rulers. The most powerful nobles were those able to gain the allegiance of warriors, often symbolized in an oath-swearing ceremony of homage and fealty that grew out of earlier Germanic oaths of loyalty. In this ceremony a warrior (knight) swore his loyalty as a **vassal**—from a Celtic term meaning "servant"—to the more powerful individual, who became his lord. In return for the vassal's loyalty, aid, and military assistance, the lord promised him protection and material support. This support might be a place in the lord's household, but was more likely a piece of land called a *feudum* or **fief** (feef). In the Roman Empire soldiers had been paid for their services with money, but in the cash-poor early Middle Ages their reward was instead a piece of land. Most legal scholars and historians have seen these personal ties of loyalty cemented by grants of land rather than allegiance to an abstract state as a political and social system they term **feudalism**. They have traced its spread from Frankish areas to other parts of Europe.

In the last several decades, increasing numbers of medieval historians have found the idea of a "feudal system" problematic. They note that the word *feudalism* was a later invention, and that vassalage ceremonies, military obligations, and the ownership rights attached to fiefs differed widely from place to place and changed considerably in form and pattern over time. Thus, to these historians, "feudalism" is so varied that it doesn't really have a clear meaning, and it would be better not to use the term at all. The problem is that no one has come up with a better term for the loose arrangements of personal and property ties that developed in the ninth century.

Whether one chooses to use the word *feudalism* or not, these relationships provided some degree of cohesiveness in a society that lacked an adequate government bureaucracy or method of taxation. In fact, because vassals owed administrative as well as military service to their lords, vassalage actually functioned as a way to organize political authority. Vassals were expected to serve as advisers to their lord, and also to pay him fees for important family events, such as the marriage of the vassal's children.

Along with granting land to knights, lords gave land to the clergy for spiritual services or promises of allegiance. In addition, the church held its own lands, and bishops, archbishops, and abbots and abbesses of monasteries sometimes granted fiefs to their own knightly vassals. Thus the "lord" in a feudal relationship was sometimes an institution. Women other than abbesses were generally not granted fiefs, but in most parts of Europe daughters could inherit them if their fathers had no sons. Occasionally, women did go through ceremonies swearing homage and fealty and swore to send fighters when the lord demanded them. More commonly, when their husbands were away women acted as surrogates, defending the territory from attack and carrying out administrative duties.

Some of the problems associated with the word *feudal* come from the fact that it is sometimes used by nonhistorians as a synonym for "medieval," or to describe relations between landholders and the peasants who lived and worked on their estates. (The latter use comes from Karl Marx, who used "feudalism" to describe a stage of economic development between slavery and capitalism.) Medieval historians on all sides of the debate about feudalism agree, however, that peasants did not swear oaths of vassalage; if there was a feudal system, peasants were not part of it.

Manorialism, Serfdom, and the Slave Trade

In feudal relationships, the "lord" was the individual or institution that had authority over a vassal, but the word *lord* was also used to describe the person or institution that had economic and political authority over peasants who lived in villages and farmed the land. Thus a vassal in one relationship was a slightly different type of lord in another. Most European people in the early Middle Ages were peasants who lived in family groups in villages or small towns and made their living predominantly by raising crops and animals. The village and the land surrounding it were called a manor, from the Latin word for "dwelling" or "homestead." Some fiefs might include only one manor, while great lords or kings might have hundreds of manors under their direct control. Residents of manors worked for the lord in exchange for protection, a system that was later referred to as **manorialism**. Free peasants surrendered themselves and their lands to the lord's jurisdiction. The land was given back, but the peasants became tied to it by various kinds of payments and services. Thus, like vassalage, manorialism involved an exchange. Because the economic power of the warring class rested on landed estates worked by peasants, feudalism and manorialism were linked, but they were not the same system.

Local custom determined precisely what services villagers would provide to their lord, but certain practices became common throughout Europe. The peasant was obliged to give the lord a percentage of the annual harvest, usually in produce, sometimes in cash. The peasant paid a fee to marry someone from outside the lord's estate. To inherit property, the peasant paid a fine, often the best beast the person owned. Above all, the peasant became part of the lord's permanent labor force. With vast stretches of uncultivated virgin land and a tiny labor population, manorial lords encouraged population growth and immigration. The most profitable form of capital was not land but laborers.

In entering into a relationship with a manorial lord, free farmers lost status. Their position became servile, and they became **serfs**. That is, they were bound to the land and could not leave it without the lord's permission. Serfdom was not the same as slavery in that lords did not own the person of the serf, but serfs were subject to the jurisdiction of the lord's court in any dispute over property and in any case of suspected criminal behavior.

The transition from freedom to serfdom was slow. In the late eighth century there were still many free peasants. And within the legal category of serfdom there were many economic levels, ranging from the highly prosperous to the desperately poor. Nevertheless, a social and legal revolution was taking place. By the year 800 perhaps 60 percent of the population of western Europe—completely free a century before—had been reduced to serfdom. The ninth-century Viking assaults on Europe created extremely unstable conditions and individual insecurity, increasing the need for protection, accelerating the transition to serfdom, and leading to additional loss of personal freedom.

Though serfdom was not slavery, the Carolingian trade in actual slaves was extensive, generally involving persons captured in war or raids. Merchants in early medieval towns used slaves to pay the suppliers of the luxury goods their noble and clerical customers desired, most of which came into Europe from the East. The Muslim conquest of Spain produced thousands of prisoner-slaves, as did Charlemagne's long wars and the Viking raids. When Frankish conquests declined in the tenth century, German and Viking merchants obtained people on the empire's eastern border who spoke Slavic languages, the origin of our word *slave*. Slaves sold across the Mediterranean fetched three or four times the amounts brought within the Carolingian Empire, so most slaves were sold to Muslims. For Europeans and Arabs alike, selling captives and other slaves was standard procedure. Christian moralists sometimes complained about the sale of Christians to non-Christians, but they did not object to slavery itself.

NOTES

1. F. E. Peters, *A Reader on Classical Islam* (Princeton, N.J.: Princeton University Press, 1994), pp. 208–209.
2. Quoted in R. McKitterick, *The Frankish Kingdoms Under the Carolingians, 751–987* (New York: Longman, 1983), p. 34.
3. Quoted ibid., p. 77.
4. Quoted in B. D. Hill, ed., *Church and State in the Middle Ages* (New York: John Wiley & Sons, 1970), pp. 46–47.
5. From Charles Melville and Ahmad Ubaydli, eds. and trans., *Christians and Moors in Spain*, vol. 3 (New York: Oxbow Books, 1992), p. 54.
6. Quoted in R. Pipes, *Russia Under the Old Regime* (New York: Charles Scribner's Sons, 1974), p. 48.

■ **manorialism** A system in which peasant residents of manors, or farming villages, provided work and goods for their lord in exchange for protection.

■ **serfs** Peasants bound to the land by a relationship with a manorial lord.

LOOKING BACK LOOKING AHEAD

The culture that emerged in Europe in the early Middle Ages has justifiably been called the first "European" civilization. While it was by no means "civilized" by modern standards, it had definite characteristics that were shared across a wide region. Other than in Muslim Spain and the pagan areas of northern and eastern Europe, almost all people were baptized Christians. Everywhere — including Muslim and pagan areas — most people lived in small villages, supporting themselves and paying their obligations to their superiors by raising crops and animals. These villages were on pieces of land increasingly granted to knights in exchange for loyalty and service to a noble lord. The educated elite was infused with Latin ideas and models, for Latin was the common language — written as well as spoken — of educated people in most of Europe.

In the several centuries after 1000, these characteristics — Christianity, village-based agriculture, vassalage, and Latin culture — would not disappear. Historians conventionally term the era from 1000 to about 1300 the "High Middle Ages," but this era built on a foundation that had already been established. The soaring Gothic cathedrals that were the most glorious architectural feature of the High Middle Ages were often constructed on the footings of early medieval churches, and their walls were built of stones that had once been part of Carolingian walls and castles. Similarly, political structures grew out of the institutions established in the Carolingian period, and later literary and cultural flowerings followed the model of the Carolingian Renaissance in looking to the classical past. Less positive developments also had their roots in the early Middle Ages, including hostilities between Christians and Muslims that would motivate the Crusades, and the continued expansion of serfdom and other forms of unfree labor.

Make Connections

Think about the larger developments and continuities within and across chapters.

1. In both Christianity and Islam, political leaders played an important role in the expansion of the faith into new territory. How would you compare the actions of Constantine and Clovis (both in Chapter 7) with those of the Muslim caliphs and Charlemagne (in this chapter) in promoting, extending, and establishing their chosen religion?

2. Charlemagne considered himself to be the reviver of the Roman Empire. Thinking about Roman and Carolingian government and society, do you think this is an accurate self-description? Why or why not?

3. How were the ninth-century migrations and invasions of the Vikings, Magyars, and Muslims similar to the earlier barbarian migrations discussed in Chapter 7? How were they different?

8 REVIEW & EXPLORE

Identify Key Terms

Identify and explain the significance of each item below.

Qur'an (p. 220)

Five Pillars of Islam (p. 222)

caliph (p. 223)

al-Andalus (p. 223)

infidel (p. 225)

civitas (p. 228)

comites (p. 228)

Treaty of Verdun (p. 237)

Kievan Rus (p. 243)

boyars (p. 244)

vassal (p. 245)

fief (p. 245)

feudalism (p. 245)

manorialism (p. 246)

serfs (p. 246)

Review the Main Ideas

Answer the focus questions from each section of the chapter.

- What were the origins of Islam, and what impact did it have on Europe as it spread? (p. 220)

- How did the Franks build and govern a European empire? (p. 228)

- What were the significant intellectual and cultural changes in Charlemagne's era? (p. 234)

- What were the consequences of the ninth-century invasions and migrations? (p. 237)

- How did internal conflict and outside threats shape European political and economic development in this period? (p. 245)

Suggested Reading and Media Resources

BOOKS

- Barbero, Allesandro. *Charlemagne: Father of a Continent*. 2004. A wonderful biography of Charlemagne and study of the times in which he lived that argues for the complexity of his legacy.

- Barford, P. M. *The Early Slavs: Culture and Society in Early Medieval Eastern Europe*. 2001. An excellent survey of developments in much of eastern Europe.

- Bitel, Lisa. *Women in Early Medieval Europe, 400–1100*. 2002. Uses literary works and archaeological evidence as well as more traditional sources to trace all aspects of women's lives: social, intellectual, political, and economic.

- Esposito, John L. *Islam: The Straight Path*, updated ed. 2004. An informed and balanced work on Islam based on the best modern scholarship and original sources.

- Heather, Peter. *Empires and Barbarians: The Fall of Rome and the Birth of Europe*. 2010. Evaluates the dynamics of migration and the social, economic, and ethnic interactions that created Europe.

- James, Edward. *The Origins of France: From Clovis to the Capetians, 500–1000*, 2d ed. 2006. A solid introductory survey of early French history with an emphasis on family relationships.

- McKitterick, Rosamond. *Charlemagne: The Formation of a European Identity*. 2008. Analyzes Charlemagne's understanding of his role and methods of rule.

- Reynolds, Susan. *Fiefs and Vassals: The Medieval Evidence Reconsidered*. 1996. A comprehensive challenge to traditional conceptions of feudalism, the fief, and vassalage that has led to a rethinking of medieval political relationships.

- Riche, Pierre. *Daily Life in the World of Charlemagne*. Trans. JoAnn McNamara. 1988. A detailed study of many facets of Carolingian society.

- Verhulst, Adriaan. *The Carolingian Economy*. 2002. A brief survey, designed for students, of all aspects of the Carolingian economy, including agrarian production, crafts, and commerce.

- Watt, W. Montgomery, and Pierre Cachea. *A History of Islamic Spain.* 2007. A succinct analysis of Islam's influence on Spain.
- Wickham, Chris. *Framing the Early Middle Ages: Europe and the Mediterranean, 400–800.* 2007. A massive, yet accessible, survey of economic and social changes in many regions, with great attention to ordinary people.
- Winroth, Anders. *The Age of the Vikings.* 2014. Insightful look at all aspects of Viking society: raiding, trade, religion, art, poetry, and life at home in early medieval Scandinavia.
- Wood, Ian. *The Merovingian Kingdoms, 450–751.* 1994. The best general treatment of the Merovingians.

DOCUMENTARIES

- *Cities of Light: The Rise and Fall of Islamic Spain* (PBS, 2007). A documentary focusing on the culture of pluralism in tenth-century Muslim Spain, especially in the city of Córdoba, and its collapse because of internal and external forces. With an accompanying Web site at **www.islamicspain.tv**.
- *The Dark Ages* (History Channel, 2007). A blood-and-gore-filled documentary of the violence and instability of the early Middle Ages that also looks at Charlemagne and others as heroic creators of new institutions.
- *The Vikings* (*Nova*, 2000). A two-hour special that presents the Vikings as merchants, shipbuilders, artisans, and colonizers, and that re-creates Viking voyages in the Atlantic and eastern Europe using replicas of their ships.

FEATURE FILMS

- *Beowulf and Grendel* (Sturla Gunnarsson, 2005). A version of the *Beowulf* story with some new plot elements; loaded with violence and shot in the bleak landscape of Iceland.
- *The 13th Warrior* (John McTiernen, 1999). A fictional retelling of the story of the real tenth-century Arab traveler and writer Ibn Fadlan, who was sent as an ambassador to the king of the Volga Bulgars, at whose court there were eastern Vikings. Based on a novel by Michael Crichton, the film also mixes in stories from *Beowulf.*

WEB SITES

- *Internet Medieval Sourcebook.* The definitive location for primary sources from the Middle Ages. Most of the texts are in English and are organized chronologically and thematically. **www.fordham.edu/halsall/sbook.html**
- *The Labyrinth: Resources for Medieval Studies.* Run by Georgetown University, this site provides free access to electronic resources in medieval studies, which are organized thematically. **labyrinth.georgetown.edu**
- *The Viking Answer Lady.* In addition to being fun for Viking enthusiasts and historical re-enactors, this site offers bibliographies, visual materials, links to original texts, and accurate information on a range of topics. **www.vikinganswerlady.com/**

9

State and Church in the High Middle Ages

1000–1300

The concept of the state had been one of Rome's great legacies to Western civilization, but for almost five hundred years after the disintegration of the Roman Empire in the West, the state did not exist. Political authority was decentralized, with power spread among many lords, bishops, abbots, and other types of local rulers. The deeply fragmented political units that covered the early medieval European continent did not have the characteristics or provide the services of a modern state.

Beginning in the last half of the tenth century, the invasions and migrations that had contributed to European fragmentation gradually ended, and domestic disorder slowly subsided. Rulers began to develop new institutions of law and government that enabled them to assert their power over lesser lords and the general population. Although nobles remained the dominant class, centralized states slowly crystallized, first in western Europe, and then in eastern and northern Europe. At the same time, energetic popes built their power within the Western Christian Church and tried to assert their superiority over kings and emperors. Monks, nuns, and friars played significant roles in medieval society, both as individuals and as members of institutions. A papal call to retake the holy city of Jerusalem led to nearly two centuries of warfare between Christians and Muslims. Christian warriors, clergy, and settlers moved out from western and central Europe in all directions, so that through conquest and colonization border regions were gradually incorporated into a more uniform Christian realm. ■

TRAhVNT:CARRVM
CVMVINO:ETARM IS:

CHAPTER PREVIEW

Life in the High Middle Ages
In this detail from the Bayeux
tapestry, men pull a cart loaded with
wine and spears to the ships with
which Duke William of Normandy
crossed the English Channel in his
invasion of England in 1066. Medieval
chronicles, songs, and stories focus on
the heroic glories of battle, but
logistics and supply were just as
important to a medieval army as they
are today. Now on display in Bayeux,
France, the Bayeux tapestry is actually
not a tapestry, but an embroidery
panel measuring 231 feet by 19 inches
that records the entire conquest.
(Musée de la Tapisserie, Bayeux, France/
Bridgeman Images)

Political Revival and the Origins of the Modern State

FOCUS QUESTION *How did monarchs try to centralize political power?*

The modern state is an organized territory with definite geographical boundaries, a body of law, and institutions of government. The modern national state provides its citizens with order and protection, supplies a currency that permits financial and commercial transactions, and conducts relations with foreign governments. To accomplish these functions, the state must have officials, bureaucracies, laws, courts of law, soldiers, information, and money. Early medieval governments had few of these elements, but beginning in the eleventh century rulers in some parts of Europe began to manipulate existing institutions to build up their power, becoming kings over growing and slowly centralizing states. As rulers expanded their territories and extended their authority, they developed larger bureaucracies, armies, judicial systems, and other institutions of state to maintain control and ensure order. Because these institutions cost money, rulers also initiated systems for generating revenue and handling financial matters. Some rulers were more successful than others, and the solutions they found to these problems laid the foundations for modern national states.

England

Throughout the ninth century the Vikings had made a concerted effort to conquer and rule all of Anglo-Saxon England. Because of its proximity to Scandinavia and its lack of unity under a single ruler, England probably suffered more from Viking invasions than any other part of Europe. In 878 Alfred, king of the West Saxons (or Wessex), defeated the Vikings, inaugurating a period of recovery and stability in England. Alfred and his immediate successors built a system of local defenses and slowly extended royal rule beyond Wessex to other Anglo-Saxon peoples until one law, royal law, took precedence over local custom. England was divided into local units called shires, or counties, each under the jurisdiction of a shire-reeve (a word that soon evolved into *sheriff*) appointed by the king. Sheriffs were unpaid officials from well-off families responsible for collecting taxes, catching and trying criminals, and raising infantry when the king required it.

The Viking invasions of England resumed, however, and the island eventually came under Viking rule. The Viking Canute (r. 1016–1035) made England the center of his empire while promoting a policy of assimilation and reconciliation between Anglo-Saxons and Vikings. When Canute's heir Edward died childless, there were three claimants to the throne of England—the Anglo-Saxon noble Harold Godwinson (ca. 1022–1066), who had been crowned by English nobles; the Norwegian king Harald III (r. 1045–1066), the grandson of Canute; and Duke William of Normandy, the illegitimate son of Edward's cousin.

In 1066 the forces of Harold Godwinson crushed Harald's invading army in northern England, then quickly marched south when they heard that William had invaded England with his Norman vassals. Harold was decisively defeated by William at the Battle of Hastings—an event now known as the Norman Conquest. In both England and Normandy, William the Conqueror limited the power of the nobles and church officials, and built a unified monarchy. In England he retained the office of sheriffs, but named Normans to the posts. William wanted to determine how much wealth there was in his new kingdom and who held what land. Royal officials were sent to every part of the country, and in every village local men were put under oath to answer the questions of these officials. In the words of a contemporary chronicler:

> So very narrowly did he have it investigated, that there was no single hide [a hide was a measure of land large enough to support one family], nor yard of land, nor indeed . . . one ox nor one cow nor one pig was there left out, and not put down in his record: and all these records were brought to him afterwards.[1]

The resulting record, called the ***Domesday Book*** (DOOMZ-day) from the Anglo-Saxon word *doom*, meaning "judgment," helped William and his descendants tax land appropriately. The book still survives and is an invaluable source of social and economic information about medieval England. It also helped William and future English kings regard their country as one unit.

William's son Henry I (r. 1100–1135) established a bureau of finance called the Exchequer that became the first institution of the government bureaucracy of England. In addition to various taxes and annual gifts, Henry's income came from money paid to the Crown for settling disputes and as penalties for crimes, as well as money due to him in his private position as landowner and lord. Henry, like other medieval kings, made no distinction between his private income and state revenues, and the officials of the Exchequer began to keep careful records of all monies paid into and out of

■ **Domesday Book** A general inquiry about the wealth of his lands ordered by William of Normandy.

■ **primogeniture** An inheritance system in which the oldest son inherits all land and noble titles.

the royal treasury. (See "Evaluating the Evidence 9.1: Marriage and Wardship in the Norman Exchequer," page 254.)

In 1128 Henry's daughter Matilda was married to Geoffrey of Anjou; their son became Henry II of England and inaugurated the Angevin (AN-juh-vuhn; from Anjou, his father's county) dynasty. Henry II inherited the French provinces of Anjou, Normandy, Maine, and Touraine in northwestern France, and in 1152 he married Eleanor of Aquitaine, heir to Aquitaine, Poitou (pwah-TOO), and Gascony in southwestern France. As a result, Henry claimed nearly half of today's France, and the histories of England and France became closely intertwined, leading to disputes and conflicts down to the fifteenth century.

France

French kings overcame the Angevin threat to expand and increasingly unify their realm. Following the death of the last Carolingian ruler in 987, an assembly of nobles selected Hugh Capet (kah-PAY) as his successor. Soon after his own coronation, Hugh crowned his oldest surviving son Robert as king to ensure the succession and prevent disputes after his death. This broke with the earlier practices of elective kingship or dividing a kingdom among one's sons, establishing instead the principle of **primogeniture** (prigh-muh-JEH-nuh-choor), in which the king's eldest son received the Crown as his rightful inheritance. Primogeniture became the standard pattern of succession in medieval western Europe, and also became an increasingly common pattern of inheritance for noble titles as well as land and other forms of wealth among all social classes.

The Capetian (kuh-PEE-shuhn) kings were weak, but they laid the foundation for later political stability. This stability came slowly. In the early twelfth century France still consisted of a number of virtually independent provinces, and the king of France maintained clear jurisdiction over a relatively small area, the Île-de-France. Over time medieval French kings worked to increase the royal domain and extend their authority over the provinces.

The work of unifying France began under Louis VI's grandson Philip II (r. 1180–1223), also known

Chronology

936–973	Reign of Otto I in Germany; facilitates spread of Christianity in the Baltics and eastern Europe
1059	Lateran Council restricts election of the pope to the college of cardinals
1061–1091	Normans defeat Muslims and Byzantines in Sicily
1066	Norman conquest of England
1073–1085	Pontificate of Pope Gregory VII, proponent of Gregorian reforms
1095–1291	Crusades
1098	Cistercian order established
1100–1135	Reign of Henry I of England; establishment of the Exchequer, England's bureau of finance
1100–1200	Establishment of canon law
1154–1189	Reign of Henry II of England; revision of legal procedure; beginnings of common law
1170	Thomas Becket assassinated in England
1180–1223	Reign of Philip II (Philip Augustus) in France; territory of France greatly expanded
1198–1216	Innocent III; height of the medieval papacy
1215	Magna Carta
1216	Papal recognition of Dominican order
1221	Papal recognition of Franciscan order
1290	Jews expelled from England
1298	Pope Boniface VIII orders all nuns to be cloistered
1302	Pope Boniface VIII declares all Christians subject to the pope in *Unam Sanctam*
1306	Jews expelled from France
1397	Queen Margrete establishes Union of Kalmar

as Philip Augustus. He took Normandy by force from King John of England in 1204, and gained other northern provinces as well. In the thirteenth century Philip Augustus's descendants acquired important holdings in the south. By the end of the thirteenth century most of the provinces of modern France had been added to the royal domain through diplomacy, marriage, war, and inheritance (Map 9.1).

In addition to expanding the royal territory, Philip Augustus devised a method of governing the provinces and providing for communication between the central government in Paris and local communities.

Marriage and Wardship in the Norman Exchequer

After the Norman Conquest, the kings of England held the right to control the marriages of their vassals, and also held wardship over the widow and children of any vassal who had died. They often sold these rights for cash, which gave the buyer control of the marriage or control over the ward's lands until he or she came of age. The records of the Exchequer include many such payments.

Alice, countess of Warwick, renders account of £1000 and 10 palfreys [the type of horse ridden by women] to be allowed to remain a widow as long as she pleases, and not to be forced to marry by the king. And if perchance she should wish to marry, she shall not marry except with the assent and on the grant of the king, where the king shall be satisfied; and to have the custody of her sons whom she has from the earl of Warwick her late husband.

Hawisa, who was wife of William Fitz Robert, renders account of 130 marks and 4 palfreys that she may have peace from Peter of Borough to whom the king has given permission to marry her; and that she may not be compelled to marry.

Geoffrey de Mandeville owes 20,000 marks to have as his wife Isabella, countess of Gloucester, with all the lands and tenements and fiefs which fall to her.

Thomas de Colville renders an account of 100 marks for having the custody of the sons of Roger Torpel and their land until they come of age.

William, bishop of Ely, owes 220 marks for having the custody of Stephen de Beauchamp with his inheritance and for marrying him where he wishes.

William of St. Mary's church renders an account of 500 marks for having the custody of the heir of Robert Young, son of Robert Fitzharding, with all his inheritance and all its appurtenances and franchises; that is to say with the services of knights and gifts of churches and marriages of women, and to be allowed to marry him to whatever one of his relatives he wishes; and that all his land is to revert to him freely when he comes of age.

Batholomew de Muleton renders an account of 100 marks for having the custody of the land and the heiress of Lambert of Ibtoft, and for marrying the wife of the same Lambert to whomsoever he wishes where she shall not be disparaged and that he may be able to confer her (the heiress) upon whom he wishes.

EVALUATE THE EVIDENCE

1. What types of individuals pay the king for power over marriage or wardship?
2. What do these payments reveal about marriage and family relationships among wealthier groups in medieval society?

Source: Edward P. Cheyney, ed., *Translations and Reprints from the Original Sources of European History*, vol. 4, part 3 (Philadelphia: The Department of History of the University of Pennsylvania, 1897), pp. 26–27.

Each province retained its own institutions and laws, but royal agents were sent from Paris into the provinces as the king's official representatives with authority to act for him. These agents were never natives of the provinces to which they were assigned, and they could not own land there. This policy reflected the fundamental principle of French administration that officials should gain their power from their connection to the monarchy, not from their own wealth or local alliances.

Philip Augustus and his successors were slower and less effective than were English kings at setting up an efficient bureau of finance. There was no national survey of property like the *Domesday Book* to help determine equitable levels of taxation, and French nobles resisted paying any taxes or fees. Not until the fourteenth century, as a result of the Hundred Years' War, did a national financial bureau emerge — the Chamber of Accounts — and even after that French nobles continued to pay little or no taxes, a problem that would help spark the French Revolution centuries later.

Central Europe

In central Europe the German king Otto I (r. 936–973) defeated many other lords to build his power from his original base in Saxony. Some of our knowledge of Otto derives from *The Deeds of Otto*, a history of his reign in heroic verse written by a nun, Hroswitha of Gandersheim (ca. 935–ca. 1003). Hroswitha viewed Otto's victories as part of God's plan: "As often as he set out for war, there was not a people, though haughty because of its strength, that could harm or conquer him, supported as he was by the consolation of the heavenly King."[2]

Otto garnered financial support from church leaders and also asserted the right to control ecclesiastical appointments. Before receiving religious consecration and being invested with the staff and ring symbolic of their offices, bishops and abbots had to perform feudal homage for the lands that accompanied the church office. This practice, later known as "lay investiture," created a grave crisis between the church and the monarchy in the eleventh century (see page 266).

In 955 Otto I inflicted a crushing defeat on the Magyars in the Battle of Lechfeld (see Chapter 8), which made Otto a great hero to the Germans. In 962 he used this victory to have himself crowned emperor by the pope in Aachen, which had been the capital of the Carolingian Empire. He chose this site to symbolize his intention to continue the tradition of Charlemagne and to demonstrate papal support for his rule. Though it was not exactly clear what Otto was the emperor of, by the eleventh century people were increasingly using the term **Holy Roman Empire** to refer to a loose confederation of principalities, duchies, cities, bishoprics, and other types of regional governments stretching from Denmark to Rome and from Burgundy to Poland (Map 9.2).

In this large area of central Europe and northern Italy, the Holy Roman emperors shared power with princes, dukes, archbishops, counts, bishops, abbots, and cities. The office of emperor remained an elected one, though the electors numbered seven — four secular rulers of large territories within the empire and three archbishops.

None of Otto's successors were as forceful as he had been, and by the first half of the twelfth century civil wars wracked the empire. The electors decided the only alternative to continued chaos was the selection of a strong ruler. They chose Frederick Barbarossa of the house of Hohenstaufen (HOH-uhn-shtow-fuhn) (r. 1152–1190). Like William the Conqueror in England and Philip in France, Frederick required vassals to take an oath of allegiance to him as emperor and appointed officials to exercise full imperial authority over local communities. He forbade the regional rulers to engage in war with one another and established sworn peace associations with them. These peace associations punished criminals and those who breached the peace.

Between 1154 and 1188 Frederick made six military expeditions into Italy in an effort to assert his imperial rights over the increasingly wealthy towns of northern Italy. While he initially made significant conquests, the Italian cities formed leagues to oppose him, and also allied with the papacy. In 1176 Frederick suffered a crushing defeat at Legnano, where the

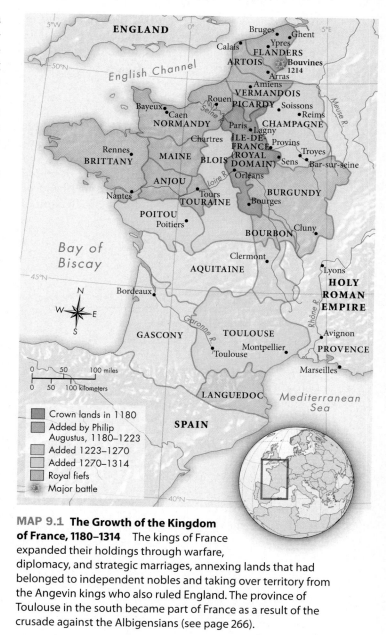

MAP 9.1 The Growth of the Kingdom of France, 1180–1314 The kings of France expanded their holdings through warfare, diplomacy, and strategic marriages, annexing lands that had belonged to independent nobles and taking over territory from the Angevin kings who also ruled England. The province of Toulouse in the south became part of France as a result of the crusade against the Albigensians (see page 266).

league armies took massive amounts of booty and many prisoners (see Map 9.2). This battle marked the first time a cavalry of armed knights was decisively defeated by an army largely made of infantrymen from the cities. Frederick was forced to recognize the municipal autonomy of the northern Italian cities and the pope's sovereignty in central Italy. His campaigns in Italy took him away from the parts of the empire north of the Alps, and regional rulers there reasserted their authority toward the end of Frederick's reign

■ **Holy Roman Empire** The loose confederation of principalities, duchies, cities, bishoprics, and other types of regional governments stretching from Denmark to Rome and from Burgundy to Poland.

and in the reigns of his successors. Thus, in contrast to France and England, Germany did not become a unified state in the Middle Ages, and would not until the nineteenth century.

Italy

The emperor and the pope also came into conflict over Sicily and southern Italy, disputes that eventually involved the kings of France and Spain as well. Between 1061 and 1091 a bold Norman knight, Roger de Hauteville, with papal support and a small band of mercenaries, defeated the Muslims and Byzantines

who controlled the island of Sicily. Roger then faced the problem of governing Sicily's heterogeneous population of native Sicilians, Italians, Greeks, Jews, Arabs, and Normans. Roger distributed scattered lands to his followers so no vassal would have a centralized power base. He took an inquest of royal property and forbade his followers to engage in war with one another. To these Norman practices, Roger fused Arab and Greek institutions, such as the bureau for record keeping and administration that had been established by the previous Muslim rulers.

In 1137 Roger's son and heir, Count Roger II, took the city of Naples and much of the surrounding territory in southern Italy. The entire area came to be known as the kingdom of Sicily (or sometimes the Kingdom of the Two Sicilies).

Roger II's grandson Frederick II (r. 1212–1250) was also the grandson of Frederick Barbarossa of Germany. He was crowned king of the Germans at Aachen (1216) and Holy Roman emperor at Rome (1220), but he concentrated all his attention on the southern parts of the empire. Frederick had grown up in multicultural Sicily, knew six languages, wrote poetry, and supported scientists, scholars, and artists, whatever their religion or background. In 1224 he founded the University of Naples to train officials for his growing bureaucracy, sending them out to govern the towns of the kingdom. He tried to administer justice fairly to all his subjects, declaring, "We cannot in the least permit Jews and Saracens [Muslims] to be defrauded of the power of our protection and to be deprived of all other help, just because the difference of their religious practices makes them hateful to Christians," implying a degree of toleration exceedingly rare at the time.[3]

Because of his broad interests and abilities, Frederick's contemporaries called him the "Wonder of the World." But Sicily required constant attention, and Frederick's absences on the Crusades—holy wars sponsored by the papacy for the recovery of Jerusalem from the Muslims (see page 274)—and on campaigns in mainland Italy took their toll. Shortly after he died, the unsupervised bureaucracy fell to pieces. The pope,

MAP 9.2 The Holy Roman Empire and the Kingdom of Sicily, ca. 1200 Frederick Barbarossa greatly expanded the size of the Holy Roman Empire, but it remained a loose collection of various types of government. The Christian kingdom of Sicily was created when Norman knights overthrew the Muslim rulers, but was later ruled by Frederick II, who was also the Holy Roman emperor.

worried about being encircled by imperial power, called in a French prince to rule the kingdom of Sicily. Like Germany, Italy would remain divided until the nineteenth century.

The Iberian Peninsula

From the eleventh to the thirteenth centuries, power in the Iberian Peninsula shifted from Muslim to Christian rulers. In the eleventh century divisions and civil war in the caliphate of Córdoba allowed Christian armies to conquer an increasingly large part of the Iberian Peninsula. Castile, in the north-central part of the peninsula, became the strongest of the growing Christian kingdoms, and Aragon, in the northeast, the second most powerful. In 1085 King Alfonso VI of Castile and León captured Toledo in central Spain. The following year forces of the Almoravid dynasty that ruled much of northwestern Africa defeated Christian armies and halted Christian advances southward, though they did not retake Toledo. The Almoravids reunified and strengthened the Muslim state for several generations, but the Christians regrouped, and in their North African homeland the Almoravids were overthrown by a rival dynasty, the Almohads, who then laid claim to the remaining Muslim territories in southern Spain.

Alfonso VIII (1158–1214) of Castile, aided by the kings of Aragon, Navarre, and Portugal, crushed the

Emperor Frederick II Granting Privileges   A young and handsome Frederick II, with a laurel wreath symbolizing his position as emperor, signs a grant of privileges for a merchant of the Italian city of Asti in this thirteenth-century manuscript. Frederick wears the flamboyant and fashionable clothing of a high noble — long-toed shoes, slit sleeves, and a cape of ermine tails — while the merchant seeking his favor is dressed in more sober and less expensive garb. (Miniature from the *Codex of Astensis*, Archivio Municipale, Asti, Italy/Scala/Art Resource, NY)

Córdoba Mosque and Cathedral The huge arches of the Great Mosque at Córdoba dwarf the cathedral built in the center after the city was conquered by Christian armies in 1236. During the reconquista, Christian kings often transformed mosques into churches, often by simply adding Christian elements such as crosses and altars to the existing structures. (Allen Brown/© dbimages/Alamy)

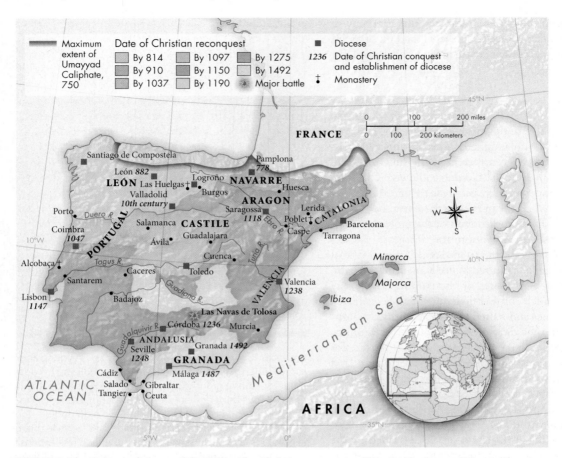

MAP 9.3 **The Reconquista, ca. 750–1492**   The Christian conquest of Muslim Spain was followed by ecclesiastical reorganization, with the establishment of dioceses, monasteries, and the Latin liturgy, which gradually tied the peninsula to the heartland of Christian Europe and to the Roman papacy.

Almohad-led Muslims in 1212, accelerating the Christian push southward. Over the next several centuries, successive popes gave Christian warriors in the Iberian Peninsula the same spiritual benefits that they gave those who traveled to Jerusalem, such as granting them forgiveness for their sins, transforming this advance into a crusade. Christian troops captured the great Muslim cities of Córdoba in 1236 and Seville in 1248. With this, Christians controlled nearly the entire Iberian Peninsula, save for the small state of Granada (Map 9.3). The chief mosques in Muslim cities became cathedrals, and Christian rulers recruited immigrants from western and southern Europe. The cities quickly became overwhelmingly Christian, and gradually rural areas did as well. Fourteenth-century clerical writers would call the movement to expel the Muslims the **reconquista** (reconquest), a sacred and patriotic crusade to wrest the country from "alien" Muslim hands. This idea became part of Spanish political culture and of the national psychology.

Law and Justice

FOCUS QUESTION *How did the administration of law evolve in this period?*

In the early Middle Ages society perceived major crimes as acts against an individual, and such crimes were settled when the accused made a cash payment to the victim or his or her kindred. In the High Middle Ages suspects were pursued and criminals punished for acting against the public interest. Throughout Europe, however, the law was a hodgepodge of local customs and provincial practices. In this period national rulers tried to blend these elements into a uniform system of rules acceptable and applicable to all their peoples, though their success at doing so varied.

Local Laws and Royal Courts

In France, this effort to create a royal judicial system was launched by Louis IX (r. 1226–1270). Each French province, even after being made part of the

■ **reconquista** The Christian term for the conquest of Muslim territories in the Iberian Peninsula by Christian forces.

kingdom of France, had retained its unique laws and procedures, but Louis IX published laws for the entire kingdom and sent royal judges to hear complaints of injustice. He established the Parlement of Paris, a kind of supreme court that heard appeals from local administrators and regional courts, and also registered (or announced) royal laws. By the very act of appealing the decisions of local courts to the Parlement of Paris, French people in far-flung provinces were recognizing the superiority of royal justice.

In the Holy Roman Empire, justice was administered at multiple levels. The manorial or seigneurial court, presided over by the local lay or ecclesiastical lord, dealt with such matters as damage to crops and fields, trespass, boundary disputes, and debt. Dukes, counts, bishops, and abbots possessed authority over larger regions, and they dispensed justice in serious criminal cases there. The Holy Roman emperors established a court of appeal similar to that of the French kings, but in their disunited empire it had little power.

England also had a variety of local laws with procedures and penalties that varied from one part of the country to another. Henry I occasionally sent out circuit judges, royal officials who traveled a given circuit or district, to hear civil and criminal cases. Henry II (r. 1154–1189) made this way of extending royal justice an annual practice. Every year royal judges left London and set up court in the counties. These courts regularized procedures in civil cases, gradually developing the idea of a **common law**, one that applied throughout the whole country. Over the next two or three centuries common law became a reality as well as a legal theory. Common law relied on precedent: a decision in an important case served as an authority for deciding similar cases. Thus written codes of law played a less important role in England than they did elsewhere. (This practice has continued to today; in contrast to the United States and most other countries, the United Kingdom does not have a written constitution.)

Henry also improved procedure in criminal justice. In 1166 he instructed the sheriffs to summon local juries to conduct inquests and draw up lists of known or suspected criminals. These lists, or indictments, sworn to by the juries, were to be presented to the royal judges when they arrived in the community. This accusing jury is the ancestor of the modern grand jury. Gradually, in the course of the thirteenth century, the king's judges adopted the practice of calling on twelve people (other than the accusing jury) to consider the question of innocence or guilt; this was the forerunner of the trial jury.

One aspect of Henry II's judicial reforms encountered stiff resistance from an unexpected source. In 1164 Henry insisted that everyone, including clerics, be subject to the royal courts. The archbishop of Canterbury Thomas Becket, who was Henry's friend and former chief adviser, vigorously protested that church law required clerics to be subject to church courts.

The disagreement between king and archbishop dragged on for years. Late in December 1170, in a fit of rage, Henry expressed the wish that Becket be destroyed. Four knights took the king at his word. They rode to Canterbury Cathedral and, as the archbishop was leaving evening services, murdered him, slashing off the crown of his head and scattering his brains on the floor of the cathedral. The assassination of an archbishop turned public opinion in England and throughout western Europe against the king, and Henry had to back down. He did public penance for the murder and gave up his attempts to bring clerics under the authority of the royal courts. Miracles were recorded at Becket's tomb; Becket was made a saint; and in a short time Canterbury Cathedral became a major pilgrimage and tourist site.

The Magna Carta

In the later years of Henry's reign, his sons, spurred on by their mother, Eleanor of Aquitaine, fought against their father and one another for power and land. Richard I, known as the Lion-Hearted (r. 1189–1199), won this civil war and acceded to the throne on Henry's death. Soon after, however, he departed on one of the Crusades, and during his reign he spent only six months in England. Richard was captured on his way back from the Crusades and held by the Holy Roman emperor for a very high ransom, paid primarily through loans and high taxes on the English people.

John (r. 1199–1216) inherited his father's and brother's heavy debts, and his efforts to squeeze money out of his subjects created an atmosphere of resentment. In July 1214 John's cavalry suffered a severe defeat at the hands of Philip Augustus of France, which ended English hopes for the recovery of territories from France and strengthened the opposition to John back in England. A rebellion begun by northern barons eventually grew to involve many key members of the English nobility. After lengthy negotiations, John met the barons in 1215 at Runnymede and was forced to approve the charter of rights later called **Magna Carta**.

The charter was simply meant to assert traditional rights enjoyed by certain groups, including the barons, the clergy, and the merchants of London, and thus state limits on the king's power. In time, however, it came to signify the broader principle that everyone, including the king and the government, must obey the

■ **common law** A body of English law established by King Henry II's court that in the next two or three centuries became common to the entire country.

■ **Magna Carta** A peace treaty intended to redress the grievances that particular groups had against King John; it was later viewed as the source of English rights and liberty more generally.

Punishment of Adulterers
Preceded by heralds
blowing horns and
followed by men carrying
sticks, a man and a woman
found guilty of adultery are
led naked through the
streets in this thirteenth-
century French manuscript.
This procession may be
driving the couple out of
town; banishment was a
very common punishment
for a number of crimes,
including theft and assault.
(Bibliothèque Municipale, Agen,
France/Bridgeman Images)

law. In the later Middle Ages references to Magna Carta underlined the Augustinian theory that a government, to be legitimate, must promote law, order, and justice (see Chapter 6). The Magna Carta also contains the germ of the idea of "due process of law," meaning that a person has the right to be heard and defended in court and is entitled to the protection of the law. Because later generations referred to Magna Carta as a written statement of English liberties, it gradually came to have an almost sacred symbolic importance.

Law in Everyday Life

Statements of legal principles such as the Magna Carta were not how most people experienced the law in medieval Europe. Instead they were involved in or witnessed something judged to be a crime, and then experienced or watched the determination of guilt and the punishment. Judges determined guilt or innocence in a number of ways. In some cases, particularly those in which there was little clear evidence, they ordered a trial by ordeal. An accused person could be tried by fire or water. In the latter case, the accused was tied hand and foot and dropped in a lake or river. People believed that water was a pure substance and would reject anything foul or unclean. Thus a person who sank was considered innocent; a person who floated was found guilty. Trial by ordeal was a ritual that appealed to the supernatural for judgment.

Trials by ordeal are fascinating to modern audiences, but they were relatively rare, and their use declined over the High Middle Ages as judges and courts increasingly favored more rational procedures. Judges heard testimony, sought witnesses, and read written evidence if it was available. A London case in 1277 provides a good example of how law worked. Around Easter, a man was sent to clean a house that had been abandoned, "but when he came to a dark and narrow place where coals were usually kept, he there found [a] headless body; upon seeing which, he sent word to the chamberlain and sheriffs." These officials went to the house and interviewed the neighbors. The men who lived nearby said that the headless body belonged to Symon de Winten, a tavern owner, whom they had seen quarreling with his servant Roger in early December. That night Roger "seized a knife, and with it cut the throat of Symon quite through, so that the head was entirely severed from the body." He had stuffed the body in the coal room, stolen clothes and a silver cup, and disappeared.[4] The surviving records don't indicate whether Roger was ever caught, but they do indicate that the sheriffs took something as "surety" from the neighbors who testified, that is, cash or goods as a pledge that their testimony was true. Taking sureties from witnesses was a common practice, which may be why the neighbors had not come forward on their own even though they seemed to have detailed knowledge of the murder. People were supposed to report crimes, and they could be fined for not doing so, but it is clear from this case that such community involvement in crime fighting did not always happen.

■ **chivalry** Code of conduct in which fighting to defend the Christian faith and protecting one's countrymen was declared to have a sacred purpose.

Had Roger been caught and found guilty, his punishment would have been as public as the investigation. Murder was a capital crime, as were a number of other violent acts, and executions took place outdoors on a scaffold. Hanging was the most common method of execution, although nobles might be beheaded because hanging was seen as demeaning. Minor crimes were punished by fines, corporal punishments such as whipping, or banishment from the area.

Nobles

FOCUS QUESTION *What were the roles of nobles, and how did they train for these?*

The expansion of centralized royal power and law involved limiting the power of the nobility, but rulers also worked through nobles, who retained their privileged status and cultural importance. In fact, despite political, scientific, and industrial revolutions, the nobility continued to hold real political and social power in Europe into the nineteenth century. In order to account for this continuing influence, it is important to understand the development of the nobility in the High Middle Ages.

Origins and Status of the Nobility

In the early Middle Ages noble status was generally limited to a very few families who either were descended from officials at the Carolingian court or were leading families among Germanic tribes. Beginning in the eleventh century, knights in the service of higher nobles or kings began to claim noble status. Although nobles were only a small fraction of the total population, the noble class grew larger and more diverse, ranging from poor knights who held tiny pieces of land (or sometimes none at all) to dukes and counts with vast territories.

Originally, most knights focused solely on military skills, but around 1200 there emerged a different ideal of knighthood, usually termed **chivalry** (SHIH-vuhl-ree). Chivalry was a code of conduct in which fighting to defend the Christian faith and protecting one's countrymen were declared to have a sacred purpose. Other qualities gradually became part of chivalry: bravery, generosity, honor, graciousness, mercy, and eventually gallantry toward women, which came to be called "courtly love." The chivalric ideal created a new standard of masculinity for nobles, in which loyalty and honor remained the most important qualities, but graceful dancing and intelligent conversation were not considered unmanly.

Training, Marriage, and Inheritance

For children of aristocratic birth, the years from infancy to around the age of seven or eight were primarily years of play. At about the age of seven, a boy of the noble class who was not intended for the church was placed in the household of one of his father's friends or relatives. There he became a servant to the lord and received formal training in arms. The boy learned to ride and to manage a horse. He had to acquire skill in wielding a sword, hurling a lance, shooting with a bow and arrow, and caring for armor and other equipment. Increasingly, noble youths learned to read and write some Latin. Formal training was concluded around the age of twenty-one, often with the ceremony of knighthood.

The ceremony of knighthood did not necessarily mean attainment of adulthood, power, and responsibility. Sons were completely dependent on their fathers for support. A young man remained a youth until he was in a financial position to marry—that is, until his

Saint Maurice This sandstone statue from Magdeburg Cathedral, carved around 1250, shows the warrior Saint Maurice. Some of the individuals who were held up to young men as models of ideal chivalry were probably real, but their lives were embellished with many stories. One example was Saint Maurice (d. 287), a soldier from Thebes in Egypt apparently executed by the Romans for refusing to renounce his Christian faith. He first emerges in the Carolingian period, and later he was held up as a model knight and declared a patron of the Holy Roman Empire and protector of the imperial army in wars against the pagan Slavs. His image was used on coins, and his cult was promoted by the archbishops of Magdeburg, who moved his relics to their cathedral. This statue is the first surviving portrayal of him as a black man, which became common in Germany until the late sixteenth century, although elsewhere he continued to be depicted as light skinned. He was (and, in some cases, still is) the patron saint of several military orders, including the Order of Saint Maurice of the National Infantry Association in the United States, and so his role as a model soldier lives on. (Markus Hilbich/akg-images)

Castles served nobles as places from which they could oppose royal authority, but they also served kings seeking to build up and maintain their power. Recognizing this value, William the Conqueror and his successors ordered the building of castles at strategic points around England. Edward I, for example, built Harlech Castle on a cliff overlooking the sea on the west coast of Wales as part of his campaign to conquer Wales and destroy the power of the Welsh nobility. The inner buildings of the castle were often built in wood originally, and then in stone, and the towers and outer walls were built in stone as well, all of which required extensive quarrying and hauling, part of the labor obligations of the peasants who lived in the surrounding area.

Castles were built for military purposes, but they were also places of residence. The lord and his family lived in the inner halls and towers, and their servants and supporters often lived there as well. During times of unrest or attack, peasants from nearby villages sometimes moved within the walls, living in the yard in the open or in hastily erected cloth and wood shelters with their animals. No one was very comfortable. Stone walls were cold and damp, and the small windows, designed for security, let in little light, augmented only by torches, oil lamps, and candles. While "medieval banquets" today offer exotic food and sumptuous settings, most meals in a castle such as Harlech—for those in the hall or in the yard—were simple, and were served in ceramic or wooden dishes and pitchers, not elegant plates and silver flagons.

QUESTIONS FOR ANALYSIS

1. What strategic value is gained by placing a castle on a hill or cliff? What other features of Harlech Castle increase its military functions? Looking at the photograph of the castle and the floor plan, what features of a castle, other than those mentioned above, do you think might make life difficult for residents?

2. The dishes shown here were for everyday use and were quite common, but few have survived. Why might this be? Even more often, medieval dishes were made out of wood, but almost none of these have survived. Why might this be?

3. How do these illustrations and objects fit with the view of life in a medieval castle presented in contemporary movies and other media?

Pottery pitcher for wine or ale, made in Lincolnshire, 1000–1200. (© The Trustees of the British Museum/Art Resource, NY)

Pottery baking dish, from Norman England, ca. 1000. (Ashmolean Museum, University of Oxford, UK/Bridgeman Images)

father died. That might not happen until he was in his late thirties, and marriage at forty was not uncommon. Increasingly, families adopted primogeniture, with property passing to the oldest son. Younger sons might be forced into the clergy or simply forbidden to marry.

Once knighted, the young man traveled for two to three years. His father selected a group of friends to accompany, guide, and protect him. If the young knight and his companions did not depart on a crusade, they hunted, meddled in local conflicts, and did the tournament circuit. The tournament, in which a number of men competed from horseback (in contrast to the joust, which involved only two competitors), gave the young knight experience in pitched battle and a way to show off his masculinity before an audience. Since the horses and equipment of the van-

Harlech Castle, with stone walls and towers, and floor plan. (castle: De Agostini/Getty Images; plan: © Crown copyright 2015, Cadw)

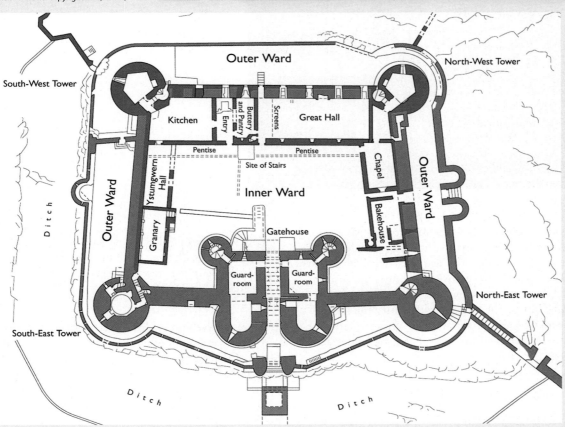

quished were forfeited to the victors, the knight could also gain a profit. Everywhere they went, young knights stirred up trouble, for chivalric ideals of honorable valor and gallant masculinity rarely served as a check on actual behavior.

While noble girls were also trained in preparation for their future tasks, that training was quite different. They were often taught to read the local language and perhaps some Latin and to write and do enough arith-

metic to keep household accounts. They also learned music, dancing, and embroidery and how to ride and hunt, both common noble pursuits. Much of this took place in the girl's own home, but, like boys, noble girls were often sent to the homes of relatives or higher nobles to act as servants or ladies in waiting or to learn how to run a household.

Parents often wanted to settle daughters' futures as soon as possible. Men tended to prefer young brides

Female Donor in Chartres Cathedral Windows Nobles and other wealthy people who paid for stained-glass windows often had their portraits included. In the south transept of Chartres Cathedral at the foot of the prophet Isaiah is the portrait of Alix of Thouars, hereditary duchess of Brittany. The windows were made in 1221–1230, right after Alix's death in childbirth, and were donated by her husband, who is also shown in one of the windows; the remaining windows show their son and daughter, though as young adults rather than as the small children they would have been at the time the windows were made. (Chartres Cathedral, Chartres, France/ Bridgeman Images)

who would have more years to produce children. Therefore, aristocratic girls in the High Middle Ages were married at around the age of sixteen, often to much older men. In the early Middle Ages the custom was for the groom to present a dowry to the bride and her family, but by the late twelfth century the process was reversed because men were in greater demand. Thereafter, the sizes of dowries offered by brides and their families rose higher and higher.

Power and Responsibility

A male member of the nobility became fully adult when he came into the possession of property. He then acquired authority over lands and people, protecting them from attack, maintaining order, and settling disputes. (See "Living in the Past: Life in an English Castle," page 262.) With this authority went responsibility. In the words of Honorius of Autun:

> Soldiers: You are the arm of the Church, because you should defend it against its enemies. Your duty is to aid the oppressed, to restrain yourself from rapine and fornication, to repress those who impugn the Church with evil acts, and to resist those who are rebels against priests. Performing such a service, you will obtain the most splendid of benefices from the greatest of Kings.[5]

Nobles rarely lived up to this ideal, however, and there are countless examples of nobles' stealing church lands instead of defending them, tyrannizing the oppressed rather than aiding them, and regularly engaging in "rapine and fornication" rather than resisting them.

Women played a large and important role in the functioning of the estate. They were responsible for the practical management of the household's "inner economy"—cooking, brewing, spinning, weaving, caring for yard animals. When the lord was away for long periods, the women frequently managed the herds, barns, granaries, and outlying fields as well. Often the responsibilities of the estate fell to them permanently, as the number of men slain in medieval warfare ran high.

Throughout the High Middle Ages, fighting remained the dominant feature of the noble lifestyle. The church's preaching and condemnations reduced but did not stop violence, and the military values of the nobles' social class encouraged petty warfare and disorder. The nobility thus represented a constant source of trouble for the monarchy.

The Papacy

FOCUS QUESTION *How did the papacy reform the church, and what were the reactions to these efforts?*

Kings and emperors were not the only rulers consolidating their power in the High Middle Ages; popes did so as well, through a series of measures that made the church more independent of secular control. In the ninth and tenth centuries secular lords like Otto I controlled the appointment of church officials. Popes and bishops were appointed to advance the political ambitions of their own families rather than for special spiritual qualifications. Under the leadership of a series of reforming popes in the eleventh century, the church tried to end this practice, but the popes' efforts were sometimes challenged by medieval kings and emperors, and the wealth of the church came under sharp criticism.

The Gregorian Reforms

During the ninth and tenth centuries the local church had come under the control of kings and feudal lords, who chose priests and bishops in their territories, granting them land and expecting loyalty and service in return. Church offices from village priest to pope were sources of income as well as positions of authority. Officeholders had the right to collect taxes and fees and often the profits from the land under their control. Church offices were thus sometimes sold outright—a practice called **simony** (SIGH-muh-nee). Not surprisingly, clergy at all levels who had bought their positions or had been granted them for political reasons provided little spiritual guidance, and their personal lives were rarely models of high moral standards. Although the Roman Church officially required men to be unmarried in order to be ordained, there were many married priests and others simply living with women. Popes were chosen by wealthy Roman families from among their members, and after gaining the papal office, they paid more attention to their families' political fortunes than to the health of the church.

Serious efforts to change all this began under Pope Leo IX (pontificate 1049–1054). Leo ordered clergy in Rome to dismiss their wives and invalidated the ordination of church officials who had purchased their offices. Pope Leo and several of his successors believed that secular or lay control over the church was largely responsible for its lack of moral leadership, so in a radical shift they proclaimed the church independent of secular rulers. The Lateran Council of 1059 decreed that the authority and power to elect the pope rested solely in the **college of cardinals**, a special group of priests from the major churches in and around Rome. The college retains that power today, though the membership has grown and become international.

Leo's successor Pope Gregory VII (pontificate 1073–1085) was even more vigorous in his championing of reform and expansion of papal power; for that reason, the eleventh-century movement is frequently called the "Gregorian reform movement." He denounced clerical marriage and simony in harsh language and ordered **excommunication** (being cut off from the sacraments and all Christian worship) for those who disagreed. He believed that the pope, as the successor of Saint Peter, was the vicar of God on earth and that papal orders were thus the orders of God. Gregory was particularly opposed to lay investiture—the selection and appointment of church officials by secular authority. In February 1075 he held a council at Rome that decreed that clerics who accepted investiture from laymen were to be deposed and laymen who invested clerics were to be excommunicated.

In the late eleventh century and throughout the twelfth and thirteenth, the papacy pressed Gregory's campaign for reform of the church. The popes held a series of councils, known as the Lateran Councils, that ratified decisions ending lay investiture, ordered bishops to live less extravagantly, and ordered married priests to give up their wives and children or face dismissal. Most church officials apparently obeyed, though we have little information on what happened to the families. In other reforms, marriage was defined as a sacrament—a ceremony that provided visible evidence of God's grace—and divorce was forbidden.

Gregory's reforms had a profound effect on nuns and other women in religious orders. The movement built a strict hierarchical church structure with bishops and priests higher in status than nuns, who could not be ordained. The double monasteries of the early Middle Ages were placed under the authority of male abbots. Church councils forbade monks and nuns to sing church services together and ordered priests to limit their visits to convents. The reformers' emphasis

---

■ **simony** The buying and selling of church offices, a policy that was officially prohibited but often practiced.

■ **college of cardinals** A special group of high clergy with the authority and power to elect the pope and the responsibility to govern the church when the office of the pope is vacant.

■ **excommunication** A penalty used by the Christian Church that meant being cut off from the sacraments and all Christian worship.

on clerical celibacy and chastity led them to portray women as impure and lustful. Thus, in 1298 in the papal decree *Periculoso*, Pope Boniface VIII ordered all nuns to be strictly cloistered, that is, to remain permanently inside the walls of the convent, and for visits with people from outside the house, including family members, to be limited. *Periculoso* was not enforced everywhere, but it did mean that convents became more cut off from medieval society than monasteries were.

Emperor Versus Pope

Gregory thought that the threat of excommunication would compel rulers to abide by his move against lay investiture. Immediately, however, Henry IV in the Holy Roman Empire, William the Conqueror in England, and Philip I in France protested, as the reform would deprive them not only of church income but also of the right to choose which monks and clerics would help them administer their kingdoms. The strongest reaction came from the Holy Roman Empire. Pope Gregory accused Henry IV of lack of respect for the papacy and insisted that disobedience to the pope was disobedience to God. Henry argued that Gregory's type of reform undermined royal authority. Within the empire, religious and secular leaders took sides to pursue their own advantage. In January 1076 many of the German bishops who had been invested by Henry withdrew their allegiance from the pope. Gregory promptly suspended them and excommunicated Henry. The pope told German nobles they no longer owed allegiance to Henry, which obviously delighted them. When powerful nobles invited the pope to come to Germany to settle their dispute with Henry, Gregory traveled to the north. Christmas of 1076 thus witnessed an ironic situation in Germany: the clergy supported the emperor while the great nobility favored the pope.

Henry managed to outwit the pope temporarily. In January 1077 he approached the castle of Countess Matilda of Tuscany (ca. 1046–1115) at Canossa in the Apennines (AH-puh-nighnz), where the pope was staying. According to a letter later sent by Gregory to his German noble allies, Henry stood for three days in the snow, imploring the pope to lift the excommunication. Henry's pleas for forgiveness won him public sympathy, and the pope readmitted the emperor to the Christian community. When the sentence of excommunication was lifted, however, Henry regained the emperorship and authority over his rebellious subjects, but continued his moves against papal power. In 1080 Gregory again excommunicated and deposed the emperor. In return, when Gregory died in 1085, Henry invaded Italy and captured Rome.

But Henry won no lasting victory. Gregory's successors encouraged Henry's sons to revolt against their father.

Finally, in 1122 at a conference held at Worms, the issue was settled by compromise. Bishops were to be chosen by the clergy. But since lay rulers were permitted to be present at ecclesiastical elections and to accept or refuse homage from the new prelates, they still possessed an effective veto over ecclesiastical appointments. Papal power was enhanced, but neither side won a clear victory.

The long controversy over lay investiture had tremendous social and political consequences in Germany. The lengthy struggle between papacy and emperor allowed emerging noble dynasties to enhance their position. To control their lands, the great lords built castles, symbolizing their increased power and growing independence. When the papal-imperial conflict ended in 1122, the nobility held the balance of power in Germany, and later German kings, such as Frederick Barbarossa, would fail in their efforts to strengthen the monarchy. For these reasons, division and local independence characterized the Holy Roman Empire in the High Middle Ages.

Criticism and Heresy

The Gregorian reform movement contributed to dissatisfaction with the church among townspeople as well as monarchs. Papal moves against simony, for example, led to widespread concern about the role of money in the church just as papal tax collectors were becoming more efficient and sophisticated. Papal efforts to improve the sexual morality of the clergy led some laypersons to assume they could, and indeed should, remove priests for any type of immorality.

Criticism of the church emerged in many places but found its largest audience in the cities, where the contrast between wealth and poverty could be seen more acutely. In northern Italian towns, the monk Arnold of Brescia (BREH-shah) (ca. 1090–1155), a vigorous advocate of strict clerical poverty, denounced clerical wealth. In France, Peter Waldo (ca. 1140–ca. 1218), a rich merchant of the city of Lyons, gave his money to the poor and preached that only prayers, not sacraments, were needed for salvation. The Waldensians (wawl-DEHN-shuhnz)—as Peter's followers were called—bitterly attacked the sacraments and church hierarchy, and they carried these ideas across Europe. In the towns and cities of southern France, the Albigensians (al-buh-JEHN-see-uhns), also known as the Cathars, used the teachings of Jesus about the evils of material goods to call for the church to give up its property. They asserted that the material world was created not by the good

Bishop Ending a Marriage In this thirteenth-century illumination from a legal manual, a bishop ends a marriage. Marriage was first declared a sacrament by officials in the Catholic Church in the late eleventh century as part of the condemnation of the Cathars, and confirmed as such at the Fourth Lateran Council. Because of this, divorce was prohibited, although marriages could be annulled — that is, declared never to have been valid in the first place — for a variety of reasons, and annulments did occur, particularly for members of the nobility. (Illustration on vellum from *Digeste*, 13th century/Bibliothèque Sainte-Geneviève, Paris, France/Archives Charmet/Bridgeman Images)

God of the New Testament, but by a different evil God of the Old Testament. People who rejected worldly things, not wealthy bishops or the papacy, should be the religious leaders.

Critical of the clergy and spiritually unfulfilled, townspeople joined the Waldensians and the Albigensians. The papacy denounced supporters of both movements as heretics and began extensive campaigns to wipe them out. In 1208 Pope Innocent III proclaimed a crusade against the Albigensians, and the French monarchy and northern French knights willingly joined in, eager to gain the lands and wealth of southern French cities. After years of fighting, the leaders agreed to terms of peace, which left the French monarchy the primary beneficiary. Later popes sent inquisitors with the power to seek out and eliminate the remaining heretics.

The Popes and Church Law

Pope Urban II laid the foundations for the papal monarchy by reorganizing the papal *curia* (the central government of the Roman Church) and recognizing the college of cardinals as a definite consultative body. The papal curia had its greatest impact as a court of law. As the highest ecclesiastical tribunal, it formulated church law, termed **canon law**. The church developed a system of courts separate from

those of secular rulers that handled disputes over church property and ecclesiastical elections and especially questions of marriage and annulment. Most of the popes in the twelfth and thirteenth centuries were canon lawyers who expanded the authority of church courts.

The most famous of the lawyer-popes was Innocent III (pontificate 1198–1216), who became the most powerful pope in history. During his pontificate the church in Rome declared itself to be supreme, united, and "catholic" (worldwide), responsible for the earthly well-being as well as the eternal salvation of Christians everywhere. Innocent pushed the kings of Europe to do his will, compelling King Philip Augustus of France to take back his wife, Ingeborg of Denmark, and King John of England to accept as archbishop of Canterbury a man John did not want.

Innocent called the Fourth Lateran Council in 1215, which affirmed the idea that ordained priests had the power to transform bread and wine during church ceremonies into the body and blood of Christ (a change termed transubstantiation). According to papal doctrine, priests now had the power to mediate for everyone with God, setting the spiritual hierarchy of the church above the secular hierarchies of kings and other rulers. The council affirmed that Christians should confess their sins to a priest at least once a year, and that marriage was a sacrament, and thus indissol-

■ **canon law** Church law, which had its own courts and procedures.

Pope Boniface VIII, *Unam Sanctam*

In late 1302, after several years of bitter conflict with King Philip IV of France over control and taxation of the clergy in France, Pope Boniface VIII issued a papal bull declaring the official church position on the proper relationships between church and state. Throughout, the pope uses the "royal we," that is, the plural "we" instead of "I" when talking about himself.

We are obliged by the faith to believe and hold — and we do firmly believe and sincerely confess — that there is one Holy Catholic and Apostolic Church, and that outside this Church there is neither salvation nor remission of sins. . . . In which Church there is "one Lord, one faith, one baptism." . . . Of this one and only Church there is one body and one head — not two heads, like a monster — namely Christ, and Christ's vicar is Peter, and Peter's successor, for the Lord said to Peter himself, "Feed my sheep." "My sheep" He said in general, not these or those sheep; wherefore He is understood to have committed them all to him. . . .

And we learn from the words of the Gospel that in this Church and in her power are two swords, the spiritual and the temporal. . . . Truly he who denies that the temporal sword is in the power of Peter, misunderstands the words of the Lord, "Put up thy sword into the sheath." Both are in the power of the Church, the spiritual sword and the material. But the latter is to be used for the Church, the former by her; the former by the priest, the latter by kings and captains but at the will and by the permission of the priest. The one sword, then, should be under the other, and temporal authority subject to spiritual. . . .

If, therefore, the earthly power err, it shall be judged by the spiritual power; and if a lesser power err, it shall be judged by a greater. But if the supreme power [the papacy] err, it can only be judged by God, not by man. . . . For this authority, although given to a man and exercised by a man, is not human, but rather divine, given at God's mouth to Peter and established on a rock for him and his successors in Him whom he confessed, the Lord saying to Peter himself, "Whatsoever thou shalt bind," etc. Whoever therefore resists this power thus ordained of God, resists the ordinance of God. . . . Furthermore, we declare, state, define, and pronounce that it is altogether necessary to salvation for every human creature to be subject to the Roman pontiff.

EVALUATE THE EVIDENCE

1. According to Pope Boniface, what is the proper relationship between the authority of the pope and the authority of earthly rulers? What is the basis for that relationship?
2. How might the earlier conflicts between popes and secular rulers traced in this chapter have influenced Boniface's declaration?

Source: Henry Bettenson, ed., *Documents of the Christian Church* (Oxford: Oxford University Press, 1963), 385w from pp. 115–116. Used by permission of Oxford University Press.

---

uble. It also ordered Jews and Muslims to wear special clothing that set them apart from Christians.

By the early thirteenth century papal efforts at reform begun more than a century earlier had attained phenomenal success, and the popes ruled a powerful, centralized institution. At the end of the century, however, the papacy again came into a violent dispute with secular rulers. Pope Boniface VIII (pontificate 1294–1303), arguing from precedent, insisted that King Edward I of England and Philip IV of France obtain his consent for taxes they had imposed on the clergy. Edward immediately denied the clergy the protection of the law, and Philip halted the shipment of all ecclesiastical revenue to Rome. Boniface had to back down.

The battle for power between the papacy and the French monarchy became a bitter war of propaganda, with Philip at one point calling the pope a heretic. Finally, in 1302, in a formal written statement known as a papal bull, Boniface insisted that all Christians — including kings — were subject to the pope. (See "Evaluating the Evidence 9.2: Pope Boniface VIII, *Unam Sanctam*," above.) Philip maintained that he was completely sovereign in his kingdom and responsible to God alone. French mercenary troops assaulted and arrested the aged pope at Anagni in Italy. Although Boniface was soon freed, he died shortly afterward. The confrontation at Anagni foreshadowed further difficulties in the Christian Church in the fourteenth century.

■ **religious orders** Groups of monastic houses following a particular rule.

Monks, Nuns, and Friars

FOCUS QUESTION *What roles did monks, nuns, and friars play in medieval society?*

While the reforming popes transformed the Christian Church into an institution free of lay control at the highest level, leaders of monasteries and convents asserted their independence from secular control on the local level as well. Monks, nuns, and friars played significant roles in medieval society, both as individuals and as members of institutions. Medieval people believed that monks and nuns performed an important social service when they prayed, for their prayers and chants secured God's blessing for society. The friars worked in the cities, teaching and preaching Christian doctrine, but also investigating heretics.

Monastic Revival

In the early Middle Ages many religious houses followed the Benedictine *Rule*, while others developed their own patterns (see Chapter 7). In the High Middle Ages this diversity became more formalized, and **religious orders**, groups of monastic houses following a particular rule, were established. Historians term the foundation, strengthening, and reform of religious orders in the High Middle Ages the "monastic revival."

In Carolingian times, the best Benedictine monasteries had been centers of learning, copying and preserving manuscripts, maintaining schools, and setting high standards of monastic observance. In the period of political disorder that followed the disintegration of the Carolingian Empire, many religious houses fell under the control and domination of local lords. Powerful laymen appointed themselves or their relatives as abbots, took the lands and goods of monasteries, and seized monastic revenues. Accordingly, the level of spiritual observance and intellectual activity in monasteries and convents declined. The local lords also compelled abbots from time to time to provide contingents of soldiers, an obligation stemming from the abbots' judicial authority over knights and peasants on monastic lands. The conflict between an abbot's religious duties on the one hand and his judicial and military obligations on the other posed a serious dilemma.

The first sign of reform came in 909, when William the Pious, duke of Aquitaine, established the abbey of Cluny in Burgundy. Duke William declared that the monastery was to be free from any feudal responsibilities to him or any other lord, its members subordinate only to the pope. The monastery at Cluny, which initially held high standards of religious behavior, came to exert vast religious influence. In the eleventh century Cluny was fortunate in having a series of highly able abbots who ruled for a long time. In a disorderly world, Cluny gradually came to represent stability. Therefore, laypersons placed lands under its custody and monastic priories under its jurisdiction (a priory is a religious house, with generally fewer residents than an abbey, governed by a prior or prioress). In this way, hundreds of religious houses, primarily in France and Spain, came under Cluny's authority.

Deeply impressed laypeople showered gifts on monasteries with good reputations, such as Cluny and its many daughter houses. But as the monasteries became richer, the lifestyle of the monks grew increasingly luxurious. Monastic observance and spiritual fervor declined. Soon fresh demands for reform were heard, resulting in the founding of new religious orders in the late eleventh and early twelfth centuries.

Monastery and Convent Life Life in monasteries and convents involved physical labor as well as spiritual activities. In this twelfth-century French manuscript, a monk and a lay brother chop down a tree. Such work was a common part of monastic life because monasteries, especially those of the Cistercians, were often built in heavily forested wilderness areas. (Bibliothèque Municipale, Dijon, France, Ms. 173 f 41/Bridgeman Images)

The Cistercians (sihs-TUHR-shuhnz) best represent the new reforming spirit because of their phenomenal expansion and great economic, political, and spiritual influence. In 1098 a group of monks left the rich abbey of Molesmes in Burgundy and founded a new house in the swampy forest of Cîteaux (see-TOH). They planned to avoid all involvement with secular society and decided to accept only uncultivated lands far from regular habitation. The early Cistercians (the word is derived from Cîteaux) determined to keep their services simple and their lives austere, returning to work in the fields and other sorts of manual labor. As with Cluny, their high ideals made them a model, and 525 Cistercian monasteries were founded in the course of the twelfth century all over Europe. The Cistercians' influence on European society was profound, for they used new agricultural methods and technology and spread them throughout Europe. Their improvements in farming and animal raising brought wealth, however, and wealth brought power. By the later twelfth century, as with Cluny earlier, economic prosperity and political power had begun to compromise the original Cistercian ideals.

Life in Convents and Monasteries

Medieval monasteries were religious institutions whose organization and structure fulfilled the social needs of the nobility. The monasteries provided noble boys with education and opportunities for ecclesiastical careers. Although a few men who rose in the ranks of church officials were of humble origins, most were from high-status families. Many had been given to the monastery by their parents. Beginning in the thirteenth century an increasing number of boys and men from professional and merchant families became monks, seeking to take advantage of the opportunities monasteries offered.

Throughout the Middle Ages social class also defined the kinds of religious life open to women. Kings and nobles usually established convents for their daughters, sisters, aunts, or aging mothers, and other women of their class. Like monks, many nuns came into the convent as children, and very often sisters, cousins, aunts, and nieces could all be found in the same place. Thus, though nuns were to some degree cut off from their families by being cloistered, family relationships were maintained within the convent.

The office of abbess or prioress was the most powerful position a woman could hold in medieval society. (See "Individuals in Society: Hildegard of Bingen," at right.) Abbesses were part of the political structure in the same way that bishops and abbots were, with manors under their financial and legal control. They appointed tax collectors, bailiffs, judges, and often priests in their lands. Some abbesses in the Holy Roman Empire even had the right to name bishops and send representatives to imperial assemblies. Abbesses also opened and supported hospitals, orphanages, and schools and hired builders, sculptors, and painters to construct and decorate residences and churches.

Monasteries for men were headed by an abbot or a prior, who was generally a member of a noble family, often a younger son in a family with several. The main body of monks, known as "choir monks" because one of their primary activities was reciting prayers and services while sitting in the part of the church called the choir, were largely of noble or middle-class background, and they did not till the land themselves. Men from peasant families sometimes became choir monks, but more often they served as lay brothers, doing the manual labor essential to running the monastery. The novice master or novice mistress was responsible for the training of recruits. The efficient operation of a monastic house also required the services of cooks, laundresses, gardeners, seamstresses, mechanics, blacksmiths, pharmacists, and others whose essential work has left, unfortunately, little written trace.

The pattern of life within individual monasteries varied widely from house to house and from region to region. One central activity, however, was performed everywhere. Daily life centered on the liturgy or Divine Office, psalms and other prayers prescribed by Saint Benedict that monks and nuns prayed seven times a day and once during the night. Prayers were offered for peace, rain, good harvests, the civil authorities, and the monks' families and benefactors. Everything connected with prayer was understood as praise of God, so abbeys spent a large percentage of their income on splendid objects to enhance the service, including sacred vessels of embossed silver or gold, altar cloths of the finest silks or velvets, embroideries, and beautiful reliquaries to house the relics of the patron saint.

In some abbeys monks and nuns spent much of their time copying books and manuscripts and then illuminating them, decorating them with human and animal figures or elaborate designs, often painted in bright colors or gold. A few monasteries and convents became centers of learning where talented residents wrote their own works as well as copying those of others.

Monks and nuns also performed a variety of social services in an age when there was no state and no conception of social welfare as a public responsibility. Monasteries often ran schools that gave primary

INDIVIDUALS IN SOCIETY

Hildegard of Bingen

The tenth child of a lesser noble family, Hildegard (1098–1179) was given as a child to an abbey in the Rhineland when she was eight years old; there she learned Latin and received a good education. She spent most of her life in various women's religious communities, two of which she founded herself. When she was a child, she began having mystical visions, often of light in the sky, but told few people about them. In middle age, however, her visions became more dramatic: "And it came to pass . . . when I was 42 years and 7 months old, that the heavens were opened and a blinding light of exceptional brilliance flowed through my entire brain. And so it kindled my whole heart and breast like a flame, not burning but warming . . . and suddenly I understood of the meaning of expositions of the books."* She wanted the church to approve of her visions and wrote first to Bernard of Clairvaux, who answered her briefly and dismissively, and then to Pope Eugenius, who encouraged her to write them down. Her first work was *Scivias* (Know the Ways of the Lord), a record of her mystical visions that incorporates vast theological learning.

Possessed of leadership and administrative talents, Hildegard left her abbey in 1147 to found the convent of Rupertsberg near Bingen. There she produced *Physica* (On the Physical Elements) and *Causa et Curae* (Causes and Cures), scientific works on the curative properties of natural elements, as well as poems, a mystery play, and several more works of mysticism. She carried on a huge correspondence with scholars, prelates, and ordinary people. When she was over fifty, she left her community to preach to audiences of clergy and laity, and she was the only woman of her time whose opinions on religious matters were considered authoritative by the church.

Hildegard's visions have been explored by theologians and also by neurologists, who judge that they may have originated in migraine headaches, as she reports many of the same phenomena that migraine sufferers do: auras of light around objects, areas of blindness, feelings of intense doubt and intense euphoria. The interpretations that she develops come from her theological insight and learning, however, not illness. That same insight also emerges in her music, for which she is best known today. Eighty of her compositions survive—a huge number for a medieval composer—most of them written to be sung by the nuns in her convent, so they have strong lines for female voices. Many of her songs and chants have been recorded and are available on CD, as downloads, and on several Web sites.

Inspired by heavenly fire, Hildegard begins to dictate her visions to her scribe. The original of this elaborately illustrated twelfth-century copy of *Scivias* disappeared from Hildegard's convent during World War II, but fortunately a facsimile copy had already been made. (Private Collection/Bridgeman)

QUESTIONS FOR ANALYSIS

1. Why do you think Hildegard sought church approval for her visions after keeping them secret for so many years?
2. In what ways is Hildegard's life representative of nuns' lives in the High Middle Ages? In what ways were her accomplishments extraordinary?

*From *Scivias*, trans. Mother Columba Hart and Jane Bishop, *The Classics of Western Spirituality* (New York/Mahwah: Paulist Press, 1990), p. 65.

Saint Francis Gives Up His Worldly Possessions   After Francis had given money to a church, his wealthy father ordered Francis to give him back the money. Francis instead took off all his clothes and returned them to his father, signifying his dependence on his father in Heaven rather than his earthly father. The fresco of this event, painted seventy years after Francis's death for the church erected in his honor in Assisi, captures the consternation of Francis's father and the confusion of the local bishop (holding the cloth in front of the naked Francis), who had told the young man to obey his earthly father. By the time the church was built, members of the Franciscan order were in violent disagreement over what Francis would have thought about a huge church built in his honor and other issues of clerical wealth. (Fresco by Giotto di Bondone [ca. 1266–1337]/San Francesco, Upper Church, Assisi, Italy/Bridgeman Images)

education to young boys; convents did the same for girls. Monasteries served as hotels and resting places for travelers, and frequently operated hospitals and leprosariums, which provided care and attention to the sick, the aged, and the afflicted.

The Friars

Monks and nuns carried out their spiritual and social services largely within the walls of their institutions, but in the thirteenth century new types of religious orders were founded whose members lived out in the world. Members of these new groups were **friars**, not monks. They thought that more contact with ordinary Christians, not less, was a better spiritual path. Friars stressed apostolic poverty, a life based on the teaching

of the Gospels in which they would own no property and depend on Christian people for their material needs. Hence they were called mendicants, from the Latin word for begging. The friars' service to the towns and the poor, their ideal of poverty, and their compassion for the human condition made them popular.

One order of friars was started by Domingo de Gúzman (1170?–1221), born in Castile. Domingo (later called Dominic), a well-educated priest, accompanied his bishop in 1206 on an unsuccessful mission to win the Albigensians in southern France back to orthodox teaching. Determined to succeed through ardent preaching, he subsequently returned to France with a few followers. In 1216 the group—officially known as the Preaching Friars, though often called Dominicans— won papal recognition as a new religious order.

Francesco di Bernardone (1181–1226), son of a wealthy Italian cloth merchant of Assisi, had a reli-

■ **friars** Men belonging to certain religious orders who lived not in monasteries but out in the world.

Brother Henry as Composer and Singer

Toward the end of his life, the Italian Franciscan friar Salimbene of Parma (1221–ca. 1290) wrote a chronicle that includes character sketches of many people he had met. Salimbene traveled widely throughout Italy and France, meeting both important figures such as Emperor Frederick II and less well-known folk such as the fellow Franciscan he describes here.

Brother Henry of Pisa was a handsome man, of medium height, generous, amiable, charitable, and merry. He knew how to get along well with everyone, . . . adapting himself to the personality of each one, and he won the love of his own brethren as well as that of the laymen, which is given to few. Moreover, he was a celebrated preacher, beloved by both the clergy and the laity. He knew how to write beautifully, and to paint, which some call illuminate, to write music, and to compose the sweetest and loveliest songs, both in harmony and in plain song. He himself was an excellent singer, and had a strong and sonorous voice, so that it filled the whole choir. And his treble sounded light, very high and clear, but sweet, lovely, and pleasing beyond measure. . . .

That Brother Henry of Pisa was a man of admirable manners, devoted to God and to the Holy Virgin, and to the Blessed Magdalene. No wonder, for the church of his quarter of Pisa bore the name of this saint; the cathedral of the city, in which he had been ordained by the archbishop of Pisa, bore the name of the Blessed Virgin. Brother Henry composed many *cantilena* and many sequences, for example, the words and melody of the following song:

O Christ, my God,
O Christ, my Refuge
O Christ, King and Lord,

[which he patterned] after the song of a maid who was going through the cathedral church of Pisa, singing in the popular tongue:

If thou carest not for me,
I'll no longer care for thee.

He made, moreover, the three-part song: "Wretched man, think thou on thy Creator's works!" . . .

He composed a noble melody to the sequence: "He had watered the tree of Jesse," which until then had had a crude one, discordant for singing. Richard of St. Victor wrote the words of this sequence, as well as those of many others.

EVALUATE THE EVIDENCE

1. What qualities of Brother Henry and his songs does Salimbene find worthy of praise?
2. Friars were active out in the world and did not live in monasteries. How did Brother Henry's position as a friar shape the music he created?

Source: "Two Musical Friars" by Salimbene, translated by Mary Martin McLaughlin, from *The Portable Medieval Reader* by James Bruce Ross and Mary Martin McLaughlin, eds., copyright 1949 by Viking Penguin, Inc. Copyright renewed © 1976 by James Bruce Ross and Mary Martin McLaughlin. Used by permission of Viking Books, an imprint of Penguin Publishing Group, a division of Penguin Random House LLC.

gious conversion and decided to live and preach the Gospel in absolute poverty. Francis of Assisi, as he came to be known, emphasized not withdrawal from the world, but joyful devotion. In contrast to the Albigensians, who saw the material world as evil, Francis saw all creation as God-given and good. He was widely reported to perform miracles involving animals and birds, and wrote hymns to natural objects. "Be praised, my Lord, through our sister Mother Earth" went one, "who feeds us and rules us and produces various fruits with colored flowers and herbs." This song also praises the sun, wind, air, water, and fire, and it was one of the first religious works ever written in a vernacular dialect. It also provides an example of how Franciscans and other friars used music to convey religious teachings. (See "Evaluating the Evidence 9.3: Brother Henry as Composer and Singer," above.)

The simplicity, humility, and joyful devotion with which Francis carried out his mission soon attracted others. Although he resisted pressure to establish an order, his followers became so numerous that he was obliged to develop some formal structure. In 1221 the papacy approved the Rule of the Little Brothers of Saint Francis, generally called the Franciscans (frahn-SIHS-kuhnz).

Friars worked among the poor, but also addressed the spiritual and intellectual needs of the middle classes and the wealthy. The Dominicans preferred that their friars be university graduates in order to better preach to a sophisticated urban society. Dominicans soon held professorial chairs at leading universities, and the Franciscans followed suit.

Beginning in 1231 the papacy also used friars to investigate heretics, sometimes under the auspices of a new ecclesiastical court, the Inquisition, in which accused people were subjected to lengthy interrogations and torture could be used to extract confessions. It is ironic that groups whose teachings were similar in so many ways to those of heretics were charged with rooting them out. That irony deepened in the case of the Spiritual Franciscans, a group that broke away from the main body of Franciscans to follow Francis's original ideals of absolute poverty. When they denied the pope's right to countermand that ideal, he ordered them tried as heretics.

Women sought to develop similar orders devoted to active service out in the world. Clare of Assisi (1193–1253) became a follower of Francis, who established a place for her to live in a church in Assisi. She was joined by other women, and they attempted to establish a rule that would follow Francis's ideals of absolute poverty and allow them to serve the poor. This rule was accepted by the papacy only after many decades, and then only because she agreed that the order, the Poor Clares, would be cloistered.

In the growing cities of Europe, especially in the Netherlands, groups of laywomen seeking to live religious lives came together as what later came to be known as Beguines (bay-GEENS). They lived communally in small houses called *beguinages*, combining lives of prayer with service to the needy. Beguine spirituality emphasized direct personal communication with God, sometimes through mystical experiences, rather than through the intercession of a saint or official church rituals. Initially some church officials gave guarded approval of the movement, but the church grew increasingly uncomfortable with women who were neither married nor cloistered nuns. By the fourteenth century Beguines were declared heretical, and much of their property was confiscated.

The Crusades and the Expansion of Christianity

FOCUS QUESTION *What were the causes, course, and consequences of both the Crusades and the broader expansion of Christianity?*

The Crusades of the eleventh and twelfth centuries were the most obvious manifestation of the papal claim to the leadership of Christian society. The **Crusades** were wars sponsored by the papacy for the recovery of the holy city of Jerusalem from the Muslims. The enormous popular response to papal calls for crusading reveals the influence of the reformed papacy and the depth of religious fervor among many different types of people. The Crusades also reflected the church's new understanding of the noble warrior class, for whom war against the church's enemies was understood as a religious duty. The word *crusade* was not actually used at the time and did not appear in English until the late sixteenth century. It means literally "taking the cross," from the cross that soldiers sewed on their garments as a Christian symbol. At the time people going off to fight simply said they were taking "the way of the cross" or "the road to Jerusalem."

Background and Motives of the Crusades

The medieval church's attitude toward violence was contradictory. On the one hand, church councils threatened excommunication for anyone who attacked peasants, clerics, or merchants or destroyed crops and unfortified places, a movement termed the Peace of God. Councils also tried to limit the number of days on which fighting was permitted, prohibiting it on Sundays, on special feast days, and in the seasons of Lent and Advent. On the other hand, popes supported armed conflict against kings and emperors if this worked to their advantage, thus encouraging warfare among Christians. After a serious theological disagreement in 1054 split the Orthodox Church of Byzantium and the Roman Church of the West, the pope also contemplated invading the Byzantine Empire, an idea that subsequent popes considered as well.

Although conflicts in which Christians fought Christians were troubling to many thinkers, war against non-Christians was another matter. By the ninth century popes and other church officials encouraged war in defense of Christianity, promising spiritual benefits to those who died fighting. By the eleventh century these benefits were extended to all those who simply joined a campaign: their sins would be remitted without having to do penance, that is, without having to confess to a priest and carry out some action to make up for the sins. Around this time, Christian thinkers were developing the concept of purgatory, a place where those on their way to Heaven stayed for a while to do any penance they had not completed while alive. (Those on their way to Hell went straight there.) Engaging in holy war could shorten one's time in purgatory, or, as many people understood the promise, allow one to head straight to paradise. Popes signified this by providing **indulgences**, grants with the pope's name on them that lessened earthly penance and postmortem purgatory. Popes promised these spiritual benefits, and also provided financial support, for Christian armies in the reconquista in Spain and the Norman campaign against the Muslims in Sicily. Preachers communicated these ideas widely and told

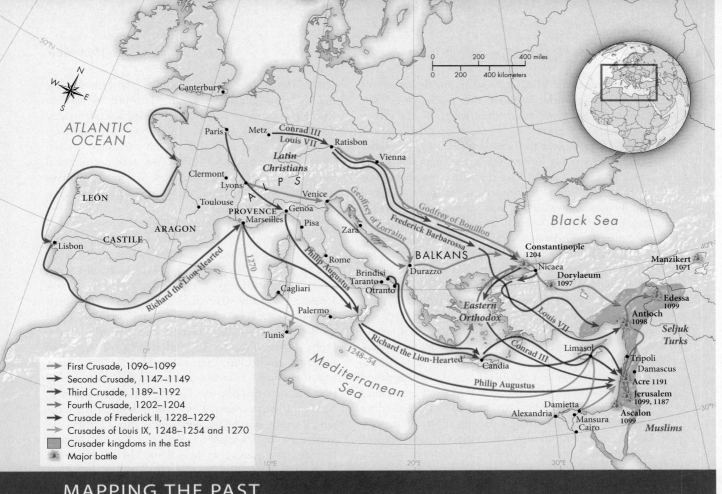

MAP 9.4 The Crusades

This map shows the many different routes that Western Christians took over the centuries to reach Jerusalem.

ANALYZING THE MAP How were the results of the various Crusades shaped by the routes that the Crusaders took?

CONNECTIONS How did the routes and Crusader kingdoms offer opportunities for profit?

stories about warrior-saints who slew hundreds of enemies.

Religious devotion had long been expressed through pilgrimages to holy places, and these were increasingly described in military terms, as battles against the hardships along the way. Pilgrims to Jerusalem were often armed, so the line between pilgrimage and holy war on this particular route was increasingly blurred. In the midst of these developments came a change in possession of Jerusalem. The Arab Muslims who had ruled Jerusalem and the surrounding territory for centuries had generally allowed Christian pilgrims to travel freely, but in the late eleventh century the Seljuk (SEHL-jook) Turks took over Palestine, defeating both Arab and Byzantine armies and pillaging in Christian and Muslim parts of Asia Minor (Map 9.4). They harassed pilgrims and looted churches, and the emperor at Constantinople appealed to the West for support. The emperor's appeal fit well with papal aims,

and in 1095 Pope Urban II called for a great Christian holy war against the infidels — a term Christians and Muslims both used to describe the other. Urban offered indulgences to those who would fight for and regain the holy city of Jerusalem.

The Course of the Crusades

Thousands of Western Christians of all classes joined the First Crusade, which began in 1096. Of all the developments of the High Middle Ages, none better reveals Europeans' religious and emotional fervor and the influence of the reformed papacy than the extraordinary outpouring of support for the First Crusade.

■ **Crusades** Wars sponsored by the papacy for the recovery of Jerusalem and surrounding territories from the Muslims in the late eleventh to the late thirteenth centuries.

■ **indulgences** Grants by the pope that lessened or eliminated the penance that sinners had to pay on earth and in purgatory before ascending to Heaven.

The First Crusade was successful, mostly because of the dynamic enthusiasm of the participants. The Crusaders had little more than religious zeal. They knew nothing about the geography or climate of the Middle East. Although there were several nobles with military experience among them, the Crusaders could never agree on a leader, and the entire expedition was marked by disputes among the great lords. Lines of supply were never set up, and starvation and disease wracked the army. Nevertheless, the army pressed on, defeating the Turks in several land battles and besieging a few larger towns, including Antioch. Finally, in 1099, three years after departing Europe, the Crusaders reached Jerusalem. After a month-long siege they got inside the city, where they slaughtered the Muslim defenders. (See "Thinking Like a Historian: Christian and Muslim Views of the Crusades," page 278.)

In the aftermath of the First Crusade, four small "Crusader kingdoms"—Jerusalem, Edessa, Tripoli, and Antioch—were established. Castles and fortified towns were built to defend against Muslim reconquest (see Map 9.4). Between 1096 and 1270 the crusading ideal was expressed in eight papally approved expeditions, though none after the First Crusade accomplished very much. Despite this lack of success, members of European noble families from nearly every generation took up the cross for roughly two hundred years.

The Crusades inspired the establishment of new religious orders, particularly military orders dedicated to protecting the Christian kingdoms. The most important was the Knights Templars, founded in 1119. Many people going off to the Holy Land put their property in Europe under Templar protection, and by the end of the thirteenth century the order was extremely wealthy, with secret rituals in which members pledged obedience to their leaders. The Templars began serving as moneylenders and bankers, which further increased their wealth. In 1307 King Philip IV of France sought to grab that wealth for himself; he arrested many Templars, accusing them of heresy, blasphemy, and sodomy. They were tortured, a number were burned at the stake, Philip took much of their money, and the Templars were disbanded.

Women from all walks of life participated in the Crusades. When King Louis IX of France was captured on the Seventh Crusade (1248–1254), his wife, Queen Marguerite, negotiated the surrender of the Egyptian city of Damietta to the Muslims. Some women concealed their sex by donning chain mail and helmets and fought with the knights. Some joined in the besieging of towns and castles by assisting in filling the moats surrounding fortified places with earth so that ladders and war engines could be brought close. More typically, women provided water to fighting men, a

service not to be underestimated in the hot, dry climate of the Middle East. They worked as washerwomen, foraged for food, and provided sexual services. There were many more European men than women, however, so marriage and sexual relations between Christian men and Muslim women were not unheard of, although marriages between Western Christian men and Orthodox Christian women who lived in the area were more common.

The Muslim states in the Middle East were politically fragmented when the Crusaders first came, and it took about a century for them to reorganize. They did so dramatically under Saladin (Salah al-Dihn), who first unified Egypt and Syria, and then retook Jerusalem in 1187. Christians immediately attempted to take it back in what was later called the Third Crusade (1189–1192). Frederick Barbarossa of the Holy Roman Empire, Richard the Lion-Hearted of England, and Philip Augustus of France participated, and the Third Crusade was better financed than the previous two. But disputes among the leaders and strategic problems prevented any lasting results. The Crusaders could not retake Jerusalem, though they did keep their hold on port towns, and Saladin allowed pilgrims safe passage to Jerusalem. He also made an agreement with Christian rulers for keeping the peace. From that point on, the Crusader states were more important economically than politically or religiously, giving Italian and French merchants direct access to Eastern products such as perfumes and silk.

In 1202 Innocent III sent out preachers who called on Christian knights to retake Jerusalem. Those who responded—in what would become the Fourth Crusade—negotiated with the Venetians to take them by boat to Cairo, but Venetian interests combined with a succession struggle over the Byzantine throne led the fleet to go to Constantinople instead. Once there, the Crusaders decided to capture and sack Constantinople, destroying its magnificent library and seizing gold, silver, and relics to send home. The Byzantines reasserted their control over the empire in 1261, but it was much smaller and weaker and soon consisted of little more than the city of Constantinople. Moreover, the assault by one Christian people on another helped discredit the entire crusading movement and obviously had no effect on Muslim control of Jerusalem and other areas.

Nonetheless, there were a few more efforts. The Seventh Crusade in 1248, led by King Louis IX of France (r. 1223–1270), tried unsuccessfully to come in through Egypt. Louis also sent monks to the court of the Mongols in Central Asia, who were at this point led by Chinggis Khan, to forge an alliance that would encircle the Muslims. The monks were unsuccessful, but they brought back geographical knowledge of Asia and the peoples they had encountered. In the end, the Mamluk rulers of Egypt conquered the Crusader states, and in 1291 their last stronghold, the port of Acre, fell. Some knights continued their crusading efforts by joining the reconquista in Spain.

Consequences of the Crusades

The Crusades gave kings and the pope opportunities to expand their bureaucracies. They also provided kings with the perfect opportunity to get rid of troublemaking knights, particularly restless younger sons for whom the practice of primogeniture meant few prospects. Some of them were able to carve out lordships in Palestine, Syria, and Greece. Even some members of the middle class who stayed at home profited from the Crusades. Nobles often had to borrow money from city residents to pay for their expeditions, and they put up part of their land as security. If a noble did not return home or could not pay the interest on the loan, the middle-class creditor took over the land.

The Crusades introduced some Europeans to Eastern luxury goods, but their immediate cultural impact on the West remains debatable. Strong economic and intellectual ties with the East had already been developed by the late eleventh century. The Crusades did greatly benefit Italian merchants, who profited from outfitting military expeditions, the opening of new trade routes, and the establishment of trading communities in the Crusader states. Since commerce with the West benefited both Muslims and Europeans, it continued to flourish even after the Crusader states collapsed.

The Crusades proved to be a disaster for Jewish-Christian relations. In many parts of Europe, Jews lent money to peasants, townspeople, and nobles, and indebtedness bred resentment. Inspired by the ideology of holy war and resentment of Jewish economic activities, Christian armies on their way to Jerusalem on the First Crusade joined with local people to attack Jewish families and sometimes entire Jewish communities. In the German cities along the Rhine River, for example, an army of Crusaders under the leadership of a German noble forced Jews to convert through mass baptisms and killed those who resisted; more than eight hundred Jews were killed in Worms and more than a thousand in Mainz. Later Crusades brought similar violence, enhanced by rumors that Jews engaged in the ritual murder of Christians to use their blood in religious rites. As a result of growing hostility, legal restrictions on Jews gradually increased throughout Europe. In 1290 King Edward I of England expelled the Jews from England and confiscated their property and goods; it

would be four centuries before they would be allowed back in. King Philip IV of France followed Edward's example in 1306.

The long-term cultural legacy of the Crusades may have been more powerful than their short-term impact. The ideal of a sacred mission to conquer or convert Muslim peoples entered some Europeans' consciousness, and was later used in other situations. When Christopher Columbus sailed west in 1492, he hoped to reach India in part to establish a Christian base from which a new crusade against Islam could be launched. Muslims later looked back on the Crusades as expansionist and imperialist, the beginning of a long trajectory of Western attempts to limit or destroy Islam.

The Expansion of Christianity

The Crusades were not the only example of Christian expansion in the High Middle Ages. As we saw earlier, Christian kingdoms were established in the Iberian Peninsula through the reconquista. This gradual Christian advance was replicated in northern and eastern Europe in the centuries after 1000. People and ideas moved from western France and western Germany into Ireland, Scandinavia, the Baltic lands, and eastern Europe, with significant consequences for those territories. Wars of expansion, the establishment of new Christian bishoprics, and the vast migration of colonists, together with the papal emphasis on a unified Christian world, brought about the gradual Christianization of a larger area. By 1350 Roman Catholic Europe was double the size it had been in 950.

Ireland had been Christian since the days of Saint Patrick (see Chapter 7), but in the twelfth century Norman knights crossed from England, defeated Irish lords, and established bishoprics with defined territorial dioceses. Latin Christian influences also entered the Scandinavian and Baltic regions primarily through the erection of dioceses. Otto I established the first Scandinavian dioceses in Denmark. In Norway Christianity spread in coastal areas beginning in the tenth century, and King Olaf II (r. 1015–1028) brought in clergy and bishops from England and Germany to establish the church more firmly. From Norway Christianity spread to Iceland; from Denmark it spread to Sweden and Finland. In all of these areas, Christian missionaries preached, baptized, and built churches. Royal power advanced institutional Christianity, and traditional Norse religions practiced by the Vikings were outlawed.

In 1397 Queen Margrete I (1353–1412) united the crowns of Denmark, Sweden-Finland, and Norway in the Union of Kalmar. She continued royal support of bishops and worked toward creating a stronger state by

Christian and Muslim Views of the Crusades

Both Christians and Muslims wrote accounts of the Crusades as they happened, which circulated among those who could read and served as the basis for later histories and visual depictions. How do Christian and Muslim views differ, and how are they similar?

1 **Peter Tudebode on the fall of Antioch, 1098.** Peter Tudebode was a French priest who accompanied the First Crusade and later wrote an account of it.

〜 There was a Turkish emir [high-ranking army officer], Firuz, who became very friendly with Bohemond [a Norman noble, one of the leaders of the First Crusade]. Often through mutual messengers Bohemond suggested that Firuz admit him to Antioch; and, in turn, the Norman offered him the Christian religion along with great wealth from many possessions. Firuz, in accepting these provisions, replied: "I pledge freely the delivery of three towers of which I am a custodian."... The knights took to the plain and the footmen to the mountain, and all night they maneuvered and marched until almost daybreak, when they came to the towers which Firuz guarded. Bohemond immediately dismounted and addressed the group: "Go in daredevil spirit and great *elan*, and mount the ladder into Antioch, which shall soon be in our hands if God so wills." They then went to a ladder, which was raised and lashed to the walls of the city, and almost sixty of our men scaled the ladder and divided their forces in the towers guarded by Firuz. ... [W]e crashed down the gate, and poured into Antioch.... At sunup the crusaders who were outside Antioch in their tents, upon hearing piercing shrieks arising from the city, raced out and saw the banner of Bohemond flying high on the hill. Thereupon they rushed forth and each one speedily came to his assigned gate and entered Antioch, killing Turks and Saracens whom they found. ... Yaghi Siyan, commander of Antioch, in great fear of the Franks, took to heel along with many of his retainers.... All of the streets of Antioch were choked with corpses so that the stench of rotting bodies was unendurable, and no one could walk the streets without tripping over a cadaver.

2 **Ibn al-Athir on the fall of Antioch.** Ali Ibn al-Athir (1160–1223), a Kurdish scholar and historian who lived in Mosul (today's Iraq), wrote a history of the First Crusade that relied on Arab sources.

〜 Yaghi Siyan, the ruler of Antioch, showed unparalleled courage and wisdom, strength and judgment. If all the Franks who died had survived they would have overrun all the lands of Islam. He protected the families of the Christians in Antioch and would not allow a hair of their heads to be touched. After the siege had been going on for a long time the Franks made a deal with...an armor-maker called Ruzbih whom they bribed with a fortune in money and lands. He worked in the tower that stood over the riverbed, where the river flowed out of the city into the valley. The Franks sealed their pact with the armor-maker, God damn him! and made their way to the watergate. They opened it and entered the city. Another gang of them climbed the tower with their ropes. At dawn, when more than 500 of them were in the city and the defenders were worn out after the night watch, they sounded their trumpets.... Panic seized Yaghi Siyan and he opened the city gates and fled in terror, with an escort of thirty pages.... This was of great help to the Franks, [who] entered the city by the gates and sacked it, slaughtering all the Muslims they found there....

It was the discord between the Muslim princes ...that enabled the Franks to overrun the country.

3 **Fulcher of Chartres on the fall of Jerusalem to the Crusaders, 1099.** Fulcher was a chaplain to military leaders on the First Crusade and over several decades wrote a long and influential chronicle.

〜 Soon thereafter the Franks gloriously entered the city at noon on the day known as Dies Veneris, the day in which Christ redeemed the whole world on the Cross. [That is, a Friday.] Amid the sound

ANALYZING THE EVIDENCE

1. How do Sources 1 and 2 differ in how they portray Yaghi Siyan and the man who opened the towers of Antioch to Christian forces? How do these and other differences influence the story?
2. In Sources 3 and 4, how is the course of the two battles for Jerusalem different? How is the aftermath different?
3. How does the artist who painted Source 5 convey his ideas about why the battle ended as it did?
4. How do these accounts balance the various aims—religious devotion, military glory, economic gain—of the two sides?

of trumpets and with everything in an uproar they attacked boldly, shouting "God help us!" At once they raised a banner in the city on the top of the wall. . . . They ran with the greatest exultation as fast as they could into the city and joined their companions in pursuing and slaying their wicked enemies without cessation. . . . If you had been there your feet would have been stained to the ankles in the blood of the slain. What shall I say? None of them were left alive. Neither women nor children were spared. How astonishing it would have seemed to you to see our squires and footmen, after they discovered the trickery of the Saracens, split open the bellies of those they had just slain in order to extract from the intestines the bezants [gold coins minted in Byzantium] which the Saracens had gulped down their loathsome throats while still alive! . . . After this great slaughter they entered the houses of the citizens, seizing whatever they found in them. This was done in such a way that whoever first entered a house, whether he was rich or poor, was not challenged by any other Frank. In this way many poor people became wealthy.

4 **Al-Isfahani on Saladin's retaking of Jerusalem, 1187.** Imad ad-Din al-Isfahani (1125–1187) was a Persian scholar who served as secretary to Saladin and accompanied him on many of his military campaigns.

Saladin marched forward to take the reins of Jerusalem. . . . [T]he Franks despaired of finding any relief from their situation and decided all to give their lives (in defense of Jerusalem). . . . The Sultan mounted catapults, and by this means milked the udders of slaughter. . . . [I]n every heart on either side burned the fire of longing, faces were exposed to the blade's kiss, hearts were tormented with longing for combat. . . . Every onslaught was energetic and achieved its object, the goal was reached, the enemy wounded. . . . The city became Muslim and the infidel belt around it was

cut. . . . By striking coincidence the date of the conquest of Jerusalem was the anniversary of the Prophet's ascension to heaven. Great joy reigned for the brilliant victory won, and words of prayer and invocation to God were on every tongue. . . . Ibn Barzun [Balian of Ibelin, one of the Crusader leaders] came out to secure a treaty with the Sultan, and asked for an amnesty for his people. . . . [A]n amount was fixed for which they were to ransom themselves and their possessions . . . ten dinar for every man, five for a woman, and two for a boy or girl. . . . Every man who paid left his house in safety, and the rest were to be enslaved. . . . The Franks began selling their possessions and taking their precious things out of safe-keeping. . . . They scavenged in their own churches and stripped them of their ornaments of gold and silver. . . . Then I said to the Sultan, "These are things of great riches; do not allow these rascals to keep this in their grasp." But he replied, "If we interpret the treaty to their disadvantage they will accuse us of breaking faith." So they carried away the most precious and lightest [objects] and shook from their hands the dust of their heritage.

(From the *Estoire d'Outremer* (vellum) by William of Tyre [ca. 1130–1185]/ Bibliothèque Municipale de Lyon, France/Bridgeman Images)

5 **Capture of Antioch.** This illustration comes from a 1280 version of William of Tyre's *A History of Deeds Beyond the Sea,* the most widely read account of the Crusades, which drew extensively on earlier histories.

PUTTING IT ALL TOGETHER

Using the sources above, along with what you have learned in class and in this chapter, write a short essay that analyzes Christian and Muslim views of the Crusades. How did they differ, and how were they similar? How did the Crusades help shape the understanding that Christians and Muslims had of each other?

Sources: (1) Peter Tudebode, *Historia de Hierosolymitano Itinere,* trans. and ed. John H. Hill and Laurita L. Hill (Philadelphia: American Philosophical Society, 1974), pp. 56–57; (2) Francesco Gabrieli, trans. and ed., *Arab Historians of the Crusades,* pp. 3–5. Translation © 1969 by Routledge & Kegan Paul Ltd. Published by the University of California Press. Used by permission of the University of California Press and by permission of Taylor & Francis Books UK; (3) Fulcher of Chartres, *A History of the Expedition to Jerusalem, 1095–1127,* trans. Frances Rita Ryan and ed. Harold S. Fink (Knoxville: University of Tennessee, 1969), pp. 121–122; (4) Gabrieli, *Arab Historians of the Crusades,* pp. 147, 150, 154, 155, 156, 157–158, 162.

checking the power of the nobility and creating a stronger financial base for the monarchy.

In eastern Europe, the German emperor Otto I planted a string of dioceses along his northern and eastern frontiers, hoping to pacify the newly conquered Slavs. German nobles built castles and ruthlessly crushed revolts by Slavic peoples, sometimes using the language of crusade to describe their actions. Albert the Bear, for example, a German noble, proclaimed a crusade against the Slavs and invited German knights to colonize conquered territories, just as earlier the French king had used French knights to crush the Albigensians. A military order of German knights founded in Palestine, the Teutonic (too-TAH-nihk) Knights, moved their operations to eastern Europe and waged wars against the pagan Prussians in the Baltic region, again terming these "crusades." After 1230, from a base in Poland, they established a new Christian territory, Prussia, and gradually the entire eastern shore of the Baltic came under their hegemony.

The church also moved into central Europe, first in Bohemia in the tenth century and from there into Poland and Hungary in the eleventh. In the twelfth and thirteenth centuries, thousands of settlers poured into eastern Europe. These immigrants were German in descent, name, language, and law. Larger towns such as Kraków and Riga engaged in long-distance trade and gradually grew into large urban centers.

Christendom

Through the actions of the Roman emperors Constantine and Theodosius (see Chapter 7), Christianity became in some ways a state as well as a religion. Early medieval writers began to use the word **Christendom** to refer to this Christian realm. Sometimes notions of Christendom were linked directly to specific states, such as Charlemagne's empire and the Holy Roman Empire. More often, however, Christendom was vague, a sort of loose sense of the body of all people who were Christian. When the pope called for holy war against the Muslims, for example, he spoke not only of the retaking of Jerusalem, but also of the defense of Christendom. When missionaries, officials, and soldiers took Christianity into the Iberian Peninsula, Scandinavia, or the Baltic region, they understood their actions as aimed at the expansion of Christendom.

From the point of view of popes such as Gregory VII and Innocent III, Christendom was a unified hierarchy with the papacy at the top. They pushed for uniformity of religious worship and campaigned continually for use of the same religious service, the Roman liturgy in Latin, in all countries and places. They forbade vernacular Christian rituals or those that differed in their pattern of worship. Under Innocent III papal directives and papal legates flowed to all parts of Europe. Twelve hundred church officials obediently came to Rome from the borderlands as well as the heartland for the Fourth Lateran Council of 1215.

As we have seen in this chapter, however, not everyone had the same view. Kings and emperors may have accepted the Roman liturgy in their lands, but they had their own ideas of the way power should operate in Christendom, even if this brought them into conflict with the papacy. They remained loyal to Christendom as a concept, but they had a profoundly different idea about how it should be structured and who could best defend it. The battles in the High Middle Ages between popes and kings and between Christians and Muslims were signs of how deeply religion had replaced tribal, political, and ethnic structures as the essence of Western culture.

NOTES

1. D. C. Douglas and G. E. Greenaway, eds., *English Historical Documents*, vol. 2 (London: Eyre & Spottiswoode, 1961), p. 853.
2. *Hrosvithae Liber Tertius, a Text with Translation*, ed. and trans. Mary Bernardine Bergman (Covington, Ky.: The Sisters of Saint Benedict, 1943), p. 45.
3. J. Johns, *Arabic Administration in Norman Sicily: The Royal Dīwān* (New York: Cambridge University Press, 2002), p. 293.
4. H. T. Riley, ed., *Memorials of London* (London: Longmans Green, 1868).
5. Honorius of Autun, "Elucidarium sive Dialogus," vol. 172, col. 1148.

■ **Christendom** The term used by early medieval writers to refer to the realm of Christianity.

LOOKING BACK LOOKING AHEAD

The High Middle Ages were a time when kings, emperors, and popes expanded their powers and created financial and legal bureaucracies to support those powers. With political expansion and stability came better communication of information, more uniform legal systems, and early financial institutions. Nobles remained the dominant social group, but as monarchs developed new institutions, their kingdoms began to function more like modern states than disorganized territories. Popes made the church more independent of lay control, established the papal curia and a separate system of canon law, approved new religious orders that provided spiritual and social services, and developed new ways of raising revenue. They supported the expansion of Christianity in southern, northern, and eastern Europe and proclaimed a series of Crusades against Muslims to extend still further the boundaries of a Christendom under their control.

Many of the systems of the High Middle Ages expanded in later centuries and are still in existence today: the financial department of the British government remains the Exchequer; the legal systems of Britain and many former British colonies (including the United States) are based on common law; the pope is still elected by the college of cardinals and assisted by the papal curia; the Roman Catholic, Eastern Orthodox, and Anglican Churches still operate law courts that make rulings based on canon law. These systems also contained the seeds of future problems, however, for wealthier nations could sustain longer wars, independent popes could more easily abuse their power, and leaders who espoused crusading ideology could justify the enslavement or extermination of whole peoples.

Despite the long-lived impact of the growth of centralized political and ecclesiastical power — for good or ill — most people who lived during the high medieval period did not have direct experience of centralized institutions. Kings and popes sent tax collectors, judges, and sometimes soldiers, but they themselves remained far away. For most people, what went on closer to home in their families and local communities was far more important.

Make Connections

Think about the larger developments and continuities within and across chapters.

1. What similarities and differences do you see between the institutions and laws established by medieval rulers and those of Roman and Byzantine emperors (Chapters 6 and 7)?

2. What factors over the centuries enabled the Christian Church to become the most powerful and wealthy institution in Europe, and what problems did this create?

3. How would you compare the privileges and roles of medieval nobles with those of earlier hereditary elites, such as those of ancient Mesopotamia and Egypt (Chapter 1) or the patricians of republican Rome (Chapter 5)?

⁹ REVIEW & EXPLORE

Identify Key Terms

Identify and explain the significance of each item below.

Domesday Book (p. 252)

primogeniture (p. 253)

Holy Roman Empire (p. 255)

reconquista (p. 258)

common law (p. 259)

Magna Carta (p. 259)

chivalry (p. 261)

simony (p. 265)

college of cardinals (p. 265)

excommunication (p. 265)

canon law (p. 267)

religious orders (p. 269)

friars (p. 272)

Crusades (p. 274)

indulgences (p. 274)

Christendom (p. 280)

Review the Main Ideas

Answer the focus questions from each section of the chapter.

◆ How did monarchs try to centralize political power? (p. 252)

◆ How did the administration of law evolve in this period? (p. 258)

◆ What were the roles of nobles, and how did they train for these? (p. 261)

◆ How did the papacy reform the church, and what were the reactions to these efforts? (p. 265)

◆ What roles did monks, nuns, and friars play in medieval society? (p. 269)

◆ What were the causes, course, and consequences of both the Crusades and the broader expansion of Christianity? (p. 274)

Suggested Reading and Media Resources

BOOKS

◆ Bartlett, Robert. *England Under the Norman and Angevin Kings, 1075–1225.* 2000. An excellent synthesis of social, cultural, and political history in highly readable prose.

◆ Edgington, Susan B., and Sarah Lambert, eds. *Gendering the Crusades.* 2002. Articles that look at the roles of men and women.

◆ Holt, J. C. *Magna Carta,* 2d ed. 1992. The authoritative study of the Magna Carta.

◆ Kaeuper, Richard W. *Chivalry and Violence in Medieval Europe.* 2006. Examines the role chivalry played in promoting violent disorder.

◆ Karras, Ruth M. *From Boys to Men: Formations of Masculinity in Late Medieval Europe.* 2002. Explores the way boys of different social groups were trained in what it meant to be a man; designed for students.

◆ Lambert, Malcolm. *Medieval Heresy: Popular Movements from the Gregorian Reform to the Reformation,* 3d ed. 2000. Analyzes the development and suppression of heresy over several centuries.

◆ Lawrence, C. H. *Medieval Monasticism: Forms of Religious Life in Western Europe in the Middle Ages.* 1988. Provides a solid introduction to monastic life as it was practiced.

◆ Madden, Thomas. *The New Concise History of the Crusades.* 2005. A highly readable brief survey by the pre-eminent American scholar of the Crusades.

◆ Moore, R. I. *The Formation of a Persecuting Society.* 1990. Sets the Inquisition and medieval heresy within a broad cultural, social, and political context.

◆ Newman, Barbara. *Voice of the Living Light: Hildegard of Bingen and Her World.* 1998. A book designed for general readers that places the medieval mystic within her social, intellectual, and political contexts.

◆ O'Callaghan, Joseph. *Reconquest and Crusade in Medieval Spain.* 2004. A broad survey that situates the Spanish reconquista within the context of crusading efforts.

- Rubin, Miri. *Gentile Tales: The Narrative Assault on Late Medieval Jews*. 2004. Explores the way that stories that were spread about Jews contributed to violence against them.

- Tyerman, Christopher. *Fighting for Christendom: Holy War and the Crusades*. 2005. Assesses the impact of the Crusades on modern times.

DOCUMENTARIES

- *Battle Castle* (Parallax, 2012). A six-part interactive documentary, first shown on Canadian television, with an accompanying Web site and computer game, that examines sieges and battles involving six formidable castles in Syria, France, Spain, Wales, Poland, and England. Reflects high production values and excellent scholarship.

FEATURE FILMS

- *Becket* (Peter Glenville, 1964). Richard Burton stars as Thomas Becket and Peter O'Toole as King Henry II of England in a widely acclaimed film that focuses on the conflict between the two and the growth of royal power.

- *Braveheart* (Mel Gibson, 1995). Loosely based on the story of the thirteenth-century Scottish nobleman William Wallace, this historical epic regularly shows up on lists of best medieval films (for its battle scenes) and worst medieval films (for its historical inaccuracy).

- *The Lion in Winter* (Anthony Harvey, 1968) (Andrey Konchalovskiy, 2003). Two award-winning film versions of the same play, centering on the intense and hostile relationships among Henry II, his wife Eleanor of Aquitaine, and their sons. The 1968 version stars Katharine Hepburn and Peter O'Toole, and the 2003 version stars Glenn Close and Patrick Stewart.

- *Vision: From the Life of Hildegard von Bingen* (Margarethe von Trotta, 2010). A German film, with English subtitles, that focuses on the famed twelfth-century Benedictine nun, mystic, composer, and philosopher. Shot on location in the convent of Bingen and the surrounding countryside.

WEB SITES

- *De Re Militari*. The official site of the Society for the Study of Medieval Military History, with primary sources, articles, dissertations, and other resources for the study of military actions, technology, and topics from the fall of Rome to the early seventeenth century. **deremilitari.org/**

- *Monastic Matrix*. A database site designed to make available all existing data about nuns and other women in religious communities in Christian Europe between 400 and 1600. Organized thematically and very easy to use. **monasticmatrix.osu.edu/**

- *Medievalists.Net*. This medieval-oriented blog provides news, articles, videos, reviews, and general information about the Middle Ages and medieval society. **www.medievalists.net**

10

Life in Villages and Cities of the High Middle Ages

1000–1300

Kings, emperors, nobles, and their officials created political and legal institutions that structured many aspects of life in the High Middle Ages, but ordinary people typically worked and lived without paying much attention to the political developments that took place at faraway centers of power. Similarly, the conflicts between popes and secular leaders were dramatic, but for most people religion was primarily a matter of joining with neighbors and family members in rituals to express beliefs, thanks, and hopes.

While the routines of medieval life followed familiar rhythms for centuries, this does not mean that life in the High Middle Ages was unchanging. Agricultural improvements such as better plows and water mills increased the amount and quality of food, and the population grew. Relative security and the increasing food supply allowed for the growth and development of towns and a revival of long-distance trade. Some urban merchants and bankers became as wealthy as great nobles. Trade brought in new ideas as well as merchandise, and cities developed into intellectual and cultural centers. The university, a new type of educational institution, came into being, providing advanced training in theology, medicine, and law. Traditions and values were spread orally and in written form through poems, stories, and songs. Gothic cathedrals, where people saw beautiful stained-glass windows and listened to complex music, were physical manifestations of medieval people's deep faith and pride in their own community. ∎

AM CRISTI · VI TI

CHAPTER PREVIEW

Life in the High Middle Ages
In this detail from a magnificent gold mosaic in the ceiling of the Basilica of Saint Clement in Rome, made in the twelfth century, a woman feeds her chickens. Scenes from everyday life often feature in the margins of paintings, mosaics, and books, and provide information about the lives of ordinary people that is unavailable elsewhere. (Detail from the mosaic *The Triumph of the Cross*, Basilica of St. Clement, Rome, Italy/De Agostini Picture Library/Gianni Dagli Orti/ Bridgeman Images)

Village Life

FOCUS QUESTION *What was village life like in medieval Europe?*

The vast majority of people in medieval Europe were peasants who lived in small villages and rarely traveled very far, but since villagers did not perform what were considered "noble" deeds, the aristocratic monks and clerics who wrote the records that serve as historical sources did not spend time or precious writing materials on the peasantry. When common people were mentioned, it was usually with contempt or in terms of the services and obligations they owed. There were exceptions. In the early twelfth century Honorius, a monk and teacher at the monastery of Autun, wrote: "What do you say about the agricultural classes? Most of them will be saved because they live simply and feed God's people by means of their sweat."[1] Today's scholars are far more interested than were their medieval predecessors in the lives of ordinary people, however, and are using archaeological, artistic, and material sources to fill in details that are rarely mentioned in written documents.

Slavery, Serfdom, and Upward Mobility

Honorius lumps together everyone who worked the land, but in fact there were many levels of peasants ranging from outright slaves to free but poor peasants to very rich farmers. The number of slaves who worked the land declined steadily in the High Middle Ages, and those who remained tended to live with wealthier peasant families or with lords. Most rural people in western Europe during this period were serfs rather than slaves, though the distinction between slave and serf was not always clear. Both lacked freedom and both were subject to the will of one person, the manorial lord. Serfs remained bound to the land when their lords died, but unlike slaves they could not be bought and sold outright.

Most serfs worked small plots of land; in addition, all serfs were required to provide a certain number of days of labor a week — more in planting and harvest seasons — on a lord's land. Serfs were also often obliged to pay fees on common occurrences, such as marriage or the inheritance of land from one generation to the next.

Serfdom was a hereditary condition. A person born a serf was likely to die a serf, though many serfs did secure their freedom. As money became more widely available and widely used, some serfs bought their freedom. Some gained it when manorial lords organized groups of villagers to cut down forests or fill in swamps and marshes to make more land available for

farming. A serf could clear a patch of fen or forestland, make it productive, and, through prudent saving, buy more land and eventually purchase freedom. Serfs who migrated longer distances, such as German peasants who moved eastward into Slavic lands, were often granted a reduction in labor services as a reward. Thus both internal and external frontier lands in the High Middle Ages provided some opportunities for upward mobility.

The Manor

Most peasants, free and serf, lived in family groups in small villages. One or more villages and the land surrounding them made up a manor controlled by a noble lord or a church official such as a bishop, abbot, or abbess. Peasant dwellings were clumped together, with the fields stretching out beyond. Most villages had a church. In some the lord's large residence was right next to the small peasant houses, while in others the lord lived in a castle or manor house separate from the village. Manors varied greatly in size; some contained a number of villages, and some were very small.

The arable land of the manor was divided between the lord and the peasantry, with the lord's portion known as the demesne (dih-MAYN), or home farm. The manor usually also held pasture or meadowland for the grazing of cattle, sheep, and sometimes goats and often had some forestland as well. Forests were valuable resources, providing wood, ash, and resin for a variety of purposes. Forests were also used for feeding pigs, cattle, and domestic animals on nuts, roots, and wild berries.

Lords generally appointed officials, such as bailiffs, to oversee the legal and business operations of their manors, collect taxes and fees, and handle disputes. Villages in many parts of Europe also developed institutions of self-government to handle issues such as crop rotation, and villagers themselves chose additional officials such as constables, jurors, and ale-tasters. Women had no official voice in running the village, but they did buy, sell, and hold land independently, especially as widows who headed households. In areas of Europe where men left seasonally or more permanently in search of work elsewhere, women played a larger decision-making role, though they generally did not hold official positions. (See "Thinking Like a Historian: Social and Economic Relations in Medieval English Villages," page 290.)

Manors did not represent the only form of medieval rural economy. In parts of Germany and the Netherlands and in much of southern France, free independent farmers owned land outright, free of rents and service obligations. In Scandinavia the soil was so poor and the climate so harsh that people tended to live on widely scattered farms rather than in villages.

Work

The peasants' work was typically divided according to gender. Men cleared new land, plowed, and cared for large animals; women cared for small animals, spun yarn, and prepared food. Both sexes planted and harvested, though often there were gender-specific tasks within these major undertakings.

Once children were able to walk, they helped their parents in the hundreds of chores that had to be done. Small children collected eggs if the family had chickens or gathered twigs and sticks for firewood. As they grew older, children had more responsible tasks, such as weeding the family's vegetable garden, milking the cows, and helping with the planting or harvesting.

In many parts of Europe, medieval farmers employed the **open-field system**, a pattern that differs sharply from modern farming practices. In the open-field system, the arable land of a manor was divided into two or three fields without hedges or fences to mark the individual holdings of the lord, serfs, and free men. The village as a whole decided what would be planted in each field, rotating the crops according to tradition and need. Some fields would be planted with crops such as wheat, rye, peas, or barley for human consumption, some with oats or other crops for both animals and humans, and some left unworked or fallow to allow the soil to rejuvenate. In addition, legume crops such as peas and beans helped the soil rebuild nutrients and also increased the villagers' protein consumption. In most areas with open-field agriculture, the holdings farmed by any one family did not consist of a whole field but consisted, instead, of strips in many fields. If one strip held by a family yielded little, those in different fields might be more bountiful. Families worked their own land and the lord's, but also cooperated with other families if they needed help, particularly during harvest time. This meant that all shared in any disaster as well as in any large harvest.

Meteorologists think that a slow but steady retreat of polar ice occurred between the ninth and eleventh centuries, and Europe experienced a significant warming trend from 1050 to 1300. The mild winters and dry summers that resulted helped increase agricultural output throughout Europe, particularly in the north.

The tenth and eleventh centuries also witnessed a number of agricultural improvements, especially in the development of mechanisms that replaced or aided human labor. Mills driven by wind and water power dramatically reduced the time and labor required to grind grain, crush seeds for oil, and carry out other tasks. This change had a significant impact on women's productivity. In the ancient world, slaves had been responsible for grinding the grain for bread; as slavery was replaced by serfdom, grinding became women's work. When water- and wind-driven mills were introduced into an area, women were freed from the task of grinding grain and could turn to other tasks, such as raising animals, working in gardens or vineyards, and raising and preparing flax to make linen. They could also devote more time to spinning yarn, which was the bottleneck in cloth production, as each weaver needed at least six spinners. Thus the spread of wind and water power indirectly contributed to an increase in cloth production in medieval Europe.

Another change, which came in the early twelfth century, was a significant increase in the production of iron. Much of this was used for weapons and

Chronology

1050–1300	Steady rise in population; period of milder climate
ca. 1100	Merchant guilds become rich and powerful in many cities; artisans begin to found craft guilds
1100s	Hospitals and other homes for the sick begin appearing
1100–1300	Height of construction of cathedrals in Europe
1160s	Silver mines opened in Germany, allowing for more coinage
ca. 1200	Founding of first universities
1215	Fourth Lateran Council orders Jews and Muslims to wear distinctive clothing
1225–1274	Life of Thomas Aquinas; *Summa Theologica*
1241	Contract between Lübeck and Hamburg, first in the Hanseatic League
ca. 1300	Bill of exchange becomes most common method of commercial payment in western Europe
1300s	Clocks in general use throughout Europe

■ **open-field system** System in which the arable land of a manor was divided into two or three fields without hedges or fences to mark individual holdings.

Harvesting Hay   A peasant with his socks rolled down to stay cool mows hay with a long scythe, while in the background a mill along a stream stands ready to grind grain or carry out other tasks. This illustration comes from a book of hours made in France in the early fifteenth century, probably for the duke of Bedford. Books of hours were devotional books with psalms, prayers, and calendars of church holidays, sometimes lavishly decorated. They often included cycles of months that linked seasonal rural activities to signs of the zodiac; here Cancer the crab shows that this is June. (From the *Bedford Hours*, 1414–1423, Bedford Master Workshop [fl. ca. 1430–1465]/British Library, London, UK/© British Library Board. All Rights Reserved/Bridgeman Images)

armor, but it also filled a growing demand in agriculture. Iron was first used for plowshares (the part of the plow that cuts a deep furrow), and then for pitchforks, spades, and axes. Harrows—cultivating instruments with heavy teeth that broke up and smoothed the soil after plowing—began to have iron instead of wooden teeth, making them more effective and less likely to break. Peasants needed money to buy iron implements from village blacksmiths, and they increasingly also needed money to pay their obligations to their lords. To get the cash they needed, they sold whatever surplus they produced in nearby towns, transporting it there in wagons with iron parts.

In central and northern Europe, peasants made increasing use of heavy wheeled iron plows pulled by teams of oxen to break up the rich, clay-filled soil common there, and agricultural productivity increased. Further technological improvements allowed horses to be used for plowing as well as oxen. The development of the padded horse collar that rested on the horse's shoulders and was attached to the load by shafts meant that the animal could put its entire weight into the task of pulling. Iron horseshoes prevented horses' hooves from splitting, and better harness systems allowed horses to be hitched together

in teams. The use of horses spread in the twelfth century because their greater speed brought greater efficiency to farming and reduced the amount of human labor involved. Horses were also used to haul goods to markets, where peasants sold any excess vegetables, grain, and animals.

By modern standards, medieval agricultural yields were very low, but there was striking improvement between the fifth and the thirteenth centuries. Increased output had a profound impact on society, improving Europeans' health, commerce, industry, and general lifestyle. More food meant that fewer people suffered from hunger and malnourishment and that devastating famines were rarer. Higher yields brought more food for animals as well as people, and the amount of meat that people ate increased slightly. A better diet had an enormous impact on women's lives in particular. More food meant increased body fat, which increased fertility, and more meat—which provided iron—meant that women were less anemic and less subject to disease. Some researchers believe that it was during the High Middle Ages that Western women began to outlive men. Improved opportunities also encouraged people to marry somewhat earlier, which meant larger families and further population growth.

Home Life

In western and central Europe, villages were generally made up of small houses for individual families. Households consisted of a married couple, their children (including stepchildren), and perhaps one or two other relatives. Some homes contained only an unmarried person, a widow, or several unmarried people living together. In southern and eastern Europe, extended families were more likely to live in the same household.

The size and quality of peasants' houses varied according to their relative prosperity, which usually depended on the amount of land held. Poorer peasants lived in windowless cottages built of wood and clay or wattle (poles interwoven with branches or reeds) and thatched with straw. These cottages consisted of one large room that served as both kitchen and living quarters. A shed attached to the house provided storage for tools and shelter for animals. Prosperous peasants added rooms; some wealthy peasants in the early fourteenth century had two-story houses with separate bedrooms for parents and children. For most people, however, living space—especially living space close enough to a fire to feel some warmth in cold weather—was cramped, dark, smoky, and smelly, with animals and people both sharing tight quarters, sometimes with each other.

Every house had a small garden and an outbuilding. Onions, garlic, turnips, and carrots were grown and stored through the winter. Cabbage was shredded, salted, and turned into kraut for storage. The mainstay of the diet for peasants—and for all other classes—was bread. It was a hard, black substance made of barley, millet, and oats, rarely of expensive wheat, which they were more likely to use to pay their taxes and fees to the lord than for their own bread. Most households did not have ovens, which were expensive to build and posed a fire danger; their bread was baked in communal ovens or purchased from households that specialized in bread-baking. The main meal was often bread and a thick soup of vegetables and grains eaten around noon. Peasants ate vegetables not because they appreciated their importance for good health but because there was usually little else available. Animals were too valuable to be used for food on a regular basis, but weaker animals were often slaughtered in the fall so that they did not need to be fed through the winter. Their meat was salted for preservation and eaten on great feast days such as Christmas and Easter.

The diet of people with access to a river, lake, or stream would be supplemented with fish, which could be eaten fresh or preserved by salting. People living close to the sea gathered shellfish. Many places had severe laws against hunting and trapping in the forests. Deer, wild boars, and other game were reserved for the king and nobles. These laws were flagrantly violated, however, and rabbits and wild game often found their way to peasants' tables.

Medieval households were not self-sufficient but bought cloth, metal, leather goods, and even some food in village markets. They also bought ale, the universal drink of the common people in northern Europe. Women dominated in the production of ale. Ale not only provided needed calories but also provided some relief from the difficult, monotonous labor that filled people's lives. Medieval men and women often drank heavily. Brawls and violent fights were frequent at taverns, and English judicial records of the thirteenth century reveal a surprisingly large number of "accidental" deaths in which people drowned, got lost, or fell from horses, often, as the court records say, "coming from an ale," meaning that the victims were probably drunk.

The steady rise in population between the mid-eleventh and fourteenth centuries was primarily the result of warmer climate, increased food supply, and a reduction of violence with growing political stability, rather than dramatic changes in health care. Most treatment of illness was handled by home remedies handed down orally or perhaps through a cherished handwritten family herbal, cookbook, or household guide. Treatments were often mixtures of herbal remedies, sayings, specific foods, prayers, amulets, and ritual healing activities. People suffering from wounds, skin diseases, or broken bones sometimes turned to barber-surgeons. For internal ailments, people consulted apothecaries, who suggested and mixed compounds taken internally or applied orally as a salve or ointment; these were generally mixtures of plants, minerals, and other natural products.

Beginning in the twelfth century in England, France, and Italy, the clergy, noble men and women, and newly rich merchants also established institutions to care for the sick or for those who could not take care of themselves. Within city walls they built hospitals, where care was provided for those with chronic diseases that were not contagious, poor expectant mothers, the handicapped, people recovering from injuries, and foundling children. Outside city walls they built leprosariums or small hospices for people with leprosy and other contagious diseases. Such institutions might be staffed by members of religious orders or by laymen and laywomen who were paid for their work.

Childbirth and Child Abandonment

The most dangerous period of life for any person, peasant or noble, was infancy and early childhood. In normal years perhaps as many as one-third of all children died before age five from illness, malnutrition,

Social and Economic Relations in Medieval English Villages

Medieval villages have often been portrayed as squalid hamlets where downtrodden peasants lived in an unchanging equality of misery under the harsh control of a lord. Do sources about actual rural life support this view of village social and economic relations, do they refute it, or do they make it more complex?

1 **Extent of the village of Alwalton, 1279.** Extents were surveys taken by landholders that listed the land and obligations of each household in a village.

〜The abbot of Peterborough holds the manor at Alwalton and village from the lord king directly. . . . Hugh Miller holds 1 virgate [about 25–30 acres] of land in villeinage by paying thence to the abbot 3 s. 1 d. [3 shillings, 1 denarius, or pence; there were 12 pence per shilling]. Likewise the same Hugh works through the year except 1 week at Christmas, 1 week at Easter, and 1 at Whitsuntide that is in each week 3 days, each day with 1 man, and in autumn each day with 2 men, performing the said works at the will of the said abbot as in plowing and other work. Likewise he gives 1 bushel of wheat for seed and 18 sheaves of oats for foddercorn. Likewise he gives 3 hens and 1 cock yearly and 5 eggs at Easter. Likewise he does carrying to Peterborough and to Jakele and nowhere else, at the will of the said abbot. Likewise if he sells a brood mare in his courtyard for 6 s. or more, he shall give to the said abbot 4 d., and if for less he shall give nothing. He gives also merchet [a payment when his daughters marry] and heriot [a payment when a family member dies] and is taxed at the feast of St. Michael, at the will of the said abbot. There are also 17 other villeins . . . paying and doing in all things, each for himself, to the said abbot yearly just as the said Hugh Miller. . . .

Henry, son of the miller, holds a cottage with a croft which contains 1 rood [¼ acre, a square about 100 feet on a side], paying thence yearly to the said abbot 2 s. Likewise he works for 3 days in carrying hay and in other works at the will of the abbot, each day with 1 man and in autumn 1 day in cutting grain with 1 man. . . . Likewise William Drake holds a cottage with a croft which contains half a rood [⅛ acre], paying to the abbot 6 d.; and he works just as the said Henry. There are also 18 other crofters . . . doing all things just as the said Henry.

2 **Extent of the manor of Bernehorne, 1307.**

〜John of Cayworth holds a house and 30 acres of land and owes yearly 2 s., at Easter and Michaelmas; and he owes a cock and two hens at Christmas, of the value of 4 d.

And he ought to harrow for 2 days at the Lenten sowing with one man and his own horse and his own harrow; the value of the work being 4 d.; and he is to receive from the lord on each day 3 meals, of the value of 5 d., and then his food will be at a loss of 1 d. Thus his harrowing is of no value to the service of the lord.

And he ought to carry the manure of the lord for 2 days with one cart, with his own 2 oxen, the value of the work being 8 d.; and he is to receive from the lord each day 3 meals of the price as above. And thus the service is worth 3 d. clear.

And he shall find one man for 2 days of mowing the meadow of the lord, who can mow, by estimation 1 acre and a half, the value of the mowing of an acre being 6 d.: the sum is therefore 9 d. and he is to receive each day 3 meals of the value given above; and thus that mowing is worth 4 d. clear. . . .

And he ought to carry the hay of the lord with a cart and 3 animals of his own . . . and in autumn carry beans and oats for 2 days with a cart . . . and carry wood from the woods of the lord as far as the manor house for two days in summer. . . . And he ought to find 1 man for 2 days to cut heath [for fuel] . . . and carry the heath that he has cut . . . and carry to Battle [a nearby town] twice in the summer season, each time a half a load of grain.

ANALYZING THE EVIDENCE

1. What types of obligations did peasants owe their lord? What types of obligations did they have to each other? How were these enforced?
2. What concerns of the villagers themselves emerge in the bylaws in Source 4? What do these concerns suggest about village society?
3. Are all villagers equal? What social and economic differences do you see among them?
4. What evidence do you see of growing commercialization, such as money, wage labor, market exchange, and considerations of market value?

3 **Cart being pulled and pushed up a hill.** This marginal illustration comes from the *Luttrell Psalter,* an illuminated manuscript commissioned by Sir Geoffrey Luttrell (1276–1345), the lord of a manor in Lincolnshire, and made by scribes and artists whose identity is unknown.

(From the *Luttrell Psalter*, ca. 1325–1335, vellum/British Library, London, UK/© British Library Board. All Rights Reserved/Bridgeman Images)

4 **Village bylaws, Great Horwood, 1306 and 1319.** Villagers themselves set rules regarding activities that they saw as problems. ("Gleaning" was picking up small bits of grain that had fallen from the stalks, an activity reserved for the elderly, small children, and ill or handicapped people.)

No one shall accept any outsider as a gleaner in autumn nor any man or woman to glean who is able to earn a penny a day for reaping if he finds someone who wishes to hire him.

Nor shall anyone pay in the field with whole sheaves, only handfuls of grain.

Nor shall anyone reap or cart except by day.

Nor shall anyone allow his calves or foals to go into the common fields of grain.

Nor shall anyone gather straw in the fields unless it be each from his own land. . . .

And if anyone is found guilty he shall pay the lord 4 d.

5 **Court records from the village of Broughton, 1286.** Several times a year villagers gathered for court proceedings during which the legal and financial affairs of both the lord and village were handled; this is a small part of the records from one day in one village.

John Nuncium le Mung [was fined] 12 d. because he did not send to the first day of service for the lord as many men as he had at his own work. . . .

William de Broughton is compelled to answer at the next court for the damage done by his two horses in the lord's peas.

Richard de Broughton [is compelled to answer] because he did not come to work for the lord in ditching. . . .

Alice Robynes is compelled to pay 6 d. for her geese damaging the lord's grain. . . .

Thomas Prat acknowledges that he is in debt to Agnes Gylot for goods to the value of 6 d. Therefore he shall make satisfaction to her for the aforesaid 6 d.

The chief pledges [male villagers responsible to know what was going on] say that the bailiff of the lord abbot made two pits in the town, to its nuisance. Therefore the bailiff is ordered to put them right. . . . And they say that Hugh Knyt harbored a strange woman who is not profitable to the town. Fined 6 d. . . . And they say that Robert Strypling pastured the grass of the neighbors by night. Fined 12 d. . . . And they say that the wife of Thomas le Hund was a gleaner against the common statute of the town. Fined 12 d. . . . And they say that Reginald Gylbert overused the pasture with twenty sheep. Fined 12 d. And they say that William Kepline paid with sheaves in the field in autumn contrary to the common statute of the town. Fined 12 d.

PUTTING IT ALL TOGETHER

Using the sources above, along with what you have learned in class and in this chapter and Chapters 8 and 9, write a short essay that analyzes social and economic relations in an English village in the High Middle Ages. To what extent is the traditional view of village life as uniformly oppressive warranted? If you believe that the traditional view is not accurate, what would be a better description?

Sources: (1, 2) *Translations and Reprints from the Original Sources of European History,* vol. 3, no. 5 (Philadelphia: University of Pennsylvania Department of History, 1897), pp. 4–7, 10–11; (4, 5) Warren O. Ault, *Open Field Farming in Medieval England: A Study of Village By-Laws* (London: George Allen and Unwin, 1972), pp. 86, 89, 155–159.

LIVING IN THE PAST
Child's Play

Historians used to paint a grim picture of medieval childhood. Childhood, they argued, was not recognized as a distinct stage in life until at least the late eighteenth century, and children were raised harshly or received little parental attention because so many died. These views were derived largely from advice about raising children provided by priests and educators who advocated strict discipline and warned against coddling, and from portraits of children that showed them dressed as little adults.

This bleak view has been relieved more recently by scholars using sources that reveal how children were actually treated. They have discovered that many parents showed great affection for their children and experienced deep grief when they died young. Parents left children to monasteries not because they were indifferent, but because they hoped thereby to ensure them a better material and spiritual future. Parents made toys for children: balls, dolls, rattles, boats, hobbyhorses, tops, and many other playthings. They tried to protect their children with religious amulets and pilgrimages to special shrines and sang them lullabies. Even practices that to us may seem cruel, such as tight swaddling, were motivated by a concern for the child's safety and health at a time when most households had open fires, domestic animals wandered freely, and mothers and older siblings engaged in labor-intensive work that prevented them from continually watching a toddler.

A mother carrying her tightly swaddled infant in a cradle, from a marginal illustration in a fourteenth-century French book of poetry. (Marginalia from *Les voeux du paon*, by Jacques de Longuyon, Northern France or Flanders, possibly Tournai, ca. 1350. MS. G.24, f. 34/The Pierpont Morgan Library, New York, NY, USA/Art Resource, NY)

QUESTIONS FOR ANALYSIS

1. In the illustration of the mother and infant, how does the manuscript illuminator portray the relationship between parent and child? Does this support or challenge the notion that medieval parents treated their children coldly?

2. How do the toys shown here prepare children for their later roles in life? Do these seem to be toys for nobles or for less elite children?

3. How does the material from which these toys were made contribute to the fact that few have survived? What else might account for this? (To answer the latter question, think about your own toys: which ones were in good shape when you outgrew them, and which were not?)

An assortment of medieval toys, including a knight, a rattle, and miniature figurines. Most medieval children's toys have long vanished, and we know them only from paintings or written descriptions, but a few have survived. (toy knight: Museum of London, UK/The Art Archive at Art Resource, NY; rattle: Musée de Normandie–Ville de Caen; figurine: National Museum of Iceland, Reykjavik, Iceland/Werner Forman/Art Resource, NY)

and accidents, and this death rate climbed to more than half in years with plagues, droughts, or famines. However, once people reached adulthood, many lived well into their fifties and sixties.

Childbirth was dangerous for mothers as well as infants. Village women helped one another through childbirth, and women who were more capable acquired midwifery skills. In larger towns and cities, such women gradually developed into professional midwives who were paid for their services and who trained younger women as apprentices. For most women, however, childbirth was handled by female friends and family.

Many infants were abandoned by parents or guardians, who left their children somewhere, sold them, or legally gave authority over them to some other person or institution. Sometimes parents believed that someone of greater means or status might find the child and bring him or her up in better circumstances than they could provide. Christian parents gave their children to monasteries as religious acts, donating them to the service of God in the same way they might donate money. (See "Living in the Past: Child's Play," at left.)

Toward the end of his *Ecclesiastical History*, written when he was well into his sixties, Orderic Vitalis (ca. 1075–ca. 1140), a monk of the Norman abbey of Saint Evroul, explained movingly how he became a monk:

> And so, O glorious God, you didst inspire my father Odeleric to renounce me utterly and submit me in all things to thy governance. So, weeping, he gave me, a weeping child, into the care of the monk Reginald, and sent me away into exile for love of thee, and never saw me again. . . . I crossed the English channel and came into Normandy as an exile, unknown to all, knowing no one. . . . But thou didst suffer me through thy grace to find nothing but kindness among strangers. . . . The name of Vitalis was given me in place of my English name, which sounded harsh to the Normans.[2]

Orderic had no doubt that God wanted him to be a monk, but even half a century later he still remembered his grief. Orderic's father was a Norman priest, and his Anglo-Saxon mother perhaps gave him his "English" name. Qualms of conscience over clerical celibacy may have led Orderic's father to place his son in a monastery.

Donating a child to a monastery was common among the poor until about the year 1000, but less common in the next three hundred years, which saw relative prosperity for peasants. On the other hand, the incidence of noble parents giving their younger sons and daughters to religious houses increased dramatically. This resulted from and also reinforced the system of primogeniture, in which estates were passed intact to the eldest son instead of being divided among heirs (see Chapter 9). Monasteries provided noble younger sons and daughters with career opportunities, and their being thus disposed of removed them as contenders for family land.

Popular Religion

FOCUS QUESTION *How did religion shape everyday life in the High Middle Ages?*

Apart from the land, the weather, and local legal and social conditions, religion had the greatest impact on the daily lives of ordinary people in the High Middle Ages. Religious practices varied widely from country to country and even from province to province. But nowhere was religion a one-hour-a-week affair. Most people in medieval Europe were Christian, but there were small Jewish communities scattered in many parts of Europe, and Muslims lived in the Iberian Peninsula, Sicily, and other Mediterranean islands.

Christian Life in Medieval Villages

For Christians the village church was the center of community life—social, political, and economic, as well as religious—with the parish priest in charge of a host of activities. From the side of the church, he read orders and messages from royal and ecclesiastical authorities to his parishioners. The front of the church, typically decorated with scenes of the Last Judgment, was the background against which royal judges traveling on circuit disposed of civil and criminal cases. In busy cities such as London, business agreements were made in the square in front of the church or even inside the church itself.

Although church law placed the priest under the bishop's authority, the manorial lord appointed the priest. Rural priests were peasants and often worked in the fields with the people during the week. On Sundays and holy days, they put on a robe and celebrated mass, or Eucharist, the ceremony in which the priest consecrated bread and wine and distributed it to believers, in a re-enactment of Jesus's Last Supper. They recited the mass in Latin, a language that few commoners, sometimes including the priest himself, could understand. At least once a year villagers were expected to take part in the ceremony and eat the consecrated bread. This usually happened at Easter, after they had confessed their sins to the priest and been assigned a penance.

In everyday life people engaged in rituals and used language heavy with religious symbolism. Before planting, the village priest customarily went out and sprinkled the fields with water, symbolizing refreshment and life. Everyone participated in village processions to honor the saints and ask their protection. The entire calendar was filled with reference to events in the life of Jesus and his disciples, such as Christmas, Easter, and Pentecost. Scriptural references and proverbs dotted everyone's language. The English *good-bye*, the French *adieu*, and the Spanish *adios* all derive from words meaning "God be with you." The signs and symbols of Christianity were visible everywhere, but so, people believed, was the Devil, who lured them to evil deeds. In some medieval images and literature, the Devil is portrayed as black, an identification that shaped Western racial attitudes.

Saints and Sacraments

Along with days marking events in the life of Jesus, the Christian calendar was filled with saints' days. Veneration of the saints had been an important tool of Christian conversion since late antiquity (see Chapter 7), and the cult of the saints was a central feature of popular culture in the Middle Ages. People believed that the saints possessed supernatural powers that enabled them to perform miracles, and the saint became the special property of the locality in which his or her relics rested. In return for the saint's healing and support, peasants offered the saint prayers, loyalty, and gifts.

In the later Middle Ages popular hagiographies (ha-gee-AH-gruh-fees)—biographies of saints based on myths, legends, and popular stories—attributed specialized functions to the saints. Saint Elmo (ca. 300), who supposedly had preached unharmed during a thunder and lightning storm, became the patron of sailors. Saint Agatha (third century), whose breasts were torn with shears because she rejected the attentions of a powerful suitor, became the patron of wet nurses, women with breast difficulties, and bell-ringers (because of the resemblance of breasts to bells). Every occupation had a patron saint, as did cities and even realms.

How were saints chosen? Since the early days of Christianity, individuals whose exemplary virtue was proved by miracles had been venerated by laypeople. Church officials in Rome insisted that they had the exclusive right to determine sainthood, but ordinary people continued to declare people saints. Between 1185 and 1431 only seventy persons were declared saints at Rome, but hundreds of new saints were venerated across Europe. Some clergy preached against the veneration of saints' relics and called it idolatry, but their appeals had little effect.

The Virgin Mary, Christ's mother, was the most important saint. In the eleventh century theologians began to emphasize Mary's spiritual motherhood of all Christians. Special masses commemorated her, churches were built in her honor, and hymns and prayers to her multiplied. Villagers listened intently to sermons telling stories about her life and miracles. One favorite story told of a minstrel and acrobat inspired to perform tumbling feats in Mary's honor:

> [He performed] until from head to heel sweat stood upon him, drop by drop, as blood falls from meat turning on a hearth. . . . [Then] there came down from the heavens a Dame so glorious, that certainly no man had seen one so precious, nor so richly crowned. . . . Then the sweet and courteous Queen herself took a white napkin in her hand, and with it gently fanned her minstrel before the altar. . . . She blesses her minstrel with the sign of God.[3]

Statue of Saint Anne, the Virgin Mary, and the Christ Child   Nearly every church had at least one image of the Virgin Mary, the most important figure of Christian devotion in medieval Europe. In this thirteenth-century wooden sculpture, she is shown holding the infant Jesus, and is herself sitting on the lap of her mother, Anne. Statues such as this reinforced people's sense that the heavenly family was much like theirs, with grandparents who sometimes played important roles. (Museo Nazionale del Bargello, Florence, Italy/Scala/Art Resource, NY)

People reasoned that if Mary would even bless tumbling (a disreputable form of popular entertainment) as long as it was done with a reverent heart, she would certainly bless their lives of hard work and pious devotion even more.

Along with the veneration of saints, sacraments were an important part of religious practice. Twelfth-century theologians expanded on Saint Augustine's understanding of sacraments (see Chapter 7) and created an entire sacramental system. In 1215 the Fourth Lateran Council formally accepted seven sacraments (baptism, penance, the Eucharist, confirmation, marriage, priestly ordination, anointment of the dying). Medieval Christians believed that these seven sacraments brought God's grace, the divine assistance or help needed to lead a good Christian life and to merit salvation. Most sacraments had to be dispensed by a priest, although spouses officially administered the sacrament of marriage to each other, and laypeople could baptize a dying infant or anoint a dying person if no priest could be found. In this way, the sacramental system enhanced the authority of priests over people's lives, but did not replace strong personal devotion to the saints.

Muslims and Jews

The centrality of Christian ceremonies to daily life for most Europeans meant that those who did not participate were clearly marked as outsiders. Many Muslims left Spain as the Christian "reconquest" proceeded and left Sicily when this became a Christian realm (see Chapter 9), but others converted. In more isolated villages, people simply continued their Muslim rituals and practices, including abstaining from pork, reciting verses from the Qur'an, praying at specified times of the day, and observing Muslim holy days, though they might hide this from the local priest or visiting officials.

Islam was geographically limited in medieval Europe, but by the late tenth century Jews could be found in many areas, often brought in from other areas as clients of rulers to help with finance. There were Jewish communities in Italian and French cities and in the cities along the Rhine. Jewish dietary laws require meat to be handled in a specific way, so Jews had their own butchers; there were Jewish artisans in many other trades as well. Jews held weekly religious services on Saturday, the Sabbath, and celebrated their own annual cycle of holidays. Each of these holidays involved special prayers, services, and often foods, and many of them commemorated events from Jewish history, including various times when Jews had been rescued from captivity.

Jews could supply other Jews with goods and services, but rulers and city leaders increasingly restricted their trade with Christians to banking and money-lending. This enhanced Christian resentment, as did the ideology of holy war that accompanied the Crusades (see Chapter 9). Violence against Jews and restrictions on their activities increased further in much of Europe. Jews were expelled from England and later from France. However, Jews continued to live in the independent cities of the Holy Roman Empire and Italy, and some migrated eastward into new towns that were being established in Slavic areas.

Rituals of Marriage and Birth

Increasing suspicion and hostility marked relations between religious groups throughout the Middle Ages, but there were also important similarities in the ways Christians, Jews, and Muslims understood and experienced their religions. In all three traditions, every major life transition was marked by a ceremony that included religious elements.

Christian weddings might be held in the village church or at the church door, though among well-to-do families the ceremony took place in the house of the bride or bridegroom. A priest's blessing was often sought, though it was not essential to the marriage. Muslim weddings were also finalized by a contract between the bride and groom and were often overseen by a wedding official. Jewish weddings were guided by statements in Talmudic law that weddings were complete when the bride had entered the *chuppah*, which medieval Jewish authorities interpreted to mean a room in the groom's house.

In all three faiths, the wedding ceremony was followed by a wedding party that often included secular rituals. Some rituals symbolized the proper hierarchical relations between the spouses—such as placing the husband's shoe on the bedstead over the couple, symbolizing his authority—or were meant to ensure the couple's fertility—such as untying all the knots in the household, for it was believed that people possessing magical powers could tie knots to inhibit a man's reproductive power. All this came together in what was often the final event of a wedding: the religious official blessed the couple in their marriage bed, often with family and friends standing around or banging on pans, yelling, or otherwise making as much noise as possible to make fun of the couple's first sexual encounter. (Tying cans on the back of the car in which a couple leaves the wedding is a modern remnant of such rituals.)

The friends and family members had generally been part of the discussions, negotiations, and activities leading up to the marriage; marriage united two families and was far too important to leave up to two people alone. Among serfs the manorial lord's permission was often required, with a special fee required to obtain it. (This permission did not, as often alleged, give the lord the right to deflower the bride. Though lords certainly forced sex on female serfs, there is no evidence in any legal sources that lords had the "right of first night," the *jus primae noctis*.) The involvement of family and friends in choosing one's spouse might lead to conflict, but more often the wishes of the couple and their parents, kin, and community were quite similar: all hoped for marriages that provided economic security, honorable standing, and a good number of healthy children. The best marriages offered companionship, emotional support, and even love, but these were understood to grow out of the marriage, not necessarily precede it. Breaking up a marriage meant breaking up the basic production and consumption unit, a very serious matter. The church forbade divorce, and even among non-Christians marital dissolution by any means other than the death of one spouse was rare.

Wedding Door of the Cathedral in Strasbourg   Medieval cathedrals, such as this one from the thirteenth century, sometimes had a side door depicting a biblical story of ten young women who went to meet a bridegroom. Five of them wisely took extra oil for their lamps, while five foolishly did not (Matthew 25:1–13). In the story, which is a parable about being prepared for the end of the world, the foolish maidens were out of oil when the bridegroom arrived and missed the wedding feast. The "maidens' door" became a popular site for weddings, which were held right in front of it. (Paul M. R. Maeyaert/akg-images)

Most brides hoped to be pregnant soon after the wedding. Christian women hoping for children said special prayers to the Virgin Mary or her mother, Anne. Some wore amulets of amber, bone, or mistletoe, thought to increase fertility. Others repeated charms and verses they had learned from other women, or, in desperate cases, went on pilgrimages to make special supplications. Muslim and Jewish women wore small cases with sacred verses or asked for blessings from religious leaders. Women continued these prayers and rituals throughout pregnancy and childbirth, often combining religious traditions with folk beliefs. Women in southern France, for example, offered prayers for easy childbirth and healthy children to Saint Guinefort, a greyhound who had been mistakenly killed by his owner after saving the owner's child from a poisonous snake. The fact that Guinefort was a dog meant he could never become an official saint, but women saw him as a powerful and martyred protector of children.

Judaism, Christianity, and Islam all required women to remain separate from the community for a short time after childbirth and often had special ceremonies welcoming them back once this period was over. These rituals often included prayers, such as this one from the Christian ritual of thanksgiving and purification, called churching, which a woman celebrated six weeks after giving birth: "Almighty and everlasting God, who has freed this woman from the danger of bearing a child, consider her to be strengthened from every pollution of the flesh so that with a clean heart and pure mind she may deserve to enter into the bosom of our mother, the church, and make her devoted to Your service."[4]

Religious ceremonies also welcomed children into the community. Among Christian families, infants were baptized soon after they were born to ensure that they could enter Heaven. Midwives who delivered children who looked especially weak and sickly often baptized them in an emergency service. In normal baptisms, the women who had assisted the mother in the birth often carried the baby to church, where godparents vowed their support. Godparents were often close friends or relatives, but parents might also choose prominent villagers or even the local lord in the hope that he might later look favorably on the child and provide for him or her in some way.

Within Judaism, a boy was circumcised by a religious official and given his name in a ceremony on his eighth day of life. This *brit milah*, or "covenant of circumcision," was viewed as a reminder of the Covenant between God and Abraham described in Hebrew Scripture. Muslims also circumcised boys in a special ritual, though the timing varied from a few days after birth to adolescence.

Death and the Afterlife

Death was similarly marked by religious ceremonies, and among Europeans of all faiths death did not sever family obligations and connections. Christians called for a priest to perform the sacrament of extreme unction when they thought the hour of death was near. The priest brought holy water, holy oil, a crucifix, and a censer with incense, all objects regarded as having power over death and the sin related to it.

Once the person had died, the body was washed and dressed in special clothing—or a sack of plain cloth—and buried within a day or two. Family and friends joined in a funeral procession, marked by the ringing of church bells; sometimes extra women were hired so that the mourning and wailing were especially loud and intense, a sign of the family's devotion. The wealthy were sometimes buried inside the church—in the walls, under the floor, or under the building itself in a crypt—but most people were buried in the churchyard or a cemetery close by. At the graveside, the priest asked for God's grace for the soul of the deceased and also asked that soul to "rest in peace." This final request was made not only for the benefit of the dead, but also for that of the living. The souls of the dead were widely believed to return to earth: mothers who had died in childbirth might come back seeking to take their children with them; executed criminals might return to gain revenge on those who had brought them to justice (to prevent that return, they were buried at crossroads, permanently under the sign of the cross, or under the gallows itself); ordinary people came seeking help from surviving family members in achieving their final salvation. Priests were hired to say memorial masses on anniversaries of family deaths, especially one week, one month, and one year afterward.

During the High Middle Ages, learned theologians increasingly emphasized the idea of purgatory, the place where souls on their way to Heaven went after death to make amends for their earthly sins. Souls in purgatory did not wander the earth, but they could still benefit from earthly activities; memorial masses, prayers, and donations made in their names could shorten their time in purgatory. So could indulgences (see Chapter 9), those papal grants that relieved a person from earthly penance. Indulgences were initially granted for performing meritorious acts, such as going on a pilgrimage or crusade, but later on they could be obtained by paying a small fee. (See "Evaluating the Evidence 10.1: The Pilgrim's Guide to Santiago de Compostela," page 298.) With this development, their spiritual benefits became transferable, so indulgences could be purchased to shorten the stay in purgatory of one's deceased relatives, as well as to lessen one's own penance or time in purgatory.

The living also had obligations to the dead among Muslims and Jews. In both groups deceased people were buried quickly, and special prayers were said by mourners and family members. Muslims fasted on behalf of the dead and maintained a brief period of official mourning. The Qur'an promises an eternal paradise with flowing rivers to "those who believe and do good deeds" (Qur'an, 4:57) and a Hell of eternal torment to those who do not.

Jews observed specified periods of mourning during which the normal activities of daily life were curtailed. Every day for eleven months after a death and every year after that on the anniversary of the death, a son of the deceased was to recite Kaddish, a special prayer of praise and glorification of God. Judaism emphasized life on earth more than an afterlife, so beliefs about what happens to the soul after death were more varied; the very righteous might go directly to a place of spiritual reward, but most souls went first to a place of punishment and purification generally referred to as *Gehinnom*. After a period that did not exceed twelve months, the soul ascended to the world to come. Those who were completely wicked during their lifetimes might simply go out of existence or continue in an eternal state of remorse.

Towns and Economic Revival

FOCUS QUESTION *What led to Europe's economic growth and reurbanization?*

Most people continued to live in villages in the High Middle Ages, but the rise of towns and the growth of a new business and commercial class was a central part of Europe's recovery after the disorders of the tenth century. The growth of towns was made possible by some of the changes already described: a rise in population; increased agricultural output, which provided an adequate food supply for town dwellers; and a degree of peace and political stability, which allowed merchants to transport and sell goods. As towns gained legal and political rights, merchant and craft guilds grew more powerful, and towns became centers of production as well as commerce.

The Rise of Towns

Medieval towns began in many different ways. Some were fortifications erected as a response to ninth-century invasions; the peasants from the surrounding countryside moved within the walls when their area was attacked. Other towns grew up around great cathedrals (see page 316) and monasteries whose schools drew students from distant areas. Many other

The Pilgrim's Guide to Santiago de Compostela

Making pilgrimages to holy shrines is a common practice in many religions. Medieval Christians of all social classes made pilgrimages, often to shrines understood to contain the body of a saint. The shrine of Santiago de Compostela (Saint James at Compostela) in the kingdom of Galicia in the Iberian Peninsula, said to contain the bones of the biblical Saint James, was one of the most popular. In the twelfth century an unknown French author gathered many of the pilgrims' experiences and put these together in a sort of guidebook.

The church, however, was begun in the year 1116 of the Spanish era [1078 c.e.]. . . . From the time when it was begun up to the present day, this church is renewed by the light of the miracles of the blessed James. In it, indeed, health is given to the sick, sight restored to the blind, the tongue of the mute is loosened, hearing is given to the deaf, soundness of limb is granted to cripples, the possessed are delivered, and what is more, the prayers of the faithful are heard, their vows are accepted, the bonds of sin are broken, heaven is opened to those who knock, consolation is given to the grieving, and all the people of foreign nations, flocking from all parts of the world, come together here in crowds bearing with them gifts of praise to the Lord. . . .

The land of Navarre . . . abounds in bread and wine, milk and cattle. . . . The Navarrese wear short black garments extending just down to the knee, like the Scots, and they wear sandals which they call *lavarcas* made of raw hide with the hair on and are bound around the foot with thongs, covering only the soles of the feet and leaving the upper foot bare. In truth, they wear black woollen hooded and fringed capes, reaching to their elbows, which they call *saias*. These people, in truth, are repulsively dressed, and they eat and drink repulsively.

For in fact all those who dwell in the household of a Navarrese, servant as well as master, maid as well as mistress, are accustomed to eat all their food mixed together from one pot, not with spoons but with their own hands, and they drink with one cup. If you saw them eat you would think them dogs or pigs. If you heard them speak, you would be reminded of the barking of dogs. For their speech is utterly barbarous. . . .

Then comes Galicia [guh-LIH-shee-uh]. . . . [T]his is wooded and has rivers and is well-provided with meadows and excellent orchards, with equally good fruits and very clear springs; there are few cities, towns or cornfields. It is short of wheaten bread and wine, bountiful in rye bread and cider, well-stocked with cattle and horses, milk and honey, ocean fish both gigantic and small, and wealthy in gold, silver, fabrics, and furs of forest animals and other riches, as well as Saracen [Muslim] treasures. The Galicians, in truth, more than all the other uncultivated Spanish peoples, are those who most closely resemble our French race by their manners, but they are alleged to be irascible and very litigious.

EVALUATE THE EVIDENCE

1. How would you evaluate the author's opinion of the people of Navarre? Of Galicia? How does he compare these people to his own countrymen, the French?
2. Pilgrimages were in many ways the precursors of modern tourism. What similarities do you see between this guide and those for today's travelers?

Source: *The Pilgrim's Guide to Santiago de Compostela*, critical edition and annotated translation by Paula Gerson, Jeanne Krochalis, Annie Shaver-Crandell, and Alison Stones. Copyright © 1997. Reprinted by permission of the authors.

towns grew from the sites of Roman army camps or cities, which had shrunk in the early Middle Ages but never entirely disappeared. Still others arose where a trade route crossed a river or a natural harbor allowed ships to moor easily.

Regardless of their origins, medieval towns had a few common characteristics. Each town had a marketplace, and most had a mint for the coining of money. The town also had a court to settle disputes. In addition, medieval towns were enclosed by walls. The terms *burgher* (BUHR-guhr) and *bourgeois* derive from the Old English and Old German words *burg*, *burgh*, *borg*, and *borough* for "a walled or fortified place." Thus a

burgher or bourgeois originally was a person who lived or worked inside the walls. Townspeople supported themselves primarily by exchanging goods and services with one another, becoming artisans, shopkeepers, and merchants. They bought their food from the surrounding countryside, and purchased goods from far away brought by traveling merchants.

No matter where people congregated, they settled on someone's land and had to secure permission to live there from the king, count, abbot, or bishop. Aristocratic nobles and churchmen were sometimes hostile to the towns set up on their land, but they soon realized that these could be a source of profits and benefits.

The growing towns of medieval Europe slowly gained legal and political rights, including the rights to hold municipal courts, select the mayor and other municipal officials, and tax residents and visitors. Lords were often reluctant to grant towns self-government, fearing loss of authority and revenue if they gave the residents full independence. When burghers bargained for a town's political independence, however, they offered sizable amounts of ready cash and sometimes promised payments for years to come. Consequently, lords ultimately agreed to self-government.

In addition to working for the independence of the towns, townspeople tried to acquire liberties for themselves. In the Middle Ages the word *liberties* meant special privileges. The most important privilege a medieval townsperson could gain was personal freedom. It gradually developed that an individual who fled his or her manor and lived in a town for a year and a day was free of servile obligations and status. Thus the growth of towns contributed to a slow decline of serfdom in western Europe, although this took centuries.

Towns developed throughout much of Europe, but the concentration of the textile industry led to the growth of many towns in the Low Countries (present-day Holland, Belgium, and French Flanders): Ghent with about 56,000 people, Bruges (broozh) with 27,000, and Tournai and Brussels with perhaps 20,000 each. In 1300 Paris was the largest city in western Christian Europe, with a population of about 200,000, and Venice, Florence, and Milan each had about 100,000 people (Map 10.1). Constantinople was larger still, with perhaps 300,000 people. Córdoba, the capital of Muslim Spain, may have been the largest city in the world, with a population that might have been nearly half a million, although this declined steeply when the city was conquered by Christian forces in 1236 and many people fled southward, swelling the population of Granada.

Merchant and Craft Guilds

The merchants, who were influential in winning towns' independence from feudal lords, also used their power and wealth to control life within the city walls. The merchants of a town joined together to form a **merchant guild** that prohibited nonmembers from trading in the town. Guild members often made up the earliest town government, serving as mayors and members of the city council, which meant that a town's economic policies were determined by its merchants' self-interest. By the late eleventh century, especially in the towns of the Low Countries and northern Italy, the leaders of the merchant guilds were rich and politically powerful.

While most towns were initially established as trading centers, they quickly became centers of production

as well. Peasants looking for better opportunities moved to towns—either with their lord's approval or without it—providing both workers and mouths to feed. Some townspeople began to specialize in certain types of food and clothing production: they bought cloth and sewed it into clothing, or purchased and butchered cattle, selling the meat to others who made small meat pies and selling the leather to those who made shoes or bags. Over time some cities specialized in certain items, becoming known for their fine fabrics, their reliable arms and armor, or their elegant gold and silver work.

Like merchants, producers recognized that organizing would bring benefits, and beginning in the twelfth century in many cities they formed **craft guilds** that regulated most aspects of production. Guilds set quality standards for their particular product and regulated the size of workshops and the conduct of members. In most cities individual guilds, such as those of shoemakers or blacksmiths, achieved a monopoly in the production of one particular product, forbidding nonmembers to work. The craft guild then chose some of its members to act as inspectors and set up a court to hear disputes between members, though the city court remained the final arbiter.

Each guild set the pattern by which members were trained and the length of the training period. A boy who wanted to become a weaver, for instance, or whose parents wanted him to, spent four to seven years as an apprentice, often bound by a contract such as the following from thirteenth-century Marseilles in southern France:

> April the ninth. I, Peter Borre, in good faith and without guile, place with you, Peter Feissac, weaver, my son Stephen, for the purpose of learning the trade and craft of weaving, to live at your house, and to do work for you from the feast of Easter next for four continuous years, promising you by this agreement to take care that my son does the said work, and that he will be faithful and trustworthy in all that he does, and that he will neither steal nor take anything away from you, nor flee nor depart from you for any reason, until he had completed his apprenticeship.[5]

When the apprenticeship was finished, a young artisan spent several years as a journeyman, working in the shop of a master artisan. He then could make his

---

■ **merchant guild** A band of merchants in a town that prohibited nonmembers from trading in that town.

■ **craft guild** A band of producers in a town that regulated most aspects of production of a good in that town.

MAPPING THE PAST

MAP 10.1 European Population Density, ca. 1300

The development of towns and the reinvigoration of trade were directly related in medieval Europe. Using this map, Maps 10.2 and 10.3, and the information in this chapter, answer the following questions.

ANALYZING THE MAP What were the four largest cities in Europe? What part of Europe had the highest density of towns?

CONNECTIONS What role did textile and other sorts of manufacturing play in the growth of towns? How was the development of towns related to that of universities, monastery schools, and cathedral schools?

"masterpiece"—in the case of weavers, a long piece of cloth. If the other masters judged the cloth acceptable, and if they thought the market in their town was large enough to support another weaver, the journeyman could then become a master and start a shop. If the guild decided there were already enough masters, he would need to leave that town and try elsewhere. Many guilds required masters to be married, as they recognized the vital role of the master's wife. She assisted in running the shop, often selling the goods her husband had produced. Their children, both male and female,

also worked alongside the apprentices and journeymen. The sons were sometimes formally apprenticed, but the daughters were generally not apprenticed, because many guilds limited formal membership to males.

Most guilds allowed a master's widow to continue operating a shop for a set period of time after her husband's death, for they recognized that she had the necessary skills and experience. Such widows paid all guild dues, but they were not considered full members and could not vote or hold office in the guild. In a handful of cities there were a few all-female guilds, especially in spinning gold thread or weaving silk ribbons for luxury clothing, trades in which girls were formally apprenticed in the same way boys were.

Both craft and merchant guilds were not only economic organizations, but also systems of social support. They took care of elderly masters who could no longer work, and they often supported masters' widows and orphans. They maintained an altar at a city church and provided for the funerals of members and baptisms of their children. Guild members marched together in city parades and reinforced their feelings of solidarity with one another by special ceremonies and distinctive dress. Merchant guilds in some parts of Europe, such as the German cities of Hamburg, Lübeck, and Bremen, had special buildings for celebrations and ceremonies.

The Revival of Long-Distance Trade

The growth of towns went hand in hand with a revival of trade as artisans and craftsmen manufactured goods for both local and foreign consumption (Map 10.2). Most trade centered in towns and was controlled by professional traders. Long-distance trade was risky and required large investments of capital. Robbers and thieves roamed virtually all of the overland trade routes. Pirates infested the sea-lanes, and shipwrecks were common. Since the risks were so great, merchants preferred to share them. A group of people would thus pool their capital to finance an expedition to a distant place. When the ship or caravan returned and the cargo was sold, these investors would share the profits. If disaster struck the caravan, an investor's loss was limited to the amount of that individual's investment.

In the late eleventh century the Italian cities, especially Venice, led the West in trade in general and completely dominated trade with the East. Venetian ships carried salt from the city's own lagoon, pepper and other spices from India and North Africa, silks and carpets from Central Asia, and slaves from many places. In northern Europe, the towns of Bruges, Ghent, and Ypres (EE-pruh) in Flanders built a vast cloth industry, becoming leaders in both the manufacture and trade of textiles.

Two circumstances help explain the lead Venice and these Flemish towns gained in long-distance trade. Both areas enjoyed a high degree of peace and political stability. Geographical factors were equally, if not more, important. Venice, at the northwestern end of the Adriatic Sea, had easy access to transalpine land routes as well as the Adriatic and Mediterranean sea-lanes connected to the markets of North Africa, Byzantium, and Russia. Merchants from Venice and Genoa also seized the commercial opportunities of-

fered by the great fairs (large periodic gatherings that attracted buyers, sellers, and goods) held in the county of Champagne in northern France. Champagne was on the main north-south trade routes, and the counts who ruled the area provided security and enforced contracts. Directly north of Champagne were the towns of Flanders, which also offered unusual possibilities for merchants: just across the Channel from England, Flanders had easy access to English wool. Because the weather in England was colder than in most of Europe, English sheep grew longer and denser wool than sheep elsewhere. With this wool, clothmakers could produce high-quality cloth, which was the most important manufactured product handled by merchants and one of the few European products for which there was a market in the East.

From the late eleventh through the thirteenth centuries, Europe enjoyed a steadily expanding volume of international trade. Trade surged markedly with demand for sugar from the Mediterranean islands to replace honey; spices from Asia to season a bland diet; and fine wines from the Rhineland, Burgundy, and Bordeaux to make life more pleasant. Other consumer goods included luxury woolens from Flanders and Tuscany, furs from Ireland and Russia, brocades and tapestries from Flanders, and silks from Constantinople and even China. Nobles prized fancy household furnishings such as silver plate, as well as swords and armor for their battles. As the trade volume expanded, the use of cash became more widespread. Beginning in the 1160s the opening of new silver mines in Germany, Bohemia, northern Italy, northern France, and western England led to the minting and circulation of vast quantities of silver coins.

Increased trade also led to a higher standard of living. Contact with Eastern civilizations introduced Europeans to eating utensils, and table manners improved. Nobles learned to eat with forks and knives instead of tearing the meat from a roast with their hands. They began to use napkins instead of wiping their greasy fingers on their clothes or on the dogs lying under the table.

Business Procedures

The economic surge of the High Middle Ages led merchants to invent new business procedures. Beginning in Italy, merchants formalized their agreements with new types of contracts, including temporary contracts for land and sea trading ventures and permanent partnerships termed *compagnie* (kahm-pah-NYEE; literally "bread together," that is, sharing bread; the root of the word *company*). Many of these agreements were initially between brothers or other relatives and in-laws, but they quickly grew to include people who were not family members. In addition, they began to involve individuals—including a few women—who invested only their money, leaving the actual running of the business to the active partners. Commercial correspondence, unnecessary when one businessperson oversaw everything and made direct bargains with buyers and sellers, proliferated. Accounting and record keeping became more sophisticated, and credit facilitated business expansion.

The ventures of the German Hanseatic League illustrate these new business procedures. The **Hanseatic League** (often called simply the Hansa) was a mercantile association of towns. It originated in agreements between merchants for mutual security and exclusive trading rights, and it gradually developed into agreements among towns themselves, often sealed with a

contract. The first such contract was between the towns of Lübeck and Hamburg in 1241, and during the next century perhaps two hundred cities from Holland to Poland joined the league. From the fourteenth to the sixteenth centuries, the Hanseatic League controlled the trade of northern Europe. In cities such as Bruges and London, Hansa merchants secured special trading concessions, exempting them from all tolls and allowing them to trade at local fairs. These merchants established foreign trading centers, called "factories" because the commercial agents in them were called "factors."

The dramatic increase in trade ran into two serious difficulties in medieval Europe. One was the problem of minting money. Despite investment in mining operations to increase the production of

MAP 10.2 Trade and Manufacturing in Thirteenth-Century Europe Note the overland and ocean lines of trade and the sources of silver, iron, copper, lead, paper, wool, carpets and rugs, and slaves.

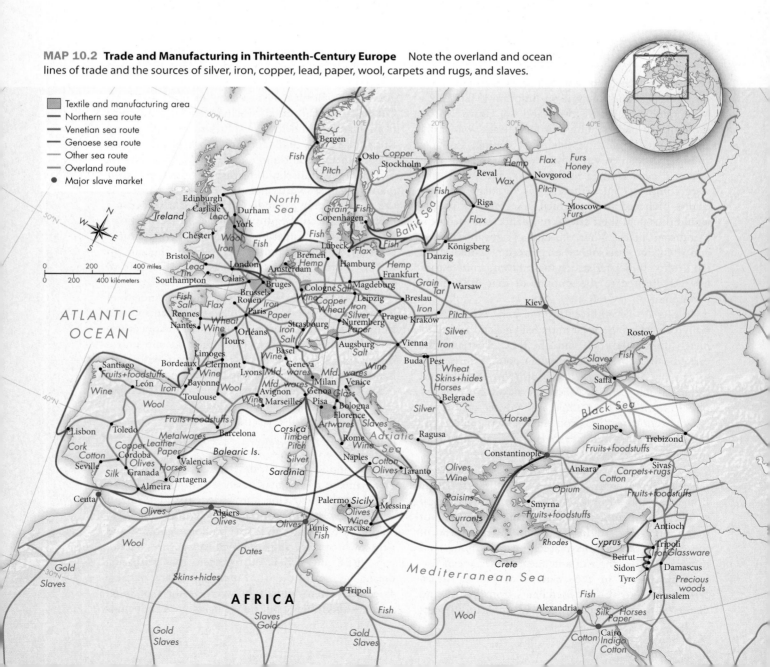

Lübeck   Gabled houses and shops line the river Trave in the old merchants' quarter of Lübeck, the "Queen of the Hanseatic League," while the brick spires of Saint Mary's and Saint Peter's churches, begun in the thirteenth century by prosperous citizens, loom above. Much of the central city and many of the churches were destroyed in World War II, but they have been rebuilt following medieval plans, and this photo provides a good sense of what a Hansa city centered on commerce would have looked like. (Insights/UIG via Getty Images)

metals, the amount of gold, silver, and copper available for coins was not adequate for the increased flow of commerce. Merchants developed paper bills of exchange, in which coins or goods in one location were exchanged for a sealed letter (much like a modern deposit statement), which could be used in place of metal coinage elsewhere. This made the long, slow, and very dangerous shipment of coins unnecessary, and facilitated the expansion of credit and commerce. By about 1300 the bill of exchange was the normal method of making commercial payments among the cities of western Europe, and it proved to be a decisive factor in their later economic development.

The second problem was a moral and theological one. Church doctrine frowned on lending money at interest, termed *usury* (YOO-zhuh-ree). This doctrine was developed in the early Middle Ages when loans were mainly for consumption, for instance, to tide a farmer over until the next harvest. Theologians reasoned that it was wrong for a Christian to take advantage of the bad luck or need of another Christian. This restriction on Christians' charging interest is one reason why Jews were frequently the moneylenders in early medieval society; it was one of the few occupations not forbidden them. As money-lending became more important to commercial ventures, the church relaxed its position. It declared that some interest was legitimate as a payment for the risk the investor was taking, and that only interest above a certain level would be considered usury. (Even today, governments generally set limits on the rate businesses may charge for loaning money.) The church itself then got into the money-lending business, opening pawnshops in cities.

The stigma attached to lending money was in many ways attached to all the activities of a merchant. Medieval people were uneasy about a person making a profit merely from the investment of money rather than labor, skill, and time. Merchants themselves shared these ideas to some degree, so they gave generous donations to the church and to charities, and took pains not to flaunt their wealth through flashy dress and homes.

The Hanseatic League, 1300–1400

■ **Hanseatic League**   A mercantile association of towns begun in northern Europe that allowed for mutual protection and trading rights.

Mirrors The commercial revolution brought new consumer goods into Europe, including exotic materials such as African ivory, here made into an intricately carved mirror case showing a knight honoring his lady while a groom holds his horses, created for a wealthy customer (left). More ordinary people used mirrors as well, as seen in this wooden carving of a woman admiring herself in a mirror (right). The carving, called a *misericord*, decorated the underside of the seat in a choir stall in a church in Beauvais, France. Secular scenes of everyday life were often shown in misericords, but the carving may also represent the sin of vanity, often symbolized by a woman holding a mirror. (ivory: © V & A Images/Alamy Stock Photo; woman: Musée national du Moyen Âge–Thermes et hôtel de Cluny/© RMN–Grand Palais/Art Resource, NY)

The Commercial Revolution

Changes in business procedures, combined with the growth in trade, led to a transformation of the European economy often called the **commercial revolution** by historians, who see it as the beginning of the modern capitalist economy. In using this label, historians point not only to increases in the sheer volume of trade and in the complexity and sophistication of business procedures, but also to the development of a new "capitalist spirit" in which making a profit is regarded as a good thing in itself, regardless of the uses to which that profit is put. (See "Individuals in Society: Francesco Datini," at right.) Because capitalism in the Middle Ages primarily involved trade rather than production, it is referred to as mercantile capitalism.

Part of this capitalist spirit was a new attitude toward time. Country people needed only approximate times—dawn, noon, sunset—for their work. Monasteries needed more precise times to call monks together for the recitation of the Divine Office. In the early Middle Ages monks used a combination of hourglasses, sundials, and water-clocks to determine the time, and then rang bells by hand. In about 1280 new types of mechanical mechanisms seem to have been devised in which weights replaced falling water and

bells were rung automatically. Records begin to use the word *clock* (from the Latin word for bell) for these machines, which sometimes indicated the movement of astronomical bodies as well as the hours. The merchants who ran city councils quickly saw clocks as useful, as these devices allowed the opening and closing of markets and shops to be set to certain hours. Through regulations that specified times and bells that marked the day, city people began to develop a mentality that conceived of the universe in quantitative terms. Clocks were also symbols of a city's prosperity. Beautiful and elaborate mechanical clocks, usually installed on the cathedral or town church, were in general use in Italy by the 1320s, in Germany by the 1330s, in England by the 1370s, and in France by the 1380s.

The commercial revolution created a great deal of new wealth, which did not escape the attention of kings and other rulers. Wealth could be taxed, and through taxation kings could create strong and centralized states. The commercial revolution also provided the opportunity for thousands of serfs to improve their social position. The slow but steady transformation of European society from almost completely rural and isolated to urban and relatively more sophisticated constituted the greatest effect of the commercial revolution that began in the eleventh century.

Even so, merchants and business people did not run medieval communities other than in central and

commercial revolution The transformation of the European economy as a result of changes in business procedures and growth in trade.

In 1348, when he was a young teenager, Francesco Datini (1335–1410) lost his father, his mother, a brother, and a sister to the Black Death epidemic that swept through Europe (see Chapter 11). Leaving his hometown of Prato in northern Italy, he apprenticed himself to merchants in nearby Florence for several years to learn accounting and other business skills. At fifteen, he moved to Avignon (ah-veen-YOHN) in southern France. The popes were at this point living in Avignon instead of Rome, and the city offered many opportunities for an energetic and enterprising young man. Datini first became involved in the weapons trade, which offered steady profits, and then became a merchant of spices, wool and silk cloth, and jewels. He was very successful, and at thirty-one he married the young daughter of another merchant in an elaborate wedding that was the talk of Avignon.

In 1378 the papacy returned to Italy, and Datini soon followed, setting up trading companies in Prato, Pisa, and Florence. He focused on cloth and leather and sought to control the trade in products used for the preparation of these materials as well, especially the rare dyes that created the brilliant colors favored by wealthy noblemen and townspeople. He eventually had offices all over Europe and became one of the richest men of his day, opening a mercantile bank and a company that produced cloth.

Datini was more successful than most businessmen, but what makes him particularly stand out was his record keeping. He kept careful account books and ledgers, all of them headed by the phrase "in the name of God and profit." He wrote to the managers of each of his offices every week, providing them with careful advice and blunt criticism: "You cannot see a crow in a bowl of milk." Taking on the son of a friend as an employee, he wrote to the young man: "Do your duty well, and you will acquire honor and profit, and you can count on me as if I were your own father. But if you do not, then do not count on me; it will be as if I had never known you."

When Datini was away from home, which was often, he wrote to his wife every day, and she sometimes responded in ways that were less deferential than we might expect of a woman who was many years younger. "I think it is not neces-

Statue of Francesco Datini located outside the city hall in Prato. (Marble statue by Nicolo Lamberti [ca. 1375–1451], 1409, Piazza del Comune, Prato, Italy/Bridgeman Images)

sary," she wrote at one point, "to send me a message every Wednesday to say that you will be here on Sunday, for it seems to me that on every Friday you change your mind."

Datini's obsessive record keeping lasted beyond his death, for someone saved all of his records—hundreds of ledgers and contracts, eleven thousand business letters, and over a hundred thousand personal letters—in sacks in his opulent house in Prato, where they were found in the nineteenth century. They provide a detailed picture of medieval business practices and also reveal much about Datini as a person. Ambitious, calculating, luxury loving, and a workaholic, Datini seems similar to a modern CEO. Like many of today's self-made billionaires, at the end of his life Datini began to think a bit more about God and less about profit. In his will, he set up a foundation for the poor in Prato and a home for orphans in Florence, both of which are still in operation. In 1967 scholars established an institute for economic history in Prato, naming it in Datini's honor; the institute now manages the collection of Datini's documents and gathers other relevant materials in its archives.

QUESTIONS FOR ANALYSIS

1. How would you evaluate Datini's motto, "In the name of God and profit"? Is it an honest statement of his aims, a hypocritical justification of greed, a blend of both, or something else?
2. Changes in business procedures in the Middle Ages have been described as a "commercial revolution." Do Datini's business ventures support this assessment? How?

Source: Iris Origo, *The Merchant of Prato: Francesco di Marco Datini, 1335–1410* (New York: Alfred A. Knopf, Inc., 1957).

northern Italy and in the county of Flanders. Kings and nobles maintained ultimate control over most European cities, such as Paris, London, and Córdoba. Most towns remained small, and urban residents never amounted to more than 10 percent of the total European population. The commercial changes of the eleventh through thirteenth centuries did, however, lay the economic foundations for the development of urban life and culture.

Urban Life

FOCUS QUESTION *What was life like in medieval cities?*

In their backgrounds and abilities, townspeople represented diversity and change. Their occupations and their preoccupations were different from those of nobles and peasants. Cities were crowded and polluted, though people flocked into them because they offered the possibility of economic advancement, social mobility, and improvement in legal status. Some urban residents grew spectacularly rich, but the numbers of poor swelled as well.

City Life

Walls surrounded almost all medieval towns and cities, and constant repair of these walls was usually the town's greatest expense. Gates pierced the walls, and visitors waited at the gates to gain entrance to the town. Most streets in a medieval town were marketplaces as much as passages for transit. Poor people selling soap, candles, wooden dishes, and similar cheap products stood next to farmers from the surrounding countryside selling eggs, chickens, or vegetables; people selling firewood or mushrooms they had gathered; and pawnbrokers selling used clothing and household goods. Because there was no way to preserve food easily, people—usually female family members or servants—had to shop every day, and the market was where they met their neighbors, exchanged information, and talked over recent events, as well as purchased needed supplies.

Some selling took place not in the open air but in the craftsman's home. A window or door in the home opened onto the street and displayed the finished products made within to attract passersby. The family lived above the business on the second or third floor. As the business and the family expanded, additional stories were added. Second and third stories jutted out over the ground floor and thus over the street. Since the streets were narrow to begin with, houses lacked fresh air and light. Initially, houses were made of wood and thatched with straw. Fire was a constant danger;

because houses were built so close to one another, fires spread rapidly. Municipal governments consequently urged construction in stone or brick.

Most medieval cities developed with little planning. As the population increased, space became increasingly limited. Air and water pollution presented serious problems. Horses and oxen, the chief means of transportation and power, dropped tons of dung on the streets every year. It was universal practice in the early towns to dump household waste, both animal and human, into the road in front of one's house. The stench must have been abominable. In 1298 the citizens of the town of Boutham in Yorkshire, England, received the following order:

> To the bailiffs of the abbot of St. Mary's York, at Boutham. Whereas it is sufficiently evident that the pavement of the said town of Boutham is so very greatly broken up . . . , and in addition the air is so corrupted and infected by the pigsties situated in the king's highways and in the lanes of that town and by the swine feeding and frequently wandering about . . . and by dung and dunghills and many other foul things placed in the streets and lanes, that great repugnance overtakes the king's ministers staying in that town and also others there dwelling and passing through . . . : the king, being unwilling longer to tolerate such great and unbearable defects there, orders the bailiffs to cause the pavement to be suitably repaired . . . before All Saints next, and to cause the pigsties, aforesaid streets and lanes to be cleansed from all dung . . . and to cause them to be kept thus cleansed hereafter.[6]

People of all sorts, from beggars to wealthy merchants, regularly rubbed shoulders in the narrow streets and alleys of crowded medieval cities. This interaction did not mean that people were unaware of social differences, however, for clothing clearly indicated social standing and sometimes occupation. Friars wore black, white, or gray woolen clothing that marked them as members of a particular religious order, while priests and bishops wore layers of specialized clothing, especially when they were officiating at religious services. Military men and servants who lived in noble households dressed in the nobles' distinctive colors known as livery (LIH-vuh-ree). Wealthier urban residents wore bright colors, imported silk or fine woolen fabrics, and fancy headgear, while poorer ones wore darker clothing made of rough linen or linen and wool blends. In university towns, students wore clothing and headgear that marked their status. University graduates—lawyers, physicians, and professors—often wore dark robes, trimmed with fur if they could afford it.

Young Men Playing Stickball
With their tunics hitched up in their belts so that they could move around more easily, young men play a game involving hitting a ball with a stick. Games involving bats and balls were popular, for the equipment needed was made from simple, inexpensive materials. (Playing game of pelota, illuminated page from *Cantigas de Santa Maria*, manuscript made under the direction of Alfonso X [1221–1284], King of Castile and León/DEA/De Agostini/Getty Images)

In the later Middle Ages many cities attempted to make clothing distinctions a matter of law as well as of habit. City councils passed **sumptuary laws** that regulated the value of clothing and jewelry that people of different social groups could wear; only members of high social groups could wear velvet, satin, pearls, or fur, for example, or wear clothing embroidered with gold thread or dyed in colors that were especially expensive to produce, such as the purple dye that came from mollusk shells. Along with enforcing social differences, sumptuary laws also attempted to impose moral standards by prohibiting plunging necklines on women or doublets (fitted buttoned jackets) that were too short on men. Their limits on imported fabrics or other materials also served to protect local industries.

Some of these laws called for marking certain individuals as members of groups not fully acceptable in urban society. Many cities ordered prostitutes to wear red or yellow bands on their clothes that were supposed to represent the flames of Hell, and the Fourth Lateran Council required Jews and Muslims to dress in ways that distinguished them from their Christian neighbors. (Many Jewish communities also developed their own sumptuary laws prohibiting extravagant or ostentatious dress.) In some cities, sumptuary laws were expanded to include restrictions on expenditures for parties and family celebrations, again set by social class. Sumptuary laws were frequently broken and were difficult to enforce, but they provide evidence of the many material goods available to urban dwellers as well as the concern of city leaders about the social mobility and extravagance they saw all around them.

Servants and the Poor

Many urban houses were larger than the tiny village dwellings, so families took in domestic servants. A less wealthy household employed one woman who assisted in all aspects of running the household; a wealthier one employed a large staff of male and female servants with specific duties. When there was only one servant, she generally lived and ate with the family, for there was rarely enough space for separate quarters. Even in wealthier households that had many rooms, servants were rarely separated from their employers the way they would be in the nineteenth century, but instead lived on intimate terms with them. In Italian cities, household servants included slaves, usually young women brought in from areas outside of Western Christianity, such as the Balkans.

Along with live-in servants, many households hired outside workers to do specific tasks. These workers laundered clothing and household linens, cared for children or invalids, repaired houses and walls, and carried messages or packages around the city or the surrounding countryside. Urban workers had to buy all their food, so they felt any increase in the price of ale or bread immediately. Their wages were generally low, and children from such families sought work at very young ages.

■ **sumptuary laws** Laws that regulated the value and style of clothing and jewelry that various social groups could wear as well as the amount they could spend on celebrations.

Illegal activities offered another way for people to support themselves. They stole merchandise from houses, wagons, and storage facilities, fencing it to pawnbrokers or taking it to the next town to sell. They stole goods or money directly from people, cutting the strings of their bags or purses. They sold sex for money, standing on street corners or moving into houses that by the fifteenth century became official brothels. They made and sold mixtures of herbs and drugs claimed to heal all sorts of ailments, perhaps combining this venture with a puppet show, trained animals, magic tricks, or music to draw customers. Or they did all these things and also worked as laundresses, day laborers, porters, peddlers, or street vendors when they could. Cities also drew in orphans, blind people, and the elderly, who resorted to begging for food and money.

Popular Entertainment

Games and sports were common forms of entertainment and relaxation. There were wrestling matches and games akin to modern football, rugby, stickball, and soccer in which balls were kicked, hit, and thrown. People played card and board games of all types. They played with dice carved from stone or bone, or with the knucklebones of animals or wood carved in knucklebone shapes, somewhat like modern jacks. They trained dogs to fight each other or put them in an enclosure to fight a captured bear. In Spain, Muslim knights confronted and killed bulls from horseback as part of religious feast days, developing a highly ritualized ceremony that would later be further adapted by Spain's Christians. All these sports and games were occasions for wagering and gambling, which preachers sometimes condemned (especially when the games were attached to a holiday or saint's day celebration) but had little power to control.

Religious and family celebrations also meant dancing, which the church also had little success banning or regulating. Men and women danced in lines toward a specific object, such as a tree or a maypole, or in circles, groups, or pairs with specific step patterns. They were accompanied by a variety of instruments: reed pipes such as the chalumeau (an ancestor of the clarinet) and shawm (predecessor to the oboe); woodwinds such as flutes, panpipes, and recorders; stringed instruments including dulcimers, harps, lyres, lutes, zithers, and mandolins; brass instruments such as horns and trumpets; and percussion instruments like drums and tambourines. Many of these instruments were simple and were made by their players. Musicians playing string or percussion instruments often sang as well, and people sang without instrumental accompaniment on festive occasions or while working.

Medieval Universities

FOCUS QUESTION *How did universities serve the needs of medieval society?*

Just as the first strong secular states emerged in the thirteenth century, so did the first universities. This was no coincidence. The new bureaucratic states and the church needed educated administrators, and universities were a response to this need.

Origins

In the early Middle Ages, monasteries and cathedral schools had offered most of the available formal instruction. Monastery schools were small, but cathedral schools, run by the bishop and his clergy in bustling cities, gradually grew larger. In the eleventh century in Italian cities like Bologna (boh-LOH-nyuh), wealthy businessmen established municipal schools. In the course of the twelfth century, cathedral schools in France and municipal schools in Italy developed into educational institutions that attracted students from a wide area (Map 10.3). These schools were often called *universitas magistrorum et scholarium* (universal society of teachers and students), the origin of the English word *university*. The first European universities appeared in Italy in Bologna, where the specialty was law, and Salerno, where the specialty was medicine.

Legal and Medical Training

The growth of the University of Bologna coincided with a revival of interest in Roman law during the investiture controversy. The study of Roman law as embodied in the Code of Justinian (see Chapter 7) had never completely died out in the West, but in the late eleventh century a complete manuscript of Justinian's Code was discovered in a library in Pisa. This discovery led scholars in nearby Bologna, beginning with Irnerius (ehr-NEH-ree-uhs) (ca. 1055–ca. 1130), to study and teach Roman law intently.

Irnerius and other teachers at Bologna taught law as an organic whole related to the society it regulated, an all-inclusive system based on logical principles that could be applied to difficult practical situations. Thus, as social and economic structures changed, law would change with them. Jurists educated at Bologna—and later at other universities—were hired by rulers and city councils to systematize their law codes and write legal treatises. In the 1260s the English jurist Henry Bracton wrote a comprehensive treatise bringing together the laws and customs of England, and King Alfonso X of Castile had scholars write the *Siete*

Legend:
◆ University
⊥ Monastery school
▪ Cathedral school
<u>Aix</u> Law school

MAP 10.3 Intellectual Centers of Medieval Europe Universities provided more sophisticated instruction than did monastery and cathedral schools, but all these institutions served to educate males who had the money to attend.

Partidas (Book in Seven Parts), a detailed plan for administering his whole kingdom according to Roman legal principles.

Canon law (see Chapter 9) was also shaped by the reinvigoration of Roman law, and canon lawyers in ever-greater numbers were hired by church officials or became prominent church officials themselves. In about 1140 the Benedictine monk Gratian put together a collection of nearly 3,800 texts covering all areas of canon law. His collection, known as the *Decretum*, became the standard text on which teachers of canon law lectured and commented.

Jewish scholars also produced elaborate commentaries on law and religious tradition. Medieval universities were closed to Jews, but in some cities in the eleventh century special rabbinic academies opened

that concentrated on the study of the Talmud, a compilation of legal arguments, proverbs, sayings, and folklore that had been produced in the fifth century in Babylon (present-day Iraq). Men seeking to become rabbis—highly respected figures within the Jewish community, with authority over economic and social as well as religious matters—spent long periods of time studying the Talmud, which served as the basis for their decisions affecting all areas of life.

Professional medical training began at Salerno. Individuals there, such as Constantine the African (1020?–1087)—who was a convert from Islam and later a Benedictine monk—began to translate medical works out of Arabic. These translations included writings by the ancient Greek physicians and Muslim medical writers, a blending of knowledge that

Healthy Living

In this illustration from a very popular fourteenth-century Latin handbook on maintaining health and well-being, women with their sleeves rolled up prepare cloth for medical uses; the woman on the left is trimming small threads off with a one-bladed shear, and the woman on the right is boiling the cloth to bleach it. The men in the background eat a meal and drink wine. The text of this handbook was a translation of an Arabic medical treatise, made in the kingdom of Sicily, the site of much cultural borrowing.

(From *Tacuinum Sanitatis* [vellum]/Österreichische Nationalbibliothek, Vienna, Austria/Alinari/Bridgeman Images)

EVALUATE THE EVIDENCE

1. Cleanliness and moderation were recommended as essential to healthy living in this handbook. How does the artist convey these values in this scene?
2. Given what you have learned about medieval medical care, why might a handbook like this have been popular with literate urban residents?

---

later occurred on the nearby island of Sicily as well. (See "Evaluating the Evidence 10.2: Healthy Living," above.) Students of medicine poured into the city.

Medical studies at Salerno were based on classical ideas, particularly those of Hippocrates and Aristotle (see Chapter 3). For the ancient Greeks, ideas about the human body were very closely linked to philosophy and to ideas about the natural world in general. Prime among these was the notion of the four bodily humors—blood, phlegm, black bile, and yellow bile—fluids in the body that influenced bodily health. Each individual was thought to have a characteristic temperament or complexion determined by the balance of these humors, just as today we might describe a person as having a "positive outlook" or a "type A" personality. Disease was generally regarded as an imbalance of humors, which could be diagnosed by

taking a patient's pulse or examining his or her urine. Treatment was thus an attempt to bring the humors back into balance, which might be accomplished through diet or drugs—mixtures of herbal or mineral substances—or by vomiting, emptying the bowels, or bloodletting. The bodily humors were somewhat gender related—women were regarded as tending toward cold and wet humors and men toward hot and dry—so therapies were also gender distinctive. Men's greater heat, scholars taught, created other gender differences: heat caused men's hair to burn internally so that they went bald, and their shoulders and brains to become larger than those of women (because heat rises and causes things to expand).

These ideas spread throughout Europe from Salerno and became the basis of training for physicians at other universities. University training gave physicians high social status and allowed them to charge high fees.

They were generally hired directly by patients as needed, though some had more permanent positions as members of the household staffs of especially wealthy nobles or rulers.

Theology and Philosophy

Law and medicine were important academic disciplines in the Middle Ages, but theology was "the queen of sciences" because it involved the study of God, who made all knowledge possible. Paris became the place to study theology. In the first decades of the twelfth century, students from across Europe crowded into the cathedral school of Notre Dame (NOH-truh DAHM) in Paris.

University professors (a term first used in the fourteenth century) were known as "schoolmen" or **Scholastics**. They developed a method of thinking, reasoning, and writing in which questions were raised and authorities cited on both sides of a question. The goal of this method was to arrive at definitive answers and to provide rational explanations for what was believed on faith.

The Scholastic approach rested on the recovery of classical philosophical texts. Ancient Greek and Arabic texts entered Europe in the early twelfth century by way of Islamic intellectual centers at Baghdad, Córdoba, and Toledo (see Chapter 8). The major contribution of Arab culture to the new currents of Western thought rested in the stimulus Arab philosophers and commentators gave to Europeans' reflections on ancient Greek texts and the ways these texts fit with Christian teachings. One of the young men drawn to Paris was Peter Abelard (1079–1142), the son of a minor Breton knight. Abelard was fascinated by logic, which he believed could be used to solve most problems. He was one of the first Scholastics, and commented, "By doubting we come to questioning, and by questioning we perceive the truth." Abelard was severely censured by a church council, but his cleverness, boldness, and imagination made him a highly popular figure among students.

Abelard's reputation for brilliance drew the attention of one of the cathedral canons, Fulbert, who hired Abelard to tutor his intelligent niece Heloise. The relationship between teacher and pupil passed beyond the intellectual. Heloise became pregnant, and Fulbert pressured the couple to marry. The couple agreed, but wanted the marriage kept secret for the sake of Abelard's career. Furious at Abelard, Fulbert hired men to castrate him. Abelard persuaded Heloise to enter a convent, and he became a monk. Their baby, baptized Astrolabe for a recent Muslim navigational invention, was given to Heloise's family for adoption. The two became leaders of their communities—Abelard an

abbot and Heloise a prioress—but they never saw each other again, though they wrote letters, which have become examples of the new self-awareness of the period.

In the thirteenth century Scholastics devoted an enormous amount of time to collecting and organizing knowledge on all topics. Such a collection was published as a *summa* (SOO-muh), or reference book. There were *summae* on law, philosophy, vegetation, animal life, and theology. Saint Thomas Aquinas (1225–1274), a Dominican friar and professor at the University of Paris, produced the most famous of these collections, the *Summa Theologica*, a summation of Christian ideas on a vast number of theological questions, including the nature of God and Christ, moral principles, and the role of the sacraments. In this, and many of his other writings, Aquinas used arguments that drew from ancient Greek philosophers, especially Aristotle, as well as earlier Christian writers. Aquinas was both a theologian and a philosopher: he wrote sermons, prayers, commentaries on books of the Bible, and argumentative works on aspects of Christian theology such as the nature of evil and the power of God, but also commentaries on several of Aristotle's works.

In these, he investigated the branch of philosophy called epistemology, which is concerned with how a person knows something. Aquinas stated that first one knows through sensory perception of the physical world—seeing, hearing, touching, and so on. He maintained that there can be nothing in the mind that is not first in the senses. The second way knowledge comes is through reason, through the mind exercising its natural abilities.

In all these works, Aquinas stressed the power of human reason to demonstrate many basic Christian principles, including the existence of God. To obtain true Christian understanding, he wrote, one needed both reason and faith. His ideas have been extremely influential in both philosophy and theology: in the former through the philosophical school known as Thomism, and in the latter especially through the Catholic Church, which has affirmed many times that they are foundational to Roman Catholic doctrine.

University Students

The influx of students eager for learning, together with dedicated and imaginative teachers, created the atmosphere in which universities grew. (See "The Past Living Now: University Life," page 312.) By the end of the fifteenth century there were at least eighty universities in Europe. Some universities also offered

■ **Scholastics** University professors in the Middle Ages who developed a method of thinking, reasoning, and writing in which questions were raised and authorities cited on both sides of a question.

Fairs and banquets with medieval or Renaissance themes offer us the opportunity to watch jousts and jugglers, eat meat pies, listen to singers with lutes, buy stained-glass windows, and perhaps even wear chain mail. But you do not have to go to such a fair to experience the Middle Ages; all you have to do is look around you. Almost every aspect of contemporary university and college life has its roots in the universities that grew up in medieval European cities.

Professors established the curriculum and set the requirements for courses and the length of time for study. That curriculum typically consisted of a core of ancient texts—such as the Bible, Justinian's Code, and the works of Aristotle—that all students had to master. The standard method of teaching was a lecture in which a professor talked about a topic—often a passage from one of those key texts—while standing in front of a class of students taking notes. Professors explained and interpreted the passage; this interpretation was called a gloss. Texts and glosses were sometimes collected and reproduced as textbooks. Because books had to be copied by hand, they were extremely expensive, and few students could afford them. Students therefore depended on their own or friends' notes. Lecture courses were augmented by seminars in which students debated key issues in what they were studying. Professors determined the form and content of examinations, which were oral and, students lamented, very difficult. Students all wanted to know exactly what would be on each examination.

Students lived in rented rooms or, by the late thirteenth century, in residential colleges, both of which could be costly. The money sent by parents or patrons was often not sufficient for all expenses, so students augmented it by doing odd jobs. If a candidate passed all exams, he was awarded a license to teach, the earliest form of academic degree. Initially these licenses granted the title of master or doctor, both derived from Latin words meaning "teach." The lower bachelor's degree was developed later. All degrees came to be certified by pieces of parchment with elegant seals and Latin phrases. The difference in status among the degrees was reflected in differences in the garments scholars wore and can be seen in the robes worn at graduations today. Robes of those with a doctorate often have velvet bands, more ornate than master's or bachelor's robes; master's robes, in turn, include hoods, making them fancier than the simple bachelor's robe. So look around at the next graduation you attend—which could be your own!—and you will be surrounded by more things with their origins in the Middle Ages than at any medieval fair.

Lecture at the University of Paris Students with somewhat dour expressions take notes while the professor lectures from a book, in this illustration from a history of France made about 1400. (From the *Grandes Chroniques de France*, ca. 1400, vellum/Bibliothèque Nationale, Paris, France/Bridgeman Images)

QUESTIONS FOR ANALYSIS

1. In what ways were medieval universities similar to those of today? In what ways were they different?
2. Why do you think universities have retained so many features over the centuries?

younger students training in what were termed the seven liberal arts—grammar, rhetoric, logic, mathematics, geometry, music, and astronomy—that could serve as a foundation for more specialized study in all areas.

University students were generally considered to be lower-level members of the clergy—this was termed being in "minor orders"—so any students accused of legal infractions were tried in church, rather than in city, courts. This clerical status, along with widely held ideas about women's lesser intellectual capabilities, meant that university education was restricted to men. Even more than feudal armies—which were often accompanied by women who did laundry, found provisions, cooked meals, and engaged in sex for money—universities were all-male communities. (Most European universities did not admit women until after World War I.)

Though university classes were not especially expensive, the many years that a university education required meant that the sons of peasants or artisans could rarely attend, unless they could find wealthy patrons who would pay their expenses. Most students were the sons of urban merchants or lower-level nobles, especially the younger sons who would not inherit family lands. University degrees were initially designed as licenses to teach at the university, but most students staffed the expanding diocesan, royal, and papal administrations as lawyers and officials.

Students did not spend all their time preparing for their degrees. Much information about medieval students concerns what we might call "extracurricular" activities: university regulations forbidding them to throw rocks at professors; sermons about breaking and entering, raping local women, attacking town residents, and disturbing church services; and court records discussing their drunken brawls, riots, and fights and duels. Students also delayed finishing their studies because life as a student could be pleasant, without the responsibilities that came with becoming fully adult. Student life was described by students in poems, usually anonymous, that celebrated the joys of Venus (the goddess of love) and other gods:

> When we are in the tavern,
> we do not think how we will go to dust,
> but we hurry to gamble,
> which always makes us sweat.
> . . .
> Here no-one fears death,
> but they throw the dice in the name of Bacchus.
> . . .
> To the Pope as to the king
> they all drink without restraint.[7]

Literature and Architecture

FOCUS QUESTION *How did literature and architecture express medieval values?*

The High Middle Ages saw the creation of new types of literature, architecture, and music. Technological advances in such areas as papermaking and stone masonry made some of these innovations possible, as did the growing wealth and sophistication of patrons. Artists and artisans flourished in the more secure environment of the High Middle Ages, producing works that celebrated the glories of love, war, and God.

Vernacular Literature and Drama

Latin was the language used in university education, scholarly writing, and works of literature. By the High Middle Ages, however, no one spoke Latin as his or her original mother tongue. The barbarian invasions, the mixture of peoples, and the usual changes in language that occur over time had resulted in a variety of local dialects that blended words and linguistic forms in various ways. As kings increased the size of their holdings, they often ruled people who spoke many different dialects.

In the High Middle Ages, some authors departed from tradition and began to write in their local dialect, that is, in the everyday language of their region, which linguistic historians call the vernacular. This new **vernacular literature** gradually transformed some local dialects into literary languages, such as French, German, Italian, and English, while other local dialects, such as Breton and Bavarian, remained (and remain to this day) means of oral communication.

Facilitating this vernacular writing was a technological advance. By the thirteenth century techniques of making paper from old linen cloth and rags began to spread from Spain, where they had been developed by the Arabs, providing a much cheaper material on which to write than parchment or vellum (see Chapter 8). People started to write down the more mundane and the less serious—personal letters, lists, songs, recipes, rules, instructions—in their dialects, using spellings that were often personal and idiosyncratic. These writings included fables, legends, stories, and myths that had circulated orally for generations, adding to the growing body of written vernacular literature.

Stories and songs in the vernacular were composed and performed at the courts of nobles and rulers. In Germany and most of northern Europe, the audiences

■ **vernacular literature** Writings in the author's local dialect, that is, in the everyday language of the region.

Courtly Love Poetry

Whether female or male, the troubadour poets celebrated fin'amor, a Provençal word for the pure or perfect love a knight was supposed to feel for his lady, which has in English come to be called "courtly love." In courtly love poetry, the writer praises his or her love object, idealizing the beloved and promising loyalty and great deeds. Most of these songs are written by, or from the perspective of, a male lover who is socially beneath his female beloved; her higher status makes her unattainable, so the lover's devotion can remain chaste and pure, rewarded by her handkerchief, or perhaps a kiss, but nothing more.

Scholars generally agree that poetry praising pure and perfect love originated in the Muslim culture of the Iberian Peninsula, where heterosexual romantic love had long been the subject of poems and songs. Spanish Muslim poets sang at the courts of Christian nobles, and Provençal poets picked up their romantic themes.

Other aspects of courtly love are hotly debated. Was it simply a literary convention, or did it shape actual behavior? Did it celebrate adultery, or was true courtly love pure (and unrequited)? How should we interpret medieval physicians' reports of people (mostly young men) becoming gravely ill from "lovesickness"? Were there actually "courts of love" in which women judged lovers based on a system of rules? Did courtly love lead to greater respect for women or toward greater misogyny, as desire for a beloved so often ended in frustration? It is very difficult to know whether courtly love literature influenced the treatment of real women to any great extent, but it did introduce a new ideal of heterosexual romance into Western literature. Courtly love ideals still shape romantic conventions and often appear in movies, songs, and novels that explore love between people of different social groups.

The following poem was written by Arnaut Daniel, a thirteenth-century troubadour praised by poets from Dante in the thirteenth century to Ezra Pound in the twentieth. Not much is known about him, but his surviving songs capture courtly love conventions perfectly.

I only know the grief that comes to me,
to my love-ridden heart, out of over-loving,
since my will is so firm and whole
that it never parted or grew distant from her
whom I craved at first sight, and afterwards:
and now, in her absence, I tell her burning words;
then, when I see her, I don't know, so much I have to,
   what to say.

To the sight of other women I am blind, deaf to hearing
   them
since her only I see, and hear and heed,

and in that I am surely not a false slanderer,
since heart desires her more than mouth may say;
wherever I may roam through fields and valleys, plains
   and mountains
I shan't find in a single person all those qualities
which God wanted to select and place in her.

I have been in many a good court,
but here by her I find much more to praise:
measure and wit and other good virtues,
beauty and youth, worthy deeds and fair disport;
so well kindness taught and instructed her
that it has rooted every ill manner out of her:
I don't think she lacks anything good.

No joy would be brief or short
coming from her whom I endear to guess [my intentions],
otherwise she won't know them from me,
if my heart cannot reveal itself without words,
since even the Rhone [River], when rain swells it,
has no such rush that my heart doesn't stir
a stronger one, weary of love, when I behold her.

Joy and merriment from another woman seems false and
   ill to me,
since no worthy one can compare with her,
and her company is above the others'.
Ah me, if I don't have her, alas, so badly she has taken me!
But this grief is amusement, laughter and joy,
since in thinking of her, of her am I gluttonous and
   greedy:
ah me, God, could I ever enjoy her otherwise!

And never, I swear, I have liked game or ball so much,
or anything has given my heart so much joy
as did the one thing that no false slanderer
made public, which is a treasure for me only.
Do I tell too much? Not I, unless she is displeased:
beautiful one, by God, speech and voice
I'd lose ere I say something to annoy you.

And I pray my song does not displease you
since, if you like the music and lyrics,
little cares Arnaut whether the unpleasant ones like them
   as well.

Far fewer poems by female trobairitz have survived than by male troubadours, but those that have survived express strong physical and emotional feelings. The following song was written in the twelfth century by the Countess of Dia. She was purportedly the wife of a Provençal nobleman, though biographies of both troubadours and trobairitz were often made up to fit the conventions of courtly love, so we don't know for sure. The words to at least four of her songs have survived, one of them with the melody, which is very rare.

~

I've suffered great distress
From a knight whom I once owned.
Now, for all time, be it known:
I loved him — yes, to excess. His jilting I've regretted,
Yet his love I never really returned. Now for my sin I
    can only burn:
Dressed, or in my bed.

O if I had that knight to caress
Naked all night in my arms,
He'd be ravished by the charm
Of using, for cushion, my breast. His love I more
    deeply prize
Than Floris did Blancheor's
Take that love, my core, My sense, my life, my eyes!

Lovely lover, gracious, kind,
When will I overcome your fight?
O if I could lie with you one night!
Feel those loving lips on mine! Listen, one thing sets
    me afire:
Here in my husband's place I want you,
If you'll just keep your promise true: Give me
    everything I desire.

EVALUATE THE EVIDENCE

1. Both of these songs focus on a beloved who does not return the lover's affection. What similarities and differences do you see in them?
2. How does courtly love reinforce other aspects of medieval society? Are there aspects of medieval society it contradicts?
3. Can you find examples from current popular music that parallel the sentiments expressed in these two songs?

Sources: First poem: From "Sol sui qui sai lo sobrafan qu'em sortz" by Arnaut Daniel, translated by Leonardo Malcovati, www.trobar.org. Used by permission of Leonardo Malcovati, editor and translator of *Prosody in England and Elsewhere: A Comparative Approach* (London: Gival Press, 2006), and online at www.trobar.org; second poem: Three verses from lyrics by the Countess of Dia, often called Beatritz, the Sappho of the Rhone, in *Lyrics of the Middle Ages: An Anthology*, edited and translated by James J. Wilhelm. Reproduced with permission of GARLAND PUBLISHING, INC., in the format Book via Copyright Clearance Center.

favored stories and songs recounting the great deeds of warrior heroes. These epics, known as *chansons de geste* (SHAN-suhn duh JEHST; songs of great deeds), celebrate violence, slaughter, revenge, and physical power. In southern Europe, especially in Provence in southern France, poets who called themselves **troubadours** (TROO-buh-dorz) wrote and sang lyric verses celebrating love, desire, beauty, and gallantry. (See "Evaluating the Evidence 10.3: Courtly Love Poetry," at left.) Troubadours included a few women, called *trobairitz*, most of whose exact identities are not known.

The songs of the troubadours were widely imitated in Italy, England, and Germany, so they spurred the development of vernacular literature there as well. At the court of his patron, Marie of Champagne, Chrétien de Troyes (ca. 1135–ca. 1190) used the legends of the fifth-century British king Arthur (see Chapter 7) as the basis for innovative tales of battle and forbidden love. His most popular story is that of the noble Lancelot, whose love for Guinevere, the wife of King Arthur, his lord, became physical as well as spiritual. Most of the troubadours came from and wrote for the aristocratic classes, and their poetry suggests the interests and values of noble culture. Their influence extended to all social groups, however, for people who could not read heard the poems and stories from people who could, so that what had originally come from oral culture was recycled back into it.

Drama, derived from the church's liturgy, emerged as a distinct art form during the High Middle Ages. Amateurs and later professional actors performed plays based on biblical themes and on the lives of the saints; these dramas were presented in the towns, first in churches and then at the marketplace. Members of the craft guilds performed "mystery" plays, so called because guilds were sometimes called "mysteries." By combining comical farce based on ordinary life with serious religious scenes, plays gave ordinary people an opportunity to identify with religious figures and think about their faith.

Churches and Cathedrals

The development of secular vernacular literature focusing on human concerns did not mean any lessening of the importance of religion in medieval people's lives. As we have seen, religious devotion was expressed through daily rituals, holiday ceremonies, and the creation of new institutions such as universities and religious orders. People also wanted permanent visible representations of their piety, and both church and city leaders wanted physical symbols of their wealth and

---

■ **troubadours** Poets who wrote and sang lyric verses celebrating love, desire, beauty, and gallantry.

Notre Dame Cathedral, Paris This view offers a fine example of the twin towers (left), the spire and great rose window over the south portal (center), and the flying buttresses that support the walls and the vaults. Like hundreds of other churches in medieval Europe, it was dedicated to the Virgin Mary. With a spire rising more than 300 feet, Notre Dame was the tallest building in Europe. (David R. Frazier/Science Source)

power. These aims found their outlet in the building of tens of thousands of churches, chapels, abbeys, and, most spectacularly, **cathedrals** in the twelfth and thirteenth centuries. A cathedral is the church of a bishop and the administrative headquarters of a diocese. The word comes from the Greek word *kathedra*, meaning seat, because the bishop's throne, a symbol of the office, is located in the cathedral.

Most of the churches in the early Middle Ages had been built primarily of wood, which meant they were susceptible to fire. They were often small, with a flat roof, in a rectangular form with a central aisle; this structure, called a basilica, was based on earlier Roman public buildings. With the increasing political stability of the eleventh century, bishops and abbots supported the construction of larger and more fire-resistant churches made almost completely out of stone. As the size of the church grew horizontally, it

also grew vertically. Builders adapted Roman-style rounded barrel vaults made of stone for the ceiling; this use of Roman forms led the style to be labeled **Romanesque**.

The next architectural style was **Gothic**, so named by later Renaissance architects who thought that only the uncouth Goths could have invented such a disunified style. In Gothic churches the solid stone barrel-vaulted roof was replaced by a roof made of stone ribs with plaster in between. Because this ceiling was much lighter, side pillars and walls did not need to carry as much weight. Exterior arched stone supports called flying buttresses also carried some of the weight of the roof, so solid walls could be replaced by windows, which let in great amounts of light. Originating in the Île-de-France in the twelfth century, Gothic architecture spread throughout France with the expansion of royal power. From France the new style spread to England, Germany, Italy, Spain, and eastern Europe.

Extraordinary amounts of money were needed to build these houses of worship. The economic growth of the period meant that merchants, nobles, and the church could afford the costs of this unparalleled

■ **cathedral** The church of a bishop and the administrative headquarters of a diocese.

■ **Romanesque** An architectural style with rounded arches and small windows.

■ **Gothic** An architectural style typified by pointed arches and large stained-glass windows.

building boom. Moreover, money was not the only need. A great number of artisans had to be assembled: quarrymen, sculptors, stonecutters, masons, mortar makers, carpenters, blacksmiths, glassmakers, roofers. Each master craftsman had apprentices, and unskilled laborers had to be recruited for the heavy work. Bishops and abbots sketched out what they wanted and set general guidelines, but they left practical needs and aesthetic considerations to the master mason. He held overall responsibility for supervision of the project.

Since cathedrals were symbols of civic pride, towns competed to build the largest and most splendid church. In 1163 the citizens of Paris began Notre Dame Cathedral, planning it to reach the height of 114 feet from the floor to the ceiling at the highest point inside. Many other cathedrals well over 100 feet tall on the inside were built as each bishop and town sought to outdo the neighbors. Towers and spires jutted up another several hundred feet. Medieval people built cathedrals to glorify God—and if mortals were impressed, all the better. Construction of a large cathedral was rarely completed in a lifetime; many were never finished at all. Because generation after generation added to the buildings, many of these churches show the architectural influences of two or even three centuries.

Stained glass beautifully reflects the creative energy of the High Middle Ages. It is both an integral part of Gothic architecture and a distinct form of visual art. From large sheets of colored glass made by glassblowers, artisans cut small pieces, linked them together with narrow strips of lead, and set them in an iron frame prepared to fit the window opening. Windows showed scenes from the Old and New Testaments and the lives of the saints, designed to teach people doctrines of the Christian faith. They also showed scenes from the lives of the artisans and merchants who paid for them.

Once at least part of a cathedral had been built, the building began to be used for religious services. Town residents gathered for masses, baptisms, funerals, and saint's day services, and also used it for guild meetings and other secular purposes. Services became increasingly complex to fit with their new surroundings. Originally, services were chanted by the clergy in unison, in a form of liturgical music termed plainsong or Gregorian chant, but by the eleventh century additional voices singing in different pitches were added, creating what is called polyphony. Church leaders sometimes fumed that polyphony made the text impossible to understand but—along with incense, candles, stained-glass windows, statuary, tapestry wall hangings, and the building itself—music made services in a Gothic cathedral a rich experience.

The frenzy to create the most magnificent Gothic cathedrals eventually came to an end. Begun in 1247, the cathedral in Beauvais reached a height of 157 feet in the interior, exceeding all others. Unfortunately, the weight imposed on the vaults was too great, and the building collapsed in 1284. The collapse was viewed as an aberration, for countless other cathedrals were in various stages of completion at the same time, and none of them fell. In hindsight, however, it can be viewed as a harbinger. Very few cathedrals not yet completed at the time of its collapse were ever finished, and even fewer were started. In the fourteenth century the church itself splintered, and the cities that had so proudly built cathedrals were decimated by famine and disease.

NOTES

1. Honorius of Autun, "Elucidarium sive Dialogus de Summa Totius Christianae Theologiae," in *Patrologia Latina*, ed. J. P. Migne (Paris: Garnier Brothers, 1854), vol. 172, col. 1149.
2. M. Chibnall, ed. and trans., *The Ecclesiastical History of Ordericus Vitalis* (Oxford: Oxford University Press, 1972), 2.xiii.
3. Thirteenth-century sermon story, in David Herlihy, ed., *Medieval Culture and Society* (New York: Harper and Row, 1968), pp. 295, 298.
4. Translated and quoted in Susan C. Karant-Nunn, *The Reformation of Ritual: An Interpretation of Early Modern Germany* (London: Routledge, 1997), p. 77.
5. Roy C. Cave and Hervet H. Coulson, *A Source Book for Medieval Economic History* (New York: Biblio and Tannen, 1965), p. 257.
6. H. Rothwell, ed., *English Historical Documents*, vol. 3 (London: Eyre & Spottiswoode, 1975), p. 854.
7. www.classical.net/music/comp.lst/works/orff-cb/carmlyr.php#track14. This verse is from one of the songs known as the Carmina Burana, which are widely available as recordings, downloadable files, and even cell phone ring tones.

LOOKING BACK LOOKING AHEAD

The High Middle Ages represent one of the most creative periods in the history of Western society. Institutions that are important parts of the modern world, including universities, jury trials, and investment banks, were all developed in this era. Advances were made in the mechanization of labor, business procedures, architectural design, and education. Through the activities of merchants, Europeans again saw products from Africa and Asia in city marketplaces, as they had in Roman times, and wealthier urban residents bought them. Individuals and groups such as craft guilds provided money for building and decorating magnificent Gothic cathedrals, where people heard increasingly complex music and watched plays that celebrated both the lives of the saints and their own daily struggles.

Toward the end of the thirteenth century, however, there were increasing signs of impending problems. The ships and caravans bringing exotic goods also brought new pests. The new vernacular literature created a stronger sense of national identity, which increased hostility toward others. The numbers of poor continued to grow, and efforts to aid their suffering were never enough. As the century ended, villagers and city residents alike continued to gather for worship, but they also wondered whether God was punishing them.

Make Connections

Think about the larger developments and continuities within and across chapters.

1. How was life in a medieval city different from life in a Hellenistic city (Chapter 4), or life in Rome during the time of Augustus (Chapter 6)? In what ways was it similar? What problems did these cities confront that are still issues for cities today?

2. Historians have begun to turn their attention to the history of children and childhood. How were children's lives in the societies you have examined shaped by larger social structures and cultural forces? What commonalities do you see in children's lives across time?

3. Chapter 4 and this chapter both examine ways in which religion and philosophy shaped life for ordinary people and for the educated elite. How would you compare Hellenistic religious practices with those of medieval Europe? How would you compare the ideas of Hellenistic philosophers such as Epicurus or Zeno with those of Scholastic philosophers such as Thomas Aquinas?

10 REVIEW & EXPLORE

Identify Key Terms

Identify and explain the significance of each item below.

open-field system (p. 287)

merchant guild (p. 299)

craft guild (p. 299)

Hanseatic League (p. 302)

commercial revolution (p. 304)

sumptuary laws (p. 307)

Scholastics (p. 311)

vernacular literature (p. 313)

troubadours (p. 315)

cathedral (p. 316)

Romanesque (p. 316)

Gothic (p. 316)

Review the Main Ideas

Answer the focus questions from each section of the chapter.

◆ What was village life like in medieval Europe? (p. 286)

◆ How did religion shape everyday life in the High Middle Ages? (p. 293)

◆ What led to Europe's economic growth and reurbanization? (p. 297)

◆ What was life like in medieval cities? (p. 306)

◆ How did universities serve the needs of medieval society? (p. 308)

◆ How did literature and architecture express medieval values? (p. 313)

Suggested Reading and Media Resources

BOOKS

◆ Bennett, Judith M. *A Medieval Life: Cecelia Peni-fader of Brigstock, c. 1297–1344*. 1998. An excellent brief introduction to all aspects of village life from the perspective of one woman; designed for students.

◆ Coldstream, Nicola. *Medieval Architecture*. 2002. A beautifully illustrated discussion of all types of buildings and how they reflect the material and spiritual concerns of the people who built and used them.

◆ Epstein, Steven A. *An Economic and Social History of Later Medieval Europe, 1000–1500*. 2009. Examines European social and economic history in its cultural setting.

◆ Gaunt, Simon, and Sarah Kay, eds. *The Troubadours: An Introduction*. 1999. A collection of essays that trace the development of troubadour song and the reception of troubadour poetry.

◆ Glick, Leonard B. *Abraham's Heirs: Jews and Christians in Medieval Europe*. 1999. Provides information on many aspects of Jewish life and Jewish-Christian relations.

◆ Mews, Constant. *Abelard and Heloise*. 2005. Examines the lives and ideas of these two thinkers in the context of their times.

◆ Moore, R. I. *The First European Revolution: 970–1215*. 2000. A bold assessment of the long-term significance of the changes discussed in this chapter.

◆ Pedersen, Olaf. *The First Universities: Studium Generale and the Origins of University Education in Europe*. 1997. Traces the development of education in Europe from antiquity to the fourteenth century, with attention to the lives of students.

◆ Shahar, Shulamit. *The Fourth Estate: A History of Women in the Middle Ages*, 2d ed. 2003. Provides information on the lives of women, including nuns, peasants, noblewomen, and townswomen.

◆ Shinners, John. *Medieval Popular Religion, 1000–1500*, 2d ed. 2006. A wide variety of sources that provide evidence about the beliefs and practices of ordinary Christians.

◆ Siraisi, Nancy. *Medieval and Early Renaissance Medicine: An Introduction to Knowledge and Practice*. 1990. The best place to start for information about both the theory and practice of medicine.

◆ Spufford, Peter. *Power and Profit: The Merchant in Medieval Europe*. 2003. A comprehensive history of medieval commerce, designed for general readers.

DOCUMENTARIES

◆ *Inside the Medieval Mind* (BBC, 2008). Professor Robert Bartlett of St. Andrew's University in Scotland examines the ways in which medieval people understood the world, including knowledge systems, religious beliefs, and ideas about sexuality.

◆ *Terry Jones' Medieval Lives* (BBC, 2004). Award-winning eight-part documentary series that focuses on the real experiences of certain kinds of medieval people often portrayed stereotypically, including the peasant, the damsel, the minstrel, the knight, and the outlaw.

FEATURE FILMS

◆ *Monty Python and the Holy Grail* (Terry Gilliam and Terry Jones, 1975). A spoof of the King Arthur legend and a send-up of popular views of many aspects of the Middle Ages (chivalry, dirt, disease, witchcraft). The basis for Eric Idle's 2005 Tony Award–winning musical *Spamalot*, and the source of countless pop culture references.

◆ *Sorceress* (Suzanne Schiffman, 1987). Written by a medieval historian and shot in both French and English, this wonderful film is based on an actual text by a thirteenth-century Dominican friar investigating the cult of Saint Guinefort, the holy greyhound, near Lyons in France. The film addresses issues relating to healing, popular religion, and the role of women.

WEB SITES

◆ *Epistolae: Medieval Women's Letters*. A collection of letters to and from women in the Middle Ages, from the fourth to the thirteenth centuries, on a range of topics including religion, diplomacy, family, and politics. Includes both the original Latin and English translations and, where available, information about the writer and the historical context of the letter. **epistolae.ccnmtl.columbia.edu/**

◆ *Index of Medieval Medical Images*. Provides access to a huge variety of images related to medicine in the Middle Ages. Most easily used through the "Browse" function, the site includes topics ranging from "Abortion" to "Zodiac." **digital.library.ucla.edu/immi/**

◆ *TEAMS Middle English Texts*. Run by the Consortium for Teaching the Middle Ages (TEAMS), this site provides a well-organized portal into the world of medieval English literature through more than 350 poems, prose narratives, sermons, books of advice, and other works. Each text has an introduction giving the cultural context. **www.lib.rochester.edu/camelot/teams/tmsmenu.htm**

11

The Later Middle Ages

1300–1450

During the later Middle Ages the last book of the New Testament, the book of Revelation, inspired thousands of sermons and hundreds of religious tracts. The book of Revelation deals with visions of the end of the world, with disease, war, famine, and death—often called the "Four Horsemen of the Apocalypse"—triumphing everywhere. It is no wonder this part of the Bible was so popular in this period, for between 1300 and 1450 Europeans experienced a frightful series of shocks. The climate turned colder and wetter, leading to poor harvests and famine. People weakened by hunger were more susceptible to disease, and in the middle of the fourteenth century a new disease, probably the bubonic plague, spread throughout Europe. With no effective treatment, the plague killed millions of people. War devastated the countryside, especially in France, leading to widespread discontent and peasant revolts. Workers in cities also revolted against dismal working conditions, and violent crime and ethnic tensions increased as well. Massive deaths and preoccupation with death make the fourteenth century one of the most wrenching periods of Western civilization. Yet, in spite of the pessimism and crises, important institutions and cultural forms, including representative assemblies and national literatures, emerged. Even institutions that experienced severe crisis, such as the Christian Church, saw new types of vitality. ■

CHAPTER PREVIEW

Life and Death in the Late Middle Ages

In this French manuscript illumination from 1465, armored knights kill peasants while they work in the fields or take refuge in a castle. Aristocratic violence was a common feature of late medieval life, although nobles would generally not have bothered to put on their armor to harass villagers. (From *Cas de Nobles Hommes et Femmes*, 1465/ Musée Condé, Chantilly, France/Bridgeman Images)

Prelude to Disaster

FOCUS QUESTION *How did climate change shape the late Middle Ages?*

Toward the end of the thirteenth century the expanding European economy began to slow down, and in the first half of the fourteenth century Europe experienced ongoing climate change that led to lower levels of food production, which had dramatic and disastrous ripple effects. Rulers attempted to find solutions but were unable to deal with the economic and social problems that resulted.

Climate Change and Famine

The period from about 1000 to about 1300 saw a warmer-than-usual climate in Europe, which underlay all the changes and vitality of the High Middle Ages. Around 1300, however, the climate changed for the worse, becoming colder and wetter. Historical geographers refer to the period from 1300 to 1450 as a "little ice age," which they can trace through both natural and human records.

Evidence from nature emerges through the study of Alpine and polar glaciers, tree rings, and pollen left in bogs. Human-produced sources include written reports of rivers freezing and crops never ripening, as well as archaeological evidence such as the collapsed houses and emptied villages of Greenland, where ice floes cut off contact with the rest of the world and the harshening climate meant that the few hardy crops grown in earlier times could no longer survive. The Viking colony on Greenland died out completely, though Inuit people who relied on hunting sea mammals continued to live in the far north, as they had before the arrival of Viking colonists.

Across Europe, an unusual number of storms brought torrential rains, ruining the wheat, oat, and hay crops on which people and animals almost everywhere depended. Since long-distance transportation of food was expensive and difficult, most urban areas depended for grain, produce, and meat on areas no more than a day's journey away. Poor harvests—and one in four was likely to be poor—led to scarcity and starvation. Almost all of northern Europe suffered a **Great Famine** in the years 1315 to 1322, which contemporaries interpreted as a recurrence of the biblical "seven lean years" that afflicted Egypt.

Even in non-famine years, the cost of grain, livestock, and dairy products rose sharply, in part because diseases hit cattle and sheep. Increasing prices meant that fewer people could afford to buy food. Reduced

Death from Famine   In this fifteenth-century painting, dead bodies lie in the middle of a path, while a funeral procession at the right includes a man with an adult's coffin and a woman with the coffin of an infant under her arm. People did not simply allow the dead to lie in the street in medieval Europe, though during famines and epidemics it was sometimes difficult to maintain normal burial procedures. (From *Chroniques d'Angleterre*, ca. 1470–1480/British Library, London, UK/© British Library Board. All Rights Reserved/Bridgeman Images)

caloric intake meant increased susceptibility to disease, especially for infants, children, and the elderly. Workers on reduced diets had less energy, which meant lower productivity, lower output, and higher grain prices.

Social Consequences

The changing climate and resulting agrarian crisis of the fourteenth century had grave social consequences. Poor harvests and famine led to the abandonment of homesteads. In parts of the Low Countries and in the Scottish-English borderlands, entire villages were deserted, and many people became vagabonds, wandering in search of food and work. In Flanders and eastern England, some peasants were forced to mortgage, sublease, or sell their holdings to richer farmers in order to buy food. Throughout the affected areas, young men and women sought work in the towns, delaying marriage. Overall, the population declined because of the deaths caused by famine and disease, though the postponement of marriages and resulting decline in offspring may have also played a part.

As the subsistence crisis deepened, starving people focused their anger on the rich, speculators, and the Jews, who were often targeted as creditors fleecing the poor through pawnbroking. (As explained in Chapter 10, Jews often became moneylenders because Christian authorities restricted their ownership of land and opportunities to engage in other trades.) Rumors spread of a plot by Jews and their agents, the lepers, to kill Christians by poisoning wells. Based on "evidence" collected by torture, many lepers and Jews were killed, beaten, or heavily fined.

Meanwhile, the international character of trade and commerce meant that a disaster in one country had serious implications elsewhere. For example, the infection that attacked English sheep in 1318 caused a sharp decline in wool exports in the following years. Without wool, Flemish weavers could not work, and thousands were laid off. Without woolen cloth, the businesses of Flemish, Hanseatic, and Italian merchants suffered. Unemployment encouraged people to turn to crime.

Government responses to these crises were ineffectual. The three sons of Philip the Fair who sat on the French throne between 1314 and 1328 condemned speculators who held stocks of grain back until conditions were desperate and prices high, and they forbade the sale of grain abroad. These measures had few actual results, however. In England, Edward II (r. 1307–1327)

Chronology

1300–1450	Little ice age
1309–1376	Babylonian Captivity; papacy in Avignon
1310–1320	Dante writes *Divine Comedy*
1315–1322	Great Famine in northern Europe
1320s	First large-scale peasant rebellion in Flanders
1337–1453	Hundred Years' War
1347	Black Death arrives in Europe
1358	Jacquerie peasant uprising in France
1366	Statute of Kilkenny
1378–1417	Great Schism
1381	English Peasants' Revolt
1387–1400	Chaucer writes *Canterbury Tales*

also condemned speculators after his attempts to set price controls on livestock and ale proved futile. He did try to buy grain abroad, but little was available, and such grain as reached southern English ports was stolen by looters and sold on the black market. The king's efforts at famine relief failed.

The Black Death

FOCUS QUESTION *How did the plague reshape European society?*

Colder weather, failed harvests, and resulting malnourishment left Europe's population susceptible to disease, and unfortunately for the continent, a virulent one appeared in the mid-fourteenth century. Around 1300 improvements in ship design had allowed year-round shipping for the first time. European merchants took advantage of these advances, and ships continually at sea carried all types of cargo. They also carried vermin of all types, especially insects and rats, both of which often harbored pathogens. Rats, fleas, and cockroaches could live for months on the cargo carried along the coasts, disembarking at ports with the grain, cloth, or other merchandise. Just as modern air travel has allowed diseases such as AIDS and the H1N1 virus to spread quickly over very long distances, medieval shipping allowed the diseases of the time to do the same. The most frightful of these diseases, carried on Genoese ships, first emerged in western Europe in 1347; the disease was later called the **Black Death**.

■ **Great Famine** A terrible famine in 1315–1322 that hit much of Europe after a period of climate change.

■ **Black Death** Plague that first struck Europe in 1347 and killed perhaps one-third of the population.

Pathology

Most historians and microbiologists identify the disease that spread in the fourteenth century as the bubonic plague, which is caused by the bacillus *Yersinia pestis*. The disease normally afflicts rats. Fleas living on the infected rats drink their blood and then pass the bacteria that cause the plague on to the next rat they bite. Usually the disease is limited to rats and other rodents, but at certain points in history—perhaps when most rats have been killed off—the fleas have jumped from their rodent hosts to humans and other animals. One of these instances appears to have occurred in the Eastern Roman Empire in the sixth century, when a plague killed millions of people. Another was in China and India in the 1890s, when millions again died. Doctors and epidemiologists closely studied this outbreak, identified the bacillus as bubonic plague, and learned about the exact cycle of infection for the first time.

The fourteenth-century outbreak showed many similarities to the nineteenth-century one, but also some differences. There are no reports of massive rat die-offs in fourteenth-century records. The medieval plague was often transmitted directly from one person to another through coughing and sneezing (what epidemiologists term *pneumonic* transmission) as well as through fleabites. The fourteenth-century outbreak spread much faster than the nineteenth-century epidemic and was much more deadly, killing as much as one-third of the population when it first reached an area. These differences have led a few historians to speculate that the Black Death was actually not the bubonic plague but a different disease, perhaps something like the Ebola virus. Other scholars counter that the differences could be explained by variant strains of the disease or improvements in sanitation and public health that would have significantly limited the mortality rate of later outbreaks, even in poor countries such as India. These debates fuel continued study of medical aspects of the plague, with scientists using innovative techniques such as studying the tooth pulp of bodies in medieval cemeteries to see if it contains DNA from plague-causing agents.

Though there is some disagreement about exactly what kind of disease the plague was, there is no dispute about its dreadful effects on the body. The classic symptom of the bubonic plague was a growth the size of a nut or an apple in the armpit, in the groin, or on the neck. This was the boil, or *bubo*, that gave the disease its name and caused agonizing pain. If the bubo was lanced and the pus thoroughly drained, the victim had a chance of recovery. If the boil was not lanced, however—and in the fourteenth century, it rarely was—the next stage was the appearance of black spots or blotches caused by bleeding under the skin. (This syndrome did not give the disease its common name; contemporaries did not call the plague the Black Death. Sometime in the fifteenth century the Latin phrase *atra mors*, meaning "dreadful death," was translated as "black death," and the phrase stuck.) Finally, the victim began to cough violently and spit blood. This stage, indicating the presence of millions of bacilli in the bloodstream, signaled the end, and death followed in two or three days. The coughing also released those pathogens into the air, infecting others when they were breathed in and beginning the deadly cycle again on new victims.

Spread of the Disease

Plague symptoms were first described in 1331 in southwestern China, then part of the Mongol Empire. Plague-infested rats accompanied Mongol armies and merchant caravans carrying silk, spices, and gold across Central Asia in the 1330s. The rats then stowed away on ships, carrying the disease to the ports of the Black Sea by the 1340s. One Italian chronicler told of more dramatic means of spreading the disease as well: Mongol armies besieging the city of Kaffa on the shores of the Black Sea catapulted plague-infected corpses over the walls to infect those inside. The city's residents dumped the corpses into the sea as fast as they could, but they were already infected.

In October 1347 Genoese ships brought the plague from Kaffa to Messina, from which it spread across Sicily. Venice and Genoa were hit in January 1348, and from the port of Pisa the disease spread south to Rome and east to Florence and all of Tuscany. By late spring southern Germany was attacked. Frightened French authorities chased a galley bearing plague victims away from the port of Marseilles, but not before plague had infected the city, from which it spread to southern France and Spain. In June 1348 two ships entered the Bristol Channel and introduced it into England, and from there it traveled northeast into Scandinavia. The plague seems to have entered Poland through the Baltic seaports and spread eastward from there (Map 11.1).

Medieval urban conditions were ideal for the spread of disease. Narrow streets were filled with refuse, human excrement, and dead animals. Houses whose upper stories projected over the lower ones blocked light and air. Houses were beginning to be constructed of brick, but many wood, clay, and mud houses remained. A determined rat had little trouble entering such a house. In addition, people were already weakened by famine, standards of personal hygiene remained frightfully low, and the urban

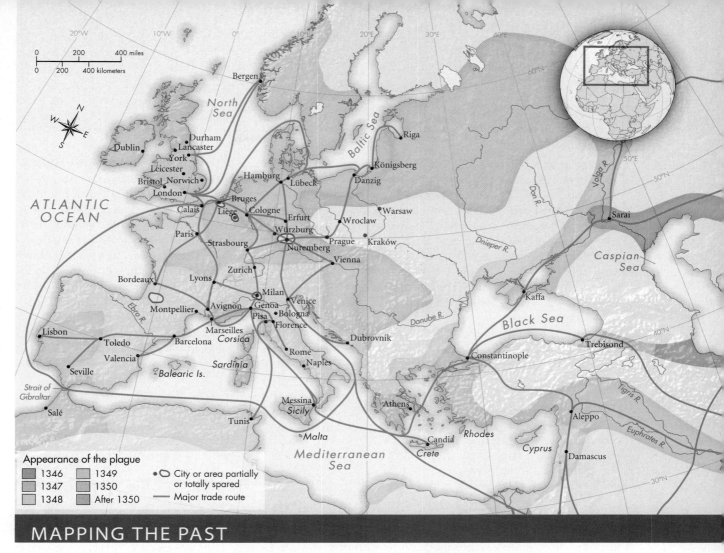

MAP 11.1 The Course of the Black Death in Fourteenth-Century Europe

The bubonic plague spread across Europe after beginning in the mid-1340s, with the first cases of disease reported in Black Sea ports.

ANALYZING THE MAP When did the plague reach Paris? How much time passed before it spread to the rest of northern France and southern Germany? Which cities and regions were spared?

CONNECTIONS How did the expansion of trade contribute to the spread of the Black Death?

populace was crowded together. Fleas and body lice were universal afflictions: everyone from peasants to archbishops had them. One more bite did not cause much alarm, and the association between rats, fleas, and the plague was unknown. Mortality rates can be only educated guesses because population figures for the period before the arrival of the plague do not exist for most countries and cities. Of a total English population of perhaps 4.2 million, probably 1.4 million died of the Black Death. Densely populated Italian cities endured incredible losses. Florence lost between one-half and two-thirds of its population when the plague visited in 1348. Islamic parts of Europe were not spared, nor was the rest of the Muslim world. The most widely accepted estimate for western Europe

and the Mediterranean is that the plague killed about one-third of the population in the first wave of infection. (Some areas, including such cities as Milan, Liège, and Nuremberg, were largely spared, primarily because city authorities closed the gates to all outsiders when plague was in the area and enough food had been stored to sustain the city until the danger had passed.)

Nor did central and eastern Europe escape the ravages of the disease. One chronicler records that, in the summer and autumn of 1349, between five hundred and six hundred died every day in Vienna. As the Black Death took its toll on the Holy Roman Empire, waves of emigrants fled to Poland, Bohemia, and Hungary, taking the plague with them. In the Byzantine Empire

LIVING IN THE PAST
Treating the Plague

Medieval physicians based treatments for the plague on their understanding of how the body worked, as do doctors in any era. Fourteenth-century people — lay, scholarly, and medical — attributed the disease to "poisons" in the air that caused the fluids in the body to become unbalanced. The imbalance in fluids led to illness, an idea that had been the core of Western ideas about the primary cause of disease since the ancient Greeks. Certain symptoms of the plague, such as boils that oozed and blood-filled coughing, were believed to be the body's natural reaction to too much fluid.

Doctors thus recommended preventive measures that would block the poisoned air from entering the body, such as burning incense or holding strong-smelling herbs or other substances, like rosemary, juniper, or sulfur, in front of the nose. Treatment concentrated on ridding the body of poisons and bringing the fluids into balance. As one fifteenth-century treatise put it, "everyone over seven should be made to vomit daily" and twice a week wrap up in sheets to "sweat copiously." The best way to regain health, however, was to let blood: "as soon as [the patient] feels an itch or pricking in his flesh [the physician] must use a goblet or cupping horn to let blood and draw down the blood from his heart, and this should be done two or three times at intervals of one or two days at the most." Letting blood was considered the most effective way to rebalance the fluids and to flush the body of poisons.

From ancient times to the nineteenth century, physicians often used cups such as this (above) to aid in bloodletting. The cup was heated to create a vacuum and then placed on the skin, where it would draw blood to the surface before a vein was cut. (cup: © Trustees of the British Museum/Art Resource, NY; doctor: From *Tractatus de Pestilencia*, by M. Albik/Private Collection/ Archives Charmet/Bridgeman Images)

328

A plague doctor is depicted in a seventeenth-century German engraving published during a later outbreak of the dreaded disease. The doctor is fully covered, with a coat waxed smooth so that poisons just slide off. The beaked mask contains strong-smelling herbs, and the stick, beaten on the ground as he walks along, warns people away. (Ca. 1656 engraving by Furst, after J. Colombina/Hulton Archive/Getty Images)

QUESTIONS FOR ANALYSIS

1. In the background of the plague doctor engraving, the artist shows a group of children running away as the plague doctor approaches. What aspects of his appearance or treatment methods contributed to this reaction?
2. Many people who lived through the plague reported that it created a sense of hopeless despair. Do the quotations from medical treatises and the objects depicted here support this idea? Why or why not?

Source: Quotations from Rosemary Horrox, *The Black Death* (Manchester: Manchester University Press, 1994), p. 194.

the plague ravaged the population. The youngest son of Emperor John VI Kantakouzenos died just as his father took over the throne in 1347. "So incurable was the evil," wrote John later in his history of the Byzantine Empire, "that neither any regularity of life, nor any bodily strength could resist it. Strong and weak bodies were all similarly carried away, and those best cared for died in the same manner as the poor."[1]

Across Europe the Black Death recurred intermittently from the 1360s to 1400. It reappeared from time to time over the following centuries as well, though never with the same virulence because by then Europeans had some resistance. Improved standards of hygiene and strictly enforced quarantine measures also lessened the plague's toll, but only in 1721 did it make its last appearance in Europe, in the French port of Marseilles. And only in 1947, six centuries after the arrival of the plague in Europe, did the American microbiologist Selman Waksman discover an effective treatment, streptomycin. Plague continues to infect rodent and human populations sporadically today.

Care of the Sick

Fourteenth-century medical literature indicates that physicians tried many different methods to prevent and treat the plague. People understood that plague and other diseases could be transmitted person to person, and they observed that crowded cities had high death rates, especially when the weather was warm and moist. We now understand that warm, moist conditions make it easier for germs to grow and spread, but fourteenth-century people thought in terms of "poisons" in the air or "corrupted air" coming from swamps, unburied animals, or the positions of the stars. Their treatments thus focused on ridding the air and the body of these poisons and on rebalancing bodily fluids. (See "Living in the Past: Treating the Plague," at left.)

People tried anything they thought might help. Perhaps loud sounds like ringing church bells or firing the newly invented cannon would clean poisoned air. Medicines made from plants that were bumpy or that oozed liquid might work, keeping the more dangerous swelling and oozing of the plague away. Magical letter and number combinations, called cryptograms, were especially popular in Muslim areas. They were often the first letters of words in prayers or religious sayings, and they gave people a sense of order when faced with the randomness with which the plague seemed to strike.

It is noteworthy that, in an age of mounting criticism of clerical wealth (see page 339), the behavior of the clergy during the plague was often exemplary. Priests, monks, and nuns cared for the sick and buried the dead. In places like Venice, from which even physicians fled, priests remained to give what ministrations they could. Consequently, their mortality rate was phenomenally high. The German clergy, especially, suffered a severe decline in personnel in the years after 1350.

There were limits to care, however. The Italian writer Giovanni Boccaccio (1313–1375), describing the course of the disease in Florence in the preface to his book of tales, *The Decameron*, identified what many knew — that the disease passed from person to person:

> This pestilence was so powerful that it was transmitted to the healthy by contact with the sick, the way a fire close to dry or oily things will set them aflame. And the evil of the plague went even further: not only did talking to or being around the sick bring infection and a common death, but also touching the clothes of the sick or anything touched or used by them seemed to communicate this very disease to the person involved.[2]

To avoid contagion, wealthier people often fled cities for the countryside, though sometimes this simply spread the plague faster. Some cities tried shutting their gates to prevent infected people and animals from coming in, which worked in a few cities. They also walled up houses in which there was plague, trying to isolate those who were sick from those who were still healthy. In Boccaccio's words, "Almost no one cared for his neighbor . . . brother abandoned brother . . . and — even worse, almost unbelievable — fathers and mothers neglected to tend and care for their children."[3]

Economic, Religious, and Cultural Effects

Economic historians and demographers sharply dispute the impact of the plague on the economy in the late fourteenth century. The traditional view that the plague had a disastrous effect has been greatly modified. By the mid-1300s the population of Europe had grown somewhat beyond what could easily be supported by available agricultural technology, and the dramatic drop in population allowed less fertile land to be abandoned. People turned to more specialized types of agriculture, such as raising sheep or wine grapes, which in the long run proved to be a better use of the land.

The Black Death did bring on a general European inflation. High mortality produced a fall in production, shortages of goods, and a general rise in prices. The price of wheat in most of Europe increased, as did the costs of meat, sausage, and cheese. This inflation continued to the end of the fourteenth century. But labor shortages resulting from the high mortality caused by the plague meant that workers could demand better wages, and the broad mass of people who survived enjoyed a higher standard of living. The greater demand for labor also meant greater mobility

Flagellants   In this manuscript illumination from 1349, shirtless flagellants scourge themselves with whips as they walk through the streets of the Flemish city of Tournai. The text notes that they are asking for God's grace to return to the city after it has been struck with the "most grave" illness. (The Flagellants of Doornik in 1349, copy of a miniature from *The Chronicle of Aegidius Li Muisis*/Private Collection/Bridgeman Images)

Dance of Death

In this fifteenth-century fresco from a tiny church in Croatia, skeletons lead people from all social classes in a procession.

(Fresco, 1475, Chapel of Our Lady of the Rocks, Croatia/Stuart Black/© Robert Harding World Imagery/Alamy Stock Photo)

EVALUATE THE EVIDENCE

1. Based on their clothing and the objects they are carrying, who are the people shown in the fresco? What does this suggest was the artist's message about death?
2. Paintings such as this clearly provide evidence of the preoccupation with death in this era, but does this work highlight other social issues as well? If so, what are they?

for peasants in rural areas and for artisans in towns and cities.

The plague also had effects on religious practices. Despite Boccaccio's comments about family members' coldness, people were saddened by the loss of their loved ones, especially their children. Not surprisingly, some people sought release from the devastating affliction in wild living, but more became more deeply pious. Rather than seeing the plague as a medical issue, they interpreted it as the result of an evil within themselves. God must be punishing them for terrible sins, they thought, so the best remedies were religious ones: asking for forgiveness, praying, trusting in God, making donations to churches, and trying to live better lives. John VI Kantakouzenos reported that in Constantinople, "many of the sick turned to better things in their minds . . . they abstained from all vice during that time and they lived virtuously; many divided their property among the poor, even before they were attacked by the disease."[4] In Muslim areas, religious leaders urged virtuous living in the face of death: give to the poor, reconcile with your enemies, free your slaves, and say a proper good-bye to your friends and family.

Believing that the Black Death was God's punishment for humanity's wickedness, some Christians turned to the severest forms of asceticism and frenzied religious fervor, joining groups of **flagellants** (FLA-juh-luhnts), who whipped and scourged themselves as penance for their and society's sins. Groups of flagellants traveled from town to town, often growing into unruly mobs. Officials worried that they would provoke violence and riots, and ordered groups to disband or forbade them to enter cities.

Along with seeing the plague as a call to reform their own behavior, however, people also searched for scapegoats, and savage cruelty sometimes resulted. As in the decades before the plague, many people believed that the Jews had poisoned the wells of Christian communities and thereby infected the drinking water. Others thought that killing Jews would prevent the plague from spreading to their town, a belief encouraged by flagellant groups. These charges led to the murder of thousands of Jews across Europe, especially in the cities of France and Germany. In Strasbourg, for example, several hundred Jews were publicly burned alive. Their houses were looted, their property was confiscated, and the remaining Jews were expelled from the city.

The literature and art of the late Middle Ages reveal a people gripped by morbid concern with death. One highly popular literary and artistic motif, the Dance of Death, depicted a dancing skeleton leading away living people, often in order of their rank. (See "Evaluating the Evidence 11.1: Dance of Death," page 331.) In the words of one early-fifteenth-century English poem:

> Death spareth not low nor high degree
> Popes, Kings, nor worthy Emperors
> When they shine most in felicity
> He can abate the freshness of their flowers
> Eclipse their bright suns with his showers . . .
> Sir Emperor, lord of all the ground,
> Sovereign Prince, and highest of nobles
> You must forsake your round apples of gold
> Leave behind your treasure and riches
> And with others to my dance obey.[5]

The years of the Black Death witnessed the foundation of new colleges at old universities and of entirely new universities. The foundation charters explain the shortage of priests and the decay of learning as the reasons for their establishment. Whereas older universities such as those at Bologna and Paris had international student bodies, these new institutions established in the wake of the Black Death had more national or local constituen-

cies. Thus the international character of medieval culture weakened, paving the way for schism (SKIH-zuhm) in the Catholic Church even before the Reformation.

As is often true with devastating events, the plague highlighted central qualities of medieval society: deep religious feeling, suspicion of those who were different, and a view of the world shaped largely by oral tradition, with a bit of classical knowledge mixed in among the educated elite.

The Hundred Years' War

FOCUS QUESTION *What were the causes, course, and consequences of the Hundred Years' War?*

The plague ravaged populations in Asia, North Africa, and Europe; in western Europe a long international war that began a decade or so before the plague struck and lasted well into the next century added further misery. England and France had engaged in sporadic military hostilities from the time of the Norman Conquest in 1066, and in the middle of the fourteenth century these became more intense. From 1337 to 1453 the two countries intermittently fought one another in what was the longest war in European history, ultimately dubbed the **Hundred Years' War**, though it actually lasted 116 years.

Causes

The Hundred Years' War had a number of causes, including disagreements over rights to land, a dispute over the succession to the French throne, and economic conflicts. Many of these revolved around the duchy of Aquitaine, a province in southern France that became part of the holdings of the English crown when Eleanor of Aquitaine married King Henry II of England in 1152 (see Chapter 9; a duchy is a territory ruled by a duke). In 1259 Henry III of England had signed the Treaty of Paris with Louis IX of France, affirming English claims to Aquitaine in return for becoming a vassal of the French crown. French policy in the fourteenth century was strongly expansionist, however, and the French kings resolved to absorb the duchy into the kingdom of France. Aquitaine therefore became a disputed territory.

The immediate political cause of the war was a disagreement over who would inherit the French throne after Charles IV of France, the last surviving son of Philip the Fair, died childless in 1328. With him ended the Capetian dynasty of France. Charles IV had a sister—Isabella—but her son was Edward III, king of England. An assembly of French high nobles, meaning to exclude Isabella and Edward from the French throne, proclaimed that "no woman nor her son could

■ **flagellants** People who believed that the plague was God's punishment for sin and sought to do penance by flagellating (whipping) themselves.

■ **Hundred Years' War** A war between England and France from 1337 to 1453, with political and economic causes and consequences.

succeed to the [French] monarchy." French lawyers defended the position with the claim that the exclusion of women from ruling or passing down the right to rule was part of Salic law, a sixth-century law code of the Franks (see Chapter 7), and that Salic law itself was part of the fundamental law of France. They used this invented tradition to argue that Edward should be barred from the French throne. (The ban on female succession became part of French legal tradition until the end of the monarchy in 1789.) The nobles passed the crown to Philip VI of Valois (r. 1328–1350), a nephew of Philip the Fair.

In 1329 Edward III formally recognized Philip VI's lordship over Aquitaine. Eight years later, Philip, eager to exercise full French jurisdiction there, confiscated the duchy. Edward III interpreted this action as a gross violation of the treaty of 1259 and as a cause for war. Moreover, Edward argued, as the eldest directly surviving male descendant of Philip the Fair, he deserved the title of king of France. Edward III's dynastic argument upset the feudal order in France: to increase their independent power, many French nobles abandoned Philip VI, using the excuse that they had to transfer their loyalty to a different overlord, Edward III. One reason the war lasted

The Hundred Years' War

1337	Philip VI of France confiscates Aquitaine; war begins
1346	English longbowmen defeat French knights at Crécy
1356	English defeat French at Poitiers
1370s–1380s	French recover some territory
1415	English defeat the French at Agincourt
1429	French victory at Orléans; Charles VII crowned king
1431	Joan of Arc declared a heretic and burned at the stake
1440s	French reconquer Normandy and Aquitaine
1453	War ends
1456	Joan cleared of charges of heresy and declared a martyr

Isabella of France and Her Son Edward Enter Oxford In this illustration for the chronicles of the counts of Flanders (made in 1477 by the artist known as the Master of Mary of Burgundy) Isabella, the sister of Charles IV of France and the wife of Edward II of England, and her son Edward are welcomed by clergy into the city of Oxford in 1326. Isabella and Edward, who was only fourteen at the time, along with her lover Roger Mortimer, had just invaded England with a small army to overthrow her husband and end the influence of his male favorite, Hugh le Despenser. They captured and imprisoned both men, executed Despenser, deposed the king, and may have ordered his murder. Isabella ruled as regent for her son for three years before he assumed personal rule by force and had Mortimer executed. She lived another twenty-eight years in high style as a wealthy woman, watching her son lead successful military ventures in France in the first decades of the Hundred Years' War. These events add further complexity to the complicated dynastic disputes that led to the war and have been the subject of plays, novels, ballets, TV miniseries, and films. (By kind permission of Viscount Coke and the Trustees of Holkham Estate, Norfolk/Bridgeman Images)

so long was that it became a French civil war, with some French nobles, most important the dukes of Burgundy, supporting English monarchs in order to thwart the centralizing goals of the French kings. On the other side, Scotland—resisting English efforts of assimilation—often allied with France; the French supported Scottish raids in northern England, and Scottish troops joined with French armies on the continent.

The governments of both England and France manipulated public opinion to support the war. The English public was convinced that the war was waged for one reason: to secure for King Edward the French crown he had been unjustly denied. Edward III issued letters to the sheriffs describing the evil deeds of the French in graphic terms and listing royal needs. Philip VI sent agents to warn communities about the dangers of invasion. Kings in both countries instructed the clergy to deliver sermons filled with patriotic sentiment. Royal propaganda on both sides fostered a kind of early nationalism, and both sides developed a deep hatred of the other.

Economic factors involving the wool trade and the control of Flemish towns were linked to these political issues. The wool trade between England and Flanders served as the cornerstone of both countries' economies; they were closely interdependent. Flanders technically belonged to the French crown, and the Flemish aristocracy was highly sympathetic to that monarchy. But the wealth of Flemish merchants and cloth manufacturers depended on English wool, and Flemish burghers strongly supported the claims of Edward III. The disruption of commerce with England threatened their prosperity.

The war also presented opportunities for wealth and advancement. Poor and idle knights were promised regular wages. Criminals who enlisted were granted pardons. The great nobles expected to be rewarded with estates. Royal exhortations to the troops before battles repeatedly stressed that, if victorious, the men might keep whatever they seized.

English Successes

The war began with a series of French sea raids on English coastal towns in 1337, but the French fleet was almost completely destroyed when it attempted to land soldiers on English soil, and from that point on the war was fought almost entirely in France and the Low Countries (Map 11.2). It consisted mainly of a series of random sieges and cavalry raids, fought in fits and starts, with treaties along the way to halt hostilities.

During the war's early stages, England was highly successful. At Crécy in northern France in 1346, English longbowmen scored a great victory over French knights and crossbowmen. Although the aim

of longbowmen was not very accurate, the weapon allowed for rapid reloading, and an English archer could send off three arrows to the French crossbowman's one. The result was a blinding shower of arrows that unhorsed the French knights and caused mass confusion. The roar of English cannon—probably the first use of artillery in the Western world—created further panic. This was not war according to the chivalric rules that Edward III would have preferred. Nevertheless, his son, Edward the Black Prince, used the same tactics ten years later to smash the French at Poitiers, where he captured the French king and held him for ransom. Edward was not able to take all of France, but the English held Aquitaine and other provinces, and allied themselves with many of France's nobles. After a brief peace, the French fought back and recovered some territory during the 1370s and 1380s, and then a treaty again halted hostilities as both sides concentrated on conflicts over power at home.

War began again in 1415 when the able English soldier-king Henry V (r. 1413–1422) invaded France. At Agincourt (AH-jihn-kort), Henry's army defeated a much larger French force, again primarily through the skill of English longbowmen. Henry followed up his triumph at Agincourt with the reconquest of Normandy, and by 1419 the English had advanced to the walls of Paris (see Map 11.2). Henry married the daughter of the French king, and a treaty made Henry and any sons the couple would have heir to the French throne. It appeared as if Henry would indeed rule both England and France, but he died unexpectedly in 1422, leaving an infant son as heir. The English continued their victories, however, and besieged the city of Orléans (or-lay-AHN), the only major city in northern France not under their control. But the French cause was not lost.

Joan of Arc and France's Victory

The ultimate French success rests heavily on the actions of Joan, an obscure French peasant girl whose vision and military leadership revived French fortunes and led to victory. (Over the centuries, she acquired the name "of Arc"—*d'Arc* in French—based on her father's name; she never used this name for herself, but called herself "the maiden"—*la Pucelle* in French.) Born in 1412 to well-to-do peasants in the village of Domrémy in Champagne, Joan grew up in a religious household. During adolescence she began to hear voices, which she later said belonged to Saint Michael, Saint Catherine, and Saint Margaret. In 1428 these voices spoke to her with great urgency, telling her that the dauphin (DOH-fuhn), the uncrowned King Charles VII, had to be crowned and the English

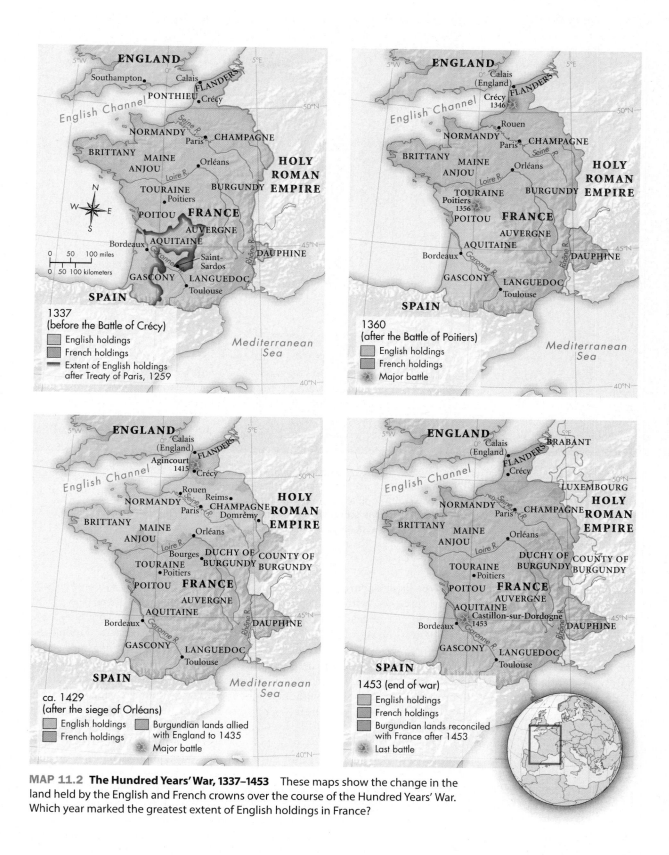

MAP 11.2 The Hundred Years' War, 1337–1453   These maps show the change in the land held by the English and French crowns over the course of the Hundred Years' War. Which year marked the greatest extent of English holdings in France?

Siege of the Castle of Mortagne   Medieval warfare usually consisted of small skirmishes and attacks on castles. This miniature shows the 1377 French siege of an English-held castle near Bordeaux that held out for six months. Most of the soldiers use longbows, although at the left two men shoot primitive muskets above a pair of cannon. Painted in the late fifteenth century, the scene reflects the military technology available at the time it was painted, not at the time of the actual siege. (British Library, London, UK/© British Library Board. All Rights Reserved/ Bridgeman Images)

expelled from France. Joan traveled to the French court wearing male clothing. She had an audience with Charles, who had her questioned about her angelic visions and examined to make sure she was the virgin she said she was. She secured his support to travel with the French army to Orléans dressed as a knight—with borrowed armor and sword. There she dictated a letter to the English ordering them to surrender:

> King of England . . . , do right in the King of Heaven's sight. Surrender to The Maid sent hither by God the King of Heaven, the keys of all the good towns you have taken and laid waste in France. She comes in God's name to establish the Blood Royal, ready to make peace if you agree to abandon France and repay what you have taken. And you, archers, comrades in arms, gentles and others, who are before the town of Orléans, retire in God's name to your own country.[6]

Such words coming from a teenage girl—even one inspired by God—were laughable given the recent course of the conflict, but Joan was amazingly successful. She inspired and led French attacks, forcing the English to retreat from Orléans. The king made Joan co-commander of the entire army, and she led it to a string of victories; other cities simply surrendered without a fight and returned their allegiance to France. In July 1429, two months after the end of the siege of Orléans, Charles VII was crowned king at Reims.

Joan and the French army continued their fight against the English and their Burgundian allies. In 1430 the Burgundians captured Joan. Charles refused to ransom her, and she was sold to the English. A church court headed by a pro-English bishop tried her for heresy, and though nothing she had done was heretical by church doctrine, she was found guilty and burned at the stake in the marketplace at Rouen. (See "Evaluating the Evidence 11.2: The Trial of Joan of Arc," at right.)

The Trial of Joan of Arc

Joan's interrogation was organized and led by Bishop Pierre Cauchon, one of many French clergy who supported the English. In a number of sessions that took place over several months, she was repeatedly asked about her voices, her decision to wear men's clothing, and other issues. This extract is from the fourth session, on Tuesday, February 27, 1431; Joan is here referred to with the French spelling of her name, Jeanne.

In their presence Jeanne was required by my lord the Bishop of Beauvais to swear and take the oath concerning what touched her trial. To which she answered that she would willingly swear as to what touched her trial, but not as to everything she knew. . . .

Asked whether she had heard her voice since Saturday, she answered: "Yes, indeed, many times." . . . Asked what it said to her when she was back in her room, she replied: "That I should answer you boldly." . . . Questioned as to whether it were the voice of an angel, or of a saint, or directly from God, she answered that the voices were those of Saint Catherine and of Saint Margaret. And their heads are crowned with beautiful crowns, most richly and preciously. And [she said] for [telling you] this I have leave from our Lord. . . .

Asked if the voice ordered her to wear a man's dress, she answered that the dress is but a small matter; and that she had not taken it by the advice of any living man; and that she did not take this dress nor do anything at all save by the command of Our Lord and the angels.

Questioned as to whether it seemed to her that this command to take male dress was a lawful one, she answered that everything she had done was at Our Lord's command, and if He had ordered Jeanne to take a different dress, she would have done so, since it would have been at God's command. . . .

Asked if she had her sword when she was taken prisoner, she said no, but that she had one which was taken from a Burgundian. . . . Asked whether, when she was before the city of Orleans, she had a standard, and of what colour it was, she replied that it had a field sown with fleurs-de-lis, and showed a world with an angel on either side, white in colour, of linen or *boucassin* [a type of fabric], and she thought that the names JESUS MARIA were written on it; and it had a silk fringe. . . . Asked which she preferred, her sword or her standard, she replied that she was forty times fonder of her standard than she was of her sword. . . . She said moreover that she herself bore her standard during an attack, in order to avoid killing anyone. And she added that she had never killed anyone at all. . . .

She also said that during the attack on the fort at the bridge she was wounded in the neck by an arrow, but she was greatly comforted by Saint Catherine, and was well again in a fortnight. . . . Asked whether she knew beforehand that she would be wounded, she said that she well knew it, and had informed her king of it; but that notwithstanding she would not give up her work.

EVALUATE THE EVIDENCE

1. How does Joan explain the way that she chose to answer the interrogators' questions, and her decisions about clothing and actions in battle?
2. Thinking about the structures of power and authority in fifteenth-century France, how do you believe the interrogators would have regarded Joan's answers?

Source: *The Trial of Joan of Arc*, translated with an introduction by W. S. Scott (Westport, Conn.: Associated Booksellers, 1956), 76, 77, 79–80, 82, 83. © 1956, The Folio Society.

The French army continued its victories without her. Sensing a shift in the balance of power, the Burgundians switched their allegiance to the French, who reconquered Normandy and, finally, ejected the English from Aquitaine in the 1440s. As the war dragged on, loss of life mounted, and money appeared to be flowing into a bottomless pit, demands for an end increased in England. Parliamentary opposition to additional war grants stiffened, fewer soldiers were sent, and more territory passed into French hands. At the war's end in 1453, only the town of Calais (KA-lay) remained in English hands.

What of Joan? A new trial in 1456—requested by Charles VII, who either had second thoughts about his abandonment of Joan or did not wish to be associated with a condemned heretic—was held by the pope. It cleared her of all charges and declared her a martyr. She became a political symbol of France from that point on, and sometimes also a symbol of the Catholic Church in opposition to the government of France. In 1920, for example, she was canonized as a saint shortly after the French government declared separation of church and state in France. Similarly, Joan has been (and continues to be) a symbol of deep religious piety to some, of conservative nationalism to others, and of gender-bending cross-dressing to others. Beneath the pious and popular legends is a teenage girl who saved the French monarchy, the embodiment of France.

Aftermath

In France thousands of soldiers and civilians had been slaughtered and hundreds of thousands of acres of rich farmland ruined, leaving the rural economy of many areas a shambles. These losses exacerbated the dreadful losses caused by the plague. The war had disrupted trade and the great trade fairs, resulting in the drastic reduction of French participation in international commerce. Defeat in battle and heavy taxation contributed to widespread dissatisfaction and aggravated peasant grievances.

The war had wreaked havoc in England as well, even though only the southern coastal ports saw actual battle. England spent the huge sum of over £5 million on the war effort, and despite the money raised by some victories, the net result was an enormous financial loss. The government attempted to finance the war by raising taxes on the wool crop, which priced wool out of the export market.

In both England and France, men of all social classes had volunteered to serve in the war in the hope of acquiring booty and becoming rich, and some were successful in the early years of the war. As time went on, however, most fortunes seem to have been squandered as fast as they were made. In addition, the social order was disrupted because the knights who ordinarily served as sheriffs, coroners, jurymen, and justices of the peace were abroad.

The war stimulated technological experimentation, especially with artillery. Cannon revolutionized warfare, making the stone castle no longer impregnable. Because only central governments, not private nobles, could afford cannon, their use strengthened the military power of national states.

The long war also had a profound impact on the political and cultural lives of the two countries. Most notably, it stimulated the development of the English Parliament. Between 1250 and 1450 **representative assemblies** flourished in many European countries. In the English Parliament, German *diets*, and Spanish *cortes*, deliberative practices developed that laid the foundations for the representative institutions of modern democratic nations. While representative assemblies declined in most countries after the fifteenth century, the English Parliament endured. Edward III's constant need for money to pay for the war compelled him to summon not only the great barons and bishops, but knights of the shires and citizens from the towns as well. Parliament met in thirty-seven of the fifty years of Edward's reign.

The frequency of the meetings is significant. Representative assemblies were becoming a habit. Knights and wealthy urban residents — or the "Commons," as they came to be called — recognized their mutual interests and began to meet apart from the great lords. The Commons gradually realized that they held the country's purse strings, and a parliamentary statute of 1341 required parliamentary approval of most new taxes. By signing the law, Edward III acknowledged that the king of England could not tax without Parliament's consent.

In England, theoretical consent to taxation and legislation was given in one assembly for the entire country. France had no such single assembly; instead, there were many regional or provincial assemblies. Why did a national representative assembly fail to develop in France? Linguistic, geographical, economic, legal, and political differences remained very strong. People tended to think of themselves as Breton, Norman, Burgundian, and so on, rather than French. In addition, provincial assemblies, highly jealous of their independence, did not want a national assembly. The costs of sending delegates to it would be high, and the result was likely to be increased taxation and a lessening of their own power. Finally, the initiative for convening assemblies rested with the king, but some monarchs lacked the power to call them, and others, including Charles VI, found the very idea of representative assemblies thoroughly distasteful.

In both countries, however, the war did promote the growth of nationalism — the feeling of unity and identity that binds together a people. After victories, each country experienced a surge of pride in its military strength. Just as English patriotism ran strong after Crécy and Poitiers, so French national confidence rose after Orléans. French national feeling demanded the expulsion of the enemy not merely from Normandy and Aquitaine but from all French soil. Perhaps no one expressed this national consciousness better than Joan when she exulted that the enemy had been "driven out of *France*."

Challenges to the Church

FOCUS QUESTION *Why did the church come under increasing criticism?*

In times of crisis or disaster, people of all faiths have sought the consolation of religion. In the fourteenth century, however, the official Christian Church offered little solace. Many priests and friars helped the sick and the hungry, but others paid more attention to worldly matters, and the leaders of the church added to the sorrow and misery of the times. In response to this lack of leadership, members of the clergy challenged the power of the pope, and laypeople challenged the authority of the church itself. Women and men increasingly relied on direct approaches to God, often through mystical encounters, rather than on the institutional church.

The Babylonian Captivity and Great Schism

Conflicts between the secular rulers of Europe and the popes were common throughout the High Middle Ages, and in the early fourteenth century the dispute between King Philip the Fair of France and Pope Boniface VIII became particularly bitter (see Chapter 9). After Boniface's death, in order to control the church and its policies, Philip pressured the new pope, Clement V, to settle permanently in Avignon in southeastern France. The popes lived in Avignon from 1309 to 1376, a period in church history often called the **Babylonian Captivity** (referring to the seventy years the ancient Hebrews were held captive in Mesopotamian Babylon).

The Babylonian Captivity badly damaged papal prestige. The seven popes at Avignon concentrated on bureaucratic and financial matters to the exclusion of spiritual objectives, and the general atmosphere was one of luxury and extravagance, which was also the case at many bishops' courts. Raimon de Cornet, a troubadour poet from southern France who was himself a priest, was only one among many criticizing the church. He wrote:

> I see the pope his sacred trust betray,
> For while the rich his grace can gain alway,
> His favors from the poor are aye withholden.
> He strives to gather wealth as best he may,
> Forcing Christ's people blindly to obey,
> So that he may repose in garments golden.
>
> . . .
>
> Our bishops, too, are plunged in similar sin,
> For pitilessly they flay the very skin
> From all their priests who chance to have fat
>   livings.
> For gold their seal official you can win
> To any writ, no matter what's therein.
> Sure God alone can make them stop their
>   thievings.[7]

The leadership of the church was cut off from its historic roots and the source of its ancient authority, the city of Rome. In 1377 Pope Gregory XI brought the papal court back to Rome but died shortly afterward. Roman citizens pressured the cardinals to elect an Italian, and they chose a distinguished administrator, the archbishop of Bari, Bartolomeo Prignano, who took the name Urban VI.

Urban VI (pontificate 1378–1389) had excellent intentions for church reform, but he went about it in a tactless manner. He attacked clerical luxury, denouncing individual cardinals and bishops by name, and even threatened to excommunicate some of them. The cardinals slipped away from Rome and met at Anagni. They declared Urban's election invalid because it had come about under threats from the Roman mob, and excommunicated the pope. The cardinals then elected Cardinal Robert of Geneva, the cousin of King Charles V of France, as pope. Cardinal Robert took the name Clement VII. There were thus two popes in 1378 — Urban at Rome and Clement VII (pontificate 1378–1394) at Avignon. So began the **Great Schism**, which divided Western Christendom until 1417.

The powers of Europe aligned themselves with Urban or Clement along strictly political lines. France naturally recognized the French pope, Clement. England, France's long-time enemy, recognized the Italian pope, Urban. Scotland, an ally of France, supported Clement. Aragon, Castile, and Portugal hesitated before deciding for Clement as well. The German emperor, hostile to France, recognized Urban. At first the Italian city-states recognized Urban; later they opted for Clement.

John of Spoleto, a professor at the law school at Bologna, eloquently summed up intellectual opinion of the schism: "The longer this schism lasts, the more it appears to be costing, and the more harm it does; scandal, massacres, ruination, agitations, troubles and disturbances."[8] The schism weakened the religious faith of many Christians and brought church leadership into serious disrepute.

Critiques, Divisions, and Councils

Criticism of the church during the Avignon papacy and the Great Schism often came from the ranks of highly learned clergy and lay professionals. One of these was William of Occam (1289?–1347?), a Franciscan friar

■ Allegiance to Rome
■ Allegiance to Avignon
☐ Official allegiance to Rome but with shifting local allegiances

The Great Schism, 1378–1417

■ **representative assemblies** Deliberative meetings of lords and wealthy urban residents that flourished in many European countries between 1250 and 1450.

■ **Babylonian Captivity** The period from 1309 to 1376 when the popes resided in Avignon rather than in Rome. The phrase refers to the seventy years when the Hebrews were held captive in Babylon.

■ **Great Schism** The division, or split, in church leadership from 1378 to 1417 when there were two, then three, popes.

and philosopher who predated the Great Schism but saw the papal court at Avignon during the Babylonian Captivity. Occam argued vigorously against the papacy and also wrote philosophical works in which he questioned the connection between reason and faith that had been developed by Thomas Aquinas (see Chapter 10). All governments should have limited powers and be accountable to those they govern, according to Occam, and church and state should be separate.

The Italian lawyer and university official Marsiglio of Padua (ca. 1275–1342) agreed with Occam. In his *Defensor Pacis* (The Defender of the Peace), Marsiglio argued against the medieval idea of a society governed by both church and state, with church supreme. Instead, Marsiglio claimed, the state was the great unifying power in society, and the church should be subordinate to it. Church leadership should rest in a general council made up of laymen as well as priests and superior to the pope. Marsiglio was excommunicated for these radical ideas, and his work was condemned as heresy — as was Occam's — but in the later part of the fourteenth century many thinkers agreed with these two critics of the papacy. They believed that reform of the church could best be achieved through periodic assemblies, or councils, representing all the Christian people. Those who argued this position were called **conciliarists**.

The English scholar and theologian John Wyclif (WIH-klihf) (ca. 1330–1384) went further than the conciliarists in his argument against medieval church structure. He wrote that the Scriptures alone should be the standard of Christian belief and practice and that papal claims of secular power had no foundation in the Scriptures. He urged that the church be stripped of its property. He also wanted Christians to read the Bible for themselves and produced the first complete translation of the Bible into English. Wyclif's followers, dubbed Lollards, from a Dutch word for "mumble," by those who ridiculed them, spread his ideas and made many copies of his Bible. Lollard teaching allowed women to preach, and women played a significant role in the movement. Lollards were persecuted in the fifteenth century; some were executed, some recanted, and others continued to meet secretly in houses, barns, and fields to read and discuss the Bible and other religious texts in English. Bohemian students returning from study at the University of Oxford around 1400 brought Wyclif's ideas with them to Prague, the capital

The Hussite Revolution, 1415–1436

□ Area under Hussite control

of what was then Bohemia and is now the Czech Republic. There another university theologian, Jan Hus (ca. 1372–1415), built on them. He also denied papal authority, called for translations of the Bible into the local Czech language, and declared indulgences — papal offers of remission of penance — useless. Hus gained many followers, who linked his theological ideas with their opposition to the church's wealth and power and with a growing sense of Czech nationalism in opposition to the pope's international power. Hus's followers were successful at defeating the combined armies of the pope and the emperor many times. In the 1430s the emperor finally agreed to recognize the Hussite Church in Bohemia, which survived into the Reformation and then merged with other Protestant churches.

The ongoing schism threatened the church, and in response to continued calls throughout Europe for a council, the cardinals of Rome and Avignon summoned a council at Pisa in 1409. That gathering of prelates and theologians deposed both popes and selected another. Neither the Avignon pope nor the Roman pope would resign, however, and the appalling result was the creation of a threefold schism.

Finally, under pressure from the German emperor Sigismund, a great council met at the imperial city of Constance (1414–1418). It had three objectives: to wipe out heresy, to end the schism, and to reform the church. Members included cardinals, bishops, abbots, and professors of theology and canon law from across Europe. The council moved first on the first point: despite being granted a safe-conduct to go to Constance by the emperor, Jan Hus was tried, condemned, and burned at the stake as a heretic in 1415. The council also eventually healed the schism. It deposed both the Roman pope and the successor of the pope chosen at Pisa, and it isolated the Avignon pope. A conclave elected a new leader, the Roman cardinal Colonna, who took the name Martin V (pontificate 1417–1431).

Martin proceeded to dissolve the council. Nothing was done about reform, the third objective of the council. In the later part of the fifteenth century the papacy concentrated on Italian problems to the exclusion of universal Christian interests. But the schism and the conciliar movement had exposed the crying need for ecclesiastical reform, thus laying the foundation for the great reform efforts of the sixteenth century.

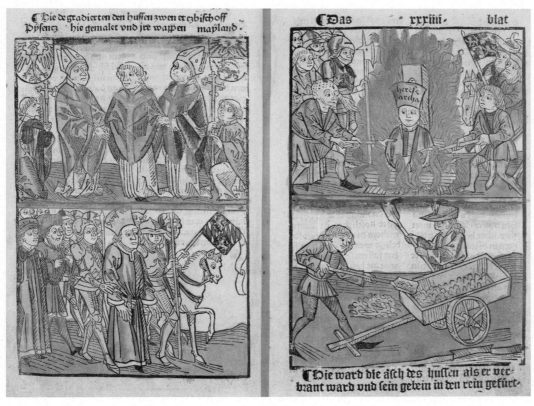

The Arrest and Execution of Jan Hus   In this woodcut from Ulrich of Richental's chronicle of the Council of Constance, Hus is arrested by bishops, led away by soldiers while wearing a hat of shame with the word "arch-heretic" on it, and burned at the stake. The final panel shows executioners shoveling his ashes and burned bones into the Rhine. Ulrich of Richental was a merchant in Constance and an eyewitness to Hus's execution and many of the other events of the council. He wrote his chronicle in German shortly after the council ended and paid for it to be illustrated. The original is lost, but many copies were made later in the fifteenth century, and the volume was printed in 1483 with many woodcuts, including this one. Hus became an important symbol of Czech independence, and in 1990 the Czech Republic declared July 6, the date of his execution in 1415, a national holiday. (From *History of the Council of Constance*, 1483/Bibliothèque Polonaise, Paris, France/Archives Charmet/Bridgeman Images)

Lay Piety and Mysticism

The failings of the Avignon papacy followed by the scandal of the Great Schism did much to weaken the spiritual mystique of the clergy in the popular mind. Laypeople had already begun to develop their own forms of piety somewhat separate from the authority of priests and bishops, and these forms of piety became more prominent in the fourteenth century.

In the thirteenth century lay Christian men and women had formed **confraternities**, voluntary lay groups organized by occupation, devotional preference, neighborhood, or charitable activity. Some confraternities specialized in praying for souls in purgatory, either for specific individuals or for the anonymous mass of all souls. In England they held dances, church festivals, and collections to raise money to clean and repair church buildings and to supply churches with candles and other liturgical objects. Like craft guilds, most confraternities were groups of men, but separate women's confraternities were formed in some towns, often to oversee the production of vestments, altar cloths, and other items made of fabric. All confraternities carried out special devotional practices such as prayers or processions, often without the leadership of a priest. Famine, plague, war, and other crises led to an expansion of confraternities in larger cities and many villages.

In Holland beginning in the late fourteenth century, a group of pious laypeople called the Brethren and Sisters of the Common Life lived in stark simplicity while daily carrying out the Gospel teaching of feeding

■ **conciliarists** People who believed that the authority in the Roman Church should rest in a general council composed of clergy, theologians, and laypeople, rather than in the pope alone.

■ **confraternities** Voluntary lay groups organized by occupation, devotional preference, neighborhood, or charitable activity.

INDIVIDUALS IN SOCIETY

Meister Eckhart

Mysticism—the direct experience of the divine—is an aspect of many world religions and has been part of Christianity throughout its history. During the late Middle Ages, however, the pursuit of mystical union became an important part of the piety of many laypeople, especially in the Rhineland area of Germany. In this they were guided by the sermons of the churchman generally known as Meister Eckhart. Born into a German noble family, Eckhart (1260–1329?) joined the Dominican order and studied theology at Paris and Cologne, attaining the academic title of "master" (*Meister* in German). The leaders of the Dominican order appointed him to a series of administrative and teaching positions, and he wrote learned treatises in Latin that reflected his Scholastic training and deep understanding of classical philosophy.

He also began to preach in German, attracting many listeners through his beautiful language and mystical insights. God, he said, was "an oversoaring being and an overbeing nothingness," whose essence was beyond the ability of humans to express: "if the soul is to know God, it must know Him outside time and place, since God is neither in this or that, but One and above them." Only through "unknowing," emptying oneself, could one come to experience the divine. Yet God was also present in individual human souls, and to a degree in every creature, all of which God had called into being before the beginning of time. Within each human soul there was what Eckhart called a "little spark," an innermost essence that allows the soul—with God's grace and Christ's redemptive action—to come to God. "Our salvation depends upon our knowing and recognizing the Chief Good which is God Himself," preached Eckhart; "the Eye with which I see God is the same Eye with which God sees me." "I have a capacity in my soul for taking in God entirely," he went on, a capacity that was shared by all humans, not only members of the clergy or those with special spiritual gifts. Although Eckhart did not reject church sacraments or the hierarchy, he frequently stressed that union with God was best accomplished through quiet detachment and simple prayer rather than pilgrimages, extensive fasts, or other activities: "If the only prayer you said in your whole life was 'thank you,' that would suffice."*

Eckhart's unusual teachings led to charges of heresy in 1327, which he denied. The pope—who was at this point in Avignon—presided over a trial condemning him, but Eckhart appears to have died during the course of the proceedings or shortly thereafter. His writings were ordered destroyed, but his followers preserved many and spread his teachings.

A sixteenth-century woodcut of Meister Eckhart teaching.
(Visual Connection Archive)

In the last few decades, Meister Eckhart's ideas have been explored and utilized by philosophers and mystics in Buddhism, Hinduism, and neo-paganism, as well as by Christians. His writings sell widely for their spiritual insights, and quotations from them—including the one above about thank-you prayers—can be found on coffee mugs, tote bags, and T-shirts.

QUESTIONS FOR ANALYSIS

1. Why might Meister Eckhart's preaching have been viewed as threatening by the leaders of the church?
2. Given the situation of the church in the late Middle Ages, why might mysticism have been attractive to pious Christians?

*Meister Eckhart's Sermons, trans. Claud Field (London: n.p., 1909).

the hungry, clothing the naked, and visiting the sick. They sought to both ease social problems and make religion a personal inner experience. The spirituality of the Brethren and Sisters of the Common Life found its finest expression in the classic *The Imitation of Christ* by the Dutch monk Thomas à Kempis (1380?–1471), which gained wide appeal among laypeople. It urges Christians to take Christ as their model, seek perfection in a simple way of life, and look to the Scriptures for guidance in living a spiritual life. In the mid-fifteenth century the movement had founded houses in the Netherlands, in central Germany, and in the Rhineland.

For some individuals, both laypeople and clerics, religious devotion included mystical experiences. (See "Individuals in Society: Meister Eckhart," at left.) Bridget of Sweden (1303–1373) was a noble-woman who journeyed to Rome after her husband's death. She began to see visions and gave advice based on these visions to both laypeople and church officials. At the end of her life Bridget made a pilgrimage to Jerusalem, where she saw visions of the Virgin Mary, who described to her exactly how she was standing "with [her] knees bent" when she gave birth to Jesus, and how she "showed to the shepherds the nature and male sex of the child."[9] Bridget's visions provide evidence of the ways in which laypeople used their own experiences to enhance their religious understanding; Bridget's own experiences of childbirth shaped the way she viewed the birth of Jesus, and she related to the Virgin Mary in part as one mother to another.

The confraternities and mystics were generally not considered heretical unless they began to challenge the authority of the papacy the way Wyclif, Hus, and some conciliarists did. However, the movement of lay piety did alter many people's perceptions of their own spiritual power.

Social Unrest in a Changing Society

FOCUS QUESTION *What explains the social unrest of the late Middle Ages?*

At the beginning of the fourteenth century famine and disease profoundly affected the lives of European peoples. As the century wore on, decades of slaughter and destruction, punctuated by the decimating visits of the Black Death, added further woes. In many parts of France and the Low Countries, fields lay in ruin or untilled for lack of labor. In England, as taxes increased, criticisms of government policy and mismanagement multiplied. Crime and new forms of

business organization aggravated economic troubles, and throughout Europe the frustrations of the common people erupted into widespread revolts.

Peasant Revolts

Nobles and clergy lived on the food produced by peasant labor, thinking little of adding taxes to the burden of peasant life. While peasants had endured centuries of exploitation, the difficult conditions of the fourteenth and fifteenth centuries spurred a wave of peasant revolts across Europe. Peasants were sometimes joined by those low on the urban social ladder, resulting in a wider revolution of poor against rich. (See "Thinking Like a Historian: Popular Revolts in the Late Middle Ages," page 344.)

The first large-scale rebellion was in the Flanders region of present-day Belgium in the 1320s (Map 11.3). In order to satisfy peace agreements, Flemish peasants were forced to pay taxes to the French, who claimed fiscal rights over the county of Flanders. Monasteries also pressed peasants for additional money above their customary tithes. In retaliation, peasants burned and pillaged castles and aristocratic country houses. A French army crushed the peasant forces, however, and savage repression and the confiscation of peasant property followed in the 1330s.

In the following decades, revolts broke out in many other places. In 1358, when French taxation for the Hundred Years' War fell heavily on the poor, the frustrations of the French peasantry exploded in a massive uprising called the **Jacquerie** (zhah-kuh-REE), after a mythical agricultural laborer, Jacques Bonhomme (Good Fellow). Peasants blamed the nobility for oppressive taxes, for the criminal banditry of the countryside, for losses on the battlefield, and for the general misery. Crowds swept through the countryside, slashing the throats of nobles, burning their castles, raping their wives and daughters, and killing or maiming their horses and cattle. Artisans and small merchants in cities and parish priests joined the peasants. Rebels committed terrible destruction, and for several weeks the nobles were on the defensive. Then the upper class united to repress the revolt with merciless ferocity. Thousands of the "Jacques," innocent as well as guilty, were cut down. That forcible suppression of social rebellion, without any effort to alleviate its underlying causes, served to drive protest underground.

In England the Black Death drastically cut the labor supply, and as a result peasants demanded higher wages and fewer manorial obligations. Their lords countered in 1351 with the Statute of Laborers, a law issued by the king that froze wages and bound workers to their manors. This attempt to freeze wages could not be enforced,

■ **Jacquerie** A massive uprising by French peasants in 1358 protesting heavy taxation.

Popular Revolts in the Late Middle Ages

Famine, plague, and war led to population decline and economic problems in the fourteenth century, which fueled both resentment and fear. How did such crises, and the response of those in power to these, spur calls for reform and revolts among peasants and workers?

1 **The Statute of Laborers, 1351.** After the English population declined by one-third because of the Black Death, rural and urban workers demanded higher wages and better working conditions, which led the English Parliament and King Edward III to pass the following law.

Because a great part of the people and especially of the workmen and servants has now died in that pestilence, some, seeing the straights of the masters and the scarcity of servants, are not willing to serve unless they receive excessive wages, and others, rather than through labour to gain their living, prefer to beg in idleness: We, considering the grave inconveniences which might come from the lack especially of ploughmen and such labourers . . . have seen fit to ordain: that every man and woman of our kingdom of England, of whatever condition, whether bond or free, who is able bodied and below the age of sixty years, . . . shall be bound to serve him who has seen fit so to seek after him; and he shall take only the wages . . . or salary which, in the places where he sought to serve, were accustomed to be paid in the twentieth year of our reign of England [1346], . . . and if any man or woman, being thus sought after in service, will not do this, the fact being proven by two faithful men before the sheriffs or the bailiffs of our lord the king, or the constables of the town where this happens . . . shall be taken and sent to the next jail, and there he shall remain in strict custody until he shall find surety for serving in the aforesaid form. . . .

Likewise saddlers, skinners, white-tawers, cordwainers, tailors, smiths, carpenters, masons, tilers, shipwrights, carters and all other artisans and labourers shall not take for their labour and handiwork more than what, in the places where they happen to labour, was customarily paid to such persons in [1346]; and if any man take more, he shall be committed to the nearest jail in the manner aforesaid.

2 **John Ball preaches to the peasants.** Beginning in the 1360s, the priest John Ball traveled around England delivering radical sermons, such as this one, reported in a chronicle by Jean Froissart. In the aftermath of the 1381 English Peasants' Revolt, Ball was arrested, imprisoned, and executed; his body was drawn and quartered; and his head was stuck on a pike on London Bridge.

John Ball was accustomed to assemble a crowd around him in the marketplace and preach to them. On such occasions he would say: "My good friends, matters cannot go on well in England until all things shall be in common; where there shall be neither vassals nor lords; when the lords shall be no more masters than ourselves. How ill they behave to us! For what reasons do they thus hold us in bondage? Are we not all descended from the same parents, Adam and Eve? When Adam delved and Eve span, who was then the gentleman? What reason can they give, why they should be more masters than ourselves? They are clothed in velvet and rich stuffs, ornamented with ermine and other furs, while we are forced to wear poor clothing. They have wines, spices, and fine bread, while we have only rye and the refuse of straw, and when we drink it must be water. They have handsome seats and manors, while we must brave the wind and rain in our labors in the field; and it is by our labor they have wherewith to support their pomp. We are called slaves, and if we do not perform our service we are beaten, and we have no sovereign to whom we can complain or who would be willing to hear us. Let us go to the King and remonstrate with him; he is young, and from him we may obtain a favorable answer, and if not we must ourselves seek to amend our condition."

ANALYZING THE EVIDENCE

1. In Source 1, what does the law require laborers to do, and what penalties does it provide if they do not do so? How did laws such as this contribute to growing social tensions?
2. What do John Ball in Source 2 and the peasants mentioned in Source 3 view as wrong in English society, and what do they want done about it?
3. In Sources 4 and 5, what do the wool workers in Florence want? How do the authors of these sources differ in their opinions about these demands?
4. What was the response of those in power to the demands of peasants and workers?

3 **English peasants meet with the king.** In 1381 peasants angered by taxes imposed to pay for the war with France seized the city of London and forced the young king Richard II to meet with them, as reported in this contemporary chronicle by Henry Knighton, an Augustinian priest.

The King advanced to the assigned place, while many of the wicked mob kept following him.... They complained that they had been seriously oppressed by many hardships and that their condition of servitude was unbearable, and that they neither could nor would endure it longer. The King, for the sake of peace, and on account of the violence of the times, yielding to their petition, granted to them a charter with the great seal, to the effect that all men in the kingdom of England should be free and of free condition, and should remain both for themselves and their heirs free from all kinds of servitude and villeinage forever.... [But] the charter was rejected and decided to be null and void by the King and the great men of the kingdom in the Parliament held at Westminster [later] in the same year.

4 **Judicial inquiry of a labor organizer in Florence, 1345.** The rulers of Florence investigated the actions of a man seeking to organize a guild of carders and combers, the lowest-paid workers in the cloth industry; he was arrested and executed by hanging.

This is the inquisition which the lord captain and his judge ... have conducted ... against Ciuto Brandini, of the parish of S. Piero Maggiore, a man of low condition and evil reputation.... Together with many others who were seduced by him, he planned to organize an association ... of carders, combers, and other laborers in the woolen cloth industry, in the largest number possible. In order that they might have the means to congregate and to elect consuls and leaders of their association ... he organized meetings on several occasions and on various days of many persons of lowly condition.... Moving from bad to worse, he sought ... to accomplish similar and even worse things, seeking always [to incite] noxious disorders, to the harm, opprobrium, danger, and destruction of the citizens of Florence, their persons and property, and of the stable regime of that city.

5 **Chronicle of the Ciompi Revolt, 1378.** An anonymous chronicle describes the 1378 revolt of the *ciompi*, the lowest-paid workers in the wool trade in Florence, against the Lana guild of wool merchants, which controlled all aspects of cloth production and dominated the city government. The changes described lasted four years, until an army organized by the wool merchants overthrew the new government.

When the *popolo* [common people, that is, the *ciompi*] and the guildsmen had seized the palace, they sent a message ... that they wished to make certain demands by means of petitions, which were just and reasonable.... They said that, for the peace and repose of the city, they wanted certain things which they had decided among themselves.... The first chapter [of the petition] stated that the Lana guild would no longer have a [police] official of the guild. Another was that the combers, carders, trimmers, washers, and other cloth workers would have their own [guild].... Moreover, all penalties involving a loss of a limb would be cancelled, and those who were condemned would pay a money fine instead.... Furthermore, for two years none of the poor people could be prosecuted for debts of 50 florins or less.

The *popolo* entered the palace and the podestà [the highest official in Florence] departed, without any harm being done to him.... Then the banners of the other guilds were unfurled from the windows ... and also the standard of justice [the city's official banner]. Those inside the palace threw out and burned ... every document that they found ... and they entered all the rooms and they found many ropes which [the authorities] had bought to hang the poor people.... Several young men climbed the bell tower and rang the bells to signal the victory which they had won in seizing the palace, in God's honor.... Then [the *popolo*] decided to call priors who would be good comrades ... and these priors called together the colleges and consuls of the guilds.... And this was done to give a part to more people, and so that each would be content, and each would have a share of the offices, and so that all of the citizens would be united. Thus poor men would have their due, for they have always borne the expenses [of government] and only the rich have profited.... And they deliberated to expand the lower guilds, and where there had been fourteen, there would now be seventeen, and thus they would be stronger, and this was done.... So all together, the lower guilds increased by some thirteen thousand men.

PUTTING IT ALL TOGETHER

Using the sources above, along with what you have learned in class and in this chapter and Chapters 9 and 10, write a short essay that analyzes popular revolts in the late Middle Ages. How did population decline and economic crisis, and the response of those in power to these challenges, spur calls for reform and revolts among peasants and workers? Why do you think the response of those in power to these revolts was so brutal?

Sources: (1) Ernest F. Henderson, trans. and ed., *Select Historical Documents of the Middle Ages* (London: George Bell and Sons, 1892), pp. 165–167; (2) Sir John Froissart, *The Chronicles of England, France, Spain, etc.* (London: Everyman's Library, 1911), pp. 207–208; (3) Edward P. Cheyney, *Readings in English History Drawn from the Original Sources* (Boston: Ginn, 1935), p. 263; (4, 5) Gene Brucker, ed., *The Society of Renaissance Florence: A Documentary Study* (New York: Harper Torchbooks, 1971), pp. 235, 237–239. Used by permission of the author.

but a huge gap remained between peasants and their lords, and the peasants sought release for their economic frustrations in revolt. Other factors combined with these economic grievances to fuel the rebellion. The south of England, where the revolt broke out, had been subjected to destructive French raids during the Hundred Years' War. The English government did little to protect the region, and villagers grew increasingly frightened and insecure. Moreover, decades of aristocratic violence against the weak peasantry had bred hostility and bitterness. Social and religious agitation by the popular preacher John Ball fanned the embers of discontent.

The English revolt was ignited by the reimposition of a tax on all adult males to pay for the war with France. Despite widespread opposition to the tax, the royal council ordered sheriffs to collect unpaid taxes by force in 1381. This led to a major uprising later termed the **English Peasants' Revolt**, which involved thousands of people, including artisans and the poor in cities as well

as rural residents. Beginning with assaults on the tax collectors, the revolt in England followed a course similar to that of the Jacquerie in France. Castles and manors were sacked. Manorial records were destroyed. Many nobles, including the archbishop of Canterbury who had ordered the collection of the tax, were murdered. The center of the revolt lay in the highly populated and economically advanced south and east, but sections of the north also witnessed rebellions (see Map 11.3).

The boy-king Richard II (r. 1377–1399) met the leaders of the revolt, agreed to charters ensuring peasants' freedom, tricked them with false promises, and then crushed the uprising with terrible ferocity. In the aftermath of the revolt, the nobility tried to restore the labor obligations of serfdom, but they were not successful, and the conversion to money rents continued. The English Peasants' Revolt did not bring social equality to England, but rural serfdom continued to decline, disappearing in England by 1550.

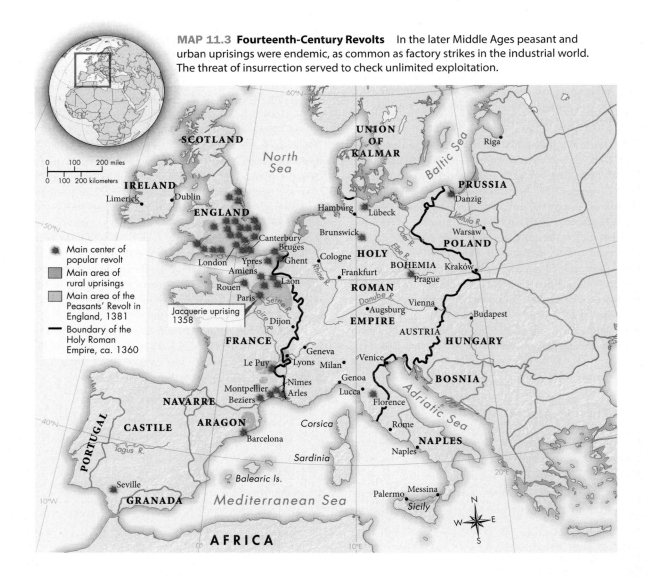

MAP 11.3 Fourteenth-Century Revolts In the later Middle Ages peasant and urban uprisings were endemic, as common as factory strikes in the industrial world. The threat of insurrection served to check unlimited exploitation.

Urban Conflicts

In Flanders, France, and England, peasant revolts often blended with conflicts involving workers in cities. Unrest also occurred in Italian, Spanish, and German cities. The urban revolts had their roots in the changing conditions of work. In the thirteenth century craft guilds had organized the production of most goods, with masters, journeymen, and apprentices working side by side. In the fourteenth century a new system evolved to make products on a larger scale. Capitalist investors hired many households, with each household performing only one step of the process. Initially these investors were wealthy bankers and merchants, but eventually shop masters themselves embraced the system. This promoted a greater division within guilds between wealthier masters and the poorer masters and journeymen they hired. Some masters became so wealthy from the profits of their workers that they no longer had to work in a shop themselves, nor did their wives and family members, though they still generally belonged to the craft guild.

While capitalism provided opportunities for some artisans to become investors and entrepreneurs, especially in cloth production, for many it led to a decrease in income and status. Guilds sometimes responded to crises by opening up membership, as they did in some places immediately after the Black Death, but they more often responded to competition by limiting membership to existing guild families, which meant that journeymen who were not master's sons or who could not find a master's widow or daughter to marry could never become masters themselves. Remaining journeymen their entire lives, they lost their sense of solidarity with the masters of their craft. Resentment led to rebellion.

Urban uprisings were also sparked by issues involving honor, such as employers' requiring workers to do tasks they regarded as beneath them. As their actual status and economic prospects declined and their work became basically wage labor, journeymen and poorer masters emphasized skill and honor as qualities that set them apart from less skilled workers.

Guilds increasingly came to view the honor of their work as tied to an all-male workplace. When urban economies were expanding in the High Middle Ages, the master's wife and daughters worked alongside him, and female domestic servants also carried out productive tasks. (See "Evaluating the Evidence 11.3: Christine de Pizan, Advice to the Wives of Artisans," page 348.) Masters' widows ran shops after the death of their husbands. But in the fourteenth century women's participation in guilds declined, despite labor shortages caused by the plague. First, masters' widows were limited in the amount of time they could keep operating a shop or were prohibited from hiring journeymen; later, female domestic servants were excluded from any productive tasks; finally, the number of daughters a master craftsman could employ was limited. When women were allowed to work, it was viewed as a substitute for charity.

Sex in the City

Peasant and urban revolts and riots had clear economic bases, but some historians have suggested that late medieval marital patterns may have also played a role. In northwestern Europe, people believed that couples should be economically independent before they married. Thus not only during times of crisis such as the Great Famine, but also in more general circumstances, men and women spent long periods as servants or workers in other households, saving money for married life and learning skills, or they waited until their own parents had died and the family property was distributed.

The most unusual feature of this pattern was the late age of marriage for women. Unlike in earlier time periods and in most other parts of the world, a woman in late medieval northern and western Europe generally entered marriage as an adult in her twenties and took charge of running a household immediately. She was thus not as dependent on her husband or mother-in-law as was a woman who married at a younger age. She also had fewer pregnancies than a woman who married earlier, though not necessarily fewer surviving children.

Men of all social groups had long tended to be older than women when they married. In general, men were in their middle or late twenties at first marriage, with wealthier urban merchants often much older. Journeymen and apprentices were often explicitly prohibited from marrying, as were the students at universities, who were understood to be in "minor orders" and thus like clergy, even if they were not intending to have careers in the church.

The prohibitions on marriage for certain groups of men and the late age of marriage for most men meant that cities and villages were filled with large numbers of young adult men with no family responsibilities who often formed the core of riots and unrest. Not surprisingly, this situation also contributed to a steady market for sexual services outside of marriage, services that in later centuries were termed prostitution. Research on the southern French province of Languedoc in the fourteenth and fifteenth centuries has revealed the establishment of legal houses of prostitution in many cities. Municipal authorities set up houses or districts for prostitution either outside the city walls or away from respectable neighborhoods. For example, authorities in Montpellier set aside Hot Street for prostitution, required women who sold sex to live there, and forbade anyone to molest them. Prostitution thus passed from

■ **English Peasants' Revolt** Revolt by English peasants in 1381 in response to changing economic conditions.

Christine de Pizan, Advice to the Wives of Artisans

Christine de Pizan (1364?–1430) was the daughter and wife of highly educated men who held positions at the court of the king of France. She was widowed at twenty-five with young children and an elderly mother to care for, and she decided to support her family through writing, an unusual choice for anyone in this era and unheard of for a woman. She began to write prose works and poetry, and gained commissions to write a biography of the French king Charles V, several histories, a long poem celebrating Joan of Arc's victory, and a book of military tactics. She became the first woman in Europe to make her living as a writer.

Among Christine's many works were several in which she considered women's nature and proper role in society, a topic of debate since ancient times. Among these was The Treasure of the City of Ladies *(1405, also called* The Book of Three Virtues*), which provides moral suggestions and practical advice on behavior and household management for women of all social classes. Most of the book is directed toward princesses and court ladies, but she also includes shorter sections for more ordinary women. Excerpted here is her advice to the wives of artisans, whose husbands were generally members of urban craft guilds, such as black-smiths, bakers, or shoemakers.*

All wives of artisans should be very painstaking and diligent if they wish to have the necessities of life. They should encourage their husbands or their workmen to get to work early in the morning and work until late, for mark our words, there is no trade so good that if you neglect your work you will not have difficulty putting bread on the table. And besides encouraging the others, the wife herself should be involved in the work to the extent that she knows all about it, so that she may know how to oversee his workers if her husband is absent, and to reprove them if they do not do well. She ought to oversee them to keep them from idleness, for through careless workers the master is sometimes ruined. And when customers come to her husband and try to drive a hard bargain, she ought to warn him solicitously to take care that he does not make a bad deal. She should advise him to be chary of giving too much credit if he does not know precisely where and to whom it is going, for in this way many come to poverty, although sometimes the greed to earn more or to accept a tempting proposition makes them do it.

In addition, she ought to keep her husband's love as much as she can, to this end: that he will stay at home more willingly and that he may not have any reason to join the foolish crowds of other young men in taverns and indulge in unnecessary and extravagant expense, as many tradesmen do, especially in Paris. By treating him kindly she should protect him as well as she can from this. It is said that three things drive a man from his home: a quarrelsome wife, a smoking fireplace and a leaking roof. She too ought to stay at home gladly and not go every day traipsing hither and yon gossiping with the neighbours and visiting her chums to find out what everyone is doing. That is done by slovenly housewives roaming about the town in groups. Nor should she go off on these pilgrimages got up for no good reason and involving a lot of needless expense. Furthermore, she ought to remind her husband that they should live so frugally that their expenditure does not exceed their income, so that at the end of the year they do not find themselves in debt.

If she has children, she should have them instructed and taught first at school by educated people so that they may know how better to serve God. Afterwards they may be put to some trade by which they may earn a living, for whoever gives a trade or business training to her child gives a great possession. The children should be kept from wantonness and from voluptuousness above all else, for truly it is something that most shames the children of good towns and is a great sin of mothers and fathers, who ought to be the cause of the virtue and good behavior of their children, but they are sometimes the reason (because of bringing them up to be finicky and indulging them too much) for their wickedness and ruin.

EVALUATE THE EVIDENCE

1. How would you describe Christine's view of the ideal artisan's wife?
2. The regulations of craft guilds often required that masters who ran workshops be married. What evidence does Christine's advice provide for why guilds would have stipulated this?
3. How are economic and moral virtues linked for Christine?

Source: Excerpts from pp. 167–168 in Christine de Pisan, *The Treasure of the City of Ladies*, translated with an Introduction by Sarah Lawson (Penguin Classics, 1985). This translation copyright © 1985 by Sarah Lawson. Reproduced by permission of Penguin Books Ltd. For more on Christine, see C. C. Willard, *Christine de Pisan: Her Life and Works* (1984), and S. Bell, *The Lost Tapestries of the City of Ladies: Christine de Pizan's Renaissance Legacy* (2004).

being a private concern to being a social matter requiring public supervision. The towns of Languedoc were not unique. Public authorities in Amiens, Dijon, Paris, Venice, Genoa, London, Florence, Rome, most of the larger German towns, and the English port of Sandwich set up brothels.

Young men associated visiting brothels with achieving manhood; for the women themselves, of course, their activities were work. Some women had no choice, for they had been traded to the brothel manager by their parents or some other person as payment for debt, or had quickly become indebted to the manager (most managers were men) for the clothes and other finery regarded as essential to their occupation. The small amount they received from their customers did not equal what they had to pay for their upkeep in a brothel. Poor women—and men—also sold sex illegally outside of city brothels, combining this with other sorts of part-time work such as laundering or sewing. Prostitution was an urban phenomenon because only populous towns had large numbers of

unmarried young men, communities of transient merchants, and a culture accustomed to a cash exchange.

Though selling sex for money was legal in the Middle Ages, the position of women who did so was always marginal. In the late fifteenth century cities began to limit brothel residents' freedom of movement and choice of clothing, requiring them to wear distinctive head coverings or bands on their clothing so that they would not be mistaken for "honorable" women. Cities also began to impose harsher penalties on women who did not live in the designated house or section of town. A few women who sold sex did earn enough to donate money to charity or buy property, but most were very poor.

Along with buying sex, young men also took it by force. Unmarried women often found it difficult to avoid sexual contact. Many worked as domestic servants, where their employers or employers' sons or male relatives could easily coerce them, or they worked in proximity to men. Notions of female honor kept upperclass women secluded in their homes, particularly in

Public Bath In this fanciful scene of a medieval public bath from a 1470 illuminated manuscript, men and women soak in tubs while they eat and drink, entertained by a musician, and a king and church official look on. At the left is a couple about to hop in a bed for sex in what might be a brothel. Normal public baths were far less elaborate, and while they did sometimes offer food, wine, and sex, their main attraction was hot water. This painting is not meant to be realistic but a commentary on declining morals. (Miniature from a manuscript, *Factorum et dictorum memorabilium*, by Valerius Maximus for Antoine of Burgundy, ca. 1470/akg-images)

Same-Sex Relations   This illustration from a fourteenth-century manuscript of Dante's *Divine Comedy* (see page 352) depicts those who engaged in same-sex relations in the seventh circle of Hell, with murderers and those who committed suicide. Dante regarded all of these as violent: murderers against others; suicides against themselves; and men who engaged in sex with men against nature and against their family line because they did not father children. They are condemned to run forever on burning sand, which represented their sterility; note that one of the men wears a bishop's hat. Dante's work was written and this illustration was painted at the time that religious and political authorities were increasingly criminalizing same-sex relations. (Detail, Cantica del Inferno from *Divina Commedia* by Dante Alighieri [1265–1321], vellum/Musée Condé, Chantilly, France/Bridgeman Images)

southern and eastern Europe, but there was little attempt anywhere to protect female servants or day laborers from the risk of seduction or rape. Rape was a capital crime in many parts of Europe, but the actual sentences handed out were more likely to be fines and brief imprisonment, with the severity of the sentence dependent on the social status of the victim and the perpetrator.

According to laws regarding rape in most parts of Europe, the victim had to prove that she had cried out and had attempted to repel the attacker, and she had to bring the charge within a short period of time after the attack had happened. Women bringing rape charges were often more interested in getting their own honorable reputations back than in punishing the perpetrators. For this reason, they sometimes asked the judge to force their rapists to marry them.

Same-sex relations—what in the late nineteenth century would be termed "homosexuality"—were another feature of medieval urban life (and of village life, though there are very few sources relating to sexual relations of any type in the rural context). Same-sex relations were of relatively little concern to church or state authorities in the early Middle Ages, but this attitude changed beginning in the late twelfth century. By 1300 most areas had defined such actions as "crimes against nature," with authorities seeing them as particularly reprehensible because they thought they did not occur anywhere else in creation. Same-sex relations, usually termed "sodomy," became a capital crime in most of Europe, with adult offenders threatened with execution by fire. The Italian cities of Venice, Florence, and Lucca created special courts to deal with sodomy, which saw thousands of investigations.

How prevalent were same-sex relations? This is difficult to answer, even in modern society, but the city of Florence provides a provocative case study. In 1432 Florence set up a special board of adult men, the Office of the Night, to "root out . . . the abominable vice of sodomy."[10] Between 1432 and the abolition of the board in 1502, about seventeen thousand men came to its attention, which, even over a seventy-year period, represents a great number in a population of about forty thousand. The men came from all classes of society, but almost all cases involved an adult man and an adolescent boy; they ranged from sex exchanged for money or gifts to long-term affectionate relationships. Florentines believed in a generational model in which different roles were appropriate to different stages in life. In a socially and sexually hierarchical world, the boy in the passive role was identified as subordinate, dependent, and mercenary, words usually applied to women. Florentines, however, never described the dominant partner in feminine terms, for he had not compromised his masculine identity or violated a gender ideal; in fact, the adult partner might be married or have female sexual partners as well as male. Only if an adult male assumed the passive role was his masculinity jeopardized.

Thus in Florence, and no doubt elsewhere in Europe, sodomy was not a marginal practice, which may account for the fact that, despite harsh laws and special courts, actual executions for sodomy were rare. Same-sex relations often developed within the context of all-male environments, such as the army, the craft shop, and the artistic workshop, and were part of the collective male experience. Homoerotic relationships played important roles in defining stages of life, expressing distinctions of status, and shaping masculine gender identity. Same-sex relations involving women almost never came to the attention of legal authorities, so it is difficult to find out how common they were. However, female-female desire was expressed in songs, plays, and stories, as was male-male desire, offering evidence of the way people understood same-sex relations.

Fur-Collar Crime

The Hundred Years' War had provided employment and opportunity for thousands of idle and fortune-seeking knights. But during periods of truce and after the war finally ended, many nobles once again had little to do. Inflation hurt them. Although many were living on fixed incomes, their chivalric code demanded lavish generosity and an aristocratic lifestyle. Many nobles thus turned to crime as a way of raising money. The fourteenth and fifteenth centuries witnessed a great deal of what we might term "fur-collar crime," a medieval version of today's white-collar crime in which those higher up the social scale prey on those who are less well-off.

This "fur-collar crime" involved both violence and fraud. Groups of noble bandits roamed the English countryside, stealing from both rich and poor. Operating like modern urban racketeers, knightly gangs demanded that peasants pay protection money or else have their hovels burned and their fields destroyed. They seized wealthy travelers and held them for ransom. Corrupt landowners, including some churchmen, pushed peasants to pay higher taxes and extra fees. When accused of wrongdoing, fur-collar criminals intimidated witnesses, threatened jurors, and used their influence to persuade judges to support them — or used cash to bribe them outright.

Aristocratic violence led to revolt, and it also shaped popular culture. The ballads of Robin Hood, a collection of folk legends from late medieval England, describe the adventures of the outlaw hero and his merry men as they avenge the common people against fur-collar criminals — grasping landlords, wicked sheriffs, and mercenary churchmen. Robin Hood was a popular figure because he symbolized the deep resentment of aristocratic corruption and abuse; he represented the struggle against tyranny and oppression.

Ethnic Tensions and Restrictions

Large numbers of people in the twelfth and thirteenth centuries migrated from one part of Europe to another in search of land, food, and work: the English into Scotland and Ireland; Germans, French, and Flemings into Poland, Bohemia, and Hungary; Christians into Muslim Spain. Everywhere in Europe, towns recruited people from the countryside as well (see Chapter 10). In frontier regions, townspeople were usually long-distance

immigrants and, in eastern Europe, Ireland, and Scotland, ethnically different from the surrounding rural population. In eastern Europe, German was the language of the towns; in Irish towns, French, the tongue of Norman or English settlers, predominated. As a result of this colonization and movement to towns, peoples of different ethnic backgrounds lived side by side.

In the early periods of conquest and colonization, and in all regions with extensive migrations, a legal dualism existed: native peoples remained subject to their traditional laws; newcomers brought and were subject to the laws of the countries from which they came. On the Prussian and Polish frontier, for example, the law was that "men who come there . . . should be judged on account of any crime or contract engaged in there according to Polish custom if they are Poles and according to German custom if they are Germans."[11] Likewise, the conquered Muslim subjects of Christian kings in Spain had the right to be judged under Muslim law by Muslim judges.

The great exception to this broad pattern of legal pluralism was Ireland. From the start, the English practiced an extreme form of discrimination toward the native Irish. The English distinguished between the free and the unfree, and the entire Irish population, simply by the fact of Irish birth, was unfree. When English legal structures were established beginning in 1210, the Irish were denied access to the common-law courts. In civil (property) disputes, an English defendant did not need to respond to an Irish plaintiff; no Irish person could make a will. In criminal procedures, the murder of an Irishman was not considered a felony. Other than in Ireland, although native peoples commonly held humbler positions, both immigrant and native townspeople prospered during the expanding economy of the thirteenth century. But with the economic turmoil of the fourteenth century, ethnic tensions multiplied.

The later Middle Ages witnessed a movement away from legal pluralism or dualism and toward legal homogeneity and an emphasis on blood descent. The dominant ethnic group in an area tried to bar others from positions of church leadership and guild membership. Marriage laws were instituted that attempted to maintain ethnic purity by prohibiting intermarriage, and some church leaders actively promoted ethnic discrimination. As Germans moved eastward, for example, German bishops refused to appoint non-Germans to any church office, while Czech bishops closed monasteries to Germans.

The most extensive attempt to prevent intermarriage and protect ethnic purity is embodied in the **Statute of Kilkenny** (1366), a law the ruling English imposed on Ireland, which states that "there were to be

■ **Statute of Kilkenny** Law issued in 1366 that discriminated against the Irish, forbidding marriage between the English and the Irish, requiring the use of the English language, and denying the Irish access to ecclesiastical offices.

no marriages between those of immigrant and native stock; that the English inhabitants of Ireland must employ the English language and bear English names; that they must ride in the English way [that is, with saddles] and have English apparel; that no Irishmen were to be granted ecclesiastical benefices or admitted to monasteries in the English parts of Ireland."[12]

Late medieval chroniclers used words such as *gens* (race or clan) and *natio* (NAH-tee-oh; species, stock, or kind) to refer to different groups. They held that peoples differed according to language, traditions, customs, and laws. None of these were unchangeable, however, and commentators increasingly also described ethnic differences in terms of "blood," which made ethnicity heritable. As national consciousness grew with the Hundred Years' War, for example, people began to speak of "French blood" and "English blood." Religious beliefs came to be conceptualized in terms of blood as well, with people regarded as having Jewish blood, Muslim blood, or Christian blood. The most dramatic expression of this was in Spain, where "purity of blood"—having no Muslim or Jewish ancestors—became an obsession. Blood also came to be used as a way to talk about social differences, especially for nobles. Just as the Irish and English were prohibited from marrying each other, those of "noble blood" were prohibited from marrying commoners in many parts of Europe. As Europeans increasingly came into contact with people from Africa and Asia, and particularly as they developed colonial empires, these notions of blood also became a way of conceptualizing racial categories.

Literacy and Vernacular Literature

The development of ethnic identities had many negative consequences, but a more positive effect was the increasing use of the vernacular, that is, the local language that people actually spoke, rather than Latin (see Chapter 10). Two masterpieces of European culture, Dante's *Divine Comedy* (1310–1320) and Chaucer's *Canterbury Tales* (1387–1400), illustrate a sophisticated use of the rhythms and rhymes of the vernacular.

The *Divine Comedy* of Dante Alighieri (DAHN-tay ah-luh-GYEHR-ee) (1265–1321) is an epic poem of one hundred cantos (verses), each of whose three equal parts describes one of the realms of the next world: Hell, Purgatory, and Paradise. The Roman poet Virgil, representing reason, leads Dante through Hell, where Dante observes the torments of the damned and denounces the disorders of his own time. Passing up into Purgatory, Virgil shows the poet how souls are purified of their disordered inclinations. From Purgatory, Beatrice, a woman Dante once loved and who serves as the symbol of divine revelation in the poem, leads him to Paradise.

The *Divine Comedy* portrays contemporary and historical figures, comments on secular and ecclesiastical affairs, and draws on the Scholastic philosophy of uniting faith and reason. Within the framework of a symbolic pilgrimage, the *Divine Comedy* embodies the psychological tensions of the age. A profoundly Christian poem, it also contains bitter criticism of some church authorities. In its symmetrical structure and use of figures from the ancient world such as Virgil, the poem perpetuates the classical tradition, but as the first major work of literature in the Italian vernacular, it is distinctly modern.

Geoffrey Chaucer (1342–1400) was an official in the administrations of the English kings Edward III and Richard II and wrote poetry as an avocation. His *Canterbury Tales* is a collection of stories in lengthy rhymed narrative. On a pilgrimage to the shrine of Saint Thomas Becket at Canterbury (see Chapter 9), thirty people of various social backgrounds tell tales. In depicting the interests and behavior of all types of people, Chaucer presents a rich panorama of English social life in the fourteenth century. Like the *Divine Comedy*, the *Canterbury Tales* reflects the cultural tensions of the times. Ostensibly Christian, many of

Chaucer's Wife of Bath   Chaucer's *Canterbury Tales* were filled with memorable characters, including the often-married Wife of Bath, shown here in a fifteenth-century manuscript. In the prologue that details her life, she denies the value of virginity and criticizes her young and handsome fifth husband for reading a book about "wicked wives." "By God, if women had but written stories . . . ," she comments, "They would have written of men more wickedness / Than all the race of Adam could redress." (Private Collection/Bridgeman Images)

the pilgrims are also materialistic, sensual, and worldly, suggesting the ambivalence of the broader society's concern for the next world and frank enjoyment of this one.

Beginning in the fourteenth century, a variety of evidence attests to the increasing literacy of laypeople. Wills and inventories reveal that many people, not just nobles, possessed books—mainly devotional texts, but also romances, manuals on manners and etiquette, histories, and sometimes legal and philosophical texts. In England the number of schools in the diocese of York quadrupled between 1350 and 1500. Information from Flemish and German towns is similar: children were sent to schools and were taught the fundamentals of reading, writing, and arithmetic. Laymen increasingly served as managers or stewards of estates and as clerks to guilds and town governments; such positions obviously required the ability to keep administrative and financial records.

The penetration of laymen into the higher positions of governmental administration, long the preserve of clerics, also illustrates rising lay literacy. With growing frequency, the upper classes sent their daughters to convent schools, where, in addition to instruction in singing, religion, needlework, deportment, and household management, they gained the rudiments of reading and sometimes writing.

The spread of literacy represents a response to the needs of an increasingly complex society. Trade, commerce, and expanding government bureaucracies required an increasing number of literate people. Late medieval culture remained a decidedly oral culture. But by the fifteenth century the evolution toward a more literate culture was already perceptible, and craftsmen would develop the new technology of the printing press in response to the increased demand for reading materials.

NOTES

1. Christos S. Bartsocas, "Two Fourteenth Century Descriptions of the 'Black Death,'" *Journal of the History of Medicine* (October 1966): 395.
2. Giovanni Boccaccio, *The Decameron*, trans. Mark Musa and Peter Bondanella (New York: W. W. Norton, 1982), p. 7.
3. Ibid., p. 9.
4. Bartsocas, "Two Fourteenth Century Descriptions," p. 397.
5. Florence Warren, ed., *The Dance of Death* (Oxford: Early English Text Society, 1931), 10 lines from p. 8. Spelling modernized. Used by permission of the Council of the Early English Text Society.
6. W. P. Barrett, trans., *The Trial of Jeanne d'Arc* (London: George Routledge, 1931), pp. 165–166.
7. James Harvey Robinson, *Readings in European History*, vol. 1 (Boston: Ginn and Company, 1904), pp. 375–376.
8. Quoted in J. H. Smith, *The Great Schism, 1378: The Disintegration of the Medieval Papacy* (New York: Weybright & Talley, 1970), p. 15.
9. Quoted in Katharina M. Wilson, ed., *Medieval Women Writers* (Athens: University of Georgia Press, 1984), p. 245.
10. Michael Rocke, *Forbidden Friendships: Homosexuality and Male Culture in Renaissance Florence* (New York: Oxford University Press, 1996), p. 45.
11. Quoted in R. Bartlett, *The Making of Europe: Conquest, Colonization and Cultural Change, 950–1350* (Princeton, N.J.: Princeton University Press, 1993), p. 205.
12. Quoted ibid., p. 239.

LOOKING BACK LOOKING AHEAD

The fourteenth and early fifteenth centuries were certainly times of crisis in western Europe, meriting the label "calamitous" given to them by one popular historian. Famine, disease, and war decimated the European population, and traditional institutions, including secular governments and the church, did little or nothing or, in some cases, made things worse. Trading connections that had been reinvigorated in the High Middle Ages spread the most deadly epidemic ever experienced through western Asia, North Africa, and almost all of Europe. No wonder survivors experienced a sort of shell shock and a fascination with death.

The plague did not destroy the prosperity of the medieval population, however, and it may in fact have indirectly improved the European economy. Wealthy merchants had plenty of money to spend on luxuries and talent. In the century after the plague, Italian artists began to create new styles of painting, writers to pen new literary forms, educators to found new types of schools, and philosophers to develop new ideas about the purpose of human life. These cultural changes eventually spread to the rest of Europe, following the same paths that the plague had traveled.

Make Connections

Think about the larger developments and continuities within and across chapters.

1. The Black Death has often been compared with later pandemics, including the global spread of HIV/AIDS, which began in the 1980s. It is easy to note the differences between these two, but what similarities do you see in the course of the two diseases and their social and cultural consequences?

2. Beginning with Chapter 7, every chapter in this book has discussed the development of the papacy and relations between popes and secular rulers. How were the problems facing the papacy in the fourteenth century the outgrowth of long-term issues? Why had attempts to solve these issues not been successful?

3. In Chapter 3 you learned about the Bronze Age Collapse, and in Chapter 7 about the end of the Roman Empire in the West, both of which have also been seen as "calamitous." What similarities and differences do you see in these earlier times of turmoil and those of the late Middle Ages?

11 REVIEW & EXPLORE

Identify Key Terms

Identify and explain the significance of each item below.

Great Famine (p. 324)

Black Death (p. 325)

flagellants (p. 332)

Hundred Years' War (p. 332)

representative assemblies (p. 338)

Babylonian Captivity (p. 339)

Great Schism (p. 339)

conciliarists (p. 340)

confraternities (p. 341)

Jacquerie (p. 343)

English Peasants' Revolt (p. 346)

Statute of Kilkenny (p. 351)

Review the Main Ideas

Answer the focus questions from each section of the chapter.

◆ How did climate change shape the late Middle Ages? (p. 324)

◆ How did the plague reshape European society? (p. 325)

◆ What were the causes, course, and consequences of the Hundred Years' War? (p. 332)

◆ Why did the church come under increasing criticism? (p. 338)

◆ What explains the social unrest of the late Middle Ages? (p. 343)

Suggested Reading and Media Resources

BOOKS

- Allmand, Christopher. *The Hundred Years War: England and France at War, ca. 1300–1450*, rev. ed. 2005. Designed for students; examines the war from political, military, social, and economic perspectives, and compares the way England and France reacted to the conflict.

- Cohn, Samuel K. *Lust for Liberty: The Politics of Social Revolt in Medieval Europe*. 2006. Analyzes a number of revolts from across Europe in terms of the aims of their leaders and participants.

- Dunn, Alastair. *The Peasants' Revolt: England's Failed Revolution of 1381*. 2004. Offers new interpretations of the causes and consequences of the English Peasants' Revolt.

- Dyer, Christopher. *Standards of Living in the Later Middle Ages*. 1989. Examines economic realities and social conditions more generally.

- Herlihy, David. *The Black Death and the Transformation of the West*, 2d ed. 1997. A fine treatment of the causes and cultural consequences of the Black Death; the best starting point for study of the great epidemic.

- Jordan, William Chester. *The Great Famine: Northern Europe in the Early Fourteenth Century*. 1996. Discusses catastrophic weather, soil exhaustion, and other factors that led to the Great Famine and the impact of the famine on community life.

- Karras, Ruth M. *Sexuality in Medieval Europe: Doing unto Others*. 2005. A brief overview designed for undergraduates that incorporates the newest scholarship.

- Keen, Maurice. *Medieval Warfare: A History*. 1999. Traces actual battles and the art of warfare from Charlemagne to 1500.

- Lehfeldt, Elizabeth, ed. *The Black Death*. 2005. Includes excerpts from scholarly articles about many aspects of the Black Death.

- McGinn, Bernard. *The Varieties of Vernacular Mysticism, 1350–1550*. 2012. A comprehensive survey that demonstrates how this period gave rise to mystical writers who remain influential even today.

- Swanson, R. N. *Religion and Devotion in Europe, c. 1215–c. 1515*. 2004. Explores many aspects of spirituality.

- Tanner, Norman. *The Church in the Later Middle Ages*. 2008. A concise survey of institutional and intellectual issues and developments.

- Tuchman, Barbara. *A Distant Mirror: The Calamitous Fourteenth Century*. 1978. Written for a general audience, it remains a vivid description of this tumultuous time.

DOCUMENTARIES

- *The Hundred Years' War* (BBC, 2012). This three-part series examines the military, political, and cultural aspects of the Hundred Years' War.

- *Michael Wood's Story of England* (BBC, 2010). This series focuses on the village of Kibworth in central England, for which extensive archives survive that give insight into daily life. Episode 3 examines the Great Famine and the Black Death, and episode 4 the Hundred Years' War and economic change.

- *The Plague* (History Channel, 2005). A documentary examining the path and impact of the plague in Europe, with firsthand accounts taken from diaries and journals.

FEATURE FILMS

- *Henry V* (Kenneth Branagh, 1989). A widely acclaimed film adaptation of Shakespeare's play about the English king and the Battle of Agincourt, with nearly every well-known English actor.

- *The Name of the Rose* (Jean-Jacques Annaud, 1986). Based on the novel by Umberto Eco about a fourteenth-century monk (played by Sean Connery), this is both a murder mystery and a commentary on issues facing the church.

- *The Reckoning* (Paul McGuigan, 2003). The story of a troupe of actors who perform a morality play for the villagers of a fourteenth-century English town, combined with a murder mystery about the death of a child.

- *The Seventh Seal* (Ingmar Bergman, 1957). A classic film about a knight who comes home from war to find plague and religious suspicion, and engages in a chess game with Death.

WEB SITES

- *Brought to Life.* A fascinating Web site on the history of medicine sponsored by the Science Museum, London, featuring thousands of objects from its medical collections. Provides multimedia introductions to topics and themes in medical history, including one on the Black Death. **www.sciencemuseum.org.uk/broughttolife /themes/diseases/black_death.aspx**

12

European Society in the Age of the Renaissance

1350–1550

While the Hundred Years' War gripped northern Europe, a new culture emerged in southern Europe. The fourteenth century witnessed remarkable changes in Italian intellectual, artistic, and cultural life. Artists and writers thought that they were living in a new golden age, but not until the sixteenth century was this change given the label we use today—the *Renaissance*, derived from the French word for "rebirth." That word was first used by art historian Giorgio Vasari (1511–1574) to describe the art of "rare men of genius" such as his contemporary Michelangelo. Through their works, Vasari judged, the glory of the classical past had been reborn after centuries of darkness. Over time, the word's meaning was broadened to include many aspects of life during that period. The new attitude had a slow diffusion out of Italy, so that the Renaissance "happened" at different times in different parts of Europe. The Renaissance was a movement, not a time period.

Later scholars increasingly saw the cultural and political changes of the Renaissance, along with the religious changes of the Reformation (see Chapter 13) and the European voyages of exploration (see Chapter 14), as ushering in the "modern" world. Some historians view the Renaissance as a bridge between the medieval and modern eras because it corresponded chronologically with the late medieval period and because there were many continuities with that period along with the changes that suggested aspects of the modern world. Others have questioned whether the word *Renaissance* should be used at all to describe an era in which many social groups saw decline rather than advance. The debates remind us that these labels—medieval, Renaissance, modern—are intellectual constructs devised after the fact, and all contain value judgments. ■

CHAPTER PREVIEW

Life in the Renaissance
In this detail from a fresco of the birth of the Virgin Mary in the Church of San Michele al Pozzo Bianco in Bergamo, Italian painter Lorenzo Lotto depicts a birth scene that would have been common among upper-class urban residents in Renaissance Italy. The birth occurs at home, with lots of women bustling about, including servants, dressed simply, and female relatives, in fancier clothing. A professional midwife sits by the side of the bed, and the mother looks quite content, a sign that this has been a successful and fairly easy childbirth, which was not always the case. (By Lorenzo Lotto [ca. 1480–1556], Church of San Michele al Pozzo Bianco, Bergamo, Italy/Mauro Ranzani Archive/Alinari Archives/Bridgeman Images)

Wealth and Power in Renaissance Italy

FOCUS QUESTION *How did politics and economics shape the Renaissance?*

The magnificent art and new ways of thinking in the **Renaissance** rested on economic and political developments in the city-states of northern Italy. Economic growth laid the material basis for the Italian Renaissance, and ambitious merchants gained political power to match their economic power. They then used their money and power to buy luxuries and hire talent in a system of **patronage**, through which cities, groups, and individuals commissioned writers and artists to produce specific works. Political leaders in Italian cities admired the traditions and power of ancient Rome, and this esteem shaped their commissions. Thus economics, politics, and culture were interconnected.

Trade and Prosperity

Northern Italian cities led the way in the great commercial revival of the eleventh century (see Chapter 10). By the middle of the twelfth century Venice, supported by a huge merchant marine, had grown enormously rich through overseas trade, as had Genoa and Milan, which had their own sizable fleets. These cities made important strides in shipbuilding that allowed their ships to sail all year long at accelerated speeds and carrying ever more merchandise.

Another commercial leader, and the city where the Renaissance began, was Florence, situated on fertile soil along the Arno River. Its favorable location on the main road northward from Rome made Florence a commercial hub, and the city grew wealthy buying and selling all types of goods throughout Europe and the Mediterranean — grain, cloth, wool, weapons, armor, spices, glass, and wine.

Florentine merchants also loaned and invested money, and they acquired control of papal banking toward the end of the thirteenth century. Florentine mercantile families began to dominate European banking on both sides of the Alps, setting up offices in major European and North African cities. The profits

from loans, investments, and money exchanges that poured back to Florence were pumped into urban industries such as clothmaking, and by the early fourteenth century the city had about eighty thousand people, about twice the population of London at that time. Profits contributed to the city's economic vitality and allowed banking families to control the city's politics and culture.

By the first quarter of the fourteenth century, the economic foundations of Florence were so strong that even severe crises could not destroy the city. In 1344 King Edward III of England repudiated his huge debts to Florentine bankers, forcing some of them into bankruptcy. Soon after, Florence suffered frightfully from the Black Death, losing at least half its population, and serious labor unrest shook the political establishment (see Chapter 11). Nevertheless, the basic Florentine economic structure remained stable, and the city grew again. In the fifteenth century the Florentine merchant and historian Benedetto Dei (DAY-ee) boasted proudly of his city in a letter to an acquaintance from Venice:

> Our beautiful Florence contains within the city in this present year two hundred seventy shops belonging to the wool merchants' guild . . . eighty-three rich and splendid warehouses of the silk merchants' guild. . . . The number of banks amounts to thirty-three; the shops of the cabinet-makers, whose business is carving and inlaid work, to eighty-four . . . there are forty-four goldsmiths' and jewellers' shops.[1]

In Florence and other thriving Italian cities, wealth allowed many people greater material pleasures, a more comfortable life, imported luxuries, and leisure time to appreciate and patronize the arts. Merchants and bankers commissioned public and private buildings from architects, and hired sculptors and painters to decorate their homes and churches. The rich, social-climbing residents of Venice, Florence, Genoa, and Rome came to see life more as an opportunity to be enjoyed than as a painful pilgrimage to the City of God.

Communes and Republics of Northern Italy

The northern Italian cities were **communes**, sworn associations of free men who, like other town residents, began in the twelfth century to seek political and economic independence from local nobles. The merchant guilds that formed the communes built and maintained the city walls and regulated trade, collected taxes, and kept civil order within them. The local nobles frequently moved into the cities, marrying the daughters of rich commercial families and starting their own businesses, often with money they had gained through the dowries provided by their wives.

■ **Renaissance** A French word meaning "rebirth," used to describe the rebirth of the culture of classical antiquity in Italy during the fourteenth to sixteenth centuries.

■ **patronage** Financial support of writers and artists by cities, groups, and individuals, often to produce specific works or works in specific styles.

■ **communes** Sworn associations of free men in Italian cities led by merchant guilds that sought political and economic independence from local nobles.

■ **popolo** Disenfranchised common people in Italian cities who resented their exclusion from power.

This merger of the northern Italian nobility and the commercial elite created a powerful oligarchy, a small group that ruled the city and surrounding countryside. Yet because of rivalries among competing powerful families within this oligarchy, Italian communes were often politically unstable.

Unrest from below exacerbated the instability. Merchant elites made citizenship in the communes dependent on a property qualification, years of residence within the city, and social connections. Only a tiny percentage of the male population possessed these qualifications and thus could hold political office. The common people, called the **popolo**, were disenfranchised and heavily taxed, and they bitterly resented their exclusion from power. Throughout most of the thirteenth century, in city after city, the popolo used armed force to take over the city governments. At times republican government—in which political power theoretically resides in the people and is exercised by their chosen representatives—was established in numerous Italian cities, including Bologna, Siena, Parma, Florence, Genoa, and other cities. These victories of the popolo proved temporary, however, because they could not establish civil order within their cities. Merchant oligarchies reasserted their power and sometimes brought in powerful military leaders to establish order. These military leaders, called *condottieri* (kahn-duh-TYER-ee; singular

Chronology

ca. 1350	Petrarch develops ideas of humanism
1434–1737	Medici family in power in Florence
1440s	Invention of movable metal type
1447–1535	Sforza family in power in Milan
1455–1471	Wars of the Roses in England
1469	Marriage of Isabella of Castile and Ferdinand of Aragon
1477	Louis XI conquers Burgundy
1478	Establishment of the Inquisition in Spain
1492	Spain conquers Granada, ending reconquista; practicing Jews expelled from Spain
1494	Invasion of Italy by Charles VIII of France
1508–1512	Michelangelo paints ceiling of Sistine Chapel
1513	Machiavelli writes *The Prince*
1563	Establishment of first formal academy for artistic training in Florence

A Florentine Bank Scene Originally a "bank" was just a counter; money changers who sat behind the counter became "bankers," exchanging different currencies and holding deposits for merchants and business people. In this scene from fifteenth-century Florence, the bank is covered with an imported Ottoman geometric rug, one of many imported luxury items handled by Florentine merchants. Most cities issued their own coins, but the gold coins of Florence, known as florins (above), were accepted throughout Europe as a standard currency. (bank scene: Detail from the fresco *The Story of St. Matthew*, San Francesco, Prato, Italy/ Scala/Art Resource, NY; coins: Museo Nazionale del Bargello, Florence, Italy/Scala/ Art Resource, NY)

condottiero), had their own mercenary armies, and in many cities they took over political power once they had supplanted the existing government.

Many cities in Italy became **signori** (seen-YOHR-ee), in which one man—whether condottiero, merchant, or noble—ruled and handed down the right to rule to his son. Some signori (the word is plural in Italian and is used for both persons and forms of government) kept the institutions of communal government in place, but these had no actual power. As a practical matter, there wasn't much difference between oligarchic regimes and signori. Oligarchies maintained a façade of republican government, but the judicial, executive, and legislative functions of government were restricted to a small class of wealthy merchants.

In the fifteenth and sixteenth centuries the signori in many cities and the most powerful merchant oligarchs in others transformed their households into **courts**. Courtly culture afforded signori and oligarchs the opportunity to display and assert their wealth and power. They built magnificent palaces in the centers of cities and required all political business to be done there. Ceremonies connected with family births, baptisms, marriages, and funerals offered occasions for magnificent pageantry and elaborate ritual. Cities welcomed rulers who were visiting with magnificent entrance parades that often included fireworks, colorful banners, mock naval battles, decorated wagons filled with people in costume, and temporary triumphal arches modeled on those of ancient Rome. Rulers of nation-states later copied and adapted all these aspects of Italian courts.

City-States and the Balance of Power

Renaissance Italians had a passionate attachment to their individual city-states: they were politically loyal and felt centered on the city. This intensity of local feeling perpetuated the dozens of small states and hindered the development of one unified state.

In the fifteenth century five powers dominated the Italian peninsula: Venice, Milan, Florence, the Papal States, and the kingdom of Naples (Map 12.1). The major Italian powers controlled the smaller city-states, such as Siena, Mantua, Ferrara, and Modena, and competed furiously among themselves for territory. While the states of northern Europe were moving toward centralization and consolidation, the world of Italian politics resembled a jungle where the powerful dominated the weak. Venice, with its enormous trade empire, ranked as an international power. Though Venice was a

republic in name, an oligarchy of merchant-aristocrats actually ran the city. Milan was also called a republic, but the condottieri-turned-signori of the Sforza (SFORT-sah) family ruled harshly and dominated Milan and several smaller cities in the north from 1447 to 1535. Likewise, in Florence the form of government was republican, with authority vested in several councils of state, but the city was effectively ruled by the great Medici (MEH-duh-chee) banking family for three centuries, beginning in 1434. Though not public officials, Cosimo (1389–1464), his son Piero, and his grandson Lorenzo (1449–1492), called Lorenzo the Magnificent by his contemporaries, ruled from behind the scenes from 1434 to 1492. The Medici were then in and out of power for several decades, and in 1569 Florence became no longer a republic but the hereditary Grand Duchy of Tuscany, with the Medici as the Grand Dukes until 1737. The Medici family produced three popes, and most other Renaissance popes were also members of powerful Italian families, selected for their political skills, not their piety. Along with the Italians was one Spaniard, Pope Alexander VI (pontificate 1492–1503), who was the most ruthless; aided militarily and politically by his illegitimate son Cesare Borgia, he reasserted papal authority in the papal lands. South of the Papal States, the kingdom of Naples was under the control of the king of Aragon.

In one significant respect, however, the Italian city-states anticipated future relations among competing European states after 1500. Whenever one Italian state appeared to gain a predominant position within the peninsula, other states combined against it to establish a balance of power. In the formation of these alliances, Renaissance Italians invented the machinery of modern diplomacy: permanent embassies with resident ambassadors in capitals where political relations and commercial ties needed continual monitoring. The resident ambassador was one of the great political achievements of the Italian Renaissance.

At the end of the fifteenth century Venice, Florence, Milan, and the papacy possessed great wealth and represented high cultural achievement. Wealthy and divided, however, they were also an inviting target for invasion. When Florence and Naples entered into an agreement to acquire Milanese territories, Milan called on France for support, and the French king Charles VIII (r. 1483–1498) invaded Italy in 1494.

Prior to this invasion, the Dominican friar Girolamo Savonarola (1452–1498) had preached to large crowds in Florence a number of fiery sermons predicting that God would punish Italy for its moral vice and corrupt leadership. Florentines interpreted the French invasion as the fulfillment of this prophecy and expelled the Medici dynasty. Savonarola became the political and religious leader of a new Florentine republic and promised Florentines even greater glory

---

■ **signori** Government by one-man rule in Italian cities such as Milan; also refers to these rulers.

■ **courts** Magnificent households and palaces where signori and other rulers lived, conducted business, and supported the arts.

MAP 12.1 The Italian City-States, ca. 1494 In the fifteenth century the Italian city-states represented great wealth and cultural sophistication, though the many political divisions throughout the peninsula invited foreign intervention.

in the future if they would reform their ways. (See "Evaluating the Evidence 12.1: A Sermon of Savonarola," page 362.) He reorganized the government; convinced it to pass laws against same-sex relations, adultery, and drunkenness; and organized groups of young men to patrol the streets looking for immoral dress and behavior. He held religious processions and what became known as "bonfires of the vanities," huge fires on the main square of Florence in which fancy clothing, cosmetics, pagan books, musical instruments, paintings, and poetry that celebrated human beauty were gathered together and burned.

For a time Savonarola was wildly popular, but eventually people tired of his moral denunciations, and he was excommunicated by the pope, tortured, and

burned at the very spot where he had overseen the bonfires. The Medici returned as the rulers of Florence.

The French invasion inaugurated a new period in Italian and European power politics. Italy became the focus of international ambitions and the battleground of foreign armies, particularly those of the Holy Roman Empire and France in a series of conflicts called the Habsburg-Valois wars (named for the German and French dynasties). The Italian cities suffered severely from continual warfare, especially in the frightful sack of Rome in 1527 by imperial forces under the emperor Charles V. Thus the failure of the city-states to consolidate, or at least to establish a common foreign policy, led to centuries of subjection by outside invaders. Italy was not to achieve unification until 1870.

A Sermon of Savonarola

In the autumn of 1494 French armies under Charles VIII surrounded Florence. The Dominican friar Girolamo Savonarola met with the French king and convinced him to spare the city and keep moving his huge army southward. He preached a series of sermons that winter saying that God had chosen Florence to achieve even greater heights under his leadership than it had in the past, provided that it followed his instructions.

O Florence . . . I tell you, do first those two things I told you another time, that is, that everyone go to confession and be purified of sins, and let everyone attend to the common good of the city; and if you will do this, your city will be glorious because in this way she will be reformed spiritually as well as temporally, that is, with regard to her people, and from you will issue the reform of all Italy. Florence will become richer and more powerful than she has ever been, and her empire will expand into many places. But if you will not do what I tell you, God will elect those who, as I said, want to see you divided, and this will be your final destruction. If you would do what I have told you, here is the fire and here is the water: now do it! . . .

But, Florence, if you want your government to be stable and strong and to endure a long time, you must return to God and to living uprightly; otherwise, you will come to ruin. . . . *Furthermore*, it is necessary that the Magnificent Signory [the government of the city] ordain that all those things contrary to godly religion be removed from the city, and in the first place, to act and ordain that the clergy must be good, because priests have to be a mirror to the people wherein everyone beholds and learns righteous living. But let the bad priests and religious be expelled. . . . They should not puff themselves up with so much material wealth, but give it to the very poor for God's sake. . . .

It is necessary that the Signory pass laws against that accursed vice of sodomy [same-sex relations], for which you know that Florence is infamous throughout the whole of Italy; this infamy arises perhaps from your talking and chattering about it so much, so that there is not so much in deeds, perhaps, as in words. Pass a law, I say, and let it be without mercy; that is, let these people be stoned and burned. On the other hand, it is necessary that you remove from among yourselves these poems and games and taverns and the evil fashion of women's clothes, and, likewise, we must throw out everything that is noxious to the health of the soul. Let everyone live for God and not for the world. . . .

The second [resolution]: attend to the common good. O citizens, if you band together and with a good will attend to the common welfare, each shall have more temporal and spiritual goods than if he alone attended to his own particular case. Attend, I say, to the common good of the city, and if anyone would elevate himself, let him be deprived of all his goods.

EVALUATE THE EVIDENCE

1. What does Savonarola tell Florentines they must do, and what will be their reward if they follow his instructions?
2. Savonarola initially had many followers, including well-known writers and artists. Why might his words have found such a ready audience in Florence at that time?

Source: *Selected Writings of Girolamo Savonarola: Religion and Politics, 1490–1498*, trans. and ed. Anne Borelli and Maria Pastore Passaro (New Haven: Yale University Press, 2006), pp. 153, 157, 158. Copyright © 2006 Yale University. Used by permission of Yale University Press.

Intellectual Change

FOCUS QUESTION *What new ideas were associated with the Renaissance?*

The Renaissance was characterized by self-conscious conviction among educated Italians that they were living in a new era. Somewhat ironically, this idea rested on a deep interest in ancient Latin and Greek literature and philosophy. Through reflecting on the classics, Renaissance thinkers developed new notions of human nature, new plans for education, and new concepts of political rule. The advent of the printing press with movable type would greatly accelerate the spread of these ideas throughout Europe.

Humanism

Giorgio Vasari was the first to use the word *Renaissance* in print, but he was not the first to feel that something was being reborn. Two centuries earlier the Florentine poet and scholar Francesco Petrarch (1304–1374) spent long hours searching for classical Latin manuscripts in dusty monastery libraries and wandering around the many ruins of the Roman Empire remaining in Italy. He became obsessed with the classical past and felt that the writers and artists of ancient Rome had reached a level of perfection in their work that had not since been duplicated. Writers of his own day should follow these ancient models, thought Petrarch, and ignore the thousand-year period between his own time and that of Rome, which he called the "dark ages" ushered in by the barbarian invasions. Petrarch believed that the recovery of classical texts would bring about a new golden age of intellectual achievement, an idea that many others came to share.

Petrarch clearly thought he was witnessing the dawning of a new era in which writers and artists would recapture the glory of the Roman Republic. Around 1350 he proposed a new kind of education to help them do this, in which young men would study the works of ancient Roman authors, using them as models of how to write clearly, argue effectively, and speak persuasively. The study of Latin classics became known as the *studia humanitates* (STOO-dee-uh oo-mahn-ee-TAH-tayz), usually translated as "liberal studies" or the "liberal arts." People who advocated it were known as *humanists* and their program as **humanism**. Humanism was the main intellectual component of the Renaissance. Like all programs of study, humanism contained an implicit philosophy: that human nature and achievements, evident in the classics, were worthy of contemplation.

The glory of Rome had been brightest, in the opinion of the humanists, in the works of the Roman author and statesman Cicero (106–43 B.C.E.). Cicero had lived during the turbulent era when Julius Caesar and other powerful generals transformed the Roman Republic into an empire (see Chapter 5). In forceful and elegantly worded speeches, letters, and treatises, Cicero supported a return to republican government. Petrarch and other humanists admired Cicero's use of language, literary style, and political ideas. Many humanists saw Caesar's transformation of Rome as a betrayal of the great society, marking the beginning of a long period of decay that the barbarian migrations then accelerated. In his history of Florence written in 1436, the humanist historian and Florentine city official Leonardo Bruni (1374–1444) closely linked the decline of the Latin language after the death of Cicero to the decline of the Roman Republic: "After the liberty of the Roman people had been lost through the rule of the emperors . . . the flourishing condition of studies and of letters perished, together with the welfare of the city of Rome."[2] In this same book, Bruni was also very clear that by the time of his writing, the period of decay had ended and a new era had begun. He was the first to divide history into three eras—ancient, medieval, and modern—though it was another humanist historian who actually invented the term "Middle Ages."

In the fifteenth century Florentine humanists became increasingly interested in Greek philosophy as well as Roman literature, especially in the ideas of Plato. Under the patronage of the Medici, the scholar Marsilio Ficino (1433–1499) began to lecture to an informal group of Florence's cultural elite; his lectures became known as the Platonic Academy, but they were not really a school. Ficino regarded Plato as a divinely inspired precursor to Christ. He translated Plato's dialogues into Latin and wrote commentaries attempting to synthesize Christian and Platonic teachings. Plato's emphasis on the spiritual and eternal over the material and transient fit well with Christian teachings about the immortality of the soul. The Platonic idea that the highest form of love was spiritual desire for pure, perfect beauty uncorrupted by bodily desires could easily be interpreted as Christian desire for the perfection of God.

For Ficino and his most gifted student, Giovanni Pico della Mirandola (1463–1494), both Christian and classical texts taught that the universe was a hierarchy of beings from God down through spiritual beings to material beings, with humanity, right in the middle, as the crucial link that possessed both material and spiritual natures. Pico developed his ideas in a series of 900 theses, or points of argumentation, and offered to defend them against anyone who wanted to come to Rome. The pope declared some of the ideas heretical and arrested Pico, though he was freed through the influence of Lorenzo de' Medici. At Lorenzo's death, Pico became a follower of Savonarola, renounced his former ideas and writings, and died of arsenic poisoning, perhaps at the hands of the recently ousted Medici family.

Man's divinely bestowed nature meant there were no limits to what he could accomplish. Families, religious brotherhoods, neighborhoods, workers' organizations, and other groups continued to have meaning in people's lives, but Renaissance thinkers increasingly viewed these groups as springboards to far greater individual achievement. They were especially interested in individuals who had risen above their background to become brilliant, powerful, or unique. (See "Individuals in Society: Leonardo da Vinci," page 376.) Such individuals had the admirable quality of **virtù** (vihr-TOO), a word that had not the conventional meaning of virtue as moral goodness, but instead the ability to shape the world around according to one's will. Bruni and other historians included biographies of individuals with virtù in their histories of cities and nations, describing ways in which these people had affected the course of history. Through the quality of their works and their influence on others, artists could also exhibit virtù, an idea that Vasari

---

■ **humanism** A program of study designed by Italians that emphasized the critical study of Latin and Greek literature with the goal of understanding human nature.

■ **virtù** The quality of being able to shape the world according to one's own will.

captures in the title of his major work, *The Lives of the Most Excellent Painters, Sculptors, and Architects*. His subjects had achieved not simply excellence but the pinnacle of excellence.

The last artist included in Vasari's book is Vasari himself, for Renaissance thinkers did not exclude themselves when they searched for models of talent and achievement. Vasari begins his discussion of his own works modestly, saying that these might "not lay claim to excellence and perfection" when compared with those of other artists, but he then goes on for more than thirty pages, clearly feeling he has achieved some level of excellence.

Leon Battista Alberti (1404–1472) had similar views of his own achievements. He had much to be proud of: he wrote novels, plays, legal treatises, a study of the family, and the first scientific analysis of perspective; he designed churches, palaces, and fortifications effective against cannon; he invented codes for sending messages secretly and a machine that could cipher and decipher them. In his autobiography—written late in his life, and in the third person, so that he calls himself "he" instead of "I"—Alberti described his personal qualities and accomplishments:

> Assiduous in the science and skill of dealing with arms and horses and musical instruments, as well as in the pursuit of letters and the fine arts, he was devoted to the knowledge of the most strange and difficult things. . . . He played ball, hurled the javelin, ran, leaped, wrestled. . . . He learned music without teachers . . . and then turned to physics and the mathematical arts. . . . Ambition was alien to him. . . . When his favorite dog died he wrote a funeral oration for him.[3]

His achievements in many fields did make Alberti a "Renaissance man," as we use the term, though it may be hard to believe his assertion that "ambition was alien to him."

Biographies and autobiographies presented individuals that humanist authors thought were worthy models, but sometimes people needed more direct instruction. The ancient Greek philosopher Plato, whom humanists greatly admired, taught that the best way to learn something was to think about its perfect, ideal form. If you wanted to learn about justice, for example, you should imagine what ideal justice would be, rather than look at actual examples of justice in the world around you, for these would never be perfect. Following Plato's ideas, Renaissance authors speculated about perfect examples of many things. Alberti wrote about the ideal country house, which was to be useful, convenient, and elegant. The English humanist Thomas More described a perfect society, which he called Utopia (see page 369).

Education

Humanists thought that their recommended course of study in the classics would provide essential skills for future politicians, diplomats, lawyers, military leaders, and businessmen, as well as writers and artists. It would provide a much broader and more practical type of training than that offered at universities, which at the time focused on theology and philosophy or on theoretical training for lawyers and physicians. Humanists poured out treatises, often in the form of letters, on the structure and goals of education and the training of rulers and leaders. (See "Thinking Like a Historian: Humanist Learning," page 366.)

Humanists put their ideas into practice. Beginning in the early fifteenth century, they opened schools and academies in Italian cities and courts in which pupils began with Latin grammar and rhetoric, went on to study Roman history and political philosophy, and then learned Greek in order to study Greek literature and philosophy. Gradually, humanist education became the basis for intermediate and advanced education for well-to-do urban boys and men. Humanist schools were established in Florence, Venice, and other Italian cities, and by the early sixteenth century across the Alps in Germany, France, and England.

Humanists disagreed about education for women. Many saw the value of exposing women to classical models of moral behavior and reasoning, but they also wondered whether a program of study that emphasized eloquence and action was proper for women, whose sphere was generally understood to be private and domestic. In his book on the family, Alberti stressed that a wife's role should be restricted to the orderliness of the household, food preparation and the serving of meals, the education of children, and the supervision of servants. (Alberti never married, so he never put his ideas into practice in his own household.) Women themselves were bolder in their claims about the value of the new learning. Although humanist academies were not open to women, a few women did become educated in the classics, and wrote and published poetry, fiction, and essays in Latin and vernacular languages.

No book on education had broader influence than Baldassare Castiglione's *The Courtier* (1528). This treatise sought to train, discipline, and fashion the young man into the courtly ideal, the gentleman. According to Castiglione (kahs-teel-YOH-nay), himself a courtier serving several different rulers, the educated man should have a broad background in many academic subjects, and should train his spiritual and physical faculties as well as his intellect. Castiglione envisioned a man who could compose a sonnet, wrestle, sing a song while accompanying himself on an instrument, ride expertly, solve difficult mathematical problems, and, above all, speak and write eloquently. Castiglione also included discussion of the perfect court lady, who, like the courtier, was to be well educated and able to paint, dance, and play a musical instrument. Physical beauty, delicacy, affability, and modesty were also important qualities for court ladies.

In the sixteenth and seventeenth centuries *The Courtier* was translated into most European languages and widely read. It influenced the social mores and patterns of conduct of elite groups in Renaissance and early modern Europe and became a how-to manual for people seeking to improve themselves and rise in the social hierarchy as well. Echoes of its ideal for women have perhaps had an even longer life.

Political Thought

Ideal courtiers should preferably serve an ideal ruler, and biographies written by humanists often described rulers who were just, wise, pious, dignified, learned, brave, kind, and distinguished. In return for such flattering portraits of living rulers or their ancestors, authors sometimes received positions at court, or at least substantial payments. Particularly in Italian cities, however, which often were divided by political factions, taken over by homegrown or regional despots, and attacked by foreign armies, such ideal rulers were hard to find. Humanists thus looked to the classical past for their models. Some, such as Bruni, argued that republicanism was the best form of government. Others used the model of Plato's philosopher-king in the *Republic* to argue that rule by an enlightened individual might be best. Both sides agreed that educated men should be active in the political affairs of their city, a position historians have since termed "civic humanism."

The most famous (or infamous) civic humanist, and ultimately the best-known political theorist of this era, was Niccolò Machiavelli (1469–1527). After the ouster of the Medici with the French invasion of 1494, Machiavelli was secretary to one of the governing bodies in the city of Florence; he was responsible for diplomatic missions and organizing a citizen army. Almost two decades later, power struggles in Florence between rival factions brought the Medici family back to power, and Machiavelli was arrested, tortured, and imprisoned on suspicion of plotting against them. He was released but had no government position, and he spent the rest of his life writing—political theory, poetry, prose works, plays, and a multivolume history of Florence—and making fruitless attempts to regain employment.

The first work Machiavelli finished—though not the first to be published—is his most famous: *The Prince* (1513), which uses the examples of classical and contemporary rulers to argue that the function of a ruler (or any government) is to preserve order and security. Weakness only leads to disorder, which might

end in civil war or conquest by an outsider, situations clearly detrimental to any people's well-being. To preserve the state, a ruler should use whatever means he needs—brutality, lying, manipulation—but should not do anything that would make the populace turn against him; stealing or cruel actions done for a ruler's own pleasure would lead to resentment and destroy the popular support needed for a strong, stable realm. "It is much safer for the prince to be feared than loved," Machiavelli advised, "but he ought to avoid making himself hated."[4]

Like the good humanist he was, Machiavelli knew that effective rulers exhibited the quality of virtù. He presented examples from the classical past of just the type of ruler he was describing, but also wrote about contemporary leaders. Cesare Borgia (1475?–1507), Machiavelli's primary example, was the son of Rodrigo Borgia, a Spanish nobleman who later became Pope Alexander VI. Cesare Borgia combined his father's power and his own ruthlessness to build up a state of

Portrait of Baldassare Castiglione In this portrait by Raphael, the most sought-after portrait painter of the Renaissance, Castiglione is shown dressed exactly as he advised courtiers to dress, in elegant but subdued clothing that would enhance the splendor of the court, but never outshine the ruler. (By Raphael [Raffaello Sanzio of Urbino] [1483–1520]/Art Media/Print Collector/Getty Images)

Humanist Learning

Renaissance humanists wrote often and forcefully about education, and learning was also a subject of artistic works shaped by humanist ideas. What did humanists see as the best course of study and the purpose of education, and how were these different for men and women?

1 Peter Paul Vergerius, letter to Ubertinus of Padua, 1392. The Venetian scholar and church official Vergerius (1370–1445) advises the son of the ruler of Padua about the proper education for men.

We call those studies liberal which are worthy of a free man; those studies by which we attain and practise virtue and wisdom; that education which calls forth, trains and develops those highest gifts of body and of mind which ennoble men, and which are rightly judged to rank next in dignity to virtue only. . . . Amongst these I accord the first place to History, on grounds both of its attractiveness and of its utility, qualities which appeal equally to the scholar and to the statesman. Next in importance ranks Moral Philosophy, which indeed is, in a peculiar sense, a "Liberal Art," in that its purpose is to teach men the secret of true freedom. History, then, gives us the concrete examples of the precepts inculcated by philosophy. The one shews what men should do, the other what men have said and done in the past, and what practical lessons we may draw therefrom for the present day. I would indicate as the third main branch of study, Eloquence, which indeed holds a place of distinction amongst the refined Arts. By philosophy we learn the essential truth of things, which by eloquence we so exhibit in orderly adornment as to bring conviction to differing minds. And history provides the light of experience — a cumulative wisdom fit to supplement the force of reason and the persuasion of eloquence. For we allow that soundness of judgment, wisdom of speech, integrity of conduct are the marks of a truly liberal temper.

2 Leonardo Bruni, letter to Lady Baptista Malatesta, ca. 1405. The Florentine humanist and city official Leonardo Bruni advises the daughter of the duke of Urbino about the proper education for women.

There are certain subjects in which, whilst a modest proficiency is on all accounts to be desired, a minute knowledge and excessive devotion seem to be a vain display. For instance, subtleties of Arithmetic and Geometry are not worthy to absorb a cultivated mind, and the same must be said of Astrology. You will be surprised to find me suggesting (though with much more hesitation) that the great and complex art of Rhetoric should be placed in the same category. My chief reason is the obvious one, that I have in view the cultivation most fitting to a woman. To her neither the intricacies of debate nor the oratorical artifices of action and delivery are of the least practical use, if indeed they are not positively unbecoming. Rhetoric in all its forms — public discussion, forensic argument, logical fence, and the like — lies absolutely outside the province of woman. What Disciplines then are properly open to her? In the first place she has before her, as a subject peculiarly her own, the whole field of religion and morals. The literature of the Church will thus claim her earnest study. . . . Moreover, the cultivated Christian lady has no need in the study of this weighty subject to confine herself to ecclesiastical writers. Morals, indeed, have been treated of by the noblest intellects of Greece and Rome. [Then] I place History: a subject which must not on any account be neglected by one who aspires to true cultivation. For it is our duty to understand the origins of our own history and its development; and the achievements of Peoples and of Kings.

ANALYZING THE EVIDENCE

1. According to these sources, what should people learn? Why should they learn?
2. Renaissance humanism has sometimes been viewed as opposed to religion, especially to the teachings of the Catholic Church at the time. Do these sources support this idea?
3. How are the programs of study recommended for men and women similar? How and why are they different?
4. How does the gender of the author shape his or her ideas about the human capacity for reason and learning?

3 **Luca della Robbia, *Grammar*, 1437–1439.** In this hexagonal panel made for the bell tower of the cathedral of Florence, Luca della Robbia conveys ideas about the course and goals of learning with the open classical door in the background.

(*Grammar*, 1437–1439, marble by Luca della Robbia [1401–1482]/Museo Opera del Duomo, Florence, Italy/De Agostini/Getty Images)

4 **Giovanni Pico della Mirandola, "Oration on the Dignity of Man," 1486.** Pico, the brilliant son of an Italian count and protégé of Lorenzo de' Medici, wrote an impassioned summary of human capacities for learning that ends with this.

⌇O sublime generosity of God the Father! O highest and most wonderful felicity of man! To him it was granted to have what he chooses, to be what he wills. At the moment when they are born, beasts bring with them from their mother's womb, as Lucilius [the classical Roman author] says, whatever they shall possess. From the beginning or soon afterwards, the highest spiritual beings have been what they are to be for all eternity. When man came into life, the Father endowed him with all kinds of seeds and the germs of every way of life. Whatever seeds each man cultivates will grow and bear fruit in him. If these seeds are vegetative, he will be like a plant; if they are sensitive, he will become like the beasts; if they are rational, he will become like a heavenly creature; if intellectual, he will be an angel and a son of God. And if, content with the lot of no created being, he withdraws into the centre of his own oneness, his spirit, made one with God in the solitary darkness of the Father, which is above all things, will surpass all things. Who then will not wonder at this chameleon of ours, or who could wonder more greatly at anything else?

5 **Cassandra Fedele, "Oration on Learning," 1487.** The Venetian Cassandra Fedele (1465–1558), the best-known female scholar of her time, gave an oration in Latin at the University of Padua in honor of her (male) cousin's graduation.

⌇I shall speak very briefly on the study of the liberal arts, which for humans is useful and honorable, pleasurable and enlightening since everyone, not only philosophers but also the most ignorant man, knows and admits that it is by reason that man is separated from beasts. For what is it that so greatly helps both the learned and the ignorant? What so enlarges and enlightens men's minds the way that an education in and knowledge of literature and the liberal arts do? . . . But erudite men who are filled with the knowledge of divine and human things turn all their thoughts and considerations toward reason as though toward a target, and free their minds from all pain, though plagued by many anxieties. These men are scarcely subjected to fortune's innumerable arrows and they prepare themselves to live well and in happiness. They follow reason as their leader in all things; nor do they consider themselves only, but they are also accustomed to assisting others with their energy and advice in matters public and private. . . . The study of literature refines men's minds, forms and makes bright the power of reason, and washes away all stains from the mind, or at any rate, greatly cleanses it. . . . States, however, and their princes who foster and cultivate these studies become more humane, more gracious, and more noble. . . . But enough on the utility of literature since it produces not only an outcome that is rich, precious, and sublime, but also provides one with advantages that are extremely pleasurable, fruitful, and lasting — benefits that I myself have enjoyed. And when I meditate on the idea of marching forth in life with the lowly and execrable weapons of the little woman — the needle and the distaff [the rod onto which yarn is wound after spinning] — even if the study of literature offers women no rewards or honors, I believe women must nonetheless pursue and embrace such studies alone for the pleasure and enjoyment they contain.

PUTTING IT ALL TOGETHER

Using the sources above, along with what you have learned in class and in this chapter, write a short essay that analyzes humanist learning. What were the goals and purposes of humanist education, and how were these different for men and women? How did these differences reflect Renaissance society more generally?

Sources: (1, 2) W. H. Woodward, ed. and trans., *Vittorino da Feltre and Other Humanist Educators* (London: Cambridge University Press, 1897), pp. 102, 106–107, 126–127; (4) Translated by Mary Martin McLaughlin, in *The Portable Renaissance Reader*, edited by James Bruce Ross and Mary Martin McLaughlin, copyright 1953, 1968, renewed © 1981 by Penguin Random House LLC. Used by permission of Viking Books, an imprint of Penguin Publishing Group, a division of Penguin Random House LLC; (5) Cassandra Fedele, *Letters and Orations*, ed. and trans. Diana Robin. Copyright © 2000 by The University of Chicago Press. All rights reserved. Used with permission of the publisher.

his own in central Italy. He made good use of new military equipment and tactics, hiring Leonardo da Vinci (1452–1519) as a military engineer, and murdered his political enemies, including the second husband of his sister, Lucrezia. Despite Borgia's efforts, his state fell apart after his father's death, which Machiavelli ascribed not to weakness, but to the operations of fate (*fortuna*, for-TOO-nah, in Italian), whose power even the best-prepared and most merciless ruler could not fully escape, though he should try. Fortuna was personified and portrayed as a goddess in ancient Rome and Renaissance Italy, and Machiavelli's last words about fortune are expressed in gendered terms: "It is better to be impetuous than cautious, for fortune is a woman, and if one wishes to keep her down, it is necessary to beat her and knock her down."[5]

The Prince is often seen as the first modern guide to politics, though Machiavelli was denounced for writing it, and people later came to use the word *Machiavellian* to mean cunning and ruthless. Medieval political philosophers had debated the proper relation between church and state, but they regarded the standards by which all governments were to be judged as emanating from moral principles established by God. Machiavelli argued that governments should instead be judged by how well they provided security, order, and safety to their populace. A ruler's moral code in maintaining these was not the same as a private individual's, for a leader could—indeed, should—use any means necessary. Machiavelli put a new spin on the Renaissance search for perfection, arguing that ideals needed to be measured in the cold light of the real world. This more pragmatic view of the purposes of government, along with Machiavelli's discussion of the role of force and cruelty, was unacceptable to many.

Even today, when Machiavelli's more secular view of the purposes of government is widely shared, scholars debate whether Machiavelli actually meant what he wrote. Most regard him as realistic or even cynical, but some suggest that he was being ironic or satirical, showing princely government in the worst possible light to contrast it with republicanism, which he favored, and also wrote about at length in the *Discourses on Livy*. He dedicated *The Prince* to the new Medici ruler of Florence, however, so any criticism was deeply buried within what was, in that era of patronage, essentially a job application.

Christian Humanism

In the last quarter of the fifteenth century, students from the Low Countries, France, Germany, and England flocked to Italy, absorbed the "new learning," and carried it back to their own countries. Northern humanists shared the ideas of Ficino and Pico about the wisdom of ancient texts, but they went beyond Italian efforts to synthesize the Christian and classical traditions to see humanist learning as a way to bring about reform of the church and deepen people's spiritual lives. These **Christian humanists**, as they were later called, thought that the best elements of classical and Christian cultures should be combined. For example, the classical ideals of calmness, stoical patience, and broadmindedness should be joined in human conduct with the Christian virtues of love, faith, and hope.

The English humanist Thomas More (1478–1535) began life as a lawyer, studied the classics, and entered government service. Despite his official duties, he had time to write, and he became most famous for his controversial dialogue *Utopia* (1516), a word More invented from the Greek words for "nowhere." *Utopia* describes a community on an island somewhere beyond Europe where all children receive a good education, primarily in the Greco-Roman classics, and adults divide their days between manual labor or business pursuits and intellectual activities. The problems that plagued More's fellow citizens, such as poverty and hunger, have been solved by a beneficent government. (See "Evaluating the Evidence 12.2: Thomas More, *Utopia*," at right.) There is religious toleration, and order and reason prevail. Because Utopian institutions are perfect, however, dissent and disagreement are not acceptable.

More's purposes in writing *Utopia* have been debated just as much as have Machiavelli's in penning *The Prince*. Some view it as a revolutionary critique of More's own hierarchical and violent society, some as a call for an even firmer hierarchy, and others as part of the humanist tradition of satire. It was widely read by learned Europeans in the Latin in which More wrote it, and later in vernacular translations, and its title quickly became the standard word for any imaginary society.

Better known by contemporaries than Thomas More was the Dutch humanist Desiderius Erasmus (dehz-ih-DARE-ee-us ih-RAZ-muhs) (1466?–1536) of Rotterdam. His fame rested on both scholarly editions and translations and popular works. Erasmus's long list of publications includes *The Education of a Christian Prince* (1504), a book combining idealistic and practical suggestions for the formation of a ruler's character through the careful study of the Bible and classical authors; *The Praise of Folly* (1509), a witty satire poking fun at political, social, and especially religious institutions; and, most important, a new Latin translation of the New Testament alongside the first printed edition of the Greek text (1516). In the preface to the New Testament, Erasmus expressed his ideas about Bible translations: "I wish that even the weakest woman should read the Gospel—should read the epistles of Paul. And I wish these were translated into all languages, so that they might be read and understood, not

■ **Christian humanists** Northern humanists who interpreted Italian ideas about and attitudes toward classical antiquity and humanism in terms of their own religious traditions.

Thomas More, *Utopia*

Published in 1516, Utopia *is written as a dialogue between Thomas More and Raphael Hythloday, a character More invented who has, in More's telling, recently returned from the newly discovered land of Utopia somewhere in the New World. More and Hythloday first discuss the problems in Europe, and then Hythloday describes how these have been solved in Utopia, ending with a long discussion of the Utopians' ban on private property.*

Well, that's the most accurate account I can give you of the Utopian Republic. To my mind, it's not only the best country in the world, but the only one that has the right to call itself a republic. Elsewhere, people are always talking about the public interest, but all they really care about is private property. In Utopia, where there's no private property, people take their duty to the public seriously. And both attitudes are perfectly reasonable. In other "republics" practically everyone knows that, if he doesn't look out for himself, he'll starve to death, however prosperous his country may be. He's therefore compelled to give his own interests priority over those of the public; that is, of other people. But in Utopia, where everything's under public ownership, no one has any fear of going short, as long as the public storehouses are full. Everyone gets a fair share, so there are never any poor men or beggars. Nobody owns anything, but everyone is rich — for what greater wealth can there be than cheerfulness, peace of mind, and freedom from anxiety? Instead of being worried about his food supply, upset by the plaintive demands of his wife, afraid of poverty for his son, and baffled by the problem of finding a dowry for his daughter, the Utopian can feel absolutely sure that he, his wife, his children, his grandchildren, his great-grandchildren, and as long a line of descendants as the proudest peer could wish to look forward to, will always have enough to eat and enough to make them happy.

There's also the further point that those who are too old to work are just as well provided for as those who are still working.

Now, will anyone venture to compare these fair arrangements in Utopia with the so-called justice of other countries? — in which I'm damned if I can see the slightest trace of justice or fairness. For what sort of justice do you call this? People like aristocrats, gold-smiths, or money-lenders, who either do no work at all, or do work that's really not essential, are rewarded for their laziness or their unnecessary activities by a splendid life of luxury. But labourers, coachmen, carpenters, and farmhands, who never stop working like cart-horses, at jobs so essential that, if they *did* stop working, they'd bring any country to a standstill within twelve months — what happens to them? They get so little to eat, and have such a wretched time, that they'd be almost better off if they *were* cart-horses. Then at least, they wouldn't work quite such long hours, their food wouldn't be very much worse, they'd enjoy it more, and they'd have no fears for the future. As it is, they're not only ground down by unrewarding toil in the present, but also worried to death by the prospect of a poverty-stricken old age.

EVALUATE THE EVIDENCE

1. How does the Utopians' economic system compare with that of Europe, in Hythloday's opinion?
2. Hythloday's comments about wealth have been seen by some scholars as More's criticism of his own society, and by others as proof that More wrote this as a satire, describing a place that could never be. Which view seems most persuasive to you?

Source: Thomas More, *Utopia*, trans. Paul Turner (London: Penguin Books, 1965), pp. 128–129. Reproduced by permission of Penguin Books Ltd.

only by Scots and Irishmen, but also by Turks and Saracens."[6]

Two fundamental themes run through all of Erasmus's work. First, education in the Bible and the classics is the means to reform, the key to moral and intellectual improvement. Erasmus called for a renaissance of the ideals of the early church to accompany the renaissance in classical education that was already going on, and criticized the church of his day for having strayed from these ideals. Second, renewal should be based on what he termed "the philosophy of Christ," an emphasis on inner spirituality and personal morality rather than Scholastic theology or outward observances

such as pilgrimages or venerating relics. His ideas, and Christian humanism in general, were important roots of the Protestant Reformation, although Erasmus himself denied this and never became a follower of Luther (see Chapter 13).

The Printed Word

The fourteenth-century humanist Petrarch and the sixteenth-century humanist Erasmus had similar ideas on many topics, but the immediate impact of their ideas was very different because of one thing: the invention of the printing press with movable metal type. The ideas of Petrarch were spread slowly from person to person by hand copying. The ideas of Erasmus were spread quickly through print, allowing hundreds or thousands of identical copies to be made in a short time.

Printing with movable metal type developed in Germany in the 1440s as a combination of existing technologies. Several metal-smiths, most prominently Johann Gutenberg, recognized that the metal stamps used to mark signs on jewelry could be covered with ink and used to mark symbols onto a surface in the same way that other craftsmen were using carved wood stamps to print books. (This woodblock printing technique originated in China and Korea centuries earlier.) Gutenberg and his assistants made metal stamps—later called *type*—for every letter of the alphabet and built racks that held the type in rows. This type could be rearranged for every page and so used over and over.

The printing revolution was also made possible by the ready availability of paper, which was also produced using techniques that had originated in China, though, unlike the printing press, this technology had been brought into Europe through Muslim Spain rather than developing independently.

By the fifteenth century the increase in urban literacy, the development of primary schools, and the opening of more universities had created an expanding market for reading materials (see Chapter 11). When Gutenberg developed what he saw at first as a faster way to copy,

professional copyists writing by hand and block-book makers, along with monks and nuns, were already churning out reading materials on paper as fast as they could for the growing number of people who could read.

Gutenberg was not the only one to recognize the huge market for books, and his invention was quickly copied. Other craftsmen made their own type, built their own presses, and bought their own paper, setting themselves up in business (Map 12.2). Historians estimate that, within a half century of the publication of Gutenberg's Bible in 1456, somewhere between 8 million and 20 million books were printed in Europe. Whatever the actual figure, the number is far greater than the number of books produced in all of Western history up to that point.

The effects of the invention of movable-type printing were not felt overnight. Nevertheless, movable type radically transformed both the private and the public lives of Europeans by the dawn of the sixteenth century. Print shops became gathering places for people interested in new ideas. Though printers were trained through apprenticeships just like blacksmiths or butchers were, they had connections to the world of politics, art, and scholarship that other craftsmen did not.

Printing gave hundreds or even thousands of people identical books, allowing them to more easily discuss the ideas that the books contained with one another in person or through letters. Printed materials reached an invisible public, allowing silent individuals to join causes and groups of individuals widely separated by geography to form a common identity; this new group consciousness could compete with and transcend older, localized loyalties.

Government and church leaders both used and worried about printing. They printed laws, declarations of war, battle accounts, and propaganda, and they also attempted to censor books and authors whose ideas they thought challenged their authority or were incorrect. Officials developed lists of prohibited books and authors, enforcing their prohibitions by confiscating books, arresting

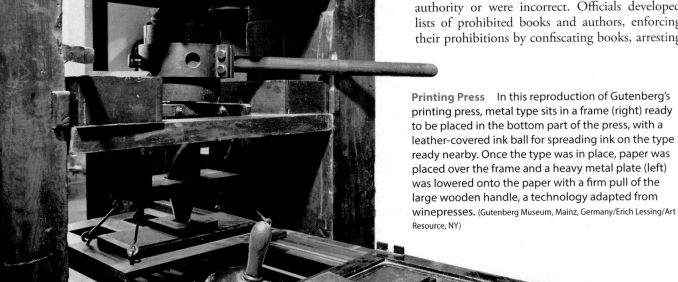

Printing Press In this reproduction of Gutenberg's printing press, metal type sits in a frame (right) ready to be placed in the bottom part of the press, with a leather-covered ink ball for spreading ink on the type ready nearby. Once the type was in place, paper was placed over the frame and a heavy metal plate (left) was lowered onto the paper with a firm pull of the large wooden handle, a technology adapted from winepresses. (Gutenberg Museum, Mainz, Germany/Erich Lessing/Art Resource, NY)

Printing centers with
date of establishment
◆ 15th century
▲ 16th century
— Political boundaries
  in 1490

Gutenberg establishes first printing press, 1448

MAPPING THE PAST

MAP 12.2 The Growth of Printing in Europe, 1448–1552

The speed with which artisans spread printing technology across Europe provides strong evidence for the growing demand for reading material. Presses in the Ottoman Empire were first established by Jewish immigrants who printed works in Hebrew, Greek, and Spanish.

ANALYZING THE MAP What part of Europe had the greatest number of printing presses by 1550? What explains this?

CONNECTIONS Printing was developed in response to a market for reading materials. Use Maps 10.2 and 10.3 (pages 302 and 309) to help explain why printing spread the way it did.

printers and booksellers, or destroying the presses of printers who disobeyed. None of this was very effective, and books were printed secretly, with fake title pages, authors, and places of publication, and smuggled all over Europe.

Printing also stimulated the literacy of laypeople and eventually came to have a deep effect on their private lives. Although most of the earliest books and pamphlets dealt with religious subjects, printers produced anything that would sell. They printed professional reference sets for lawyers, doctors, and students,

and historical romances, biographies, and how-to manuals for the general public. They discovered that illustrations increased a book's sales, so they published books on a wide range of topics—from history to pornography—full of woodcuts and engravings. Single-page broadsides and fly sheets allowed great public events and "wonders" such as comets and two-headed calves to be experienced vicariously by a stay-at-home readership. Since books and other printed materials were read aloud to illiterate listeners, print bridged the gap between the written and oral cultures.

Art and the Artist

FOCUS QUESTION *How did art reflect new Renaissance ideals?*

No feature of the Renaissance evokes greater admiration than its artistic masterpieces. The 1400s (*quattrocento*) and 1500s (*cinquecento*) bore witness to dazzling creativity in painting, architecture, and sculpture. In all the arts, the city of Florence led the way. But Florence was not the only artistic center, for Rome and Venice also became important, and northern Europeans perfected their own styles.

Patronage and Power

In early Renaissance Italy, powerful urban groups often flaunted their wealth by commissioning works of art. The Florentine cloth merchants, for example, delegated Filippo Brunelleschi (broo-nayl-LAYS-kee) to build the magnificent dome on the cathedral of Florence and selected Lorenzo Ghiberti (gee-BEHR-tee) to design the bronze doors of the adjacent Baptistery, a separate building in which baptisms were performed. These works represented the merchants' dominant influence in the community.

Increasingly in the late fifteenth century, wealthy individuals and rulers, rather than corporate groups, sponsored works of art. Patrician merchants and bankers, popes, and princes spent vast sums on the arts to glorify themselves and their families. Writing in about 1470, Florentine ruler Lorenzo de' Medici declared that his family had spent hundreds of thousands of gold florins for artistic and architectural commissions, but commented, "I think it casts a brilliant light on our estate [public reputation] and it seems to me that the monies were well spent and I am very pleased with this."[7]

Patrons varied in their level of involvement as a work progressed; some simply ordered a specific subject or scene, while others oversaw the work of the artist or architect very closely, suggesting themes and styles and demanding changes while the work was in progress. For example, Pope Julius II (pontificate 1503–1513), who commissioned Michelangelo to paint the ceiling of the Vatican's Sistine Chapel in 1508, demanded that the artist work as fast as he could and frequently visited him at his work with suggestions and criticisms. Michelangelo, a Florentine who had spent his young adulthood at the court of Lorenzo de' Medici, complained in person and by letter about the pope's meddling, but his reputation did not match the power of the pope, and he kept working until the chapel was finished in 1512.

In addition to power, art reveals changing patterns of consumption among the wealthy elite in European society. In the rural world of the Middle Ages, society had been organized for war, and men of wealth spent their money on military gear. As Italian nobles settled in towns (see Chapter 10), they adjusted to an urban culture. Rather than employing knights for warfare, cities hired mercenaries. Accordingly, expenditures on military hardware by nobles declined. For the noble recently arrived from the countryside or the rich merchant of the city, a grand urban palace represented the greatest outlay of cash. Wealthy individuals and families ordered gold dishes, embroidered tablecloths, wall tapestries, paintings on canvas (an innovation), and sculptural decorations to adorn these homes. By the late sixteenth century the

Plate Showing the Abduction of Helen of Troy   Filled with well-muscled men, curvaceous women, and exotic landscapes, this colorful plate with a gold rim depicts a well-known scene from Greek mythology, the abduction of Helen, which sparked the Trojan War. Such tin-glazed pottery, known as maiolica and made in many places in Italy beginning in the late fifteenth century, was sold throughout Europe to wealthy consumers, who favored designs with family crests or legendary or historical scenes, known as *istoriato* ("painted with stories"). (Museo Nazionale del Bargello, Florence, Italy/Bridgeman Images)

Strozzi banking family of Florence spent more on household goods than they did on clothing, jewelry, or food, though these were increasingly elaborate as well.

After the palace itself, the private chapel within the palace symbolized the largest expenditure for the wealthy of the sixteenth century. Decorated with religious scenes and equipped with ecclesiastical furniture, the chapel served as the center of the household's religious life and its cult of remembrance of the dead.

Changing Artistic Styles

Both the content and style of Renaissance art often differed from those of the Middle Ages. Religious topics, such as the Annunciation of the Virgin and the Nativity, remained popular among both patrons and artists, but frequently the patron had himself and his family portrayed in the scene. As the fifteenth century advanced and humanist ideas spread more widely, classical themes

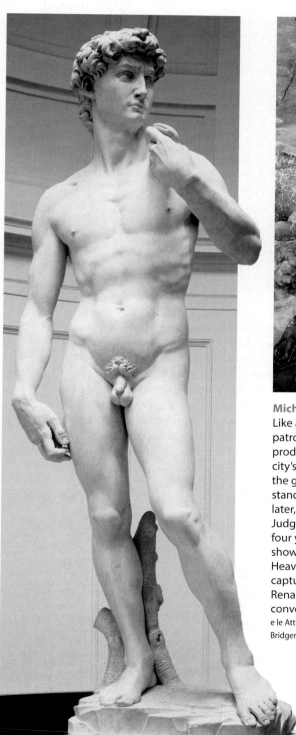

Michelangelo's *David* **(1501–1504) and the** *Last Judgment* **(detail, 1537–1541)** Like all Renaissance artists, Michelangelo worked largely on commissions from patrons. Officials of the city of Florence contracted the young sculptor to produce a statue of the Old Testament hero David (left) to be displayed on the city's main square. Michelangelo portrayed David anticipating his fight against the giant Goliath, and the statue came to symbolize the republic of Florence standing up to its larger and more powerful enemies. More than thirty years later, Michelangelo was commissioned by the pope to paint a scene of the Last Judgment on the altar wall of the Sistine Chapel, where he had earlier spent four years covering the ceiling with magnificent frescoes. The massive work shows a powerful Christ standing in judgment, with souls ascending into Heaven while others are dragged by demons into Hell (above). The *David* captures ideals of human perfection and has come to be an iconic symbol of Renaissance artistic brilliance, while the dramatic and violent *Last Judgment* conveys both terror and divine power. (sculpture: Accademia, Florence, Italy/Ministero per i Beni e le Attività Culturali/Scala/Art Resource, NY; painting: Vatican Museums and Galleries, Vatican State/Alinari/ Bridgeman Images)

The Madonna of Chancellor Rolin, **ca. 1435** This exquisitely detailed oil painting by Jan van Eyck, commissioned by Nicolas Rolin, the chancellor of the duchy of Burgundy, shows the Virgin Mary presenting the infant Jesus to Rolin, whose portrait in a brocade fur-lined robe takes up the entire left side. The foreground is an Italian-style loggia with an inlaid floor, while the background shows Rolin's hometown of Autun, where he was a major landowner and where the painting was displayed in his parish church. Renaissance paintings from southern and northern Europe often show their patrons together with biblical figures and highlight exactly the qualities the patron wanted: wealth, learning, piety, and power. (*La Vierge au Chancelier*, ca. 1435, panel by Jan van Eyck [ca. 1390–1441]/Musée du Louvre, Paris, France/Bridgeman Images)

and motifs, such as the lives and loves of pagan gods and goddesses, figured increasingly in painting and sculpture, with the facial features of the gods sometimes modeled on living people.

The individual portrait emerged as a distinct artistic genre in this movement. Rather than reflecting a spiritual ideal, as medieval painting and sculpture tended to do, Renaissance portraits showed human ideals, often portrayed in the more realistic style increasingly favored by both artists and patrons. The Florentine painter Giotto (JAH-toh) (1276–1337) led the way in the use of realism; his treatment of the human body and face replaced the formal stiffness and artificiality that had long characterized representation of the human body. Piero della Francesca (frahn-CHAY-skah) (1420–1492) and Andrea Mantegna (mahn-TEHN-yuh) (1430/31–1506) pioneered perspective, the linear representation of distance and space on a flat surface, which enhanced the realism of paintings and differentiated them from the flatter and more stylized images of medieval art. The sculptor Donatello (1386–1466) revived the classical figure, with its balance and self-awareness. In architecture, Filippo Brunelleschi (1377–1446) looked to the classical past for inspiration, designing a hospital for orphans and

foundlings in which all proportions—of the windows, height, floor plan, and covered walkway with a series of rounded arches—were carefully thought out to achieve a sense of balance and harmony.

Art produced in northern Europe tended to be more religious in orientation than that produced in Italy. Some Flemish painters, notably Rogier van der Weyden (1399/1400–1464) and Jan van Eyck (1366–1441), were considered the artistic equals of Italian painters and were much admired in Italy. Van Eyck was one of the earliest artists to use oil-based paints successfully, and his religious scenes and portraits all show great realism and remarkable attention to human personality. Albrecht Dürer (1471–1528), from the German city of Nuremberg, studied with artists in Italy, and produced woodcuts, engravings, and etchings that rendered the human form and the natural world in amazing detail. He was fascinated with the theoretical and practical problems of perspective, and designed mechanical devices that could assist artists in solving these. Late in his life he saw the first pieces of Aztec art shipped back to Europe from the New World and commented in his diary about how amazing they were.

In the early sixteenth century the center of the new art shifted from Florence to Rome, where wealthy cardinals and popes wanted visual expression of the church's and their own families' power and piety. Renaissance popes expended enormous enthusiasm and huge sums of money to beautify the city. Pope Julius II tore down the old Saint Peter's Basilica and began work on the present structure in 1506. Michelangelo went to Rome from Florence in about 1500 and began the series of statues, paintings, and architectural projects from which he gained an international reputation: the *Pietà, Moses*, the redesigning of the plaza and surrounding palaces on the Capitoline Hill in central Rome, and, most famously, the dome for Saint Peter's and the ceiling and altar wall of the nearby Sistine Chapel.

Raphael Sanzio (1483–1520), another Florentine, got the commission for frescoes in the papal apartments, and in his relatively short life he painted hundreds of portraits and devotional images, becoming the most sought-after artist in Europe. Raphael also oversaw a large workshop with many collaborators and apprentices—who assisted on the less difficult sections of some paintings—and wrote treatises on his philosophy of art in which he emphasized the importance of imitating nature and developing an orderly sequence of design and proportion.

Venice became another artistic center in the sixteenth century. Titian (TIH-shuhn) (1490–1576) produced portraits, religious subjects, and mythological scenes, developing techniques of painting in oil without doing elaborate drawings first, which speeded up the process and pleased patrons eager to display their acquisitions. Titian and other sixteenth-century painters developed an artistic style known in English as "mannerism" (from *maniera* or "style" in Italian) in which artists sometimes distorted figures, exaggerated musculature, and heightened color to express emotion and drama more intently. (Paintings by Titian can be found on pages 380 and 382; this is also the style in which Michelangelo painted the *Last Judgment* in the Sistine Chapel, shown on page 373.)

The Renaissance Artist

Some patrons rewarded certain artists very well, and some artists gained great public acclaim as, in Vasari's words, "rare men of genius." This adulation of the artist has led many historians to view the Renaissance as the beginning of the concept of the artist as having a special talent. In the Middle Ages people believed that only God created, albeit through individuals; the medieval conception recognized no particular value in artistic originality. Renaissance artists and humanists came to think that a work of art was the deliberate creation of a unique personality who transcended traditions, rules, and theories. A genius had a peculiar gift, which ordinary laws should not inhibit. Michelangelo and Leonardo da Vinci perhaps best embody the new concept of the Renaissance

Villa Capra   Architecture as well as literature and art aimed to re-create classical styles. The Venetian architect Andrea Palladio modeled this country villa, constructed for a papal official in 1566, on the Pantheon of ancient Rome (see Chapter 6). Surrounded by statues of classical deities, it is completely symmetrical, capturing humanist ideals of perfection and balance. This villa and other buildings that Palladio designed influenced later buildings all over the world, including the U.S. Capitol in Washington, D.C., and countless state capitol buildings. (age-fotostock/Superstock)

What makes a genius? A deep curiosity about an extensive variety of subjects? A divine spark that emerges in talents that far exceed the norm? Or is it just "one percent inspiration and ninety-nine percent perspiration," as Thomas Edison said? However it is defined, Leonardo da Vinci counts as a genius. In fact, Leonardo was one of the individuals whom the Renaissance label "genius" was designed to describe: a special kind of human being with exceptional creative powers. Leonardo (who, despite the title of a popular novel and film, is always called by his first name) was born in Vinci, near Florence, the illegitimate son of Caterina, a local peasant girl, and Ser Piero da Vinci, a notary public. When Ser Piero's marriage to Donna Albrussia produced no children, he and his wife took in Leonardo, whose mother had married another man. Ser Piero secured Leonardo an apprenticeship with the painter and sculptor Andrea del Verrocchio in Florence. In 1472, when Leonardo was just twenty years old, he was already listed as a master in Florence's "Company of Artists."

Leonardo's most famous portrait, *Mona Lisa*, shows a woman with an enigmatic smile that Giorgio Vasari described as "so pleasing that it seemed divine rather than human." The portrait, probably of the young wife of a rich Florentine merchant (her exact identity is hotly debated), may be the best-known painting in the history of art. One of its competitors for that designation would be another work of Leonardo, *The Last Supper*, which has been called "the most revered painting in the world."

Leonardo's reputation as a genius does not rest on his paintings, however, which are actually few in number, but rather on the breadth of his abilities and interests. He is considered by many the first "Renaissance man," a phrase still used for a multitalented individual. Hoping to reproduce what the eye can see, he drew everything he saw around him, including executed criminals hanging on gallows as well as the beauties of nature. Trying to understand how the human body worked, Leonardo studied live and dead bodies, doing autopsies and dissections to investigate muscles and circulation. He carefully analyzed the effects of light, and he experimented with perspective.

Leonardo used his drawings not only as the basis for his paintings but also as a tool of scientific investigation. He drew

Vitruvian Man, a drawing by Leonardo showing correlations between the ideal human proportions and the geometric shapes of the circle and square, is based on the ideas of the ancient Roman architect Vitruvius, whose works Leonardo read. (Galleria dell'Accademia, Venice, Italy/Bridgeman Images)

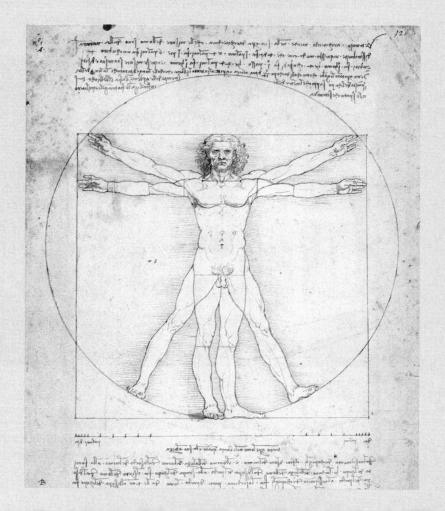

plans for hundreds of inventions, many of which would become reality centuries later, such as the helicopter, tank, machine gun, and parachute. He was hired by one of the powerful new rulers in Italy, Duke Ludovico Sforza of Milan, to design weapons, fortresses, and water systems, as well as to produce works of art. Leonardo left Milan when Sforza was overthrown, and spent the last years of his life painting, drawing, and designing for the pope and the French king.

Leonardo experimented with new materials for painting and sculpture, not all of which worked. The experimental method he used to paint *The Last Supper* caused the picture to deteriorate rapidly, and it began to flake off the wall as soon as it was finished. Leonardo regarded it as never quite completed, for he could not find a model for the face of Christ who would evoke the spiritual depth he felt the figure deserved. His gigantic equestrian statue in honor of Ludovico's father, Duke Francesco Sforza, was never made, and the clay model collapsed. He planned to write books on many subjects but never finished any of them, leaving only notebooks. Leonardo once said that "a painter is not admirable unless he is universal." The patrons who supported him—and he was supported very well—perhaps wished that his inspirations would have been a bit less universal in scope, or at least accompanied by more perspiration.

QUESTIONS FOR ANALYSIS

1. In what ways do the notions of a "genius" and of a "Renaissance man" both support and contradict each other? Which better fits Leonardo?
2. Has the idea of artistic genius changed since the Renaissance? How?

Sources: Giorgio Vasari, *Lives of the Artists*, vol. 1, trans. G. Bull (London: Penguin Books, 1965); S. B. Nuland, *Leonardo da Vinci* (New York: Lipper/Viking, 2000).

artist as genius. (See "Individuals in Society: Leonardo da Vinci," at left.)

It is important not to overemphasize the Renaissance notion of genius. As certain artists became popular and well known, they could assert their own artistic styles and pay less attention to the wishes of patrons, but even major artists like Raphael generally worked according to the patron's specific guidelines. Whether in Italy or northern Europe, most Renaissance artists trained in the workshops of older artists; Botticelli, Raphael, Titian, and at times even Michelangelo were known for their large, well-run, and prolific workshops. Though they might be men of genius, artists were still expected to be well trained in proper artistic techniques and stylistic conventions; the notion that artistic genius could show up in the work of an untrained artist did not emerge until the twentieth century. Beginning artists spent years mastering their craft by copying drawings and paintings; learning how to prepare paint and other artistic materials; and, by the sixteenth century, reading books about design and composition. Younger artists gathered together in the evenings for further drawing practice; by the later sixteenth century some of these informal groups had turned into more formal artistic "academies," the first of which was begun in 1563 in Florence by Vasari under the patronage of the Medici.

As Vasari's phrase indicates, the notion of artistic genius that developed in the Renaissance was gendered. All the most famous and most prolific Renaissance artists were male. The types of art in which more women were active, such as textiles, needlework, and painting on porcelain, were regarded not as "major arts," but only as "minor" or "decorative" arts. (The division between "major" and "minor" arts begun in the Renaissance continues to influence the way museums and collections are organized today.) Like painting, embroidery changed in the Renaissance to become more naturalistic, more visually complex, and more classical in its subject matter. Embroiderers were not trained to view their work as products of individual genius, however, so they rarely included their names on the works, and there is no way to discover their identities.

There are no female architects whose names are known and only one female sculptor, though several women did become well known as painters in their day. Stylistically, their works are different from one another, but their careers show many similarities. The majority of female painters were the daughters of painters or of minor noblemen with ties to artistic circles. Many were eldest daughters or came from families in which there were no sons, so their fathers took unusual interest in their careers. Many women painters began their careers before they were twenty and either produced far fewer paintings after they married or stopped painting entirely. Women were

Botticelli, *Primavera* (Spring), ca. 1482   Framed by a grove of orange trees, Venus, goddess of love, is flanked on the right by Flora, goddess of flowers and fertility, and on the left by the Three Graces, goddesses of banquets, dance, and social occasions. Above, Venus's son Cupid, the god of love, shoots darts of desire, while at the far right the wind-god Zephyrus chases the nymph Chloris. The entire scene rests on classical mythology, though some art historians claim that Venus is an allegory for the Virgin Mary. Botticelli captured the ideal for female beauty in the Renaissance: slender, with pale skin, a high forehead, red-blond hair, and sloping shoulders. (Galleria degli Uffizi, Florence, Italy/Bridgeman Images)

not allowed to study the male nude, a study that was viewed as essential if one wanted to paint large history or biblical paintings with many figures. Women also could not learn the technique of fresco, in which colors are applied directly to wet plaster walls, because such work had to be done in public, which was judged inappropriate for women. Joining a group of male artists for informal practice was also seen as improper, so women had no access to the newly established artistic academies. Like universities, humanist academies, and most craft guild shops, artistic workshops were male-only settings in which men of different ages came together for training and created bonds of friendship, influence, patronage, and sometimes intimacy.

Women were not alone in being excluded from the institutions of Renaissance culture. Though a few rare men of genius such as Leonardo and Michelangelo emerged from artisanal backgrounds, most scholars and artists came from families with at least some money. The ideas of the highly educated humanists did not influence the lives of most people in cities and did not affect life in the villages at all. For rural people

and for less well-off town residents, work and play continued much as they had in the High Middle Ages: religious festivals and family celebrations provided people's main amusements, and learning came from one's parents, not through formal schooling (see Chapter 10).

Social Hierarchies

FOCUS QUESTION *What were the key social hierarchies in Renaissance Europe?*

The division between educated and uneducated people was only one of many social hierarchies evident in the Renaissance. Every society has social hierarchies; in ancient Rome, for example, there were patricians and plebeians (see Chapter 5). Such hierarchies are to some degree descriptions of social reality, but they are also idealizations—that is, they describe how people imagined their society to be, without all the messy reality of social-climbing plebeians or groups that did not fit the standard categories. Social

***The Chess Game*, 1555**   In this oil painting, the Italian artist Sofonisba Anguissola (1532–1625) shows her three younger sisters playing chess, a game that was growing in popularity in the sixteenth century. Each sister looks at the one immediately older than herself, with the girl on the left looking out at her sister, the artist. Anguissola's father, a minor nobleman, recognized his daughter's talent and arranged for her to study with several painters. She became a court painter at the Spanish royal court, where she painted many portraits. Returning to Italy, she continued to be active, painting her last portrait when she was over eighty. (Museum Narodowe, Poznan, Poland/Bridgeman Images)

hierarchies in the Renaissance were built on those of the Middle Ages that divided nobles from commoners, but they also developed new concepts that contributed to modern social hierarchies, such as those of race, class, and gender.

Race and Slavery

Renaissance people did not use the word *race* the way we do, but often used *race*, *people*, and *nation* interchangeably for ethnic, national, religious, or other groups—the French race, the Jewish nation, the Irish people, "the race of learned gentlemen," and so on. They did make distinctions based on skin color that provide some of the background for later conceptualizations of race, but these distinctions were interwoven with other characteristics when people thought about human differences.

Ever since the time of the Roman Republic, a small number of black Africans had lived in western Europe. They had come, along with white slaves, as the spoils of war. Even after the collapse of the Roman Empire, Muslim and Christian merchants continued to import them. Unstable political conditions in many parts of Africa enabled enterprising merchants to seize people and sell them into slavery. Local authorities afforded these Africans no protection. Long tradition, moreover, sanctioned the practice of slavery. The evidence of medieval art attests to the continued presence of Africans in Europe throughout the Middle Ages and to Europeans' awareness of them.

Beginning in the fifteenth century sizable numbers of black slaves entered Europe. Portuguese sailors brought perhaps a thousand Africans a year to the mar-

kets of Seville, Barcelona, Marseilles, and Genoa. In the late fifteenth century this flow increased, with thousands of people taken from the west coast of Africa. By 1530 between four thousand and five thousand were sold to the Portuguese each year. By the mid-sixteenth century blacks, both slave and free, constituted about 10 percent of the population of the Portuguese cities of Lisbon and Évora and roughly 3 percent of the Portuguese population overall. Cities such as Lisbon also had significant numbers of people of mixed African and European descent, as African slaves intermingled with the people they lived among and sometimes intermarried.

Although blacks were concentrated in the Iberian Peninsula, some Africans must have lived in northern Europe as well. In the 1580s, for example, Queen Elizabeth I of England complained that there were too many "blackamoores" competing with needy English people for places as domestic servants. Black servants were much sought after; the medieval interest in curiosities, the exotic, and the marvelous continued in the Renaissance. Italian aristocrats had their portraits painted with their black page boys to indicate their wealth (as in the painting on page 380). Blacks were so greatly in demand at the Renaissance courts of northern Italy, in fact, that the Venetians defied papal threats of excommunication to secure them. In 1491 Isabella d'Este, the duchess of Mantua and a major patron of the arts, instructed her agent to secure a black girl between four and eight years old, "shapely and as black as possible." She hoped the girl would become "the best buffoon in the world," and noted, "[W]e shall make her very happy and shall have great fun with her."[8] The girl would join musicians, acrobats, and

Laura de Dianti, 1523 The Venetian artist Titian portrays a young Italian woman with a gorgeous blue dress and an elaborate pearl and feather headdress, accompanied by a young black page with a gold earring. Both the African page and the headdress connect the portrait's subject with the exotic, though slaves from Africa and the Ottoman Empire were actually common in wealthy Venetian households. (Private Collection/© Human Bios International AG)

dancers at Isabella's court as a source of entertainment, her status similar to that of the dwarves who could be found at many Renaissance courts.

Africans were not simply amusements at court. In Portugal, Spain, and Italy slaves supplemented the labor force in virtually all occupations—as servants, agricultural laborers, craftsmen, and seamen on ships going to Lisbon and Africa. Agriculture in Europe did not involve large plantations, so large-scale agricultural slavery did not develop there as it would in the late fifteenth century in the New World.

Until the voyages down the African coast in the late fifteenth century, Europeans had little concrete knowledge of Africans and their cultures. They perceived Africa as a remote place, the home of strange people isolated by heresy and Islam from superior European civilization. Africans' contact, even as slaves, with Christian Europeans could only "improve" the blacks, they thought. The expanding slave trade reinforced negative preconceptions about the inferiority of black Africans.

■ **debate about women** Debate among writers and thinkers in the Renaissance about women's qualities and proper role in society.

Wealth and the Nobility

The word *class*—as in working class, middle class, and upper class—was not used in the Renaissance to describe social divisions, but by the thirteenth century, and even more so by the fifteenth, the idea of a hierarchy based on wealth was emerging. This was particularly true in cities, where wealthy merchants who oversaw vast trading empires lived in splendor that rivaled the richest nobles. As we saw earlier, in many cities these merchants had gained political power to match their economic might, becoming merchant oligarchs who ruled through city councils. This hierarchy of wealth was more fluid than the older divisions into noble and commoner, allowing individuals and families to rise—and fall—within one generation.

The development of a hierarchy of wealth did not mean an end to the prominence of nobles, however, and even poorer nobility still had higher status than wealthy commoners. Thus wealthy Italian merchants enthusiastically bought noble titles and country villas in the fifteenth century, and wealthy English or Spanish merchants eagerly married their daughters and sons into often-impoverished noble families. The nobility maintained its status in most parts of Europe not by maintaining rigid boundaries, but by taking in and integrating the new social elite of wealth.

Along with being tied to hierarchies of wealth and family standing, social status was linked to considerations of honor. Among the nobility, for example, certain weapons and battle tactics were favored because they were viewed as more honorable. Among urban dwellers, certain occupations, such as city executioner or manager of the municipal brothel, might be well paid but were understood to be dishonorable and so of low status. In cities, sumptuary laws reflected both wealth and honor (see Chapter 10); merchants were specifically allowed fur and jewels, while prostitutes were ordered to wear yellow bands that would remind potential customers of the flames of Hell.

Gender Roles

Renaissance people would not have understood the word *gender* to refer to categories of people, but they would have easily grasped the concept. Toward the end of the fourteenth century, learned men (and a few women) began what was termed the **debate about women** (*querelle des femmes*), a debate about women's character and nature that would last for centuries. Misogynist (muh-SAH-juh-nihst) critiques of women from both clerical and secular authors denounced females as devious, domineering, and demanding. In answer, several authors compiled long lists of famous and praiseworthy women exemplary for their loyalty, bravery, and morality. Christine de Pizan was among the writers who were interested not only in defending women, but also in exploring the reasons behind women's secondary status—that is, why the great philosophers, statesmen, and poets had generally been men. In this they were anticipating discussions about the "social construction of gender" by six hundred years. (See "Evaluating the Evidence 11.3: Christine de Pizan, Advice to the Wives of Artisans," page 348.)

With the development of the printing press, popular interest in the debate about women grew, and works were translated, reprinted, and shared around Europe. Prints that juxtaposed female virtues and vices were also very popular, with the virtuous women depicted as those of the classical or biblical past and the vice-ridden dressed in contemporary clothes. The favorite metaphor for the virtuous wife was either the snail or the tortoise, both animals that never leave their "houses" and are totally silent, although such images were never as widespread as those depicting wives beating their husbands or hiding their lovers from them.

Beginning in the sixteenth century, the debate about women also became a debate about female rulers, sparked primarily by dynastic accidents in many countries, including Spain, England, Scotland, and France, which led to women's ruling in their own right or serving as advisers to child-kings. The questions were vigorously and at times viciously argued. They directly concerned the social construction of gender: Could a woman's being born into a royal family and educated to rule allow her to overcome the limitations of her sex? Should it? Or stated another way: which was (or should be) the stronger determinant of character and social role, gender or rank? Despite a prevailing sentiment that women were not as fit to rule as men, there were no successful rebellions against female rulers simply because they were women, but in part this was because female rulers, especially Queen Elizabeth I of England, emphasized qualities regarded as masculine—physical bravery, stamina, wisdom, duty—whenever they appeared in public.

Ideas about women's and men's proper roles determined the actions of ordinary men and women even more forcefully. The dominant notion of the "true" man was that of the married head of household, so men whose social status and age would have normally conferred political power but who remained unmarried did not participate in politics at the same level as their married brothers. Unmarried men in Venice, for example, could not be part of the ruling council. (See "Living in the Past: Male Clothing and Masculinity," page 382.)

Women were also understood as either "married or to be married," even if the actual marriage patterns in Europe left many women (and men) unmarried until quite late in life (see Chapter 11). This meant that

Phyllis Riding Aristotle   Among the many scenes that expressed the debate about women visually were woodcuts, engravings, paintings, and even cups and plates that showed the classical philosopher Aristotle as an old man being ridden by the young, beautiful Phyllis (shown here in a German woodcut). The origins of the story are uncertain, but in the Renaissance everyone knew the tale of how Aristotle's infatuation with Phyllis led to his ridicule. Male moralists used it as a warning about the power of women's sexual allure, though women may have interpreted it differently. (Musée du Louvre, Paris, France/© RMN–Grand Palais/Art Resource, NY)

In the Renaissance wealthy people displayed their power and prosperity on their bodies as well as in their houses and household furnishings. Expanded trade brought in silks, pearls, gemstones, feathers, dyes, and furs, which tailors, goldsmiths, seamstresses, furriers, and hatmakers turned into magnificent clothing and jewelry. Nowhere was fashion more evident than on the men in Renaissance cities and courts. Young men favored multicolored garments that fit tightly, often topping the ensemble with a matching hat on carefully combed long hair. The close-cut garments emphasized the male form, which was further accentuated by tight hose stylishly split to reveal a brightly colored codpiece. Older men favored more subdued colors but with multiple padded shirts, vests, and coats that emphasized real or simulated upper-body strength and that allowed the display of many layers of expensive fabrics. Golden rings, earrings, pins, and necklaces provided additional glamour.

The Venetian painter Titian's portrait of Emperor Charles V with one of his hunting dogs. (Prado, Madrid, Spain/Bridgeman Images)

Doublet and hose worn by a groom at a wedding in the mid-sixteenth century. (© Staatliche Kunstsammlungen Dresden/Bridgeman Images)

women's work was not viewed as financially supporting a family—even if it did—and was valued less than men's. If they worked for wages, and many women did, women earned about half to two-thirds of what men did, even for the same work. Regulations for vineyard workers in the early sixteenth century, for example, specified:

> Men who work in the vineyards, doing work that is skilled, are to be paid 16 pence per day; in addition, they are to receive soup and wine in the morning, at midday beer, vegetables and meat, and in the evening soup, vegetables and wine. Young boys are to be paid 10 pence per day. Women who work as haymakers are to be given 6 pence a day. If the employer wants to have them doing other work, he may make an agreement with them to pay them 7 or 8 pence. He may also give them soup and vegetables to eat in the morning—but no wine—milk and bread at midday, but nothing in the evening.[9]

Two young men, who are side figures in *The Adoration of the Magi,* by Luca Signorelli (1445–1523). (Galleria degli Uffizi, Florence, Italy/Scala/Art Resource, NY)

QUESTIONS FOR ANALYSIS

1. Male clothing in any era communicates social values and ideas about masculinity. What does Renaissance fashion suggest about notions of manhood in this era?

2. In *The Prince*, Machiavelli used the word *effeminate* to describe the worst kind of ruler, though the word carried different connotations than it does today. Strong heterosexual passion was not a sign of manliness and could make one "effeminate"— that is, dominated by women as well as similar to them. Look at the portrait of Charles V here and at the other portraits in this chapter. How did male rulers visually symbolize their masculinity?

The maintenance of appropriate power relationships between men and women, with men dominant and women subordinate, served as a symbol of the proper functioning of society as a whole. Disorder in the proper gender hierarchy was linked with social upheaval and was viewed as threatening. Of all the ways in which Renaissance society was hierarchically arranged—social rank, age, level of education, race, occupation—gender was regarded as the most "natural" and therefore the most important to defend.

Politics and the State in Western Europe

FOCUS QUESTION *How did nation-states develop in this period?*

The High Middle Ages had witnessed the origins of many of the basic institutions of the modern state. Sheriffs, inquests, juries, circuit judges, professional bureaucracies, and representative assemblies all trace their origins to the twelfth and thirteenth centuries. The linchpin for the development of states, however, was strong monarchy, and during the period of the Hundred Years' War no ruler in western Europe was able to provide effective leadership. The resurgent power of feudal nobilities weakened the centralizing work begun earlier.

Beginning in the fifteenth century, however, rulers utilized aggressive methods to rebuild their governments. First in the regional states of Italy, then in the expanding monarchies of France, England, and Spain, rulers began the work of reducing violence, curbing unruly nobles, and establishing domestic order. They attempted to secure their borders and enhanced methods of raising revenue. The monarchs of western Europe emphasized royal majesty and royal sovereignty and insisted on the respect and loyalty of all subjects, including the nobility. In central Europe the Holy Roman emperors attempted to do the same, but they were not able to overcome the power of local interests to create a unified state (see Chapter 13).

France

The Black Death and the Hundred Years' War left France drastically depopulated, commercially ruined, and agriculturally weak. Nonetheless, the ruler whom Joan of Arc had seen crowned at Reims, Charles VII (r. 1422–1461), revived the monarchy and France. He seemed an unlikely person to do so. Frail, indecisive, and burdened with questions about his paternity (his father had been deranged; his mother, notoriously promiscuous), Charles VII nevertheless began France's long recovery.

Charles reconciled the Burgundians and Armagnacs (ahr-muhn-YAKZ), who had been waging civil war for thirty years. By 1453 French armies had expelled the English from French soil except in Calais. Charles reorganized the royal council, giving increased influence to lawyers and bankers, and strengthened royal finances through taxes on certain products and on land, which remained the Crown's chief sources of income until the Revolution of 1789.

By establishing regular companies of cavalry and archers—recruited, paid, and inspected by the state—Charles created the first permanent royal army anywhere in Europe. His son Louis XI (r. 1461–1483),

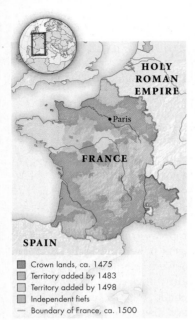

Crown lands, ca. 1475
Territory added by 1483
Territory added by 1498
Independent fiefs
Boundary of France, ca. 1500

The Expansion of France, 1475–1500

called the "Spider King" because of his treacherous character, improved upon Charles's army and used it to control the nobles' separate militias and to curb urban independence. The army was also employed in 1477 when Louis conquered Burgundy upon the death of its ruler Charles the Bold. Three years later, the extinction of the house of Anjou with the death of its last legitimate male heir brought Louis the counties of Anjou, Bar, Maine, and Provence.

Two further developments strengthened the French monarchy. The marriage of Louis XII (r. 1498–1515) and Anne of Brittany added the large western duchy of Brittany to the state. Then King Francis I and Pope Leo X reached a mutually satisfactory agreement about church and state powers in 1516. The new treaty, the Concordat of Bologna, approved the pope's right to receive the first year's income of newly named bishops and abbots in France. In return, Leo X recognized the French ruler's right to select French bishops and abbots. French kings thereafter effectively controlled the appointment and thus the policies of church officials in the kingdom.

England

English society also suffered severely from the disorders of the fifteenth century. The aristocracy dominated the government of Henry IV (r. 1399–1413) and indulged in disruptive violence at the local level, fighting each other, seizing wealthy travelers for ransom, and plundering merchant caravans (see Chapter 11). Population continued to decline. Between 1455 and 1471 adherents of the ducal houses of York and Lancaster contended for control of the Crown in a civil war, commonly called the Wars of the Roses because the symbol of the Yorkists was a white rose and that of the Lancastrians a red one. The chronic disorder hurt trade, agriculture, and domestic industry. Under the pious but mentally disturbed Henry VI (r. 1422–1461), the authority of the monarchy sank lower than it had been in centuries.

The Yorkist Edward IV (r. 1461–1483) began establishing domestic tranquillity. He succeeded in defeating the Lancastrian forces and after 1471 began to recon-

struct the monarchy. Edward, his brother Richard III (r. 1483–1485), and Henry VII (r. 1485–1509) of the Welsh house of Tudor worked to restore royal prestige, to crush the power of the nobility, and to establish order and law at the local level. All three rulers used methods that Machiavelli himself would have praised—ruthlessness, efficiency, and secrecy.

Edward IV and subsequently the Tudors, except Henry VIII, conducted foreign policy on the basis of diplomacy, avoiding expensive wars. Thus the English monarchy did not have to depend on Parliament for money, and the Crown undercut that source of aristocratic influence.

Henry VII did summon several meetings of Parliament in the early years of his reign, primarily to confirm laws, but the center of royal authority was the royal council, which governed at the national level. There Henry VII revealed his distrust of the nobility: though not completely excluded, very few great lords were among the king's closest advisers. Instead he chose men from among the smaller landowners and urban residents trained in law. The council conducted negotiations with foreign governments and secured international recognition of the Tudor dynasty through the marriage in 1501 of Henry VII's eldest son, Arthur, to Catherine of Aragon, the daughter of Ferdinand and Isabella of Spain. The council dealt with real or potential aristocratic threats through a judicial offshoot, the Court of Star Chamber, so called because of the stars painted on the ceiling of the room. The court applied methods that were sometimes terrifying: accused persons were not entitled to see evidence against them, sessions were secret, juries were not called, and torture could be applied to extract confessions. These procedures ran directly counter to English common-law precedents, but they effectively reduced aristocratic troublemaking.

When Henry VII died in 1509, he left a country at peace both domestically and internationally, a substantially augmented treasury, an expanding wool trade, and a crown with its dignity and role much enhanced. He was greatly missed after he died "by all his subjects," wrote the historian Polydore Vergil, "who had been able to conduct their lives peaceably, far removed from the assaults and evildoings of scoundrels."[10]

Spain

While England and France laid the foundations of unified nation-states during the Middle Ages, Spain remained a conglomerate of independent kingdoms. By the middle of the fifteenth century, the kingdoms of Castile and Aragon dominated the weaker Navarre, Portugal, and Granada; and the Iberian Peninsula, with the exception of Granada, had been won for Christianity (Map 12.3). The wedding in 1469 of the dynamic and aggressive Isabella of Castile

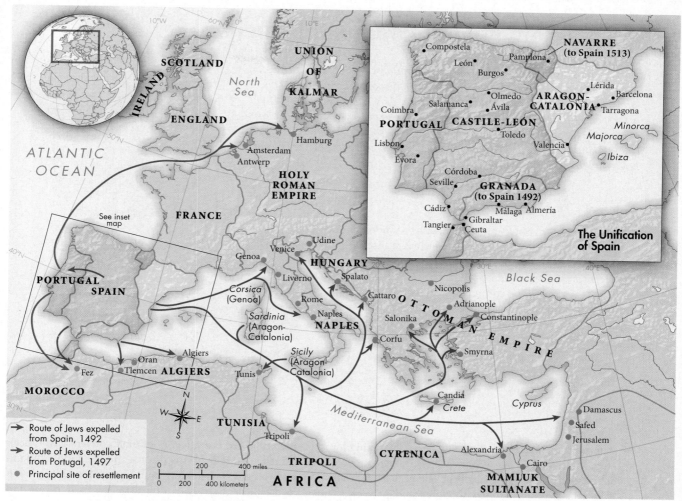

MAP 12.3 The Unification of Spain and the Expulsion of the Jews, Fifteenth Century   The marriage of Ferdinand of Aragon and Isabella of Castile in 1469 brought most of the Iberian Peninsula under one monarchy, although different parts of Spain retained distinct cultures, languages, and legal systems. In 1492 Ferdinand and Isabella conquered Granada, where most people were Muslim, and expelled the Jews from all of Spain. Spanish Jews resettled in cities of Europe and the Mediterranean that allowed them in, including Muslim states such as the Ottoman Empire. Muslims were also expelled from Spain over the course of the sixteenth and early seventeenth centuries.

(r. 1474–1504) and the crafty and persistent Ferdinand of Aragon (r. 1479–1516) did not bring about administrative unity, as each state maintained its own cortes (parliament), laws, courts, and systems of coinage and taxation until about 1700. But the two rulers pursued a common foreign policy, and under their heirs Spain became a more unified realm.

Ferdinand and Isabella were able to exert their authority in ways similar to the rulers of France and England. They curbed aristocratic power by excluding high nobles from the royal council, which had full executive, judicial, and legislative powers under the monarchy, instead appointing lesser landowners. The council and various government boards recruited men trained in Roman law, which exalted the power of the Crown. (See "Evaluating the Evidence 12.3: A Gold Coin of

Ferdinand and Isabella," page 386.) They also secured from the Spanish Borgia pope Alexander VI—Cesare Borgia's father—the right to appoint bishops in Spain and in the Hispanic territories in America, enabling them to establish the equivalent of a national church. With the revenues from ecclesiastical estates, they were able to expand their territories to include the remaining land held by Arabs in southern Spain. The victorious entry of Ferdinand and Isabella into Granada on January 6, 1492, signaled the conclusion of the reconquista (see Map 9.3, page 258). Granada was incorporated into the Spanish kingdom, and after Isabella's death Ferdinand conquered Navarre in the north.

There still remained a sizable and, in the view of the majority of the Spanish people, potentially dangerous minority, the Jews. When the kings of France and

A Gold Coin of Ferdinand and Isabella

Minting coins provided a way for Renaissance monarchs to enhance their economies and also to show royal might and communicate other messages. This large gold coin, known as the "double excelente," was issued by the Seville mint in 1475, one year after Isabella had become queen in her own right of Castile and Ferdinand had become king because he was her husband. (Ferdinand would become king of Aragon in 1479 when his father died.) The eagle on the reverse holds both their coats of arms.

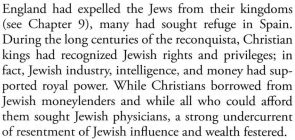

EVALUATE THE EVIDENCE

1. What symbols of power are shown with the monarchs on the coin? How does the coin convey the fact that their marriage was the union of two rulers?
2. Rulers sometimes stipulated that all major transactions within their realms be carried out with certain coins, much the same way governments today allow only the national currency. What was their aim in doing this, and why might such policies have been hard to enforce?

(photos: Seville mint, 1475/Fitzwilliam Museum, University of Cambridge, UK/Bridgeman Images)

England had expelled the Jews from their kingdoms (see Chapter 9), many had sought refuge in Spain. During the long centuries of the reconquista, Christian kings had recognized Jewish rights and privileges; in fact, Jewish industry, intelligence, and money had supported royal power. While Christians borrowed from Jewish moneylenders and while all who could afford them sought Jewish physicians, a strong undercurrent of resentment of Jewish influence and wealth festered.

In the fourteenth century anti-Semitism in Spain was aggravated by fiery anti-Jewish preaching, by economic dislocation, and by the search for a scapegoat during the Black Death. Anti-Semitic pogroms swept the towns of Spain, and perhaps 40 percent of the Jewish population was killed or forced to convert. Those converted were called *conversos* or **New Christians**. Conversos were often well educated and held prominent positions in government, the church, medicine, law, and business. Numbering perhaps 200,000 in a total Spanish population of about 7.5 million, New Christians and Jews in fifteenth-century Spain exercised influence disproportionate to their numbers.

Such successes bred resentment. Aristocratic grandees resented the conversos' financial independence, the poor hated the converso tax collectors, and church-

men doubted the sincerity of their conversions. Queen Isabella shared these suspicions, and she and Ferdinand had received permission from Pope Sixtus IV in 1478 to establish their own Inquisition to "search out and punish converts from Judaism who had transgressed against Christianity by secretly adhering to Jewish beliefs and performing rites of the Jews."[11] Investigations and trials began immediately, as officials of the Inquisition looked for conversos who showed any sign of incomplete conversion, such as not eating pork.

Recent scholarship has carefully analyzed documents of the Inquisition. Most conversos identified themselves as sincere Christians; many came from families that had received baptism generations before. In response to conversos' statements, officials of the Inquisition developed a new type of anti-Semitism. A person's status as a Jew, they argued, could not be changed by religious conversion, but was in the person's blood and was heritable, so Jews could never be true Christians. In what were known as "purity of blood" laws, having pure Christian blood became a requirement for noble status. Ideas about Jews developed in Spain were important components in European concepts of race, and discussions of "Jewish blood" later expanded into notions of the "Jewish race."

In 1492, shortly after the conquest of Granada, Isabella and Ferdinand issued an edict expelling all

■ **New Christians** A term for Jews and Muslims in the Iberian Peninsula who accepted Christianity; in many cases they included Christians whose families had converted centuries earlier.

practicing Jews from Spain. Of the community of perhaps 200,000 Jews, 150,000 fled. Many Muslims in Granada were forcibly baptized and became another type of New Christian investigated by the Inquisition. Absolute religious orthodoxy and purity of blood served as the theoretical foundation of the Spanish national state.

The Spanish national state rested on marital politics as well as military victories and religious courts. Following their own example, the royal couple made astute marriages for their children with every country that could assist them against France, their most powerful neighbor. In 1496 Ferdinand and Isabella married their second daughter, Joanna, heiress to Castile, to the archduke Philip, heir to the Burgundian Netherlands and the Holy Roman Empire. Philip and Joanna's son Charles V (r. 1519–1556) thus succeeded to a vast inheritance. When Charles's son Philip II joined Portugal to the Spanish crown in 1580, the Iberian Peninsula was at last politically united.

NOTES

1. In Gertrude R. B. Richards, *Florentine Merchants in the Age of the Medici* (Cambridge: Harvard University Press, 1932).
2. From *The Portable Renaissance Reader*, p. 27, by James B. Ross and Mary Martin McLaughlin, editors, copyright 1953, 1968, renewed © 1981 by Penguin Random House LLC. Used by permission of Viking Books, an imprint of Penguin Publishing Group, a division of Penguin Random House LLC.
3. Ibid., pp. 480–481, 482, 492.
4. Niccolò Machiavelli, *The Prince*, trans. Leo Paul S. de Alvarez (Prospect Heights, Ill.: Waveland Press, 1980), p. 101.
5. Ibid., p. 149.
6. Quoted in F. Seebohm, *The Oxford Reformers* (London: J. M. Dent & Sons, 1867), p. 256.
7. Quoted in Lauro Martines, *Power and Imagination: City-States in Renaissance Italy* (New York: Vintage Books, 1980), p. 253.
8. Quoted in J. Devisse and M. Mollat, *The Image of the Black in Western Art*, vol. 2, trans. W. G. Ryan (New York: William Morrow, 1979), pt. 2, pp. 187–188.
9. Stuttgart, Württembergische Hauptstaatsarchiv, Generalreskripta, A38, Bü. 2, 1550; trans. Merry Wiesner-Hanks.
10. Denys Hay, ed. and trans., *The Anglia Historia of Polydore Vergil*, AD 1485–1537, book 74 (London: Camden Society, 1950), p. 147.
11. Quoted in Benzion Netanyahu, *The Origins of the Inquisition in Fifteenth Century Spain* (New York: Random House, 1995), p. 921.

LOOKING BACK LOOKING AHEAD

The art historian Giorgio Vasari, who first called this era the Renaissance, thought that his contemporaries had both revived the classical past and gone beyond it. Vasari's judgment was echoed for centuries as historians sharply contrasted the art, architecture, educational ideas, social structures, and attitude toward life of the Renaissance with those of the Middle Ages: in this view, whereas the Middle Ages were corporate and religious, the Renaissance was individualistic and secular. More recently, historians and other scholars have stressed continuity as well as change. Families, kin networks, guilds, and other corporate groups remained important in the Renaissance, and religious belief remained firm. This re-evaluation changes our view of the relationship between the Middle Ages and the Renaissance. It may also change our view of the relationship between the Renaissance and the dramatic changes in religion that occurred in Europe in the sixteenth century. Those religious changes, the Reformation, used to be viewed as a rejection of the values of the Renaissance and a return to the intense concern with religion of the Middle Ages. This idea of the Reformation as a sort of counter-Renaissance may be true to some degree, but there are powerful continuities as well. Both movements looked back to a time people regarded as purer and better than their own, and both offered opportunities for strong individuals to shape their world in unexpected ways.

Make Connections

Think about the larger developments and continuities within and across chapters.

1. The word *Renaissance*, invented to describe the cultural flowering in Italy that began in the fifteenth century, has often been used for other periods of advances in learning and the arts, such as the "Carolingian Renaissance" that you read about in Chapter 8. Can you think of other, more recent "Renaissances"? How else is the word used today?

2. Many artists in the Renaissance consciously modeled their works on those of ancient Greece (Chapters 3 and 4) and Rome (Chapters 5 and 6). Comparing the art and architecture shown in those chapters with those in this chapter, what similarities do you see? Are there aspects of classical art and architecture that were *not* emulated in the Renaissance? Why do you think this might be?

3. The Renaissance was clearly a period of cultural change for educated men. Given what you have read about women's lives and ideas about women in this and earlier chapters, did women have a Renaissance? (This question was posed first by the historian Joan Kelly in 1977 and remains a topic of great debate.) Why or why not?

12 REVIEW & EXPLORE

Identify Key Terms

Identify and explain the significance of each item below.

Renaissance (p. 358)

patronage (p. 358)

communes (p. 358)

popolo (p. 359)

signori (p. 360)

courts (p. 360)

humanism (p. 363)

virtù (p. 363)

Christian humanists (p. 368)

debate about women (p. 380)

New Christians (p. 386)

Review the Main Ideas

Answer the focus questions from each section of the chapter.

◆ How did politics and economics shape the Renaissance? (p. 358)

◆ What new ideas were associated with the Renaissance? (p. 362)

◆ How did art reflect new Renaissance ideals? (p. 372)

◆ What were the key social hierarchies in Renaissance Europe? (p. 378)

◆ How did nation-states develop in this period? (p. 383)

Suggested Reading and Media Resources

BOOKS

- Earle, T. F., and K. J. P. Lowe, eds. *Black Africans in Renaissance Europe.* 2005. Includes essays discussing many aspects of ideas about race and the experience of Africans in Europe.
- Eisenstein, Elizabeth. *The Printing Press as an Agent of Change: Communications and Cultural Transformations in Early Modern Europe.* 1979. The definitive study of the impact of printing.
- Ertman, Thomas. *The Birth of Leviathan: Building States and Regimes in Medieval and Early Modern Europe.* 1997. A good introduction to the creation of nation-states.
- Hartt, Frederick, and David Wilkins. *History of Italian Renaissance Art*, 7th ed. 2010. A comprehensive survey of painting, sculpture, and architecture in Italy.
- Jardine, Lisa. *Worldly Goods: A New History of the Renaissance.* 1998. Discusses changing notions of social status, artistic patronage, and consumer goods.
- Johnson, Geraldine. *Renaissance Art: A Very Short Introduction.* 2005. An excellent brief survey that includes male and female artists, and sets the art in its cultural and historical context.
- King, Ross. *Machiavelli: Philosopher of Power.* 2006. A brief biography that explores Machiavelli's thought in its social and political context.
- Man, John. *Gutenberg Revolution: The Story of a Genius and an Invention That Changed the World.* 2002. Presents a rather idealized view of Gutenberg, but has good discussions of his milieu and excellent illustrations.
- Najemy, John M. *A History of Florence, 1200–1575.* 2008. A comprehensive survey of cultural, political, and social developments, based on the newest research.
- Nauert, Charles. *Humanism and the Culture of Renaissance Europe*, 2d ed. 2006. A thorough introduction to humanism throughout Europe.
- Rummel, Erica. *Desiderius Erasmus.* 2006. An excellent short introduction to Erasmus as a scholar and Christian thinker.
- Waley, Daniel, and Trevor Dean. *The Italian City States*, 4th ed. 2004. Analyzes the rise of independent city-states in northern Italy, including discussion of the artistic and social lives of their inhabitants.
- Wiesner-Hanks, Merry E. *Women and Gender in Early Modern Europe*, 3d ed. 2008. Discusses all aspects of women's lives and ideas about gender.

DOCUMENTARIES

- *Leonardo da Vinci* (BBC, 2004). A three-part documentary telling the life story of Leonardo as an artist, inventor, and engineer. Features tests of his designs for the parachute, tank, diving suit, and glider, and an investigation of the *Mona Lisa*.
- *The Medici: Godfathers of the Renaissance* (PBS, 2004). A four-part documentary examining the power and patronage of the Medici family, shot on location, with extensive coverage of art and architecture.

FEATURE FILMS AND TELEVISION

- *The Agony and the Ecstasy* (Carol Reed, 1965). A classic film highlighting the conflict between Michelangelo and Pope Julius II over the painting of the Sistine Chapel, with Charlton Heston as the artist and Rex Harrison as the pope.
- *The Borgias* (Showtime, 2011). A fictionalized docudrama of the rise of the Borgia family to power in the church and in Italy, with Jeremy Irons as Pope Alexander VI.
- *Dangerous Beauty* (Marshall Herskovitz, 1998). A biographical drama about the life of Veronica Franco, a well-educated courtesan in sixteenth-century Venice, based on the biography of Franco written by Margaret Rosenthal.

WEB SITES

- *Heilbrunn Timeline of Art History.* A chronological, geographical, and thematic exploration of the history of art from around the world, run by the Metropolitan Museum of Art. Includes numerous special topics sections on nearly every aspect of Renaissance art, and also on book production, musical instruments, clothing, household furnishings, and political and economic developments. **www.metmuseum.org/toah/**
- *Medici Archive Project.* A database for researching the nearly three million letters held by the archives on the Medici Grand Dukes of Tuscany, who ruled Florence from 1537 to 1743. Includes topical "document highlights" in English and Italian, accompanied by illustrations. **www.medici.org/**

Glossary

al-Andalus The part of the Iberian Peninsula under Muslim control in the eighth century, encompassing most of modern-day Spain. (p. 223)

apostolic succession The doctrine that all bishops can trace their spiritual ancestry back to Jesus's apostles. (p. 190)

aqueducts Canals, channels, and pipes that brought freshwater into cities. (p. 170)

Arianism A theological belief that originated when Arius, a priest of Alexandria, denied that Christ was co-eternal with God the Father. (p. 189)

Babylonian Captivity The period from 1309 to 1376 when the popes resided in Avignon rather than in Rome. The phrase refers to the seventy years when the Hebrews were held captive in Babylon. (p. 339)

barracks emperors The emperors of the middle of the third century, so called because they were military commanders. (p. 181)

bishops Christian Church officials with jurisdiction over certain areas and the power to determine the correct interpretation of Christian teachings. (p. 179)

Black Death Plague that first struck Europe in 1347 and killed perhaps one-third of the population. (p. 325)

Book of the Dead Egyptian funerary manuscripts, written to help guide the dead through the difficulties they would encounter on the way to the afterlife. (p. 25)

boyars The highest-ranking members of the Russian nobility. (p. 244)

Bronze Age The period in which the production and use of bronze implements became basic to society. (p. 11)

caliph A successor, as chosen by a group of Muhammad's closest followers. (p. 223)

canon law Church law, which had its own courts and procedures. (p. 267)

cathedral The church of a bishop and the administrative headquarters of a diocese. (p. 316)

chivalry Code of conduct in which fighting to defend the Christian faith and protecting one's countrymen was declared to have a sacred purpose. (p. 261)

Christendom The term used by early medieval writers to refer to the realm of Christianity. (p. 280)

Christian humanists Northern humanists who interpreted Italian ideas about and attitudes toward classical antiquity and humanism in terms of their own religious traditions. (p. 368)

civilization A large-scale system of human political, economic, and social organizations; civilizations have cities, laws, states, and often writing. (p. 5)

civitas The city and surrounding territory that served as a basis of the administrative system in the Frankish kingdoms, based on Roman models. (p. 228)

college of cardinals A special group of high clergy with the authority and power to elect the pope and the responsibility to govern the church when the office of the pope is vacant. (p. 265)

comitatus A war band of young men in a barbarian tribe who were closely associated with the chief, swore loyalty to him, and fought with him in battle. (p. 196)

comites A senior official or royal companion, later called a count, who presided over the civitas. (p. 228)

commercial revolution The transformation of the European economy as a result of changes in business procedures and growth in trade. (p. 304)

common law A body of English law established by King Henry II's court that in the next two or three centuries became common to the entire country. (p. 259)

communes Sworn associations of free men in Italian cities led by merchant guilds that sought political and economic independence from local nobles. (p. 358)

conciliarists People who believed that the authority in the Roman Church should rest in a general council composed of clergy, theologians, and laypeople, rather than in the pope alone. (p. 340)

confraternities Voluntary lay groups organized by occupation, devotional preference, neighborhood, or charitable activity. (p. 341)

consuls Primary executives in the Roman Republic, elected for one-year terms, who commanded the army in battle, administered state business, and supervised financial affairs. (p. 125)

courts Magnificent households and palaces where signori and other rulers lived, conducted business, and supported the arts. (p. 360)

Covenant An agreement that the Hebrews believed to exist between themselves and Yahweh, in which he would consider them his chosen people if they worshipped him as their only god. (p. 41)

craft guild A band of producers in a town that regulated most aspects of production of a good in that town. (p. 299)

Crusades Wars sponsored by the papacy for the recovery of Jerusalem and surrounding territories from the Muslims in the late eleventh to the late thirteenth centuries. (p. 274)

cuneiform Sumerian form of writing; the term describes the wedge-shaped marks made by a stylus. (p. 13)

debate about women Debate among writers and thinkers in the Renaissance about women's qualities and proper role in society. (p. 380)

Delian League A military alliance led by Athens aimed at protecting the Aegean Islands, liberating Ionia from Persian rule, and keeping the Persians out of Greece. (p. 73)

democracy A type of Greek government in which all citizens administered the workings of government. (p. 68)

G-1

diocese An administrative unit in the later Roman Empire; adopted by the Christian Church as the territory under the authority of a bishop. (p. 186)

Domesday Book A general inquiry about the wealth of his lands ordered by William of Normandy. (p. 252)

English Peasants' Revolt Revolt by English peasants in 1381 in response to changing economic conditions. (p. 346)

Epicureanism A system of philosophy based on the teachings of Epicurus, who viewed a life of contentment, free from fear and suffering, as the greatest good. (p. 110)

excommunication A penalty used by the Christian Church that meant being cut off from the sacraments and all Christian worship. (p. 265)

Fertile Crescent An area of mild climate and abundant wild grain where agriculture first developed, in present-day Lebanon, Israel, Jordan, Turkey, and Iraq. (p. 7)

feudalism A term devised by later scholars to describe the political system in which a vassal was generally given a piece of land in return for his loyalty. (p. 245)

fief A piece of land granted by a feudal lord to a vassal in return for service and loyalty. (p. 245)

First Triumvirate The name later given to an informal political alliance among Caesar, Crassus, and Pompey in which they agreed to advance one another's interests. (p. 145)

"five good emperors" The five Roman emperors (Nerva, Trajan, Hadrian, Antoninus Pius, and Marcus Aurelius) of the second century C.E. whose reigns were relatively prosperous and stable. (p. 165)

Five Pillars of Islam The five practices Muslims must fulfill according to the shari'a, or sacred law, including the profession of faith, prayer, fasting, giving alms to the poor, and pilgrimage to Mecca. (p. 222)

flagellants People who believed that the plague was God's punishment for sin and sought to do penance by flagellating (whipping) themselves. (p. 332)

friars Men belonging to certain religious orders who lived not in monasteries but out in the world. (p. 272)

Gothic An architectural style typified by pointed arches and large stained-glass windows. (p. 316)

Great Famine (Europe) A terrible famine in 1315–1322 that hit much of Europe after a period of climate change. (p. 324)

Great Schism The division, or split, in church leadership from 1378 to 1417 when there were two, then three, popes. (p. 339)

gynaeceum Women's quarters at the back of an Athenian house where the women of the family and the female slaves worked, ate, and slept. (p. 81)

Hammurabi's law code A proclamation issued by Babylonian king Hammurabi to establish laws regulating many aspects of life. (p. 20)

Hanseatic League A mercantile association of towns begun in northern Europe that allowed for mutual protection and trading rights. (p. 302)

Hellenistic A term that literally means "like the Greek," used to describe the period after the death of Alexander the Great, when Greek culture spread. (p. 97)

Hellenization The spread of Greek ideas, culture, and traditions to non-Greek groups across a wide area. (p. 98)

helots Unfree residents of Sparta forced to work state lands. (p. 70)

heresy A religious practice or belief judged unacceptable by church officials. (p. 179)

Holy Roman Empire The loose confederation of principalities, duchies, cities, bishoprics, and other types of regional governments stretching from Denmark to Rome and from Burgundy to Poland. (p. 255)

hoplites Heavily armed citizens who served as infantrymen and fought to defend the polis. (p. 68)

humanism A program of study designed by Italians that emphasized the critical study of Latin and Greek literature with the goal of understanding human nature. (p. 363)

Hundred Years' War A war between England and France from 1337 to 1453, with political and economic causes and consequences. (p. 332)

imperator Title given to a Roman general after a major victory that came to mean "emperor." (p. 154)

indulgence A document issued by the Catholic Church lessening penance or time in purgatory, widely believed to bring forgiveness of all sins. (p. 274)

infidel A disparaging term used for a person who does not believe in a particular religion. (p. 225)

Iron Age Period beginning about 1100 B.C.E., when iron became the most important material for tools and weapons. (p. 36)

Jacquerie A massive uprising by French peasants in 1358 protesting heavy taxation. (p. 343)

Kievan Rus A confederation of Slavic territories, with its capital at Kiev, ruled by descendants of the Vikings. (p. 243)

Kush Kingdom in Nubia that adopted hieroglyphics and pyramids, and later conquered Egypt. (p. 37)

latifundia Huge agricultural estates owned by wealthy absentee landowners and worked by slaves. (p. 140)

ma'at The Egyptian belief in a cosmic harmony that embraced truth, justice, and moral integrity; it gave the kings the right and duty to govern. (p. 23)

Magna Carta A peace treaty intended to redress the grievances that particular groups had against King John; it was later viewed as the source of English rights and liberty more generally. (p. 259)

manorialism A system in which peasant residents of manors, or farming villages, provided work and goods for their lord in exchange for protection. (p. 246)

manumission The freeing of individual slaves by their masters. (p. 135)

merchant guild A band of merchants in a town that prohibited nonmembers from trading in that town. (p. 299)

Messiah In Jewish belief, a savior who would bring a period of peace and happiness for Jews. (p. 176)

Minoan A wealthy and vibrant culture on Crete from around 1900 B.C.E. to 1450 B.C.E., ruled by a king with a large palace at Knossos. (p. 63)

Mycenaean A Bronze Age culture that flourished in Greece from about 1650 B.C.E. to 1100 B.C.E., building fortified palaces and cities. (p. 64)

mystery religions Belief systems that were characterized by secret doctrines, rituals of initiation, and sometimes the promise of rebirth or an afterlife. (p. 87)

natural law A Stoic concept that a single law that was part of the natural order of life governed all people. (p. 111)

Neolithic era The period after 9000 B.C.E., when people developed agriculture, domesticated animals, and used tools made of stone and wood. (p. 6)

New Christians A term for Jews and Muslims in the Iberian Peninsula who accepted Christianity; in many cases they included Christians whose families had converted centuries earlier. (p. 386)

oligarchy A type of Greek government in which citizens who owned a certain amount of property ruled. (p. 68)

open-field system System in which the arable land of a manor was divided into two or three fields without hedges or fences to mark individual holdings. (p. 287)

Orthodox Church Eastern Christian Church in the Byzantine Empire. (p. 214)

pagan Originally referring to those who lived in the countryside, it came to mean those who practiced religions other than Judaism or Christianity. (p. 176)

Paleolithic era The period of human history up to about 9000 B.C.E., when tools were made from stone and bone and people gained their food through foraging. (p. 5)

pastoralism An economic system based on herding flocks of goats, sheep, cattle, or other animals beneficial to humans. (p. 8)

paterfamilias The oldest dominant male of the family, who held great power over the lives of family members. (p. 133)

patriarchy A society in which most power is held by older adult men, especially those from the elite groups. (p. 9)

patricians The Roman hereditary aristocracy, who held most of the political power in the republic. (p. 128)

patronage Financial support of writers and artists by cities, groups, and individuals, often to produce specific works or works in specific styles. (p. 358)

patron-client system An informal system of patronage in which free men promised their votes to a more powerful man in exchange for his help in legal or other matters. (p. 130)

pax Romana The "Roman peace," a period during the first and second centuries C.E. of political stability and relative peace. (p. 159)

Petrine Doctrine A doctrine stating that the popes (the bishops of Rome) were the successors of Saint Peter and therefore heirs to his highest level of authority as chief of the apostles. (p. 191)

pharaoh The title given to the king of Egypt in the New Kingdom, from a word that meant "great house." (p. 23)

Phoenicians Seafaring people from Canaan who traded and founded colonies throughout the Mediterranean and spread the phonetic alphabet. (p. 38)

Platonic ideals In Plato's thought, the eternal unchanging ideal forms that are the essence of true reality. (p. 88)

plebeians The common people of Rome, who were free but had few of the patricians' advantages. (p. 128)

polis Generally translated as "city-state," it was the basic political and institutional unit of Greece in the Hellenic period. (p. 66)

polytheism The worship of many gods and goddesses. (p. 11)

popolo Disenfranchised common people in Italian cities who resented their exclusion from power. (p. 359)

Praetorians Imperial bodyguard created by Augustus. (p. 164)

primogeniture An inheritance system in which the oldest son inherits all land and noble titles. (p. 253)

principate Official title of Augustus's form of government, taken from *princeps*, meaning "first citizen." (p. 154)

Punic Wars A series of three wars between Rome and Carthage in which Rome emerged the victor. (p. 130)

Qur'an The sacred book of Islam. (p. 220)

reconquista The Christian term for the conquest of Muslim territories in the Iberian Peninsula by Christian forces. (p. 258)

regular clergy Men and women who lived in monastic houses and followed sets of rules, first those of Benedict and later those written by other individuals. (p. 191)

relics Bones, articles of clothing, or other objects associated with the life of a saint. (p. 209)

religious orders Groups of monastic houses following a particular rule. (p. 269)

Renaissance A French word meaning "rebirth," used to describe the rebirth of the culture of classical antiquity in Italy during the fourteenth to sixteenth centuries. (p. 358)

representative assemblies Deliberative meetings of lords and wealthy urban residents that flourished in many European countries between 1250 and 1450. (p. 338)

Roma et Augustus Patriotic cult encouraged by Augustus and later emperors in which the good of Rome and the good of the emperor were linked. (p. 158)

Romanesque An architectural style with rounded arches and small windows. (p. 316)

runic alphabet Writing system developed in some barbarian groups that helps give a more accurate picture of barbarian society. (p. 195)

sacraments Certain rituals defined by the church in which God bestows benefits on the believer through grace. (p. 195)

satraps Administrators in the Persian Empire who controlled local government, collected taxes, heard legal cases, and maintained order. (p. 54)

Scholastics University professors in the Middle Ages who developed a method of thinking, reasoning, and writing in which questions were raised and authorities cited on both sides of a question. (p. 311)

Second Triumvirate A formal agreement in 43 B.C.E. among Octavian, Mark Antony, and Lepidus to defeat Caesar's murderers. (p. 149)

secular clergy Priests and bishops who staffed churches where people worshipped and who were not cut off from the world. (p. 192)

Senate The assembly that was the main institution of power in the Roman Republic, originally composed only of aristocrats. (p. 125)

serfs Peasants bound to the land by a relationship with a manorial lord. (p. 246)

signori Government by one-man rule in Italian cities such as Milan; also refers to these rulers. (p. 360)

simony The buying and selling of church offices, a policy that was officially prohibited but often practiced. (p. 265)

Socratic method A method of inquiry used by Socrates based on asking questions, through which participants developed their critical thinking skills and explored ethical issues. (p. 88)

Sophists A group of thinkers in fifth-century-B.C.E. Athens who applied philosophical speculation to politics and language and were accused of deceit. (p. 88)

Statute of Kilkenny Law issued in 1366 that discriminated against the Irish, forbidding marriage between the English and the Irish, requiring the use of the English language, and denying the Irish access to ecclesiastical offices. (p. 351)

Stoicism A philosophy, based on the ideas of Zeno, that people could be happy only when living in accordance with nature and accepting whatever happened. (p. 110)

Struggle of the Orders A conflict in which the plebeians sought political representation and safeguards against patrician domination. (p. 129)

sumptuary laws Laws that regulated the value and style of clothing and jewelry that various social groups could wear as well as the amount they could spend on celebrations. (p. 307)

tetrarchy Diocletian's four-part division of the Roman Empire. (p. 186)

Torah The first five books of the Hebrew Bible, containing the most important legal and ethical Hebrew texts; later became part of the Christian Old Testament. (p. 41)

Treaty of Verdun Treaty signed in 843 by Charlemagne's grandsons dividing the Carolingian Empire into three parts and setting the pattern for political boundaries in Europe still in use today. (p. 237)

tribunes Plebeian-elected officials; tribunes brought plebeian grievances to the Senate for resolution and protected plebeians from the arbitrary conduct of patrician magistrates. (p. 129)

troubadours Poets who wrote and sang lyric verses celebrating love, desire, beauty, and gallantry. (p. 315)

tyranny Rule by one man who took over an existing government, generally by using his wealth to gain a political following. (p. 68)

vassal A warrior who swore loyalty and service to a noble in exchange for land, protection, and support. (p. 245)

vernacular literature Writings in the author's local dialect, that is, in the everyday language of the region. (p. 313)

virtù The quality of being able to shape the world according to one's own will. (p. 363)

wergeld Compensatory payment for death or injury set in many barbarian law codes. (p. 200)

Yahweh The sole god in Hebrew monotheism; later anglicized as Jehovah. (p. 40)

Zoroastrianism Religion based on the ideas of Zoroaster that stressed devotion to the god Ahuramazda alone, and that emphasized the individual's responsibility to choose between good and evil. (p. 55)

Index

I-16　　Index

Timeline | A History of Western Society: A Brief Overview

	Government	Society and Economy
3000 B.C.E.	Emergence of first cities in Mesopotamia, ca. 3800 Unification of Egypt; Archaic Period, ca. 3100–2600 Old Kingdom of Egypt, ca. 2660–2180 Dominance of Akkadian empire in Mesopotamia, ca. 2331–2200 Middle Kingdom in Egypt, ca. 2080–1640	Neolithic peoples rely on settled agriculture, while others pursue nomadic life, ca. 7000–3000 Expansion of Mesopotamian trade and culture into the modern Middle East and Turkey, ca. 2600
2000 B.C.E.	Babylonian empire, ca. 2000–1595 Code of Hammurabi, ca. 1755 Hyksos invade Egypt, ca. 1640–1570 Hittite Empire, ca. 1600–1200 New Kingdom in Egypt, ca. 1570–1075	First wave of Indo-European migrants, by ca. 2000 Extended commerce in Egypt, by ca. 2000 Horses introduced into Asia and North Africa, by ca. 2500
1500 B.C.E.	Third Intermediate Period in Egypt, ca. 1070–712 Unified Hebrew kingdom under Saul, David, and Solomon, ca. 1025–925	Use of iron increases in western Asia, by ca. 1300–1100 Second wave of Indo-European migrants, by ca. 1200 "Dark Age" in Greece, ca. 1100–800
1000 B.C.E.	Hebrew kingdom divided into Israel and Judah, 925 Assyrian Empire, ca. 900–612 Phoenicians found Carthage, 813 Kingdom of Kush conquers and reunifies Egypt, ca. 800–700 Roman monarchy, ca. 753–509 Medes conquers Persia, 710 Babylon wins independence from Assyria, 626 Dracon issues law code at Athens, 621 Solon's reforms at Athens, ca. 594 Cyrus the Great conquers Medes, founds Persian Empire, 550 Persians complete conquest of ancient Near East, 521–464 Reforms of Cleisthenes in Athens, 508	Phoenician seafaring and trading in the Mediterranean, ca. 900–550 First Olympic games, 776 Concentration of landed wealth in Greece, ca. 750–600 Greek overseas expansion, ca. 750–550 Beginning of coinage in western Asia, ca. 640
500 B.C.E.	Persian wars, 499–479 Struggle of the Orders in Rome, ca. 494–287 Growth of the Athenian Empire, 478–431 Peloponnesian War, 431–404 Rome captures Veii, 396 Gauls sack Rome, 387 Roman expansion in Italy, 390–290 Philip II of Macedonia conquers Greece, 338 Conquests of Alexander the Great, 334–324 Punic Wars, 264–146 Reforms of the Gracchi, 133–121	Growth of Hellenistic trade and cities, ca. 330–100 Beginning of Roman silver coinage, 269 Growth of slavery, decline of small farmers in Rome, ca. 250–100 Agrarian reforms of the Gracchi, 133–121

Religion and Philosophy	Science and Technology	Arts and Letters
Growth of anthropomorphic religion in Mesopotamia, ca. 3000–2000	Development of wheeled transport in Mesopotamia, by ca. 3000	Cuneiform and hieroglyphic writing, ca. 3200
Emergence of Egyptian polytheism and belief in personal immortality, ca. 2660	Use of widespread irrigation in Mesopotamia and Egypt, ca. 3000	
Spread of Mesopotamian and Egyptian religious ideas as far north as modern Turkey and as far south as central Africa, ca. 2600	Construction of Stonehenge monument in England, ca. 2500	
	Construction of first pyramid in Egypt, ca. 2600	
Emergence of Hebrew monotheism, ca. 1700	Construction of first ziggurats in Mesopotamia, ca. 2100	*Epic of Gilgamesh*, ca. 1900
Mixture of Hittite and Near Eastern religious beliefs, ca. 1595	Widespread use of bronze in ancient Near East, ca. 1900	
	Babylonian mathematical advances, ca. 1800	
Exodus of the Hebrews from Egypt into Palestine, ca. 1300–1200	Hittites introduce iron technology, ca. 1400	Phoenicians develop alphabet, ca. 1400
		Naturalistic art in Egypt under Akhenaten, 1367–1350
		Egyptian *Book of the Dead*, ca. 1300
Era of the prophets in Israel, ca. 1100–500	Babylonian astronomical advances, ca. 750–400	Homer, traditional author of *Iliad* and *Odyssey*, ca. 800
Beginning of the Hebrew Bible, ca. 950–800	Construction of Parthenon in Athens begins, 447	Hesiod, author of *Theogony* and *Works and Days*, ca. 800
Intermixture of Etruscan and Roman religious cults, ca. 753–509		Aeschylus, first significant Athenian tragedian, ca. 525–456
Growing popularity of local Greek religious cults, ca. 700 B.C.E.–337 C.E.		
Introduction of Zoroastrianism, ca. 600		
Babylonian Captivity of the Hebrews, 587–538		
Pre-Socratic philosophers, ca. 500–400	Hippocrates, formal founder of medicine, ca. 430	Sophocles, tragedian whose plays explore moral and political problems, ca. 496–406
Socrates executed, 399	Building of the Via Appia begins, 312	
Plato, student of Socrates, 427–347	Aristarchos of Samos, advances in astronomy, ca. 310–230	Herodotus, "father of history," ca. 485–425
Diogenes, leading proponent of cynicism, ca. 412–323	Euclid codifies geometry, ca. 300	Euripides, most personal of the Athenian tragedians, ca. 480–406
Aristotle, student of Plato, 384–322	Herophilus, discoveries in medicine, ca. 300–250	Thucydides, historian of Peloponnesian War, ca. 460–440
Epicurus, founder of Epicurean philosophy, 340–270	Archimedes, works on physics and hydrologics, ca. 287–212	Aristophanes, greatest Athenian comic playwright, ca. 445–386
Zeno, founder of Stoic philosophy, 335–262		
Emergence of Mithraism, ca. 300		
Greek cults brought to Rome, ca. 200		
Spread of Hellenistic mystery religions, ca. 200–100		

Government	Society and Economy
100 B.C.E. Dictatorship of Sulla, 88–79 B.C.E. Civil war in Rome, 88–31 B.C.E. Dictatorship of Caesar, 45–44 B.C.E. Principate of Augustus, 31 B.C.E.–14 C.E. "Five Good Emperors" of Rome, 96–180 C.E. "Barracks Emperors'" civil war, 235–284 C.E.	Reform of the Roman calendar, 46 B.C.E. "Golden age" of Roman prosperity and vast increase in trade, 96–180 C.E. Growth of serfdom in Roman Empire, ca. 200–500 C.E. Economic contraction in Roman Empire, ca. 235–284 C.E.
300 C.E. Constantine removes capital of Roman Empire to Constantinople, ca. 315 Visigoths defeat Roman army at Adrianople, 378 Bishop Ambrose asserts church's independence from the state, 380 Odoacer deposes last Roman emperor in the West, 476 Clovis issues Salic law of the Franks, ca. 490	Barbarian migrations throughout western and northern Europe, ca. 378–600
500 Law code of Justinian, 529 Spread of Islam across Arabia, the Mediterranean region, Spain, North Africa, and Asia as far as India, ca. 630–733	Gallo-Roman aristocracy intermarries with Germanic chieftains, ca. 500–700 Decline of towns and trade in the West; agrarian economy predominates, ca. 500–1800
700 Charles Martel defeats Muslims at Tours, 732 Pippin III anointed king of the Franks, 754 Charlemagne secures Frankish crown, r. 768–814	Height of Muslim commercial activity with western Europe, ca. 700–1300
800 Imperial coronation of Charlemagne, Christmas 800 Treaty of Verdun divides Carolingian kingdom, 843 Viking, Magyar, and Muslim invasions, ca. 850–1000 Establishment of Kievan Rus, ca. 900	Invasions and unstable conditions lead to increase of serfdom in western Europe, ca. 800–900 Height of Byzantine commerce and industry, ca. 800–1000
1000 Seljuk Turks conquer Muslim Baghdad, 1055 Norman conquest of England, 1066 Penance of Henry IV at Canossa, 1077	Decline of Byzantine free peasantry, ca. 1025–1100 Growth of towns and trade in the West, ca. 1050–1300 *Domesday Book* in England, 1086
1100 Henry I of England, r. 1100–1135 Louis VI of France, r. 1108–1137 Frederick I of Germany, r. 1152–1190 Henry II of England, r. 1154–1189	Henry I of England establishes the Exchequer, 1130 Beginnings of the Hanseatic League, 1159

Religion and Philosophy	Science and Technology	Arts and Letters
Mithraism spreads to Rome, 27 B.C.E.–270 C.E. Life of Jesus, ca. 3 B.C.E.–29 C.E.	Engineering advances in Rome, ca. 100 B.C.E.–180 C.E.	Flowering of Latin literature: Virgil, 70–19 B.C.E.; Livy, ca. 59 B.C.E.–17 C.E.; Ovid, 43 B.C.E.–17 C.E.
Constantine legalizes Christianity, 312 Theodosius declares Christianity the official state religion, 380 Donatist heretical movement at its height, ca. 400 St. Augustine, *Confessions*, ca. 390; *The City of God*, ca. 425 Clovis adopts Roman Christianity, 496	Construction of Arch of Constantine, ca. 315	St. Jerome publishes Latin *Vulgate*, late 4th c. Byzantines preserve Greco-Roman culture, ca. 400–1000
Rule of St. Benedict, 529 Life of the Prophet Muhammad, ca. 571–632 Pope Gregory the Great publishes *Dialogues*, *Pastoral Care*, *Moralia*, 590–604 Monasteries established in Anglo-Saxon England, ca. 600–700 Publication of the Qur'an, 651 Synod of Whitby, 664	Using watermills, Benedictine monks exploit energy of fast-flowing rivers and streams, by 600 Heavy plow and improved harness facilitate use of multiple-ox teams; harrow widely used in northern Europe, by 600 Byzantines successfully use "Greek fire" in naval combat against Arab fleets attacking Constantinople, 673, 717	Boethius, *The Consolation of Philosophy*, ca. 520 Justinian constructs church of Santa Sophia, 532–537
Bede, *Ecclesiastical History of the English Nation*, ca. 700 Missionary work of St. Boniface in Germany, ca. 710–750 Iconoclastic controversy in Byzantine Empire, 726–843 Pippin III donates Papal States to the papacy, 756		Lindisfarne Gospel Book, ca. 700 *Beowulf*, ca. 700 Carolingian Renaissance, ca. 780–850
Foundation of abbey of Cluny, 909 Byzantine conversion of Russia, late 10th c.	Stirrup and nailed horseshoes become widespread in combat, 900–1000 Paper (invented in China, ca. 150) enters Europe through Muslim Spain, ca. 900–1000	Byzantines develop Cyrillic script, late 10th c.
Schism between Roman and Greek Orthodox churches, 1054 Lateran Council restricts election of pope to College of Cardinals, 1059 Pope Gregory VII, 1073–1085 Theologian Peter Abelard, 1079–1142 First Crusade, 1095–1099 Founding of Cistercian order, 1098	Arab conquests bring new irrigation methods, cotton cultivation, and manufacture to Spain, Sicily, southern Italy, by 1000 Avicenna, Arab scientist, d. 1037	Muslim musicians introduce lute, rebec (stringed instruments, ancestors of violin), ca. 1000 Romanesque style in architecture and art, ca. 1000–1200 *Song of Roland*, ca. 1095
Universities begin, ca. 1100–1300 Concordat of Worms ends investiture controversy, 1122 Height of Cistercian monasticism, 1125–1175	Europeans, copying Muslim and Byzantine models, construct castles with rounded towers and crenellated walls, by 1100	Troubadour poetry, especially of Chrétien de Troyes, circulates widely, ca. 1100–1200 *Rubaiyat of Umar Khayyam*, ca. 1120 Dedication of abbey church of Saint-Denis launches Gothic style, 1144

	Government	Society and Economy
1100 (CONT.)	Thomas Becket, archbishop of Canterbury, murdered 1170 Philip Augustus of France, r. 1180–1223	
1200	Spanish victory over Muslims at Las Navas de Tolosa, 1212 Frederick II of Germany and Sicily, r. 1212–1250 Magna Carta, charter of English political and civil liberties, 1215 Louis IX of France, r. 1226–1270 Mongols end Abbasid caliphate, 1258 Edward I of England, r. 1272–1307 Philip IV (the Fair) of France, r. 1285–1314	European revival, growth of towns; agricultural expansion leads to population growth, ca. 1200–1300 Crusaders capture Constantinople (Fourth Crusade) and spur Venetian economy, 1204
1300	Philip IV orders arrest of Pope Boniface at Anagni, 1303 Hundred Years' War between England and France, 1337–1453 Political disorder in Germany, ca. 1350–1450 Merchant oligarchies or despots rule Italian city-states, ca. 1350–1550	"Little ice age," European economic depression, ca. 1300–1450 Black Death appears ca. 1347; returns intermittently until ca. 1720 Height of the Hanseatic League, 1350–1450 Peasant and working-class revolts: Flanders, 1328; France, 1358; Florence, 1378; England, 1381
1400	Joan of Arc rallies French monarchy, 1429–1431 Medici domination of Florence begins, 1434 Princes in Germany consolidate power, ca. 1450–1500 Ottoman Turks under Mahomet II capture Constantinople, May 1453 Wars of the Roses in England, 1455–1471 Establishment of the Inquisition in Spain, 1478 Ferdinand and Isabella complete reconquista in Spain, 1492 French invasion of Italy, 1494	Population decline, peasants' revolts, high labor costs contribute to decline of serfdom in western Europe, ca. 1400–1650 Flow of Balkan slaves into eastern Mediterranean, of African slaves into Iberia and Italy, ca. 1400–1500 Christopher Columbus reaches the Americas, 1492 Portuguese gain control of East Indian spice trade, 1498–1511
1500	Charles V, Holy Roman emperor, 1519–1556 Habsburg-Valois Wars, 1521–1559 Philip II of Spain, r. 1556–1598 Revolt of the Netherlands, 1566–1598 St. Bartholomew's Day massacre in France, 1572 English defeat of the Spanish Armada, 1588 Henry IV of France issues Edict of Nantes, 1598	Consolidation of serfdom in eastern Europe, ca. 1500–1650 Balboa discovers the Pacific, 1513 Magellan's crew circumnavigates the earth, 1519–1522 Spain and Portugal gain control of regions of Central and South America, ca. 1520–1550 Peasants' Revolt in Germany, 1524–1525 "Time of Troubles" in Russia, 1598–1613

Religion and Philosophy	Science and Technology	Arts and Letters
Aristotle's works translated into Latin, ca. 1140–1260 Third Crusade, 1189–1192 Pope Innocent III, height of the medieval papacy, 1198–1216	Underground pipes with running water and indoor latrines installed in some monasteries, such as Clairvaux and Canterbury Cathedral Priory, by 1100; elsewhere rare until 1800 Windmill invented, ca. 1180	
Founding of the Franciscan order, 1210 Fourth Lateran Council accepts seven sacraments, 1215 Founding of Dominican order, 1216 Thomas Aquinas, height of scholasticism, 1225–1274	*Notebooks* of architect Villard de Honnecourt, a major source for Gothic engineering, ca. 1250 Development of double-entry bookkeeping in Florence and Genoa, ca. 1250–1340 Venetians purchase secrets of glass manufacture from Syria, 1277 Mechanical clock invented, ca. 1290	*Parzifal, Roman de la rose, King Arthur and the Round Table* celebrate virtues of knighthood and chivalry, ca. 1200–1300 Height of Gothic style, ca. 1225–1300
Pope Boniface VIII declares all Christians subject to the pope in *Unam Sanctam*, 1302 Babylonian Captivity of the papacy, 1309–1376 Theologian John Wyclif, ca. 1330–1384 Great Schism in the papacy, 1378–1417	Edward III of England uses cannon in siege of Calais, 1346 Clocks in general use throughout Europe, by 1400	Paintings of Giotto mark emergence of Renaissance movement in the arts, ca. 1305–1337 Dante, *Divine Comedy*, ca. 1310 Petrarch develops ideas of humanism, ca. 1350 Boccaccio, *The Decameron*, ca. 1350 Jan van Eyck, Flemish painter, 1366–1441 Brunelleschi, Florentine architect, 1377–1446 Chaucer, *Canterbury Tales*, ca. 1387–1400
Council of Constance ends the schism in the papacy, 1414–1418 Pragmatic Sanction of Bourges affirms special rights of French crown over French church, 1438 Expulsion of Jews from Spain, 1492	Water-powered blast furnaces operative in Sweden, Austria, the Rhine Valley, Liège, ca. 1400 Leonardo Fibonacci's *Liber Abaci* popularizes use of Hindu-Arabic numerals, important in rise of Western science, 1402 Paris and largest Italian cities pave streets, making street cleaning possible, ca. 1450 European printing and movable type, ca. 1450	Height of Renaissance movement: Masaccio, 1401–1428; Botticelli, 1444–1510; Leonardo da Vinci, 1452–1519; Albrecht Dürer, 1471–1528; Michelangelo, 1475–1564; Raphael, 1483–1520
Machiavelli, *The Prince*, 1513 More, *Utopia*, 1516 Luther, *Ninety-five Theses*, 1517 Henry VIII of England breaks with Rome, 1532–1534 Merici establishes Ursuline order for education of women, 1535 Loyola establishes Society of Jesus, 1540 Calvin establishes theocracy in Geneva, 1541 Council of Trent shapes essential character of Catholicism until the 1960s, 1545–1563 Peace of Augsburg, official recognition of Lutheranism, 1555	Scientific revolution in western Europe, ca. 1540–1690: Copernicus, *On the Revolutions of the Heavenly Bodies*, 1543; Galileo, 1564–1642; Kepler, 1571–1630; Harvey, 1578–1657	Erasmus, *The Praise of Folly*, 1509 Castiglione, *The Courtier*, 1528 Baroque movement in arts, ca. 1550–1725: Rubens, 1577–1640; Velasquez, 1599–1660 Shakespeare, West's most enduring and influential playwright, 1564–1616 Montaigne, *Essays*, 1598

	Government	Society and Economy
1600	Thirty Years' War begins, 1618 Richelieu dominates French government, 1624–1643 Frederick William, Elector of Brandenburg, r. 1640–1688 English Civil War, 1642–1649 Louis XIV, r. 1643–1715 Peace of Westphalia ends the Thirty Years' War, 1648 The Fronde in France, 1648–1660	Chartering of British East India Company, 1600 English Poor Law, 1601 Chartering of Dutch East India Company, 1602 Height of Dutch commercial activity, ca. 1630–1665
1650	Anglo-Dutch wars, 1652–1674 Protectorate in England, 1653–1658 Leopold I, Habsburg emperor, r. 1658–1705 English monarchy restored, 1660 Ottoman siege of Vienna, 1683 Glorious Revolution in England, 1688–1689 Peter the Great of Russia, r. 1689–1725	Height of mercantilism in Europe, ca. 1650–1750 Agricultural revolution in Europe, ca. 1650–1850 Principle of peasants' hereditary subjugation to their lords affirmed in Prussia, 1653 Colbert's economic reforms in France, ca. 1663–1683 Cossack revolt in Russia, 1670–1671
1700	War of the Spanish Succession, 1701–1713 Peace of Utrecht redraws political boundaries of Europe, 1713 Frederick William I of Prussia, r. 1713–1740 Louis XV of France, r. 1715–1774 Maria Theresa of Austria, r. 1740–1780 Frederick the Great of Prussia, r. 1740–1786	Foundation of St. Petersburg, 1701 Last appearance of bubonic plague in western Europe, ca. 1720 Growth of European population, ca. 1720–1789 Enclosure movement in England, ca. 1730–1830
1750	Seven Years' War, 1756–1763 Catherine the Great of Russia, r. 1762–1796 Partition of Poland, 1772–1795 Louis XVI of France, r. 1774–1792 American Revolution, 1775–1783 French Revolution, 1789–1799 Slave insurrection in Saint-Domingue, 1791	Growth of illegitimate births in Europe, ca. 1750–1850 Industrial Revolution in western Europe, ca. 1780–1850 Serfdom abolished in France, 1789
1800	Napoleonic era, 1799–1815 Haitian republic declares independence, 1804 Congress of Vienna re-establishes political power after defeat of Napoleon, 1814–1815 Greece wins independence from Ottoman Empire, 1830 French conquest of Algeria, 1830 Revolution in France, 1830 Great Britain: Reform Bill of 1832; Poor Law reform, 1834; Chartists, repeal of Corn Laws, 1838–1848 Revolutions in Europe, 1848	British takeover of India complete, 1805 British slave trade abolished, 1807 German Zollverein founded, 1834 European capitalists begin large-scale foreign investment, 1840s Great Famine in Ireland, 1845–1851 First public health law in Britain, 1848

Religion and Philosophy	Science and Technology	Arts and Letters
Huguenot revolt in France, 1625	Further development of scientific method: Bacon, *The Advancement of Learning*, 1605; Descartes, *Discourse on Method*, 1637	Cervantes, *Don Quixote*, 1605, 1615 Flourishing of French theater: Molière, 1622–1673; Racine, 1639–1699 Golden age of Dutch culture, ca. 1625–1675: Rembrandt van Rijn, 1606–1669; Vermeer, 1632–1675
Social contract theory: Hobbes, *Leviathan*, 1651; Locke, *Second Treatise on Civil Government*, 1690 Patriarch Nikon's reforms split Russian Orthodox Church, 1652 Test Act in England excludes Roman Catholics from public office, 1673 Revocation of Edict of Nantes, 1685 James II tries to restore Catholicism as state religion, 1685–1688	Tull (1674–1741) encourages innovation in English agriculture Newton, *Principia Mathematica*, 1687	Construction of baroque palaces and remodeling of capital cities, central and eastern Europe, ca. 1650–1725 Bach, great late baroque German composer, 1685–1750 Enlightenment begins, ca. 1690: Fontenelle, *Conversations on the Plurality of Worlds*, 1686; Voltaire, French philosopher and writer whose work epitomizes Enlightenment, 1694–1778 Pierre Bayle, *Historical and Critical Dictionary*, 1697
Wesley, founder of Methodism, 1703–1791 Montesquieu, *The Spirit of Laws*, 1748	Newcomen develops steam engine, 1705 Charles Townsend introduces four-year crop rotation, 1730	
Hume, *The Natural History of Religion*, 1755 Rousseau, *The Social Contract* and *Emile*, 1762 Fourier, French utopian socialist, 1772–1837 Papacy dissolves Jesuits, 1773 Smith, *The Wealth of Nations*, 1776 Church reforms of Joseph II in Austria, 1780s Kant, *What Is Enlightenment?*, 1784 Reorganization of church in France, 1790s Wollstonecraft, *A Vindication of the Rights of Woman*, 1792 Malthus, *Essay on the Principle of Population*, 1798	Hargreaves's spinning jenny, ca. 1765 Arkwright's water frame, ca. 1765 Watt's steam engine promotes industrial breakthroughs, 1780s Jenner's smallpox vaccine, 1796	*Encyclopedia*, edited by Diderot and d'Alembert, published 1751–1765 Classical style in music, ca. 1770–1830: Mozart, 1756–1791; Beethoven, 1770–1827 Wordsworth, English romantic poet, 1770–1850 Romanticism in art and literature, ca. 1790–1850
Napoleon signs Concordat with Pope Pius VII regulating Catholic Church in France, 1801 Spencer, Social Darwinist, 1820–1903 Comte, *System of Positive Philosophy*, 1830–1842 Height of French utopian socialism, 1830s–1840s List, *National System of Political Economy*, 1841 Nietzsche, radical and highly influential German philosopher, 1844–1900 Marx, *Communist Manifesto*, 1848	First railroad, Great Britain, 1825 Faraday studies electromagnetism, 1830–1840s	Staël, *On Germany*, 1810 Balzac, *The Human Comedy*, 1829–1841 Delacroix, *Liberty Leading the People*, 1830 Hugo, *The Hunchback of Notre Dame*, 1831

	Government	Society and Economy
1850	Second Empire in France, 1852–1870 Crimean War, 1853–1856 Britain crushes Great Rebellion in India, 1857–1858 Unification of Italy, 1859–1870 U.S. Civil War, 1861–1865 Bismarck leads Germany, 1862–1890 Unification of Germany, 1864–1871 Britain's Second Reform Bill, 1867 Third Republic in France, 1870–1940	Crédit Mobilier founded in France, 1852 Japan opened to European influence, 1853 Russian serfs emancipated, 1861 First Socialist International, 1864–1871
1875	Congress of Berlin, 1878 European "scramble for Africa," 1880–1900 Britain's Third Reform Bill, 1884 Dreyfus affair in France, 1894–1899 Spanish-American War, 1898 South African War, 1899–1902	Full property rights for women in Great Britain, 1882 Second Industrial Revolution; birthrate steadily declines in Europe, ca. 1880–1913 Social welfare legislation, Germany, 1883–1889 Second Socialist International, 1889–1914 Witte directs modernization of Russian economy, 1892–1899
1900	Russo-Japanese War, 1904–1905 Revolution in Russia, 1905 Balkan wars, 1912–1913	Women's suffrage movement, England, ca. 1900–1914 Social welfare legislation, France, 1904, 1910; Great Britain, 1906–1914 Agrarian reforms in Russia, 1907–1912
1914	World War I, 1914–1918 Armenian genocide, 1915 Easter Rebellion, 1916 U.S. declares war on Germany, 1917 Bolshevik Revolution, 1917–1918 Treaty of Versailles, World War I peace settlement, 1919	Planned economics in Europe, 1914 Auxiliary Service Law in Germany, 1916 Bread riots in Russia, March 1917
1920	Mussolini seizes power in Italy, 1922 Stalin comes to power in U.S.S.R., 1927 Hitler gains power in Germany, 1933 Rome-Berlin Axis, 1936 Nazi-Soviet Non-Aggression Pact, 1939 World War II, 1939–1945	New Economic Policy in U.S.S.R., 1921 Dawes Plan for reparations and recovery, 1924 Great Depression, 1929–1939 Rapid industrialization in U.S.S.R., 1930s Start of Roosevelt's New Deal in U.S., 1933
1940	United Nations founded, 1945 Decolonization of Asia and Africa, 1945–1960s Cold War begins, 1947 Founding of Israel, 1948 Communist government in China, 1949 Korean War, 1950–1953 De-Stalinization of Soviet Union under Khrushchev, 1953–1964	Holocaust, 1941–1945 Marshall Plan enacted, 1947 European economic progress, ca. 1950–1970 European Coal and Steel Community founded, 1952 European Economic Community founded, 1957

Religion and Philosophy	Science and Technology	Arts and Letters
Decline in church attendance among working classes, ca. 1850–1914	Modernization of Paris, ca. 1850–1870	Realism in art and literature, ca. 1850–1870
Mill, *On Liberty*, 1859	Great Exhibition in London, 1851	Flaubert, *Madame Bovary*, 1857
Pope Pius IX, *Syllabus of Errors*, denounces modern thoughts, 1864	Freud, founder of psychoanalysis, 1856–1939	Tolstoy, *War and Peace*, 1869
Marx, *Das Capital*, 1867	Darwin, *On the Origin of Species*, 1859	Impressionism in art, ca. 1870–1900
Doctrine of papal infallibility, 1870	Pasteur develops germ theory of disease, 1860s	Eliot (Mary Ann Evans), *Middlemarch*, 1872
	Suez Canal opened, 1869	
	Mendeleev develops periodic table, 1869	
Growth of public education in France, ca. 1880–1900	Emergence of modern immunology, ca. 1875–1900	Zola, *Germinal*, 1885
Growth of mission schools in Africa, 1890–1914	Electrical industry: lighting and streetcars, ca. 1880–1900	Kipling, "The White Man's Burden," 1899
	Trans-Siberian Railroad, 1890s	
	Marie Curie, discovery of radium, 1898	
Separation of church and state in France, 1901–1905	Planck develops quantum theory, ca. 1900	Modernism in art and literature, ca. 1900–1929
Hobson, *Imperialism*, 1902	First airplane flight, 1903	Conrad, *Heart of Darkness*, 1902
Schweitzer, *Quest of the Historical Jesus*, 1906	Einstein develops theory of special relativity, 1905–1910	Cubism in art, ca. 1905–1930
		Proust, *Remembrance of Things Past*, 1913–1927
Keynes, *Economic Consequences of the Peace*, 1919	Submarine warfare introduced, 1915	Spengler, *The Decline of the West*, 1918
	Ernest Rutherford splits atom, 1919	
Emergence of modern existentialism, 1920s	"Heroic age of physics," 1920s	Gropius, Bauhaus, 1920s
Revival of Christianity, 1920s–1930s	First major public radio broadcasts in Great Britain and U.S., 1920	Dadaism and surrealism, 1920s
Wittgenstein, *Essay on Logical Philosophy*, 1922	First talking movies, 1930	Woolf, *Jacob's Room*, 1922
Heisenberg's principle of uncertainty, 1927	Radar system in England, 1939	Joyce, *Ulysses*, 1922
		Eliot, *The Waste Land*, 1922
		Remarque, *All Quiet on the Western Front*, 1929
		Picasso, *Guernica*, 1937
De Beauvoir, *The Second Sex*, 1949	U.S. drops atomic bombs on Japan, 1945	Cultural purge in Soviet Union, 1946–1952
Communists fail to break Catholic Church in Poland, 1950s	Big Science in U.S., ca. 1945–1965	Van der Rohe, Lake Shore Apartments, 1948–1951
	Watson and Crick discover structure of DNA molecule, 1953	Orwell, *1984*, 1949
	Russian satellite in orbit, 1957	Pasternak, *Doctor Zhivago*, 1956
		"Beat" movement in U.S., late 1950s

Government	Society and Economy
1960	
Building of Berlin Wall, 1961	Civil rights movement in U.S., 1960s
U.S. involvement in Vietnam War, 1964–1973	Stagflation, 1970s
Student rebellion in France, 1968	Feminist movement, 1970s
Soviet tanks end Prague Spring, 1968	Collapse of postwar monetary system, 1971
Détente between U.S. and U.S.S.R., 1970s	OPEC oil price increases, 1973, 1979
Soviet occupation of Afghanistan, 1979–1989	
1980	
U.S. military buildup, 1980s	Growth of debt in the West, 1980s
Solidarity in Poland, 1980	Economic crisis in Poland, 1988
Unification of Germany, 1989	Maastricht Treaty proposes monetary union, 1990
Revolutions in eastern Germany, 1989–1990	European Community becomes European Union, 1993
Persian Gulf War, 1990–1991	Migration to western Europe increases, 1990s
Dissolution of Soviet Union, 1991	Former Soviet bloc nations adopt capitalist economies, 1990s
Civil war in Yugoslavia, 1991–2001	
Separatist war breaks out in Chechnya, 1991	
2000	
Vladimir Putin elected president of Russian Federation, 2000	Same-sex marriage legalized in the Netherlands, 2001
Terrorist attacks on U.S., Sept. 11, 2001	Euro enters circulation, 2002
War in Afghanistan begins, 2001	Voters reject new European Union constitution, 2005
Iraq War, 2003–2011	Immigrant riots in France, 2005, 2009
Angela Merkel elected chancellor of Germany, 2005	Worldwide financial crisis begins, 2008
Growing popularity of anti-immigrant, far-right political parties across Europe, 2010s	European financial crisis intensifies, 2010
NATO intervenes in Libyan civil war, 2011	Anti-austerity protests across Europe begin, 2010
Al-Qaeda leader Osama bin Laden killed, 2011	Arab Spring uprisings in the Middle East and North Africa, 2011
Vladimir Putin re-elected, 2012	France legalizes same-sex marriage, 2013
Ex-NSA contractor Edward Snowden leaks classified U.S. government information, 2013	Occupy Movement begins in the United States, spreads to Europe, 2011
Russia annexes Crimea (southern Ukraine) and supports pro-Russian Ukrainian rebels, 2014	Greek debt crisis, 2015
Growth of Islamic State, 2014–2015	Massive influx of refugees from the Middle East, 2015–2016
Terrorist attacks in Paris organized by Islamic State kill 130 people, 2015	Refugee crisis undermines European unity, 2016
Terrorist attacks in Brussels organized by Islamic State kill 32 people, 2016	

Religion and Philosophy	Science and Technology	Arts and Letters
Second Vatican Council announces sweeping Catholic reforms, 1962–1965 Pope John II, 1978–2005	European Council for Nuclear Research founded, 1960 Space race, 1960s Russian cosmonaut first to orbit globe, 1961 American astronaut first person on moon, 1969	The Beatles, 1960s Solzhenitsyn, *One Day in the Life of Ivan Denisovich*, 1962 Carson, *Silent Spring*, 1962 Friedan, *The Feminine Mystique*, 1963 Servan-Schreiber, *The American Challenge*, 1967
Revival of religion in Soviet Union, 1985– Growth of Islam in Europe, 1990s Fukuyama proclaims "end of history," 1991	Reduced spending on Big Science, 1980s Computer revolution continues, 1980s–1990s U.S. Genome Project begins, 1990 First World Wide Web server and browser, 1991 Pentium processor invented, 1993 First genetically cloned sheep, 1996	Consolidation and popularization of postmodernism in fine arts and literature, 1980s Solzhenitsyn returns to Russia, 1994; dies 2008 Author Salman Rushdie exiled from Iran, 1989 Gehry, Guggenheim Museum, Bilbao, 1997
Number of Europeans who claim to be religious continues to decline, 2000– UN announces first World Philosophy Day to "honor philosophical reflection" across the globe, 2002 Ramadan, *Western Muslims and the Future of Islam*, 2004 Pontificate of Benedict XVI, 2005–2013 Jorge Mario Bergoglio elected as Pope Francis, 2013 Noted Slovenian philosopher Slavoj Žižek critiques contemporary Western notions of freedom, 2014	Google emerges as popular Internet search engine, 2000s Growing concern about global warming, 2000s First hybrid car, 2003 Facebook founded, 2004 YouTube founded, 2005 iPhone introduced to consumers, 2007 Copenhagen summit on climate change, 2009 Paris summit on climate change, 2015	Middle East conflict leads to looting and destruction of archaeological sites and museums, 2000– Growing importance of artists and art centers outside of Europe: in Latin America, Africa, and Asia, 2000– Digital methods of production and display grow increasingly popular in works of art, 2000– Movies and books exploring clash between immigrants and host cultures popular: *Bend It Like Beckham*, 2002; *The Namesake*, 2003; *White Teeth*, 2003; *The Class*, 2008; *Brooklyn*, 2015

About the Authors

John P. McKay (Ph.D., University of California, Berkeley) is professor emeritus at the University of Illinois. He has written or edited numerous works, including the Herbert Baxter Adams Prize–winning book *Pioneers for Profit: Foreign Entrepreneurship and Russian Industrialization, 1885–1913.*

Bennett D. Hill (Ph.D., Princeton University), late of Georgetown University, published *Church and State in the Middle Ages* and numerous articles and reviews, and he was one of the contributing editors to *The Encyclopedia of World History*. He taught for many years at the University of Illinois and was a Benedictine monk of St. Anselm's Abbey in Washington, D.C.

John Buckler (Ph.D., Harvard University), late of the University of Illinois, published numerous works, including *Theban Hegemony, 371–362 B.C.*; *Philip II and the Sacred War*; and *Aegean Greece in the Fourth Century B.C.* With Hans Beck, he published *Central Greece and the Politics of Power in the Fourth Century.*

Clare Haru Crowston (Ph.D., Cornell University) teaches at the University of Illinois, where she is currently professor of history and department chair. She is the author of *Credit, Fashion, Sex: Economies of Regard in Old Regime France* and *Fabricating Women: The Seamstresses of Old Regime France, 1675–1791*, which won the Berkshire and Hagley Prizes. She edited two special issues of the *Journal of Women's History*, has published numerous journal articles and reviews, and is one of the editors of the *Journal of Social History* and past president of the Society for French Historical Studies.

Merry E. Wiesner-Hanks (Ph.D., University of Wisconsin–Madison) taught first at Augustana College in Illinois, and since 1985 at the University of Wisconsin–Milwaukee, where she is currently UWM Distinguished Professor in the department of history. She is the senior editor of the *Sixteenth Century Journal*, one of the editors of the *Journal of Global History*, and the author or editor of more than twenty books, including *A Concise History of the World* (2015). She is the former Chief Reader for Advanced Placement World History.

Joe Perry (Ph.D., University of Illinois at Urbana-Champaign) is associate professor of modern German and European history at Georgia State University. He has published numerous articles and is author of *Christmas in Germany: A Cultural History*. His current research interests focus on issues of consumption, gender, and popular culture in West Germany and Western Europe after World War II.